OXFORD STUDIES IN AFRICAN AFFAIRS

POLITICAL PARTIES
IN FRENCH-SPEAKING
WEST AFRICA

Oxford University Press, Ely House, London, W.1

GLASGOW NEW YORK TORONTO MELBOURNE WELLINGTON
CAPE TOWN SALISBURY IBADAN NAIROBI LUSAKA ADDIS ABABA
BOMBAY CALCUTTA MADRAS KARACHI LAHORE DACCA
KUALA LUMPUR HONG KONG TOKYO

POLITICAL PARTIES
IN FRENCH-SPEAKING
WEST AFRICA

BY

RUTH SCHACHTER MORGENTHAU

CLARENDON PRESS · OXFORD

©*Oxford University Press, 1964*

FIRST PUBLISHED 1964
REPRINTED LITHOGRAPHICALLY IN GREAT BRITAIN
FROM CORRECTED SHEETS OF THE FIRST EDITION
1967
BY WILLIAM CLOWES AND SONS, LIMITED
LONDON AND BECCLES

TO HENRY

PREFACE

THIS book could not have been written without help from many friends and institutions. In Africa, the late President Ouëzzin Coulibaly showed me where to look and how to ask questions. MM. Mamby Sidibé, Hampaté Bâ, Madany Mountaga Tall, and Baidy Guèye taught me that the parties rested on the work of many generations, and of villagers, not just townsmen. President Touré of Guinea opened the doors to union and party headquarters; so did Ambassador Diallo Seydou. Minister Keïta N'Famara and my friends Ambassador Diallo Telli and Fofana Karim guided me in Guinea. In Mali, US Political Secretary Idrissa Diarra gave precious time and encouragement, as did President Mahamane Alassane Haidara, Ministers Mamadou Aw, Seydou Badian Kouyaté, and Abdoulaye Sangaré. Elsewhere Bernard Dadié showed me the poet's side of party history. Urbain Nicoué and Issoufou Seydou Djermakoye, Sénou Adande, Émile Zinsou, and Doudou Guèye gave valuable advice and hospitality. In Senegal, President Lamine Guèye, former President Mamadou Dia, Minister Doudou Thiam, Assane and Ursula Seck, and Abdoulaye Guèye shared their knowledge and thoughts. Dr. Abdoulaye Ly did me the special honour of advising me on the manuscript. All these and many more made my work in Africa possible; they shared ideas, food, and friendship and made me feel their world was part of mine.

Mlle. Claude Gérard of Paris gave generously of her time, her files, and her knowledge. M. Bernard Cornut-Gentille gave me sound advice. Professor Kenneth E. Robinson, now Director of the Institute of Commonwealth Studies, University of London, encouraged me steadily when I first came to him with this subject ten years ago. He guided me into the shelter of Nuffield College, Oxford, to whose Warden and Fellows I owe special thanks. Thomas Hodgkin, now Director of the Institute of African Studies, University of Ghana, gave an immense amount of time to the manuscript in its several stages; I was indeed fortunate to find in him a teacher—my *marabout* —in the full sense.

Immanuel Wallerstein gave valuable criticism of the entire manuscript. William Foltz helped with the Mali chapter, and Aristede Zolberg with the chapter on the Ivory Coast. Finally my thanks go to the African Studies Program of Boston University and particularly to the Director, Professor William O. Brown, who made it possible for me to teach and earn and learn while writing the final version of this book. There Lydia Zemba was a painstaking editor and Lucy Creevey

Behrman helped with the long task of checking references, while Janis Hall worked tirelessly on the typing. Elinor Halprin spent many hours on the index.

This book is published the year of the 75th anniversary of Barnard College. I was a student there when I first became interested in African parties and Barnard encouraged me to further study on a Fulbright grant in Paris. The work led to a doctoral dissertation accepted in 1958 at Oxford University and was the purpose of my trips to Africa in 1952, 1956, and 1961. Most of the documentation was in French; I have translated citations into English. In references to parties and institutions I give the full name the first time only. In Appendix XII there are lists of African parties and their initials.

R. S. M.

Boston, March 1963

CONTENTS

APPENDICES

LIST OF FIGURES AND MAPS

MAPS

LIST OF ABBREVIATIONS

A.N.	Assemblée Nationale
AOF	Afrique Occidentale Française
A.U.F.	Assemblée de l'Union Française
J.O.A.N.C.I *Débats.*	*Journal Officiel, Assemblée Nationale Constituante, Débats Parlementaires*
J.O.A.N.C.II *Débats.*	*Journal Officiel, Deuxième Assemblée Nationale Constituante, Débats Parlementaires.*
J.O.A.N. *Débats.*	*Journal Officiel, Assemblée Nationale, Débats Parlementaires.*
J.O.C.R. *Débats.*	*Journal Officiel, Conseil de la République, Débats Parlementaires.*
J.O.C.D. *Débats.*	*Journal Officiel, Chambre des Députés, Débats Parlementaires.*
p.v.	Procès-verbal

INTRODUCTION

IN writing this book I had three goals: to contribute to the general study of politics, particularly of parties; to add to the small though growing number of studies of contemporary African politics; and to relate the history of parties in the French-speaking West African states of Senegal, the Ivory Coast, Guinea, Mali, and (much more briefly) in Niger, Upper Volta, Dahomey, and Mauretania.[1] Between 1958 and 1960 these states became independent republics, but before they were French dependencies, administered in the federation of *Afrique Occidentale Française* (AOF), known as 'colonies' under the Third Republic, and 'overseas territories' under the Fourth.

The approach is from the specific to the general. Only after completing four case studies do I pose in the final parts of this book broader questions of relations among all the West African states, and of party theory. Specific historical events come first for several reasons. The French-speaking West African parties are little known; it is necessary to study them in themselves, before placing them in a more general framework. They have a special place in African societies, which are so different from Western ones; in time, African parties became 'as much African institutions as lineages, age sets or secret societies'.[2] African parties interlocked with the extended family, with age groups, warrior groups, groups of captives; with lower castes of artisans, such as shoemakers, blacksmiths, jewellers, pedlars, and *griots* (hereditary praise-singers); with traditional leaders such as chiefs and their rivals, *marabouts* (Muslim teachers), fetish priests, heads of clans, and headmen of migrant workers. The parties used traditional points of assembly: births, circumcisions, weddings, funerals, prayers, markets, feasts, and dances. The historical chapters seek to confirm these points.

Another reason for moving from the specific to the general is to bring out what I believe to be a necessary connexion between the study of politics and action; I do not agree with those who set up analytic categories leaving no room for values or for the concept of time. Hence I try to set parties in historical context. They could take root in Africa only after the Second World War had marked a new stage in international politics, indicating that the colonial era was

[1] The former French United Nations trust territory of Togo, now an independent Republic, is not included here.

[2] Hodgkin, Thomas. 'A Note on West African Political Parties', *What are the Problems of Parliamentary Government in West Africa?*, The Hansard Society, London, 1958, p. 51.

over. Then Africa became involved in the universal attempt of the poorer nations to reduce the gap separating them from the richer. The birth of parties can be seen as steps in this direction. Africans first sought to become politically independent because they believed that only thus could they take active part in their own development. This is the standpoint of most modernizing African townsmen.

I proceed from the specific to the general, furthermore, in the hope that the historical data can overcome some of the problems of terminology and concepts which confront students of politics. The discipline rests mainly on the data of western institutions. We must use language to communicate, but how are we to choose the right words, since these reflect the state of western society? Even the word 'parties' has its roots there. A 'progressive', in the French political context, is close to the Communist position; in French-speaking West Africa it means 'anti-colonial modernizer', and carries no suggestion of the cold war. We are accustomed to discuss the pattern of authority within parties as collective, or personal, charismatic, institutionalized, but each word has a history and a set of associations, mostly western. How are we to understand references to *Fama*, roughly 'king' in Malinke, used in referring to Sékou Touré of Guinea?

The standard thinking on evidence among students of politics also reflects western society—there is a preference for lots of documents and reports written in impersonal language. Europeans drew up most of the documents on contemporary Africa, which Africans considered to be biased. In the colonial era few Africans shared the western idea that papers and machines produce reliable information. There were few party archives; party records, correspondence and newspapers were scattered and often hidden. Most African party organizers felt that documents might be seized by the colonial administration and used against them; they passed the more important messages by word of mouth. Telegrams were too expensive and most Africans believed that these as well as letters and telephone calls were censored by European officials. This does not mean there are no documents, but rather that the student must go to the scene, hear, and if possible witness events so as to be in a position to find and to evaluate what papers are available.

To indicate what they consider most certain, Africans frequently touch their eyes, meaning, 'I know, for I myself have seen.' This emphasis on personal experience rather than on written or mechanical records is only partly due to the difference in power between Europeans and Africans; it is due also to differences in social structure and technology. Africans building parties after the Second World War had to do so among people mostly ignorant of French. Yet this was the language expressing the modern constitutional decisions, including the decisions to make the franchise universal. Few had ever been to a large town and most had never lived in one; almost all handled money rarely and lived far from roads or railroads. The African party organizer who came into a village to solicit votes was at the same time a transmitter of news from a modern world. This world was symbolized by the airport, located perhaps fifty miles from the village if the distance is reckoned in physical mileage, but if the distance is plotted against the timetable of European economic and social history, then several hundred years away.

African party organizers came to the village first with the call, 'Become masters in your own home.' Behind the drive against colonialism there was another issue, modernization. Behind the struggle for power between Europeans and Africans there was a struggle among Africans, sharpest between modernizers who believed in social equality, and traditionalists who believed in social distinctions based on heredity. Many African modernizers believed that the colonial administration, by making use of co-operating African traditionalists, 'grafted modern abuses on ancient injustice',[1] and combined being anti-colonial with being anti-'chief'.

These issues were involved in varying degrees in the growth of all the parties in all the West African states. That is why the first part of the book is about the African social setting, and emphasizes the background of those who took the lead in the parties. Most French-speaking West African leaders, like their English-speaking counterparts, were products of the educational system introduced by the Europeans. They belonged to that still comparatively small group of people earning regular money incomes. Their professions and education gave them a direct interest in the new political units whose frontiers, mostly drawn by Europeans during the nineteenth century, bore no resemblance to traditional African political divisions. To achieve political power, African party leaders had to displace the colonial rulers. They succeeded, owing not only to the efforts of their parties, but also to the European colonizers, who, shortly before withdrawing, introduced representative institutions to which they transferred a growing amount of power leading to independence. The representative institutions allowed the growth of African parties, and moreover favoured the educated Africans as leaders.

Within this broadly similar process of simultaneous African pressure and European reforms, political parties and nations were born in both French-speaking and English-speaking West Africa. Seen in

[1] Césaire, Aimé. *Discours sur le colonialisme*, Présence Africaine, Paris, 1955, p. 27.

greater detail, however, striking differences existed, before independence, between the frameworks for African political movements set by the French and those set by the British colonizers. In so far as British concessions were made to African political demands, they followed an established pattern, whose most important feature was the progressive transfer of power to democratically elected African governments. The changes that transformed the Gold Coast into the state of Ghana in 1957 conformed to the precedents of independence for India, Pakistan, Ceylon, and Burma. At no time was there any serious question of admitting African political leaders into British metropolitan parliamentary institutions. An African leader like Kwame Nkrumah was never in the position of having to lead a minority party in the British House of Commons, as the Irish nationalists had been some fifty years earlier. He did not have to decide whether his chances of achieving his political aims in Africa might increase by an alliance with one particular British party. Moreover, while British party divisions had their importance within Britain, and occasionally had direct relevance for the course of events in British colonial territories, these divisions had relatively little influence on the behaviour of British colonial administrators. Differences were not so deep that British civil servants could not abandon their private political views during their exercise of public tasks. British colonial officials in general carried out official policy; they did not behave as representatives of British political parties.

Almost directly opposite statements applied to the French post-war colonial framework. In spite of the deep political divisions in France under the Fourth Republic a negative consensus existed on one issue: for a dozen years independence, or a national existence for the French West African territories separate from that of France, was firmly rejected. The October 1946 Constitution placed tropical Africa squarely within a unitary Republic. Africans obtained limited representation in the French Parliament. Their minority position obliged them to contract alliances with one or other of the rival partners in the French multi-party system. In Parliament their votes affected decisions on major and minor French domestic and foreign policy issues: NATO, the Saar, Vietnam, North Africa, or subsidies to French brewers. Furthermore, their alliances drew them into French inter-party and internal party controversies: such as those between the Socialists and the MRP over state support to church schools, and between André Philip and Guy Mollet over Socialist party policy. Participation in the French Parliament made African leaders even more aware of political divisions in France. They already had experience of these in their dealings with French administrators in Africa, where ministerial changes in France were frequently reflected either by changes among the higher civil servants or by shifts in their political allegiances. Africans also realized that at times French administrators placed political party loyalty above loyalty to French official policy.

These contrasting generalizations help to explain why, although a study of parties which were born in British West Africa needs to take relatively little account of internal British politics, a study of French West African parties must give adequate attention to French metropolitan institutions and party alignments. The first phase of French-speaking West African party history was one in which power remained located in Paris and metropolitan politics reached into Africa. Elections and the birth of parties preceded by more than a decade responsible government located in Africa. This formative phase, which left deposits in party ideas, structure, and practice is discussed in the second and third parts of this book. It drew abruptly to a close with the adoption of the Constitution of the Fifth Republic, the independence of the Republic of Guinea in September 1958, and of the other seven states of 'ex-AOF' by 1960.

Independence created fresh conditions. It meant a change in relations with the rest of the world and with France; a change in relations with West African neighbours; new constitutions and institutions within each state, and therefore new tasks and adjustment for people and the parties. When the obvious ties of colonialism were broken one goal of the first generation of French-speaking West African party leaders was achieved. But only one. Independence changed the political rulers. It did not wipe out the differences—economic, cultural and political—between the rulers and the ruled. After independence, to meet the expectations of the mass of the people and provide occasions for further social mobility, economic development became the order of the day. It was the goal of the generation which aspired to the succession.

This book is mainly about the work of the first generation, the 'founding fathers' of the parties and the new states. Into their active lives many crises and a remarkable amount of work have been compressed. Those who knew the sleepy towns which were Abidjan, Bamako, Conakry, or Dakar in 1939 would hardly recognize now the bustling cities which bear the same names. Those who saw the verandas or tumbledown rooms which were the first meeting places of the African parties would not know the large, well lit headquarters of the parties which took credit for the transition to independence. In the countryside, too, old methods changed, and the *indigénat* (European administrative justice) or the French *rois de la brousse* (kings of the bush) faded into the past.

It was not the party leaders alone who awakened among their

people the energies and the talents needed to adapt to and create new conditions. But they have contributed to this awakening, to the emergence of a climate of opinion favouring, indeed glorifying in rapid change. They have channelled most of these energies constructively towards the reorganization of public life in West Africa and towards building a few African nations out of what were previously many tribes under foreign rule.

An outside observer, who enjoyed the hospitality of the leaders of different parties in French-speaking West Africa, cannot but feel a profound respect for what they have accomplished in a short time. Mindful of the complexity of African problems, and above all of the temptation to illuminate events in Africa with the false light of conceptions formed in Europe or America, I feel impelled to begin these pages with a reference to the reproachful litany written by an African poet:

> From experts on African questions,
> Deliver us, O Lord.[1]

[1] From Dadié, Bernard. 'Litanie d'un sujet français', *Afrique debout!*, Pierre Seghers, Paris, *c*. 1950, p. 25.

The African Social Setting

THOUGH French contact with West Africa goes back to the seventeenth century, colonial rule really began only at the end of the nineteenth. Not until the beginning of the twentieth century was it firmly established: in 1904, for example, the federation of Afrique Occidentale Française became a legal entity.[1] The usual official indication that the phase of conquest had ended and colonial authority was assured was the transfer from military to civil administration. Though technically this took place in 1920 for Mauretania and in 1922 for Niger, even afterwards on occasion the military took over in the Saharan regions. Thus French authority did not last very long in West Africa. Yet it did set the immediate conditions of the 'colonial situation'[2] in which political parties were born.

Except in Senegal, all French-speaking West African parties were born after July 1943, when the Gaullist governor–general, Pierre Cournarie, took over the administration from the Vichy supporter Pierre Boisson. Educated Africans everywhere demanded changes in the pre-war system of autocratic French colonial rule. Their sharpest complaints were against the policy of forced labour, the *indigénat* or special colonial system of justice, and the poverty accentuated by the war-time paralysis of the economy.

Forced Labour and the Indigénat
The term *travail forcé* covered several different legal categories of compulsory work: *travail publique obligatoire*, defined as 'village works, sanctioned by the customs of the group concerned, which are part of the normal obligations of community life';[3] *prestations*, or tax in labour for public works, generally levied through the chiefs and redeemable in cash; and military conscripted labour, or the

---

[1] Newbury, C. W. 'The Formation of the Government General of French West Africa', *The Journal of African History*, vol. 1, no. 1, London, Cambridge University Press, 1960, p. 111.

[2] Balandier, Georges. 'La Situation coloniale: approche théorique', *Cahiers Internationaux de Sociologie*, vol. xi, 1951, pp. 44 f.

[3] Hailey, Lord. *An African Survey*, Oxford University Press, London, 1938, p. 622, quoting from the decree of 21 August 1930; see also Rolland, Louis and Pierre Lampué. *Précis de droit des pays d'outre-mer*, 2nd Edition, Librairie Dalloz, Paris, 1952, p. 271.

deuxième contingent of the colonial army, used to carry on public works.[1] From 1919 universal military training was on the statute books for French West Africa. Only a very small proportion of the eligible men could in fact be drafted for ordinary military service in the *premier contingent*. Others were placed in the *deuxième contingent* and set to construction of public works.[2] Laws forbidding vagrancy, allowing requisitioning of porters, providing for employment of tax defaulters, and allowing local administrators to imprison and subject to forced labour those who broke the law, gave additional legal bases for requiring every able-bodied African to work as and where officials determined.

The forced-labour system had its defenders, who claimed that future generations would be grateful for the work accomplished.[3] That it had its abuses was recognized before the war by some French Catholics,[4] and by the Popular Front parties. Marcel de Coppet, named governor-general of French West Africa, under the Popular Front, recorded his opposition to the system.[5] So did Léon Blum.[6]

Chiefs were known to take revenge on their enemies when they drew up the lists for the *prestations*. Women and children were put to work in some areas, as well as the men. Short-term service frequently meant that little or no provision for health, nutrition, housing or transport was made. Punishments were often harsh. In the sparsely settled territories, like Niger, Mauretania, and parts of the Soudan, most of the drafted workers did their labour service near home, and if they were fortunate, near hospitable relatives who spoke the same language. But from the more highly populated Upper Volta, parts of the Ivory Coast, Guinea and Soudan, forced labourers frequently had to work far from home, in a strange climate, at unfamiliar tasks, under managers and among workers who did not speak their language, know their customs, or even their names. Forced labourers at times had to travel more than five hundred miles, at their own cost, from the recruiting centres to their place of

[1] Hailey, 1938, op. cit., pp. 624–8; Delavignette, Robert. *Freedom and Authority in French West Africa*, Oxford University Press, London, 1950, p. 123.
[2] See protest by Soudanese Socialist deputy Jean Silvandre, and response by the Overseas Under-Secretary, Tony Révillon, J.O.A.N., *Débats*, 28 January 1949, pp. 238 f.
[3] A pioneer inquiry into the history and economics of labour recruitment in Africa was made by Elliot Berg in his doctoral dissertation for Harvard University, *The Recruitment of a Labor Force in Sub-Sahara Africa*, Cambridge, 1960.
[4] An account of and a protest against forced labour by a French Catholic scholar are to be found in Joseph Folliet's *Le Travail forcé aux colonies*, Les Éditions du Cerf, Paris, c. 1936. See.also *Bulletin Catholique International*, 1 June 1928.
[5] Delavignette, op. cit., p. 113, and Hailey, 1938, op. cit., p. 626.
[6] *Le Populaire*, 5 and 7 July 1927.

work, e.g. from Bobo-Dioulasso to Gagnoa in the Ivory Coast
territory.[1]
   The most severe system of forced labour existed where Europeans
required the largest labour force, particularly in the fertile forest
zone of the Ivory Coast, where European planters and timber
merchants had settled. European organization of the timber industry
started early in this century in the Ivory Coast; European cocoa
planting started about 1920; coffee planting after 1930; banana
planting about 1933. The forest zone had a low density of population, about nine to the square mile. Europeans had to import labour
to cut trees, plant cocoa, coffee, or bananas, from the more populated northern Ivory Coast, Guinea, and most of all from Upper
Volta. Official estimates were that about 190,000 Upper Volta men
went into forced labour brigades between 1920 and 1930,[2] representing between a third and a quarter of the able-bodied men of the
population of some three million.[3] The Europeans hired recruiting
agents who bargained with northern chiefs for men and transported
them to the plantations. Already before 1925 forced labour, which
by law was required to be used only for limited periods of time and
for public works, was in practice placed at the disposal of European
plantations and other private enterprises. The rare French administrator who opposed this as illegal, such as Governor Brunot of the
Ivory Coast, was quickly transferred.[4]
   The decree of 25 October 1925[5] regulated the flow of labour from
the poor northern savannah regions to the more fertile south. This
decree recognized both that European planters needed African
labour, and that the administration who did not need to pay wages
and planters who did, were competing with each other for labour.
The decree fixed conditions for recruitment and employment of

[1] Fréchou, Hubert. *Les Plantations européennes en Côte d'Ivoire*, Thesis typescript,
University of Bordeaux, c. 1955, pp. 128 f; Berg, Elliot. 'French West Africa',
Labor and Economic Development, Walter Galenson, ed., Wiley, New York, 1959,
chapter 5.
[2] Delavignette, op. cit., p. 113.
[3] Berg. 'French West Africa', op. cit., p. 195. An interesting study of migration
from Upper Volta is Jean Rouch's 'Migrations au Ghana', *Journal de la Société
des Africanistes*, tome xxvi, fasc. i and ii, Musée de l'Homme, Paris, 1956, pp. 33–
196.
[4] Annex 11348 to J.O.A.N. Records, 21 November 1950, *Rapport fait au nom de la
commission chargée d'enquêter sur les incidents survenus en Côte d'Ivoire*, M.
Damas, 3 vols., p. 14. (Henceforth cited as *Annex 11348*.) Also report by Inspec-
teur des Colonies Maret, Bouaké, 26 May 1931, ts. (Henceforth cited as Maret
Report.) Brunot's successor, Reste, favoured use of forced labour for European
plantations. He was elected a first college representative to the first Constituent
Assembly.
[5] Later somewhat amended.

African labour on European plantations, and required administrative authorization for recruiting. Soon the administration not only authorized, but also stated how and where workers were to be recruited and stationed, and how much pressure could be used on Africans to obtain the authorized number of workers. The distinction between forced labour for public works and free labour for private enterprises disappeared; 'workers were drafted by the administration and attached to an enterprise; only after they finished their period of forced labour could they freely choose, if they wanted, a new employer'.[1] Payment for free labour, regulated by the administration, was extremely low; 1927 salaries. for men were 2 francs a day for 3 months, and 2.50 francs a day afterwards, while women received 1 franc a day for 3 months, and 1.25 francs afterwards.[2] Only half was paid during the period of work, and the rest after the contract time had expired, in order that workers should not run away. The terminal half of the salary more often than not went to the administration as taxes, or to chiefs in repayment of debts.[3] In law, workers were to receive food and housing. This was not really enforced, and 'all depended on the goodwill of the planter, who could count on the indulgence of the authorities'.[4]

The migrant labourers worked during the southern harvest season, which in their homes was usually the dry season; at the end of the harvest, they returned home to cultivate their own fields. Since labourers rarely stayed more than six months with the same employer, whether the administration or a European entrepreneur, employers had little incentive to know personally or to care for the workers. 'The whip and the stick were therefore in current practice.' If any died, 'the climate or change of surroundings was blamed . . . and if the administrator heard of it, the whole thing cost 300 francs'.[5]

Obviously this system brought Africans great hardships and gave them little incentive for work.[6] Many have not forgotten their experiences in this period, and still tell of the flight of their families, sometimes of their villages, to escape labour levies. President Houphouët-Boigny said after the war:

> One has to have seen these used-up workers, skeletons covered with sores, wandering or in the fields; one has to have seen assembled for recruitment these thousands of men, their whole bodies trembling before the medical inspectors; one has to have watched the distracted flights from the *chefs de village* or *chefs de canton* into the bush; one has to have read the eyes of planters forced to abandon their own land to work for starvation wages; one has to have seen the long lines of men, women and children,

[1] Fréchou thesis, op. cit., p. 133.   [2] Ibid., p. 135.
[3] Maret report, op. cit., p. 5.   [4] Fréchou thesis, op. cit., p. 135.
[5] Maret report, op. cit., p. 16.   [6] *Annex 11348*, op. cit., p. 2.

brows furrowed, march silently along the road to the fields; one has to have seen the recruiting agents, the modern slave traders, crowd people heedlessly in trucks, exposed to all climates, or lock them into baggage cars like animals; one must have lived, as chief, through the poignant, heartrending scenes, when old women ask for their sons, their only source of support, orphans ask for their fathers, women weighed down by children for their husbands, their only providers, to understand the drama of forced labour in Ivory Coast.[1]

Until 1937 the system had many abuses, but they reached a new height afterwards and during the Second World War, when for many reasons the number of workers available decreased appreciably. Africans had started plantations in the Ivory Coast in their own right, and were competing with the administration and European entrepreneurs for labour, especially after world prices rose in 1936–7.[2] Africans who needed to earn tax money and wanted to escape forced labour went to work instead in British colonies, particularly the Gold Coast. There are no exact pre-war figures, though officials estimated 20,000 to 30,000 Mossi farm labourers who would ordinarily have gone to the Ivory Coast went instead to the Gold Coast in 1944.[3] Some planters, both European and African, were drafted into the army, and the administration tried to maintain the abandoned European but not the African plantations. Goods, machinery, replacement parts, gasoline, and other imports became scarcer as the war continued and the communication system collapsed.

The administration increasingly used force to make Africans work harder and compensate for the deterioration of the money economy. Labour was conscripted to build defence installations along the Gold Coast frontier. It was not unusual for a village to be encircled, and for men to be taken from the villages under military guard to do the work the administration thought necessary. By 1944 the forced labour system had almost broken down, since the vicious circle of brutality and flight gradually meant that less and less men were available, and less work was done.[4]

The *indigénat* was another important source of African resentment against the pre-war political system. The *indigénat* referred to the special provisions in the penal code which permitted governors or French administrators to take speedy punitive action against African 'subjects'.[5] As codified in 1924 the *indigénat* in some cases authorized deportation, imposition of individual or collective fines, and dispossession by simple administrative decision. The powers granted

[1] Houphouët, J.O.A.N.C. I, *Débats*, 23 March 1946, pp. 1028 f.
[2] Fréchou thesis, op. cit., p. 136. See Figure 5, p. 168.   [3] Ibid., p. 140.
[4] Ibid., pp. 136–9, 182 f., and 221 f.   [5] See pp. 61 f.

under the *indigénat* were invoked by administrators to punish persons who moved without authorization from one territory to another or who attended meetings of more than twenty-four men. The extreme provision of the *indigénat*, applicable in Cameroun, allowed imprisonment for up to ten years.[1] In West Africa, however, the usual provisions of the *indigénat* in the late thirties stated that administrators could imprison for not more than fifteen days, and exact fines of no more than 100 fr. (1939).[2]

These administrative disciplinary powers existed over and above the normal provisions of the native penal code, applicable to the 'subjects'. Mê Lamine Guèye attacked it by citing this example:

We pass two men fighting with knives. We say to ourselves 'These gentlemen have matters to settle. This does not concern us.' We continue on our way. If we are French citizens, it is not a crime for us to take no interest in the fight. But if we are 'subjects', not intervening—even at the risk of being stabbed—makes us liable to 5 years imprisonment and 5 years of exile.[3]

Nor were the native courts dealing with civil and criminal cases independent of the administrators. In the first-degree courts of the subdivision, and in the second-degree courts of the largè administrative unit, the *cercle*, the local French administrator presided over proceedings. These native courts could inflict the death penalty, or penal servitude for life. 'It hardly needs great imagination to realize what Africans thought of this system.'[4]

Unrest

The absence of outlets to express African protest or political aspirations was another major source of grievance against the prewar colonial system. Africans had no access to political power or responsibility, no right of assembly or freedom of speech. Outside of the 'old communes' of Senegal[5] no African parties were permitted. In the countryside, among illiterate peasants and herdsmen, there was little expressed desire for, and little knowledge of modern representative institutions. There were, however, many sporadic indications of protest.

[1] Guèye, Lamine. *Étapes et perspectives de l'Union française*, Éditions de l'Union Française, Paris, 1955, pp. 37–8.
[2] Robinson, K. E. 'The Public Law of Overseas France Since the War', Oxford University, Institute of Colonial Studies, Reprint no. 1a, p. 3; Rolland and Lampué, op. cit., pp. 294–7; Devèze, Michel, *La France d'outre-mer*, Hachette, Paris, 1948, pp. 76–77.
[3] J.O.A.N.C. I, 22 March 1946, pp. 1000 f. See also Hailey, 1938, op. cit., pp. 290–1.
[4] Guèye, *Étapes et perspectives . . .*, op. cit., p. 36.   [5] See pp. 58 f.

There was periodic unrest among the nomads of Soudan in the northern regions of Niger and Mauretania, where French control was uncertain even after the First World War. To escape forced labour levies, occasionally the entire population of villages took flight. Observers estimated that hundreds of thousands abandoned their villages in the Ivory Coast, which then included most of Upper Volta.[1] Villagers showed their discontent by refusing to furnish requisitioned goods, resisting expropriation of land, not paying taxes, and rejecting the authority of officially appointed chiefs.

There is a special background to these controversies about 'chiefly' authority. French colonizers redrew the boundaries of local administration with little reference to pre-European political frontiers. French administrators directly responsible to a governor commanded each of the 188 *cercles* of French West Africa, where they were assisted by members of the regular civil service. They had further auxiliaries in the African chiefs, members of the *commandement indigène* composed of some 2,200 cantonal chiefs and their subordinates, 48,000 village chiefs.[2] Most of these official chiefs were distinguished from the regular, mobile civil service by being illiterate and serving only among their kinsmen. They were appointed and dismissed by the European administrators, had no tenure, and their income was precarious. Of them, Governor Deschamps says:

> The French do not have, as do the English, a superstitious regard for monarchy; nowhere did they consolidate the power of the chiefs, by granting them tribunals or autonomous treasuries. The chief is not considered a potentate, but rather a useful administrative auxiliary. The cantonal chiefs (in the subdivisions of the administrative districts or *cercles*) are appointed only to transmit orders and to collect taxes. The French administrator does not shrink in the least from personal contact, and instinctively practices direct administration. He is the 'commandant', the 'king of the bush', whose very presence creates a new political unit.[3]

Since it was official French policy to rule directly rather than indirectly, the official chiefs were not necessarily men with a traditional claim to chieftaincy. Often villagers preferred other leaders to the official chiefs. Conflicts over chieftaincy resulted, and these multiplied as tension mounted in the countryside.

Religious protest movements sprang up. An illustration among Muslims was the spread of Hamalliya, particularly in the Soudan. The administration suppressed the Hamallists,[4] deported some

---

[1] Folliet, op. cit., p. 43–9.　　　　　　[2] Delavignette, op. cit., p. 71–84.
[3] Deschamps, Hubert. *L'Éveil politique africain*, Presses Universitaires de France, Paris, 1952, p. 81.
[4] Grivot, R. *Réactions dahoméennes*, Éditions Berger-Levrault, Paris, 1954, p. 145, reflects official fear of the radical tendencies in Hamallism.

leaders in the twenties and thirties, and unwittingly helped spread the doctrine.[1] By 1937, however, French Popular Front leaders 'took a less hostile view of Islam', and came at least to tolerate Hamalliya.[2] Religious protest among the Christianized coastal peoples of the Ivory Coast and Dahomey took the form of the separatist Harrist movement, which was said to have baptized 120,000 in the Ivory Coast in 1914–15.[3]

Yet a further example of village protest was the *Nana Vo* movement which flourished in 1934 in the traditionally 'anarchic' Bobo region of Upper Volta.[4] *'Nana,'* in the language of the Bobo's, means 'taking without paying'. *'Vo'* means 'end'. The people of the region resisted 'the arbitrary requisitioning of food and animals by the chiefs, with the agreement of the administration'.[5] Incidents took place, especially around Bobo-Dioulasso, Dédougou, Boromo, Tougan, and Koutiala, and French control was reasserted only by the use of force. (The official inquiry concluded that the Bobos were encouraged in their protest by the White Father missions.)

Such unco-ordinated, largely spontaneous protests in the country-side multiplied during the war when officials harshly applied the *indigénat* and forced labour laws and the economy deteriorated. Before the war there were almost no industries, even for partial transformation of local agricultural and mining exports. African peasant growers earned some money income from peanuts in Senegal and to a smaller extent in Soudan and Niger, from coffee and cocoa in the Ivory Coast, from rice in Guinea, Soudan and Niger, and from vegetable oils in Dahomey and the Ivory Coast. This money—used for taxes, for the purchase of imported manufactured goods, and for the redemption of some villagers from forced labour— lost its value during the war. The necessarily regular banana transport and therefore trade, disappeared. Under Vichy, the AOF economy, controlled by the administration, furnished some crops and raw materials to France. After the North African landing in November 1942, however, even this trickle of trade with France stopped until the Liberation.[6] Crops remained stocked locally, imports were almost unobtainable. Salaries, where paid, had little meaning because money had hardly any purchasing power. Workers

---

[1] Gouilly, Alphonse. *L'Islam dans l'Afrique occidentale française*, Éditions Larose, Paris, 1952, p. 145.
[2] Ibid., p. 140.
[3] Hodgkin, Thomas. *Nationalism in Colonial Africa*, Muller, London, 1956, p. 107.
[4] See the note, signed D.O., in *Esprit*, Paris, September 1953.
[5] From an unpublished typescript by an eye witness.
[6] See Figure 5, p. 168, and Appendix XI.

deserted villages and fields.[1] The Algiers government, in control of West Africa in 1943, requisitioned new commodities, such as rubber, which required a large labour force. Richard-Molard left the following graphic record of the war effort demanded of African colonies by the Free French:

One *cercle* is required to produce so many tons of liana rubber, even though no liana grows in the territory. The native is therefore forced to travel on foot, sometimes over long distances, to buy rubber elsewhere, regardless of cost. He must sell this to the commandant at the official price, which is several times lower than the purchasing price, in order to escape the hand of 'justice'. Another *cercle* is ordered to produce honey. None is available. The commandant is punished for telegraphing his superiors 'AGREE TO HONEY. STOP. SEND BEES.'[2]

Thus the points of friction multiplied during the Second World War between villagers and those in authority: the French administrators or their African associates, the chiefs, the police, the army and the *gardes de cercle*. In 1941 Prince Adingra, traditional leader of the Brong on the frontier of the Ivory Coast and the Gold Coast, went with his people to the Gold Coast to escape the Vichy administration.[3] In 1943 the cluster of Bobo, Lobi, Dafing, and Gourounsi peoples in the Western region of what is now Upper Volta again rioted against the administration, and were subdued with considerable force. By 1944, in spite of heavy pressure, villagers were not paying taxes, not appearing for forced labour service, and made fewer and fewer compulsory crop deliveries. Smuggling increased across international frontiers, for example near Man and Danané in Ivory Coast, and Nzérékoré in Guinea, both close to the Liberian frontier. Agricultural produce found its way to the black market.[4] There

a piece of percale costing officially 195 francs, cost 600 francs from the *dioula* [trader in Malinke] and was resold at 1100 to 1200 francs by itinerant pedlars . . .[5]

In the Kankan region of Guinea, a religiously inspired rebellion, directed by the Muslim leader Lamine Kaba, led to violent clashes in 1945–6. Incidents about successors to chiefs—such as those between 1942 and 1947 in Abengourou, on the Ivory Coast[6]—took place in many other regions.

[1] See d'Arboussier's discussion of inflation in Africa during the war, J.O.A.N.C. I, *Débats*, 22 March 1946, pp. 889 f.
[2] Richard-Molard, Jacques. *Afrique Occidentale Française*, Paris, Éditions Berger-Levrault, 1952, p. 167.
[3] See d'Aby, F. J. Amon. *La Côte d'Ivoire dans la cité africaine*, Larose, Paris, 1951, p. 41, and Devèze, op. cit., p. 158.   [4] *Afrique Nouvelle*, 10 August 1947.
[5] Ibid., 5 October 1947.   [6] *Annex 11348*, op. cit., pp. 25–9.

Under the pre-war colonial regime, since no political parties yet existed, Africans used traditional and neo-traditional institutions to express both political protest and aspirations. To some extent, therefore, the traditional African social, economic, and religious institutions were the forerunners of the political parties and other modern organizations which took over these tasks after 1945. Although traditional and neo-traditional African forms of organization often expressed village discontent, these institutions did not of themselves change into modern political parties. Nor can it be said that the unco-ordinated incidents, which multiplied during the war, were specifically directed against the lack of freedom to organize or to acquire political power. The work of enlarging the scale of political units, of generalizing from individual local grievances, of expressing these in modern terms, of demanding changes in the colonial political system, was carried out by educated African town dwellers. Their associations were the immediate forerunners of African political parties.

The Educated Africans

As the war ended, the Africans educated in the schools introduced by the French persistently spoke up for reforms. After 1945 the French government made concessions to these demands and Africans decided to use the legal channels to present their candidates for elections. During some fifteen years in which roughly 1,500 seats in representative institutions above the local level were filled by successive popular elections, the vast majority of the candidates were literate. Africans reasoned that their representatives had to be equipped to deal with the Europeans, their language and their institutions.

They had learned to read and write before 1945, when educational facilities were still very limited, and less than 5 per cent. of AOF's school age children were actually in school.[1] They began their formal political careers right after the war, and in the fifties and sixties achieved top positions as deputies, ministers, party leaders and trade unionists. As the colonies moved towards independence, not only the formal institutions of government, but parties and other modern organizations often changed their labels and other specifications. Yet the educational facilities expanded far more slowly, as did, therefore, the size and composition of the educated group. Regardless how often persons holding office were replaced, these always came from the tiny minority of educated people.

[1] Service des Statistiques d'Outre-mer, *Outre-mer 1958*, Imprimerie Paul Dupont, Paris, 1959, p. 189.

The products of the pre-Liberation educational system were locally educated; practically none had ever been outside Africa. In French, unlike British West Africa, there existed almost no university graduates in 1945. The handful of exceptions came almost exclusively from Senegal, and primarily there from among the pre-war 'citizens' living in Dakar, Saint-Louis, Rufisque, and Gorée. Only among this comparatively privileged community could some select families point in 1960 to as many as three generations of educated men. Among the 'citizens' most who had acquired pre-war French university degrees were trained as veterinary surgeons—for example the novelist and Socialist mayor of Rufisque, Ousmane Socé Diop. The grammarian and poet, Léopold Senghor, and the doctor of law, Mê Lamine Guèye—both naturalized pre-war 'citizens'—were also among the Senegalese exceptions.

These men apart, only in the late 'fifties have any significant number of French-speaking West African graduates returned from their universities in France or in the post-war University of Dakar. They were at their books while their countrymen were passing through the important first phase of the struggle for political power. Armed with their degrees and ready for jobs, they found filled the most important political posts in government, in parties or in other modern institutions. Most had to content themselves with second-level posts in the civil service. Some, indeed, were in the peculiar position of working under African ministers who were contemporaries and had failed secondary school or college entrance examinations. The failure had left the locally educated men free to take part in the first crucial years of political activity after 1945; and so to become 'founding fathers'.

What were they like? Part of the answer is to be found in the educational system of pre-war French West Africa, which trained people to occupy subordinate positions in the administration. Practically none had ever been out of Africa or had university degrees; practically all were the first of their families to learn reading and writing in a language other than Arabic; their degrees were local, without equivalents elsewhere; their instruction was always in French.[1]

Those who managed to go from the local village or nomad school to the regional (rural) or urban primary school, and from there respectively to technical schools or to the few existing upper primary schools, had through approximately eight years of successful study achieved the right to be very junior clerks, or assistants to teachers or

[1] For surveys of pre-war education, see Guernier, Eugène, editor, *Afrique Occidentale Française*, Encyclopédie Coloniale et Maritime, tome i, Paris, 1949, pp. 267–78, and Hailey, 1938, op. cit., pp. 1260–7.

technicians. Those from the upper primary schools who also managed to win one of the few coveted places in the principal federal secondary school, the École Normale William-Ponty, had won their way to the 'nerve center, the most solid link which joined the *évolués* of the French West African colonies'.[1]

The high political, civil service, and commercial posts which graduates of Ponty occupied after 1945 demonstrate that calling that institution the pre-war Oxford of French West Africa is no exaggeration.[2] But at the time the students were not trained to lead. They were trained by the state, free of charge, to be 'qualified auxiliaries'[3] to European superiors, according to a 'clearly defined policy of limiting more advanced education to demand'[4] for more clerks, teachers, and medical assistants. Practically all upper primary and secondary school graduates had to work for the administration. This was because of the terms on which their study was subsidized, and because African resources were still unexplored, the economy was largely stagnant, and the few operating European trading firms were unwilling or unable to offer Africans jobs. Therefore practically all except those who could plant cocoa or coffee in southern Ivory Coast or profit from the peanut trade in Senegal saw no alternative prospects than in the civil service to earn the income or enjoy the social status which their education made them want. Certainly none were willing to return to subsistence farming, at least partly because producing crops, which was compulsory in pre-war elementary and primary schools 'disgusted pupils forever, and inspired in them a holy terror of work on the land'.[5] Pupils in one three-class school in Ivory Coast during 1937 had to plant a hectare of coffee trees, without money or tools, though at the time 50,000 francs was considered the necessary capital investment for preparing a hectare of virgin forest for coffee production.[6]

Thus the very large majority of the principal post-war leaders were civil servants by profession, dependent on the administration for their income. Only in Senegal, until 1952 the richest territory in AOF, were there a number of exceptions.[7] The laws of eligibility for office did not disqualify most African civil servants—clerks, medical and

---

[1] From a speech by N'Diaye Babakar, president of the Ponty alumni association, the *Association William-Ponty*, reprinted in *Genèse*, the association bulletin, 1 April 1945, Imprimerie du Gouvernement, Dakar, p. v.

[2] See the pride with which Ray Autra, himself a graduate of Ponty, discusses this point in 'Historique de l'enseignement en A.O.F.', *Présence Africaine*, February–March 1956, Paris, p. 73.

[3] Dirand, A., in his report to the *Congrès International de l'Évolution Culturelle des Peuples Coloniaux*, Paris, 1938, p. 35.

[4] Hailey, 1938, op. cit., p. 1262.   [5] Autra, op. cit., p. 72.   [6] Ibid.

[7] For some substantiating details, see Appendix VIII, 'professions'.

veterinary assistants, state school teachers—from running for office. Indeed, had they been disqualified, it is difficult to see where alternative educated candidates might have been found to fill political offices.

Few places at the secondary schools meant that many able candidates fell by the wayside, including those who temperamentally could not survive the rigors implied in the official slogan of 'discipline, work, and perseverance'.[1] Very roughly, the total number of Ponty graduates from all territories between 1918 and 1945 can be estimated at less than two thousand, of whom about a third were trained as medical assistants (African doctors).[2] Few places, and difficult examinations, meant that territories with more and better primary schools—Senegal and Dahomey—filled a disproportionately high number of Ponty places, while the poor territories, Mauretania, Niger, and Upper Volta, filled very few. Standards were lower at the younger and less influential normal schools, Frédéric Assomption at Katibougou[3] in Soudan, at Dabou[4] in Ivory Coast, the girls' normal school at Rufisque,[5] and the professional technical schools. These instructed a few hundred more administrative auxiliaries. The mission schools, tightly controlled by the state, modestly increased the numbers of advanced primary or secondary school graduates, especially in southern Dahomey and the Mossi region of Upper Volta.[6]

Until 1945 this was the framework for the AOF system of education for 'subjects'. It gave only locally recognized degrees which gave access only to the lower ranks of the civil service. Metropolitan degrees were pegged to the higher ranks, and few Africans had access to schools meeting metropolitan standards. Only Europeans could attend the primary schools 'opened in the larger cities for the children of European civil servants'.[7] 'Citizens,' mainly from Senegal, had access to Lycée Faidherbe founded in 1920 at Saint-Louis, or to the classes which became in 1940 the Lycée Van Vollenhoven at Dakar. Elsewhere in AOF there were no *lycées* until 1945, when the

---

[1] *Genèse*, op. cit., p. vi. Bernard Dadié, an Ivory Coast graduate of Ponty, in his novel *Climbié*, Éditions Seghers, Paris, 1956, described a young African's reactions to pre-war school life.
[2] This estimate, given by education officials in Dakar, was confirmed by calculations based on Hailey, 1938, op. cit., pp. 1185–6, and by figures in Haut Commissariat de l'AOF, *Annuaire Statistique de l'AOF*, Édition 1951, tome ii, Imprimerie Nationale, Paris, 1951, p. 83.
[3] Started in 1934, with 99 pupils in 1937–8.
[4] Started in 1938, with 47 pupils.   [5] Started in 1939.
[6] See 'La Scolarisation de l'Afrique noire', *Tam-Tam*, Bulletin des Étudiants Catholiques en France, Paris, March–May 1955, for a discussion of the role (with supporting statistical information) of the mission schools.
[7] Guernier, op. cit., p. 271.

secondary school courses at Bamako's Terrasson de Fougères were up-graded, and gradually each territory built at least one *lycée*.

The common training of educated Africans gave to many an ambivalent outlook towards the policy of assimilation,[1] on which pre-war colonial policy of the French Left was theoretically based. Privately most condemned assimilation, which in their eyes included the assumption that Africans had little if any civilization, while France alone had a culture. Most protested energetically when schools used textbooks teaching Africans of 'our ancestors, the Gauls', and exclaimed ironically, 'what was the good Lord doing, making blond Gauls produce Blacks?'[2] Some in their spare time became serious writers, poets, and playwrights, students of African dance, legend, poetry, history, and language. Among them were active leaders of the RDA like Bernard Dadié and Coffi Gadeau from Ivory Coast;[3] Keïta Fodéba and Ray Autra from Guinea; Modibo Keïta and Madeira Keïta from Soudan; and Boubou Hama from Niger. Most attended Ponty during the years that Charles Béart, a Popular Front appointee, was director of the school. He and the director of studies, Ouëzzin Coulibaly, encouraged Ponty students to develop African culture through the use of French forms. They called this 'double assimilation', then also advocated by Léopold Senghor studying in France.[4] Ponty students carried their preoccupation with African culture—which was their reaction to the assault French education made on African values and customs—into the field of politics after the war. From this assault stemmed their later interest in *négritude* (Senghor) and the *personalité africaine* (Sékou Touré). More than their English-speaking neighbours French-speaking West Africans have persistently emphasized developing their own cultural tradition. The *Présence Africaine* group established in Paris in 1947 was dedicated to this task. At meetings and in the pages of a journal, it assembled Ponty-trained artists and the first generation of African university students who shared passionate concern with a cultural as well as a political African renaissance.[5]

Even before the war few Africans believed possible, or desirable the ultimate goal of 'assimilation', that Africans act and think like

[1] See pp. 57 f.
[2] Dadié, Bernard. 'Misère de l'enseignement en A.O.F.', *Présence Africaine*, Paris, December 1956–January 1957, p. 59.   [3] d'Aby, op. cit., pp. 154–63.
[4] See Béart in *Genèse*, op. cit., pp. 25–6, and his *Recherche des éléments d'une sociologie des peuples africains à partir de leurs jeux*, Présence Africaine, Paris, 1960.
[5] For some views of post-war African students in Paris see A. Sar, I. Fofana, and K. Banny, 'Esprit et situation de l'enseignement en Afrique noire', *Présence Africaine*, December 1956–January 1957, Paris, pp. 71–83; and by A. Wade, 'Examen critique des méthodes pédagogiques', ibid., April–May 1956, pp. 56–73.

Frenchmen. But many considered useful the implied corollary of that goal, that Africans and Frenchmen have equal rights. Those attending Ponty lived near Dakar, observed with a mixture of envy and resentment the rights which the African 'citizens' had, and learned to emulate the dexterity with which the 'citizens', in order to maintain and increase their privileges, manipulated French generalizations about equality. The educated pre-war 'subjects' pressed for concessions: as students, to argue for the then unattainable chance to study in France; as civil servants, to press for professional advancement. They were encouraged when Popular Front ministers introduced some cautious reforms in this direction. Then cultural organizations of the educated urban Africans were given somewhat wider scope; rudimentary trade unions, especially among teachers, were permitted; a few more 'subjects' became eligible for French citizenship as the conditions of acceptance were somewhat liberalized; there was even talk of abolishing forced labour, and of revising the *indigénat*. They were encouraged even further into half-believing equality between Frenchmen and Africans possible, by the lessons absorbed from the handful of eager young French Socialists, and the more influential French Communists, who took jobs as civil servants or teachers in Africa during the 'thirties. The educated Africans carried the habits of thought and expression learned before the war into their post-war political careers. Chafing under the limits set on their careers by the pre-war educational system of AOF, educated Africans pressed in 1945 to have it more closely aligned with that of France. This background may partly explain the time-lag between their post-war political demands—which, prior to 1957, did not explicitly include independence as the primary goal—and the post-war demands of British West African leaders. For a few years after the war, some educated French-speaking Africans were uncertain whether independence in fact provided the emancipation they sought.

As the war ended, this elite had many reasons for discontent. They were among the most intelligent and able of their countrymen, self-made men to a large extent. Their achievement of education probably involved more effort than the attainment of a Harvard degree by an immigrant American slum dweller during the depression. They were touchy about the limited status attached to most of their diplomas which had no equivalents outside AOF, and gave them no access to top posts even in AOF. The discriminatory practices under Vichy emphasized how precarious, indeed, were their subordinate positions. In Ivory Coast, for example, 'Natives were not tolerated in hotels run by Europeans. In the stores, counters for coloured customers were well separated from European counters.'[1] Summary

[1] d'Aby, op. cit., p. 44.

executions for suspected sabotage were not unusual; only Africans were executed for resistance to Vichy.[1] Racial discrimination under Vichy affected the African 'citizens' as well. An amusing illustration was the requirement that Africans, presumably 'citizens', had to sign declarations stating that they were not Jews. 'As if they could not see,' remarked Lamine Guèye.[2] By comparison with metropolitan soldiers, colonial soldiers had lower salaries, stricter discipline and fewer material benefits. Their anger was expressed at Tiaroye, Senegal, where they rioted, in December 1944. Many were killed before order was restored, and the case of the Tiaroye veterans became an item in the long list of African post-war grievances.[3]

The educated Africans pointed to the discrepancy between the promises of assimilation and the reality of conditions in Africa. The fall of France, the change-over to Vichy, and the further change to the Free French profoundly affected their belief in the power of France. 'It was hard to know on which side true patriotism lay.' Ivory Coast notables, accustomed to sending dutiful messages of loyalty to the French government, sent a note to Pétain which labelled the Allied landing in North Africa an 'unqualified aggression'.[4] Generally, however, educated Africans favoured the cause of de Gaulle, at least in part because the local Europeans, preoccupied with French authority and prestige, were generally pro-Vichy. At the same time, educated Africans learned of events in Asia, Europe, and elsewhere, and gathered determination to force changes. Their daily contact with the misery of their relations in the countryside helped keep this determination fresh.

Their Ties

The educated Africans had formed some associations before and during the war. Some of these associations were the 'anodyne pre-war groupings' whose object was recreation, sport, African history and art, and carefully apolitical education.[5] Most organizations of this type, where permitted by officials, had to be patronized by French citizens; all were closely controlled. Politics were forbidden and violations of this rule led to swift official reprisal. African civil servants who proved mildly disturbing to the administration were transferred to posts isolated in the Mauretanian or Niger desert. Nevertheless, most of these organizations either directly, through discreetly conducted discussions, or indirectly provided regular channels of communication among educated Africans on political matters.

[1] Senghor's speech at the Annual Congress of the French SFIO, 20 March 1947, reprinted in *l'A.O.F.*, 2 May 1947. Richard-Molard, op. cit., p. 166.
[2] J.O.A.N.C. I, *Débats*, 22 March 1946, p. 998.   [3] *L'A.O.F.*, June 1947.
[4] Both citations from d'Aby, op. cit., p. 42.   [5] d'Aby, op. cit., p. 36.

These associations were safety-valves for discontent among the educated, similar in function to religious or economic protest movements among villagers in the same period. The performance among the elite of an historical play, based on the resistance of the warrior chiefs Samory Touré or al Hajj Umar Tall to European penetration, was comparable to the ceremonial retelling of the same story by the *griots* at village celebrations.

Prior to 1945, these associations provided the only modern political training ground for educated Africans. When the first African elections were suddenly called in 1945, these organizations either became the nuclei of political parties, or furnished the candidates for office. Their historical importance is reason for examining them rather more closely.

There were urban cultural associations: the *Foyer France-Sénégal* in Dakar; the fluctuating Dahomey coastal creole groups, publishing newspapers like the *Voix du Dahomey* since the end of the First World War;[1] *Art et Travail*,[2] *Espérance*,[3] and *Foyer du Soudan*[4] in Soudan; the *Association de Défense des Intérêts des Autochtones de la Côte d'Ivoire*, the *Union Fraternelle des Originaires de la Côte d'Ivoire*, and the *Association Fraternelle des Originaires de la Haute Volta* in Abidjan. There were in most territories regional and ethnic groups, usually led by an uneasy alliance of the chiefs and the educated. Some flourished in Ivory Coast: the *Idéal* among the Malinke Muslim peoples of Odienné, in 1949–51 was used as the basis for the *Entente des Indépendants de la Côte d'Ivoire*, a party supported by the administration against the RDA;[5] the *Association des Originaires de Gagnoa* among the Bete, was later the basis of the small Socialist nucleus in Ivory Coast.[6] Similar groups were in Dahomey: the *Groupement Ethnique du Nord Dahomey* was the basis of the *Movement Démocratique du Dahomey* (later *Rassemblement Démocratique du Dahomey*), the party in northern Dahomey which supported President Hubert Maga; while the *Groupement des Fon d'Abomey* became one of the *comités électoraux* which organized the *constituante* elections in Dahomey, and later joined the *Union Progressiste Dahoméenne*.

---

[1] See Garigue, Philip. 'Changing Political Leadership in West Africa', *Africa*, vol. xxiv, no. 3, Oxford University Press, London, July 1954, pp. 228 f.

[2] Led by Modibo Keïta, Ponty graduate, teacher, secretary-general of the *Union Soudanaise* (RDA); in 1956 Soudan deputy to the French National Assembly; in 1961 President of Mali.

[3] Led by Fodé Touré, a Guinean, one of the very few pre-war African lawyers, senator from Guinea in 1955.

[4] Led by Mamadou Konaté, teacher, Ponty graduate, from 1946 RDA deputy from Soudan (d. 1956).

[5] *Annex 11348*, tome ii, op. cit., p. 463.   [6] Ibid., p. 465.

The graduates of mission schools maintained cultural and social activities in organizations like the Catholic *A·sociation des Anciens Seminaristes* of Ouagadougou, or its Dahomey counterpart. Rudimentary professional organizations also existed. As early as 1933, an African trader tried to organize the Ivory Coast African planters to defend their interests. But the authorities joined their disapproval to that of the European settlers, and the organization gave few other signs of life than the name *Cooperative des Planteurs de la Côte d'Ivoire*.[1] Eleven years later, in 1944, the far more successful *Syndicat Agricole Africain* came into existence, and gave birth to the Ivory Coast RDA. Benefit and friendly societies existed among African civil servants, such as the *Mutuelle des Fonctionnaires* in Ouagadougou. After November 1942 there were also the various patriotic resistance associations: in Ivory Coast, *Croix de Lorraine* and *Combat*. Europeans anxious to cleanse themselves of Vichy associations joined these groups more eagerly than African civil servants, who joined only because pressed to do so, and left as soon as racial lines between Africans and Europeans were tightly drawn during the municipal elections in August 1945.[2] The *Comités d'Études Franco-Africaine* (CEFA) in Dakar, Abidjan, Bobo-Dioulasso and Bouake belonged to the same 'patriotic' category, though by 1946, most CEFAs were dominated by Communist sympathizers.

For the most part, these associations existed as separate territorial entities, and had few relations with similar organizations in other territories. In addition, modern channels of communication among the African elite in the various territories existed prior to 1945, which later facilitated the creation of interterritorial parties—above all, of the *Rassemblement Démocratique Africain*. These links were of three related types, based on the state schools, the civil service, and the activities of the French Communist Party.

The officially recognized *Association des Anciens Élèves et Amis de l'École William-Ponty* was not itself very significant. From 1939 on, Ponty graduates had sought official permission to found this Association. No doubt because Ponty graduates were regarded as potentially dangerous agitators, permission was not granted until 1944. The statutes were accepted by the administration, on condition there be no professional trade union, political, and religious activities or discussions.[3] The Association had to be patronized by 'numerous high officials; its cradle was filled with so many flowers that it became a tomb'.[4]

---

[1] d'Aby, op. cit., pp. 110–11.
[2] d'Aby, op. cit., p. 42; *Climats*, 27 December 1955, no. 496.
[3] A brief history is given in *Genèse*, op. cit., pp. 3–7.
[4] Dadié, 'Misère de l'enseignement en A.O.F.', op. cit., p. 60.

Ponty ties which later proved politically significant were informal. They had their source in the modest aims which led the Guinea Fulani students, for example, to create the *Voix du Montagnard*, to help each other with their studies, leisure activities, finance, exploration of African history, with 'overcoming their shyness'. This little ethnic association was the basis of the Guinea *Amicale Gilbert Vieillard*, created in 1943 to 'modernize the Fouta Djallon'.[1] The *Amicale* became the nucleus of the Guinea Socialist party, which in turn could never overcome its exclusive ethnic origins and appeal to all Guineans.

Other politically significant ties had their origins in the informal personal and group relations among the Ponty students. From among the Ponty graduates, came most of the post-war *parlementaires* and a very large proportion of the rival post-war party leaders. Underlying their temporary post-war differences of party loyalty, was a basic identity of outlook. At Ponty, students took pride as Africans—not merely as Bambara or Baule tribesmen, as Senegalese or as Ivory Coasters—when a colleague distinguished himself as a scholar, artist, or sportsman. A large proportion of these outstanding Ponty graduates assumed party office within the RDA. The first in a class was called *major*; his standing among his peers was comparable with that of a man who has a 'first' from Oxford. Interterritorial political director Ouëzzin Coulibaly (d. 1958) was a *major* at Ponty; so were Guinea RDA leader Diallo Sayfoulaye and Ambassador Diallo Telli and Mali RDA leader Modibo Keïta. The respect which their future political opponents acquired towards them at Ponty, remained strong even during periods of intense political rivalry.

Underlying the post-war political controversies among educated leaders—in addition to their common intellectual background—was a fund of intimate common personal experiences. That at Ponty an RDA leader saved the life of an IOM man; that as students RDA Ivory Coast leaders learned to have confidence in the integrity of a *Progressiste* leader,[2] facilitated the quick transfer of partisan loyalties which occurred periodically among French West African party leaders after the war. Since 1956, for example, the dominant mass parties absorbed smaller former rival parties in the various territories, many parties merged, or changed names and forms of organization. Rival educated leaders—who only recently spoke of and acted harshly, even violently towards each other—became allies. The illiterate supporters of these post-war leaders, however, found speedy transfer of support from one party to another far more difficult to

---

[1] Citations from interviews in 1956, Conakry.
[2] *Parti Progressiste de la Côte d'Ivoire.*

achieve. They had no common intellectual background or experiences; their party loyalty was shaped largely by their loyalty to their ethnic unit or sub-unit. For many villagers, for example, the choice of membership in a particular party was largely determined by the fact that their group's traditional enemies supported a rival party. When educated party rivals became reconciled, their rural supporters were frequently unable to do the same, and remained divided by the controversies—about kinship, land, water supply, cattle, religion and so forth—which had contributed to their initial choice of parties.

On these occasions, some educated African leaders used with great skill the intellectual tools—partly derived from their modern studies, and little developed in traditional modes of thought—which enabled them to acquire 'objective knowledge of the forces determining their social organization and actuating their social behaviour'.[1] They used this knowledge in order to build parties capable of harmonizing historic differences, and of embracing wider social units than had existed previously. The most successful mass party leaders both analyzed and devised party methods to strengthen the points which hostile villagers or illiterate townsmen had in common. Mainly within regional and ethnic parties, however, some educated African leaders did not hesitate to employ techniques which they knew reinforced traditional enmities.

Like Ponty, the lower state schools, whether vocational or not, also instilled African, as against ethnic values and links, and equipped students with the tools which they used to build analytical knowledge of their own societies. The political importance of the Bamako upper primary school, Terrasson de Fougères, and the Conakry vocational École Georges Croiret was illustrated when the products became the founders and leaders of the Soudan and Guinea sections of the RDA.[2]

While the state schools helped to weaken ethnic and historical antagonism, they also created new cleavages among the educated elite. Many of the pupils of the lower secondary and upper primary schools had themselves competed for scarce Ponty places. Bitter competition and rigid discipline meant that many failed, and resented those who succeeded. This resentment of the less towards the more educated later acquired political importance in some territories. In Guinea, where Ponty graduates had little alternative but administrative politics, most joined the various officially sanctioned regional and ethnic political groups. Therefore with very few exceptions, the Guinea RDA was led by products of the lower state schools, who

---

[1] Fortes, M. and E. Evans-Pritchard. *African Political Systems*, Oxford University Press, London, 1940, p. 17.
[2] For substantiating evidence, see Appendix VIII, 'education'.

accuséd the Ponty graduates of betraying the masses, and called them the valets of the administration. In Ivory Coast, however, Ponty graduates took the lead in the RDA, as well as in rival parties. There the RDA Ponty graduates found alternatives to administrative employment in farming. In Soudan, Ponty graduates also took the lead in the two most important rival parties, usually in the *Parti Progressiste Soudanais* if they were the clients or kinsmen of officially recognized chiefs, and in the RDA if they were not.[1] Consequently the resentment of the less towards the more educated in Ivory Coast and Soudan never assumed political importance comparable to that in Guinea. This group resentment can be compared to the attitude of the 'Standard VII Boys' who built the CPP of Ghana.[2]

The second kind of territorial and interterritorial ties were among Africans in the civil service, composed essentially of graduates of state schools. According to French practice, the civil servants were frequently transferred from one territory to another. They thus gained wide experience of the Federation's problems, and built up relationships and common interests which made them a relatively cosmopolitan group. The growing tendency of the mobile civil servants to think federally, rather than territorially or ethnically did not, however, have much influence on politics at the grass roots. An unusually large proportion of the pre-war civil service posts were held by educated Senegalese, but their attempt to plant socialist parties outside of Senegal was unsuccessful even though they were sometimes helped by French civil servants. There were no obvious political consequences to the fact that many Dahomeans also held civil service posts outside their territory. Senegalese, Dahomeans, and others, when they were 'strangers', depended for political status outside of their territories upon the support of the indigenous territorial politicians. This was even more true for the mulatto civil servants, who as pre-war 'citizens' occasionally achieved high administrative posts. At the grass roots level, *militants* often accused Senegalese, Dahomeans and other 'strangers' of having acquired positions and values which separated them from the masses.

The educated civil servants who had the greatest post-war popular political success were the native educated Africans; the clerks, Ponty trained medical assistants, and most important, teachers. More teachers were members of party executives and representative assemblies, than men of any other single occupation.[3] Teachers had the advantage of close contact with the people. The teachers began

[1] For supporting statistics, see Figure 7, p. 278.
[2] Apter, David. *The Gold Coast in Transition*, Princeton University Press, Princeton, 1955, p. 167.
[3] See Appendix VIII, 'professions', for supporting statistics.

to think in federal terms and to develop a strong sense of their collective interests as early as 1937, when they formed the first French-speaking West African trade union, led by Ouëzzin Coulibaly (d. 1958) and Mamadou Konaté (d. 1956). The ties which linked civil servants across territorial frontiers naturally affected parties at the level of leadership, rather than of local organization. The African civil servants who became successful RDA leaders in the various territories knew and had confidence in their professional colleagues in other territories. This facilitated the expansion of the RDA from one territory to another. It also led many RDA native leaders to use their authority to secure acceptance of 'strangers' as RDA leaders or candidates.[1] For example, the RDA controlled territorial assembly of Ivory Coast elected the former administrator Gabriel d'Arboussier, a mulatto, councillor of the French Union in 1947. In 1957, the RDA of Niger elected him territorial councillor and grand councillor.[2] Ivory Coast between 1946 and 1957 elected a native of Upper Volta, Ouëzzin Coulibaly, deputy twice and senator once. To a lesser extent, the same generalization could be made about the Senegalese BPS leaders. In 1957 one Senegalese Minister was Mê Boissier-Palun, a mulatto from Dahomey, and the first vice-president of the Senegalese Territorial Assembly was Mê André Guillabert, also a mulatto.

The French Communists

The third kind of modern territorial and interterritorial links were created by the French Communists. Before the war, a handful of Left-wing organizations existed in France, in which Africans met with Negroes from other parts of the world, and with French marxists, especially Communists. The *Ligue de la Défense de la Race Nègre* was probably the most influential of these; as early as 1930, publications of the *Ligue* were seized by the police at Grand Popo, Dimbroko and Grand Bassam.[3] Other organizations were the *Centre de Liaison Anti-impérialist*, founded in 1939; the *Union des Travailleurs Nègres*; the *Comité Universel de l'Institut Nègre de Paris*; and the *Rassemblement des Peuples Colonisés*. The first president of the *Rassemblement*, in 1937, was the Algerian nationalist, Messali Hadj. These ephemeral groups in Paris left some traces in Africa, especially on these who read the occasional publications. Their influence was indirect, however, for in French West Africa all but a few Senegalese 'citizens' were locally educated, and had very little contact with the political or intellectual life of Paris until after 1945.

[1] See Appendix VIII, 'ethnic origins', for supporting figures.
[2] After the referendum he became a deputy in Senegal's National Assembly, and after independence, Senegal's first Minister of Justice.
[3] *L'Ami du Peuple*, 24 February 1930.

Far more important were the ties which the Communists built in Africa, in the *Groupe Social* of Senegal organized during Popular Front days, and in many other territories during and immediately after the war. These ties were based primarily upon the schools, the civil service, African urban organizations, and to some extent the colonial armed forces. Initially these ties were the scaffolding for the interterritorial RDA and the trade union movement. Since the Popular Front, French Communists, 'progressives' and their sympathizers had taken jobs in the administration, as teachers, technicians, and officers of the colonial military regiments.[1] Among the schools where Communists taught were Ponty and the upper primary and vocational schools of Dakar, Conakry and Bamako. French Communists worked among the colonial sailors stationed in Senegal. From these posts, the Communists befriended the men they considered potential leaders from among the educated Africans. The Communists won the trust of Africans by behaving in ways that Africans had never seen Europeans behave. They were personal friends and comrades, rather than superiors; they taught political ideas and doctrines which strongly attracted Africans who had had little access to any acceptable alternative political education.

The Communists encouraged the formation of *Groupes d'Études Communistes* (GEC). Immediately after the French West African administration became responsible to the provisional de Gaulle government at the end of 1943, GEC's flourished in Dakar, Abidjan, Conakry, Bamako and, for a brief time, existed in Bobo-Dioulasso.[2] The GECs, 'although not organisms of the French Communist Party, nevertheless had direct links with it, and organized the Communist elements living in tropical Africa'. A restricted number of Africans, under the guidance of French Communists, studied 'Marxist–Leninism'. The writers studied were principally Russian or French. The writings of Asian Communists, not to mention Asian nationalists, received little attention. The GECs also considered 'the social, economic, and political situation of the territory', and 'a common strategy and tactics for fighting against colonialism within the mass

---

[1] The names of some are cited in *Le Rassemblement Démocratique Africain dans la lutte anti-impérialiste*, pamphlet printed at Impressions Rapides, Paris, *c.* 1948, p. 63. (Henceforth cited as RDA 1948 pamphlet.) Among the French Communists were M. and Mme. Faure, M. and Mme. Gérard Cauche, M. Suret-Canale in Dakar; Governor Latrille's *chef de cabinet* Lambert, and Philippe Franceschi, elected senator from Ivory Coast in 1948; teachers Morlet and Fayette in Bamako.

[2] From mimeographed report by RDA secretary-general Gabriel d'Arboussier to the RDA Co-ordinating Committee, 12 April 1949, p. 16. In Bobo-Dioulasso, a French Trotskyist, Mê Robert Bailhache, exercised personal influence,

organizations (political, trade union, cultural, &c. . . .) of the territory'.[1]

In French-speaking West Africa, as in other underdeveloped areas the Communists faced the problem of leadership; they recognized that for the most part the modern elite was the 'national Bourgeoisie'.[2] The position taken in the GECs was that

The cadres of the movement will necessarily have to be furnished largely by the intellectuals who have risen out of tribal and feudal cadres. It is necessary to take into account the preponderant influence which these leaders exercise on the African masses; without them, it would be difficult, and in many cases even impossible, to penetrate the masses or even have access to them. . . . It remains for the workers, peasants and honest intellectuals to remain at the base of the movement. Once the masses are reached, we must organize them and eventually lead them away from the tribal and feudal leaders who are hesitant; when necessary we must force these leaders to obey pressure from the masses.[3]

The French Communists opposed the immediate creation of an African Communist party and cited Stalin's *Colonialism and the National Question* to explain that in a country where the national bourgeoisie has not yet divided into revolutionary and conciliatory wings, the task of the Communist elements is to create a single national front against imperialism. They explained further that

If there is no Communist Party in tropical Africa, this is no index of a lack of confidence in the African Communists; this is not because Africans are not sufficiently *évolués* and educated to be able to organize a Communist Party. This is simply because such a party would not suit the kind of battle which the Communists have to wage at present in tropical Africa.[4]

There were several less publicized reasons. First, the French Communists did not think the limited Marxist education and experience of African GEC members sufficient for the creation of an African party. The few Africans judged ready for membership cards were allowed to join the French CP. The French Communists never stated that they expected Africans eventually to have a separate party. On the contrary, their words implied that they expected Africans and Europeans to continue working within a single party, controlled from Paris. Second, the French Communists knew and

[1] From mimeographed by-laws of the GEC of Dakar.
[2] Vernon McKay in 'Communist Exploitation of Anti-Colonialism and Nationalism in Africa', *The Threat of Soviet Imperialism*, C. Grove Haines, ed., Baltimore, the Johns Hopkins Press, 1954, pp. 259–60.
[3] Senegalese GEC course No. 2, mimeographed, 1947.
[4] Ibid.

favoured only their own slow centralized methods for building a Communist party. But they did not want to follow this process exclusively, for fear of losing precious opportunities to lead in post-war Africa. Thus they hoped through the GECs to inculcate French CP techniques and ideological standards, and to attract the loyalty of the most able African leaders. They hoped that these Africans would in turn influence, and eventually dominate, the nascent modern mass organizations. Third, they were aware of African sensitivity to European control. Most African GEC members did not hesitate to state their desire to run their own affairs, and to point out that the French Communists were woefully ignorant of African political conditions. The French Communists tried to counter latent 'nationalist deviation' by arguing that colonialism was the source of African misery, that the trusts caused colonialism, that the trusts were powerful because of their position in France, that consequently the only sensible course for Africans was to ally with the French Communists, who attacked the trusts in France.[1] They also used another, more sophisticated argument. They claimed that if France were to leave immediately, economically backward Africa would but fall victim to British or American imperialism. This would be far worse than French imperialism, for in Britain and America the 'democratic progressive forces' were 'particularly feeble'. The powerful French 'democratic movement', however, could help to emancipate Africa.[2] The French Communists also hoped that the formally unattached, educational framework of the GECs would help to overcome African sensitivity to outside direction, and thus hasten their acceptance of the French Communist position.

French Communist action influenced the origin of African parties in numerous ways. By organizing and indoctrinating some of the most able African leaders, the GECs left an imprint on African political terminology. By teaching the duties of the vanguard of the revolution, the Communists deepened the sense of mission to lead the masses which many educated Africans already had. By familiarizing Africans with developments elsewhere, through press, missions, courses, discussions, conference, and opportunities for travel, the Communists increased African awareness of international events. Travel included African attendance at French and international political, peace, trade union, youth, student, women's, and other conferences. By teaching about Communist forms of organization

---

[1] The argument is reproduced from GEC 1947 course, op. cit. The same point is made in R. Barbé's circulars 41 and 55 to the GECs. Barbé was the member of the French CP's Central Committee in charge of colonial questions. He became a member of the Assembly of the French Union in 1947.
[2] GEC 1947 course, op. cit.

and political action, the French Communists influenced the structural forms of the African parties, especially the RDA. In France, the Communists drew as many of the elected African representatives as they could into study courses, some at the École des Cadres. By reporting facts and opinions and urging identical policies, the Communists hastened the process of consolidation and co-ordination of the geographically scattered modern African associations. They also did this by training GEC members to work simultaneously, or in turn, in parties, trade unions, youth, and other organizations.

This GEC practice of rotating leaders as conditions demanded, was well suited to dealing with the fluid characteristics of modern African associations in 1945. The associations frequently changed names; there was brisk competition as men who had been peers sorted themselves out into of some sort of a hierarchy. Rivals negotiated almost continually with each other, and with the representatives of the numerous existing ethnic groups; frequently the lines separating the members of one organization from those of another were hardly perceptible. The Communists encouraged the existing scattered African organizations to unify into a 'single national anti-imperialist front', soon baptised the RDA. The absolute amount of aid was not great. But not much was needed to make a difference. Previously there had been a void. Subsidized stencils, typewriters, and mimeographing machines made possible the wide circulation of documents, issued both from Paris Communist headquarters and locally, and dealing with territorial, French and international questions. By 1946, the RDA newspaper *Réveil* was printed in Dakar, one of the first African party papers.[1] That the RDA founding Congress took place in October 1946, less than a year after the first African elections were held, was at least partly due to Communist resources and to the Communist supported system of communication.

In three other ways, the French Communists influenced African parties in their formative stages, but indirectly also contributed to the subsequent African rejection of French Communist tutelage. First, by preaching the need for solidarity between the 'oppressed colonial peoples and the working classes of France', the French Communists opposed, and thus postponed the growth of African pro-independence nationalism. Instead, so long as the French Communist party wanted to appear to be like other parties in France—which worked within the French parliamentary and party system

---

[1] In Paris, the glossy propaganda journal *l'Afrique* was sporadically published. The French Communist press, which circulated in Africa, carried comments on colonial affairs, e.g. R. Barbé's 'Les Problèmes de l'Union française' and 'Où va l'Union française?', published in the October 1946 and May 1947 issues of *Cahiers du Communisme*.

—they urged African support for the French Constitution and the French Union.

> There exists in France a powerful democratic movement; thanks to the alliance of the progressive forces of the metropole with those from overseas, the present Constitution was voted, which contains undeniable progressive elements. . . . These acquired gains are not negligible, and Africans should use them by waging their fight against imperialism through fighting for the preservation and the application of the principles of the Constitution. This is why the Communists of Africa favour the maintenance and implementation of the French Union within the framework of the Constitution.[1]

This stand, and the Communist declaration that African emancipation could result only when France was controlled by the Communists, contained the implied major premise that the interests of the French CP took precedence over the interests of African political organizations. Second, by encouraging their African sympathizers to consider traitors those who opposed the Communists, the French CP for a time superimposed on Africa the divisions of French and international politics. This meant that Africans, still struggling to create a measure of unity among different, often quarrelling ethnic and religious groups, had to deal locally with another, imported source of conflict. Lastly, the Communist connexions of African leaders lent substance to the charges by French colonial officials that the anticolonial movement in Africa was Communist inspired. Subsequent history showed the fact was rather that the French Communists were benefiting from, and trying to catch up with, existing African postwar unrest.

The Impact of Reforms

The many changes taking place right after Liberation in administrative practice, in the economy and in the institutional framework stimulated rather than reduced unrest and political activity in French West Africa. Purges of Vichy supporters led to a break in the continuity of French administrative practice, and increased African awareness of instability within France. New men who rose through the Resistance movement took over high posts. An example was the nomination in 1943 of Ivory Coast Governor Latrille, whose policies in favour of the African rather than European planters were unprecedented. Partial resumption of international trade and transport meant that people again travelled, farmers earned money, traders recommenced their rounds. News and ideas travelled more freely. The presence of some American Negro troops in Dakar aroused lively interest. African war veterans returned to the towns and villages, and

[1] GEC 1947 course, op. cit.

recounted their experiences abroad. Though the number was considerably less than the 173,000 who had served in the First World War,[1] nevertheless quite a few had been abroad. In 1938 there were 30,000 in France, Syria, and North Africa and 15,000 in tropical Africa; in 1939 a special draft added 12,000 more.[2] Upon their return many were disinclined to follow the lead of village or cantonal chiefs.

The reforms resulting from the Brazzaville recommendations of 1944[3] raised African expectations, and increased the tempo of African political activities. This rather than relief of the accumulated tension, was the immediate result of the reform of the *indigénat*;[4] the end to the worst abuses of racial discrimination;[5] wider permission to organize trade unions and the creation of minimum standards for African workers;[6] the measure of freedom of assembly which permitted the creation of political organization;[7] the plan for the progressive elimination of forced labour; the proposed expansion of educational facilities.

The reforms, particularly the introduction of elections in Africa, precipitated the creation of parties.[8] The new representative institutions offered incentives which, though restricted and at first imperfectly understood, allowed African discontent to crystallize through party forms. The likelihood of violence was reduced as the holding of elections encouraged African leaders to express their grievances and achieve their ends with legal rather than clandestine underground movements. Partly before and specially after 1955, when officials relatively honestly administered elections, the reforms made possible fairly orderly transfer of political power to educated Africans who had some popular support. The transfer took place soon after, or while mass parties were forming.

This does not mean, of course, that the reforms caused the forces which crystallized into parties. Though, as French African institutions became progressively more Africanized and elections took place frequently, these became in turn stimuli to which African

[1] Delafosse, Maurice. 'L'Afrique Occidentale Française', in Hanotaux, Gabriel and Alfred Martineau, *Histoire des colonies françaises et de l'expansion de la France dans le monde*, tome iv, Société de l'Histoire Nationale, Plon, Paris, 1931, p. 351.
[2] Devèze, op. cit., p. 62. For a brief description of the role of ex-servicemen in Ghana, see Nkrumah, Kwame, *Ghana: The Autobiography of Kwame Nkrumah*, Thomas Nelson and Sons, Ltd., London, 1957, p. 76.
[3] See p. 69.
[4] Decree of 17 July 1944, and decrees of 22 December 1945 and 20 February 1946.
[5] Decree of 7 January 1944 (before the Brazzaville conference).
[6] Decree of 7 August 1944.   [7] Decree of 11 April 1945.
[8] See Coleman, James S., 'The Emergence of African Political Parties', in *Africa Today*, C. Grove Haines, ed., Johns Hopkins Press, Baltimore, 1955, pp. 225 f.

political organizations responded. On the whole, however, times of elections or institutional change coincided only partly with the periods of extraordinary social and political stress and activity in French tropical Africa. During these waves of political action— 1944–6 in most territories, 1948–51 in Ivory Coast and Senegal, 1954–6 in Guinea, 1956–9 in most territories—mass parties were usually reorganized and strengthened, though not necessarily born. The reforms prior to independence were adopted according to a French political timetable, while the waves of political activity in French Africa were produced, increasingly, by dynamics of African politics.

The elections not only channelled, they also synchronized political developments in territories where political pressure was unequal. In all the territories the first elections encouraged the rapid formation of small electoral groups aiming at filling the new offices from among their ranks. Yet Mauretania, Niger, and some parts of Upper Volta could have been and in some respects were ruled in the old paternal way some years after 1945. Elections there since 1945 certainly accelerated the formation of parties. On the other hand Senegal and Ivory Coast were in 1945 on the brink of popular explosion. There the elections also encouraged the formation of small electoral groups, but certainly did not cause the growth of new mass political movements. These already existed; the elections legalized them, and accelerated their transformation into political parties.

The reforms also strengthened the position of educated Africans in their bid for political leadership. Their bid to lead, however, had deeper causes. A consequence of colonial rule was the decline of traditional African rulers, whose power was undercut by European laws, soldiers, and administrators. The new boundaries of the territories and *cercles* took no account of the boundaries of traditional political units. The existence of official chiefs complicated issues of succession in each locality. Tribesmen found it to their advantage to seek the help of educated kinsmen rather than chiefs over matters which brought them into contact with the European administration. Increasingly people respected the educated minority. The decline of chiefs and the rise of a new educated group of leaders had been taking place since the start of European rule.[1] The reforms, by their nature, order and duration reinforced the process by making it possible for educated Africans to institutionalize their position of leadership.

[1] A fascinating picture of the many forces which led to the disintegration of traditional authority in Guinea is found in Territoire de la Guinée Française, *Conférence des commandants de cercle*, Conakry, 25–27 July 1957, Imprimerie du Gouvernement, 1957.

Most people agreed that Africans who expected to participate effectively in French or French inspired institutions needed some French education. One of the main criticisms made of the candidacy of Tenga Ouëdraogo, in the Constituent Assembly elections in Ivory Coast of 1945, was 'his almost total ignorance of the French language, which hardly qualified him to participate usefully . . . in the debates'.[1] (He was a functionary at the court of the Morho Naba, the officially designated paramount chief of the Mossi. He lost.) Furthermore, the new offices were open to all; none were reserved for the chiefs; only Europeans had for a time some reserved places. This is not to say that the status a man had in traditional society had no relevance for his status in the modern parties. In French Africa, as in other similarly rapidly changing societies, some of the most effective political leaders were those who derived or appeared to derive their position both from the traditional and modern systems. One example was Sékou Touré, a descendant of the warrior king Samory Touré whose campaigns were stopped by French military operations at the turn of the century.[2]

The voting system also helped to institutionalize the position of leadership of educated Africans. The limited franchise of 1945 restricted the immediate organizing task of parties. Few African leaders saw this restriction, however, as other than temporary. They saw it as the not very satisfactory appetizer for the universal franchise which became law in 1957. The limited franchise, moreover, was heavily weighted in favour of the towns. Those allowed to vote, by the ordinance of 22 August 1945, included 'veterans, those who had French decorations or distinctions, those who had school certificates higher than and including the primary school certificate, chiefs of ethnic groups, members of unions or professional groups and civil servants'.[3] As the franchise broadened in 1951, the majority of voters shifted from town to countryside. Then, at least partly because of administrative encouragement, traditional and neo-traditional leaders seemed for a time to assume more significant modern roles. Yet subsequent history showed their position was continually declining.

While strengthening the political position of the educated Africans, the reforms also made it their task to explain to their illiterate countrymen the vote, the choice it implied, and the concept of representation. So began a process of modern political education, democratic in form, of the whole African population. With elections came a steady accumulation of political experience—on a scale wider than

[1] d'Aby, op. cit., p. 56.
[2] For more details, see Appendix VIII, 'ethnic status'.
[3] Devèze, op. cit., pp. 219-20.

the traditional tribal unit—and growing acceptance for the idea that power must rest on renewed, expressed popular consent. Repeated elections maintained political activities at a high level. 'The result was an unprecedented political awakening, a mobilization of groups previously untouched and inert.'[1]

[1] Coleman. 'The Emergence of African Political Parties', op. cit., p. 240.

PART TWO

French Policy and African Institutions*

Pre-War Precedents

FRENCH colonial reforms in 1946 sprang from a genuine desire to make the lot of West Africans under the Fourth Republic better than it had been. After Liberation, Africans received French citizenship, representation in metropolitan institutions, some personal and political rights, and a measure of local autonomy. Striking by its absence was any legal provision for eventual African independence. The ideas and experiences behind this feature of French post-war reforms lay in the pre-war policy towards West Africa.

French colonial policy under the Third Republic oscillated between two formulae, commonly termed 'assimilation' and 'association'. By assimilation was meant 'the fiction by which the colonies were treated as parts of France';[1] 'as such, their economic relationship with France and with other French colonies, their constitutional position and their administrative organization were to be identical with those of any part of France itself.'[2] This formula, the ideal of the French Left, had its roots in the idea of the French Revolution, that 'all men are equal by nature and before the law'.[3] In theory the people of the French colonies were to be treated as Frenchmen: this presupposed that they were educated like Frenchmen. Assimilation and French education have always been entwined. French colonizers in Africa did not produce an obvious 'colour line', as did the British. Instead, Frenchmen drew a 'culture line'; limited access to French education made the 'culture line' not very different in practice from the 'colour line'.

In West Africa, the pre-war formula of assimilation was the official policy only with respect to the inhabitants of the four old communes of Senegal (Dakar, Rufisque, Gorée and Saint-Louis) who were made 'citizens' of France in 1848.[4] To French republicans,

---

* I owe a great debt to the pioneer studies by Professor Kenneth E. Robinson (see Bibliography) and could hardly have written Part Two without them.
[1] Thomson, David. *Democracy in France*, O.U.P., London, 1952, p. 165.
[2] Robinson, 'The Public Law of Overseas France Since the War', op. cit., p. 1.
[3] Article 3, Declaration of the Rights of Man, 1793, *Les Constitutions . . . de la France depuis 1789*, Librairie de Droit et de Jurisprudence, Paris, 1952, p. 62.
[4] Thiam, Doudou. *La Portée de la citoyenneté française dans les territoires d'outre-*

citizenship meant representation in Paris. Senegal briefly had one representative in the Constituent and Legislative Assemblies of the Second Republic (1848). Since 1875, one seat in the French Chamber of Deputies was continuously occupied by a representative of the old Senegalese 'citizens'.[1] Citizenship also meant that measure of self government which the French *étatist* centralizing tradition— meaning 'the subordination of local decisions to the agreement of state officials'[2]—permitted at the local level. The 'citizens' of Senegal elected representatives to govern the four *communes de plein exercice* since 1872,[3] and to deliberate in the territorial *conseil général* since 1879.[4] Citizenship entailed the additional rights to trial by French courts, to organize parties and other voluntary associations, to travel freely, to hold higher civil service posts.

The policy of association responded to the problems posed by the rapid expansion of the French Empire, by conquest and treaty, under the Third Republic. France acquired vast areas, including most of tropical Africa, and assimilation became obviously impractical. To the supporters of the French Right, association meant domination, the subordination to French interests of lands and peoples considered inferior.[5] To the supporters of the French Left, including the Socialists, Communists and Radicals, assimilation remained the ideal, and association meant 'varying degrees of concessions to existing conditions'.[6]

What did association mean for West Africans? Before 1946, out-side of the four old communes Africans were not 'citizens' but 'subjects' of France. 'Their political influence in the general system was nil.'[7] 'Subjects' had no right of representation in metropolitan institutions, no access to higher posts in the civil service, no right to organize voluntary associations. The administration could levy them

---

mer. Société d'Éditions Africaines, Paris, 1953, pp. 99–104. Senegalese were briefly granted citizenship during the French Revolution, by the decree of the 16th pluviose, An II. See Guèye, *Étapes et perspectives . . .*, op. cit., pp. 21–30.
[1] Deschamps, Hubert. *Méthodes et doctrines coloniales de la France*, Armand Colin, Paris, 1953, pp. 107–8.
[2] Chapman, Brian. *Introduction to French Local Government*, Allen & Unwin Ltd., London, 1953, p. 219.
[3] Decrees of 10 August 1872, 12 June 1880, and 17 June 1887, modified by the decree of 9 April 1929. Rolland and Lampué, op. cit., p. 478. See also Guèye, op. cit., p. 32.
[4] Hailey, 1938, op. cit., pp. 197–8; and Buell, R. L., *The Native Problem in Africa*, New York, MacMillan, 2 vols., 1928, pp. 932 f. and 967 f.
[5] Deschamps, Hubert uses the formula 'non-assimilation' to describe the tendency I describe as association. *L'Union Française*, Berger-Levrault, Paris, 1952, p. 28.
[6] Robinson. 'The Public Law of Overseas France', op. cit., p. 1.
[7] Deschamps. *Méthodes et doctrines . . .*, op. cit., p. 140.

for goods or labour, and submitted them to a legal code, the *indigénat*, with traditions based on the rights of conquest rather than on French justice. In principle the Parliament of the Third Republic could legislate on colonial, as on all other French matters. It did so rarely, however, and most colonial questions were decided by French executive decree.[1] The French government appointed the governor-general of the West African federation, and the governors of the individual colonies. These officials controlled the French admini-strators, who ruled over the African 'subjects'.

In Africa, French citizenship did not imply legal equality for all, as it did in France. When compared with the 'subjects', the old 'citizens' of Senegal were a privileged oligarchy.[2] But their privileges were insecure and depended on continued French agreement. A single Senegalese deputy in the Paris Chamber, among more than five hundred others, could hardly hope to modify general French policy. He could hope only for more modest satisfactions; special treatment at official events, personal enrichment or concessions to faithful followers.

Senegalese deputies elected before 1914 were Europeans. The first African was Blaise Diagne, elected in 1914. He voted with the parties in the majority in the Chamber, and between 1917 and 1921 held, first the title *haut commissaire de l'ouest africain* and then *commissaire général des troupes noires*.[3] His job was to travel in Africa to recruit more soldiers for France during the First World War. Diagne's travels in Africa early in 1918 added 63,000 men to the French armed forces, making the total *tirailleurs sénégalais* at the disposal of France during the First World War 173,000. Partly as a reward for service rendered, he achieved a parliamentary confirma-tion of the principle that 'the natives of the four communes of Senegal and their descendants are and remain French citizens', known as the *loi Diagne*.[4] Nevertheless, in French courts controversy about interpreting the status of these African 'citizens' continued. Though subject to French public law, could they on matters of personal civil law, such as marriage or inheritance, adhere to their own customary law?[5] The matter was not settled until 1946. The minor concession to the wishes of the Senegalese 'citizens' contained

---

[1] Robinson. 'The Public Law of Overseas France', op. cit., p. 4.
[2] In 1936, there were 80,509 African 'citizens' and 14,621,000 African 'subjects' in French West Africa. Of these, 49,124 'citizens' and 1,640,500 'subjects' lived in Senegal. Haut Commissariat de l'AOF. *Annuaire Statistique de l'A.O.F.*, Édition 1949, tome i, Imprimerie Nationale, Paris, 1950, pp. 79 and 81.
[3] I am grateful to Thomas Cassilly and G. Wesley Johnson for the exact titles. See also Hailey, 1938, op. cit., p. 196.
[4] 29 September 1916.
[5] Thiam, op. cit., pp. 104–6; Rolland and Lampué, op. cit., p. 245.

in the *loi Diagne* remained practically the only liberal colonial decision made in Paris before the Popular Front coalition came to power.

The French political trend to the Left brought victory at the polls in 1936 to the constellation of parties ranging from the Radicals to the Communists. To the extent that they thought about the colonies, the supporters of these parties still held assimilation to be the ideal policy.[1] The parties of the Popular Front affected West Africa in many ways. They influenced the political thinking and activities of the younger African Senegalese 'citizens', who had received a modern French education. Africans who had the opportunity and the ability to scale the French educational ladder, to achieve not only the *baccalauréat* but better still a university *licence*, were accepted by many Frenchmen as one of themselves. Such a man was the young Lamine Guèye, who was the first French West African to obtain a doctorate of law from the University of Paris.[2] During his student days, Lamine Guèye became familiar with the intricacies of French political divisions. He studied the French republican tradition, as expounded by the evolutionary socialists. He hoped to find ways to raise the subordinate status of all Africans, and accepted as useful the assimilationist policy which had formed him. He then conceived the aim of true assimilation which motivated him for some thirty years. He urged the extension of citizenship to all Africans, hoping in this way to achieve equality between Frenchmen and Africans, as well as among Africans between 'citizens' and 'subjects'.

The goal of true assimilation inspired Lamine Guèye and some of his African 'citizen' friends to join with European supporters of the French Left resident in Dakar, and create in the late twenties the *Parti Socialiste Sénégalais*. The PSS was a purely Senegalese party, but the use of the term socialist indicated that for the first time the 'citizens' had selected a political label which had meaning in France to help them gain concessions from their French rulers. This process went even further. In 1936 Marius Moutet, a Socialist and a friend of Lamine Guèye, became Colonial Minister. Intent on giving

---

[1] 'Generally speaking, French Socialists in the French colonies (whether of native or of European origin) have remained faithful to the old democratic tradition of 1789 and approach the problem from the standpoint of the political assimilation of the natives to Europeans and the extension to them of equal civil and political rights with all French citizens.' Citation from the 1928 Third Congress of the Labour and Socialist International in Pickles, Dorothy. *French Politics*, Royal Institute of International Affairs, Oxford University Press, London, 1953, p. 150.
[2] Lamine Guèye's doctoral dissertation was entitled *De la situation politique des sénégalais originaires des communes de plein exercice, telle qu'elle résulte des lois des 19 octobre 1915, 29 septembre 1916, et de la jurisprudence antérieure*, La Vie Universitaire, Paris, 1921.

some real content to the formula of assimilation, he travelled to
Senegal in September and October 1936. Two months afterwards,
the founding congress of the SFIO[1] federation of Senegal took place.
Lamine Guèye became the political director of this, the only tropical
African branch of any French party.

The Popular Front affected not only the old 'citizens'; but also
the African 'subjects'. Government decisions liberalized the conditions for African access to French citizenship and made it possible
for a small number of educated African 'subjects' to become citizens;[2] extended a modified form of trade union rights to Africa;[3]
there was talk of abolishing forced labour and reforming the indigénat.[4] Perhaps the most far-reaching consequence for Africans of
the French Popular Front was the change in the political views of
the Frenchmen who went to Africa. Until then, it 'was notorious
that colonial posts were often filled, from the highest to the lowest
ranks, with men whose claims were political in the narrow sense of
the word'.[5] Before 1936, Europeans in or out of the administration
in Africa had been either favourable to the ideas of the French Right,
or apolitical. From the middle thirties, however, date the first
contacts of African 'subjects' with supporters of the French anti-
clerical Left; a few Left-wing Christian missionaries were in Africa
already. Such colonial reformers as Governor-General de Coppet
and Governor-General Eboué were appointed by the Popular Front
government in 1936. In addition, some eager young French Socialists
and Communists took civil service posts, and most important, posts
as teachers in state schools not only in Senegal, but also in Soudan,
Guinea, Ivory Coast and elsewhere.

The apostles of the French Left talked to their African students
about the implications for Africa of the political philosophies which
they supported. These men never considered seriously the possibility of the separation of Africa from France. Rather, they stated
firmly that emancipation for Africa would only follow from the
assumption of power in France by the Left. Many of the pupils of
these teachers became the leaders of the African political parties
born after 1945. A practical result, therefore, of the teachings by the
spokesmen of the French Left was that some Africans knew and

---

[1] *Section Française de l'Intérnationale Ouvrière.*   [2] Decree of 23 July 1937.
[3] The decree of 11 March 1937, modified by the decree of 12 July 1939, extended
the right to join trade unions to African workers among the 'subjects' who held
the *certificat d'études primaires.* Secrétariat Social de Dakar, *Manuel pratique du
syndicaliste,* Librairie Clairafrique, Dakar, 1956, p. 18.
[4] Devèze, op. cit., p. 76. Devèze was a *Mouvement Républicain Populaire* (MRP)
deputy at the *Constituantes,* see also Fréchou thesis, op. cit., p. 139.
[5] Brogan, D. W. *The Development of Modern France,* Hamish Hamilton, London,
1940, p. 252.

partly agreed with the French Communist, evolutionary Socialist or Christian Democrat political traditions. From these traditions originated the policies of the three major post-war French parties which reformed the French Empire and built the Fourth Republic.

The representatives of the French Left were only a small group in Africa. The bulk of the European population[1] remained in favour of 'association', in practice domination. The fall of France in 1940, and the advent of the Vichy government shifted all political power back to the colonial officials who believed in autocratic administrative methods.[2] The administration in French West Africa remained loyal to Pétain until the Allied landing in North Africa. By 1943, however, the Provisional Government in Algiers took control over the administration, and started planning post-war colonial reforms.

The plans were influenced by the colonial doctrines and practices both in the 'old communes' under the Popular Front, and can be summarized under three main heads. First, French politicians of the Right and of the Left agreed that the link between France and her colonies was indissoluble. Consequently, the idea of independence for the colonies had no supporters among any groups in France. The disagreement among French political leaders centred around the kind of links which should hold the French system together. Second, to the French Left assimilation still remained the theoretical, if remote and difficult, ideal. They believed that the extension of the rights of French citizenship to African 'subjects' was the highest possible good, and accepted the implications of citizenship to the extent of favouring the inclusion of some colonial representatives in metropolitan institutions. Third, all groups in France realized that French colonial policy had to make some concessions to geographical and ethnic realities. Therefore they favoured a measure of administrative decentralization and of territorial local government. These ideas were reflected in the discussions of post-war colonial reforms held at Brazzaville from 30 January to 8 February 1944.

The Brazzaville Recommendations

The forty-four French colonial administrators, political and trade union leaders who conferred in 1944 at Brazzaville laid down the broad lines of French post-war colonial policy. There were no African delegates; the only intrusion of African opinion was in the written appendix to Félix Eboué's report. A Negro born in French Guiana, he was promoted to the rank of Governor under the Popular Front,

---

[1] In 1936, there were 17,148 French Europeans and 7,650 foreign Europeans in the West African federation. *Annuaire Statistique*, tome i, 1950, op. cit., p. 79.
[2] Deschamps, *Méthodes et doctrines* . . ., op. cit., pp. 176–8, and Robinson, 'The Public Law of Overseas France', op. cit., pp. 5–6.

and at the start of the war was Governor of Chad. He was largely responsible for Chad's early response, in August 1940, to General de Gaulle's call to resist the Vichy government. Partly as a consequence he was appointed Governor-General of Equatorial Africa that year.[1]

General de Gaulle, presiding over the first session, called for a 'noble, liberal road for the future'. He and his associates were keenly aware how significant the colonies were to France; 'a large part of the war has been fought in Africa and the absolute and relative importance of the resources, lines of communication and the troops from Africa has been apparent in the harsh light of the theatres of operations'.[2] By January 1944, all the African colonies had rallied to de Gaulle. The conference, said Colonial Commissioner René Pleven, was to suggest ways by which 'the peoples of our Empire who shared French sorrows might also be fully associated with our rebirth'.[3]

The Brazzaville delegates unanimously agreed on several points. The most important was embodied in the first resolution. 'The aims of the civilizing labours of France in the colonies exclude all possibilities of development outside of the French imperial system; the eventual formation even in the distant future of self-governments in the colonies must be dismissed.'[4] The delegates expressed partiality for 'empire in the Roman not the Anglo-Saxon sense',[5] and further stated that 'simply ameliorating the system of representation existing on 1 September 1939 . . . is inadequate and sterile'. Therefore 'it is desirable, even indispensable, that the colonies be represented at the future Constituent Assembly'.[6] Implicit in this recommendation was the belief that 'overseas France should not have a separate constitution; its constitution shall be that of France itself'.[7] This view, respected by the authors of the 1946 French Constitution, strikingly differentiated the legal framework of post-war French West Africa from that of British West Africa.

Within this broad area of agreement, there was some controversy among the Brazzaville delegates about the post-war constitutional connexion between France and the colonies.[8] Governor-General Eboué and Governor Latrille of Ivory Coast stressed the need

---

[1] Devèze, op. cit., p. 156.
[2] de Gaulle, General. *War Memoirs, Unity, 1942–4, Documents*, English translation, Weidenfeld and Nicolson, London, 1959, p. 249.
[3] *La Conférence Africaine Française, Brazzaville*, Commissariat aux Colonies, Alger, 1944, p. 19. (Henceforth termed *Brazzaville records*.)
[4] Ibid., p. 35. 'Self-governments' is used in the plural, in English, in the original text. The entire citation is printed in capitals in the original.
[5] Ibid., p. 71.   [6] Ibid., p. 36.   [7] Ibid., p. 73.
[8] Devèze, op. cit., pp. 181–2.

for flexible institutions, preferably of a federal type, and suited to harmonizing the cultural, social, and economic differences between France and her colonies in Africa, Asia, and the West Indies. On the other hand, men like Colonial Commissioner Pleven and Governor Toby emphasized the maintenance of French sovereignty, which they combined remotely with the ideal of assimilation, and immediately with institutions dominated by metropolitan France.

In the event, the Brazzaville conference compromised between these two conflicting conceptions of empire. Similarly, the members of the post-war Constituent Assemblies compromised rather than choose between the model of assimilation, closely followed by reiteration of metropolitan predominance, and the model of potentially equal autonomous units, loosely expressed by the term federation. The Brazzaville conference recommended a 'federal' parliament, but defined the term with care, so as to be certain of 'affirming and guaranteeing the unbreakable unity of the French system'.[1] Most delegates at the conference remembered their own frustrations in dealing with the Colonial Ministry in Paris, which maintained a tight control on, but paid little attention to, the territorial administrations. In the future, they urged that 'the territories . . . should gradually move towards administrative decentralization and become legal political entities'.[2] The delegates advised the creation of territorial representative assemblies, eventually elected by universal suffrage, with decisive budgetary powers, and consultative powers on other matters. They urged the democratization of local and regional councils.

The Brazzaville delegates gave advice on social, economic, and administrative matters also. The delegates urged the eventual cessation of forced labour, the regulation of free labour to assure the rights of African workers, including the right to form trade unions; the eventual replacement of the *indigénat* by a unified penal code independent both of the administration and of native custom; improved health and agricultural services; training facilities and research; the elaboration of an African development plan, as part of a French state plan, to provide for African industries and public works; increased education in French, while 'the use of local spoken dialects should be absolutely forbidden both in private and in public schools'.[3] The conference made detailed recommendations on the civil service, including its Africanization without changes in the salary or status connected with posts previously held exclusively by Europeans.

Finally, the conference was very insistent on the rights of women.

[1] *Brazzaville records*, op. cit., p. 36.   [2] Ibid.   [3] Ibid., p. 44.

Symptomatic, first, of the assimilationist bias, was the condemnation of polygamy (though not a call for outlawing it); second, of the French egalitarian tradition, was the condemnation of child brides and the call for free consent from both parties in a marriage; third, of the general approval of the Resistance role played by women, which resulted in granting them the right to vote for the first time in the metropolitan elections of 1945, was the proposal of equal rights for women in the colonial public services.

Immediately after the war, French governments accepted the comparatively liberal Brazzaville proposals at least partly in recognition of the help African soldiers and civilians had given to the Free French cause. The Provisional Government, as a reward for Resistance, nominated a 'citizen' of Senegal, Ely Manel Fall, to the Provisional Consultative Assembly[1] and gave effect to some Brazzaville suggestions by decree.[2] In particular, the Algiers government accepted the idea that representatives from the colonies take part in the 1945 Constituent Assembly. The small lobby of African students in France had the satisfaction of seeing the Provisional Government accept the principle that some 'subjects' might vote. The 'citizens' voted on a separate roll called the first electoral college, while some specially qualified 'subjects' voted in the second electoral college. After lengthy discussions,[3] the de Gaulle government called 64 colonial representatives among a total of 586 to the 1945 Constituent Assembly; 36 were to be elected by French citizens in the first electoral college, 24 by 'subjects' in the second electoral college, and 4 on common electoral rolls.[4] Of these, West Africa's share was 5 first college and 5 second college deputies; Equatorial Africa and Cameroun elected 6, half in the first and half in the second electoral college.[5]

The recommendations made at Brazzaville provided the inspira-

[1] d'Aby, op. cit., p. 54. For its composition, see Lidderdale, D. S. W., *The Parliament of France*, The Hansard Society, London, 1951, p. 40.

[2] For a list of 16 such decrees on economic, social, administrative, and judicial matters, see *Brazzaville records*, op. cit., p. 125.

[3] The Resistance organization *Combat d'outre-mer* called for 88 deputies to a two-chamber Assembly. The *États Généraux de la Renaissance Française*, wanted one-fifth of the Assembly to be overseas deputies, without counting 25 deputies from Algeria. In February 1945 a *Commission* of the Consultative Assembly was nominated by Colonial Minister Giacobbi, to examine overseas representation. The *Commission Monnerville* (named after its president) called in July 1945 for 95 overseas deputies in a single-chamber Assembly, or 66 + 29 overseas deputies in a two-chamber legislature, Devèze, op. cit., p. 218.

[4] See Appendix III for a list of West African deputies. Three deputies from Oran were never seated.

[5] *Ordonnance* No. 45–1874 of 22 August 1945 called Africans to the Constituent Assembly.

tion as well as the outlines of the French Union—the new name of the French Empire under the Fourth Republic. The men of Brazzaville expanded on the more liberal precedents which they already knew—the law of the old communes of Senegal, and the reforms enacted or planned under the Popular Front. In most essential respects these 1944 suggestions had passed into law with the implementation in 1957 of the Loi-Cadre reforms.

The April 1946 Constitution

At the first Constituent Assembly, the three main parties—Communists, Socialists, and MRP—monopolized the votes.[1] An alliance between any two of these automatically brought a majority. The Socialists voted more frequently with the Communists than with the MRP. Socialists and Communists agreed that the Fourth Republic should be governed by a single chamber legislature, headed by a responsible council of ministers, and that the president of the Republic should have only the bare minimum of ceremonial powers. The MRP on the other hand, preferred, as did the numerically feeble Centre and Rightist deputies, a two chamber legislature and a somewhat stronger executive.[2]

Most provisions for the new French Union were voted unanimously by the Constitutional Commission.[3] Indeed, on colonial questions, the only real controversy among the three main parties was on the Council of the French Union. The MRP and parties of the Right and Centre had hoped to use the Council in order to manoeuvre the Socialists and Communists into accepting a second legislative chamber with real powers. The arguments unsuccessfully presented by the minority in favour of a strong Council of the French Union were in fact quite irrelevant to the colonial problem.[4] The French Union plans of the Socialists and the Communists resembled each other from the beginning. Both parties agreed on decentralization, local autonomy, on the right of the former 'subjects' to express their views about the institutions of the French

[1] For party strengths see Appendix IV.
[2] For an interesting eye-witness account of the work of the two Constituent Assemblies, see Wright, Gordon. *The Reshaping of French Democracy*, Methuen & Co. Ltd., London, 1950.
[3] With the exception of provisions for a Council of the French Union. Senghor, J.O.A.N.C. I, *Débats*, 11 April 1946, pp. 1713 f.; see also Devèze, op. cit., pp. 225–9.
[4] Devèze, op. cit., p. 228; see also J.O.A.N.C. I, *Débats*, 15 April 1946, p. 1844, and *scrutin* no. 102, pp. 1858–60, showing 288 against and 260 for including the Council of the French Union as one of a two-chamber Parliament. The overseas deputies hardly participated in the debate, and voted with their various parliamentary groups.

Union, and on representation in the French National Assembly for the colonies. After some hesitations, the MRP agreed also to these points, which were consequently written into the Constitution.

In the April draft Constitution, the elaborate Declaration of the Rights of Man extended 'to all men and women living within the French Union the right to the individual and collective exercise' of specified rights which were not only political, but economic and social as well.[1] Africans were invited to participate in the French Union. 'France forms with the overseas territories on the one hand, and with the associated states on the other, a Union freely consented to.' This important article, contradicting the first Brazzaville recommendation (Art. 41), both left open the question whether the overseas territories were part of the Republic of France, and implied free choice of status for all constituent parts of the Union. The reporter of the Constitutional Commission, Pierre Cot (pre-war Radical who on 2 April 1946 became member of the progressive *Groupe d'Union des Républicains et Résistants—apparenté* to the Communists), made unprecedented remarks on French colonial policy.

> Its aim should be liberation . . . not only of the human being but also of peoples. We need to define a new policy which is not only a policy for the individual, but also a policy for nationalities which we want, gradually, to see come into the French Union. . . . Brazzaville lacked political sense; the historical perspective was inadequate . . . especially in regards the first resolution, which forbade the peoples living in the French Union all hope, even remote, of independence and liberty.[2]

The April Constitution provided for African representation in a single-chamber French legislature. The proposed Council of the French Union was to have consultative powers only. Local territorial assemblies were to be established. All Africans were to be citizens, and eventually to vote. The pre-war system of appointing career governors-general responsible to the Colonial Minister was to be replaced by one in which representatives of France in the territories were to be political appointees. 'The Minister in charge of all the problems of overseas France is assisted by a resident Under-Secretary of State for every federation or group of territories.' The Under-Secretary was to be responsible for defence and law and order, as well as for administration and public services.

These remarkably liberal provisions were scattered throughout the April draft Constitution. They were supplemented by several laws

---

[1] See Appendix II: A. One fourth of the time of the Constitutional Commission was spent on the Declaration, much more than on colonial matters. Wright, op. cit., p. 135.

[2] J.O.A.N.C. I, *Débats*, 23 March 1946, p. 1044.

passed during the life of the first Constituent Assembly. Forced labour was totally abolished.[1] Citizenship was extended to all 'subjects', who on civil matters could retain the use of customary law. The law made a distinction between French citizens, *citoyens français*, in private and public law, and citizens *de statut local*, who retained African customary law on marriage, inheritance and so forth.[2] The electoral law for the new National Assembly provided for one deputy from Africa for every 800,000 inhabitants:[3] a total of 21 from West Africa, elected by single electoral college. Territorial assemblies were also to be elected by single electoral colleges.[4] Decrees ended the pre-war native penal code,[5] and extended freedom of assembly and association to Africa.[6]

The final draft of the April Constitution was accepted by a majority of the *Constituante*, but the MRP had decided to oppose it.[7] On 18 April, shortly after this MRP decision, an interesting proposal was made by the African Socialist deputy from Senegal, Mê Lamine Guèye. He put forward a bill to allow the overseas peoples, both citizens and 'subjects', to vote in the constitutional referendum. He explained that only thus could the 'free consent' of the various proposed members of the French Union be determined.[8] The consequences of this bill could have been far reaching for France, had it become law. The Socialists and Communists probably hoped to compensate for the expected negative votes in France which MRP opposition to the Constitution implied, by broadening the electorate in the colonies. Indeed, had the electorate for the May 1946 constitutional referendum been the same as for representatives to the Constituent Assembly, then the one million vote majority which rejected the April Constitution might well not have existed.[9] But

---

[1] Law of 11 April 1946.
[2] Law of 7 May 1946, often called the *loi Lamine Guèye* after its sponsor. It was incorporated into Article 80 of the October 1946 Constitution.
[3] And every fraction above 400,000; at least one per territory. Law of 13 April 1946, abrogated by the more restrictive law of 5 October 1946. For debate, see J.O.A.N.C. I, *Débats*, 5 April 1946, pp. 1533 f. For categories of voters, see Devèze, op. cit., p. 238.
[4] Organic Law of 5 April 1946, by the May 1946 referendum.
[5] Decrees of 22 December 1945 and 20 February 1946 ended administrative native justice (*indigénat*). Decree of 30 April 1946 ended the native penal code.
[6] Decree of 11 April 1946 granted freedom of assembly. Decrees of 13 March 1946 and 16 April 1946 granted freedom of association.
[7] The final text was accepted by 309; against were 249, including the MRP and the Centre and Right parties. The MRP, through spokesman Paul Viard, emphasized that the opposition was unrelated to the texts on colonial questions. See J.O.A.N.C. I, *Débats*, 11 April 1946, p. 1713. See also Devèze, op. cit., pp. 231–2.
[8] J.O.A.N.C. I, *Débats*, 18 April 1946, pp. 2021 f.
[9] See Appendix VI: A.

E

the bill proposed by Lamine Guèye was illegal, according to the basic law of the Assembly adopted in the referendum of 21 October 1945. Only French citizens could vote in the referendum. Overseas, this meant first college, but not second college voters.[1]

Legally, therefore, a vote to establish the 'free consent' of the subjects could be held only after the adoption of the Constitution. The first *Constituante* decided that such a referendum might be held two months after the May referendum. But the proposed overseas referendum never took place, for the April Constitution was rejected. Once again, voters went to the polls to select members of the second French Constitutional Assembly of 1946.[2]

'To Save the Empire'

The leaders of the three major French parties had publicly agreed not to change the French Union provisions of the April Constitution, regardless of the outcome of the referendum of 5 May. Three days later, to calm the worries of Africans, the government repeated that

the provisions of the French Union were adopted unanimously at the Constituent Assembly and had the support of all parties. Therefore the Government unanimously states, at the request of M. Marius Moutet, that Sunday's vote cannot be interpreted as a disavowal of the position taken towards the overseas peoples.[3]

The Socialists and MRP reneged on this, and the decisions of the second Constituent Assembly regarding the overseas territories were far less liberal than were those of the first. The MRP and the SFIO changed their position during 1946, for several reasons. First, disturbances in North and tropical Africa and in Vietnam helped to frighten by their violence or its implications, many French politicians of the Centre and the non-Communist Left. Second, the European settlers and French commercial interests in the colonies organized a widespread publicity campaign and lobbied against the French Union provisions in the first constitutional draft. Third, the balance of French domestic politics shifted.

The three-cornered struggle in Vietnam among France, the Viet Minh and Bao Dai, was temporarily interrupted by a conference in July 1946 at Fontainbleau. The failure of this conference made French political leaders more aware of the danger of war in Vietnam. This situation brought to the fore French fear of imperial weakness;

---

[1] Law of 2 November 1945 (Article 3), as adopted in the October 1945 referendum. J.O.A.N.C. I, *Débats*, 25 April 1946, p. 2254.
[2] The electoral law was the same as for the first *Constituante*.
[3] J.O.A.N.C. II, *Débats*, 18 September 1946, cited by Senghor, pp. 3790 f.

blurred the issue of colonial nationalism by confusing it with international Communism; and showed the deep divisions within France and its tripartite Government. The Socialists moved away from the Communists and closer to the MRP and Centre parties.

Difficulties in tropical Africa, also, came to the attention of the Socialist Overseas Minister, Marius Moutet. These included riots in Cameroun and in Senegal, strikes in many cities, and desertion of European plantations by African workers freed from forced labour by the law of 11 April 1946.[1] From Madagascar came news of the growth of Malagasy nationalism, which in May 1947 was to lead to serious and armed conflict.[2]

In North Africa, nationalist demonstrations were violently suppressed by French forces in 1945. Since many nationalist leaders were in jail in 1945, the Algerians elected to represent the second electoral college at the first Constituent Assembly affiliated with metropolitan French parties were moderates.[3] But eleven of the thirteen second college Algerian deputies who came to the second Constituent Assembly were thoroughgoing nationalists, maintained effective parliamentary discipline, voted together, and did not affiliate with any French parliamentary group.[4] This irritated many French deputies, since the political balance in the second Assembly had changed, and any combination of two out of three main French parties was no longer assured on an easy majority.[5]

Throughout the deliberations of the first Constituent Assembly those who represented European overseas interests made evident their displeasure with the colonial decisions taken. They were the first college representatives who outside of Senegal represented European majorities. They opposed most colonial reforms, from the abolition of forced labour to the suppression of the double electoral colleges.[6] Their negative attitude led one of them to jest, 'You want

---

[1] See Fréchou thesis, op. cit., pp. 139–45.

[2] See J.O.A.N., *Débats*, 6 and 9 May 1947, pp. 1476 f., 6 June 1947, pp. 1987 f., and 1 August 1947, pp. 3820 f.

[3] Four second college and two first college Algerians were members of the SFIO parliamentary group; four others were *apparentés* SFIO in the first *Constituante*. In the second *Constituante*, three first college and one second college Algerian were members of the SFIO group, and one second college Algerian was *apparenté* SFIO. The SFIO had lost five Algerian votes by the second Constituent Assembly.

[4] Members of the then moderate nationalist *Union Démocratique du Manifeste Algerien*, led by Ferhat Abbas. Less than a decade later he became a member of the directorate of the *Front de Libération Nationale*, and leader of the Algerian government in exile.   [5] Devèze, op. cit., p. 265.

[6] Maurice Kaouza, first college *Résistance Démocratique et Socialiste* deputy from Soudan–Niger, labelled the MRP argument for a single electoral college in West African elections, *'jésuitisme'*. J.O.A.N.C. I, *Débats*, 5 April 1946, pp. 1533 f.

a deliberative assembly in Madagascar? But the settlers are not ripe enough for that!'[1] In the first Assembly, the first college representatives had little opportunity to make their votes count, however. They represented constituents still largely partisans of the Third Republic, and so most became members of French splinter groups of the Centre and Right. They were therefore automatically out-voted by the majority which any two of the three dominant parties could muster. Their displeasure with the April draft, and that of their European constituents in Africa, was evident from their overwhelming vote against it.

The rejection of the April Constitution gave them a second chance. As the *États Généraux de la Colonisation Française*, overseas settlers and commercial representatives had already met in Douala in September 1945. Shortly after the referendum they held a second, more important meeting (30 July to 24 August 1946), this time in Paris so as to be close to officials and public opinion. The Paris meeting was instigated by Jean Rose, the president of the Ivory Coast *Chambre d'Agriculture*, and president of the *Association des Colons de la Côte d'Ivoire*. The meetings took place at the headquarters of the *Comité de l'Empire Française*.[2] With one exception, all those present came from tropical Africa or Madagascar; among them were the first college deputies, Schock of the Ivory Coast and Ferracci of Guinea. Delegates came from 'Chambres de Commerce et d'Agriculture, des Chambres syndicales des mines, des Syndicats forestiers et usiniers du bois, des Syndicats agricoles, de grandes Associations africaines de colons, des Fédérations de producteurs, des Syndicats d'employés et d'employeurs'.[3]

'To save the Empire'[4] they collected and publicized their arguments against the overseas decisions of the April draft Constitution. They stressed the danger to France of nationalist 'separatism' in North Africa, Vietnam and tropical Africa. They questioned how far the African deputies could be regarded as representative of 'the native masses, who yearn for *la paix française dans l'ordre et le travail*.' They condemned 'the agitation of a few separatists, who are but the products of yesterday's outworn feudalism or tomorrow's tyrannies, yet who are now ironically considered to be the representatives of the overseas peoples.'[5] They set up a permanent secretariat—the *Comité d'Action de l'Union Française*—with impressive

---

[1] George Boussenot, *apparenté* Radical, first college deputy from Madagascar J.O.A.N.C. I, *Débats*, 21 March 1946, p. 942.
[2] It later changed its name to *Comité Centrale de la France d'Outre-mer.*
[3] *États Généraux de la colonisation française*, typescript, Paris meeting, 30 July–24 August 1946; see Introduction, p. i. (Henceforth cited as E.G.C. typescript.)
[4] Ibid., pp. 1–2.   [5] Ibid., p. 17.

propaganda funds to publicize the need to preserve 'the sacred principle of French sovereignty'.[1]

They produced a new plan for the colonies, which excluded representation in the French Parliament, but did allow for it in an Assembly of the French Union. It called for a 'federal' French Union, dominated by France.[2] It favoured maintaining everywhere 'at least equal representation of the two colleges',[3] strongly opposed the extension of French citizenship to colonial subjects, and wanted a clear separation between citizenship of the French Union and of France.

Among the more interesting features of the plan was a call for local territorial assemblies, with quite wide financial powers. The *États Généraux* emphasized the need for more economic freedom in the colonies, and insisted on their right as a group to have an important say in the allocation of foreign exchange earned by local products. The plan makes no claim, however, for the right of territorial assemblies to have a say in allocating sub-soil or mineral concessions. The *États Généraux* were on the whole less concerned than was the French government at the time about permitting local assemblies to make statements on political matters. Article 29 of the *États Généraux* plan allowed territorial assemblies to address any observations to the relevant French ministers and officials. But the decree of 25 October 1946, which later established local assemblies, in Article 44, carefully excluded political problems from the subjects on which the local assemblies might issue observations.

In addition, the *États Généraux* contrived a lengthy scheme to ensure that Africans—freed from forced labour by the law of 11 April 1946—would nevertheless be obliged to work. 'Work is a social duty.'[4] Each man between the ages of 18 and 55 must work at least 240 days. Naturally the *États Généraux* claimed a large part of the right to decide what kind of work would count locally towards meeting the 'social duty'. In his introductory remarks the conference president, Jean Rose, said, 'whether we want to or not we shall have to resort to coercive measures'[5] to bring in the next crop. The authors of the scheme denied perhaps a shade too vehemently that their aim was to restore forced labour. The scheme ended with the claim that it was 'inspired by modern democracy'.[6]

A further important difference between the first and second *Constituante* concerned the balance of political power in France.[7] The MRP materially strengthened its position in the 2 June 1946 elections

[1] E.G.C. typescript, pp. 18 and 65.   [2] Ibid., p. 16.
[3] Ibid., p. 12.   [4] Ibid., p. 55.
[5] Ibid., p. 6.   [6] Ibid., p. 59.
[7] For the party breakdown in the second Constituent Assembly, see Appendix IV.

and became the strongest single party. Communists, Socialists, and MRP had 161, 150 and 150 votes in the first *Constituante*; in the second, these were 153, 129 and 169 respectively. A Communist–Socialist alliance no longer brought an automatic majority in an Assembly of 586. A MRP–Socialist alliance could produce such a majority, only if both parties maintained strict discipline; any defection immediately made it necessary to seek supplementary votes elsewhere. Therefore the small free-wheeling Centre political groups, although with the Right no more than one-fifth of the total, had more bargaining power in the second Constituent Assembly than in the first. The importance of the small groups was particularly evident on issues which sharply divided the Left, such as the future organization of the French Union, whether Parliament should be composed of one or two chambers, and the executive should be weak or strong. These changes in the complexion of the Assembly pushed the Socialists closer to the MRP and marked the beginning of the slow movement of post-war French politics away from a Left and towards a Centre Majority.

The October 1946 Constitution

New and different circumstances surrounded the meeting of the second Constituent Assembly. In spite of African protests, the colonial clauses of the April Constitution were thrown out and a new text was drafted—because the MRP reversed their original decision to support the first Constitution's liberal colonial texts; because Marius Moutet often agreed with the MRP; because the European settlers had organized tightly in their fear that French domination of Africa would be reasserted constitutionally. Long and bitter negotiations among African deputies, European colonial deputies, the President of the Constituent Assembly, Vincent Auriol (Socialist), the Reporter of the Constitutional Commission, Paul Costé-Floret (MRP), and the Colonial Minister, Marius Moutet (Socialist), preceded final agreement on the colonial clauses of the Constitution. The final text of the October Constitution pleased neither European overseas nor African deputies.[1]

The October Constitution[2] made the cornerstone of the French Union not free consent but domination by France. 'Article 1. France is a Republic, indivisible, laic, democratic and social.' 'Article 60. The French Union consists, on the one hand, of the French Republic, which comprises Metropolitan France, the overseas *départements* and territories, and on the other hand, of the associated territories and States.' This article is almost identical with Article I of the

[1] Devèze, op. cit., pp. 274–7.   [2] See Appendix II: B.

États Généraux de le Colonisation constitutional draft. French West Africa, composed of eight overseas territories, was placed inside the unitary structure of the French Republic.[1] Article 75 admitted that a territory might change status within the French Union. But 'passage from one category to another within the framework set forth in Article 60, can only be brought about by a law voted by Parliament. . . .'

The dominant position of metropolitan France was evident from the allocation of power over legislation. 'Article 72. In overseas territories, legislative power belongs to Parliament, in matters of criminal law, the organisation of public freedoms and political and administrative organisation.' While in the April Constitution French metropolitan law was applicable in the former colonies, except when the contrary was expressly written into the text, in the October Constitution, this provision was reversed. Furthermore, 'special provisions for each territory can be decreed in Council of Ministers by the President of the Republic after previous consultation with the Assembly of the Union'. Article 76 restored the career Governors as 'trustees of the powers of the Republic'.[2] Local assemblies with powers to be decided by organic law, were established by Article 77. Article 78 called for the creation of federal assemblies, with powers to be fixed by law, in groups of territories like the eight West African territories.[3] Article 79 confirmed African representation in the National Assembly and the Council of the Republic. Articles 63 and 66–71 created an Assembly of the French Union, indirectly elected, with half the members representing the overseas departments, territories and associated states and half representing metropolitan France. The Assembly received purely consultative powers on any matter on which its opinion was asked by the government or the National Assembly; it could give unasked an opinion related to the overseas territories.

Compromises were eventually achieved on three questions which aroused violent controversy between overseas European and African deputies: citizenship for 'subjects'; the size of the electorate in Africa; and single or double electoral colleges. Most overseas Europeans wanted a distinction between French and French Union citizenship. African deputies wanted all 'subjects' given unconditional French citizenship. Article 81 stated: 'All French nationals and subjects of the French Union are citizens of the French Union, a title which ensures for them the enjoyment of the rights and freedoms

[1] Rolland and Lampué, op. cit., p. 84.   [2] Ibid., pp. 86–8.
[3] There were only seven West African territories until 1947, when the law of 4 September re-established Upper Volta as the separate territory it had been before 1932.

guaranteed by the Preamble . . .' and Article 82 compensated for the fact that it is not quite clear whether French Union or French citizenship was granted to 'subjects', by stating that 'Citizens who do not enjoy French civil[1] status preserve their personal status so long as they do not renounce it. This cannot, in any case, constitute grounds for refusing or restricting the rights and liberties attached to French citizenship.'[2] No compromise was possible on a constitutional text specifying the size of the African electorate or on whether overseas Europeans were entitled to special representation. Therefore these issues were left to organic laws, more easily changed than the Constitution.

The colonial provisions of both the April and the October Constitutions drew inspiration from the institutions of the pre-war communes of Senegal, from the reforms planned or introduced under the Popular Front, and from the Brazzaville recommendations. The two sets of constitutional texts and laws differed in several respects, however, primarily because the internal and the international political position of France had altered during the short interval.

One difference was in the overseas franchise. This directly related, of course, to the decision written into both Constitutions to make Africans citizens. As long as voting rights of most people overseas were less than in the metropole, Africans could and did charge that first and second class citizenship persisted, even after the legal category of French 'subject' disappeared. The first *Constituante* went considerably further in equalizing the franchise than did the second. It granted the franchise to wider categories of Africans and gave Africans more seats in Parliament. Another five years had to pass before these first *Constituante's* intentions became law.[3] Furthermore, it discarded the two-college system. Maintenance of a single college for direct elections to local assemblies[4] would have meant the elimination of most Europeans representing African constituencies a decade before the actual event.

The second *Constituante* kept the single college for elections to the French National Assembly from West Africa[5]—though not from Equatorial Africa. But the two-college system was enacted for local assembly elections (see Figure 1, p. 51) except in Senegal because

[1] 'Civilian' in the official translation of the French embassy in London.
[2] Rolland and Lampué, op. cit., pp. 250–3; also Thiam, op. cit., pp. 19–21. The decree of 24 February 1953 defines citizenship *de statut personnel* for Africans. See Brin, H. L., *La Nationalité française dans les territoires d'outre-mer*, Recueil Sirey, Paris, 1954.   [3] After the implementation of the law of 23 May 1951.
[4] Law of 5 April 1946, nullified by the law of 7 October 1946 and decrees of 25 October 1946. See J.O.A.N.C. I, *Débats*, 25 April 1946, p. 2245 for chart of projected local assembly membership.
[5] Law of 5 October 1946. See Thiam, op. cit., pp. 113–6.

FIGURE 1

Members of Representative Assemblies in Africa: From the Conseil Générale *to National Assemblies*

	CONSEIL GENERALE 1946–52ᵃ		Territorial Assembly 1952–7ᵈ		Territorial Assembly 1957–8ᵉ	AFRICAN NATIONAL ASSEMBLY 1958 onward ᵍ
	50ᵇ Single college		50 Single college		Single college 60	Single college
	1st col.	2nd col.	1st col.	2nd col.		
Senegal						80—22 Mar. 1959
						100—1 Dec. 1963
Mauretania	6	14	8	16	34	40—17 May 1959
Soudanᶠ	20	30	20	40	70	80—8 Mar. 1959
Niger	10	20	15	35	60	60—14 Dec. 1958ⁱ
Guinea	16	24	18	32	60	75—28 Sept. 1963ʰ
Dahomey	12	18	18	32	60	70—23 Apr. 1959
						—11 Dec. 1960
Upper Volta	10	40ᶜ	10	40	70	75—10 Apr. 1959
Ivory Coast	18	27	18	32	60	100—12 Apr. 1959
						70—27 Nov. 1960

a. Established by decrees of 25 October 1946.
b. Established by decree of 25 February 1946 because of the special pre-war position of Senegal.
c. Established by decree of 31 March 1948, when Upper Volta was reconstituted. Then Ivory Coast lost 5 Councillors, from 20–30 to 18–27.
d. Law of 6 February 1952.
e. The Loi-Cadre of 23 June 1956 established universal franchise. The number of councillors was set forth in law 56–1147 of 15 November 1956 and elections were in March 1957.
f. Republic of Mali after August 1960.
g. After 1958, the dates of elections in each state ceased to be uniform, and were as indicated on chart.
h. No election between 1957 and 1963.
i. Partial elections took place at Zinder, 27 June 1959.

of its special pre-war position. As a practical consequence for ten years the first college, composed principally of the tiny European minority resident in Africa, also enjoyed weighted representation in the federal Grand Council at Dakar, in the Assembly of the French Union and in the Council of the Republic. For the local territorial councillors elected the members to the first two bodies, and to the third voted together with the deputies to the French National Assembly.

By proportional representation each of the local assemblies elected from among its members five Grand Councillors to five-year terms.[1] Mauretania, because of its small population, was allotted but one seat each in the Assembly of the French Union and the Council of the Republic; it filled these seats by simple majority vote *à deux tours*. By proportional representation and party lists the other local assemblies also voted for the additional twenty-six AOF councillors serving six-year terms in the Assembly of the French Union.[2] Though technically these elections were held in single college, proportional representation assured special weight to first college votes. The two-college system was explicitly used—except in Senegal and Mauretania —to designate the West Africans serving six year terms in the French Council of the Republic. Half were re-elected every three years. There were twenty (1948–59) West African senators,[3] a number equal to the maximum (1951–9) deputies to the National Assembly. Since its total membership was practically twice that of the upper house, the West African quota of the Senate was twice that of the Assembly. Where only one senator was elected—Mauretania and the six first colleges—vote was by simple majority *à deux tours*. Where more than one senator was elected—Senegal and the six second colleges— voting was by party list and proportional representation. Consequently six senatorial seats were in practice reserved to the West African first college.

Besides making the electorate smaller, keeping the two college system for territorial elections, and allotting an even smaller number of seats to West Africans in the French Parliament than the first

[1] The law of 29 August 1947 governed the work of the Grand Council of West Africa. See J.O.A.N., *Débats*, 4 August 1947, p. 3899.
[2] The metropolitan members of Parliament elected by proportional representation half the members of the Assembly of the French Union. Of these, ⅔ were elected by the National Assembly, and ⅓ by the Council of the Republic. Total membership (1958) was 188. Law of 27 October 1946, modified by the law of 4 September 1947 and also the decree of 6 September 1947; also Articles 63, 66–72, of the October Constitution.
[3] The law of 27 October 1946 provided for election of 19; 20 came up for election in 1948, according to the law of 23 September 1948 (modified slightly by the law of 6 February 1952).

Constituent Assembly, the second took decisions which differed in yet other respects. The October Constitution was more restrictive on the possibility of autonomy, and set a firmer French parliamentary control over the constitutional status of the overseas territories. This was evident from the elimination in October of the provision written into the April draft for determining 'free consent' from the overseas peoples. Not until 1958 and the Fifth Republic was a provision for consent revived. Under the Fourth only constitutional amendment could clear the way for Africans in the overseas territories to demand a change of legal status—to associated states, for example. This constitutional restriction, coupled with the fact that the territories were placed within the centralised unitary Republic, sufficed for many French political leaders to justify labelling subversive, anti-French, anti-Republican any talk of independence by Africans. For a decade, the leaders of African parties could not press for fundamental alterations without attacking the French Constitution at least implicitly. Considerably less than the April draft was the October Constitution compatible with evolution into a federal or confederal system, composed, as is the Commonwealth, of partners who are equal.

The second Assembly restored to the French executive—both council of government and the civil servants in the administration—many of the powers distributed in April to the Legislature. By deciding that 'special provisions for each territory can be decreed in the Council of Ministers . . .' the October Constitution gave to the French executive most of the powers over colonial matters that it had before 1945. Only because consultation of the Assembly of French Union became compulsory prior to issuing a ministerial decree for the overseas territories, were executive powers differentiated after October 1946 from what they had been, when based simply on the *sénatus consulte* of 3 May 1854.[1] With the executive decree power largely intact, it was perfectly possible for the National Assembly to take up only those occasional colonial matters it had time for in a crowded agenda, and the significance of African rights of representation in the French Parliament was thereby reduced. Nor were the local territorial assemblies, as compensation, given wider powers. In line with the French *conseil général* tradition, the powers of these assemblies were severely restricted in almost all matters but budgetary.[2]

[1] For the *sénatus consulte* see Rossillion, Claude. *Le Régime législatif de la France d'outre-mer*, Éditions de l'Union Française, Paris, 1953, pp. 72–3.

[2] Guèye. *Étapes et perspectives . . .*, op. cit., pp. 106–7. See decrees of 25 October 1946. For a detailed discussion of the powers of the territorial assemblies in 1955, see Robinson, Kenneth, 'Political Development in French West Africa', in Calvin Stillman, ed., *Africa in the Modern World*, University of Chicago Press, Chicago, 1955, pp. 167–71.

There was no more talk of under-secretaries for Overseas France to reside in Africa. Power over day-to-day decisions remained with the permanent career officials. Once again the governors and governors-general represented in Africa not only the French government of the day, but also the more permanent Republic. The October Constitution limited them only to the extent of requiring consultation of the Grand Council or territorial assemblies on specified matters. They could take some measures based on previous French law or decree. Only the governor-general could correspond with the government. He had control over civil police and the military, and no French law or decree was in force until promulgated by him.[1] Therefore the permanent administration, a specially significant force while governments changed often, once again enjoyed considerable power. For some years many overseas reforms passed in Paris were challenged, or not fully implemented in Africa, as 'divided ministries, lacking effective support in the country', were 'too weak to impose the necessary sacrifice on any powerful private interest, or organized social group'.[2] The European overseas firms, the first college representatives, and a segment of the administration hoped to be able to ignore, or at least delay the implementation of reforms.

The October 1946 Constitution was adopted in referendum. For a dozen years it determined the institutional structure of AOF, even though most overseas voters rejected it. Only Senegal, where Africans were a majority of the electorate, voted for the Constitution. This was not because they were satisfied with it. Rather, seeing strong European opposition, they feared still less acceptable terms.[3]

The Early Reforms

French Africans went to the polls numerous times to elect representatives to fill the many posts the new October 1946 Constitution opened to Africans. Between 1945 and 1958, West African voters took part in four referenda.[4] They voted in direct elections to the *Constituante* and National Assembly at least five times,[5] and directly

[1] See *Annuaire Statistique*, tome i, 1950, op. cit., pp. 5–6; Haut Commissariat de l'AOF, *Annuaire Statistique de l'Afrique Occidentale, Années 1950 à 1954*, vol. 5, tome i, Imprimerie Servant-Crouzet, Paris, 1956, pp. 7–8; and Guèye, *Étapes et perspectives . . .*, op. cit., pp. 104–5. The legal bases were the decree of 18 October 1904, its partial re-enactment in Article 76 of the Constitution, and the decree of 4 May 1948.
[2] Williams, Philip. *Politics in Post-War France*, 2nd Edition, Longmans, Green & Co., London, 1958, p. 26.   [3] For results, see Appendix VI: A.
[4] 21 October 1945, to establish the post-war Constituent Assembly; 5 May 1946, on the April Constitution; 13 October 1946, on the October Constitution; 28 September 1958, on the Constitution of the Fifth Republic.
[5] 21 October 1945; 2 June 1946; 10 November 1946; 17 June 1951; 2 January 1956.

elected territorial councillors to territorial assemblies three times.[1] The territorial councillors elected members to the Assembly of the French Union[2] at least twice; to the federal grand council at least three times;[3] together with the deputies, they elected senators at least three times.[4] Partial elections filled offices vacated by death or resignation. Some overseas representatives took part in the work of the consultative Economic Council.[5] Frequent elections maintained an almost continuous climate of electioneering in Africa. The novelty for a brief time obscured the fact that the Africans elected to posts in the French Parliament, the Assembly of the French Union and Economic Council, the Grand Council and the local territorial assemblies, had some influence but little legislative and no executive power, in France or in Africa.

The franchise provisions adopted in 1946 fell considerably short of the republican ideal of one man one vote. In the decade that followed many formal debates in the National Assembly hinged around gradual abolition of the two college system and the extension of the franchise until it became—in 1956—universal. This African goal was more easily admitted as legitimate by French political leaders, than almost any other.

In 1946 the criteria for the vote were individual identity or importance in the society: for example, notables;[6] members or former members of local assemblies, co-operatives, unions; holders of French decorations; regular wage earners in establishments recognized by law; ministers of religion; veterans; owners of legally registered property; holders of hunting or drivers' licences.[7] A 1947 law added 'all those who can prove they can read and write in French or Arabic'.[8] The electoral law for the 1951 National Assembly included a new criterion: status within the family, such as heads of

[1] Senegal in March 1946; December 1946–January 1947 in the other territories. 30 March 1952. 31 March 1957.
[2] November–December 1947; October–November 1953.
[3] September 1947; October–November 1953; May 1957.
[4] December 1946–January 1947, in all territories; October–November 1948, in all territories; May 1952, in Senegal, Upper Volta, and Niger; May 1955, in Mauretania, Guinea, Ivory Coast, Dahomey, Soudan. June 1958, in Senegal, Upper Volta, and Niger.
[5] The decree of 10 May 1951 provided for 9 economic representatives from the overseas and trust territories, and 4 representatives of African trade unions. In 1956, 3 Africans from West Africa were members of the Economic Council.
[6] See Gayet, G. 'Évolution récente des collèges électoraux en Afrique occidentale', *Comptes rendus mensuels des séances de l'Académie des Sciences Coloniales*, vol. xii, Paris, February 1952, pp. 57–73. The changing numbers of registered African voters are given in Appendix V.
[7] Law of 5 October 1946, supplementing *ordonnance* of 22 August 1945.
[8] Law of 27 August 1947.

families who pay tax, and mothers of two children living or dead in
the service of France.[1] The electoral law for the 1952 territorial
assemblies eliminated the proviso that heads of families must pay tax
to vote.[2] The 1955 municipal law made the franchise universal in the
cities,[3] and finally in 1956 the Loi-Cadre allowed every citizen over 21
the vote.[4] The 1952 law for the territorial assemblies reduced the
number of seats reserved to the first college,[5] and the Loi-Cadre
eliminated it altogether.

Even as all Africans were acquiring the vote, the electoral system
under the Fourth Republic still discriminated between overseas and
metropolitan inhabitants. It took many more overseas inhabitants to
send a man to Parliament. At best, after 1951, the ratio was 10 : 1;
roughly 900,000 overseas inhabitants, but only 90,000 metropolitan
inhabitants were entitled to one deputy. Between 1945 and 1951 the
number of seats in the National Assembly allotted to West Africans
increased slightly; 5 each for the two colleges at the *Constituantes*;
15 in the 1946,[6] and 20 in the 1951 and 1956 Legislatures. The rise
stopped there.[7] Frenchmen had no intention of allowing the deputies
from overseas in Parliament to become so numerous as to make
France a colony of her colonies[8]—at least the tropical African ones.
Not all metropolitan deputies, of course, were as tactless on the
subject as the man who complained, after a close vote, 'Ce sont les
malgaches qui font la loi!'[9]

Agreement was general, if tacit, that the African quota in Parliament would not increase much.[10] It explained the attention given to
local assemblies in the territories. Formally these territorial *conseils
généraux* set up in 1946 were based on the local government tradition
in the metropolitan departments, a tradition which explained why
the powers changed but little for some ten years. (Though in practice,
some territorial assemblies, especially of Senegal and Ivory Coast,
exercised more powers than the law provided.) By 1952, another

---

[1] Law of 23 May 1951.   [2] Law of 6 February 1952.
[3] Law of 18 November 1955.   [4] Law of 23 June 1956, Article 10.
[5] Law of 6 February 1952.
[6] This figure excludes Kabore Zinda of Ivory Coast–Upper Volta, who died
in 1947 and was not replaced; but includes 3 deputies from Upper Volta, elected
on 27 June 1948.
[7] The first reading of a bill to extend the franchise and the number of seats for
Africans had passed the National Assembly at the end of 1955, and was before
the Council of the Republic. Dissolution kept the bill from becoming law. *Le
Monde*, 25–26 December 1955.
'Edouard Herriot, veteran Radical, opened the French Union debate in the second
Constituante by mentioning this. J.O.A.N.C. II, *Débats*, 27 August 1946, pp. 3333 f.
[9] PRL deputy M. Legendre, J.O.A.N.C. II, *Débats*, 11 September 1946, p. 3657.
[10] Le Brun Kéris, Georges (MRP councillor of the French Union), 'Le Fédéralisme
sauvera-t-il l'Union française?', *Monde Nouveau*, Paris, May–June 1955, p. 44.

organic law conferred the new name of territorial assemblies, and indicated thereby a timid departure from the French departmental tradition.[1] The new law was more specific on matters of electoral regulations, partly because when these matters were left to the governors there were numerous complaints of administrative gerrymandering and interference in elections. The powers, however, apart from budgetary, were still rudimentary, and control over implementation still remained with the French administration.[2] In this the territorial assemblies reached yet another of the limits inherited from the centralizing, pre-war assimilationist tradition.

It had started as a revolutionary idea at the time of the French Revolution when communication was hard, education limited to a few who knew each other, and the economic role of the state very small. Assimilation never applied to the total relationship between France and her colonies. It had meaning in reference only to a tiny, educated African minority. A policy for elites, it was hardly suitable to post-war mass politics. Assimilation originally meant little more than an equal share for all in the administration of law and order. The welfare state changed all that. Assimilation in a unitary state then presumed sharing the resources of rich, industrialized France with poorly developed Africa.

The high cost of true assimilation was barely suggested by the few remaining overseas laws the French National Assembly had the time to adopt prior to 1954. Though many French reformers of the Left had not yet fully abandoned the ideal of assimilation, none of course suggested implementing it, for example in appropriations for the overseas sector of the annual budgets, or the fund for overseas development—the *Fond d'Investissment pour le Développement Économique et Sociale des Territoires d'Outre-mer* (FIDES).[3] The

---

[1] Law of 6 February 1952.

[2] Holleaux, A. 'Les Élections aux assemblées dans les territoires d'outre-mer', *Révue Juridique et Politique de l'Union Française*, no. 1, January–March 1956, Paris, op. cit.; Gonidec, P. F., 'Les assemblées locales des territoires d'outre-mer', in *Révue Juridique et Politique de l'Union Française*, no. 3, July–September 1952, and no. 4, October–December 1953; 'L'Évolution récente des institutions politiques dans les Territoires d'outre-mer et Territoires associés', *La Documentation Française*, 11 March 1954, no. 1847, pp. 26–32, and Robinson, 'Political Development in French West Africa', in Stillman, op. cit., p. 161.

[3] Law of 30 April 1946. FIDES was administered by the *Caisse centrale de la France d'outre-mer* (*ordonnance* of 12 February 1941), renamed under the Fifth Republic *Caisse Centrale de la Cooperation Économique*. Annual reports are published. See Oudard, George. *Union Française 1953*, Julliard, Paris, 1953, pp. 41–64; ibid., 1954, pp. 31–47; ibid., 1957, pp. 67–100; Interafrique Presse, 15 December 1955; Leduc, Gaston. 'Réflexions sur les Plans de développement des Territoires française d'outre-mer', *Civilisations*, Brussels, vol. vi, no. 4, 1956, pp. 529–52.

closest the Assembly came to accepting even some of the economic corollaries of assimilation was in the adoption of two laws tending towards equalizing the working conditions of Europeans and Africans.

The liberal Code du Travail applied to all wage earners in Africa;[1] Parliament debated four years before finally adopting it on 15 December 1952. The most serious objections to the Code came from the European overseas employers. Their last attempt to stymie it took place in the Council of the Republic, where one of their spokesmen, Senator Durand Réville of Gabon, introduced a series of amendments early in 1952. One was to Article 2, which forbids forced labour. The Council of the Republic added a definition which included reference to paragraphs 1 and 2 of the International Convention of Geneva no. 29 of 28 June 1930, as ratified 17 June 1937 by France. Someone took the trouble to look the references up, and found these permitted exceptions so wide that 'they in no way forbade forced labour, but organized it'.[2] In final reading, the National Assembly overrode the Council, and removed all qualifications from the abolition of forced labour.[3]

The law of 30 June 1950, also known after its sponsor as the *deuxième loi Lamine Guèye*, applied to higher civil servants. Those Africans who fell within its province were entitled to much the same fringe benefits—trips to France and family allowances, for example— as the Europeans. The standards reflected by this law were closer to those which could be borne by the metropolitan budget than by African ones. When adopted, that fact was relatively unimportant; it became so later. Comparatively high wage bills in French-speaking West Africa may well be one of the more enduring consequences of assimilation.

Thus with these two very limited exceptions, the post-war political system was bound by limits emphasizing that Africans and Frenchmen, though citizens of the same Republic, were far from equal: limits in the number of French parliamentary seats allotted to Africans, and limits in expenditures by the state. Assimilation had left as a heritage those restrictive features of the centralized Fourth Republic which for a decade did not permit reforms leading towards responsible self-government. As a formula for reform, assimilation was exhausted.

---

[1] Berg. 'French West Africa' in Galenson, op. cit.
[2] Abbas Guèye, Senegalese deputy and former CGT leader, J.O.A.N., *Débats*, 22 November 1952, p. 5470. The Assembly overrode the Council of the Republic, and eliminated all qualifications from the abolition of forced labour.
[3] See Secrétariat Social d'Outre-mer, *Code du Travail des territoires d'Outre-mer*; *Guide de l'usager*, Société d'Éditions Africaines, Paris, n.d.

It took some time before French political leaders publicly recognized this fact. The National Assembly was, at least up to 1954, far too busy to spend much time on the overseas territories. Many questions about the future of the overseas territories were still open, and not even considered. Empty benches were the rule when overseas questions were debated. Jacques Soustelle (UDSR, later RPF) remarked these debates reminded him of the poem describing the Champs-Elysées, 'où un valet, armé de l'ombre d'une brosse, fourbissait l'ombre d'un carosse'.[1] One explanation for neglect by the legislators was the constant crises, both domestic and foreign, which characterized French politics during the first post-war decade.

The domestic political balance moved to the Right.[2] In the November 1946 elections, both the MRP and the Socialists lost votes and the Communists once again became the largest party. The campaign tactics of the three principal parties, and the weighty anti-constitutional pronouncements by General de Gaulle, foreshadowed the end of *tripartisme*. This came on 'the most important date in the post-war history of France',[3] 5 May 1947, when the Communists left the government to begin systematic opposition. Almost simultaneously, the Gaullists organized as a separate party, and frightened the 'republican majority' at the municipal elections of October 1947, where their *Rassemblement du Peuple Français* received more votes than any other party, 40 per cent.[4] Since 1947, governments were formed 'only by the alliance of all the middle parties, loyal to the classic forms of parliamentary rule',[5] at a time when the parliamentary system was under fire from Left and Right. Consequently Centre and Conservative parties began again to take part in the formation of ministries, while the Socialists could not escape working with these governments.

The 1951 elections, held under an electoral law favouring the republican majority, increased further the strength of the Centre and the Conservatives.[6] The position of the Socialists was almost unchanged, but the MRP lost almost 70 seats, the Communists lost more than 80, while Conservatives, especially the RPF, profited from these losses. Once again, as during the Third Republic, individualist Centre politicians were firmly in the saddle. Together with the MRP they were indispensable to a majority. During the entire 1951 Legislature, the Socialists avoided ministerial portfolios, but they, or part of their group, could not avoid frequently voting with the government.

---

[1] J.O.A.N.C. I, *Débats*, 23 March 1946, p. 1033.   [2] See Appendix IV.
[3] Williams, op. cit., p. 20.   [4] Ibid., p. 32.   [5] Ibid., p. 21.
[6] See Appendix IV for the distribution of seats by parties. See also Williams, op. cit., pp. 321–6, for a discussion of the 1951 electoral law.

F

Since the end of *tripartisme*, governments were uneasy coalitions of partners co-operating to prevent a power vacuum which might otherwise be filled by one or the other of the extremes, but were divided on most other major issues. Strikes, reconstruction, economic policy, war in Vietnam, European unification and defence, inevitably crowded the agenda of the National Assembly. The French parliamentary system did not encourage the executive to deal alone with these crises, and the Assembly was both too large and too divided to be able to keep abreast, much less ahead of events.

Grave problems existed in tropical Africa, but these were misunderstood by the ordinary deputy, and left to the government and administration, as the law permitted. In practice, prior to 1954, many overseas reforms passed in Parliament were challenged or not fully implemented in Africa. Prior to 1951 in most territories and after it in some, the administration repressed the main radical political movement in tropical Africa, the *Rassemblement Démocratique Africain*. A 'tough' anti-RDA policy on the federal level was pursued by Governor-General Paul Béchard, designated in January 1948 when he was still a Socialist deputy. (He later resigned from the National Assembly.) Of the 'tough' governors, Toby had been in Niger since 1947, Mouragues came to Upper Volta in June 1948, and Péchoux was appointed to Ivory Coast in October 1948. As a result of the repressive policy, incidents began in Ivory Coast in February 1949, and continued steadily for two years. When news of clashes in Africa arrived in Paris, they were explained away as Communist inspired. This automatically brought the majority of the Assembly to agree with the government's policy. The occasional debates in Parliament provided few correctives to abuses in Africa.

Though the National Assembly spent little time prior to 1954 on such matters which preoccupied West Africans, the French executive took many extra-parliamentary decisions for the territories.[1] These were taken amid bitter battles among Communists, lobbyists of European overseas interests, politicians, and civil servants who never accepted the post-war reforms; a few French officials who honestly sought to apply the reforms; and West African representatives in Paris. While before 1951 the usual French government policy was to repress African grievances, by 1951 there were signs that those who

[1] Compare this with the experience of the Irish nationalists at Westminster in the 'nineties. 'Occasionally an Irish member's bill did pass through all its stages and become law, but none of these contributed to the settlement of any of the fundamental issues of the Irish question. Such issues indeed were far too large and complicated to be dealt with by such bills and for their adequate treatment the Irish party was forced to rely upon the promises of successive ministries.' Lyons, F. S. L. *The Irish Parliamentary Party 1890–1910*, Faber, London, 1951, pp. 223–4.

favoured a policy of conciliation overseas were winning some of these struggles in ministerial offices.

These indications included changes in the higher personnel in Africa. François Mitterrand, Overseas Minister in 1950–1, ended the official repression of the RDA in the Ivory Coast, and transferred Governor Péchoux. In September 1951, Bernard Cornut-Gentille, who favoured conciliation, succeeded Paul Béchard as Governor-General. Officials in Paris paid increasing attention to the reports of the labour and administrative inspectors. The corps of inspectors of labour in West Africa, organized independently of the overseas administration, since 1945 played a part in exposing abuses of African workers. Some administrative inspectors, responsible not to the governors but to the overseas minister, reported abuses of power by administrators in Ivory Coast, for example. The pace of economic development increased in the territories, especially after the Korean war raised the world market prices of most African exports, and the schemes sponsored by FIDES started operating. There were official concessions to African strikers by decrees implementing some of the disputed provisions of the Code du Travail, still bitterly opposed by many European overseas firms. Periodically in 1952 and 1953, African trade unions organized strikes first in favour of a liberal Code du Travail, and later for the liberal implementation, by decrees, of the provisions of the Code.

Meanwhile, during 1951–4, other French executive decisions showed that the supporters of the policy of repression were still influential. The administration falsified the results of the 1951 elections to the National Assembly in most West African territories, and exercised considerable, though less pressure on the 1952 territorial assembly elections.[1] The administration also falsified the results of the 1954 partial elections in Guinea for the National Assembly.[2] These important struggles between advocates of repression and of reform within the administration were largely ignored by Parliament, until in 1954 the tropical African territories gained new importance in French eyes.

A Policy of Autonomy

By 1954, there was a substantial decline in the international power position of France, including a dramatic contraction of the boundaries of the French Union. In June 1954, shocked by military defeats in Vietnam, the French National Assembly invested the unorthodox Premier Pierre Mendès-France. He and his successors negotiated the Geneva agreements on Vietnam and the treaties recognizing

[1] See pp. 201–2.   [2] See pp. 240–6.

independence for Tunisia and Morocco, registering the end of French hopes of integrating these nations into the French Union. Since the end of 1954, another war, against the Algerian nationalists, drained heavily on French human and material resources; the war's continuation sapped public confidence in the utility of the legal fiction which designated Algeria a part of the French Republic. The failure of the Anglo-French intervention in Suez contributed to the decline of French power in North Africa.

In this setting, most French political leaders and higher administrators grew increasingly concerned about the possible 'separatist' influence on French tropical Africa of the independence for Ghana which would soon follow the June 1954 elections there. Government supporters in the French Assembly progressively realized they could not afford to fight nationalist demands both in North and in tropical Africa.

Recurrent incidents in the overseas territories were contributing reasons why the French Parliament elaborated new institutional reforms for the overseas territories after 1954. Incidents in tropical Africa, however, did not in themselves inhibit French readiness to use force against West Africans. Little differentiated the causes of the incidents in Madagascar in 1947, in Ivory Coast in 1949–51, from the grievances which gave rise to the incidents of Guinea in 1954–6, or in Cameroun in 1955–8. Nor did French domestic political considerations substantially affect the change of French policy towards tropical Africa. Party labels were largely irrelevant to the policies of overseas ministers before and after 1954. They first consistently repressed, and after 1954 conciliated West African discontent.[1] By then it was becoming government policy to find some legitimate outlets for West African pressures in favour of self-government.

Another clue both to the resumption of French parliamentary interest in the elaboration of African reforms, and to the ascendancy within the overseas administration of those who believed in the reforms, was a general realization by 1954 that Africa might have sound economic prospects. Economic surveys pointed to the potential resources of Guinea, Mauretania, and of the rest of the Southern Sahara. The policy of conciliation which had been followed since 1951 in Ivory Coast impressed many representatives of European enterprises in tropical Africa. They slowly came to believe co-operation not only possible, but indeed indispensable, with the present generation of moderate nationalist African leaders. By the mid-

[1] See Appendix I, for a list of French overseas ministers, and their parties, 1945–58.

'fifties they began to withdraw their opposition both to a policy of conciliation, and to the elaboration of reforms.[1]

Therefore when Robert Buron, Overseas Minister in the Mendès-France government, generalized the conciliatory administrative methods which his predecessors had introduced in Ivory Coast, he met with less opposition. He removed, or transferred from West Africa, the governors known to be 'tough'. Governor Toby left Niger for Tahiti; Governor Péchoux came to Paris from Togo, and Governor Roland Pré was sent from Guinea to Cameroun. By 1956 the only 'tough' governor in West Africa was Mouragues of Mauretania. Buron appeased with assurances for the future the RDA leaders of Guinea indignant at the falsification of the 1954 elections. It was Buron's hope to create 'a climate of true understanding and fraternity'.[2]

The statute for the UN trust territory of Togo which Buron piloted through the National Assembly in 1955 set French colonial policy on a fresh course—towards self-government. Togo's constitutional position, like that of Cameroun, was determined by the UN Charter. Domestic French legal barriers to independence did not apply, but French policy was to avoid it. Until 1955 policy in Togo was aligned as much as international law permitted on that of AOF. Under the October Constitution, the French UN trust territories had been baptized 'associated territories' but could not be placed within the Republic. Togo was not part of the Grand Council of AOF, but elected representatives to the French Parliament. Togo nationalists then seeking unification with British Togoland, and independence— the *Comité de l'Unité Togolaise* (CUT) and JUVENTO—were repressed by the administration at the same time as the *Rassemblement Démocratique Africain* in neighbouring AOF. While the nationalists charged, at the United Nations, that elections were falsified against them, in 1955 the majority party in the local assembly of Togo was amenable to French wishes.

This may have made it easier for some French deputies to vote for loosening legal control over Togo. Many voted for the 1955 Togo statute in the hope of avoiding independence. There were urgent reasons for reform. Britain made clear it wanted Togoland's future

---

[1] Included in this pressure group were the *Comité de l'Empire Française*, which sponsored the *États Généraux de la Colonisation* and later became the *Comité Central de la France d'Outre-mer*, and the backers of the weeklies *Climats* and *Marchés Coloniaux du Monde*. *Climats* petered out of existence in 1955; *Marchés Coloniaux* showed by changing its name in 1956 to *Marchés Tropicaux du Monde*, acceptance of political reform in tropical Africa.

[2] Buron, Robert. 'Les Problèmes du sous-developpement et l'assistance technique', *Les Cahiers de la République*, May–June 1957, p. 21. Buron defied MRP discipline to join the Mendès-France government.

settled when Ghana became independent, and France wanted to be prepared for the action expected of the United Nations.[1]

The 1955 statute departed from French precedents by establishing an 'Autonomous Republic of Togo' with a Legislative Assembly having considerably more powers than the assemblies in neighbouring AOF and residual ones. The most radical innovation provided for an elected African executive, including a prime minister. The 1955 statute did not satisfy the Togolese nationalists; CUT and JUVENTO boycotted votes administered under it by France, and pointed out the many significant powers still reserved to the government of the French Republic.[2] Subsequent laws and decrees extended African powers, however, and United Nations supervision helped keep honest the elections won by the nationalists in April 1958. Two years later Togo was independent.

To political leaders in AOF, Parliament's acceptance of the Togo statute brought hope of reversing peacefully traditional French refusal to accept self-government. Henceforth the Togo statute was cited to back up African claims, for real powers to territorial assemblies and for elected executives. Its adoption was the first product of the reconsideration given after 1954 to the institutions of the French Union by most of the parties and organs of the French government. The Assembly of the French Union published a report on alternative changes,[3] which aided the universal suffrage commission

[1] Coleman, James, *Togoland*, International Conciliation, New York, September 1956. France organized a referendum on the new statute on 28 October 1956, as provided for in the decree of 24 August 1956. 71 per cent. of registered voters approved the statute. The report on the referendum was submitted to the UN Trusteeship Council, as T/1292, 8 December 1956. The statute set forth in the decree of 24 August 1956 was reprinted as UN/T/1290, 9 December 1956, Annex.

[2] Part V of the statute enumerated the powers regulated by the 'central organs of the French Republic'; the following is a selection: foreign affairs, defence, personal and property status of French citizens, penal, criminal investigation and commercial code, administrative disputes, justice under French law, administrative tribunals, public freedoms, currency, foreign exchange, customs, secondary and higher public education, labour code, laws relating to mineral rights. The French Republic retained control over and financed the administrative branches of: High Commissioner; the Secretary-General; magistrates, judicial police; administrative tribunals; *sûreté, sécurité générale*; labour inspectorate; radio; telephone; cables; civil aviation; customs; the treasury.

[3] Assemblée de l'Union Française, *Rapport* no. 104, Annexe au p.v., lre séance, 22 March 1955, drafted by Alfred Bour, MRP councillor. This report was followed by a remarkable discussion in the Assembly of the French Union: A.U.F., *Révision du Titre VIII de la Constitution*, compte-rendu in extenso des débats, Intercommission saisie de présenter à l'Assemblée des suggestions susceptibles d'être transmises au Parlement et au Gouvernement, 29 March–8 July 1955, mimeographed, Paris.

of the National Assembly in its draft for revision of the Constitution.[1]

Federation and confederation were widely discussed. Spokesmen of the French Right called for a system composed of 'states federated *to* France',[2] and so providing for continued French domination. The minority wing of the SFIO which supported federalism since Liberation was given more respectful attention.[3] Senghor of Senegal put forward federalist solutions since 1948,[4] as had his IOM group;[5] equality among the parts of any federation attracted them specially. In the UDSR, supporters of Mitterrand favoured, and those of Pleven opposed federalism.[6]

Still in harmony with established French policy was the reform Parliament adopted in 1955, creating twenty-six new *communes de plein exercise* to supplement the three municipalities of Senegal fully self-governing since the nineteenth century. Parliament took almost for granted voting would be universal and by single electoral college, and gave to the territorial assemblies the power to extend to other cities the same rights.[7] Everywhere, however, plans were drawn which departed from previous French post-war policy towards tropical Africa.[8] Out of this activity grew the Loi-Cadre of 1956 and 1957, and subsequently the overseas provisions of the Constitution of the Fifth Republic in 1958.

During the campaign following the abrupt decision by the Edgar Faure government to dissolve the Assembly in December 1955,

---

[1] *Assemblée Nationale* no. 4663, Annexe au p.v. 1956–7; séance du 26 mars, 1957; *Rapport fait au nom de la commission du suffrage universel, des lois constitution-nelles, du règlement et des petitions, en exécution de la résolution adopté par l'Assemblée Nationale le 24 mai, 1955, et par le Conseil de la République le 19 juillet, 1955, décidant la révision des articles 17, 49, 50, 51, 60 à 82 inclus (Titre VIII) et 90 de la Constitution.* . . . Paris.

[2] Lavergne, Bernard. *Afrique du Nord et Afrique Noire*, Larose, Paris, 1956, p. 70 (my italics).

[3] Led by Alduy, Paul. *Union française et mission de la France*, Fasquelle, Paris, 1948.

[4] See BDS paper *Condition Humaine*, Dakar, 5 October 1948. Senghor's federalist ideas were developed in 'L'Avenir de la France dans l'Outre-mer', *Politique Étrangère*. August–October 1954, Paris, pp. 419–26.

[5] *Journées d'Études des Indépendants d'Outre-mer*, Paris, July 1950, Imprimerie Mont Louis, Clermont-Ferrand (henceforth cited as IOM 1950 pamphlet).

[6] *Le Monde*, 19 June 1956.

[7] Law of 18 November 1955. The background is given in Robinson, Kenneth, 'Local Government in French Tropical Africa', *Journal of African Administration*, October 1956.

[8] The reforms embodied in the Loi-Cadre of 23 June 1956 were explained in Governor Rey's speech to the *Comité Centrale de la France d'Outre-mer* on 13 October 1955. See *La Nouvelle Révue Française d'Outre-mer*, no. 10, October, 1955, p. 550. Governor Rey had a part in drafting the Loi-Cadre.

Africans openly called for autonomy. They said, 'We want to wear our own glasses.'[1] French leaders, worried by Algeria, were willing to make concessions, and the new Legislature, slightly to the Left of its predecessor, wanted to 'act in time'.[2] The government, thanks to plans drafted by the administration, was prepared with the Loi-Cadre.[3] Defending it before Parliament, Overseas Minister Defferre (Socialist) referred to past French experiences in Morocco, Tunisia, and Vietnam.

The failure of the federalist policies pursued there was because we sulked, clipped, delayed, dilly-dallied, shilly-shallied, quibbled before we offered conditionally a degree of autonomy which would have had a very different reception, and opposite results, had it been offered in good time and good faith.

He urged Parliament to avoid 'the same error with the territories inside the Republic'.[4]

The Loi-Cadre of 23 June 1956, for West Africa, made the vote universal and by single college, authorized for the first time jail sentences (up to three months) and fines (up to 200,000 French francs) in cases involving violations of decisions by territorial assemblies. Most important, it called for executive decrees: among them specifying the powers and functions of the governor-general and of the grand council,[5] creating councils of governments, or elected executives, in the eight territories;[6] enlarging legislative powers of the territorial assemblies;[7] reorganizing the public services of West Africa into the French state services, responsible to and financed by the French government, and the territorial services, responsible to and financed by the territorial governments.[8]

The Loi-Cadre provided for a most unusual procedure. Decrees drafted by the executive were submitted simultaneously to the Assembly of the French Union, and to the National Assembly. The former had fifteen days in which to issue its opinion; the latter had

[1] From an unpublished speech by Guinea RDA deputy Sékou Touré, in Dakar, 19 February 1956.
[2] Citation from a declaration by Overseas Minister Defferre, Socialist, in *Abidjan Matin*, 22 March 1956.
[3] Several other minor reforms were also adopted, including law 56-1147 of 15 November 1956, which raised the number of territorial assembly members in each territory by 10, except in Upper Volta which increased by 20.
[4] J.O.C.R., *Débats*, 19 February 1957, p. 440, Senator Durand-Réville citing Defferre's speech to the Council, 7 June 1956.
[5] Decree 57-458, 4 April 1957.   [6] Decree 57-459, 4 April 1957.
[7] Decree 57-460, 4 April 1957.
[8] Decrees 56-1227, 3 December 1956, and 57-479, 4 April 1957. Numerous other decrees, of lesser importance, also became law, including rural and post office reforms, and Africanization of civil service training and posts.

two months in which to accept, reject, or amend. The decrees had to be promulgated within four months of their submission to the National Assembly.[1] There was no consultation of any African assembly—the grand council or the territorial assemblies. By April 1957 some two dozen decrees authorized by the Loi-Cadre became law, and basically altered the institutions of AOF.

Before 1957, the powers of the territorial assemblies were essentially budgetary and financial. Even these were severely limited because more than half the expenditures were obligatory. (The figures varied. P. Sanner calculated that in 1952 the obligatory expenditures varied between 40 per cent. and 70 per cent.,[2] while former Overseas Minister Teitgen told the National Assembly in March 1956 that between 60 per cent. and 70 per cent. of the territorial receipts were absorbed in obligatory expenditures, mostly administrative.[3]) On most other matters the assemblies were only consulted. After the Loi-Cadre, the territorial assemblies had specified legislative powers in such matters as public works, land and the public domain, soil conservation, agriculture, fisheries, most mineral rights, codification of customary law, health, co-operatives, and urbanization. The assemblies became responsible for primary and secondary education, although France still continued to set the standards required for the teaching profession, and for such state examinations as the *baccalauréat*. The assemblies became responsible for territorial public services, including their finance. There was a sharp cut in the obligatory expenditures as 22 categories were eliminated, and only 8 remained.[4] An estimated 20,000,000 French francs were thus saved by the combined overseas territories.[5] The main reduction was in territorial payments towards the state services, almost all of which were paid after the Loi-Cadre, by the metropolitan budget.[6]

Yet another departure from previous French policy in the Loi-Cadre decrees created elected territorial executives. At first the governors presided over the councils of government, composed of between 6 and 12 ministers. By party lists ministers were collectively

[1] Article 1, Law of 23 June 1956.
[2] Sanner, P. 'Budgets et fiscalité des territoires d'outre-mer', *Révue d'Économie Politique*, 1952, p. 942, cited in Kenneth Robinson's excellent study, 'Constitutional Reform in French Tropical Africa', *Political Studies*, Oxford, February 1958, vol. vi, no. 1, p. 58, n. 2.
[3] Association pour l'étude des problèmes de l'Union française, *Bulletin* 99, Paris, April 1956, p. 14.
[4] Decree 57-466, 4 April 1957.
[5] Jean Filippi, Under-Secretary for the Budget, J.O.A.N., *Débats*, 1 February 1957, p. 482.
[6] Robinson. 'Constitutional Reform in French Tropical Africa', 1, op. cit., p. 58.

elected by, but not necessarily from among the territorial assemblies. The head of the list, in the absence of the governor, presided over the council. First designated the vice-president of the council, by 1958 he took the title president.[1] Each minister was assigned one of the territorial public services, e.g. interior, labour, agriculture, for which he had to account to the assembly. Most of the decisions of the council had to be ratified by the assembly. The council could not dissolve the assembly, and was not formally responsible to it, but had 'the option of resigning if they consider that they no longer have the confidence of the assembly'.[2]

Appointed by the French government, subordinate to the Governor-general, the governor of each territory was 'the trustee of the powers of the Republic'.[3] His powers were diminished, though still great. The reforms made him responsible for 'foreign affairs, defence, the guarantee of public liberties, the monetary and fiscal system, and the maintenance of solidarity among the constituent elements of the Republic, and its expansion in the economic, social, and cultural fields'.[4] Working in fields outside the jurisdiction of the territorial assembly, he no longer controlled all execution, but only most public boards and state services—e.g. his own staff and the higher administrators, security forces ranging from army through customs, judiciary, administrative and labour inspection, treasury and related services, communications from air through television. He not only presided over the council of ministers, but also enjoyed reserved powers. He could ask the assembly to reconsider its decisions. He could refer to the French government for annulment within three months both decisions of the Assembly he believed exceeded the law,[5] and decisions of the council of government he believed illegal, exceeded the law, endangered security, national defence, public order or public liberties.[6]

In spite of many protests by both the outgoing and the newly elected grand council, there was no provision for an elected federal executive. The governor-general retained exclusive control over the execution of the decisions of the grand council and over the restricted range of federal services. Federal services included only finance, economic co-ordination, geology and mineral prospecting, higher education and cultural co-ordination, services to fight human, plant, and animal epidemics, soil conservation. The trend towards

[1] *Ordonnance* of 26 July 1958.   [2] Decree 57-459, 4 April 1957, Article 2.
[3] Decree 57-560, 4 April 1957, Article 1. The clause is identical with Article 76 of the Constitution.
[4] Decree 56-1227, 3 December 1956, Article 1. (This decree was amended by the decree 57-479, 14 April 1957.)
[5] Decree 57-460, 4 April 1957, Article 46–47.   [6] Ibid., Article 12.

reducing the federal institutions was not materially reversed by the provisions that the territorial assemblies could request the grand council to create other federal services, and that two or more bordering states could set up joint machinery for their territorial public services.[1] Some services which had in the past been administered at the federal level—broadcasting and postal services—moved to Paris and were designated state services.[2]

The governor-general could declare a state of emergency, and was to 'assure the general co-ordination of the state services, the common (interterritorial) services, and the territorial services'.[3] For this purpose he received authority to convene conferences—of governors, of territorial ministers, or of territorial assemblies[4]—required by law to discuss economic and financial decisions taken in one territory, which in the opinion of the leaders of another territory 'might prejudice their interests'.[5] If the recommendation of the conference was not accepted by the territories concerned, the issue could be resolved by decree of the French government, after consultation with the Assembly of the French Union. This new mechanism, to be occasional only, undercut the grand council.

Thus the Loi-Cadre considerably reduced the powers of the federation of AOF. The grand council received legislative powers only over strictly limited subjects, corresponding to the interterritorial services.[6] It could also deliberate on matters referred to it by two or more territorial assemblies, and recommend ways 'to assure the co-ordination and eventual unification of territorial regulations and territorial finance'.[7]

The grand council retained deliberative powers over the federal budget, but its receipts could be spent only on the restricted federal activities specified by law. The remainder became available as grants to the territorial governments.[8] Moreover, its source of revenue shrank. Before 1957, it collected all indirect taxes, most important, export and import duties. After April 1957, it collected all import and only half the export taxes, and royalties on exported minerals and oil. This change meant the territories whose exports were largely agricultural—Ivory Coast and Senegal especially—no longer paid a share of taxes from exported cocoa, coffee, and peanuts into the federal budget. The territories exporting or about to export minerals and oil —such as Guinea and Mauretania—paid revenue from these into the

[1] Decree 57-458, 4 April 1957, Article 13.
[2] Senghor, J.O.A.N., *Débats*, 29 January 1957, p. 373.
[3] Decree 57-458, 4 April 1957, Article 9e.
[4] Such a conference could also be called on request of a majority of the councils concerned.   [5] Decree 57-458, 4 April 1957, Article 17.
[6] Ibid., Article 28.   [7] Ibid., Article 17.   [8] Ibid., Article 45.

federation's budget. The representatives of European enterprises overseas, who also opposed elected executives at the level of the federation, argued for equality between agricultural and mineral exporting countries in federal taxes.[1] The African deputies, however, did not echo this claim. They knew most income from agricultural exports went to Africans who then spent it on imported goods subject to federal duty, while the income from mineral and oil exports went to expatriates who would spend little of it in Africa.

The Loi-Cadre reforms marked a turning point in the relations between France and the overseas territories. The decrees gave to elected territorial governments powers which can be compared to those granted to the Gold Coast Legislative Assembly by the Order in Council of December 1950.[2] In conception, however, the Loi-Cadre differed, because they still kept within the unitary French Republic, and the provisions of the October 1946 Constitution, although considerably reinterpreted, remained in force. In law, the Loi-Cadre reforms did not derive increased legislative and executive powers and functions for the territories from the powers of the French Parliament. Rather, the reforms transferred to the elected territorial governments some of the authority previously exercised with few democratic checks mainly by the governor, partly by the grand council and the governor-general, and partly by the overseas minister who controlled these high officials. In constitutional theory, therefore, the Loi-Cadre reforms decentralized and democratized the conduct of territorial affairs, but did not decentralize the unitary state. Seen in this light, the Loi-Cadre reforms might be, as Minister of Justice Mitterrand said, 'the final fulfilment of the thirteen year old promises of Brazzaville'.[3]

It is by no means certain that even the letter of the 1946 Constitution was respected by the Loi-Cadre decrees. Certainly its spirit was not. Article 72 reserved the right to legislate on overseas criminal law to Parliament, yet the Loi-Cadre decrees made it legal for territorial assemblies to impose fines or jail sentences. Article 72 reserved to Parliament legislation on overseas administration, while Article 76 designated the governor 'head of the administration of the territory'. Yet the Loi-Cadre divided the public services into state and territorial ones, and gave the governor charge only of the former. Article 74 stated the territorial assemblies had to be consulted before Parliament adopts laws on 'the internal organisation of each overseas

[1] See the speech by Senator Durand-Réville (first college, Gabon). J.O.C.R., *Débats*, 19 February 1957, p. 439.

[2] This comparison was also suggested by Lord Hailey in *An African Survey, Revised 1956*, Oxford University Press, London, 1957, p. 344.

[3] Mitterrand, François. *Présence française et abandon*, Plon, Paris, 1957, p. 214.

territory or of each group of territories', yet the assemblies were altogether ignored in the Loi-Cadre procedure. Finally, Article 72 expressly forbade Parliament to delegate legislative powers, and yet the Loi-Cadre did just that. Overseas Minister Defferre invoked the Constitution when he successfully argued Article 76 meant the chief African minister could not be called prime minister and the council of government could not technically be responsible to the territorial assembly. On the whole, however, in the opinion of French jurists, the Constitution was violated.[1] Only because the Constitution gave Parliament most powers to decide on the constitutionality of its own acts, could the Loi-Cadre reforms be adopted without previous constitutional revision.[2]

After the Loi-Cadre reforms were law, revision of the Constitution became essential. The chief break with past practice came with dividing between the government in Paris and in each territory the power to legislate, execute, and administer. This really divided the 'indivisible' Fourth Republic.[3] The terms of the October 1958 Constitution may have been something of a surprise in France, but not overseas.[4] It simply contitutionalized and built upon the precedents set with the Loi-Cadre reforms by differentiating between France, the Republic, and the West African territories rebaptized states within the Community. The Loi-Cadre materially reduced the number of overseas questions decided in Paris, and the disappearance of African representatives from the organs of the Fifth Republic followed logically. So did, in 1959, the adoption of individual constitutions by each of the seven French-speaking West African states which then remained in the Community.[5]

France accepted a division of power between the territories and the government in Paris during 1957, but not independence. The hope, as in Togo, was to prevent it, first through timing. Both the Loi-Cadre decrees and even more the Constitution of the Fifth Republic were drawn to French rather than African specifications and presented according to a schedule which gave Africans little opportunity to decide. At most, with the October 1958 Constitutions, Africans could express their yes or no.

[1] See Lampué, Pierre. 'Pour une réforme de l'Union française', *Les Cahiers de la République*, May–June 1957, pp. 25–6.
[2] Williams, op. cit., pp. 289–92, and Articles 91–93 of the Constitution.
[3] See Appendix II: C, for the Constitution of the Fifth Republic of 4 October 1958.
[4] In February 1958 the French government decided to convene a round table conference to discuss revision of Titre VIII of the 1946 Constitution. *Paris–Dakar*, 7 February 1958.
[5] *Constitutions des états de la communauté*; textes recueillis et présentés par P. F. Gonidec, Sirey, Paris, 1959.

Another technique used to prevent independence was dissolution of the federation of AOF—in the words of Senghor, 'Balkanization'. In contrast to recent British policy, recent French policy towards tropical Africa has been to avoid setting up responsible government at the federal level. This reversed the precedents established by France in 1904, when the AOF federation was created principally as a way to make the poorer colonies pay for the administration of the richer ones. Then, total control over the colonial administration resided in Paris, independence was unthinkable and nationalism unknown. After nationalism became the chief cause of French post-war colonial difficulties, France changed policy towards tropical Africa in 1956, and accepted territorial autonomy—partly to prevent independence. The existence of a self-governing federation was seen as a threat. French leaders realized independence for each territory, inhabited on the average by two and a half million people, was an obviously less attractive prospect than for a federation of eight territories comprising upwards of twenty million people. Since Article 78 of the 1946 Constitution specifically referred to the Grand Councils, it was impossible for the Loi-Cadre to cut out altogether the federation of AOF. This came with the Constitution of the Fifth Republic which eliminated all reference to any Grand Council, did away with the federation of AOF and but vaguely mentioned (Article 76) that those states in the Community desiring to group themselves might do so. In January 1959, four African states—Senegal, Soudan, Dahomey, and Upper Volta—took the initiative to create a federation, Mali. Once again largely, though not solely, because of French pressure Dahomey and Upper Volta dropped out even before Mali was born of Soudan and Senegal in April. This federation broke apart in August 1960. (By September Mali ceased to refer to the federation, and became the new name adopted by Soudan.) Though not all French officials opposed federation the government did and pointed in justification to the territorialist position of the Ivory Coast leaders.

Another technique France used to prevent independence was setting legal limits. The dominant position of metropolitan France was written into the Loi-Cadre reforms. Supreme powers over legislation remained with the French Parliament; its laws continued to take precedence over decisions by territorial assemblies. Though with a few designated exceptions, assemblies in Africa could repeal laws and decrees passed before the Loi-Cadre reforms in spheres assigned to the territories or the federation. The state public services, which included the *commandants des cercles* (district officers) and reached into each locality, continued to function free from territorial control. The French government retained not only the sole right to dissolve

African assemblies,[1] but also the right to annul their decisions. It remained arbiter of interterritorial disputes and supervisor of interterritorial contacts. The authority of African assemblies was specifically defined, while that of the Republic was residual.

The Constitution of the Fifth Republic also contained legal barriers to independence, only it enumerated the powers reserved in practice to France, and made residual those of the states in the Community. Article 78: 'Foreign policy, defence, currency, common economic and financial policy, policy on strategic raw materials' were assigned definitely, and 'supervision of tribunals, higher education, the general organization of external transportation and transportation within the Community, as well as of telecommunications' were assigned, unless contradicted by specific agreements, to 'the Community'. This appeared to be a federal division of powers, but it was not. For only the government of the French Republic, mainly through its President, had the power to decide on these enumerated matters. There were indeed organs of the Community—mainly the Senate, indirectly elected according to population by the members of the Community, and the Executive Council representing the Community governments. But these were purely consultative. And although article 86 of the 1958 Constitution made independence possible, it also made it incompatible with membership in the Community.

If these legal assignments of control to France were the stick used against independence, finance was the carrot. Africans observed, 'the economic content of the Loi-Cadre is more important than its political content'.[2] They appreciated, for example, payments from the metropolitan budget for the cost of the state services, for guaranteed prices and markets of many African products, and for economic development. Economic considerations featured prominently in the thinking of both Frenchmen and Africans when they took the decisions in 1958 which established the Community. General de Gaulle told those territories voting 'no' in the constitutional referendum of 28 September 1958 they had to 'take the consequences'—no aid.[3] Only one did, and in 1958 the Republic of Guinea became the first of the former French-speaking West African states to acquire independence.

That was the final blow to French resistance to independence. The remnants of French resistance to independence collapsed in 1959, as

[1] Decree 57-495, 5 April 1957, Article 17.
[2] From a speech by Soudan minister of commerce and industry, Hamaciré Douré, RDA, *Paris-Dakar*, 27 August 1957.
[3] From a speech by Charles de Gaulle at Brazzaville, 24 August 1958, during his African tour.

the war in Algeria dragged on and civil war endangered the stability of the Fifth Republic, and with Togo, Cameroun, the Belgian Congo, and Nigeria shortly to join Guinea, Ghana, and Liberia as independent states in western Africa. Speaking in Dakar on 13 December after the sixth meeting of the executive council of the Community, General de Gaulle accepted independence for the federal state of Mali created early in 1959 by the leaders of Senegal and Soudan. 'This state of Mali will take what is called the status of independence, and what I prefer to call that of international sovereignty. . . . Independence is a word signifying an intention, but the world being what it is, so small, so narrow, so intertwined with itself, that real independence, total independence belongs in truth to no one.'[1]

Little more than a year separated the spiteful treatment meted out by France to Guinea, when it chose independence—cut telephone wires, cracked state dishes, hospital shelves stripped of drugs—from the polite acceptance of independence for Mali. The contrast marked finally French acceptance of the inevitable. Without fuss in 1960 the French government sponsored a constitutional amendment of Title XII, making it possible for a state to be sovereign and yet a member of the *Communauté renovée*. Therefore the results of both French and British colonial policy in West Africa, once so different, were after all identical, and the Community became a 'Commonwealth à la française'.[2] Even this community faded, and abhorrence of the idea of colonial independence, which had for so long been the first premise of French colonial policy, disappeared 'along with much else reminiscent of a by-gone age, into the limbo of forgotten things'.[3]

[1] Merle, Marcel. 'La Communauté franco-africaine', *Révue de l'Action Populaire*, June 1960, p. 674.
[2] Senghor, Léopold Sédar. 'Rapport sur la doctrine et le program du Parti', *Congrès Constitutif du Parti de la Fédération Africaine*, Dakar, 1–3 July 1959, p. 25.
[3] Lyons, op. cit., p. 264.

PART THREE

West Africans in the French Parliament

INVITING African representatives into the French Parliament was a by-product of the revolutionary doctrine of assimilation, given first expression in 1848, when the 'citizens' from the old communes of Senegal elected one man to the French Chamber. A more meaningful number of Africans took seats in the French Parliament, ironically, only during the lifetime of the Fourth Republic, when assimilation was already outdated. The men holding these seats were known as the West African *parlementaires*. The term, under the Fourth Republic, distinguished them from the broader group of *élus* which included the councillors in the assemblies located in Africa. The *parlementaires* commuted between Paris and their African constituencies. Many helped make possible eventual French acceptance of independence for the West African states. With considerable skill they worked themselves out of their French positions and into African ones—in one of the new republics of Guinea, Mali, Mauretania, Ivory Coast, Niger, Upper Volta, or Dahomey.

Africans from tropical Africa ceased to be *parlementaires* when the Fifth Republic was born. It is useful to examine their work partly because it constitutes an interesting footnote in the history of France. More important, from the African standpoint, is the record they left of some fourteen years of negotiations with the changing governments and party leaders of France. The only counterpart of this work in English-speaking Africa was occasional, in the conferences held in London between Kenyans or Nigerians and the British government prior to independence. Since some Africans were in Paris regularly, they gained intimate experience of metropolitan politics. They learned to benefit from the changing balance of French majorities, and contracted a variety of links with different French political parties.

From the beginning, the African deputies to the French National Assembly were the most important of the *parlementaires*. They set the pattern of the alliances with French parliamentary party groups made by Africans in the Council of the Republic and the Assembly of the French Union. The occasional deviations from the pattern simply reflected the differences in the rules about minimum numbers constituting a group, in party composition, and in the time and manner of election. This explained, for example, why between 1947 and 1950 *Rassemblement Démocratique Africain* deputies in the National Assembly allied with the URR progressive group (*Union des Républicaine et Résistants*) *apparenté* with the Communists, while in the Council of the Republic and the Assembly of the French Union the RDA were *apparentés* directly with the Communists.

The most important reason why deputies set the pace for the West African *parlementaires* was the dominant position of the National Assembly. Under the Fourth Republic the initiative on colonial questions was on the whole with the French Council of Ministers, responsible only to the Assembly. It was not very important, therefore, that the Council of the Republic was more conservative on colonial questions, partly because its members were indirectly elected, mainly by local councils. From West Africa, the two college electoral system used for the territorial assemblies meant there were Senators representing the small European commercial and planter minority resident in West Africa, who after 1946 no longer had places reserved in the lower house. Furthermore, the number of electors from West Africa for Senators was small, and it was comparatively easy for French pressure groups or administrators to 'arrange' the outcome, particularly in the poorer territories. It was something of a surprise to most Soudanese to find themselves represented in the first Council of the Republic by Marius Moutet, post-war overseas minister until November 1947, who had not been re-elected to the first Legislature of the National Assembly. His successor was an even more unusual figure in Soudan, Pierre Bertaux, the former Resistance hero who resigned under a cloud as Director General of the Sûreté Nationale over the scandal of the Begum Ali Khan's jewel robbery in the South of France.[1] Nor was his successor, René Fillon, any better known. Before his election in June 1955, he could only claim 'a discreet three day stay in Soudan'.[2] Since the upper house had little power, however, West Africans paid less attention to electoral scandals surrounding Senators than deputies.

In the long run, the conservative votes of the Council of the Republic on colonial questions could only delay, not prevent laws which the majority of the National Assembly favoured. This was illustrated by the law of 18 November 1955 which provided for African municipal councils elected by universal suffrage and single electoral college. From 12 August 1954, to the final adoption of the

[1] See chapter iv in Theodore White's *Fire in the Ashes*, Sloane, New York, 1954
[2] *Le Journal du Soudan* (paper printed in Paris by associates of Bertaux), 2 July 1955.

law in November 1955, the Council of the Republic fought against the National Assembly's decision for a single electoral college. Three readings of the municipalities bill in the National Assembly, and three in the Council of the Republic took place. But the Assembly's bill became law.[1]

The assembly of the French Union was quite powerless. Centre deputies, during the early years of the Fourth Republic, considered it a waste of money. René Pleven (UDSR) said so, and suggested its replacement in whole or in part by the Council of the Republic transformed on colonial matters into an assembly of the French Union.[2] The members of the Assembly of the French Union frequently complained of neglect.[3] Not until 1954 was any one of its texts, on Togo, taken into consideration by the National Assembly, and then because a change of colonial policy was taking place under the Mendès-France government. The consultative powers of the Assembly of the French Union on occasion enabled it to influence legislation, and decrees of overseas ministers. It had more time than the National Assembly to devote to the discussion of major African issues, and made some valuable additions to hastily drafted bills or decrees. The Assembly of the French Union as a whole, with its right to issue opinions on French executive and administrative edicts, lost significance when the Loi-Cadre decrees in 1957 expanded the scope of elected territorial governments. For this reason, several alternative constitutional reforms were considered in 1958. Should the Assembly of the French Union disappear, and African representation in Parliament increase? This was rejected. Instead, the Constitution of the Fifth Republic chose to end African representation in the Parliament of France, and transform the Assembly of the French Union into the Senate of the Community, elected according to population. It shared the weakness of its predecessor: no real powers. After an initial meeting in July 1959, the Senate faded as the Community was transformed into a club of independent states.

·The work of African senators in the Council of the Republic, African councillors in the Assembly of the French Union and African councillors in the Economic Council is of some interest. Most men in these posts had prestige in Africa, regardless whether their assemblies had any real power. Furthermore, African participation in these institutions had repercussions on their operation. African parties put up their top leaders, however, for election as

---

[1] See *Interafrique Presse*, no. 53, 17 November 1955. For differences between National Assembly and Council of the Republic texts, see the *Bulletin d'information de l'Union française* (MRP), June 1955, Paris.

[2] Le Brun Kéris, op. cit., p. 45.

[3] J.O.A.N.C., *Débats*, 12 August 1947, p. 4257.

deputies. For the purpose of determining the relationship between French and African parties and institutions, West African representation in the National Assembly has most significance and is therefore specially examined here.

Upon election, West Africans deputies had to decide either to reject entirely alliances with French parties, and to retain their special African identity by refusing to behave as French deputies behave; or to act as any small group of deputies acts in a multi-party Assembly: seeking alliances, and exploiting the shifting majority. Some deputies from Madagascar[1] and nationalist second college deputies from Algeria[2] refused to bow to the rules of the National Assembly. They made no alliances and sacrificed key commission appointments and parliamentary time to maintain their independence of French parties. They frequently voted with the deputies of the Left during *tripartisme*, but refused any parliamentary group discipline other than their own. None of the West African deputies to the National Assembly acted in this way. Although some West African deputies challenged the French system in Africa, for a dozen years they made no open challenge in Paris. They used parliamentary privileges fully, and accepted the rules which encouraged individual deputies to become members of parliamentary groups.

A regular salary, and access to transportation, information, and secretaries were some of the privileges of deputies. Probably the most important privilege, parliamentary immunity, proved a boon for African leaders whose parties were opposed by the local administration. Immunity meant no deputy could be arrested for a crime or misdemeanour unless either caught in the act,[3] or the Assembly agreed to suspend his immunity, which it was most reluctant to do.[4] Immunity helped save Houphouët-Boigny, RDA Ivory Coast deputy from arrest in 1950. Immunity also meant that newspapers directed by a deputy could not in practice be sued for slander. This kept several African newspapers publishing in spite of official displeasure. For example in 1949–51, when pursuing a repressive policy against the RDA of Ivory Coast, Governor Péchoux tried to sue the RDA newspaper, *Le Démocrate*, and prosecute for slander its director, deputy Ouëzzin Coulibaly. The governor could not do so. After 1951, the National Assembly limited this attribute of immunity.

[1] The *Mouvement Démocratique de Rénovation Malgache* (MDRM) deputies in the Constituent Assemblies and the first Legislature, 1945–7.
[2] The 11 *Union Démocratique du Manifeste Algérien* deputies in the second Constituent Assembly, and the 5 *Mouvement du Triomphe des Libertés Démocratiques* (MTLD) Algerian deputies in the first Legislature.
[3] *Flagrant délit.*
[4] Williams, op. cit., pp. 193–4; Lidderdale, op. cit., pp. 94–100.

The Constitution of the Fourth Republic and the standing orders of the Assembly encouraged individual deputies to join parliamentary political groups by giving them an important role in the organization of agenda, commissions, debates, and the division of posts of Assembly command. The groups were proportionally represented in the Assembly's working commissions, and in the *bureau* which organized the work of the Assembly and its staff. Only spokesmen of groups were recognized in some debates. They had special rights in proposing bills. They alone could ask for open ballots without proxies.[1] They took part in the conference of presidents, which included also the president and vice-presidents of the Assembly, presidents of commissions and a representative of the Government. This conference organized debates, alloted debating time, and fixed the agenda of the Assembly.[2]

If they had worked alone, Africans would have had very little influence in an Assembly which with successive elections grew from 586 to 627 deputies. The number of West African deputies was 6 Africans and 4 Europeans in the Constituent Assemblies, 13 Africans in 1946–7, 15 in 1947–51, and 20 after 1951. To make the most of their presence in the Assembly, therefore, West African deputies established various types of relationships with French parliamentary groups. They did this by inscription—joining already existing groups; by *apparentement*—allying themselves indirectly to these groups; or by trying to form parliamentary groups composed solely of overseas representatives.[3]

During the two Constituent Assemblies, 4 West African deputies were members of the Socialist group and 2 were members of the *Union des Républicains et Résistants*,[4] which in turn was *apparenté* to the Communists. During the first Legislature, West African deputies changed their alliances frequently: until 1948, 7 were URR and 6 Socialist; after 1948, until October 1950, 4 were URR, 4 Socialist,

---

[1] This *scrutin publique à la tribune* was abolished in 1952, except in verification of deputies' credentials.

[2] Subject to confirmation by the Assembly. Williams, op. cit., pp. 364–6; Lidderdale, op. cit., pp. 100–16.

[3] See Appendix III, for a list of West African deputies, and their parliamentary groups, 1945–58.

[4] The URR had its origin in the Communist resistance affiliate, *Mouvement Unifié de la Renaissance Française*, Wright, op. cit., pp. 77 and 103. The URR had a majority of overseas members and added *pour l'Union Française* to its title in July 1947. Between 1949 and 1951, the URR could muster the necessary 14 members to be a parliamentary group in its own right, and was therefore not formally *apparenté* with the Communists. On almost every vote, the URR voted with the Communists. After the West African deputies left the URR at the end of 1950, the group changed its name to *Union des Républicains Progressistes*.

6 Overseas Independent (IOM)[1] and 1 was UDSR; at the end of 1950, the 4 URR deputies resigned and remained independent of any group. In the 1951 Legislature, the pattern of West African parliamentary alliances moved towards the Centre; 9 were IOM, 5 Socialist, 1 UDSR and 2 *apparentés* UDSR,[2] and 3 Conservative.[3] In 1956 the proportion of IOM and *apparentés* UDSR almost reversed: 8 UDSR-RDA;[4] 4 IOM, 2 Socialist, 4 Conservative, and 2 were independent.[5]

It is understandable that deputies representing principally European electorates did not co-operate with those representing non-European majorities from Algeria, the newly baptized overseas territories and overseas departments, and the associated U.N. (Trust) territories. There were 61 European and non-European overseas deputies in the two Constituent Assemblies. In the 1946 Legislature that number rose to 78, in 1951 to 83, and in 1956, because no elections were held in Algeria (30 deputies) or in French India (1 deputy), the number fell to 52. Of these more than 25 represented non-European majorities in the Constituent Assemblies; in time they became more than 40. Why, even among them, was there comparatively little formal co-operation? In political outlook, these non-European deputies belonged to three distinct categories: those who rejected the French framework which brought them to Paris; those who believed that co-operation either with a French political party or with the *ministrables* of France was tactically necessary to achieve their aim of ending French domination; and those elected primarily because of administrative support.

Some Malagasy and North African revolutionary nationalists—respectively MDRM deputies 1945–7, UDMA and MTLD deputies 1945–51—concentrated on direct action in their countries, not on parliamentary alliances and debate. Their aim was to sever or radically alter the ties that made them French deputies. In contrast, most West African and Equatorial African deputies, whether honestly elected or not, agreed in 1945 to play the French parliamentary game and continued to do so during the lifetime of the Fourth Republic.

[1] IOM deputies were *apparentés* to the MRP, September 1948 to January 1949, when they achieved the total of 14 members needed to constitute a parliamentary group. The *apparentement* was resumed after the 2 January 1956 elections, when the IOM again fell to under 14.

[2] RDA representatives who until 1950 had been members of the URR group.

[3] The term Conservative covers Africans who were members, or *apparentés* of the MRP parliamentary group (exclusive of the IOM), as well as groups, under various parliamentary labels, of the Radicals, Gaullists, and Independents.

[4] 7 RDA, and Condat, *apparenté* UDSR.

[5] Deputies Guissou and Conombo of Upper Volta, IOM in the 1951 Legislature, shifted to the RDA in 1956. Conombo broke with the RDA in 1957.

Even if nationalists, their approach was evolutionary. They did not emulate the nationalists among their neighbours from the trust territories of Togo and Cameroun, who on occasion refused to present candidates in election. The non-European deputies elected, only because sponsored by the administration, often had little in common with evolutionary nationalists and still less, of course, with North African or Malagasy revolutionary nationalists. Administrative *protegés* were often declared elected in Algeria;[1] the 1951 tropical African elections and the 1954 partial elections in Guinea also saw much administrative interference. Deputies elected in such conditions treated their posts as lucrative sinecures, and generally allied themselves with French parties of the Centre or Right.

Even had all non-European deputies voted together, they were too few to obtain the consent of the majority of the Assembly on issues so controversial and diverse as North Africa, Madagascar, Vietnam, and tropical Africa. Many West African deputies were attacked by their African followers when they voted against, or abstained on issues favoured by nationalists in other parts of the French Empire— particularly Togo, Cameroun, and Algeria. The tropical African deputies quickly learned they improved their chances with the majority, if they dissociated themselves from explosive nationalist demands elsewhere, and for a decade concentrated on their own narrowly defined interests. Co-operation was regular only among West and Equatorial African deputies, whose institutions and interests were usually identical, and even this was confined to specific issues.

There were a few exceptions to this general lack of co-operation among non-European deputies from geographically dispersed colonies. At the first Constituent Assembly, Gabriel d'Arboussier[2] unsuccessfully pleaded that Algeria be discussed in the Overseas Territories Commission, and thus challenged the French conception

---

[1] See Julien, Charles-André, *L'Afrique du nord en marche*, Paris, Julliard, 1952, chapter viii.

[2] J.O.A.N.C. I, *Débats*, 22 November 1945, p. 97. d'Arboussier's father was a French administrator, and his mother a Djavando from the French Soudan. Trained as a lawyer and administrator, he was for a time director of political affairs in the Ivory Coast. He was the first African deputy to speak in the Constituent Assembly. He was a first college URR deputy in the first *Constituante* from Gabon-Moyen Congo; between 1947 and 1952 he was an Ivory Coast councillor of the French Union. Between 1946 and 1950, he was secretary-general of the RDA, where he did much to stimulate Marxist modes of thought and sympathy with Communist views. He had no significant political role in Africa during the years 1951 to 1956. In 1957 he was elected first vice-president of the federal Grand Council of French West Africa, and president in 1958; he then represented Niger. In 1959 he became member of the federal assembly of Mali, and in 1960 Minister of Justice of Senegal.

that Algeria was part of metropolitan France. To the RDA deputies, one of the attractions of their *apparentement* with the Communists was the support the Communist group frequently gave to nationalist demands. Together with their group, before 1950, RDA deputies made spirited attacks upon, and voted against government policy in Algeria and Vietnam.[1] During the first *Constituante*, the tropical African deputies voted for the unsuccessful demand made by second college Algerians for a single electoral college in Algeria.[2]

In 1947 most tropical African deputies challenged French repressive measures in Madagascar. Since the start of the Algerian war in 1954, the speeches, though not the votes, of tropical African deputies on North African questions showed considerable sympathy with the Algerian nationalist cause. The war in Algeria was the best illustration of the dilemma which at times faced the West African political leaders who were also *parlementaires*. Since 1955 their parties passed increasingly emphatic resolutions favouring the nationalists. The deputies frequently helped draft the resolutions, but did not necessarily vote against government policy. The West African deputies knew their bargaining position in Parliament was strengthened by the war. They thought voting against the government's Algerian policy while not changing it, would make many French deputies unwilling to vote reforms for tropical Africa. All the West African deputies are uncomfortable to have on record such votes as those of 1956 and 1957, when not one voted against special powers to the government for the Algerian war.[3]

The pattern of changing alliances of the West African deputies reflected, with something of a time lag, the movement of the majority in France. The ties were strongest when African parties were weakest. In the first few years after the war, the alliances of the West African deputies roughly concorded with the way in which the French parties within the post-war tripartite front 'parcelled out the administration among themselves, each treating its own sector as an area to be exploited for its private purposes'.[4] In time Africans adjusted their alliances to the movement of the political majority in France from Left to Centre, and consequently from groups demanding strong

[1] For some details, see *Interafrique Presse*, no. 127, 13 September 1957, pp. 1–4.
[2] J.O.A.N.C. I, *Débats*, 11 April 1946, p. 1718.
[3] Special powers for Algeria were voted to the Guy Mollet 1956–7 Government, which included the RDA president, Félix Houphouët-Boigny. No African deputy voted against special powers. Both IOM and RDA–UDSR West African deputies split their votes:—*For:*—Diallo S., Diawadou, Dia, Houphouët, Dicko, Diori, Senghor, Sidi el Mokhtar. *Voluntary abstention:* Apithy. *Did not take part in the vote:* Konaté, Maga, Keïta, Nazi Boni, Ouëdraogo, Touré, Coulibaly, Sissoko. *Interafrique Presse*, 16 March 1956, and 19 July 1957.
[4] Williams, op. cit., p. 384, also p. 388.

discipline towards those allowing considerable freedom to individual deputies.[1] Increasingly Africans confined their relations with French groups to administrative *apparentement*, so that after the Loi-Cadre these ties simply faded away, a fact registered when the October 1958 Constitution ended African representation in the French Parliament.

Africans at the Constituent Assembly

The elections of 21 October 1945, came as a surprise to most parts of Africa. Only in Senegal and Ivory Coast were Africans at all organized for them. The timing made no concession to African distances, Lamine Guèye of Senegal complained, for sessions of the Assembly started on 6 November, even though the second ballot in some overseas areas was not cast until the 18th.[2] No wonder, therefore, that overseas representatives played a very small role in the first few weeks of session. Only Lamine Guèye and his fellow Socialist from Senegal, Léopold Sédar Senghor were present.

West African deputies learned quickly what was expected of them. They adopted protective colouring so rapidly that they earned qualified admiration from their French colleagues—'like ourselves, most of the indigenous deputies from the overseas territories are profoundly French. But they run a great risk, that their influence will disappear with that of France.'[3] The West Africans knew they were expected to praise, or be considered ungrateful. Occasionally this elicited protest. 'We are not here to sing praise and nothing but praise,' cried RDA President Félix Houphouët-Boigny of Ivory Coast during one debate.[4]

The West African representatives learned too that their position in the Assembly was marginal. Most of their metropolitan colleagues were not only ignorant about African questions, but also bored with them. Little side incidents illustrated this. When Horma Ould Babana of Mauretania said French governments changed too often to handle serious problems with Russia, Germany, and the United States, a voice from the Right cut in, 'and the problem of Mauretania'.[5] Benches were almost empty during the rare debates on colonial questions. No more than fifty, for example, attended the debate on the overseas section of the French budget during the first *Constituante*. Yet when votes were taken, almost 380 voted. 'This

[1] Campbell, Peter. 'Discipline and Loyalty in French Parliament during the Pinay Government', *Political Studies*, vol. i, no. 3, Oxford, October 1953.
[2] J.O.A.N.C. I, *Débats*, 18 April 1946, p. 2020.
[3] PRL deputy Brunhes, J.O.A.N.C. II, *Débats*, 11 September 1946, p. 3790.
[4] J.O.A.N., *Débats*, 4 August 1947, p. 3909, in a discussion on the powers of federal assemblies.
[5] J.O.A.N., *Débats*, 19 July 1948, p. 4847.

proves four Communists and twelve Socialists can put 300 ballots into the urn,' grumbled M. Denais.[1] Assembly rules allowed absentee ballots to be cast by the group's representative, the *boîtier*.[2]

West Africans were expected to keep out of purely metropolitan issues and confine their work to colonial matters. Even then they were not sure of being heeded. When the Assembly did not take into account the view of the overseas deputies regarding devaluation of the colonial franc, Lamine Guèye protested:

It seems to me the Government and the Assembly have the obligation to take our proposals into serious consideration. This alone can give the impression that we are not here simply to vote on texts that interest France; this alone can give the certainty that when the overseas territories are discussed, France knows that solidarity cannot operate only in a single direction.[3]

The West African deputies quickly contracted alliances with one of the two Marxist parties in the tripartite government. All three government parties had found posts for their supporters as senior administrators in Africa to replace those purged for collaboration— the Socialists and Communists mainly in West Africa, and the MRP principally in Equatorial Africa.[4] Most West Africans owed their election in 1945 to some administrative support. It was no accident, for example, that Governor Latrille of Ivory Coast sympathized with the Communists, and so did deputy Houphouët-Boigny. Governor Wiltord of Senegal was a Socialist, and so was Lamine Guèye. Of the six West Africans, four joined the Socialists and two the URR.

Lamine Guèye, who had founded a branch of the SFIO among the pre-war 'citizens' of Senegal in 1936, joined the Socialist group for the ideas it represented, out of loyalty, and for backing. He quickly became the 'grand old man' among African deputies; both age and experience fitted him for this. Many of his pre-war views—citizen-ship for all, abolition of the native penal code and of forced labour—found their way into the Constitutions. Lamine Guèye's junior from Senegal, Léopold Senghor, followed his lead. The other two Socialist West Africans, Sourou Migan Apithy of Dahomey and Yacine Diallo of Guinea, allied themselves with the SFIO for reasons of expediency.

[1] J.O.A.N.C. I, *Débats*, 20 April 1946, p. 2101.
[2] See Lidderdale, op. cit., p. 142.
[3] J.O.A.N., *Débats*, 12 February 1948, p. 663.
[4] Since July 1943 the Gaullist Pierre Cournarie replaced the Vichy supporter Pierre Boisson, who had held the post of governor-general of French West Africa since 26 June 1941. Cournarie, like his successor in 1946, the sometime professor of philosophy and colonial civil servant René Barthes, had no obvious partisan political affiliations beyond favouring the Marxist parties.

Both URR West African deputies, Houphouët-Boigny from the Ivory Coast and Fily Dabo Sissoko from Soudan, had links with Communist administrators and teachers. They chose their allies primarily in the hope that Communist votes in the Assembly would help them in their demands. Houphouët was cited:

I thought it advantageous to be able to count on 180 Communist votes every time we had a demand to make. My three Malgasy colleagues were always alone. Every time they had a demand to make for their country, they had great difficulty in interesting other groups; while I always had the automatic backing of the Communist Party every time I had some demand to make for AOF.[1]

The Communists were the only French party prepared both to accept West Africans in their group and to devote funds, machinery, and technicians to the training of African political leaders. Since the Communists were still partners in the government, their West African allies were not yet faced with the problems which arose with systematic opposition.

On balance, the decisions of the first Constituent Assembly satisfied the African deputies. True, they voiced countless grievances about post-war conditions in Africa.[2] They saw that the decisions made in Paris were still paper reforms, which needed implementation and above all, funds to make changes visible in Africa. Still, many of their main demands—citizenship, the franchise, the idea of free consent as the basis of their future relationship with France, the end of forced labour, a programme of development—were met.

This was true, even though the Constitutional Commission included no West African deputy until in February 1946 the Socialists replaced one of their members with Léopold Sédar Senghor of Senegal.[3] He quickly became the unofficial grammarian of the Commission. Most West African deputies congregated in the Overseas Territories Commission, where they fought with first college European overseas deputies and helped draft the liberal colonial laws that were passed by the first Constituent Assembly. So pleased, in fact, were the second college deputies with the final decisions, that the

[1] Georges Monnet, European territorial councillor of the Ivory Coast, cited this conversation he had had with RDA Ivory Coast deputy Houphouët-Boigny. *Annex 11348*, op. cit., p. 136.

[2] See the interpellations on colonial policy, 20–26 March 1946, J.O.A.N.C. I, *Débats*, pp. 899 f. which ended in adoption of a vote of confidence in the Government.

[3] Senghor replaced the Socialist deputy from Guadaloupe, Paul Valentino, who refused to follow party instructions, and insisted on larger local powers than the newly created category of overseas department allowed for the French West Indies.

tropical African deputies allied with the MRP broke group discipline to vote in favour of the April Constitution.[1]

Africans feared reaction when the April Constitution was rejected. They were not reassured by the government's circular stating that the French Union decisions of the April draft were not in question. On 2 June, all the West Africans who had been in the first Assembly were elected to the second, and made the same parliamentary alliances as before. But only one of the four Europeans from West Africa was re-elected, an index of local European displeasure with the April draft. The speech General de Gaulle made at Bayeux on 16 June added to African worries. He advocated federalism for the 'more advanced' colonies, but for the tropical African colonies he suggested rule by presidential decree.[2] Africans knew the era of good feeling was over, when the *États Généraux de la Colonisation Française* met in Paris 'to save the Empire'. Even ten years after that meeting the term Africans used to sum up what they hated in colonial practices was *États Généraux*. To combat this organized lobby of overseas Europeans, the African deputies organized in July an inter-group of non-European overseas deputies; they made Lamine Guèye their president. Throughout the second Constituent Assembly, this inter-group maintained discipline across party lines on all matters considered vital to non-European interests.

What did the overseas inter-group propose? They claimed the right within twenty years to decide among three alternatives: independence, federation with France, or integration into the French Republic. (In 1958, the referendum on the Constitution of the Fifth Republic gave Africans a somewhat similar set of choices.) To write a constitution for the French Union the African deputies of 1946 called for a third Constituent Assembly where each representative was elected by universal suffrage and represented an equal number of voters. This implied that non-Europeans would outnumber Europeans. Wrote an MRP deputy: 'Such a project was certainly unacceptable: . . . French colonization itself, already pushed aside by a single electoral college in the colonies and by immediate universal suffrage could (at a third French Union *Constituante*, R.S.M.) receive a mortal blow.'[3] French deputies could not agree to the demands of the overseas colonies, and institutions based on equal representation and free consent.

[1] *Scrutin* 121, J.O.A.N.C. I, *Débats*, 19 April 1946, p. 2070; 309 for, 249 against. The MRP voted against the Constitution, but Douala Manga Bell, second college deputy from Cameroun, and le R. P. Bertho, first college deputy from Dahomey, broke party discipline and voted for the Constitution; J. P. Aujoulat, first college MRP deputy from Cameroun, was absent on leave. See also Wright, op. cit., p. 167.
[2] Ibid., pp. 194–9.   [3] Devèze, op. cit., p. 268.

Controversy was sharp in the Constitutional Commission, where conflicting plans of the non-European and European deputies were discussed. The MRP made clear almost from the start they wanted the April Constitution revised in order to reinforce French sovereignty. Within the Commission, therefore, the non-European inter-group had a chance of preventing a reversal of the liberal colonial provisions of the April Constitution only as long as the Communists and Socialists held out against the MRP and the Right. A change of mind by Minister Marius Moutet proved decisive. After the failure of the Vietnamese negotiations at Fontainbleau, Moutet persuaded his fellow Socialists to support some of the MRP's more conservative colonial proposals. This swung the Commission's majority to the side of the MRP, and the French Union texts which resulted were unacceptable to the non-European inter-group. Only the Communists supported the non-European minority.

Disgusted, all Africans walked out of the debates.[1] Long corridor negotiations took place, among the MRP reporter of the Constitutional Commission Paul Coste-Floret, Marius Moutet, the Socialist President of the Constitutional Assembly Vincent Auriol, and the non-European inter-group, led by Lamine Guèye and Ivory Coast deputy Félix Houphouët-Boigny. The walk-out of the overseas non-Europeans had the effect of persuading the Government not to write the double electoral college into the Constitution; to accept the principle of citizenship for Africans; and to agree to a slightly larger overseas representation in the 1946.National Assembly than for the *Constituantes*.

All the African deputies finally voted for the October Constitution, but they were angry and disappointed.[2] Many African observers considered only the Communists were their friends, and recognized their marginal position in Parliament. They had, on several overseas issues, broken discipline with their parliamentary groups. They resented the part played by the Socialist overseas minister in defeating their hopes for a more liberal constitution. The tension within the Socialist group was evident from the fact that Lamine Guèye presided over the overseas inter-group which fought against Moutet.[3]

[1] Discussion of the French Union sections of the Constitution was postponed in plenary session (J.O.A.N.C. II, *Débats*, 20 September 1946, pp. 3888 f.) since no overseas non-European deputies were present.

[2] *Scrutin* 72, J.O.A.N.C. II, *Débats*, 28 September 1946, p. 4259. The Communists, Socialists, and MRP voted for the Constitution. The Algerian UDMA deputies, and the Malgasy MDRM deputies abstained or did not take part in the vote.

[3] In the first week of October 1946 most West African deputies broke discipline with their groups on African issues. Even the RDA–URR deputies did this once: *Scrutin* 89, J.O.A.N.C. II, *Débats*, 4 October 1946, p. 4567, on the electoral

Bad feeling among Africans and Europeans, however, did not prevent extra-parliamentary negotiations from taking place. Houphouët-Boigny left on a mission to Africa, to settle some of the pressing manpower problems which resulted from the abolition of forced labour.[1] African deputies succeeded in obtaining the transfer of some French administrators they considered particularly obnoxious in Africa. Handling such individual local questions, outside of Parliament, was among the most important tasks of the overseas deputies. The French executive retained power both over issues arising out of or not referred to by post-war reforms, and over administration. Most tropical African deputies, representing relatively weak, new parties, found it convenient to co-operate with the government happening to be in power in France.[2]

The tropical African deputies allied with the Communists and Socialists carried their inter-group co-operation beyond the term of the second Constituent Assembly into the electoral campaign for the first Legislature. Their object was to organize against 'reaction'. In a manifesto of September 1946,[3] they called an inter-party tropical African Congress in Bamako, Soudan to form an interterritorial movement to work for African emancipation, soon baptized the *Rassemblement Démocratique Africain* (RDA). They invited observers from all the metropolitan parties.

At first, Overseas Minister Marius Moutet hoped the new African movement, the *Rassemblement Africain*,[4] might join forces with the

law for the National Assembly: 295 for, 245 against. The Communists and URR voted against, but the tropical African deputies who usually voted with the URR —Félix Houphouët-Boigny, Fily–Dabo Sissoko, and the Equatorial African Félix Tchicaya—voted with the majority.

[1] Mentioned by Moutet, J.O.A.N., *Débats*, 9 May 1947, pp. 1543 f.

[2] Compare this with the observations made by Lyons, op. cit., in his chapter describing the actions of the Irish leaders at Westminster. He states that they 'understood that the whole question of home rule was so intimately bound up with English politics, that there were certain to be long periods when the complexities of those politics would crowd the issue of self-government for Ireland into the wings of the parliamentary stage. This fact had been fully realized . . . and its logical consequences had been duly grasped. If the Irish party was obliged to mark time in the matter of self-government, then it was essential that it should have alternative aims to pursue and that while acquiescing in the temporary abandonment of home rule, it should be able to extract from whatever government was in power legislation which might improve social and economic conditions in Ireland.' p. 218.

[3] It was signed by all six West African deputies (Senghor signed after the others, since he was away when the Manifesto was issued) and by the first and second college deputies of Gabon–Moyen–Congo, Gabriel d'Arboussier, and Félix Tchicaya.

[4] Before the Congress, the first mimeographed draft of the RDA statutes spoke of *Rassemblement Africain*; *Démocratique* was inserted later.

Socialists. Soon he concluded it would not, and citing Communist tactics in Africa and France, as well as signs of increasing anti-colonial ferment, called the Bamako Congress dangerous to France. His influence prevented all French parties except the Communists from accepting the invitation to the Bamako meeting of 19–21 October 1946. Had either several or no French parties attended the Bamako conference, then much of the subsequent history of French West Africa might have been different. In the event, French parties both contributed to the failure of the immediate aim at Bamako of unifying all French African parties and party leaders; and the French Communists were left a clear field at Bamako to consolidate an alliance with the RDA.

Perhaps the most important consequence of metropolitan man-oeuvres at the time of the Bamako Congress was the divorce of the modern leaders with mass support in Senegal, from their counterparts in the other French West African territories. The French SFIO had a branch in Senegal, led by Lamine Guèye and Léopold Senghor. At Moutet's instructions they did not attend the meeting. Eleven years afterwards Léopold Senghor still sought to repair:

the fault committed by the Senegalese deputies . . . in refusing to attend the Bamako Congress of the RDA. Certainly I personally wanted to go there, and I did not hesitate to say so at the time to the leaders of the metropolitan party to which I belonged. But I must modestly take my self-criticism to its conclusion. My error was in obeying orders which were imposed on me from outside. Let this be a lesson to you, comrades.[1]

Both Senghor in Senegal, and most RDA leaders at the Bamako Congress were committed not only to political emancipation, but also to economic and social reform. Senegalese absence from the Bamako conference added to already existing tension between them and other French West African political groups, based much more on rivalry for leadership, and a different political history, than on fundamental policy issues.

There were several other West African deputies who, under French pressure, either did not attend or, soon afterwards, abandoned the RDA movement founded at Bamako. Yacine Diallo of Guinea, Sourou Migan Apithy of Dahomey were among these. Fily-Dabo Sissoko wanted to stay away, as Moutet had instructed, but his Soudanese electors forced him to attend and preside the first session. Shortly after the meeting he again repudiated the RDA.[2] Said RDA President Houphouët-Boigny:

[1] January 1957 constituent congress of *Convention Africaine* in Dakar, mimeo-graphed conference records, Dakar, p. 3. (Henceforth cited as CAF records.)
[2] Until 23 January 1946 he was *apparenté* Paysan *apparenté* RDS; until 28 January 1947, URR; then he moved to the Socialist parliamentary group.

All these betrayals of Fily-Dabo Sissoko find their reward in his ephemeral stay at the Under Secretariat of Commerce and Industry, and in his participation in the French delegation at the United Nations. Thus this sad figure is a puppet of the French government and used against the overseas peoples and democratic nations.[1]

The absence of these men from the RDA group was less important, however, than that of the Senegalese. Their supports turned out to be largely ethnic alliances, forged through the officially designated chiefs and backed by the administration. RDA leaders called them *administratifs*. These supports dwindled over time. Attendance at and fidelity to the decisions of the Bamako Congress was for some twelve years a major theme in elections.

Largely because the French Communists had a clear field at Bamako, the RDA, grouping the most important territorial parties outside Senegal and Mauretania in AOF, was allied to the French Communists in Parliament between 1946 and 1950. Slowly, Communist influence deepened. In May 1947, when they began systematically to oppose the French government, so did the RDA. As the domestic cold war cut the French Communists from the republican majority, the French government began actively to repress the RDA in Africa. The most serious consequences were in Ivory Coast, where numerous incidents occurred between 1949 and 1951, involving the administration, local European settlers, and the African supporters of the strongest RDA branch then existing in Africa. A good deal of the zeal with which the RDA was pursued by some administrators and European planters and businessmen had little to do with Communism, except in that it gave them an internationally acceptable excuse for squashing local upstarts and delaying implementation of the constitutional reforms.

French Pressure on African Deputies

After the Liberation, Communists and Socialists both increased activities in West Africa. At Bamako, the Communists clearly defeated the Socialists in the battle for influence over the RDA. After the November 1946 elections, 7 West Africans became indirectly *apparentés* with the Communists, and 6 became members of the Socialist group. The elections moved the French metropolitan majority towards the Centre, especially after the Communists left the government. By November 1947 Moutet stepped out of the Overseas Ministry, and his successors for three years were members of the MRP. At the end of 1947, therefore, the MRP was in a position to make a bid for influence in Africa. It did so as a

[1] RDA 1948 pamphlet, op. cit., p. 19 n.

by-product of the anti-RDA policy which Overseas Minister Paul Coste-Floret claimed was fighting Communism.

The French parties in the government majority not only wrote electoral laws in their own favour,[1] but also put pressure upon the African deputies to change their political alliances. The votes of the overseas deputies at times seemed of great importance in the second Constituent Assembly. Several important votes had been decided by single figure margins.[2] These votes were on amendments to the Constitution or to laws which made no direct reference to the colonies. It is difficult to justify singling out the non-European deputies rather than any others as responsible for swinging the narrow majority one way or another. Certainly there is no proof that the non-European deputies consciously used their vote to influence these decisions. In debates on these issues, non-European deputies did not speak. It was not necessary even to be present at the vote, since ballots could be cast by the *boîtiers*. It could only be said, therefore, that the non-European deputies generally preferred, during the *Constituantes* to vote with the Left on matters that did not directly concern them. Leaders of the republican majority counted the overseas deputies as floating votes to be wooed. It took but little to believe, and then to act upon the belief that Africans who refused overtures from the *ministrables* were enemies of France—a threat both internally, as were the Communists, and externally, as were nationalists in Vietnam, Madagascar, and North Africa.

Official pressure on the RDA was applied both in Africa and in France. To repress the RDA Minister Coste-Floret designated 'tough' men to head the administration. The Socialist deputy Béchard became governor-general, and at first tried, in May 1948, to persuade the RDA, as Moutet had tried, to join with the Socialists.[3] Orselli was still governor of Ivory Coast. Appointed in February, he relates:

Coste-Floret received me for several moments, and the few phrases which he spoke to me can be resumed in the following manner: 'you are going there to suppress the RDA'.[4]

---

[1] See Chapter 19 in Williams, op. cit., pp. 309–26.
[2] Some examples are *scrutin* 25, 29 August 1946, where two votes killed an amendment on education to the preamble of the Constitution proposed by the pro-clerical parties of the Assembly; in *scrutin* 38, 11 September 1946, two votes prevented writing an indirect electoral procedure for the Council of the Republic into the Constitution, as favoured by MRP and the Right; on another Council of the Republic electoral controversy of 28 September 1946, two votes defeated MRP and the Right in *scrutin* 82; in *scrutin* 83 on the electoral law for the Economic Council, 2 October 1946, six votes defeated a proposal by the MRP and the Right to have representatives from Chambers of Commerce directly appointed by the Chambers.
[3] *Annex 11348*, op. cit., Houphouët-Boigny, p. 35.   [4] Ibid., Orselli, p. 98.

Béchard failed to persuade, and Orselli did not suppress satisfactorily. Therefore, in October 1948 Governor Péchoux replaced him. The first of the Ivory Coast incidents began in February 1949.

A policy of repression meant imprisonment for RDA militants, insults and attempts at bribery for RDA *élus*, banning of RDA meetings. In some areas, especially Ivory Coast, incidents and clashes took place involving RDA supporters, French security forces, officially backed African opponents of the RDA, and occasionally European settlers. The authorities brushed aside interventions on behalf of their followers made by RDA *parlementaires*. When Governor Mouragues banned RDA meetings in Upper Volta in 1948, for example, he told RDA leaders that not even the overseas minister could countermand the order, since the Constitution made the governor alone responsible for maintaining law and order.[1] Civil servants, both African and European, learned that promotion or tenure was incompatible with support of the RDA.

The administration falsified elections. Between the first and second round of the *conseil général* elections in the newly reconstituted territory of Upper Volta, Mouragues became governor. Ouëzzin Coulibaly, RDA deputy from Ivory Coast and a native of Upper Volta, reported to Parliament that Mouragues made very clear he intended to defeat the RDA. Yet RDA complaints in the Assembly met with indifference. There was no reaction when Ouëzzin Coulibaly charged Coste-Floret refused to sign the usually automatic decree to fill a vacant Assembly of the French Union seat in the Soudan until after the Upper Volta elections had been validated.[2] In 1950, the Council of Ministers was reported to have outlawed all RDA meetings in Africa.[3] Even the RDA claim that the Constitution be fully implemented was treated by officials in Africa as a slur upon their prestige. One of the official charges, recognized by the courts, made against RDA militants who attended a meeting ending in incidents in Treichville, Ivory Coast, on 9 February 1949, was 'singing the *Marseillaise*'. (At a retrial in 1953, the court decided 'if, after the dissolution of the meeting, the accused sang the *Marseillaise* and returned home, the court should never have been concerned with this'.)[4]

[1] Houphouët-Boigny, J.O.A.N., *Débats*, 7 December 1948, pp. 7407 f.
[2] J.O.A.N., *Débats*, 22 March 1949, p. 1683.
[3] *Agence France-Presse*, 1 February 1950. This was not published in the *Journal Officiel*. On 24 March 1950 Soudanese RDA deputy Mamadou Konaté questioned the MRP minister Letourneau in the National Assembly about banned RDA meetings in Niger. The minister answered that the ban was imposed in accordance with the law of 30 June 1881. He did not cite any Council of Ministers decision.
[4] *La Côte d'Ivoire* (European-owned), 22 April 1953, reporting on trials of RDA leaders.

Of course little sympathy was forthcoming in France, except among Communists, when they used their considerable propaganda machine[1] to present in France their own version of the troubles the RDA were having with the administration in Africa. There were but few exceptions to the monopoly the Communists had over this publicity. On 9 July 1950 the MRP section of Dordogne voted 13 to. 4 to back the vote cast against his parliamentary group by their deputy A. Denise. Denise justified his indiscipline by citing, *inter alia*, the incidents in the Ivory Coast, for which he held the Government partly responsible. Occasional resignations from the MRP for similar reasons were announced during 1950, as by Robert Lucente, member of the *comité directeur* of the Seine federation (30 June 1950). The public relations work done by such well known left-wing Catholics as Mlle. Claude Gérard was another exception.

The National Assembly was far too busy with other matters to show any constructive interest in African difficulties. In this atmosphere it was hardly surprising that when the West African deputies did change their affiliations, many did so to the profit of the MRP in the Assembly, by joining the new MRP-sponsored *Indépendants d'Outre-mer* (IOM) group. By the end of 1948, only 4 West Africans remained RDA in opposition with the URR and the Communists; 4 were Socialists; 1 *apparenté* UDSR, while 6 had joined the IOM.

What did these new parliamentary alliances mean? The RDA–URR alliance was remarkable because four RDA deputies maintained discipline, in their own ranks and with the Communists, for almost four years after the tripartite political balance had broken down. The RDA leaders saw a wave of anti-Communism in France rise almost simultaneously with anti-RDA pressure in Africa. They found no evidence, therefore, to disprove the explanation their Communist friends gave: that the interests of the French working class and of the colonial peoples were identical; that only the rise to power of the Communists in France would bring true emancipation to Africans. RDA deputies sympathized with criticism of the war in Vietnam that was the immediate cause of Communist opposition on 5 May 1947. At first, the Communist alliance was based largely on expediency, on gratitude for Communist aid and re-

[1] The following are some of the organizations led by Communists or Communist sympathizers which, with their press, misrepresented most incidents in Africa: French Communist Party; *Union Républicaine et Résistante*; *Parti Socialiste Unitaire*; *Juristes Démocrates*; *Union des Femmes Françaises*; *Union de la Jeunesse Républicaine de France*; *Association Nationale des Anciens F.F.I.-F.T.P.F.*; *Union des Chrétiens Progressistes*; *Comité Permanent, Congrès Mondial des Partisans de la Paix*; *Combattants Paix et Liberté*; *Union Nationale des Intellectuels* (list taken from RDA cable of 11 January 1950); *Comité de Défense des Intérêts de l'Afrique Noire*, and *Secours Populaire*.

sources. But as pressure against the RDA increased, and Communist influence within and around the RDA grew, the alliance became firmer: 'an alliance in their common fight against imperialism of the democratic forces of Africa with the democratic and progressive forces of the entire world, and primarily with those of the French people, in their common fight against imperialism'.[1]

The IOM group were officially encouraged to undercut RDA influence in Africa. IOM overseas deputies had relatively little in common, beyond changing their parliamentary alliances two or three times. IOM was a parliamentary alliance of convenience, linked with the MRP, less because most IOM deputies happened to be Catholics, than because the MRP happened to be in power. IOM deputies were, however, in a better position to appeal to the Catholic minority in Africa, than were African deputies, often Muslims, allied with the anti-clerical French parties, for IOM generally followed MRP discipline on matters concerning the Catholic clergy.

The IOM leader, Dr. J.-P. Aujoulat, a European first college deputy from Cameroun,[2] alone wholeheartedly accepted the Christian Democratic ideas of the MRP. Only Senghor of Senegal was supported in Africa by the nucleus of a modern mass party. His *Bloc Démocratique Sénégalais* was formed in 1948 after a split in the Senegalese SFIO and built on Socialist, rather than Christian Democratic lines. For local reasons, Senghor left the Socialist group; for ideological as well as tactical reasons he rejected an alliance with the RDA as long as they were linked to the Communists. Within the IOM group he emphasized the specifically African—as distinct from MRP—satellite characteristics of the IOM. Mamba Sano of Guinea and Sourou Migan Apithy of Dahomey transferred from the URR and Socialist groups respectively, partly out of desire to be on the side of those in power in France, and partly for local ethnic political reasons. The three Upper Voltan deputies, Henri Guissou, Mamadou Ouëdraogo and Nazi Boni were elected, because of traditional and administrative support, at a time when the governor, Mouragues, said openly, 'I am a well-known MRP man, so is Coste-Floret, so is the President of the Council.'[3] (Schuman) Though the three Upper Volta deputies were in the same parliamentary group, this did not keep their supporters, living in different regions, from fighting each other.[4]

[1] RDA 1948 pamphlet, op. cit., p. 75, citing a 3 October 1948 RDA Co-ordinating Committee resolution. RDA deputies also publicly agreed with the Communists on the Marshall Plan. J.O.A.N., *Débats*, 3 March 1949, p. 1222 f.
[2] Elected second college deputy in 1951, but defeated on 2 January 1956.
[3] Ouëzzin Coulibaly, J.O.A.N., *Débats*, 22 March 1949, p. 1674.
[4] *Le Monde*, 12 March 1955.

There were several attempts to transform IOM from a parliamentary group into a political movement in Africa. It was discussed and rejected at the IOM parliamentary study sessions in Paris in July of 1950.[1] *A Mouvement des Indépendants d'Outre-mer* was voted into being at the IOM Congress in Bobo-Dioulasso, 12–15 February 1953. But Secretary-General Mamadou Dia[2] admitted IOM 'co-ordination showed itself to be inoperative, perhaps because it did not have very much to co-ordinate',[3] and so a fresh attempt was made, with a nationalist platform and a new name, at the *Convention Africaine* congress in Dakar, January 1957. None of these moves really succeeded, principally because IOM gathered in a loose fashion *parlementaires* who had known each other not by working side by side in Africa, but by sitting side by side in Paris. The one significant fact in all these attempts was that the West African IOM was led by, and represented the interterritorial policies of the Senegalese leaders who had a mass following. Consequently two rival interterritorial organizations existed in French West Africa: the RDA, led by the Ivory Coast deputy Félix Houphouët-Boigny, and the IOM, led by Léopold Senghor of Senegal.

Horma Ould Babana of Mauretania became an *apparenté* of the UDSR in August 1948, in the vain hope his followers might be undisturbed by the administration and therefore be able to organize. (He was less successful in the tactic than Barthélemy Boganda, who moved from the MRP to the Independent Peasants on the Right, seeking with parliamentary respectability in Paris to offset his radicalism in Oubangui-Chari.) Ould Babana, not re-elected in 1951 partly because of administrative pressure, in 1956 began supporting Moroccan claims to Mauretania.

Among the Africans voting with the Socialists, Lamine Guèye of the SFIO branch in Senegal was an exception. French SFIO leaders respected him in his own right, not merely as the *doyen* both of African political leaders and of Socialism in Africa. Since the thirties, Lamine Guèye played a distinguished part in the formulation of SFIO policy, such as the resolutions passed at the National Council meeting of 10–20 March 1947, making one of the ten declared principles of policy that, 'The French Union, founded on the free consent and on the legal equality of the associated peoples, must become a political and economic reality, and be freed of all colonialist overtones.' The Council further stated that 'Socialism, inseparable from liberty both for nations and for individuals, has always de-

---

[1] See IOM 1950 pamphlet, op. cit., p. 2.
[2] Senator from Senegal, 1948–56; deputy 1956–9; first head, as vice-president, then president of the council of government of Senegal.
[3] CAF records, op. cit., p. 5.

nounced exploitation of man by man, and the subordination of nation by nation'.[1] Fily-Dabo Sissoko and Jean Silvandre (d. 1960) of the Soudan, and Yacine Diallo (d. 1954) of Guinea, enjoyed a different type of relationship with the French Socialists. Their parties in Africa did not try to resemble SFIO branches. In Africa, their parties were officially backed ethnic alliances, and in part their parliamentary affiliations were explained by local ethnic rivalries. Yacine Diallo, *apparenté* Socialist, was in Guinea supported by the official chiefs of the Muslim Fulani kingdoms in the Fouta Djallon plateau; while Mamba Sano, IOM, had the backing in Guinea of the principally animist, ethnically diverse, loosely organized peoples from the forest region of Guinea. For a few years it appeared as if non-RDA Muslim deputies or deputies with predominantly Muslim supporters voted with the Socialists: Lamine Guèye, Yacine Diallo and Sissoko were obvious examples. Muslim Africans perhaps found the extra-parliamentary freemason atmosphere of the anti-clericals more congenial than the semi-religious atmosphere of the MRP. But this generalization cannot be carried too far. IOM leader Senghor, for example, came from a predominantly Muslim constituency. The question of private schools never excited Africans affiliated to anti-clerical parties as it excited metropolitan deputies. Some Muslims wanted state support for Muslim schools, and education was a pressing need.

While the RDA deputies were under heavy pressure, the West African deputies voting during the first Legislature with the Socialists and MRP, still sparring with each other, received some rewards. Sissoko for a brief spell was an Under-Secretary of Commerce and Industry; he and Lamine Guèye were members of French delegations to the UN. Senghor and the Senegalese Senator Ousmane Socé Diop, a Socialist 'citizen' trained as a veterinarian, went with the French delegation to the September 1950 meetings of the European Consultative Assembly in Strasbourg. Senghor was also a member of French delegations to UNESCO, and in October 1950 to the UN Trusteeship Council. By the end of the Legislature, SFIO power was waning and they were no longer able to support their African *protegés* as under *tripartisme*.

Senghor as early as 1948 managed to steal a march on Lamine Guèye on the electoral law for the Council of the Republic. Some proportional representation was specified, and this allowed Senghor's ally in Senegal, Mamadou Dia, to become Senator.[2] In September 1950, Governor Wiltord, a Socialist, in spite of Lamine

---

[1] SFIO *Bulletin Intérieur*, no. 24, March 1947.
[2] J.O.A.N., *Débats*, 20 September 1948, pp. 6747 f. and *Condition Humaine*, 19 October 1948; 30 November 1948.

Guèye's protests, was replaced by Governor Bailly, who was warmly welcomed by Senghor.[1] Evidence was accumulating that administrators in Africa, intent on defeating the RDA, planned to make the IOM the beneficiaries of the 1951 elections. The MRP successfully insisted IOM leader Aujoulat from Cameroun become Mitterrand's Under-Secretary for Overseas France. In April 1951, the Socialist Governor-General, Béchard, made the political error of prosecuting for violation of the press law the White Father missionaries who edited the Dakar weekly *Afrique Nouvelle*. This launched an avalanche of pre-electoral oratory directed against the Socialists, and gave a convenient reason for Béchard's 'interim' replacement in May by Secretary-General Chauvet. During the elections of 1951, therefore, the African Socialists were left without their powerful protector.

In the charged political atmosphere of 1947–51, the French Parliament adopted practically no liberal reforms for the African territories. Inter-group co-operation among tropical African deputies was practically at a standstill. The RDA votes, cast not in person but by the URR *boîtier*, affected the Assembly's majority but little. RDA deputies spent most of their time in Africa. During the RDA–IOM dispute on validation of the credentials of Upper Volta deputies, the IOM Cameroun deputy accused the RDA deputy, Ouëzzin Coulibaly, of spending 'winter, spring and fall' in his African constituency. In reply, the RDA Soudanese deputy, Konaté tartly explained, '. . . if some deputies remain in their territories, it is only to avoid the creation of situations as deplorable as those well known in Madagascar, and in Indochina.'[2] Parliamentary immunity kept the deputies, but not their followers out of jail. Even the African *parlementaires* risked their lives. Kaboret Zinda, Ivory Coast (Upper Volta) RDA deputy died in 1947. In popular belief he was helped to his death by local chiefs, but no evidence is available to confirm or deny this. Ouëzzin Coulibaly, RDA Ivory Coast deputy, escaped attempts on his life in 1949 and 1950. Ivory Coast RDA deputy Houphouët-Boigny was taken into hiding in the forest by his Baule kinsmen to assure his personal safety after the death in 1950 of Biaka Boda, RDA Ivory Coast Senator.[3]

Mounting evidence against the utility of the Communist alliance confronted the RDA deputies. As their organization disintegrated under the impact of administrative repression, and incident succeeded incident in Ivory Coast, the RDA deputies gave increasing thought to the view that, 'We must unite all Africans, kill the pretext, the

---

[1] *Condition Humaine*, 11 April 1950.
[2] J.O.A.N., *Débats*, 22 March 1949, p. 1679.   [3] See pp. 196 f.

false pretext of Communism, and co-operate with men of good will.' RDA leaders watched Kwame Nkrumah's work in Gold Coast, and soon speculated, 'Did Kwame refuse to collaborate with the Conservatives who replaced Labour in power? He raised no battle cry against the British in Malaya, the Atlantic Pact, English constituencies, or German rearmament. Kwame acts. He has his feet on the ground. He does not dream.' The RDA parliamentary group soon 'found that the overseas representatives cannot obtain anything for their countries while in systematic opposition to the government majority'.[1]

The Communists tried to keep the RDA within their orbit. Within the formal RDA structure, modelled partly on the French Communist pattern, the RDA parliamentary representatives 'were firmly subordinated to the Co-ordinating Committee, the supreme directing organ'[2] of the movement, after the second RDA interterritorial congress in Abidjan in February 1949. At that meeting, in part due to Communist advice, the RDA Co-ordinating Committee was reorganized, to exclude the *parlementaires* as such, and include only eight interterritorial officers and two representatives from each territorial section. (Some of these were, of course, also *parlementaires*.) This Co-ordinating Committee represented the party machine, directed by Secretary-General Gabriel d'Arboussier. He favoured maintaining the alliance with the Communists. On 23 June 1950 the parliamentary group of the RDA asked d'Arboussier to resign, as a necessary 'tactical retreat'.[3] He did so, but only, he subsequently claimed, on the condition that he remain unofficially in the post. Some doubt surrounded his resignation until it was dispelled, on 12 July 1952, by the RDA parliamentary group 'definitively excluding Gabriel d'Arboussier from its ranks'.[4]

Within the RDA, the legality of the *parlementaires'* authority remained in doubt, until finally in 1955 the Co-ordinating Committee met again and confirmed it. To circumvent the problem of structure, and to act quickly on what they believed to be 'the higher interest of the movement',[5] the RDA *parlementaires* decided in October 1950 to cut all links with the French Communist party.

[1] These three passages are from 'Réponse à d'Arboussier', a letter written by RDA President Houphouët-Boigny to the former secretary-general of the RDA, d'Arboussier, who opposed disaffiliation from the Communists. *Afrique Noire*, 24 July 1952 (d'Arboussier's letters: *Lettre Ouverte à Félix Houphouët-Boigny*, May–June 1952, and *Deuxième Lettre Ouverte à Félix Houphouët-Boigny*, September 1952, were printed in pamphlet form in Paris. These letters are henceforth cited as Houphouët–d'Arboussier correspondence).
[2] From the political resolution of the 1949 Abidjan RDA congress.
[3] Houphouët in the Houphouët–d'Arboussier correspondence, op. cit.
[4] *Afrique Noire*, 24 July 1952.   [5] Ibid.

The *Rassemblement Démocratique Africain* members of the various metropolitan assemblies, recognizing that common action among all the elected representatives of the overseas territories, in favour of a precise programme, provides the best formula for the defence of the higher interests of Africa, decide to disaffiliate from the metropolitan parliamentary groups to which they were affiliated until this date, in order to achieve the goal of unity.[1]

On 3 December 1950 Félix Tchicaya, Middle Congo, RDA, announced in the Assembly that the RDA would vote confidence in the Pleven government. Pleven thanked the RDA for their *'ralliement à la cause nationale'*, amid general applause. The RDA *parlementaires* had considerable difficulty explaining, less to the mass of their followers, than to the party leaders in Africa, both the decision and the exceptional procedure violating party statutes by which it was taken. In Africa the French Communist reporters, lawyers and other representatives urged RDA militants to condemn their *parlementaires* as 'accomplices of the oppressors, of the slave dealers and the purveyors of prisons'.[2] RDA leaders had to answer these charges, and to begin a long, slow, painful process of rebuilding. They had to cope with confusion, anger, and bitterness; to explain the new tactics; calm terrified villagers; deal with thousands of law cases; obtain a minimum of neutrality from the administration. In France, they began complicated negotiations to forge new alliances within the republican majority, and learned a new language to suit the new decision to collaborate with French officials.

The first parliamentary result of this change in RDA policy came in October 1950 with the revival of the overseas inter-group of all second college tropical African deputies, under the presidency of Lamine Guèye. Their goal was 'to translate all the constitutional promises into institutions and reality'. They agreed 'to respect entirely the independence and the originality of the political formations from which they have sprung', while using the inter-group 'to maintain among themselves the unity in outlook and action necessary for the execution of a common programme': the *Code du Travail*, reform of the local assemblies, electoral and municipal reform, reform of penal legislation, of the health service, of the legislation on citizenship in the overseas territories, a better position for chiefs, and increased credits for development.[3] Moves towards organiza-

---

[1] RDA communique, 18 October 1950. François Mitterrand, speaking at a dinner on 28 September announced some RDA leaders were ready to break their alliance. *Marchés Coloniaux*, 7 October 1950, p. 2373.
[2] Editorial by André Menetrier, secretary-general of *Secours Populaire*, in a special issue of its journal, *La Défense*, n.d., *c.* 1951, Paris, p. 1.
[3] From the inter-group's press communiqué, October 1950.

tional unity among the African deputies failed in spring of 1951, partly because they were not certain what they were unifying for. Their parliamentary programme was a minimum one, and composed of short term goals only. They knew French fear of African 'separation' was at its height, and were not prepared to add to these by challenging, rather than calling for the implementation of the Constitution.

The RDA, uninscribed, wanted to join a group. First, they considered joining forces with the IOM to form an African bloc in Parliament.[1] This failed for several reasons, the most important of which was local bitterness. Many IOM leaders, among them Mambo Sano of Guinea, Apithy of Dahomey, and some of the Senegalese supporters of Senghor against Lamine Guèye, belonged to the RDA before *la répression*;[2] mutual recrimination was too strong to allow collaboration in the approaching elections of June 1951. IOM leaders were not inclined to sacrifice the electoral victory they expected, since the French administrative machine was geared to defeat the RDA. Furthermore, the IOM leaders, opposed to Communism, demanded that the RDA not only break with, but denounce their former allies. But the RDA parliamentary group walked an ideological tightrope in explaining disaffiliation to their followers as a tactical retreat rather than capitulation. They claimed continued adherence to the programme of anti-colonial unity drawn up at the 1946 Bamako congress. They had to convince RDA members, whose formal political education came largely from Marxist and Communist party literature, to agree to disaffiliation, and so could not afford critical denunciation of their former allies, even if they were inclined to. Nor did they favour abandoning, as an alliance with the IOM presupposed, their ambition to constitute a single unified interterritorial grass roots movement. Since the 1946 Bamako Congress the RDA leaders with few exceptions built RDA branches from the ground up in each territory.

For the RDA another argument against an alliance with the IOM was it would not effect total unity even among West African party leaders, since several West Africans worked with the French Socialists. Lamine Guèye also tried to establish links with the RDA early in 1951. Since African Socialists were locally opposed not only by RDA but also IOM, joining the Socialists also did not mean the unity called for at Bamako. The sharpest IOM–Socialist rivalry was in Senegal. An alliance with Lamine Guèye against Senghor might

[1] The negotiations were described indirectly in the Houphouët–d'Arboussier correspondence of 1952. See also *Afrique Nouvelle*, 28 October 1950, and 29 January 1951.
[2] The RDA term describing official policy, 1947–50.

have strengthened the RDA temporarily in that important territory, and so in their rivalry with the IOM for West African leadership. But Socialist strength in Senegal was rapidly declining. The RDA rejected joining the Socialists for other reasons as well. The SFIO, in the persons of Marius Moutet and Governor-General Béchard, was too closely associated with an anti-RDA policy. The dominant majority among the SFIO held assimilationist views and maintained strict discipline in Parliament, both irreconcilable with the RDA desire to maintain a separate, distinctly African identity.

There was no unity, therefore, in spring of 1951. RDA leaders considered, but did not yet accept the alliance offered them by the UDSR overseas minister, François Mitterrand. He made the proposal primarily because the UDSR had lost much of its parliamentary strength when the Gaullists formed a separate party in 1948. UDSR numbers shrank to perilously near the minimum of 14 needed for a separate parliamentary group. At the end of 1946 the UDSR had 23 members and 5 *apparentés*. But on 9 December 1950 group membership was down to 17.[1] At the annual recount of January 1951 this had fallen to 13, which, but for the gallant move of Finance Minister Petsche (no party) who temporarily joined the UDSR, would have meant no commission representation for Prime Minister Pleven's party.[2] Most UDSR deputies were anxious to be or remain ministers. RDA leaders knew that, unlike the Communists or Socialists, the UDSR made no serious demands of policy or voting discipline on its members.[3] Mitterrand helped ease the RDA break with the Communists. Shortly before the 1951 elections, he somewhat reduced anti-RDA pressure in Africa and appointed some higher civil servants who favoured policies of conciliation. By February 1951 Mitterrand and Houphouët-Boigny together opened the newly constructed artificial port of Abidjan. On 1 May 1951 Governor Geay replaced Governor Péchoux.[4] The replacement of Governor-General Béchard in the same month pleased the RDA as much as the IOM.

While the RDA deputies remained uninscribed, the revived overseas inter-group made but little headway before the elections on its minimum programme. In April, after two years of protracted study, the Assembly adopted in first reading the Code du Travail, a success for the West African deputies delayed again when the Council of the Republic rejected liberal clauses of the Code. The Council of the Republic almost upset another victory on the new overseas electoral law. The inter-group played skilfully on the dwindling government majority and refused confidence until the government promised a

[1] From official lists.   [2] Williams, op. cit., p. 236, n. 6.
[3] Ibid., pp. 140, 143–6.
[4] See Mitterrand, *Présence française*, op. cit., chapter iv.

wider African franchise and a declaration of principle in favour of universal suffrage, single electoral colleges in all overseas and associated territories, and more seats in the new Assembly. With the elections only a few weeks away, the Senate turned down these provisions. The overseas inter-group refused to vote for dissolution until the Assembly's liberal electoral provisions became law. The IOM junior minister Aujoulat threatened resignation out of sympathy with the inter-group, while the Radicals shared the Senate's conservatism and threatened mutiny against the Radical Premier Queuille.[1] As usual, the result was compromise: double electoral colleges were maintained outside of West Africa, as in November 1946; the franchise widened but there was no declaration of principle favouring universal suffrage; the number of overseas deputies slightly increased.[2]

Not even non-RDA deputies could cite solid achievements during the first Legislature, of a type that could satisfy their followers.

Let us be frank. The coloured representatives obtained absolutely nothing during the five year term which is now ending. They did not even succeed in·capturing for a few moments the attention of an Assembly indifferent to the point of insolence.

wrote IOM councillor of the French Union Emile-Derlin Zinsou.[3] The reforms written into the Constitution of 1946 were far from implemented in 1951.

Marking Time

Since the new overseas electoral law was published on 24 May, and the elections took place less than a month later, on 17 June 1951, it is not surprising there were many complaints of incorrect administrative procedure, particularly in the compilation of electoral registers. Charges were also made of illegal activity in Senegal. where Lamine Guèye was unexpectedly defeated by Senghor's lieutenant Abbas Guèye. But these referred largely to actions by African party representatives rather than administrators.

In a different category were the documented charges of deliberate official tampering with the results, made particularly in connexion with elections in Mauretania, and also Niger, Soudan, Ivory Coast, and Guinea. Horma Ould Babana, in the first Legislature *apparenté* UDSR since 1948, was defeated in Mauretania less by his nominal rival Sidi el Mokhtar than by the governor, Rogué, designated under the UDSR prime minister, Pleven. In debate, UDSR deputy Pierre Chevallier cited a president of a Mauretanian polling station. 'Had a

[1] *Afrique Nouvelle*, 5 May 1951.
[2] Ibid., 19, 26 May and 2 June 1951.　　　　　[3] Ibid., 7 April 1951.

dog come before me with a voter's card, I would have made him vote.' He charged the governor showed open and declared hostility to the former deputy of Mauretania.[1] Voting against validation, 'the Communists had other allies in the division on the results of Mauretania. The division was among the first in the new Assembly in which the Catholic parties, who supported the winner, confronted the lay parties, who opposed him for various reasons.'[2] The Socialists favoured Babana, up to 1948 a Socialist, the UDSR because he had been with them, and the Radicals because they were allied with the UDSR.

In Niger, Soudan, Ivory Coast, and Guinea the RDA were the losers in the electoral falsification. Typical of the quality of the debate on these elections was a remark by the Soudanese deputy Jean Silvandre, who benefited from the RDA loss. He defended the administration and reproached the RDA as the party 'which aims at sowing trouble and disorder in the French Union'.[3] One deputy in debate unfavourably compared the elections in AOF with those in the neighbouring Gold Coast. The Socialists protested, for they were divided between principles and 'appreciation of the existing system which gave them extra seats in certain colonies under sympathetic administration'.[4] There was solid evidence to support the RDA claim that French officials worked to defeat Ouëzzin Coulibaly of Ivory Coast and Hamani Diori of Niger. Yet the National Assembly adopted a simple political, not a judicial, solution for all these challenges. It saw that on the whole the men declared elected in Africa added votes to the parties hoping to form government majorities, ignored the challenges and validated all results announced in West Africa.[5]

The parliamentary alignments of West Africans in the second Legislature were clear by January 1952: 8 were IOM;[6] 5 Social-

---

[1] J.O.A.N., *Débats*, 7 August 1951, pp. 6233 f.
[2] Campbell, Peter. 'Vérification des Pouvoirs in the French National Assembly', *Political Studies*, vol. i, no. 1, Oxford, February 1953, p. 76.
[3] *Afrique Nouvelle*, 25 August 1951.
[4] Campbell, 'Vérification . . .', op. cit., p. 69.
[5] Campbell, ibid., also concluded that political considerations governed the Assembly's votes on credentials. The Communists 'were sometimes joined by a few overseas deputies in opposing the results of Côte d'Ivoire, French India, Guinea, Niger, and Soudan. (J.O.A.N., *Débats*, 1951), pp. 6493, 5960, 6412, 6388.) The other parties were prepared to regard as inevitable the admitted irregularities in these constituencies, yet doubtless their tolerance was made easier by calculation. These five constituencies together returned twelve deputies, of whom one was RPF, one was affiliated to the MRP, three were UDSR, five were Socialist, and two belonged to the *Rassemblement Démocratique Africain*', p. 75.
[6] Excluding Zodi Ikhia of Niger, who joined the IOM in 1954.

ist;[1] 2 UDSR;[2] 2 *apparentés* UDSR; and 3 Conservative.[3] The new Assembly's majority moved to the Centre, and so did West African links with French parties. Events had eliminated the alliances based on positive preference: Lamine Guèye was defeated; RDA deputies ended their *apparentement* with the Communists. So only frank opportunism characterized the attitude of West Africans to their new parliamentary alliances. Considerations of gratitude, local African differences and mutual expediency which brought the RDA to their *apparentement* with the UDSR in January 1952, typified the reasoning behind all West African parliamentary alliances from then on.

In the 1951 Legislature the UDSR had just 14 members on 6 July. Existence as a separate group was again most precarious, partly because among the 14 were both Zodi Ikhia and Mahamane Condat whose rivalry in Niger soon resulted in Ikhia's transfer to the IOM. The RDA's *apparentement* was with deputies who looked upon the UDSR as a parliamentary home each man inhabits for his own reasons. The metropolitan members of the UDSR made small pretense at unity, as the long-standing feud between Pleven and Mitterrand indicated; the overseas deputies were also a strange mixture. During the *Constituantes*, about one third of the UDSR were first college deputies. The RDA *apparentement* caused considerable comment, including that it 'will probably prevent the ministerial candidates of the UDSR from occupying the rue d'Oudinot'[4] (overseas ministry). Indeed under the Fourth Republic the UDSR never again held the overseas portfolio. The RDA *apparentement* lost the UDSR the vote of at least one European overseas Senator, Marc Rucart of Upper Volta, whose reaction was, 'There is no longer anything I have in common with the *Rassemblement des Gauches*.[5] I want to be able to look straight in the eyes of the Africans who never stopped being loyal to France.'[6] By 1952, the overseas deputies in the UDSR almost outnumbered the metropolitan deputies, but represented the second challenge from North and tropical Africa. Only three were RDA; the others included Algerians, a lone Somali, and until 1954 both Niger deputies.

Only when convenient did the RDA deputies maintain voting discipline with the UDSR, which acted similarly on issues supported by the RDA. The RDA insisted on maintaining a separate identity,

[1] Including Yacine Diallo of Guinea, who died in 1954.
[2] Including Zodi Ikhia.
[3] Excluding Barry Diawadou of Guinea, who took Yacine Diallo's seat in 1954, and joined the Radicals.
[4] *Afrique Nouvelle*, 19 January 1952.
[5] Group which included UDSR in the Council of the Republic.
[6] *Afrique Nouvelle*, 26 January 1952.

and between 1952 and 1955 were *apparentés*, not members of the UDSR group. During the second Legislature, the RDA marked time in Paris and held no ministerial portfolios. They concentrated on their African constituencies, and settled numerous local questions. The UDSR alliance gave them, in the eyes of the administration, a measure of respectability which they used to prepare successfully the 1956 elections. In Africa, they made no effort to explain or publicize the UDSR alliance. True, the RDA usually sent observers to UDSR congresses,[1] and encouraged the European settlers of the Ivory Coast to form a UDSR branch. It was a way to keep separate. Africans did not become members of the Ivory Coast UDSR, and Europeans, with a few exceptions, did not become RDA. In Abidjan, the Paris alliance meant that RDA leaders attended UDSR dinners and vice-versa, and at elections reserved a few municipal, territorial, and metropolitan seats for the Europeans. The most important of these was the Ivory Coast senatorial seat given in 1956 to UDSR Secretary-General Joseph Perrin, who had lost in the National Assembly election.

Meanwhile, the IOM reaped the prizes to which their central position entitled them. Ties with the MRP, 'the party which can never escape office',[2] brought the IOM junior ministerial portfolios in almost every French government of the second Legislature,[3] and gave them advantage over other West African leaders in extra-parliamentary dealings with French officials on local questions. Yet this did not help the IOM in the 1956 vote.

The African Socialists in the second Legislature found themselves with many handicaps. The elections had eliminated their parliamentary leader, Lamine Guèye, who alone had the stature to command an audience in and out of the SFIO. The Socialists kept out of all French governments during the Legislature, and therefore could not help the Africans in their group through influence, as they had done previously. Except among a minority in Senegal, African Socialists had few solid roots, since they owed their election largely to official chiefs and Socialists in the administration, both declining forces in Africa as mass parties grew. Tight Socialist group discipline made it relatively hard for Socialist West Africans to join in an inter-party West African pressure group on African issues. Not unexpectedly, the 1956 elections showed further Socialist decline in Africa.

With the possible exception of Apithy from Dahomey, West Afri-

---

[1] See *Interafrique Presse*, 27 October 1955.

[2] Williams, op. cit., p. 394.

[3] Dr. Aujoulat, IOM, Cameroun, was a full minister, of health, under Mendès-France. Léopold Senghor was a Secretary of State for Scientific Research under Edgar Faure.

can Conservative deputies, like West African Socialists, were unimportant in France. There were too few Conservatives to reap posts and patronage from a Centre balancing position in the Assembly, as did the IOM. Outside of Mauretania, the official support which had brought the Conservatives to the National Assembly dwindled, as it became French policy after 1954 to seek out *interlocuteurs valables* in West Africa. (The notion referred to men, truly representative, willing to negotiate with France, and vice-versa.)

The incidents which took place in Guinea, after official falsification of by-elections there, confirmed the arguments of the AOF Governor-General Cornut-Gentille, and several influential French party leaders, that only conciliatory administrative policies, honest elections and speedy reforms could make possible a future working relationship between France and tropical Africa. In the 1954 by-election the administration in Guinea, through the official chiefs, falsified the outcome in favour of Barry Diawadou and against the RDA candidate, Sékou Touré. Popular unrest was widespread. To calm it, Robert Buron, overseas minister under Mendès-France, toured Guinea in October 1954, promising honest elections in future.

In the Assembly, the RDA deputies challenged Diawadou's credentials. Partly because not only Sékou Touré, but also the Socialist leader of Guinea, Barry III (Barry Ibrahima) was also defeated, the SFIO at their congress of 3 July 1954 condemned 'the interference of the administration', demanded the recall of the governor of Guinea and the inspector of administrative affairs 'who had been accused of participating in the electoral campaign'.[1] The UDSR also let it be known they would oppose Diawadou's validation because they were the *apparentés* of the RDA. Yet when Diawadou's election was validated on 21 January 1955 only the Communists and the RDA voted against. The Socialists abstained, and most of the UDSR managed to be out of the Assembly during the vote (by raised hands). There were new incidents in Guinea.[2]

This vote took place in the last weeks of the Mendès-France government. West African deputies almost unanimously deplored its fall. The Geneva agreements and negotiations in Tunisia caught their imagination, and renewed their hope for a peaceful French acceptance of self-government for Africa. Mendès 'appeared to us as the chivalrous president, careful to keep his word, courageous enough to step out of the worn grooves of French policy', said Mamadou Coulibaly, Ivory Coast RDA councillor of the French Union. On the day the Mendès government fell, all the West African deputies except Apithy of Dahomey voted for the government. Even

[1] *Interafrique Presse*, 30 January 1955.
[2] *Afrique Informations*, 15 March–1 April 1955.

Sékou Sanogo, the man who benefited from the falsification of the 1951 elections in Ivory Coast, broke his *apparentement* with the MRP to vote confidence.[1]

The opportunism with which aspiring governmental parties validated Diawadou's election and then scrambled for his vote confirmed the West African deputies in the belief all had acted upon since 1952, that their various French parliamentary allies were little concerned with events which took place several thousand miles from Paris. They sought alliances with different rather than one group more and more for reasons of African rather than metropolitan politics. But they chose all their French allies from within the governing majority, since they sought to influence the many overseas decisions which remained the business of the executive.

Many common interests of the West African deputies transcended their local rivalries. They co-operated across group lines to back reforms in Parliament. Their formal inter-group of 1950-1 gave way, during the second Legislature, to a similar though informal organization which also had limited, immediate aims: the Code du Travail; an extended franchise; increased financial subsidies; territorial assembly and municipal reforms; increased territorial autonomy. Apart from municipal reform and the Code du Travail, they achieved only a small proportion of these aims in the second Legislature. Major reforms for the overseas territories, widely discussed since 1954, were postponed, for new elections, following upon Edgar Faure's dissolution of the Assembly, took place unexpectedly.[2]

Africans Take the Initiative

The 1956 elections moved slightly to the Left again the balance of the Assembly's majority, which seemed impossible without the Socialists.[3] Since the numbers of the extreme Left and Right increased to 205, the need to form a government pushed the Socialists towards the Centre and Conservative groups. Of a total of 596 deputies, only 381 were likely supporters of a government; of these, 206 were divided among the numerous, often rival Centre and Conservative groups. The votes of the overseas deputies, especially in the pivotal groups of the UDSR–RDA and the IOM, appeared to have increased in value to *ministrables* seeking a majority.[4] Only 4 metropolitan UDSR deputies were elected. To them were added 14

[1] *Interafrique Presse*, 10 February 1955.
[2] See *Interafrique Presse*, 8 December 1955; *Afrique Informations*, 1–15 December 1955, and Campbell, Peter, *French Electoral Systems and Elections 1789–1957*, Faber, London, 1958, p. 124.
[3] See Appendix IV for a breakdown of party strengths.
[4] See Jacques Fauvet, *Le Monde*, 25 December 1955; Claude Delmas, *Combat*, 29 December 1955.

from overseas, including 10 RDA deputies from West and Equatorial Africa.

In the overseas territories, these elections were relatively free from administrative interference, and West African results differed considerably from those of 1951. In the French National Assembly, 8 were UDSR–RDA; 4 IOM *apparenté* MRP; 2 Socialist; 4 Conservative; 2 were independent. Thus the proportion of IOM to RDA almost reversed, and the number of West African Socialists again decreased.

The losses of the IOM indicated a new political orientation in French West African politics. Gone were the post-Liberation days when African leaders were politically inexperienced, and when French parties exercised considerable influence over African parties and the choice of African leaders. Since then, African parties became increasingly well organized, and developed their own primarily African dynamics. During the campaign, the IOM had tried to increase their standing in Africa by hardening their criticism of the French system, and by arguing in favour of autonomy, federation, and constitutional revision. In contrast, the RDA leaders, in the speeches they made in French, employed a language favourable to *la communauté franco-africaine*,[1] and made little public mention of federation or constitutional revision. Nevertheless, the RDA defeated the IOM.

This did not mean that the voters opposed the nationalism expressed by the language of the IOM, and preferred literally the moderate formulae of the RDA. The results suggested instead that West African voters, distinguishing between political slogans and the parties or persons using them, paid little attention to the sense of French political categories; that indeed the French language itself was a vehicle for the communication of ideas in Africa only on the top surface of society.

Events subsequent to the elections indicated that autonomy from France and from French organizations, had become a major criterion for political support in Africa. The RDA succeeded in altering the name of their parliamentary group to UDSR–RDA, and announced

the UDSR–RDA group in the National Assembly is composed of two distinct organizations, each with its own directing organs empowered to make decisions only for its own members.[2]

IOM, reduced to less than 14 deputies, took care to announce they were *apparentés* 'for purely administrative reasons with the MRP

[1] From speeches made by Félix Houphouët-Boigny during the 1955–6 campaign.
[2] *La Presse de Guineé*, 25 February 1956.

group'.[1] In February 1957 IOM reorganized, with a nationalist pro-gramme, as *Convention Africaine*. Moving further in the direction of autonomy, even the Socialists reorganized in January 1957. With the agreement of the SFIO a *Mouvement Socialiste Africain* (MSA) was born in Conakry, separate from the SFIO, though each group had representation on the executive of the other; MSA deputies were in Parliament *apparentés* SFIO. In February, the SFIO branch of Senegal broke the French tie it had assumed so proudly in 1936.[2] No group in Africa could resist grass roots pressure for autonomy.

The RDA electoral victory led the government to try to make RDA president Houphouët-Boigny into 'the most devoted and effective support of the French government in Africa'.[3] A war in Algeria, independence for Ghana, and continuous unrest in West Africa, as well as the perennial problem of finding a majority willing to support a French government, led Guy Mollet and his successors as prime minister to give the first full ministerial portfolio ever held by an African to Houphouët. From then on, through the establish-ment of the first Debré government of the Fifth Republic, Hou-phouët remained a full minister. Mollet also gave a post as Under-Secretary to Hammadoun Dicko, Socialist from Soudan. Bourgès-Manoury kept him and added another, Modibo Keïta, RDA, Soudan. Gaillard kept both and added a third Under-Secretary, Hubert Maga, who had links with but was not proposed for a port-folio by the *Convention*. From then on the major interterritorial political formations had at least one representative in the remaining governments of the Fourth Republic.

Once the *ministrables* in 1956 had pinned their hopes on the ability of the RDA president to convince his skeptical followers that France brought a liberal spirit to the Loi-Cadre reforms, they were lavish with concessions and prestige for the RDA deputies. They made one a vice-president of the National Assembly;[4] they included Houphouët in the French delegation to the United Nations;[5] they transferred unceremoniously French administrators disliked by the RDA. One of Mitterrand's first acts as Minister of Justice was pres-sing an amnesty law through the National Assembly which freed the remaining RDA political prisoners, and removed the limitation

---

[1] *Paris–Dakar*, 24 January 1956.
[2] *Afrique Nouvelle*, 22 and 29 January 1957.
[3] *Interafrique Presse*, 11 January 1957, citing a SFIO internal document.
[4] Mamadou Konaté, RDA, Soudan, who died in 1956, replaced by Modibo Keïta, RDA, Soudan, who resigned in 1957 to become an Under-Secretary. Hamani Diori, RDA, Niger, replaced him.
[5] There he defended French colonial policy, especially in Togo. Resumé in *La Concorde*, supplement, 20 January 1957.

of the political rights of the former RDA political prisoners.[1] The French government even ignored the fact that some RDA leaders openly contradicted the party's commitment to government policy implied by Houphouët's participation.

The West African deputies showed little interest in the policies of the Assembly's majority. Although Minister Houphouët, RDA, frequently repeated slogans like:

Between total autonomy chosen by Africans of Anglo-Saxon training and independence within a Franco-African community, we have consciously chosen the latter,[2]

the parties in Africa spoke instead of the 'inalienable right to independence'.[3] The West African deputies no longer gave their ballots to the *boîtiers* and stopped voting almost automatically for the government on issues unrelated to tropical Africa. On an issue like the government proposal to amend the finance bill for aid to Tunisia and Morocco (*scrutin* of 4 December 1956) 4 West Africans voted in favour, 3 against, and 13 did not take part in the vote.[4] In the vote of confidence to the Guy Mollet government, related to Algerian policy, at the end of March 1957, 15 out of 20 West African deputies did not take part in the vote. Among the 15 were all the IOM deputies, and 5 of the 8 RDA deputies.[5] In the vote investing Gaillard as prime minister, 6 West Africans, 4 RDA–UDSR and 2 *Convention* did not take part in the vote.[6] Heedless of issues critical to the French government in the third Legislature, most West African *parlementaires* were busy in Africa, preparing the ground for the changes planned under the Loi-Cadre, and solidifying their positions in their constituencies. For example, deputies Dia, Coulibaly, Apithy, and Touré became the first vice-presidents and then presidents of the councils of government respectively of Senegal, Upper Volta, Dahomey and Guinea, and by 1959 former deputies in Paris Houphouët, Keïta and Diori stepped into the posts of prime minister of Ivory Coast, Mali (then Soudan and Senegal), and Niger.

Most revealing of a new, aggressive stance of the West African deputies within the French Parliament and parliamentary groups during the last years of the Fourth Republic, was their role in the adoption of the Loi-Cadre reforms. They needed first to clarify their positions towards the complex drafts of decrees which came out of

[1] Law 56-353 of 27 March 1956.   [2] *La Concorde*, 6 March 1957, Abidjan.
[3] From the proceedings of the third RDA interterritorial Congress, Bamako, September 1957.
[4] *Paris–Dakar*, 11 December 1956.
[5] *Le Monde* weekly, 28 March–3 April 1957.
[6] *Paris–Dakar*, 7 November 1957.

the overseas ministry.[1] They were not prepared; at first they 'improvised',[2] determining their positions took time. The RDA deputies had been building up parties rather than defining policies. Only the Senegalese deputies, particularly Léopold Senghor, had some clear ideas what institutions they were for, not only against.

West African parliamentary strategy on the Loi-Cadre reforms was influenced by the many elections which took place in Africa during 1956 and 1957, years of remarkable political fluidity in which there was considerable turnover of leadership. National Assembly, municipal, territorial, and federal elections stirred up African political rivalries, and at times hampered co-operation among Africans in Parliament. RDA, *Convention*, and MSA delegates toured in search of support in the territories where there was no stable majority: Dahomey, Upper Volta, and Niger. These local rivalries help explain why although the African deputies achieved inter-group unity in their Loi-Cadre interventions, they remained the allies of different French political groups in the Assembly until they left the French Parliament. The political activity accompanying the elections of 1956 and 1957 also expressed and stimulated other forces, leading to closer co-operation among the West African deputies. At meetings, the West African deputies clarified their ideas about the new reforms. They attended not only their own but also each other's political rallies, and were aware of two themes which aroused enthusiastic demonstrations at all West African political meetings during 1956 and 1957.

The first was unity, among Africans, against France, to permit the most qualified people in each territory to assume the new posts opened to Africans by the Loi-Cadre reforms. 'In any meeting whatsoever it suffices to pronounce the single word UNITY to let loose thunderous applause. . . .'[3] The second theme was autonomy: in relation to French parties, French trade unions, French youth organization, French culture, international organizations, and above all French administrators and French domination. Autonomy led to the formation of the MSA; autonomy and unity were dominant themes in the 1957 congresses of CAF and the RDA. Unity among rival trade union organizations was achieved in January 1957, at Cotonou. There African trade union leaders previously linked with the French *Confédération Générale du Travail* (CGT), and some, though not all linked with the *Confédération Française des Travailleurs Chrétiens*

---

[1] Sourou-Migan Apithy, Overseas Territories Commission reporter, J.O.A.N. *Débats*, 29 January 1957, pp. 366–7.

[2] IOM senator Emile-Derlin Zinsou criticized this in *Afrique Nouvelle*, 20 November 1956.

[3] *Afrique Nouvelle*, 11 September 1956.

(CFTC), created a single African international trade union organization, the *Union Générale des Travailleurs d'Afrique Noire* (UGTAN). UGTAN decided, in order to permit unity, to remain autonomous of all French and international trade union organizations. Unity among youth organizations was achieved in October 1957 at a congress in Abidjan. There the territorial youth councils—some of which had links with French youth movements, and others in the *Conseil Fédérale de la Jeunesse d'AOF*, which rejected such links—merged into the single international *Conseil de la Jeunesse d'Afrique* (CJA). For CJA too, unity was achieved only through agreement to allow each territorial youth council to decide whether to affiliate with any international youth organizations.

The West African deputies realized their African constituents tested their work in Parliament against the two new ideals of unity and autonomy. Because they wanted to be 'Africans who are followed, not by-passed',[1] even those deputies who had previously been inclined towards the *status quo* hardened their demands for autonomy. For the same reason they abandoned sufficiently their rivalries to achieve, on the Loi-Cadre decrees, more unity than ever before in their parliamentary careers. Their activities in Paris were given backing in Africa. The Grand Council of AOF and most territorial assemblies challenged the procedure which did not consult these bodies during the drafting of the decrees. The Grand Council passed a unanimous protest, and was supported by six of the eight territorial assemblies.[2] The 'revolt of the African deputies' was how the discussions on the Loi-Cadre decrees came to be known; these had more in common with diplomatic negotiations than with parliamentary proceedings. Not once did the government pose the question of confidence. Houphouët remained a minister while the RDA joined the other West African deputies in challenging the text of the government on the decrees. During some of these discussions RDA deputy Modibo Keïta of Soudan was the Assembly's presiding officer.

The challenge began in the Overseas Territories Commission, where the overseas deputies had a majority. 'We say NO to the government drafts,' said their reporter, Apithy of Dahomey.[3] They amended the French government's proposals that the members of the councils of government be half elected, half appointed by the governor, without an African leader of government and in no way responsible to the territorial assemblies. They called instead for fully elected councils of government. They wanted elected territorial prime

---

[1] Joseph Conombo, Upper Volta, J.O.A.N., *Débats*, 29 January 1957, p. 370.
[2] Ibid., Senghor, p. 371.   [3] Ibid., pp. 366–7.

ministers to choose the other members of the councils, which in turn would be fully responsible to the territorial assemblies. The Assembly's compromise over the title of territorial prime minister, that is, its decision to create the title vice president of the council of government,[1] can be compared with the British decision of 1951 in the Gold Coast to grant the title 'Leader of Government Business' to Kwame Nkrumah.

The French government proposed both a limited list of territorial services in areas within which the territorial assembly could legislate, and a far more general list of the responsibilities of the metropolitan government administered by its state public services. The African deputies, instead, asked not only for a limited list of state services and areas reserved to the French government, but also for a definition of the territorial services giving residual powers to the elected territorial governments.[2] They cited the Togo statute as precedent.

The Overseas Territories Commission greatly amended the government drafts, and controversies between the African deputies and the government came to the floor of the Assembly on 29 January 1957. The publicity of the resulting conflict was in sharp contrast with the privacy of the decisions in the Nigerian constitutional conference in London during the same year. There were three days of intensive negotiations. Even on the compromise drafts, either most of the Africans or a few—particularly the IOM and the 2 Guinea RDA deputies—voted with the Communists against the rest of the Assembly.[3] Neither IOM nor MRP were in the government at the time, and most IOM deputies, led by Senghor and Dia of Senegal, either abstained or voted against the Loi-Cadre decrees. They did, however, specify 'we want the reforms carried out'.[4] The Assembly accepted several demands of the African deputies, who immediately made clear they intended to keep pressing the points on which they had been defeated.

The West African deputies were unified, and effective in their Assembly fight for extending the autonomy of the territorial institutions. They were less united and less clear in answering what should be the powers of the federal institutions of AOF. The political commission of the Assembly of the French Union, and the representatives of the European interests in Africa, had a clear answer:

[1] J.O.A.N., *Débats*, 29 January 1957, p. 371.
[2] See the report by Teitgen, reporter for the Overseas Territories Commission. Ibid., p. 363.
[3] See J.O.A.N., *Débats*, 1 February 1957, *scrutin 445*, p. 501 and *scrutin 446*, p. 535; 2 February 1957, *scrutin 448–52*, pp. 558–65.
[4] J.O.A.N., *Débats*, 2 February 1957, p. 557.

the barest possible minimum.[1] They wanted considerable concessions to territorial demands for autonomy, but all powers not devolved upon the territories concentrated in Paris, not Dakar. Their idea was to avoid creating and strengthening institutions which might help Africans choose independence. Even as it stood, the Loi-Cadre did not go far enough in abolishing the federation to satisfy Senator Durand-Réville, first college Senator from Gabon. He called the Loi-Cadre 'a bastard, tarred from birth as an unsuccessful hybrid, which experience will show to be impotent'.[2] The government shared most of these anti-federal ideas, and its drafts weakened the Grand Council, made no suggestion for an elected federal executive, and curtailed the federal services.

The anti-federal bias of the Loi-Cadre and the limits of the powers of elected territorial governments, led African students in France, through the organ of the *Fédération des Étudiants d'Afrique Noire en France* (FEANF), to print a cartoon representing the Loi-Cadre as an African chained hand and foot.[3] The pro-federal position of the students was largely shared by the members of the Grand Council in Dakar. On 28 June 1956 the retiring councillors, on 29 August 1957 the newly elected councillors called for a federal executive for AOF. They underlined their refusal 'to swallow' the Loi-Cadre by rejecting the budget on 12 December 1956.[4] Yet another proof that federal grand councillors were but second-echelon leaders, was that these votes were in final analysis disregarded by many of the African deputies in Paris.

The Senegalese deputies apart, the West Africans, and especially the RDA, had not even posed the fundamental questions on the federation within their parties. Only after the government had implicitly answered them through the drafts proposed to the Assembly in December 1956 did a great debate begin within all African organizations on the issue of federation; on this depended whether AOF was to become independent as many little states, or a single powerful one. In the first quarter of 1957, when the National Assembly debated the Loi-Cadre decrees, there were among the West African deputies 'federalists' and 'territorialists'.

The federalists were led by Senghor of Senegal, who wanted more rather than less powers of the Grand Council, a change from indirect to direct elections for its members, and the creation of a

[1] See Alduy, reporter of the Overseas Territories Commission, ibid., p. 365; *Afrique Nouvelle*, 11 September 1956, 30 October 1956, 20 November 1956; also Durand-Réville, J.O.C.R., *Débats*, 19 February 1957, pp. 439 f.
[2] J.O.C.R., *Débats*, 19 February 1957, p. 440.
[3] See *L'Étudiant Afrique Noire*, June–September 1956, p. 16.
[4] *Paris–Dakar*, 28 June, 12 December 1956; 30 August 1957.

responsible elected federal executive. Senghor told the Assembly, 'I tell you, be afraid; if the territories are "Balkanized", one will look to Lagos, another to Accra, a third to Rabat.'[1] He was, after all, leader of the territory which had benefited most from the existence of AOF: housed its capital, contributed a disproportionately high number of its civil servants, profited from the trade which moved through Dakar, and since 1947 controlled the grand council politically.

The 'territorialists' agreed in essence with the government; in 1957 they were led by Apithy of Dahomey and Houphouët of Ivory Coast. Apithy, leader of the state next to Togo and with much in common culturally with Nigeria, told the Assembly, 'Politically it is impossible to refuse tropical African territories the status which Togo has . . . and which Cameroun will have.'[2] Houphouët differed from Apithy in opposing both independence and federation. His opposition to a powerful West African federation had several explanations. There was the simple point of Ivory Coast self interest. His home territory was the richest in West Africa, where planters of coffee and cocoa resented the sums paid to the AOF budget. There was 'anti-senegalism'. The seat of the AOF federation was far from Houphouët's territory. Until 1957 the grand council was controlled by Senegalese, whom Houphouët regarded as political rivals. When Houphouët became president of the grand council, in June 1957, he did so only to mark yet another RDA victory over IOM. To Houphouët a strong AOF was linked with a strong interterritorial position for Senegal. While he was a minister in the French government, he called for federation in another form—of France with the separate African territories.

Since the West African deputies were still divided on the question of federal institutions, they concentrated their united challenge of the government on the composition and powers of the elected territorial governments. They took no common position on the principle of federation; though, arguing from the dictates of common sense, they successfully restored to the federation a few of the powers which the French government had removed from Dakar to Paris.[3]

The Loi-Cadre reforms as promulgated, pleased neither the 'federalists' nor the 'territorialists' among the West African deputies, and did not concede full territorial self-government. Therefore the Loi-Cadre did not remove the pressures for unity among Africans—particularly unity against France—which had characterized African politics since the 1956 elections. Yet another round of political

[1] J.O.A.N., *Débats*, 29 January 1957, p. 373.
[2] Ibid., p. 366; see also *Afrique Nouvelle*, 11 September 1956.
[3] See Alduy, J.O.A.N., *Débats*, 29 January 1957, p. 365.

debate took place; but while the debate of 1956 centred around the problems of territorial government and autonomy, that of 1957 and 1958 centred around federation and independence.

In this debate Africans questioned not only the value of links with French governmental and non-governmental institutions, but also of French culture and political tradition. This was illustrated by the proceedings of the first *Congrès des Écrivains et Artistes Noirs*, organized by the editors of *Présence Africaine*.[1] Moreover, the debate exposed almost every controversy and conflict of African society: controversies among and conflicts within persons, parties, generations, ethnic groups, territories, and interest groups. Houphouët took sharp issue with Senghor, reflecting a conflict of interest between Ivory Coast and Senegal, and between the interterritorial RDA and the *Convention Africaine*. The conflict of generations was evident in all the parties. In the RDA the younger, nationalist 'federalists' found their spokesman in Sékou Touré, the 35 year old secretary-general of the Guinea section of the RDA who challenged his senior and president, Houphouët. In the Convention the challenge to Senghor came from the 'young intellectuals' who returned from French universities. The federal co-ordinating council of youth organizations, the CJA; the *Fédération des Étudiants d'Afrique Noire Française* (FEANF) which grouped university students, and the autonomous federal trade union, UGTAN, were all led by younger men. All were of course also members of political parties, in which they expounded on their federalist and nationalist positions.[2] In the countryside, the 'federalist'–'territorialist' debate involved such frontier peoples as the Toucouleur living between Senegal and Mauretania. And in all the cities, the educated civil servants expressed concern with the prospect of a future which 'condemned them to spending their entire lives in one single territory'.[3]

In this debate, by 1958, five points were evident. First the theme of African unity was omnipresent. Organic unity had largely been achieved both territorially and federally, among previously rival African groups; among parties, and even more effectively among workers', students', and youth organizations. In spite of French efforts to the contrary, unity, where Africans achieved it, was

[1] See *Afrique Nouvelle*, 2 October 1956, for a report on what the paper believed to be the 'African Bandung', 19–22 September 1956, held in Paris. See also *Présence Africaine*, Paris, no. 8–10, June–November 1956, and 14–15 June–September 1957.

[2] See *L'Étudiant Afrique Noire*, July 1957, pp. 4 f.; *Le Travailleur d'Afrique Noire*, March 1957; and the mimeographed political resolution of the CJA congress in Abidjan, October 1957.

[3] J.O.A.N., *Débats*, 29 January 1957, p. 371. Also *Paris–Dakar*, 24 February 1958.

always at the expense of links with France or French groups. Second, African unity, initially achieved in relation to the demand for autonomy, became focused upon the claim for the 'inalienable right to independence'. Third, the social and political ferment accompanying the Loi-Cadre reforms and the assumption of new responsibilities by Africans, encouraged Africans to question other established institutions. In some areas, chiefly authority was rejected, and there were moves towards the revision of certain territorial frontiers between southern Mauretania and Senegal,[1] between northern Dahomey and Niger.[2] A fourth tendency was the increasing international prominence and activities of West African leaders, partly under the aegis of France; discussing Togo at the United Nations, discussing the Common Market with Europeans,[3] taking part in the *Organisation Commune des Régions Sahariénnes*,[4] or in FAMA.[5] Partly this occurred outside the French framework, at times without French approval. There were negotiations between representatives of Morocco and Mauretania; of Guinea and Sierra Leone; the Algerian nationalists and territories bordering upon the Sahara; Ghana and Guinea, Mali, or Ivory Coast. Fifth, in spite of the increasing demands made by the West African party leaders, a radical opposition to all the dominant parties appeared, led by young men dissatisfied with the pace and methods of leaders Lamine Guèye, Houphouët and Senghor. This Left wing pressed for closer unity, more drastic reforms, total independence, and international policies conducted in the spirit of Bandung.

Under this pressure, the African deputies, conferring in February 1958, achieved what became their high point of unity. They reached a tentative agreement, and unanimously[6] issued a statement directed not only at Africa, but also at those Frenchmen involved in constitutional revision. The tropical African leaders called for West and Equatorial African 'federations, democratically established by the territories on the bases of solidarity, equality, and voluntarily

[1] *Abidjan–Matin*, 17 October 1957; see also *Le Monde*, 13–19 March 1958.
[2] *Paris–Dakar*, 13 November 1957. For a proposal to redraw all African frontiers along ethnic lines, see Nazi Boni, *Afrique Nouvelle*, 2 October 1956.
[3] *Concorde*, 6 February 1957; *Le Monde*, 13–19 February 1958.
[4] Law of 10 January 1957. See *Le Monde*, 5–11 December 1957; *Paris–Dakar*, 5 February 1957; for revised texts see *Afrique Nouvelle*, 20 February 1959.
[5] Foundation for African Mutual Assistance; see *West Africa*, 25 January 1958; *Paris–Dakar*, 13 March 1958. Modibo Keïta led the French delegation to the 1958 FAMA conference in Accra.
[6] At the conference were the leaders of all the major tropical African parties, except the *Parti Républicain du Dahomey*, led by Sourou Migan Apithy. Also the *Parti Africain de l'Indépendance*, founded in 1957 by African orthodox Marxists in Dakar, dissented from the report because it called for 'organic' unity.

abandoned sovereignty'. They agreed that the African federations might join with a 'Federal Republic' uniting metropolitan France, the African federations and the non-federated French overseas territories[1] 'on the basis of free co-operation, absolute equality and the right to independence'. They stated that each component of the Federal Republic should have 'a central autonomous government, responsible to a Legislative Assembly, which has all the attributes of internal sovereignty except direct and exclusive control of foreign affairs, defence, currency, higher education, and the judiciary;' these matters should be 'reserved for the government of the Federal Republic'. Finally, the West African leaders agreed that 'the Federal Republic might contract into a *Confederal Union*, to unite in some form the Federal Republic and states which were either independent or about to become independent'.[2]

These proposals are indeed complicated: a confederation of states at least one of which is a federation of federations. The important feature was that the 'territorialist' Houphouët and the 'federalist' Senghor both agreed on the two outstanding points: states within the French system 'about to be independent' might acquire full sovereignty, and the principle of responsible federal government in Africa. These proposals indicated that French hesitation to accept full territorial self government in 1958 pushed the African deputies further towards a federalist position.

French officials did not hesitate for long, however. They also felt the pressures from Africa. No French leaders, regardless of party, seriously suggested that as in the past force should be used to stem West African nationalism—indeed some even suggested the total 'abandonment' of Africa.[3] The majority reaction in France was the one taken up as policy by de Gaulle—more subsidies first with the Constitution of 1958, in the hope to prevent independence. That hope was disappointed. African desire for independence was in part based on the view that 'F.I.D.E.S. is the Marshall Plan of the poor'[4] and so not enough.

France transferred power to the specifically territorial African institutions alone and broke the momentum of 'federalist' forces.

[1] Presumably French Somaliland, and possibly Togo and Cameroun.
[2] See the 'Rapport de la conférence de regroupement des partis africains', mimeographed, Paris, 17 February 1958, for the full text.
[3] Durand-Réville, J.O.C.R., *Débats*, 19 February 1957, p. 442. This view is frequently called 'Cartierisme'. The term refers to a series of articles written by a French journalist, Raymond Cartier, *Paris–Match*, 11 and 18 August and 1 September 1956, arguing that the overseas territories cost more than they were worth to France. See *Afrique Nouvelle*, 9 October 1956; see also Robinson, 'Constitutional Reform in French Tropical Africa', 1958, op. cit., p. 66.
[4] Zinsou, J.O.C.R., *Débats*, 20 February 1957, p. 468.

Nationalism was defined in territorial terms—a fact underlined by the failure of the Mali federation. Federal trade unions, youth organizations, political parties, and the federal civil service, as well as the grand council—all the interterritorial structures created or reinforced in 1958, by 1960 had dissolved. French-speaking West Africans came into the UN as eight separate states, and this represented a victory for the 'territorialists'.

This victory may be but transitional. Independence changed the frontiers and the legal position from which 'territorialists' and 'federalists' conducted their debate in West Africa. But independence did not end the debate.

Some Effects of the 'Metropolitan Axis'

The post-war reforms preceding independence in French-speaking West Africa gave to African politics a 'metropolitan axis' by providing for African representatives in the Parliament of France. What were the effects of this arrangement on French deputies? On the decisions of the National Assembly? On the African deputies? On relations between French and African parties? On African parties and party relationships?

The main effect on French deputies was educational. Since the tropical African deputies were scattered among different French parliamentary groups, French deputies came to know some elements of African politics. This must not be exaggerated: many French deputies remained uninterested by the fact that a few Africans sometimes attended parliamentary group caucuses. Yet the MRP listened to what Senghor had to say; the Socialists respected Lamine Guèye as an elder statesman; the UDSR gave courteous attention to Houphouët. There resulted a climate of parliamentary opinion conducive to the adoption of reforms for the African territories. That was important during the Fourth Republic, noted for the legislature's hostility to executive prerogative, and for frequent rotation of ministerial posts. Exchanges of views between French and African deputies were often bitter. But the mere fact that communication occurred, is one reason why French deputies have not for long supported—as they did in Vietnam or North Africa—the use of force to prevent the transfer of political power.

The effects of the tropical African votes on the majority in the French Assembly were more apparent than real. The handful of Africans looked different, which may be why outside observers developed theories exaggerating the extent to which African votes affected marginal votes, far beyond any deliberate intention of the Africans themselves. In the National Assembly, usually votes were marginal on wholly unrelated issues. It is doubtful whether in the majority of such issues, the African votes can reasonably be thought to have been more decisive than any others. The African deputies, like their French counterparts, acquired some skill in exploiting the opportunities open to small groups in the multi-party Assembly when government majorities were shrinking. Thus they too had some access to French ministerial positions and patronage. However, because they were so few, the African deputies could rarely arbitrate in the votes on colonial issues before the Assembly, which were rarely settled by slender majorities. When on African questions the African deputies walked out of the Assembly in protest, the results they achieved were due not to their own votes nor to any substantial shift in metropolitan votes within the Legislature. The results were due rather to the impact of such a demonstration upon the French executive during periods when it wished to implement reforms in Africa, and depended upon African co-operation to do so. For under the Fourth Republic, the French executive still had a virtual monopoly over tropical African policy.

What did a seat in the French Parliament mean to the West African deputies? For them, as indeed for many Frenchmen, to be a *parlementaire* was a general education. Several, taking advantage of their presence in Paris, attended schools and universities. Many travelled to see foreign lands. A *parlementaire* had more security than educated West Africans had previously known: a regular salary; status; mobility; immunity not only from colonial law but from the normal processes of French law; and a sense of partial acceptance in France, as contrasted with the normal lack of acceptance among Frenchmen in Africa. The African *parlementaires* obtained unique political experience. Some became officers of Parliament; had responsibilities as French ministers; represented France at international meetings. Although in practice they confined their active work in Parliament to African questions, they nevertheless learned a great deal about the internal affairs of France; about France's deep social divisions, international position, resources, and intentions towards Africa. They learned more about French society than the vast majority of French administrators ever learned about Africa. Their experiences altered the way in which they thought about political problems, and so differentiated them from their colleagues in Africa, making them a special group apart.

The provisions for Africans to sit in the metropolitan Parliament made relations between French and African political parties somewhat closer than they might otherwise have been, and encouraged the relations between individual French party members and Africans to crystallize into alliances. These alliances in turn resulted in a minimum common stake of the partners in their respective political success or failure in France and in Africa. For example, the election of an African bearing a Socialist ticket added to SFIO parliamentary strength, while Socialist participation in a French government was of immediate concern to the African Socialists. These alliances also meant that the major political issue confronting both French and African leaders received more discussion among each group than might otherwise have occurred: the war in Vietnam or European defence on the African side; the Loi-Cadre or the Code du Travail on the French. Within each allied party a small group specialized in the affairs of its partner and had a vested interest in maintaining the alliance.

The constitutional framework could not obscure, however, conflicts between the interests of the French and African allies. These conflicts did not arise merely from the fact that the allied parties differed in their degree of formal organization, in the number of their adherents, or in their resources. The conflicts were essentially the consequence of the colonial relationship, of the very different frames of reference, political, economic, and social, in which French and African parties developed and carried on their principal activities. These gave to many of the joint pronouncements by French and African political allies overtones reminiscent of those by the United States Army of Occupation and Japanese political leaders after V-J Day.

Growing realization that fundamental differences existed, largely accounted for the perceptible evolution in the motives behind, and the types of alliances Africans formed with French parties. The first type was the organic link between the Senegalese federation and the SFIO. To the latter in 1936, this link was a logical extension of both their ideology and political strategy. All men are equal, and that included the Senegalese; the administrators whom the Senegalese opposed in Africa came roughly from the same social group as the metropolitan opponents of the SFIO. For their part, the Senegalese leaders were interested in using the ideas, and the power of the French SFIO against official abuses in Africa. The second type was between the French Communists and the RDA. The Communists viewed the alliance as an extension of their doctrines and strategy to Africa. The RDA viewed the alliance as productive of ideas and resources useful in the struggle for 'emancipation'. The French SFIO to some, and the French Communists to a great extent interpreted the alliances as entailing extra-parliamentary activities; in these the French parties always took the initiative. Africans came gradually to view these activities as the counterpart on the level of parties of the domination of Africa by the French state.

The third type of alliance obtained for all African parties—for the RDA since the start of the second Legislature; for the Senegalese

Socialists since 1957; for the others since their representatives came to Parliament. This type was a purely parliamentary alliance based on a bargain. In return for the votes of the African deputies, the French groups gave some patronage and some political support against adversaries in Africa. To Africans, the value of the bargain depended on whether the French allies took turns in staffing French ministries. These alliances were perceptible outside Parliament merely in the exchange of delegations at party congresses, of party literature, and of patronage. All these alliances broke down on votes relating to the fundamental interests of tropical Africa. Although the African deputies—largely for reasons of personal and political rivalries in Africa —scattered their votes among different French groups, nevertheless on African questions they united against those of their French parliamentary allies supporting the government. African deputies saw that the continuity of French colonial policy transcended differences in party labels of individual overseas ministers. Clearly alliances of this type were liable to easy dissolution. They involved not parties but deputies. Their disappearance with the Fifth Republic was hardly noticed.

There were also effects on the African parties; first, on leadership. Prior to 1957, the *parlementaires* were dominant in their parties, though the revision of outlook evident in a party leader who became a *parlementaire*—moderation of vocabulary, qualification of an attitude of total opposition—gave rise to some challenges within his party. These came most often if he remained for long in Paris, and if he became a French minister. Domination of the party by the *parlementaires* was part of the more general tendency towards domination of party executives by the elected representatives.

The principle of party control over elected representatives was not yet posed in West Africa, for peculiar historical reasons. At almost every new election since 1945, more offices became open to Africans. As a result, within each party the balance of power altered among *parlementaires*, territorial elected representatives and other party leaders. Limited educational facilities meant there was but a small number of educated men on whom a party could draw as candidates for office, and the general result was that the significant leaders of most major African parties were without public office for only a brief time. These conditions altered, of course, with the first crop of graduates from expanded post-war education facilities, at the time of the implementation of the Loi-Cadre.

Most important, the domination of party executives by the *parlementaires* was largely a consequence of the decisions by the parties to present their most important leaders as candidates. No parties boycotted the elections to the French National Assembly.

Had this not been so, the tendency would probably have been far different. No one who became a *parlementaire* either for lack of organized opposition, or because he had administrative support, was able subsequently to make use of his position to gain mass support, or merely to organize a disciplined membership party. Even when the administration interfered in the elections, and secured the validation of a man lacking popular support, Africans indicated the value they attached to the position, as distinct from the man holding it, by calling their unsuccessful candidate 'the real deputy'.

Thus parties counted more than elective office; the political institutions of French West Africa were still too unstable, their legitimacy was still too frequently questioned, the elections prior to 1956 were too frequently falsified, for the reverse to be true. It was in their capacity as leaders of the RDA, rather than as deputies, that Houphouët in Ivory Coast or Sékou Touré in Guinea could be said —as their critics did—to have become 'stronger than the governor'[1] well before independence. For in these territories, as mass parties achieved dominance, people allowed themselves to be governed far more through the parties, than through the legal government, the administration. The primacy of the top party leaders was usually well established before he ever became the 'first' deputy, while the men who took second or third position on the party lists found they could consolidate their party positions as they became deputies.

Another effect of representation in the French Parliament was that the *parlementaires* could use their role in the French Parliament in order to alter occasionally the constitutional distribution of power between the administration and Africans in the overseas territories. A *parlementaire* was usually beyond the reach of the authority of the governor. Even when Governor Péchoux pursued a policy of repression of the RDA in Ivory Coast, parliamentary immunity protected the RDA deputies—unlike Kwame Nkrumah in Gold Coast—from prison. A deputy with access to the French government might succeed in having governors or administrators replaced or reprimanded. The African parties tried to use their metropolitan connexions, prior to 1957, to acquire control in fact over the territorial executive which they did not have in law. Where a deputy's party had a majority in the territorial assembly, he used his influence in Paris in order to secure for the *vœux* or 'prayers' of the assembly the force of decisions. Where his party was not in the majority, he used his influence in order to secure curtailment even of the slim legal powers of the territorial assembly. In all territories, the possibility a deputy had of influencing the French government, added to the already considerable instability of the territorial government.

[1] *Climats*, 9–15 August 1951.

K

Representation in the French Parliament led many African leaders of parties to appear ambiguous in their statements and contradictory in their actions. Party leaders adapted their methods to the very different requirements for political success in Paris and in Africa, and so led opposition demonstrations in Africa while they voted confidence to the government in Paris.

In some respects, the 'metropolitan axis' discouraged co-operation among African leaders and their parties. For the system placed French parties and ministers in the position of arbiters, indeed helped superimpose French controversies on those of Africa—for example the division between the RDA allied with the Communists and the Senegalese Socialists. Since the MRP and the SFIO served rarely in the same government, their African allies rarely enjoyed ministerial patronage at the same time, and had similar interests in changes of government. The French ally at times helped the African party against rivals in Africa, and tried by pressure on the African ally to prevent moves for co-operation among African parties. And so alliances with French parties at first sharpened and later helped maintain divisions among African parties—but did not create the divisions. When the 'metropolitan axis' disappeared after Africans left the French Parliament in 1959, so did the metropolitan labels of the divisions existing among parties in Africa. Yet divisions remained.

In other respects the 'metropolitan axis' encouraged African *parlementaires* from different parties to co-operate. Their unity of action was at times echoed in Africa. Among the leaders of the various territorial branches of the RDA and the IOM or the African Socialists, identical French parliamentary alliances maintained cohesion. Coming from different territories, the African *parlementaires* met often in Paris where, free from the immediate pressures of their environment, they developed a common outlook. They met always as equals, as the system discouraged them from reconciling their differences among themselves without French intervention. Thus the contributions the 'metropolitan axis' made to the growth of interritorial African co-operation were indirect, and from the French standpoint accidental.

After the Loi-Cadre and prior to independence the African *parlementaires* hastened to take on elective territorial offices in West Africa, for these alone remained theirs as the 'metropolitan axis' dissolved with the end of the Fourth Republic. That the African *parlementaires* were important people, who had acquired experience both unique and useful, was shown as the states of French-speaking West Africa became independent between 1958 and 1960. They took top positions in all the new states.

PART FOUR

Citizens and Subjects of Senegal

PARTY politics have a longer history in Senegal than in any other French-speaking West African territory. Since 1914 the restricted number of pre-war 'citizens' used their right to form parties; and immediately after the Liberation, the Senegalese 'citizens' alone had previous political experience. There is an historical interest, therefore, in examining the pre-war political groups, and the transition made from them to parties suited in structure and technique to the expanding electorate and the universal French citizenship introduced after the Second World War.

The social background of party leaders in Senegal differed somewhat from that of the leaders in the other French-speaking West African territories. In parts of Senegal French rule was introduced as early as the seventeenth century. There were more schools and Senegal was the one territory with no serious shortage of educated African personnel. Indeed Senegal had a tradition of exporting trained people to other territories where economic and social change had not been as extensive. While in the other territories of AOF there was at least one party founded on the power of the official chiefs supported by the French administration, in Senegal neither the administration nor the chiefs played so clear-cut a role.

Partly this has been because social change was well advanced in Senegal. Belonging to a given ethnic community had meaning. But generally men whose only claim to lead was status in an ethnic group were succeeded by men whose claim to lead was partly based on non-ethnic social standing. Some of these non-ethnic social categories developed as a direct result of European colonial rule: according to schooling, or to professions ranging from traders, to teachers, civil servants, and veterans. Other non-ethnic social categories were not at all, or only indirectly the result of European rule: for example, lower castes such as jewellers, blacksmiths, shoemakers, or *griots*. In many parts of Senegal tribal chiefs have for long been displaced by official ones, and the traditional lines of succession have become blurred. In the nineteenth century inter-African wars—led in the Senegal river area by the Toucouleur warrior al Hajj Umar Tall and later his son Ahmadou, and in the Sine-Saloum area by Mamadou Lamine—complicated problems of succession by introducing issues of recent victory or defeat. Many chiefly tribal families have kept status and wealth by becoming leading Muslim families, *marabouts* or Muslim teachers. Many live from the tribute paid by their *talibes* (pupils) who cultivate peanuts. For all these reasons, a man's status only partly derived from ethnic categories; it was usually supplemented by designations of a non-ethnic kind.

This is recognized in the political terminology of Senegal, and in the informal structure of the parties. The major parties were alliances of *clans*, a term considerably vaguer than ethnic group. It designated groups of leaders and their followers, usually living in a given region though not necessarily belonging to the same ethnic group or related by kinship. *Clans* could mean traders and their peasant customers; civil servants and their illiterate relations; fishermen and their literate spokesmen; ethnic 'collectivities' living in the towns, such as the Lebou, and led by literate men often traders or Muslim notables, 'stranger' communities come to earn money. *Clans* could designate economic interest groups, ethnic groups, religious brotherhoods, even castes. *Clans* usually combined the literate and the illiterate; those drawing most of their needs from the subsistence economy and those whose main income is in money. 'Clan politics' characterized the parties of Senegal, and joined the mass of the population to the territorial leaders.

All the Senegalese parties were led by educated Africans. Since French education was more readily available, one more generation than in the rest of AOF went to school, and a number of university graduates took an active part in post-war politics of Senegal though not in the rest of AOF. Most post-war differences among political leaders were explained by the pre-war distinction between 'citizens' and 'subjects', which often coincided with differences of generation, education, profession, religious affiliation, and place of residence. Most Senegalese party leaders were not, like their Ivory Coast counterparts, involved in farming. They were further removed from the land. They earned money rather as civil servants, in the professions, as traders dealing with peanuts, the main export crop of Senegal.[1] In consequence, the language, methods, and issues of Senegalese politics have seemed more modern, and party documents and newspapers were more frequently and regularly produced than elsewhere in AOF.[2]

Knowledge of the politics of post-war Senegal is necessary for an understanding of the interterritorial alignment of parties in French West Africa. The leaders of Senegal speak for one of the two richest

[1] See Appendix VIII: E, for supporting statistical data.
[2] See the bibliography for a list of the Senegalese newspapers.

territories.[1] It includes Dakar, the former capital of the federation, where cultural and political life is highly developed. It is the territory with the highest percentage of people living in the towns[2] and the largest number of wage earners.[3] Under the Fourth Republic the Senegalese leaders pursued—with varying political labels and uneven success—a policy opposed on the interterritorial level to that of the RDA. No examination of the federal relationship among parties in AOF is possible without prior consideration of the parties in Senegal.

Pre-war Cliques and the SFIO

Since the adoption of some 'assimilationist' colonial reforms in France during the nineteenth century, Africans born within the four old coastal communes—Dakar, Saint-Louis, Rufisque and Gorée—were 'citizens' of France. While in civil matters—marriage, inheritance—they were governed by their own usually Muslim tradition, in matters of public law they had in theory rights and obligations equal to those of Frenchmen. Their rights, when compared with those of the 'subjects', were considerable. An African 'citizen' could publish a newspaper; form a voluntary association He could strike a Frenchman and receive no more unwelcome attention from the law than a European. Under the *indigénat*, a 'subject', on the other hand, was liable to be drafted into forced labour brigades, to be exiled, and to receive very severe penalties. 'Subjects' had practically no rights of representation while the 'citizens' elected one member to the French Chamber of Deputies since the beginning of the Third Republic. (They did not, however, elect any Senators.) They elected municipal councillors who, from among their ranks, elected mayors of the old communes. They also elected councillors to the *conseil général*.

Composed of twenty people elected by the French 'citizens' in the territory, it had considerable powers, but only over the part of Senegal under direct administration. The establishment of the federation in 1904 whittled away at the powers of the *conseil général*, and gave rise to much protest from its members. In 1920, the *conseil colonial* replaced it. The *conseil colonial* had fewer powers but wider geographic coverage. It was composed of 44 members, 18 representing the 'citizens', and 26 elected by the non-citizen *chefs de canton* and the *chefs de province* in general assembly. The chiefs were appointed by the administration, and therefore voted as instructed. There was bitter wrangling between the chiefs and 'citizens' in the *conseil colonial*.[4]

[1] See Appendix XI for supporting statistical data.
[2] See Appendix IX for supporting statistical data.
[3] See Appendix X for supporting statistical data.
[4] An excellent sample is to be found in Colonie du Sénégal, *Conseil Colonial, Session ordinaire de juin 1938*, Imprimerie du Gouvernement, Saint-Louis, 1938, pp. 159 f.

The 'citizens' had comparatively easy access to French education. The École des Otages, later changed to the École des Fils des Chefs et des Interprètes, and still later replaced by the École Normale William-Ponty, though recruiting from all the territories, accepted a large proportion of students from Senegal.[1] The presence of a sizeable number of Europeans in Senegal—where France had long been established and from where the West African federation was administered—led to the creation of Lycée Van Vollenhoven at Dakar and Lycée Faidherbe at Saint-Louis. An increasing number of African 'citizens' attended the *lycées*. In 1936, the *lycée* of Dakar had 500 students; the majority were European. But in the same year, of the 230 students at the *lycée* in Saint-Louis, some two-thirds were Africans.[2] Between the wars it was French policy to allow a handful of Senegalese to obtain degrees as veterinary officers from the École Vétérinaire de Maison Alford in France.[3] Several 'citizens', considered 'Young Turks' in the 'twenties, managed to become lawyers.

Three to five per cent. of the total population of Senegal were African 'citizens'. Of all 'citizens' in Senegal, both African and European, less than one-eighth were European; therefore African 'citizens' usually elected Africans as their representatives. In 1936, 78,373 African 'citizens' lived in Senegal. Since women did not vote, and there was a high proportion of children among the 'citizens', only 20,746 African and European 'citizens' were on the electoral rolls for the 1936 parliamentary elections.[4] Most lived in the towns.

Few in number, the African 'citizens' knew each other well. They created a number of associations, ethnic, professional, social, religious, and youth. For example, the *Foyer France-Sénégal*, headed by Fall Papa Guèye, was dedicated to assimilationist cultural ideals. *Jeunesse Dorée* grouped the students of the École Normale William-Ponty. Their publications included *La Révue Africaine*, *Le Périscope Africain*, *Le Progrès*, *Le Jeune Sénégal*. Though African customs continued to play a significant part in the personal lives of the 'citizens', their social and cultural standards were strongly marked by those which they had learned of France. Ousmane Socé Diop was

[1] Delafosse in Hanotaux and Martineau, op. cit., p. 152.
[2] Cited in the report of *Congrès International de l'Évolution Culturelle des Peuples Coloniaux*, Paris, op. cit., pp. 27 f. In 1937–8, there were 15,453 students in Senegalese primary public schools and 1,557 students in private (usually Catholic mission) schools. *Annuaire Statistique*, tome ii, 1951, op. cit., pp. 83–5.
[3] See Appendix VIII: E, 'education' for evidence of the relatively higher educational level of Senegalese.
[4] The number of registered Senegalese voters in elections for the Chamber of Deputies was: in 1914, 8,674, J.O.C.D., *Débats*, 7 July 1914, p. 2735; in 1928, 16,553; in 1932, 18,797; in 1936, 20,746. Lachapelle, G., *Élections législatives*, Paris, 1928, 1932, 1936.

a pre-war 'citizen' whose novels expressed the ideals and sentiments of his group. In *Karim*, he explained the fusion of European and African mores, and the fascination of 'the legends with which our

FIGURE 2

1926–1945: Pre-war French 'citizens' (African[b] and European) in Senegal and in AOF. (Sources: Tableaux XXVII–XL, *Annuaire Statistique,* 1949, tome i, op. cit., pp. 80–81.)

	1926	1931	1936	1945[ae]
SENEGAL				
African citizens in Dakar	18,822	25,692	29,249	55,778
African citizens in Senegal	48,973	66,692	78,373	93,328
European citizens in Senegal	5,545	8,638	8,351	17,529
Total population	1,358,000	1,638,000	1,793,000	1,872,000
AOF				
African citizens in AOF	50,722	68,412	80,509	97,707
European Citizens in AOF	11,368	14,400	17,148	31,031[c]
Total population AOF[d]	13,499,000	14,576,000	14,743,000	15,955,000

[a] Estimate.
[b] African 'citizens' based on law of 29 September 1916.
[c] Including mulattos but excluding non-French Europeans.
[d] Including 'subjects', citizens, and foreigners.
[e] The sharp rise in the number of European citizens is partly because during the war a number of Europeans were stranded in tropical Africa.

mothers, grandmothers and aunts enchanted our childhood'.[1] But he also wrote of the 'citizen':

> His dearest hope . . . was to see this France whose language, history and geography he had studied with so much love. The names of cities or rivers like Anger or Lys had magic overtones which troubled him. The scent of a newly printed French catalogue . . . the smell of the items imported from France in his schoolboy's kit, attracted him as powerfully as the roads which seemed to lead to infinity, or the horizons of the ocean.[2]

The 'citizens' valued highly French education, decorations, and commodities. As Senghor explained in 1937, total assimilation was their goal. 'Therefore, the Senegalese bourgeoisie strongly resisted the popular rural school' which had no equivalent in the metropolitan educational system.[3]

The 'citizens' showed great pleasure at any indications of acceptance as equals by Europeans. When the wife of an European administrator wiped the shoes of the first African deputy, Blaise Diagne—while he travelled in Africa in 1917 on a government mission seeking

[1] Socé, Ousmane, *Karim,* Éditions 'France–Afrique', Paris, 1949, p. 82.
[2] Socé, Ousmane, *Mirages de Paris,* Éditions Latines, Paris, n.d., p. 20.
[3] Report of *Congrès International de l'Évolution Culturelles des Peuples Coloniaux,* op. cit., p. 40.

African soldiers for the First World War—the fact was discussed and repeated for many years.[1] First as a *commissaire* and in 1931-2 as under-secretary of state for the colonies, he held a higher rank than any colonial administrator, and this created conflicts for Europeans in Africa accustomed to automatic social precedence.[2]

The 'citizens' defended their special rights with eloquence and were prepared to take disputes to the highest courts of France. But they also knew their privileged status was totally dependent not upon themselves, not upon their African countrymen the 'subjects', but rather upon the pleasure of the French government. Most 'citizens' did not really challenge the system, but rather quarrelled over the spoils. Their parties are best described as cliques grouped around individual leaders, who at election time aligned themselves behind one or another candidate in accordance with the benefits they expected to reap from victory. It was in this pre-war period that Senegalese 'clan politics' began. Ideology played little part. The significant issues as well as the real power of the state were outside the scope of the parties—a characteristic of the pre-war parties of Senegal similar to that of the parties among the privileged European minority in post-war Southern Rhodesia.[3] One perceptive observer recorded:

Election meetings are sometimes so noisy that the speaker cannot make himself heard. It is the policy for one side occasionally to break up the meetings of the opposition; while the 'subjects' who cannot vote frequently vent their spleen against their privileged brethren by throwing stones at orators addressing political rallies.[4]

The resentment of the 'subjects' was not lessened by the constant evidence they saw of the 'citizens' privileges. As civil servants not only in Senegal but also in other territories of the federation, many Senegalese 'citizens' tried to behave and were regarded by the 'subjects' as Frenchmen. The politics of the 'citizens' was largely concerned with division of the fruits of public office—prestige, opportunities for material improvement such as easy loans for construction, leases for land, job promotion. In the rural provinces 'citizens' became traders and middle men in the peanut trade. And because the available benefits were comparatively few, competition among the 'citizens' was sharp. The *conseil général* of 1918 passed a resolution

[1] Mentioned in Buell, op. cit., p. 955. He cites this from the records of the December 1918 deliberations of the *conseil général*, p. 148.
[2] Delafosse in Hanotaux and Martineau, op. cit., tome iv, p. 351 See also p. 34, n. 3.
[3] Leys, Colin. *European Politics in Southern Rhodesia*, Oxford at the Clarendon Press, London, 1959.
[4] Buell, op. cit., p. 957. See also the article by Abdoulaye Thiaw in *l'Action*, 31 October 1956.

asking that Senegal be given two deputies and one senator in Parliament. In the debate, mention was made that 'the present deputy (Blaise Diagne) never comes to our defence'.[1] Another example occurred in 1925. Freshly returned with the then unique honour of a Doctorate in Law from Paris, Lamine Guèye was mayor of Saint-Louis. However, he practiced law in Dakar. The municipal councillors were quick to protest. By October of that year the council passed a resolution that 'it is altogether impossible and even dangerous for the interests of the commune to have the mayor live in Dakar and only make a few and short appearances in Saint-Louis'.[2]

Except for a brief interlude in 1848, Senegalese representation in the French Chamber of Deputies really began in 1875, with the election of a European, Alfred Gascogni.[3] The first African, Blaise Diagne, was elected deputy in 1914, and became an under-secretary in several French governments. 'A modest black customs official from Gorée,'[4] Diagne had also been a civil servant in Réunion, French Guiana, and Madagascar. Lamine Guèye claimed Diagne 'was elected only on the condition that he sponsor a law in Parliament to make the "citizens" born in the four *communes de plein exercise* eligible for compulsory military training', as were the European citizens.[5] He achieved this with the law of 29 September 1916, confirming the special position of the 'citizens', and set forth to prove the patriotism of the 'citizens' by energetically recruiting soldiers for the First World War. Most 'citizens' saw as a daring move this trade of African soldiers for the French reforms in the *loi Diagne*. Lamine Guèye was then one of the 'young Turks', a radical in the egalitarian 'Schoelcher' anti-slavery tradition. After the war many of the veterans of 1917 backed Lamine Guèye's call for real assimilation.

Diagne's followers were known as the *Diagnists*; his opponents, which included Lamine Guèye and Galandou Diouf, were known as the *parti de l'opposition*. Diouf unsuccessfully opposed Diagne in the 1928 and 1932 elections. Lamine Guèye[6] briefly defeated Blaise Diagne as mayor of Saint-Louis in 1925, then left on a tour of duty as a judge in the French West Indies. When Diagne died in 1934, the

[1] Buell, op. cit., pp. 953–4, n. 26, citing the December 1918 records, p. 147.
[2] Buell, op. cit., p. 959.
[3] Sadji, Abdoulaye. *Réalités Africaines*, 15 October 1955. See also Kenneth Robinson's excellent study of 'Senegal: The Elections to the Territorial Assembly, March 1957', in *Five Elections in Africa*, edited by W. J. M. Mackenzie and Kenneth Robinson, Oxford at the Clarendon Press, 1960, pp. 306 f.
[4] Diagne's work as Minister was cited by Lamine Guèye in J.O.A.N.C. II, *Débats*, 18 September 1946, p. 3797.
[5] Guèye thesis, op. cit., pp. 39–40. Jacobson, Alfred, 'L'Afrique Occidentale', in *La France d'outre-mer: sa situation actuelle*, Plon, Paris, 1953, p. 81.
[6] *Condition Humaine*, 8 March 1949.

opposition split. Galandou Diouf won in the by-election, and again in 1936. Lamine Guèye, just back from his overseas post, contested the by-election also, and managed to secure the support of some former Diagnists, as well as of Charles Graziani, president of the Chamber of Commerce in Dakar. In approximately 1928 Graziani, Turbé, a European radical resident in Dakar, and several others of socialist leanings, founded the *Parti Socialiste Sénégalais* (PSS), which in name reflected the rise of the Left in France. The PSS unsuccessfully tried to challenge the validation of Diouf's election, charging administrative interference.

From this failure by the PSS was born the idea of a Senegalese section of the French SFIO. The Senegalese 'citizens' already had some contact with Socialist forms and language. In Saint-Louis as early as 1912 some Frenchmen and mulattos reputedly with Socialist leanings, organized a club, *l'Aurore*. Diagne ran for office as a *Socialiste Unitaire*; in the Chamber he became a *Socialiste Républicain*; for a time he was a member of the SFIO federation of the Seine. During the early 'thirties, some Europeans in Senegal had started SFIO groups, and even contested the Dakar municipal elections.[1] Then in 1936, the Popular Front government came to power in France, and Lamine Guèye's colleague, Marius Moutet, became Colonial Minister. In September–October 1936, Moutet made an official trip to Dakar; he was received by a local *Comité du Front Populaire*, in which Mê Lamine Guèye was much in evidence.[2] Some months after Moutet's trip, the founding *grand congrès* of the Senegalese SFIO federation took place. Its birth was of some importance. The Senegalese SFIO was the first African branch of a French political party and remained unique, if by African branch is meant the majority of the members were African.[3] The Senegalese administration, still largely staffed by men favourable to the French Right, had supported Galandou Diouf. To the founders of the Senegalese SFIO, the *Dioufists* were the party of the administration; the prospect of support from the French Socialists against their local opponents was very attractive.

Who were the leaders of the SFIO? The political director was Mê Lamine Guèye, who in 1936 was also the president of the PSS. He believed in French Socialist ideas, and hoped to use his seat in the French SFIO executive in order to secure extension to the 'subjects' of the privileges which the 'citizens' alone enjoyed. This goal was already implied in his doctoral dissertation of 1921.[4] Another

[1] Information based on interviews, 1956.   [2] *Paris–Dakar*, 1 October 1936.
[3] After the war, Europeans organized some French party branches, chiefly in Senegal and Ivory Coast.
[4] Guèye thesis, op. cit., p. 14.

leader was Mê Paul Bonifay, a Socialist lawyer in Dakar, who remained after the war one of the rare Europeans to exercise any influence within an African political party. Other SFIO leaders included former supporters of the PSS. In June 1938 the majority of the PSS voted to merge with the SFIO,[1] and the SFIO was strengthened when joined by such members as the trader Ibrahima Seydou N'Daw—the most influential person in the populous peanut centre of Kaolack.[2] Only a PSS rump group, composed largely of French Radicals opposed to the French SFIO, continued until it dwindled out of existence just after the Second World War.

The pre-war Senegalese federation was Socialist far more in principle than in practice. The party had the same structure and policy as any French section of the SFIO. *L'A.O.F.*, the party's newspaper, mentioned branches, a library, the necessity for internal party democracy and discipline. The party took positions against fascism, was anti-clerical, and favoured raising the status of women. Yet Socialist terminology, and French Socialist problems, were the province of but a small educated group in the SFIO—led by Lamine Guèye—who also attended the Socialist congresses in France. There Senegalese delegates were accredited as the representatives of 3,000 members, and generally voted with the established leaders of the party.[3] (Their minority position at SFIO congresses in France was not unlike the minority position of African deputies in Parliament.) But the SFIO federation of Senegal represented privileged African citizens, included few workers or peasants. The limited franchise, and its own constitutional outlook made it, necessarily, also an alliance of 'clans.' It included ethnic associations such as the Lebous of Dakar, many of whose *notables* were illiterate; its electoral position was stiffened by such informal bodies as the *amis de Lamine Guèye*. It was after all, the *parti de l'opposition* to Galandou Diouf and his *Dioufists*. The SFIO federation favoured reforms, and the spread of citizenship as a consequence of its assimilationist doctrine. But it was careful not to attack the system, and on 14 July SFIO *tam-tams* sounded loud in all the neighbourhoods where the party had any influence.[4] Ever since a hostage of Samory was brought to Paris to watch the 14 July celebrations in 1886, these July celebrations had special importance in French-speaking Africa, as occasions for Africans to show their loyalty to France.[5]

---

[1] *L'A.O.F.*, 27 May 1939.   [2] Ibid., 25 February 1939.
[3] *L'A.O.F.*, 1 April 1939 and 14 January 1939, mentioned Senegalese interventions at the December 1938 Montrouge SFIO Congress.
[4] 'Tam-tams' refers to African popular outdoor celebrations, where there is dancing to the steady accompaniment of beating drums.
[5] Delafosse in Hanotaux and Martineau, op. cit., p. 205.

The Popular Front adopted some reforms, and planned others. Trade unions led by literate Africans became legal. The first African strike took place in 1938 among the railroad workers of Thiès, amid clashes between strikers and security forces. An unusually abundant peanut crop brought wealth not only to the 'citizen'-traders, but also to the 'subject' peasants.[1] Lamine Guèye used his legal training to defend the 'subjects' in the courts. Associations, discussing political reforms, multiplied in the towns. Meanwhile, the SFIO achieved some electoral victories over their *Dioufist* adversaries. Some of their members were elected to the *conseil colonial*; they controlled the municipality of Saint-Louis by 1937, and the other municipalities by 1939. An SFIO nucleus of Europeans and African 'citizens' existed even in Guinea.[2] Study groups, usually led by Europeans, disseminated Marxist thought among educated Africans; branches of the SFIO existed in the four communes, and in the two other urban centres of Kaolack and Thiès in Senegal. The main goal of the SFIO was to win the Senegalese parliamentary seat. But the fall of France in 1940 postponed this achievement. The Vichy administration dissolved Parliament in France, and in Senegal suppressed all representative institutions.

Liberation and the Bloc Africain

As in the other tropical African territories, in Senegal the Second World War and Vichy rule made Africans very critical of colonial rule, and very aware of international events. The 'citizens' lost most of their legal privileges, and for the first time encountered systematic racial segregation and discrimination. Not only some Europeans, but also some Africans were Gaullists. The students at the École Normale William-Ponty asked for arms to fight against Germany.[3] Africans observed that 'only Negroes were executed' for their resistance to Vichy. 'Forced labour became generalized'; rationing and official requisitioning of goods and produce caused economic hardship.[4] With the interruption of world trade the income from peanuts of the 'citizen'-traders and of the 'subject'-peasants diminished.[5] In September 1940 Dakar witnessed backwater naval engagements as the Allies tried unsuccessfully to take it from Vichy.[6] Through Dakar passed soldiers and sailors of many nations.

[1] *L'A.O.F.*, 2 May 1947.
[2] Ibid., 1 April 1939.
[3] From an unpublished manuscript by Lamine Diakhité.
[4] Both citations are from a speech by Senghor on 20 March 1947, at the SFIO national congress in France. *L'A.O.F.*, 2 May 1947.
[5] See Figure 3, p. 135.
[6] *L'A.O.F.*, 6 and 27 June 1947.

FIGURE 3

Commercialization of Peanuts in Senegal

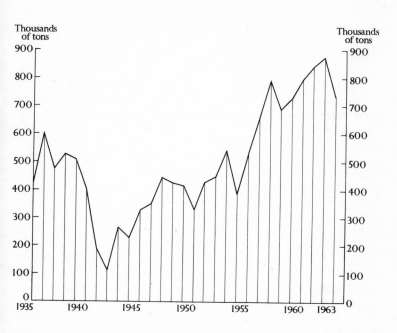

Sources: *Bulletin Statistique*, Sénégal et Mauritanie, No. 2, Saint-Louis, April
1956; *Outre-mer 1958*, op. cit., p. 731. *Bulletin Statistique et économique
mensuel*, République du Sénégal, No. 5, Dakar, May 1963, p. 3.

African soldiers fought on the side of de Gaulle. There was great resentment when African veterans, repatriated in 1944 after years in German prisoner of war camps, were shot by their French officers for mutiny at Tiaroye, just outside of Dakar. Lamine Guèye, the lawyer of the veterans involved in the incident, explained that 40 veterans were shot, another 40 gravely injured, and many others slightly injured. The veterans wanted to be paid at a higher rate, 'because they had been prisoners of war'. They were not given this payment, but told to file their request 'with their *chefs de canton*, who should pass it on to the administrator, who should pass it to the governor, who should pass it to the governor-general'. The veterans demonstrated their discontent, and incidents, less than 12 miles from Dakar, took place.[1] 'These facts were not easily forgotten,'[2] and partly explained the post-Liberation burst of political activity in Senegal.

In 1945 came the first reforms, elections began, the administration was reorganized as collaborators were tried, and Africans in Senegal spent much time discussing and publishing on political questions. The initiative for these post-war political activities came from the educated Africans in the towns who were more numerous in Senegal, than in any other territory. Immediately after Liberation, the differences between 'subjects' and 'citizens', partly wiped out during the war, were less evident than ever before. As in the other territories, the idea of African unity became dominant after the meetings of the *États Généraux de la Colonisation Française*. To effect unity, the leaders of the existing urban associations of educated Africans met in a *comité d'entente* in Dakar in 1945.

What were the most important constituent groups in the *comité d'entente*? There were the nationalists or autonomists, who discussed the prospect and desirability of African independence: members either of the small *Mouvement Nationalist Africain*,[3] or of the minor *Mouvement Autonomist Africain*.[4] There was the *Comité d'Études Franco-Africain*;[5] within its ranks some Gaullists and the rump group of the pre-war PSS struggled unsuccessfully for power with the *Groupe d'Études Communistes*. There was the GEC, known as the *Groupe Sociale* before the war. There were the members of the African section of the *Ligue des Droits de l'Homme*, at least some of whom were also freemasons. Lastly, there was the SFIO, including the *Union des Jeunes* which had connexions with the GEC, and the *Bloc Sénégalais* SFIO section of Dakar.

[1] J.O.A.N.C. I, *Débats*, 22 March 1946, pp. 1000 f.
[2] *L'A.O.F.*, 22 August 1947.
[3] Led by Pierre Diagne, and publishing the newspaper *Communauté*.
[4] Led by Amadou Bâ, and publishing the newspaper *Le Sénégal*.
[5] Publishing the newspaper *Clarté*.

A struggle for power took place within the *comité d'entente*—as in its counterparts in other territories—between the GEC and the SFIO leaders. In Senegal the SFIO won. The *comité* adopted the name which the 'citizen'-Socialists proposed, *Bloc Africain*. Lamine Guèye—elder statesman and reputed opponent of the administration, of the *Dioufists* and of the Vichy regime—became the recognized leader of the *Bloc*. The *Bloc* was praised in popular song. For the urban population, *b'loc*, *b'loc* came to symbolize progress, change, and opposition to the French system. The newest fashion for women in the towns was the *b'loc* dress, which left the right shoulder uncovered.[1] In enthusiastic public meetings, the partisans of the *Bloc*, and particularly the Socialists, hoped to extend their influence and organization to all the West African territories. They even attempted to invest candidates for Guinea and Soudan, indicating their belief in Senegal's mission to lead AOF. In all the elections until the fall of 1946, *Bloc*-sponsored candidates had overwhelming support. However, the *Bloc* had neither an effective organization, nor an agreed programme. An illustration of the confusion reigning within the *Bloc Africain* was that two lists bore its name in Rufisque elections. The SFIO—which alone had a working structure and experienced African leaders—in fact selected the candidates for the parliamentary elections.

Who were they? Lamine Guèye, whose reputation as the defender both of 'citizens' and 'subjects' was at its height, one of the first Africans to own a villa and a car, became the first college candidate as a matter of course. He chose and the SFIO invested the second college candidate, Léopold Sédar Senghor; and Senghor was presented both to the *Bloc*, and to the 'subjects', as their deputy. At first there was considerable opposition to the choice of Senghor, both from among the African students in Paris, and from among the younger leaders of the *Bloc Africain*. They protested both against Senghor's person, and against the way in which he was designated by Lamine Guèye. Nevertheless, Senghor ran.

About twenty years younger than the Wolof 'citizen' Lamine Guèye, Senghor was the son of a prosperous 'subject' Serere shopkeeper from Joal, in the Sine-Saloum, the heart of the peanut growing area of Senegal. A Catholic, partly mission educated, he spent many years in France, where he became the first African to obtain the coveted *aggrégation*, and taught grammar in *lycées* in Paris and Tours. He became a naturalized French citizen. Mobilized in 1939, he spent a short time in a German prison, but spent most of the war

[1] Mercier, P. and Balandier, G. *Les Pêcheurs lébou*, Études Sénégalaises no. 3, I.F.A.N. Saint-Louis, 1952, p. 77. Their spelling is 'b'lok'.

teaching at a *lycée* in Joinville. In France and Africa he was a recognized man of letters, and a poet. He was a spokesman for African art and culture, for *négritude*, and became one of the patrons of *Présence Africaine*.[1] While Lamine Guèye, used to living in the towns, travelled in the interior with difficulty, dressed formally in well-pressed suit and tie, Senghor wore khaki and sunglasses, sat on the floor of huts and ate what he was served. Some of the 'citizen' Socialists disdainfully called him 'the deputy in khaki', while the numerous Senegalese war veterans, who were also voters, applauded Senghor's deliberate attempt to identify with them.

The plebiscite vote for Lamine Guèye and Senghor was but partly based upon the *Bloc*, which attracted support mainly in the towns and among many who had no franchise. In addition, the SFIO and particularly Lamine Guèye, gained the backing of the Lébou and Wolof notables,[2] of the Muslim denominational leaders with some of whom he had attended Koranic school, of official 'chiefs' in the Fouta Toro and even his adversaries in the *conseil colonial*. Furthermore, while Moutet was colonial minister, the administration facilitated Lamine Guèye's successful attempt to take over the *Bloc*.

The final absorption of the *Bloc* by the Senegalese SFIO was related to the rivalry between French Socialists and Communists for influence over the nascent West African parties. Lamine Guèye and Senghor signed the call of all the African deputies to the Bamako conference, while the *Bloc* flourished and Marius Moutet still hoped that the Bamako meeting might form a great African Socialist party.[3] At the same time, the small but active group of GEC members in Senegal refrained from attacking Lamine Guèye and were joined in enthusiasm for a *rassemblement* by others, including the Socialist *Union des Jeunes*. There were a number of partisans of the RDA position at the Senegalese SFIO congress of October 1946. Soon, however, the controversy between those for a Socialist *bloc* and those for the GEC formula of a *rassemblement* became public, as Lamine Guèye and Senghor decided not to attend the Bamako Congress. By the end of 1946 the *Bloc* had disintegrated. Supporters of the RDA at the Socialist youth congress of June 1947 were suspended by the territorial executive.[4] The newly formed RDA section of Senegal— *Union Démocratique Sénégalaise* (UDS)—attacked Lamine Guèye and the Socialists and accused them of lining up with the administra-

[1] Senghor was editor and contributor of *Anthologie de la nouvelle poésie nègre et malgache de langue française*, Presses Universitaires de France, Paris, 1948, as well as of several other volumes of poetry.
[2] For the ethnic groups of Senegal, see Map 3.
[3] *L'A.O.F.*, 20 June 1947.   [4] Guèye, Doudou in *Réveil*, 22 April 1958.

tion. The Senegalese SFIO still attracted most of the voters. They charged that the RDA was Communist. How else, they asked, explain the refusal of leaders in other territories to answer the call to unity around the *Bloc*, issued even before the 1945 municipal elections?[1]

The Senegalese leaders did not then realize their lead in the *Bloc* might be resented by former subjects in other territories still rankling at the pre-war privileges of the 'citizens'. Meanwhile within Senegal the post-war unity and enthusiasm were over. The constitutional reforms had fallen far short of people's expectations; the economy was in decline; people were disillusioned with the SFIO; and opposition mounted in the countryside. At the same time, though all Africans became citizens of France in 1946, the pre-war difference in legal status between 'subjects' and 'citizens' became a major point of cleavage among the territorial leaders who had co-operated briefly in the Senegalese SFIO.

The BDS Breaks Away

While the SFIO *bureau fédéral* invested all the Senegalese representatives elected at every level—from municipal to parliamentary—there were many tensions within the party. There were both political differences and personal friction between Lamine Guèye and Senghor. Among the educated Africans, there was a struggle for power between the old 'citizens', who retained control of the SFIO executive, and the pre-war 'subjects', who resented the continued political domination of the former. There was obvious feeling in the countryside against the town 'citizens' who nominated not the local favourite sons, but rather one of themselves, as representatives to the 1946 territorial assembly.

Indications of a break between Senghor and Lamine Guèye were evident in votes recorded between 1946 and 1948 in Parliament over questions related to the revolt of Madagascar. For a short time, Lamine Guèye was legal advisor to the Malagasy political leaders implicated in the rebellion. He, as well as Senghor, broke discipline with the Socialist group and voted against the government proposal to lift parliamentary immunity on the Malagasy MDRM deputies.[2] Afterwards, Lamine Guèye diplomatically travelled to Mecca, in the hope this might rebuild his support among Senegal's Muslims. He left Senghor to explain the votes to the Socialist parliamentary group. Tight parliamentary discipline within the Socialist group, together with Socialist participation in the French government, made

[1] *L'A.O.F.*, 28 March 1947.
[2] J.O.A.N., *Débats*, 9 May 1947, pp. 1540 f., and 1982 f.; also 1 August 1947, pp. 3823 f., and *scrutins* 220 and 221, pp. 3833–5.

L

it difficult for the Senegalese Socialists to oppose the government in France or in Africa. This was acceptable to Lamine Guèye, whose loyalty to the French Socialists was built on his pre-war experiences, and who found some rewards in the post-war reforms, and the designation of Socialists as governor-general of French West Africa, and governor of Senegal.[1] But Senghor—a Socialist only since 1945, Catholic and therefore not in sympathy with SFIO anti-clericalism, philosophically preoccupied with the particular, rather than the universal characteristics of African society—found French Socialist discipline unsupportable. He broke discipline on several votes[2] and stated his doubt whether the French Socialists were the best allies for Africans interested in reforms.

Senghor knew that in Africa people were displeased with many of the provisions of the overseas reforms adopted in Paris. In most territories, this displeasure was registered at the first meetings of the newly created *conseils généraux*. There were stormy exchanges between the spokesmen of the administration and the territorial councillors chafing at the restrictions which the law placed on their powers. In Senegal, the limitations of the decrees of 25 October 1946 were particularly resented. The Senegalese took for granted that the law recognize their special position with the provisions for a single electoral college. (This mode of election of Senegalese territorial councillors was unique in AOF until the Loi-Cadre of 1956 made the single college universal.) The Senegalese particularly resented the limit in financial powers. Before the war Senegalese councillors had considerable financial powers, which had been increased by the decree of 25 February 1946, adopted during the first Constituent Assembly. But this decree was superseded, and the powers accorded to the *conseil général* under the decree of 25 October 1946 were somewhat less. The Senegalese, who had more experience fighting the French administration on points of law than had their colleagues in other territories, decided to press the matter.

On 11 January 1947, the territorial councillors unanimously refused to vote Senegal's budget. They asked Parliament to increase their autonomy, and to limit severely the federal taxation powers of the projected *grand conseil*. The Senegalese councillors took particular exception to article 85 of the parliamentary *loi de finance* of 23 December 1946. High federal taxation has been a recurrent grievance first of the Senegalese, and then of the Ivory Coast territorial councillors. For both these territories subsidized, through the

---

[1] Governor Wiltord, 1947–50, and Governor-General Béchard, 1948–51.
[2] For example, during the second *Constituante*, Senghor was one of 18 deputies who voted for, while 530 voted against a proposal for a single electoral college in Madagascar. J.O.A.N.C. II, *Débats*, 4 October 1946, p. 4566.

federal budget, the poorer West African territories.[1] The issue was taken up in Paris. 'Position unchanged. Marius Moutet does not want to understand. Be firm', cabled Lamine Guèye to the *conseil général*.[2] In June 1947 the councillors again refused to vote the budget. Not until the extraordinary session of July 1947 did they approve it. They had failed to obtain more extensive powers.

The members of the Senegalese *conseil général* had been elected while the formula of unity surrounding the *Bloc Africain* was still generally accepted and the single territorial electoral list included even one RDA councillor.[3] But the mystique of unity dissolved as French Socialists decided they could not make allies of the RDA born at the October 1946 Bamako Congress. By 1947 a *groupe socialiste* emerged and marked the beginning of partisan quarrels within the Senegalese *conseil général*. The interterritorial RDA leaders were quick to point out—and many Senegalese calling themselves SFIO could not but agree—that the French Socialists had not granted the expressed wishes of their African party colleagues.

There were personal, not only political, differences between Senghor and Lamine Guèye. These stemmed from the same causes that led the educated pre-war 'subjects' in Senegal to take exception to the 'citizens' assumption that they were the rightful political leaders of Senegal—indeed of tropical Africa. The minority of former 'subjects' within the *conseil général*, and the majority of them outside, chafed at this assumption. They saw evidence of it in the way the candidates for the *conseil général* were chosen. Although the law provided for a single electoral college, and therefore theoretically removed all distinctions between first and second-class citizens, the candidates, invested through the SFIO party machine, came principally from among former 'citizens': at least 35 out of 50. The elections were held in four large constituencies, which favoured control from Dakar; and the candidates were mainly townsmen not close to the provincial electors. While two-thirds of the candidates were Wolof, Lebou, mulatto, or European, these groups constituted less than one-third of the total population. The rural voters had no direct way of affecting the nominations or indeed the elections for the SFIO was dominated by the 'citizens' and it was the only organized party.[4]

Staffed in 1936 by 'citizens' interested in acquiring office from the *Dioufists*, the group of SFIO leaders did not expand enough to take

---

[1] *L'A.O.F.*, 15 January 1947.

[2] Territoire du Sénégal, *p.v. du conseil général, session extraordinaire de juillet 1947*, Saint-Louis, 1950, p. 9.

[3] The list of the *Bloc d'Union Socialiste et Républicain* included Guy Etcheverry, a European journalist who edited the RDA newspaper in Dakar, *Réveil*.

[4] See Appendix VIII: E.

into account the widened electorate and the post-war reforms they had helped to bring about. Party decisions continued to be taken by Lamine Guèye in consultation with his *amis*, and the 'citizens' in the party's territorial executive. Not surprisingly, in view of this personal type of SFIO leadership, Lamine Guèye accumulated offices and was at the same time political director of the party, member of the French SFIO executive, deputy, president of the *conseil général*, president of the *grand conseil*, and mayor of Dakar. The resentment of the 'subjects' outside this political oligarchy increased, as grand councillors of the French Union and senators were successively chosen from among European, West Indian, or African 'citizens'.

Senghor became the spokesman for the discontented 'subjects'. His personal break with Lamine Guèye appeared imminent, when the latter retracted his promise to assure the election as councillor of the French Union of Mamadou Dia—a 'subject' schoolteacher stationed in the Sine-Saloum region.[1] Dia became one of the first critics of the established leaders of the SFIO. The 7 March 1947 issue of *l'A.O.F.* announced that not all of Dia's articles were printed, because some of his statements 'conflicted with socialist principles'. The Kaolack Senegalese SFIO Congress of 1947 was the scene of bitter disputes. The report of the administrative secretary, Mê Paul Bonifay, was rejected by 143 votes against 91, with 83 abstentions.[2] And Senghor, supported by the delegates from the provinces—from the populous peanut region of Kaolack; the railroad centre of Thiès; the ethnically diverse and geographically isolated Casamance, the impoverished savannah region of the Senegal river—denounced the party's leader. He charged the *bureau fédéral* with employing 'clan policies', designating 'deputies of the first and second degree', with 'nepotism', and insufficient contact with the party's rank and file.[3] Only the delegates from the four old communes did not join the revolt against Lamine Guèye.

Not only within the SFIO, but through Senegal there were many grievances against existing conditions by 1947. Peanut prices, always

---

[1] Mamadou Dia, a Ponty graduate who had earned his *baccalauréat* before 1945, spent much of his time as a senator in Paris studying economics. He became secretary-general of the BDS, and of the interterritorial IOM. In 1956, he became a deputy, together with Senghor. In 1957 he became vice-president of the council of government of Senegal; and in 1960 president, a post he held until 1962. His works on African economics include: *Contribution à l'étude du mouvement coopératif en Afrique noire*, Paris, Clermont-Ferrand, 1952; *Réflexions sur l'économie de l'Afrique noire*, Éditions Africaines, Paris, c. 1954; *l'Économie africaine*, Presses Universitaires de France, Paris, 1957; *Nations africaines et solidarité mondiale*, Presses Universitaires de France, Paris, 1960.

[2] *L'A.O.F.*, 3 October 1947.

[3] Ibid., and *Afrique Nouvelle*, 12 October 1947.

an indication of rural political sentiment in Senegal, began a decline not reversed until the start of the Korean war.[1] Lamine Guèye, preoccupied with legal reforms—equality, citizenship—did not speak the language of the peasants. The SFIO leaders had no further programme beyond the reiteration of their pre-war ideas which had been written into the Constitution. Senghor realized that 'the African peasants . . . were far more affected by the suppression of forced labour and rising peanut prices, than by the right of citizenship'.[2]

Many disputes took place in the countryside. One was in Kaolack, perhaps the centre of gravity of Senegalese politics because it dominates the Sine-Saloum, the most fertile peanut growing area. About one-fifth of the population,[3] and about half the peanut crop come from there. It was a centre of farming, trading, and religion. A personal opponent of Senghor, Djim Momar Guèye, started a regional *Parti Travailliste Saloum-Saloum*. Its emergence was a direct challenge to the authority of the 'grand elector' of Kaolack, Ibrahima Seydou N'Daw, the regional SFIO leader.[4] Of the same generation as Lamine Guèye, Ibrahima Seydou N'Daw was locally called the *Diaraf*, or chief of the region. His reputation was that of a kingmaker: his support of Lamine Guèye in 1945, and subsequently of Senghor in 1949, contributed significantly to their election. He was the head of the *Syndicat des Commerçants des Indigènes du Sine-Saloum*, an organization grouping the African traders and middle men involved in the marketing of peanuts. The dispute was quite public, and in an exchange of articles in *l'A.O.F.*, N'Daw charged that the *Parti Travailliste* was 'imported from Bathurst'. Momar Guèye taunted N'Daw as 'the lawyer in a kaftan'.[5] The two men belonged to different traditions of Islam. N'Daw was closely associated with the Tidjaniya brotherhood, to which many established African trading families belonged, and whose spiritual guide, Ibrahima Niasse, also lived in Kaolack. Djim Momar Guèye, a jeweller by hereditary position, was connected with the Mouride Muslim denomination. N'Daw was not pleased to learn that Lamine Guèye was supporting Djim Momar Guèye for the Council of the French Union. From discontent with other decisions of the SFIO federation grew such separate regional and ethnic associations as the *Union Générale des Originaires de la Vallée du Fleuve* (UGOVF), the *Fédération des Originaires et Natifs du Oualo*, the *Mouvement des Forces Démocratiques de la Casamance*, the *Association des Toucouleurs du Fouta*

---

[1] See Appendix XI and Figure 3, p. 135.
[2] *Condition Humaine*, 19 October 1948.
[3] 489,400 in 1956, according to the Service Statistique, Saint-Louis.
[4] Between 1952 and 1958 he was president of the territorial assembly of Senegal.
[5] See *L'A.O.F.*, 4 April, 29 July, 15 August, 2 and 23 September 1947.

Toro pour la Défense de la Condition Humaine, and many other regional and ethnic groups.[1]

Senghor, who spent most of his time in the interior, realized there was ample scope for a new party. The question he faced was what kind of party. The young educated 'subjects' in the towns were attracted to the RDA. Some started Marxist study courses for adults in Dakar and Saint-Louis. The young men of the GEC in Senegal started a Université Populaire Africaine for adults, where workers could learn about history and Marxist theory. (This venture was similar to the *Ligue Contre l'Ignorance* of Ivory Coast.) Both groups were led by men impatient at the slow expansion of the state educational programmes. Some were the leaders of the trade unions. Labour disputes flared up in the Dakar area; a five month strike of Senegalese railroad workers took place.[2] The workers of Senegal were more numerous and better organized than those of the other territories;[3] they were attached organically to the French Communist-dominated *Confédération Générale du Travail* (CGT); and were more responsive to the RDA than the SFIO.

Senghor, however, was not inclined to join his forces—largely rural—with those of the young left-wing cadres of the RDA. It was 1947, and he saw the new balance of French politics. An MRP overseas minister replaced Moutet, and France was torn by the rivalry between the Communists—in total opposition—and the non-Communists in the government. The Socialist allies of the SFIO had decreasing political influence, while that of the MRP was growing. With this French political background in mind, Senghor moved his supporters into opposition in Senegal—but collaboration with the MRP in France. And he began this collaboration just when the MRP ministers were preparing an offensive against the RDA.

By February 1948, Senghor and his colleagues started publishing *Condition Humaine*. An editorial explained that the name was chosen with the intention of inviting reflection, rather than excitement.[4] Moderate in tone, the newspaper claimed to be an unofficial Socialist 'organ of quest and combat',[5] which sought to 'combine Socialist method with African probity'.[6] The paper defended regional associations and the striking workers;[7] it gave attention to the interests of the Muslim denominational leaders, and attacked local corruption and 'immorality'. It took no great changes to transform *Condition*

[1] Mentioned in *Condition Humaine* issues for 1948 and 1949.
[2] For details, see the 1948 issues of *Réveil*.
[3] For some supporting statistics, see Appendix X.
[4] *Condition Humaine*, 3 March 1948.
[5] Ibid., 25 February 1948.   [6] Ibid., 25 July 1948.
[7] Ibid., 26 April 1948, for an editorial supporting the railroad strikers.

Humaine into the organ of the SFIO rebels. They called themselves the *Bloc Démocratique Sénégalais* (BDS), thus continuing the familiar terminology of the *Bloc Africain*. In 1948 a *group BDS* was formed in the *conseil général*.

In Paris, Senghor broke discipline with the Socialist parliamentary group. At the 1948 French SFIO Congress he was eliminated from the executive committee,[1] on which he had served since first elected in 1945.[2] In September, he sent a letter to Guy Mollet announcing his resignation, explaining that he believed his action was in the higher interests of African socialism.[3] On 16 November he joined the MRP-sponsored *Indépendants d'Outre-mer* group in the National Assembly. One of his first concrete achievements—a victory over Lamine Guèye in the Assembly—was to gain parliamentary approval for an electoral law providing for the use of proportional representation in the selection of the overseas representatives to the Council of the Republic.[4] This electoral system allowed the minority of Senghor's supporters in the *conseil général* to elect Mamadou Dia a senator, with 18 out of 50 votes.[5] Dia became the secretary-general of the new Senegalese party.

BDS Tactics

How did the seventeen territorial councillors who became the BDS nucleus explain their revolt? They claimed to differ with the Senegalese SFIO leaders in doctrine, procedure, emphasis, and morals. Mamadou Dia, in his report to the first BDS annual Congress, criticized the French SFIO for voting with reactionary French parties in Parliament; lifting the immunity of the Malagasy deputies; refusing pensions for African veterans equal to those of French veterans; and recognizing the state of Israel, against the wishes of the Arab League.[6] Senghor asserted an African, as contrasted with a French, type of socialism. The Senegalese SFIO, he alleged, violated fundamental African precepts of behaviour; it indulged in nepotism, corruption; its leaders permitted no criticism, and worshipped 'the fetish of a man—the divine-right chief of African democracy'.[7] The BDS called the system of leadership in the SFIO 'Laminisme', and rejected it with puritan injunctions to truly democratic, honest political behaviour.

[1] *Condition Humaine*, 5 August 1948.
[2] *L'A.O.F.*, 29 August 1947.
[3] The letter was reprinted in *Condition Humaine*, 5 October 1948.
[4] J.O.A.N., *Débats*, 20 September 1948, pp. 6747 f.
[5] *Condition Humaine*, 30 November 1948.
[6] Rapport moral, typescript, 17 April 1949.   [7] Ibid.

How can we hesitate to gather together all our strength, when immorality makes successive assaults on our most sacred values, the moral values which are the condition of our survival in this terrible century of the atomic bomb? Since we cannot claim to be part of any materialistic civilisation, our policy must be to maintain scrupulously the normal standards of morality, else we risk total disintegration. Language of puritans, the jokers will cry. . . . Morality remains an eternal factor in progress, a saving and conciliating factor, always ready to save civilisation.[1]

The BDS newspaper, unlike the SFIO's *A.O.F.*, gave little space to the details of French politics. Instead, the paper printed party records and reports, and dealt with the theories of African art, literature, poetry, and philosophy. The preoccupation of the BDS leaders with African values and a truly African theory of socialism,[2] pointed as early as 1948 to the 'separatist' concerns of the Senegalese intellectuals, which in 1956 gave impetus to the transformation of the BDS into an openly nationalist party. But in 1948 the BDS firmly rejected all 'disloyalty' to France, and gave eloquent support to the French Union, limited only by occasional statements in favour of a revision of the unitary French Constitution to allow for federalism. Like the SFIO, however, the first goal of the party was electoral victory, and this gave to the BDS pronouncements constitutional overtones distinguishing them from those of the more revolutionary RDA.

The founders of the BDS tried to avoid the mistakes of the SFIO oligarchy. Their organization was based on the idea of a universal, not a restricted franchise. Mass membership was the goal, and the BDS *comité d'organisation provisoire* deliberately sought out Senegal's ethnic, religious, professional, business, and regional representatives. With Dia and Senghor worked some educated 'subjects' who had been supporters of the RDA, several mulatto lawyers, and a few 'subject' territorial councillors. They toured the provinces continuously, and their newspaper testified to their knowledge of and support for local grievances. The expressions of grievances, such as those of the *Union pour la défense des intérêts du quartier de Guet-n-Dar et des pêcheurs*—who founded their organization because they had 'no market for their salted fish, no stable prices', because they felt forgotten, their streets were ugly and unlit, their water supply was short, 'and no political party brought about any changes'[3]—has been one of the most important factors contributing to the success of the BDS, as of the other African mass parties.

[1] *Condition Humaine*, 11 August 1948.
[2] An interesting illustration of the cultural concerns of the top-level BDS leaders, is Senghor's report to the May 1956 BDS Congress, entitled 'Socialisme et culture', and reprinted in *Condition Humaine*, 31 May 1956.
[3] *Afrique Noire*, Dakar, 15 July 1954.

The leaders of the BDS entered into a series of negotiations with the major ethnic and interest groups. Perhaps the most important of these were Muslim, since at least four-fifths of the population of Senegal was Muslim.[1] The centre of gravity of the Muslim groups, as indeed of the Senegalese economy, is the rich and densely populated Sine-Saloum area. The significance of support from the Kaolack area, particularly while the franchise was restricted, was illustrated by the electoral statistics for the 1956 French parliamentary elections. Out of a total of 133,179 votes cast in the region, 121,809 were for the BDS. The total number of valid votes cast in Senegal was 454,886.[2] Similarly, within the BDS, out of a total of 1,500 mandates recognized at the 1956 BDS Congress, 746 were cast by delegates from the Kaolack region.[3] BDS cards were sold in the region while the peanut crop was being marketed.

Over the generations, through intermarriage and conversion to Islam, almost a single social category concentrating rural religious and secular power and wealth had emerged out of the maraboutic, trading and traditionally chiefly families.[4] They have a remarkable circuit of communication, and their *talibés* or student-clients send contributions from trading, or give labour and grow peanuts. These important families were concentrated in the Sine-Saloum, where unlike Casamance or the Fouta Toro, no party could hope to win in elections without either beating or joining them. The BDS tried to join them. Both Dia and Senghor were well aware the chances of winning votes depended in large measure upon the backing of the *marabouts* who, hearing the complaints of their *talibés*, were dissatisfied with Lamine Guèye and the SFIO.

Among the West African Tidjaniya stretching from Nigeria to Senegal, Ibrahima Niasse of Kaolack was of special importance. In Senegal he had a following among the established traders, and he was close to Lamine Guèye. It was a step forward when N'Daw broke with him and joined the BDS.[5] The Omarien Tidjaniya influence was strong among the Toucouleur of the Senegal river area, the birthplace of al Hajj Umar Tall and his associates. Seydou Nourou Tall, descendant of one of al Hajj Umar Tall's sons who had sided with the French, became publicly associated with the BDS. He had sided with the Vichy administration and been Muslim chaplain of the French African troops, and was thus more notable for joining whatever administration was in power at the moment than for his following.

[1] *Tam-Tam*, March–May 1955, op. cit., p. 34.
[2] Direction des Affaires Politiques, Gouvernement–Général, Dakar, 1956.
[3] Supplement, *Les Échos d'Afrique Noire*, no. 267, Dakar, 1956.
[4] Gouilly, op. cit., pp. 116–33.
[5] *Condition Humaine*, 2 November 1948.

The two most important religious dynasties were the Sy and M'Backé families. The Sy dynasty guided the Tidjaniya Hafedist from their principal place of residence in Tivaouane, one of the destinations of West Africa's religious pilgrims. Before the war the Sy had been the spiritual guides of Galandou Diouf, Lamine Guèye's rival. The Tivaouane religious leaders had a special following among the older urban workers, particularly some of the railroad workers of Thiès. The choice of Abbas Guèye as Senghor's partner in the 1951 election to the National Assembly was made partly by Ababacar Sy, engaged in rivalry with his brother who backed Lamine Guèye.

Touba, near Diourbel, is the principal place of residence of the M'Backé dynasty. At Touba is the tomb of Ahmadou Bamba, founder of the Mouride movement. Unlike the Tidjaniya the Mourides are specifically Senegalese, and their growth in the twentieth century was probably related to Senegalese protest against foreign rule. The ground-swell of protest in the countryside of Senegal added fuel to a quarrel over succession between the followers of Fadilou M'Backé who had Mouride law on his side, and Cheikh M'Backé, son of the old Khalif. Fadilou M'Backé decided to break with the Socialists, which may explain why his residence was stoned by SFIO supporters during the 1951 campaign. Cheikh M'Backé continued to support Lamine Guèye. The BDS victory gave the Fadilou M'Backé wing of the Mourides the opportunity to con- solidate their power. The Mourides of Senegal have grown faster than any other religious group, and the decision of Fadilou M'Backé to support the BDS helped it to electoral victory.[1]

What made the Mourides decide to back Senghor, a Catholic by choice and a French poet by profession who had spent many years out of Senegal? Senghor was not even particularly fluent in Wolof, the language in which the Mourides conducted most of their studies. Of the seventeen territorial councillors who originally broke with the SFIO, ten were Catholics. Partly because of these proportions the BDS leaders went out of their way to hear specific Muslim demands, to back the support of a mosque in one area, a Koranic school in another, the teaching of Arabic in the state schools, and more free trips to Mecca for the faithful. More important in obtaining Mouride backing was the position of Mamadou Dia. Dia had real eloquence in Wolof; he had learned it in the Koranic schools of the Mourides in the Baol of Senegal, and indeed could recall as a boy sitting at the feet of Ahmadou Bamba. It is probably then that Dia first formed

---

[1] The Centre de Hautes Études Administratives sur l'Afrique et l'Asie Modernes, in *Notes et études sur l'islam en Afrique noire*, Peyronnet, Paris, 1962, p. 125, estimated there were 1,029,577 Tidjaniya and 423,273 Mourides.

the habits of scholarship which helped him to what was a remarkable achievement before the war in Senegal, a *baccalauréat* degree for a 'subject'. The Mourides may have felt sure of their influence over Mamadou Dia because his traditional social status was low and he was the son of a Toucouleur-speaking veteran of the First World War who had become a policeman and died in the course of duty. While Dia and Senghor worked together in harmony, the majority of the Mouride organization felt it had a spokesman within the BDS. The Mourides had another worker-representative within the BDS, in Ibrahima Sarr of the railroad union.

There were other BDS tactics in the first campaign. They promised the peasants democratically run co-operatives, for Senghor was aware of the resentment against 'citizen' traders who held leading posts in the SFIO. The 'chiefs', moreover, were not unresponsive to the BDS suggestion of higher salaries and secure status. Senghor argued that 'the maintenance of traditional chiefs is in conformity with the spirit of scientific socialism'.[1] Veterans were wooed by promises of higher pensions, and by the unfamiliar sight of a deputy tramping around the countryside in khaki. In 1945 Lamine Guèye presented Senghor to villagers in the provinces as 'their deputy'; in 1948 Senghor asked them to adhere to the party built specifically 'in the service of the people in the bush'.[2]

BDS leaders negotiated with the ethnic unions like UGOVF from the Senegal river area, the *Union des Toucouleurs*, and the MFDC of Casamance. Senghor and his colleagues took great care to associate with the party representatives of the major groups living in the area —for they wanted to avoid duplicating the SFIO error of a leadership dominated by Wolof and Lebou townsmen. In an area like the Casamance, geographically isolated and ethnically different from the rest of Senegal, their problems were considerable. Senghor's own background brought Catholic support; it took further long negotiations to achieve the widely representative BDS regional executive illustrated in Figure 4. In spite of the close parallel between the ethnic proportions of the Casamance population as a whole, and the BDS regional executive committee, the Guinea-Mande minority was not represented in the BDS. Tension between the Guinea-Mande groups who sided with the SFIO, and the rest who supported the BDS, broke into the incidents which took place in January 1955, as BDS supporters from Bignona clashed with SFIO supporters from Sedhiou on the occasion of a tour in the region by Lamine Guèye.[3]

---

[1] Senghor's article, *Condition Humaine*, 19 October 1948.
[2] Senghor's article, ibid., 31 May 1949.
[3] *Les Échos d'Afrique Noire*, 26 April–2 May 1956.

FIGURE 4

Origins of BDS regional executive (1956) in Casamance

	BDS number	Executive proportion	Casamance proportion	Population[a] number
Total	31	1	1	400,000
Ethnic Origins				
Diola	10	1/3	1/3	
Fulani	5	1/6	1/4	
Mandingue	5	1/6	1/5	
Wolof	4	1/8	1/50	375,000
Serere	3	1/10	1/1000	
Portuguese Creole	2	1/15	1/10	
Toucouleur	1	1/31	1/45	
Mulatto	1	1/31		
Guinea-Mande Groups[b]				
Sarakole				
Baniouk				
Malinke				
Macagne	none	none	1/16	25,000
Bambara				
Diallonke				
Others				
Average Age	37			

Religion

Muslim	22
Catholic	9

Profession

Teacher	10
Government Clerk	10
Trader	3
Farmer	1
Business Clerk	2
Agricultural Officer	2
Veterinary Officer	1
Chauffeur	1
African Doctor	1

Education

Lycée	3
Ponty	8
EPS (Upper Primary)	9
CEP (Lower Primary)	9
Literate	2

Ethnic Status

Mulatto	1
Commoner	19
Chief's family	7
Jeweller	1
Shoemaker	1
Marabout family	1
Warrior	1

[a] The figures are approximations derived for the region of Casamance (except Ziguinchor) from the typewritten chart of the Service de Statistique, Senegal, 1 January 1956, Saint-Louis; for the city of Ziguinchor, the mimeographed pamphlet, *Commune Mixte de Ziguinchor*, Recensement de 1951, Service de Statistique d'A.O.F., 1953, Dakar.

[b] Of 25,000 Guinea-Mande groups, 20,000 live in the region of Sedhiou, where they form 1/5 of the total population; 5,000 live in the city of Ziguinchor, where they form about 1/4 of the total population.

Similarly, the results of the November 1956 municipal elections at Zuiguinchor—21 BDS, 6 SFIO[1]—were also partly explained by ethnic differences.

Limiting separatist inclinations of these regional groups, and generalizing the local organizational structure at the local level, became a major preoccupation of the party's territorial leaders after 1953, when they had already defeated the SFIO in elections. But prior to that, gaining maximum popular support was the chief concern of the BDS leaders. In the cities the traditional Socialist stronghold were in the older neighbourhoods, while the BDS won support in the newer neighbourhoods; the first BDS town sections had such names as *Section Guinéenne de Dakar, Section des Bijoutiers de Dakar, Comité des Jeunes Griots de la Guele Tapée, Comité des Ouvriers Indépendants de Rufisque, Section BDS des Chauffeurs de Taxis à Dakar, Comité Centrale de l'Union des Travailleurs de l'Alimentation de Dakar.*[2] Many town dwellers considered of lower status—either because of their caste, their profession, or their 'stranger' origins—joined forces with the provincial ethnic associations. This gave to the local party sub-sections of the BDS, with their *comités d'honneur* and *bureaux*, a solid basis in the major African ethnic and professional pressure groups.

Not only the party's structure, but also the selection of candidates reflected the leaders' intention to include the major groups in the territory.[3] They wanted at least the tacit support of the trade unionists of whom most were affiliated with the CGT, and some with the RDA. The BDS placed the leader of the Senegalese CGT *union*, Abbas Guèye, a Lebou from Dakar, on their list for the National Assembly elections of 1951, headed by Senghor; and assured the election of the Senegalese railroad union leader, Ibrahima Sarr, as councillor of the French Union. The BDS parliamentary alliance with the MRP assured relative administrative neutrality and the co-operation of the Catholic missions, angered at the anti-clerical bias of the Socialists.[4] Just as the Ivory Coast RDA set about presenting a unified list of the major interests of the territory for the territorial assembly elections of 1952, so did the BDS; both lists included representatives of the European business and trading firms, as well as of the French administrators. Europeans supported by the BDS included Robert Delmas, who became a territorial and grand councillor; Fousson, a senator; and Louis Rogier, a councillor of the French Union.

By carefully choosing candidates supported at the grass roots, the

---

[1] *Paris–Dakar*, 19 November 1956.   [2] *Condition Humaine*, 1948–9.
[3] For supporting statistics see Appendix VIII: E.
[4] *Afrique Nouvelle*, 11 August 1951. The newspaper is edited by the White Fathers, Catholic missionaries in Dakar.

BDS chose men capable of defeating the 'citizen' territorial councillors. Representing the BDS in the territorial assembly there were more Toucouleur (11) than the traditional leading Wolof group (9), indeed more Serere (4), and Diola (3) than Lebou (1). More of the BDS territorial councillors were schoolteachers (12) than members of any other profession. In the 1946–52 territorial assembly the SFIO had placed mostly traders (13). In most constituencies the BDS chose 'favourite sons' obviously resident in the area.[1] The BDS were helped by the expansion of the electorate in 1951. The number of registered voters more than tripled, from 196,696 to 660,931,[2] and in consequence, there was a shift in the majority from the towns to the rural provinces. The number of constituencies grew from 4 to 12 in the 1952 elections, but for the most part remained multi-member. This made it possible for the BDS leaders to place for election in the provinces some candidates normally resident in Dakar and Saint-Louis, strongholds of the SFIO. Voting was by list only, and in the multi-member constituencies the system encouraged large parties and gave 'minority opinion little prospect of representation' except within a large party.[3]

These techniques brought spectacular electoral results to the BDS. Between 1951 and 1952 they won practically all the seats previously held by the SFIO, except those for territorial and municipal councillors in the old communes. After victory, the BDS leaders made maximum use of patronge. For educated party supporters there were places in the co-operatives and peanut-control stations. For loyal civil servants there were promotions. For the Muslim dignitaries and traditional leaders there were easy loans and public decorations. For the BDS territorial councillors there were places reserved in the management boards of the local *sociétés de prévoyance* (agricultural co-operatives set up in 1919 and previously controlled by the administration).[4] Their influence extended to the elected rural councils which advised the administrators and the officially designated chiefs.

Following the electoral successes of the BDS, peanut prices rose because of the Korean war.[5] The BDS of Senegal, like the Ivory Coast RDA, benefited from rising world prices. More money meant that local improvements could be made. By 1952 the BDS leaders were so well implanted in the territory that no administrator and no

[1] See Appendix VIII: E.
[2] Figures from Direction des Affaires Politiques d'AOF, Gouvernement Général, Dakar.
[3] Robinson, 'Senegal . . .', in *Five Elections*, op. cit., p. 298.
[4] See Joseph M'Baye's discussion of the reforms of the *sociétés de prévoyance*, *Condition Humaine*, 2 March 1954.
[5] See Appendix XI, and Figure 3, p. 135.

governor could do much against the will of the party's leaders. Like the RDA *élus* in Ivory Coast, the BDS *parlementaires* and territorial councillors achieved a greater measure of *de facto* power over administration than the laws and decrees allotted to them prior to the Loi-Cadre reforms.

The effectiveness of the BDS, and the steady decline of the SFIO, were again confirmed by a resounding BDS victory in the 1956 parliamentary elections. Only the majority of the voters in Saint-Louis and Dakar remained loyal to the SFIO, which had found no other strategy against the steady ascendency of the BDS than dwelling upon the pioneer role of Lamine Guèye and the SFIO in the formulation of the post-war reforms, and accusing Senghor and his BDS colleagues of ingratitude. In spite of victory, however, the BDS leaders began an extensive process of reorganization in 1956.

Moves Towards Unity

Immediately after the BDS leaders won 76 per cent. of the votes cast,[1] they took the opportunity to reorganize their party—in structure, programme, leadership, and name. They knew their weaknesses. Though they won easily in Senegal, their affiliates of the *Indépendants d'Outre-mer* movement in the rest of AOF were defeated in the elections, mostly by sections of the *Rassemblement Démocratique Africain.* In consequence, they lost control of the *grand conseil* in 1957. They were the leaders of the territory with the most to gain from the federation, yet they were in fact in danger of isolation politically in AOF. They felt an urgent need to re-examine their interterritorial strategy, and if possible to remove the old political barriers which had made RDA and IOM political rivals. The electoral losses of the IOM altered the terms of BDS relations in France. In 1956 French leaders decided to give full backing to the RDA and appointed RDA president Houphouët-Boigny the first African to be a full minister in a French government. Thus the BDS–IOM leaders, for the first time since their parliamentary group was born with official blessing, found themselves uncommitted to a French government and able freely to reconsider their relations with France.

There were other weaknesses of the BDS. The BDS leaders knew well that 'Regionalism is an inheritance from the tribe, the clan, the caste.'[2] Occasional defections in the countryside did not seriously endanger the BDS majority, however, for the BDS leaders knew this opposition was unco-ordinated and limited here to a small ethnic

[1] In 1951 the BDS had won 69 per cent. of the votes cast. Direction des Affaires Politiques, Dakar.
[2] Tevoedjre, Albert. 'Le Régionalism . . . cette absurdité', *Afrique Nouvelle,* 24 January 1956.

sub-group, there to the immediate entourage of a 'clan' leader dis-satisfied when the party did not heed him in nominating or in proto-col. Corruption and nepotism were becoming problems, as BDS *élus* were taking on many of the attributes of the SFIO men they had defeated. Though teaching was the most important source of income of most BDS leaders in the 'forties, in the 'fifties many benefited privately from the public distribution of seeds and loans.

The most serious problem was cadres. Though the rural voters could run up sizeable BDS majorities, they could not produce the personnel needed to staff a modern government. With the implemen-tation of the Loi-Cadre reforms the BDS leaders became responsible for governing and, of course, wanted to Africanize the civil service. Yet the BDS had the least support in the towns, and was weakest precisely among those most qualified by education or by experience to make a new government work. Most members of the established professional elite in the towns—lawyers, doctors, judges, veterinary surgeons, senior African members of the army, police, and the rest of the civil service—remained loyal to the SFIO and Lamine Guèye. In addition, most of the younger Africans in the towns were outside of the BDS, openly despised the party 'bureaucrats', charged that both the BDS and the SFIO were 'stagnating', and deplored the lack of an ideological base to Senegal's politics.[1]

Among these younger men there were several related groups: returned university graduates, active members of youth organiza-tions and trade unions, radicals within Muslim reform movements, and the leaders of the small Senegalese branch of the RDA. The hostility towards the BDS of all these town groups went back to the time of the *Bloc Africain*. University graduates were returning in growing numbers to Senegal, a few years earlier than to the other territories because of Senegal's longer contact with French education. In Africa they remained for a while outside parties and organized in groups, continuing those they founded as students in Paris. Often rivalries begun in Paris outlasted the original differences in belief, as well as the move to Dakar—among different graduating classes, for example, or among those who in Paris were attracted first to the political writings of French Communists, Trotskyists, or Catho-lics.

Some were active in *Réalités Africaines*, a non-partisan discussion group publishing for some years a newspaper of the same name. It included the first of the returned post-war graduates—men like the lawyer Abdoulaye Thiaw, or the geographer Assane Seck. Seck had

---

[1] Both citations were recorded during the BDS congress at Kaolack, and the SFIO congress at Saint-Louis, in 1956.

a special position, for he was among the last to graduate from the École Normale William-Ponty, where he succeeded Ouëzzin Coulibaly as director of studies. Veteran's status helped him continue his studies in Paris, and he was, in the mid-fifties, the only African on the staff of the University of Dakar. He became the second candidate on a list headed by Lamine Guèye for the January 1956 elections to the National Assembly. Seck ran not in the name of the SFIO, but as candidate for a regional Casamance party, the *Mouvement Autonome de la Casamance*.

Among the independent Marxists were African students involved in the *Groupe Africain de Recherche Économique et Politique* (GAREP). Its leader was the brilliant young historian Dr. Abdoulaye Ly who became second in command in the Institut Français d'Afrique Noire (IFAN); he was also the director of the historical museum on the Island of Gorée.[1] The historian Amadou Moctar M'Bow, pioneer in fundamental education, was also part of this group in Paris; so was the lawyer Fadilou Diop, and Cheikh Fall, an engineer. GAREP had associated with it Africans from territories other than Senegal—for example, Fofana Karim, a Guinean graduate of the École des Mines in France.

Of those who had favoured co-operation with the orthodox Communist movement in France not all retained these beliefs. For example, Mê Valdiodio N'Diaye, member of a chiefly family from the densely populated Sine-Saloum region, joined the BPS and rapidly rose to become the minister of interior and defence in Senegal. Others, however, retained their connexions with Communism and founded, in 1957, the *Parti Africain de l'Indépendence* (PAI); among them was Diop Majhemout[2] and Ly Tidiany Baïdy.[3]

Yet another returned student group was influenced by left-wing Catholics, specially Emmanuel Mounier's philosophy of *personnalisme* and the ideas of Père L. J. Lebret. Their *Mouvement Africain de Libération Nationale* (MLN) had fewer Senegalese associated with it, than graduates from territories where Catholic education was more widespread—men like Albert Tevoedjre of Dahomey,[4] and Joseph Ki Zerbo[5] of Upper Volta. Though the MLN retained no formal links with the Catholic world, it was the logical outgrowth of the

[1] Ly's political ideas were expressed in his books, published by Présence Africaine in Paris: *Les Masses africaines et l'actuelle condition humaine* (1956) is the most important. See also *La Compagnie du Sénégal* (1958), and *Mercenaires noirs* (1957).
[2] Author of *Contribution à l'étude des problèmes politiques en Afrique noire*, Présence Africaine, Paris, 1958.
[3] Teacher at the Lycée Delafosse in Dakar.
[4] Author of *L'Afrique revoltée*, Présence Africaine, Paris, 1958, and former editor of the FEANF journal.   [5] *Agrégé* in history.

M

Étudiants Catholiques en France, a group which published the bi-monthly *Tam-Tam* in Paris.[1] Meanwhile the African students at the University of Dakar, organized in the *Union Générale des Étudiants d'Afrique Occidentale* (UGEAO), looked up to their colleagues studying in Paris and active in the *Fédération des Étudiants d'Afrique Noire en France* (FEANF). Student leaders in office continued to respect their former officers who had returned to Dakar—such as Ly Tidiani Baïdy, and Albert Tevoedjre.

This was a new generation to whom neither Senghor nor Lamine Guèye were heroes. Most returned students were uncommitted in the quarrel between the BDS and the SFIO, for they saw little reason to keep alive the differences between 'citizens' and 'subjects'. They saw Senegal's chief problem to be self-government and economic development, and continued the pan-Africanist orientation of their student days in insisting on West African federation. They were not interested in links with France, but rather in a 'vast West African Federation of Ghana or of Mali, as a step towards the United States of Black Africa'.[2]

These were the views which linked the university graduates with the other politically disaffected young Africans living in the towns of Senegal. The leaders of the Senegalese youth movements, including those associated with the SFIO and the BDS, were largely locally educated. They held middle and lower echelon posts in the civil service. Like the returned graduates, they rejected the constitutional orientation of their respective parties, and spoke of the need to end 'French occupation'[3] of Africa. They were closely associated with the Muslim reformers who opposed the *marabouts* associated with the BDS. The *Union Culturelle Musulmane*, was a reform organization led by men trained in North African universities; associated with them was the *Association Musulmane des Étudiants Africans*, at the University of Dakar. Both organizations opposed the Muslim policy of the administration. So did Cheikh Tidjane Sy, who challenged his uncle's right to become in 1957 Khalif of the Tidjaniya.

Many important leaders of the Senegalese trade unions also remained outside the BDS. This affected both the domestic position of

[1] Service Catholique des Étudiants d'Outre-mer, Paris.
[2] Manifeste du Mouvement Africain de Libération Nationale, *Libérons l'Afrique*, États-Unis d'Afrique Noire, Socialisme africain, Dakar, 25 August 1958, printed in Paris, p. 6.
[3] Citation from a speech by Kane Aly Bocar, Socialist youth leader, at the SFIO congress in Saint-Louis in 1956. Bocar was also president of the co-ordinating committee of the major Senegalese youth movements, the *Conseil de la Jeunesse du Sénégal*, and of the interterritorial *Conseil Fédéral de la Jeunesse d'A.O.F.*

the BDS and its relations with parties in other territories. Officially there were more union members in Senegal than in any other territory, some 55,700 (1955),[1] and the approximately 100,000 (1957) regular wage earners constituted the mobile active portion of the town inhabitants.[2] It was a constant source of embarrassment to BDS and SFIO leaders in Senegal that they could not count upon the co-operation of youth organizations and trade unions, nor affect strikes—even before they became the leaders of the government and thus the single most important employer of labour. The tactic of nominating a union representative to elective office did not appreciably strengthen the BDS among the workers. Abbas Guèye's election to the National Assembly of France on the BDS ticket in 1951 was followed by a decline of his influence among the workers of Senegal. They accepted the lead of men like Bassirou Guèye and Abdoulaye Guèye,[3] who had refused SFIO absorption of the *Bloc Africain* and remained unconvinced the BDS was any improvement over the SFIO.

The explanation was partly historical. Most West African union leaders had frequented the *Groupes d'Études Communistes* (GEC's), like the leaders of the RDA. Though the majority of the RDA broke parliamentary links with the French Communist party in 1950, most trade union leaders—through the West African federation belonging to the central *Confédération Générale du Travail* (CGT)—retained links with French Communist-led unions until 1956. Within Senegal, the CGT absorbed most of the energies of the leaders of the small *Union Démocratique Sénégalaise*, formed as a branch of the RDA. The UDS refused to accept the decision of the RDA parliamentary representatives to disaffiliate from the Communist group, and so remained estranged from the main RDA community. In Senegal the UDS could not muster many votes, but had the respect of the workers. This the BDS leaders knew, and criticism on their left from the UDS made them uncomfortable.

For all these reasons, the BDS took part, immediately after the January elections, in a series of private and public discussions which had the object of drawing it closer to all these opposition groups. As the BDS negotiated to fuse with these groups it successively changed names: in 1956, to the *Bloc Populaire Sénégalais* (BPS) and in April 1958, to the *Union Progressiste Sénégalaise* (UPS). The process of fusion was helped as across organizational lines younger Africans found they had more in common with each other than with

[1] *Annuaire Statistique*, vol. ii, 1957, p. 137.
[2] *Outre-mer 1958*, op. cit., p. 208.
[3] Senegalese teacher, head of the *syndicat* of West African teachers, and then vice-president of the *Fédération Internationale des Syndicats d'Enseignants* (FISE).

the older members of their individual organizations. They launched within the BDS and the SFIO, as well as outside, themes and activities impossible to ignore. Public response was overwhelming to their call for African unity and for the end of colonial rule. They discussed openly the pros and cons of independence; they favoured a strong West African federation; they bitterly criticized the restrictive aspects of the Loi-Cadre. They were influenced by the Bandung conference and the prospect of independence of Ghana. They were repelled by the idea of tropical African responsibility—through participation in the French Parliament—for the French war against the Algerian nationalists.

While they criticized the BDS, they were impressed by the effectiveness of its machinery, believed they could not replace it, and decided their best chance to bring about reforms was from within rather than outside the BDS. There began, in January 1956, a public exchange of letters between the 'young intellectuals'—Abdoulaye Ly, Amadou Moctar M'Bow, and Mê Fadilou Diop—who announced their intention to join the BDS, and Senghor who welcomed them.[1] In May Dia and Senghor, at the annual Congress meeting in Kaolack, used their authority to 'parachute'—in the words of their critics—the 'young intellectuals' into key party posts. Ly was elected propaganda and organizational secretary of the BDS, and M'Bow associate propaganda secretary.[2] Some administrators, members of the European community of Senegal, and members of the governing parties of France privately protested to BDS deputies. Within the party, some of the older 'clan' leaders—such as Ibrahima Seydou N'Daw, some of the ethnic and Muslim leaders, party 'bureaucrats', and territorial assembly members whose personal authority was threatened—were not in sympathy. They rejected the goals, methods, and Marxist language of the newcomers to the party, who were dedicated to the 'integration of their party into a larger movement'.[3] Backed by Dia and Senghor, the 'young Turks' energetically set about creating 'the first organized detachment of the West African masses of Senegal, the Senegalese section of the unified movement of workers and peasants, which *alone*' could bring about the 'destruction of all forms of domination' and the 'modernization of Africa'.[4]

Unity through fusion of all the parties was the object. Political,

[1] *Paris–Dakar*, January and February 1956, and particularly of 25 and 26 January 1956.
[2] For the reports of Senghor and Mamadou Dia to the 1956 Congress, see *Condition Humaine*, 31 May 1956.
[3] From an editorial by Senghor in *Condition Humaine*, 19 June 1956.
[4] Ibid., citing speech by Abdoulaye Ly.

administrative, trade union, and cultural autonomy from France was the programme.[1] The UDS was perhaps the most important group with which the newcomers to the BDS sought to unify. And for several reasons the UDS leaders agreed, besides the common beliefs they had with the 'young intellectuals'. In 1956 the UDS were a small group and comparatively isolated. In the 1956 elections out of almost half a million votes cast they received a scant 7,000.[2] The inter-territorial RDA Co-ordinating Committee meeting in Conakry in July 1955 had expelled the UDS for breach of discipline on the Communist issue, and given its blessings to a new orthodox RDA branch in Senegal, the *Mouvement Populaire Sénégalais* (MPS) led by the Ponty-trained doctor Doudou Guèye. The UDS felt betrayed when Gabriel d'Arboussier made his peace with Houphouët. The same RDA meeting began the chain of events which progressively estranged the UDS from the French Communists. Sékou Touré launched there the idea of an autonomous West African trade union movement. This idea was taken up again in 1956 by the three federal secretaries of the CGT in Dakar—Sékou Touré, Diallo Seydou and Bassirou Guèye. Over a period of two years the break was consolidated, and the CGT was replaced by the *Union Générale des Travailleurs d'Afrique Noire* (UGTAN). The UDS leaders were of course involved in these moves, and came to have some confidence in those 'young intellectuals'—like Abdoulaye Ly, Mê Fadilou Diop, and Dr. Naguib Accar[3]—who offered the unions their services to replace Communist technical advisers. The attitude of many UDS leaders towards the French Communists became markedly less favourable, as they watched the sharp, though unsuccessful struggle of the French CGT to retain a hold in West Africa.

The estrangement of the UDS from the French Communists became complete in the summer of 1956. A shift in international Communist strategy had occurred, in part accounted for by Bandung, the death of Stalin, and the failure of the French CGT in Africa. This shift meant the abandonment of hopes that the French Communists might regain influence in the kind of organization represented by the RDA. The international Communist movement sought new contacts, among the younger Africans who had 'effective links with the principal mass parties in the federation',[4] and paid but little attention to the UDS. The foundation in 1957 of the *Parti Africain de*

---

[1] *Condition Humaine*, 19 June 1956.
[2] Figures from the Direction des Affaires Politiques, Dakar, 1956.
[3] In 1957, he became Minister of Health in the government of Guinea.
[4] From oral reports of declarations in summer 1956, by Jacques Mitterrand, French Communist Councillor of the French Union who toured AOF in the name of the World Peace Council.

l'Indépendance marked a new phase in the connexions of orthodox Communism with French-speaking West Africa. While the PAI was probably founded without an international Communist directive, afterwards the French Communist movement was no longer the sole connecting channel to French-speaking West Africa. The PAI was an elitist party, led by former university students and not confined solely to Senegal. Though the PAI joined energetically in the general call for independence, unity, and socialism, they differed in insisting on unity of action, rather than fusion, and on retaining their separate identity.

In June 1956, it seemed the call to unity and autonomy themes would draw all Senegalese parties together—the MPS and the SFIO, if left to themselves, would have joined a new fusion party then. But by July the French SFIO and the interterritorial RDA objected to fusion by their Senegalese branches which withdrew from unity talks. In each, however, there were dissidents. The *Socialistes Unitaires* broke from the SFIO and individual MPS leaders—like the trade union leader Abdoulaye Thiaw—broke with their party to join the newly named fusion party—the *Bloc Populaire Sénégalais*. At the end of 1956 the BPS marked the unification of the BDS with the UDS and with the younger radicals who had broken with the Senegalese branches of the RDA and the SFIO. The rejuvenated BPS won overwhelming electoral victories in the March 1957 elections for the territorial assembly which designated, for the first time, a Senegalese council of ministers. The BPS won 47 of the 60 seats, leaving but 12 to the SFIO.[1]

Throughout 1957 the SFIO of Senegal tried to keep intact their party, first by breaking formal links with the French SFIO, and then by changing name. In January 1957, with the approval of the French SFIO, an autonomous interterritorial *Mouvement Socialiste Africain* (MSA) was born. In February, the Senegalese SFIO, a branch of the MSA, took on the new name of *Parti Sénégalais d'Action Socialiste* (PSAS). These changes could not halt the dissolution of the Senegalese Socialists. Shortly afterwards yet another group of dissidents broke away, forming the *Mouvement Socialiste d'Unité Sénégalaise* under the lead of the novelist-veterinarian Ousmane Socé Diop, and announced their intention to join a reorganized BPS. The 'young Turks' of the BPS were successful in pointing out that the reason for a separate Socialist party in Senegal had disappeared. Unity between the Socialists and the BPS was finally achieved in early 1958, with the creation of the *Union Progressiste Sénégalaise* (UPS). Then all but the leaders of two minor parties of Senegal—PAI and MPS—were united.

[1] There was one Independent.

Thus the reorganization of Senegalese parties was accomplished by April 1958, and the UPS was distinguished by including trade union and youth leaders. It could be argued the UPS of 1958 was a better organized *Bloc Africain*; as in 1945, in the UPS the young men of the towns again set the pace and tone of Senegalese life. Again Senghor and Lamine Guèye amicably shared the same platform. In the towns party stalwarts who in the green head-dress of the BDS or the red of the SFIO had been bitter rivals during ten years, applauded together the speeches of the 'young Turks'. In the many and enthusiastic fusion meetings, the old issues between 'citizens' and 'subjects' seemed forgotten. During the first part of 1958, the government of Senegal represented practically all the tendencies— PAI and MPS excepted. The *marabouts* sent messages of loyalty, and 'clan' leader Ibrahima Seydou N'Daw was president of the territorial assembly. 'Citizen' leaders Lamine Guèye and Ousmane Socé Diop held offices; 'subject' bureaucrats of the old BDS, like Joseph M'Baye and Badara M'Bengue were ministers. Mamadou Dia took over as president of the council of government, while Senghor held high party office. One returned graduate, strong in the Kaolack region, Valdiodio N'Diaye, became minister of interior, while further to the left Ly held the key post of minister of production and M'Bow minister of education. UGTAN and the UDS both were represented in the government in the person of men like Camara Latyr, as the Minister in charge of the civil service. The European residents of Dakar were represented, as André Peytavin (MRP) was Minister of Finance. It was indeed a government of unity, formed because—in the words of Gabriel d'Arboussier—'The need for Unity comes out of the very reality of existing divisions.'[1]

Unity and independence were the themes, also, which carried delegates through the organizing, and only, congress of the *Parti du Regroupement Africain* (PRA), an interterritorial meeting of all the parties of AOF except those of the RDA or in Mauretania. This was the Cotonou conference of July 1958, noted for the adoption of a political resolution calling for independence, just when France was passing through the crisis which marked the death of the Fourth Republic. Dia and Senghor opposed the resolution which nevertheless was rammed through the conference by its radical younger members, those whose participation distinguished the PRA from its predecessors, the IOM and the shortlived *Convention Africaine*. The adoption of this resolution at Cotonou marked the highpoint,

---

[1] Fédération du Mali, *Procès-verbaux des séances des 14 et 17 janvier 1959 de l'Assemblée Constituante Fédérale*, Dakar, 1959, p. 35. (Henceforth cited as Mali, Assemblée Constituante, p.v.)

as well as the end of the wave of unity which had begun in Senegal in 1956.

Independence Without Unity

The young newcomers to the UPS were proud of the Cotonou resolutions on independence, and wished to carry its implications into UPS instructions to vote 'no' in the referendum on the 1958 Constitution. But Senghor and Lamine Guèye, both associated with the writing of it in the French Constitutional Consultative Committee, thought otherwise. One reason why they rejected immediate independence was the price of peanuts, which France supported at a level considerably above the world market price. They argued that independence then would not have been 'real', but only 'nominal'.[1] There were stormy meetings within the UPS. The party had been under strain since Abdoulaye Ly and the other 'young Turks' trjed to undercut the economic and political power of the 'grand electors' within the UPS—the *marabouts* and men like Ibrahima Seydou N'Daw. They fought against 'nepotism and corruption' and in the process Abdoulaye Ly left the government, though not the UPS, in May 1958. The 'young Turks' nevertheless dominated the UPS delegation at Cotonou. They constituted a party within the party, and even took a colour—yellow, 'for earth, mother, sun, Africa'. They argued heatedly against the foreign aid mentality of the older UPS leaders, and called it one more example of the *mentalité de pourboire* (tipping mentality) which Senegalese students in Paris had held against Senghor back in 1945. The UPS *bureau politique* ceased to meet for the 'young Turks' had gained control of it, and Senghor and Dia called the full *comité executif* of 154 members to get backing.[2] Early in September 1958 it decided on a 'yes' in the referendum.

By then the split was in the open. It had been quite clear at the time of de Gaulle's visit to Dakar. Both Dia and Senghor had left town, and Lamine Guèye received the General and tried to explain the meaning of the many yellow banners, placarts, and signs in favour of independence. The 'young Turks' organized a demonstration in Dakar to show that many Senegalese disagreed with Dia and Senghor. In campaigning for a 'no' vote, they ran a recording of the Cotonou PRA meeting, including a passage in which Senghor, swept up by the enthusiasm of the meeting, cried 'independence by September'. The 'young Turks' had difficulty recruiting mass support against the older UPS leaders, partly, they claimed, because Senghor's speeches in Wolof were more nationalistic than in French,

---

[1] Resolution sponsored by the UPS at PRA Comité Directeur meeting, Niamey, 14 September 1958.   [2] *Paris–Dakar*, 9 April 1958.

and because in Wolof the words autonomy and independence are synonymous.

The UPS remained dominant among the rural electors and had no trouble organizing a 'yes' majority. But the party lost support at the level of leadership of most who had rejuvenated it since 1956. Once again the radicals went into opposition. In 1956 they had been divided among BDS, SFIO, UDS, youth, and student groups, to trade unions and organizations of returned graduates. By September 1958, however, they too had achieved some unity, and so organized a single opposition party. They called it *PRA-Sénégal* as a sign of their loyalty to the resolutions of Cotonou. University trained men like Abdoulaye Ly and Assane Seck were in it; so were locally trained men like Abdoulaye Guèye. They were Marxists, but rejected the orthodox position of the PAI. They believed independence and federation both necessary to the achievement of 'real promotion of the underdeveloped countries'. One month after founding their party, on 20 October 1958, they explained themselves thus:

Since the Referendum, things are becoming startlingly clear. The UPS and the other YES MEN of the PRA find they are faced with a dilemma they can no longer escape, except by simply disappearing because of an inability to adapt:—Either to become committed openly and more and more radically to the uncompromising fight for national liberation and social progress, under the murderous fire nourished from imperialism and its African valets . . .—Or to surrender totally, infamously, to surrender not only in deed by assuming the monstrous responsibility for a campaign in favour of a 'Yes' and a servile commitment to build the Community dominated by colonialists, but to surrender also in words and to renounce definitively all references . . . to the revolutionary positions taken at the Cotonou Congress, particularly independence . . .[1]

Over the next two years, the exchanges grew increasingly bitter between the government party and its critics. These were momentous years for Senegal, as it became an autonomous republic within the Community, took the initiative in the formation and the dissolution of the Mali federation, which became independent and shortly after dissolved leaving Senegal a sovereign state.

In this historical context, there were many serious consequences of the political division between UPS and the younger generation of radicals. Within Senegal, the schism had implications in the realm of personnel. The government and the UPS were dominated by older men whose political views were formed before or during the Second World War. Many highly qualified men educated in the post-war era remained alienated; some offered their services to the Republic of

[1] Both citations from the PRA-Sénégal journal, *l'Indépendance Africaine*, 11 July 1959.

Guinea where independence was accompanied by the abrupt departure of French technicians and civil servants. Africanization proceeded at a much slower pace than might have been as a result of Senegal's comparatively high number of qualified men. UPS leaders were reluctant to replace Frenchmen with Senegalese who were their opponents politically. There were other consequences. The UPS as a party began to stagnate. Party officials took on government offices and spent most of their energy there. The campaign against 'clan leaders' which men like Abdoulaye Ly and Abdoulaye Guèye had waged within the party came to an end, as did the process of revitalizing the local branches. In most rural constituencies leadership was resumed by men who had controlled the BDS, while the cities of Dakar and Saint-Louis continued to be fiefs of the former SFIO leaders. In some localities, separate 'SFIO' and 'BDS' committees continued to exist.

Though the breakup of unity within Senegal was by no means the sole cause, it contributed to the failure of the leaders of Senegal to end their 'isolation' within West Africa. Senegal's need for a federation was perhaps greater than that of any other territory in AOF. It was essential to maintain the expensive installations in the port of Dakar, to make the Dakar–Bamako railroad pay, as an outlet for the small but growing industries, to keep standards, teachers, and students at the University of Dakar, and to find employment for what was becoming a surplus of educated Senegalese. When AOF died with the Fourth Republic, Senegal had a serious problem, and a major grievance against the French policy of 'Balkanization'. Senegalese leaders could hardly envisage a future alone, though at the same time their idea was of federation dominated by Senegal.

Fear of isolation brought the UPS of Senegal into an uneasy partnership with the RDA of Soudan in January 1959, expressed at the government level in the Federation of Mali and at the party level in the *Parti de la Fédération Africaine* (PFA). In their militant egalitarianism and insistence on immediate independence, on a powerful central government dominated by a single party, on very rapid economic development, the RDA leaders of Soudan had views closer to the PRA-Sénégal than to the UPS. Meanwhile among the Tidjaniya there was a quarrel over succession, and partly as a result 'clan' leaders of whom the most notable was Ibrahima Seydou N'Daw, left the UPS and formed the *Parti de Solidarité Sénégalaise* (PSS). Some of their followers demonstrated and there were incidents. At the same time the Senegalese government feared the radical policies of their Soudanese partners who were specially opposed to voting for Senghor as President of the Mali Federation. This was the immediate issue causing the break, and in August 1960 Senegal seceded from the federation.[1] Partly as a result of the crisis, the PSS dissidents gave back their support to the Senegalese government, and their former leader Cheikh Tidjane Sy, was released from prison to become an ambassador.

Perhaps the most important consequence of the schism within the UPS in 1958, was that the young radicals—in the PRA-Sénégal, in the *Bloc des Masses Sénégalaises* founded in 1961 by Cheikh Anta Diop,[2] and in the PAI—had no responsibility for the circumstances surrounding the independence of Senegal. They had no responsibility for support of France in Algeria; for the break-up of the federation of Mali, or for the many economic problems of the new state. Many predicted, from opposition, that French membership in the Common Market would force Senegal to adjust to the world market price of peanuts, that French subsidies would not last for long, and were better done without. The young radicals of Senegal were perhaps better organized to take the succession than their counterparts in any other state of French-speaking West Africa.

Independence came to Senegal. As Lamine Guèye, who had once been the great spokesman for assimilation in West Africa, remarked, 'one cannot hold back the ocean with one's hands'.[3] But sovereignty was a hollow victory. Senegal had economic difficulties and internal dissent at home, not too different from the circumstances which led Senghor and Lamine Guèye to divide in the 'forties. By the end of 1962 Dia and Senghor were divided. Senghor, when he justified insisting on a 'yes' vote in the 1958 referendum, had said it was 'above all a yes for Negro–African unity'.[4] Yet after Senegal became independent in 1960, the leaders of its dominant party found themselves far from unity at home or in West Africa.

[1] Senghor explained the reasons in his *Conférence de presse du 23 août 1960.* Ministère de l'Information, République du Sénégal, Dakar, 1960. For a scholarly analysis of the break-up, see William J. Foltz, *From French West Africa to the Mali Federation:* The Background to Federation and Failure, Ph.D. dissertation, Yale University, 1963.

[2] Cheikh Anta Diop wrote *Nations nègres et culture, l'Unité culturelle de l'Afrique noire*, and *l'Afrique noire précoloniale*, all published in Paris by Présence Africaine, respectively 1955, 1959, and 1960.

[3] Mali, Assemblée Constituante, p.v., op. cit., p. 12.

[4] Senghor. 'Vers l'indépendance dans l'amitié', *Cahiers de la République,* no. 16, 1959.

PART FIVE

Planters and Politics in the
Ivory Coast

THE history of parties in Ivory Coast has several interesting features. One is the comparatively long life of the dominant mass party—the *Parti Démocratique de la Côte d'Ivoire*. Born in 1946, it is the oldest West African mass party, giving Ivory Coast the oldest single-party system. Moreover, the PDCI is in a special sense agrarian. Like the other successful West African parties the PDCI is composed of a vast rural majority, necessarily so, given the mass franchise and the present social structure. The PDCI has the additional special feature of growing out of a union of African planters, the *Syndicat Agricole Africain*. Its role in the PDCI is comparable to that of the trade unions in the RDA of Guinea, or the Trades Union Congress in the British Labour Party.

Furthermore, just after the war the political activities of the Africans involved in the planting and exporting of cocoa and coffee in Ivory Coast bordered upon revolt. This was a departure from the moderate tone which usually characterized African parties dominated by men involved in the growing and trading of the new export crops—the *Action Group of Nigeria*, for example. The explanation lies in the circumstances in which the *Syndicat* was born—out of African reaction against the control exercised over the economy and the administration of Ivory Coast by a small group of French settlers. The rise to power of the PDCI was also the fall of the European planters, the only such group in West Africa.

In 1949 there began a crisis in relations between the PDCI and French officials, taking the form of incidents which were among the most serious in post-war West Africa. At their close in 1951 the PDCI was in control of the Ivory Coast and changed to a policy which for a decade became a model of Franco–African co-operation. This change of policy had far-reaching effects not only on Ivory Coast but on the other French-speaking West African territories too.

For the PDCI was the base from which the interterritorial organization of the *Rassemblement Démocratique Africain* spread throughout tropical Africa under French rule. The struggle between the

PDCI and the French administration also involved RDA partisans in the other territories, and all RDA sections had in common an attitude of militant anti-colonialism. After that common denominator dissolved, and partly in consequence, the interterritorial RDA broke up in 1958. As for the PDCI, over a decade it emphasized not independence but the economic advantages of the French connexion. In 1960, in another policy shift, the PDCI led Ivory Coast to total independence from France. These events are studied here more closely.

The Plantation Economy

At the end of the Second World War conditions favourable to the rise of a mass opposition party were present in Ivory Coast. These were brought about by the official policy of discrimination against Africans in a territory characterized by very rapid economic and social changes. The rate of economic growth in Ivory Coast was faster than in any other territory in AOF. It was illustrated by the rapidly increasing share of Ivory Coast in the exports of the federation. While Ivory Coast produced in 1925 only 14.8 per cent. of the exports of AOF, by 1956 its share was 45 per cent., and of imports 30 per cent.[1] Moreover, by 1951 Ivory Coast managed to surpass Senegal, and so became the richest of the French West African territories.[2]

While the economy of Senegal rests on peanuts, that of Ivory Coast is based on coffee and cocoa. Since the end of the war these two crops constituted an average 90 per cent. of the value of exports from Ivory Coast. They grew in Ivory Coast as a result of French official policy, as of British policy in Ghana. But the administration in Ivory Coast adopted a course quite unusual for West Africa—that of attracting European planters. Some Europeans came to Ivory Coast, particularly since the thirties, and their cocoa and coffee plantations flourished in the forest belt[3]—roughly south of the 8° parallel. European plantations were installed to the west of the Badama river, near Gagnoa, Daloa, and Man; along the southern coast, near Grand Bassam, Abidjan, Grand Lahou, and Sassandra; along the railroad axis of Agboville, Dimbokro and Bouake in the

---

[1] Preface by R. Saller, Ministre du Plan, to *Inventaire économique de la Côte d'Ivoire 1947–1956*, Service de la Statistique, Abidjan, 1958. Ivory Coast figures usually include those of Upper Volta.

[2] See Appendix XI. Elliot Berg's 1960 article, op. cit., provides an excellent resume of the comparative economic position of Ivory Coast in AOF.

[3] Fréchou thesis, op. cit., Introduction; also Gouverneur Messmer, *Rapport à l'assemblée territoriale de la Côte d'Ivoire 1955*, Abidjan, p. 13. (Hereafter cited as Messmer 1955 Report.)

forest, and of Katiola and Korhogo in the northern savannah.[1] The number of Europeans who became planters was never very large. In 1953 there were only 235 according to official statistics, and owning 61,877 hectares[2] of cultivated land.[3] Though these figures may not constitute the highpoint of settler numbers and land holdings, they are a rough average, and must, of course, be viewed in relation to a total population estimated at the close of the war at 2

FIGURE 5

Principal exports of Ivory Coast, 1897–1960, in Tons

Years	Coffee	Cocoa	Bananas	Wood	Palm oil
1897	63				3,900
1910	30	6		14,448	5,955
1920	17	1,036		41,302	8,559
1930	445	22,239	2	90,902	6,439
1931	726	19,875	10	52,523	4,166
1935	5,183	43,565	4,360	46,025	2,284
1936	6,484	49,765	6,612	47,162	4,084
1938	14,076	52,720	12,271	65,683	2,971
1939	17,961	55,189	14,286	42,887	3,871
1940	15,606	45,359	6,396	23,220	2,420
1941	28,415	52,961		2,995	1,155
1942	19,798	28,592	9	8,135	1,743
1943	22,893	543	2	2,410	2,942
1944	24,103	14,672	1	11,363	2,612
1945	37,872	26,936	19	10,068	1,606
1946	36,282	28,337	1,657	41,057	137
1947	42,677	28 048	6,470	48,724	1
1948	55,391	41,220	13,447	78,959	856
1949	61,093	56,195	18,291	81,006	613
1950	54,189	61,686	23,013	108,709	999
1951	59,538	55,452	16,067	130,702	1,012
1952	64,098	50,171	17,553	76,357	1,869
1953	50,400	71,400	22,731	131,000	1,515
1954	88,292	52,703	20,939	131,455	1,300
1955	84,796	75,196	27,000	169,000	1,900
1956	118,794	75,745	24,700	212,000	1,400
1957	101,200	66,500	34,700	263,000	1,700
1958	112,500	46,300	46,100	402,300	800
1959	104,700	63,300	54,000	444,300	1,400
1960	147,500	62,900	72,600	654,900	1,600

Sources:

Through 1955: Messmer 1955 Report, op. cit., p. 48, annex.

1955–7: *AOF 1957*, op. cit., pp. 77–8; *Outre-mer 1958*, op. cit., pp. 238, 250, 256, 300, 771.

1958–60: United Nations, *African Statistics* (Annex to the Economic Bulletin for Africa) vol. ii, no. 1, January 1962, p. 62.

[1] See Fréchou, H., 'Les Plantations européennes en Côte d'Ivoire', reprint by the Institut des Hautes Études de Dakar, département de géographie, no. 3, *c.* 1955. p. 3, Figure 1. Also see Figure 5, p. 323.

[2] A hectare is about 2.47 acres.

[3] Fréchou thesis, op. cit., p. 114.

million, in 1956 at $2\frac{1}{2}$ million, but according to 1960 figures 3.1 million Africans, and 14,500 Europeans.[1]

After the Europeans expanded their enterprises from trading and wood cutting to the planting of export crops, Africans also started plantations. Their methods were different from those of the Europeans—their plots were smaller, and scattered throughout the forest. They did not fully clear their land, a practice which on some occasions saved their trees from parasites which attacked trees of the Europeans, standing on fully cleared land. Gradually in the inter-war years the African plantations spread east of the Badama river among the Baule and Agni peoples. (Baule and Agni are related; both are, like the Ashanti of Ghana, classified as Akan.)[2] More African planters installed themselves in areas where Europeans set the example.[3]

At first the number of Africans who became planters and needed workers was not very large and their average yield per person was quite small, but they quickly outstripped the production of the European planters. In 1942 the Europeans produced approximately 55 per cent. of the coffee and 8 per cent. of the cocoa of Ivory Coast; in 1952 they produced but 6 per cent. of the coffee and 4 per cent. of the cocoa. Since 1947 Africans produced 90 per cent. or more of the coffee and cocoa exported.[4]

These figures take on significance against the background of Ivory Coast history prior to 1944. Until then, and particularly during the war, the administration followed a policy which favoured the European planters, with the result that the points of conflict between European and African planters multiplied, particularly over land and labour. As early as 1925, when the cultivation of coffee and cocoa had just begun, the decree regulating forced labour was also intended to keep up a steady flow of workers for the European planters, which became necessary because Africans had started to plant.[5] Then in the thirties competition between Europeans and Africans became

[1] *Annuaire Statistique*, tome i, 1956, op. cit., p. 57; *Outre-mer 1958*, op. cit., p. 36; and *Inventaire économique et sociale de la Côte d'Ivoire*, 1947–58; Ministère des Finances, des Affaires Économique et du Plan, Service Statistique, Abidjan, 1960, pp. 35–6.

[2] Leroi-Gourhan, André and Jean Poirier. *Ethnologie de l'Union française*, Tome Premier, Afrique, Presses Universitaires de France, Paris, 1953, p. 280.

[3] Fréchou's thesis presents an excellent historical summary of the rise of African planters, op. cit., pp. 182–207.

[4] Fréchou article, op. cit., p. 24.

[5] For further details, see the *Bulletin de la Chambre de Commerce de la Côte d'Ivoire*, no. 10, 24 March 1924; no. 12, 7 December 1924; and particularly no. 14, 5 April 1925. Imprimerie du Gouvernement, Bingerville, Ivory Coast, 1925.

sharper, for more Africans began planting.[1] Prior to 1941, the African planters paid agricultural workers the same low wages as the Europeans, and indeed had some access to forced labour. This point became academic when the war began, for as the shortage of imported goods and labour became acute the administration proceeded to 'systematically favour the Europeans'.[2] The Africans were refused all labour,[3] and only the special measures adopted by the administration kept the European planters solvent.[4] There seemed little doubt that under Vichy the European planters and the administration planned to reduce the African plantations to a scale for which hired labour was unnecessary.[5] European crops earned higher prices. Africans received but 2.60 francs for each kilo of coffee, and had to pay for transport, while the Europeans received an even 4.50 for each kilo.[6] Europeans had priority rights to imported goods, which were then severely rationed, and which Africans recall with some bitterness they could only buy on the black market.[7] In 1944 a decree declared a premium of 1,000 francs per hectare for all planters who had 25 or more contiguous hectares under cultivation. All the Europeans did, but only 50 Africans, for African plantations rarely extended contiguously for more than a few hectares.[8] All the 'subjects' including the planters could be drafted for forced labour. 'So-called plant sanitation teams' destroyed African plantations because they were 'nests of parasites' and many African plantations were reclaimed by the forest.[9]

The effect of these measures of economic discrimination was to throw the African planters into determined opposition to the French administration, an attitude distinguishing them from their counterparts in Ghana, for example. The Ivory Coast planters took the initiative in the anti-colonial struggle after the war. It is doubtful whether they would have done so if the administration had followed a policy of neutrality towards them or favoured them. In Ghana there were no European planters and the African farmers were much less involved in nationalist activities. It is possible to speculate further what might have been the social composition of the *Convention People's Party* if the British authorities had not replied with 'downright refusal' to Lord Leverhulme's demands for 'freehold concessions for planting, a labour supply guaranteed by the

[1] See the *Bulletin de la Chambre d'Agriculture et d'Industrie de la Côte d'Ivoire*, no. 13, Abidjan, Ivory Coast, 1937–8, for details on the labour controversy in Ivory Coast. For the statistics confirming rising production of export crops in Ivory Coast, see Figure 5, p. 323.　　[2] Fréchou thesis, op. cit., p. 186.
[3] d'Aby, op. cit., p. 111. Before 1941 African planters paid the same low wages as the Europeans.　　[4] Fréchou thesis, op. cit., p. 187.
[5] Ibid., pp. 317 f.　　[6] *Annex 11348*, op. cit., Houphouët, p. 5.
[7] Ibid., p. 6.　　[8] Ibid., p. 5.　　[9] Fréchou thesis, op. cit., pp. 317 f.

government, and the exclusive right of purchasing fruit from Native sellers at a price fixed by his own mills'.[1] Would the Ashanti planters have been as influential in the CPP as the Baules became in the RDA? Would the CPP have been as sharply in conflict with chiefs as it became? Would the Life Chairman of the CPP have been an Ashanti planter, and his relations with the Asantehene as close as was Houphouët's with the paramount chief of the Baules, Kouakou Anoublé? The only other French West African territory where a substantial group of Africans enjoyed a steady money income in 1945 was Senegal. But the resemblance in 1945 between the 'citizens' of Senegal and the planters of Ivory Coast stops with numbers and income. It does not extend to politics. For the 'citizens' were favoured by the administration while the Ivory Coast planters had their interests ignored.

Because the Ivory Coast planters took the initiative in building the RDA immediately after the war, which had mass support within a short time, it is worth looking rather more closely at their origins. Some were educated townsmen who grew coffee and cocoa because they saw it could free them from total dependence upon the French authorities. It added or even replaced the income which their peers in other territories could earn only through the civil service. Not all who took to planting had European schooling, however. There was a 'plantation frontier' in Ivory Coast which attracted the most dynamic individuals and groups in the villages as well, particularly from the forest and coastal tribes owning the land best suited to growing the export crops. Many were commoners who saw in cocoa and coffee a way to achieve status and riches they had not inherited, and began growing—often with members of their age-group, or with kinsmen.[2] Indeed, in areas where inheritance of land was in some form matrilineal, occasionally women also started plantations.[3] Not only those traditionally commoners turned to planting. Though village land was for the most part communally owned first choice often went to the important people—to traditional chiefs where there were some, and to the officially designated chiefs also. Hence some chiefs profited directly from the new crops and most benefited at least indirectly from the increased wealth of their kinsmen.

Few pre-European cadres existed among the so-called stateless

[1] Hancock, Sir Keith. *A Survey of British Commonwealth Affairs*, vol. ii, Oxford University Press, London, 1942, p. 191.
[2] For an interesting example of co-operation among members of an age-group 'whose resources were meagre' to finance cocoa plantations, see *Étude sur la société Adioukrou et la région de Dabou*, mimeographed, Ivory Coast, 1 September 1954–31 January 1955, p. 5.　　　　　　　　　　　[3] Ibid., pp. 6–7.

N

peoples living mainly along the Liberian and Guinean frontiers—where generally 'societies . . . lack centralized authority, administrative machinery, and constituted judicial institutions . . . there are no sharp divisions of rank, status, or wealth'.[1] But a pre-colonial hierarchy existed among the diverse coastal tribes, and most important among the Baule and Agni peoples.[2] The Baule constitute the single largest ethnic group in Ivory Coast, an estimated 400,000; the Agni, about 95,000, are their relations but divided from them by historic differences.[3] Among both groups, occupying pivotal positions within Ivory Coast comparable to the position of the Ashanti in Ghana, many of the pre-colonial leaders managed to become planters. Hence they kept, sometimes enhanced, the high status they had inherited, in contrast with the general decline of chiefly status that accompanied the introduction of European rule and technology.

Thus in Ivory Coast the spread of the money economy by way of small African plantations served to blur, though not erase, social distinctions which elsewhere in West Africa remained sharp among groups frequently opposed. In Ivory Coast, unlike Senegal, through planting most of the educated elite kept deep roots in the countryside. Rivalry between traditional and modern elites was cushioned since chiefs who earned money through planting sought the best possible education for their children. The distance between traditional commoners and chiefs was also reduced, within the planter class, as both came to accept money as a sign of high status. Even the distinction between traditional and official chief faded among the planters, and a man like Félix Houphouët-Boigny, of but minor traditional status, but a *chef de canton* and Ponty-trained, came to be accepted as a spokesman of chiefs. This process whereby not only educated men but also some of the cadres from the pre-European political systems shifted to new activities—economic, political, religious—without precedent in tradition, was by no means confined simply to Ivory Coast. It occurred in various forms, for example, among the Ashanti of Gold Coast, the Baganda of Buganda, the Wolof and Serere in Senegal.

In most West African territories the post-war politics of the official chiefs were closely linked with the administration. In Ivory Coast this occurred less, mainly because many official chiefs were related to the new planter class—and therefore, as we shall see, to the RDA.

The emergence of an African planter class was but one of many social consequences of the introduction of cash crops to Ivory

---

[1] Fortes and Evans-Pritchard, op. cit., p. 5.
[2] For a description of the system of dividing land for plantations among the Baule and Gouro, see *Enquête agricole de Bouaké*, Ivory Coast, mimeographed c. 1954, pp. 10–1, 20, and 23.   [3] Leroi-Gourhan and Poirier, op. cit., p. 280.

Coast.[1] The economy became sensitive to world market prices, and the number of Africans earning money increased. People's income—'inexorable barometer of social change' in the words of a former French governor[2]—fluctuated with the depression, the rise in world prices in 1936, the decline of trade during the Second World War, and afterwards with the Korean war or frosts in Brazil. Yet another effect was the arrival of migrants. Hundreds of thousands came, especially from Upper Volta (mostly administered as part of Ivory Coast between 1932 and 1947) to work on the farms at harvest time. The relation of migrant worker to planter, whether European or African, became a perennial problem. At the close of the war the abuses of forced labour had reached their height, and those African agricultural labourers who had not fled joined the African planters in determined opposition to the system. It would be wrong to under-estimate the part of conviction in the condemnation by the African planters of Ivory Coast of forced labour. At the same time, their interests did confirm their convictions, for after 1940 labour was forced only for the convenience of the Europeans.

Some of the peaceful migrants from the savannah stayed, and became planters, calling upon their kinsmen to join them. They started their own settlements, and the geography of the forest made it easy to transfer from one plot to another, since building materials, game, water, and fertile soil for growing food were all readily available. Indeed this was yet another effect of the introduction of cash crops in Ivory Coast, the arrival of African immigrants—of 'strangers' in search of business, work, and new horizons, who added yet more variety to the heterogeneous population of Ivory Coast. Even before the Europeans came the land was inhabited by many different tribes, mostly animists who were pushed south and west into the protective foliage of the forest by invaders from the savannah kingdoms. Thus the figures on religion—some 70 per cent. animist, 23 per cent. Muslim, and 7 per cent. Christian—hide a remarkable ethnic diversity;[3] African leaders usually say some sixty different tribes.[4]

[1] For a pioneer study of the Bété and Agni African planters, see Köbben, A. J. F., *Le Planteur noir*: Essai d'une ethnographie d'aspect, Études Eburnéennes, vol. v, I.F.A.N., Centre de Côte d'Ivoire, 1956. Polly Hill has written an interesting review of this work in *West Africa*, 12 April 1958. C. R. Hiernaux has a brief discussion of the repercussions of the introduction of cash crops on Gagou social structure in 'Notes sur l'évolution des Gagous', *Bulletin de l'I.F.A.N.*, tome xii, no. 2, Dakar, April 1950, pp. 488–512.
[2] Siriex, Paul-Henri. *Une nouvelle Afrique: AOF 1957*, Paris, Plon, 1957, p. 55.
[3] See ethnic Map 4.
[4] *Tam-Tam*, March–May 1955, pp. 34–5. I.F.A.N. pamphlet, *Présentation de la Côte d'Ivoire*, Abidjan, 1953, p. 40.

As the internal market expanded still other aliens came as middle men, traders, transporters. Some were Lebanese or Syrian, others were Africans. Hence there took place in the forest and southern regions of Ivory Coast a process best described as 'rural urbanization', as the planter economy drew more and more people of different backgrounds to join an already diversified population.[1] The extent of this process remained unknown for statistics were inadequate. But it is suggested by the results of such samplings taken, for example, in 1955, in a supposedly Agni region of Bongouanou. The administrative estimates were that some 2,100 strangers lived there; the sample showed 18,000,[2] and showed further that among 8,531 people 23 different ethnic groups were represented, as well as 1,794 classified simply as 'others'.[3] One official estimate was that in 1957 60 per cent. of the wage earners were 'strangers'.[4]

Hence there were many 'strangers' in Ivory Coast. It became general practice to call all strangers 'dioula', particularly among people in the countryside.[5] The term is used even more loosely than is 'Hausa' in Ghana. 'Dioula' does not refer to any specific ethnic group, and indeed in some animist areas it is sufficient for a man to become a Muslim to be labelled a 'dioula'. In the savannah regions it has a more specific meaning. It refers to the trading families, the peddlers, many of which have traditions reaching back many centuries to the trans-Saharan trade. Their trade changed direction after the arrival of the Europeans, when goods imported to Africa came across the ocean rather than across the desert. As the volume of trade increased, the route of the *dioula* traders became more profitable. A few became very wealthy, for example, the Marka trader from Nioro in Soudan, Yacouba Sylla. In the late twenties he left Soudan due to French pressure against his Hamallist Muslim affiliations. In Ivory Coast he not only practiced Hamallism and helped spread it, but acquired trucking interests, motion picture halls, electrical installations, and plantations. From the first he expressed his family's tradition of revolt against French authorities by supporting the RDA. The interests of the African traders were closely tied to those of the African planters. They suffered from one of the by-products of the French rule—encouragement by French trading firms to European, Lebanese, and Syrian middlemen rather than African.

Yet another effect of economic change was the growth of cities—

[1] Rapport no. 5, *Enquête nutrition niveau de vie*, Bongouanou, 1955–6, mimeographed, Ivory Coast, p. 1.   [2] Ibid., p. 3.   [3] Ibid., p. 5.
[4] Haut Commissariat à Dakar, *Comptes économiques de l'Afrique occidentale française*, Rapport no. ii, Inventaire des Ressources Humaines en 1956, March 1959, p. 36.   [5] Fréchou thesis, op. cit., pp. 182 f.

particularly Abidjan and the coffee trading city of Bouaké. Abidjan grew rapidly from one-third Dakar's size in 1945, with a population of some 46,000, to half Dakar's size when in 1956 it had a population of some 127,000.[1] By then it was the second largest city in French-speaking West Africa, with double the people of the third largest, Bamako. Bouaké doubled its size between 1945 and 1955, becoming with 42,000 people almost as large as the peanut trading city of Kaolack.[2] Apart from these two cities, however, all other centres remained very small—under 10,000 except for 13,000 in Korhogo. For Ivory Coast remained essentially rural, and it was in the country-side where profound social changes were taking place. This was reflected in the official statistics on the wage earners. By 1957 Ivory Coast had 90,000, more than half its regular wage earners, in the countryside, working not for themselves but for employers on farms, fisheries, and in the forest. For Senegal, on the contrary, no more than 4,650 people were in this category, and this constituted less than 5 per cent. of the salaried wage earners. As for Ivory Coast employers, by 1957 there were 87,000 of them who were planters outside the cities, leaving only 3,200 in the cities. Senegal, on the other hand, then had no more than 6,500 employers all told.[3]

Nevertheless, the cities were the centres of contact, and had special significance just when the post-war reforms were introduced; economic change was yet less advanced, and the total number of African planters was estimated at 20,000.[4] Abidjan attracted a very varied population, including a fair number of strangers among the elite—clerks, teachers, doctors, lawyers—mainly from Senegal but also from Dahomey. In the city Africans came in touch with racial discrimination, which the settler community tightened considerably under the Vichy administration. In Abidjan some clubs, restaurants, hotels, and stores were reserved technically for 'citizens', but in practice for Europeans, since there were but a handful of African 'citizens' in the territory. One incident, still discussed among RDA militants, evokes the state of relations between the two races at the close of the war. Two founding members of the interterritorial RDA, Doudou Guèye, an African doctor from Senegal, and Ouëzzin Coulibaly, then director of studies at Ponty, decided to test the validity of the laws saying African 'citizens' had the same rights as Europeans. They went to an Abidjan restaurant patronized ex-clusively by Europeans. Almost immediately, the European employees tried to throw them out. The two Africans fought back, and there was a brawl, involving the European clients. The restaurant's owner,

[1] See Appendix IX.
[2] Ibid.
[3] *Outre-mer 1958*, op. cit., pp. 208–9.
[4] See p. 177, n. 5.

unaware that the two Africans were 'citizens', called the police, and invoked the *indigénat* applicable to African 'subjects'. But at police headquarters the two Africans proved they were 'citizens'. They knew the law, and claimed if they were jailed for the brawl, then they had to be in a common cell with the Europeans whom they had fought. In the end, the two Africans were released. Their fight against the Europeans symbolized the fight of the Ivory Coast RDA against local European privileges.[1]

Thus the post-war reforms came in Ivory Coast to a setting of rapid economic and social change. People expected wealth to grow even more rapidly than in the past, and there were great extremes of wealth. Among Africans there were many existing or potential sources of division—between townsmen and planters, between planters and agricultural or town labourers; among members of different ethnic groups; within ethnic groups; between *originaires* whose residence in Ivory Coast predated the French conquest and those who came during the twentieth century—a full fifth of the African population.[2] But Africans saw, at Liberation, ample reasons to unify against the *colons* and administrators, and tension between the Africans and Europeans mounted.

The Syndicat and the PDCI

The reforms gave Africans in Ivory Coast some opportunities to express grievances legally. Rapidly they took advantage of the new rights to organize. Only briefly in 1943, were the African and European planters partners within the *Syndicat Agricole de la Côte d'Ivoire*. The partnership broke up since the organization was dominated by the Europeans among whom Africans found 'total incomprehension'.[3] The attitude of the European planters was illustrated by the views of Jean Rose, their president who was also a prime mover in the *États Généraux de la Colonisation Française*. When the administration gave a subsidy of 1,000 francs per hectare to all who had 25 hectares or more contiguously under cultivation, Jean Rose opposed giving more than 500 francs per hectare even to the 50 Africans who qualified, on the grounds they did not 'have to worry about home leave, go to France or eat bread'. He said this while France was still occupied by the Germans and trips there were hardly possible.[4]

Liberation gave the African planters the opportunity to strike out on their own. Early in 1944 the Brazzaville conference recom-

---

[1] Information based on interviews Abidjan, 1956.
[2] *Interafrique Presse*, 11–17 July 1960, p. 1.
[3] *Annex 11348*, op. cit., Houphouët, p. 4.
[4] Ibid., pp. 5–6.

mended the end of forced labour, while the Provisional Government in Algiers replaced the administrators who had been loyal to Vichy. Governor Rey was thus replaced by Governor André Latrille. He was a Resistance leader who with his *chef de cabinet*, Lambert, a man close to the French Communists, introduced a new order in Ivory Coast. For the first time French administrators actually helped when Africans 'decided, in 1944, to take our interests in our own hands'.[1] In September the African planters set up their own organization—the *Syndicat Agricole Africain*.[2] Their first meeting took place at the Maison des Combattants, the club of veterans, to symbolize a challenge to the many European settlers who had co-operated enthusiastically with the Vichy administration. And they chose as their president the wealthy Baule planter Felix Houphouët-Boigny. Born in 1905 of a chiefly family in the village of Yamous-soukrou, he became as the war began a *chef de canton* of the Akoues. Then he abandoned his practice as an African doctor, for which he had trained in Dakar at the École de Medicine, and graduated in the mid-twenties as *major* of his class.

The SAA spread quickly with the aid of scarce cars and gasoline allocated by the administration.[3] Officials added another incentive by exempting members of the SAA from forced labour service well before Parliament passed the law of 11 April 1946 abolishing it in all the French colonies.[4] Officials ruled a man eligible for membership in the *Syndicat* if he had at least two hectares of coffee or three of cocoa under cultivation, and some 20,000 Africans qualified.[5] The SAA challenged not only the European planters but also the European middlemen, by signing contracts directly with the big trading firms, particularly the *Société Commerciale de l'Ouest Africain*. The SAA laid plans for the creation of a *Co-operative des Planteurs Africains* under the direction of Jean Delafosse. But the immediate problem was bringing in the 1944 and 1945 harvests. In the recruitment of workers there began 'the battle between settlers and Africans'[6] in Ivory Coast. First the SAA simply favoured the more equitable distribution of labourers between European and African planters. Soon, however, the SAA took a stand against the principle of forced labour. Houphouët claimed to be no more concerned about the economic consequences than the abolitionists of slavery had been in the nineteenth century.[7] The SAA proceeded to recruit

[1] *Annex 11348*, op. cit., Houphouët, p. 6. See also statement by Joseph Anoma, Houphouët's successor as president of the SAA, ibid., pp. 393 f.
[2] d'Aby, op. cit., p. 112.   [3] d'Aby, op. cit., p. 109.
[4] Fréchou thesis, op. cit., p. 139.
[5] *Annex 11348*, op. cit., Houphouët, pp. 9–10.   [6] Ibid., p. 6.
[7] Houphouët–d'Arboussier correspondence, op. cit.

workers directly for voluntary labour.[1] They did want to save at least some of the harvest from their plantations which had degenerated during the war.

Quite a few of the local agents of the *Syndicat* in the plantation belt of Ivory Coast were official chiefs.[2] This made it easier for SAA delegates to reach agreements with the northern chiefs who supplied voluntary labourers—chiefs like the Morho Naba of the Mossi and the Gbon Coulibaly of the Senoufo.[3] The SAA recruiters offered labourers part of the harvest and four times what the Europeans paid. The Europeans paid the official rate of 3.50 francs a day, plus maintenance. The Africans offered 20 francs a day, though they deducted 10 francs for maintenance, and one-third the cocoa or two-fifths the coffee harvest as well.[4] No wonder the African planters had some success in winning workers away from European and Gold Coast farms. For the 1944–5 harvest they successfully enticed 4–5,000 voluntary workers to join the estimated 35,000 forced labourers.[5]

This was not nearly enough workers for a normal full harvest—the estimated average need for seasonal workers after the war was 115,000 for African planters and 28,000 for European.[6] Nevertheless the SAA felt in 1945 they had proved the case for free labour. The European planters vehemently denied this. Their lobby in Paris claimed they would be bankrupt without forced labour and attacked the policies of the Governor. The French government heeded the complaints and replaced Governor Latrille with the Comte de Mauduit[7] who again favoured the European planters and extended the operation of the forced labour system to allow the Europeans to bring in the 1945–6 harvest.[8]

Meanwhile political reforms made it legal for Africans to form parties. As in the other territories, African town associations sought in Ivory Coast to transform themselves into parties, by forming alliances. There were in Abidjan many town groups. An organization like the *Syndicat du Personnel Africain de l'Enseignement Primaire de la Côte d'Ivoire*, defended the interests of African state school teachers. Their secretary-general, Yacé Philippe, later became secre-

---

[1] d'Aby, op. cit., p. 112.   [2] Ibid., p. 113.
[3] Houphouët's successor as SAA president. *Annex 11348*, op. cit., Anoma, pp. 393 f.   [4] Ibid., Houphouët, p. 7.
[5] The typescript of Houphouët's defence of the *Syndicat* when it was attacked in the courts of Ivory Coast, *c.* 1948, claimed 4,000 workers; but in *Annex 11348*, op. cit., p. 9, Houphouët claimed 5,000; d'Aby, op. cit., p. 109.
[6] M. Desclercs, president of the Ivory Coast Chamber of Commerce. 'Le Problème de la main-d'oeuvre en Côte d'Ivoire', S.I.A.M.O., Abidjan, 1950. Also Fréchou thesis, op. cit., p. 147.   [7] d'Aby, op. cit., pp. 108–9.
[8] Fréchou thesis, op. cit., pp. 140–5.

tary-general of the RDA *sous-section* in Treichville. There were also radical groups such as the *Groupe d'Études Communistes* (GEC), the *Comité d'Études Franco–Africain* (CEFA) and the *Union Fraternelle des Originaires de la Côte d'Ivoire* (UFOCI). These groups were linked by associations with French Communists, and by having members active in the *Syndicat*. The SAA had the advantages of funds and a structure reaching most villages in the coastal and forest regions. These related groups constituted the nuclei for the Ivory Coast *section* of the RDA, and organized the first parliamentary campaign, in 1945, with the assistance of some Senegalese 'citizens'.[1] They used the resources of the *Syndicat* and its 'regional delegates— for the most part *chefs de canton* and village chiefs'[2]—agreed to support President Houphouët.

Houphouët won only on the second ballot, by 12,980 votes against 11,621 for his nearest rival, the Baloum Naba.[3] There were several reasons why the vote was narrow. First, the attitude of the administration became distinctly unfavourable towards the *Syndicat* after the Comte de Mauduit took Latrille's place as governor. Officials worked for Houphouët's defeat. They knew he was strong among the southern and forest peoples; that of the approximately 30,000 second college voters a little more than half lived in what became, in 1947, the territory of Upper Volta; and that of these perhaps three fourths were Mossi obedient to chiefs who were responsive to administrative pressures.[4] Until the change in governors, the paramount chief of the Mossi, the Morho Naba, had agreed to support Houphouët. Then he changed his mind and presented the candidacy of his illiterate lieutenant, the Baloum Naba.[5] He was the only candidate for a seat in the French parliament not educated in French schools. With some sympathy Houphouët later described the Baloum Naba's campaign:

> He was watched, God knows he was watched. Whenever he could free himself from surveillance, he told people 'Vote for my friend Houphouët ... What will I do in that Paris, with my forty four wives and at my age? I can't speak a blasted word of French! ... He was told 'But you will have an administrator as secretary.'[6]

Administrative inspiration of the candidacy of the Baloum Naba was not the sole reason for a narrow vote. There was a genuine

---

[1] *Annex 11348*, op. cit., Houphouët, p. 13, and d'Aby, op. cit., p. 56.
[2] Ibid., p. 113.
[3] Le Monde, ed. *Élections et referendums*, des 21 octobre, 1945, 5 mai et 2 juin 1946, Le Monde, Paris, 1946, p. 249.
[4] *Annex 11348*, op. cit., Houphouët, p. 13.
[5] d'Aby, op. cit., p. 55.   [6] *Annex 11348*, op. cit., p. 14.

desire, particularly among the Mossi, for a separation from Ivory Coast. As early as 1945 the Mossi chiefs, with clients of chiefs around Bobo–Dioulasso, had formed the *Union Voltaïque*. Its primary object was separate status for the area which became, in 1947, the territory of Upper Volta; a subsidiary object was 'to see the railroad extended to Ouagadougou'.[1] Separatist feeling there, and resentment of exploitation by the southerners added heat to the electoral contest. Houphouët's agents found their way barred by guards sent by Mossi chiefs, bridges cut and cars ambushed, when they sought to enter Mossi country.[2]

It is doubtful whether Houphouët would have won this election without the support of most voters from the Bobo–Dioulasso region (subsequently in Upper Volta). There educated townsmen opposed to the 'chiefs' were active in a small CEFA nucleus—men like Famory Coulibaly and Djibril Vinama. Their leader was Ouëzzin Coulibaly, born a Bobo-fing and educated at Ponty some ten years after Houphouët. Ouëzzin decided not to compete with Houphouët at their first meeting, on a train in Ivory Coast just after the war, which began a close association that lasted until Ouëzzin died in September 1958. In 1945 he threw his energy and organizing skill behind Houphouët's campaign. It was in this first campaign that in Mossi country a French administrator seized Ouëzzin, and to discourage potential voters, stripped him and with a rope around his neck promenaded him through the town. Some twelve years later he became the head of the first African government of Upper Volta. But in the interval, it was in Ivory Coast that Ouëzzin Coulibaly spent most of his political career. From there, even after Upper Volta separated off, Coulibaly was elected a *parlementaire* and he remained Houphouët's closest companion. In Ivory Coast he represented not only the *Association des Originaires de la Haute Volta* and the wider 'stranger' community, but also the federal, indeed pan-African tendencies of the RDA.

The Bobo votes made the difference. Rival candidates from several ethnic associations of eastern and southern tribes took only a few votes from Houphouët, because support was limited to their own small groups.[3] Since the inter-war years there existed in the towns of Ivory Coast many ethnic and regional associations—such as the *Association du Sanwy*, the *Union Fraternelle des Agnis de Sahoua*, the *Association Mutuelle des Originaires d'Assinie*, the *Union Sociale des*

---

[1] Information based on interviews.
[2] *Annex 11348*, op. cit., Houphouët, p. 15; also his typewritten letter to the overseas minister asking for Latrille's return.
[3] For supporting statistics on ethnic groups, see *Annuaire Statistique*, tome i, 1956, op. cit., pp. 55–7.

Ressortissants Adioukrou de Tiébissou.[1] The small southern tribes of Ivory Coast, like those of Ghana, had a long history of contact with Europe and a fairly high proportion of educated men interested in elective office. But the *Syndicat* had the support of most of the rural voters in the south and the forest. Only within two ethnic groups did the majority refuse to back the *Syndicat* president. One was the Bete, whose leader, Dignan Bailly, became the head of the Ivory Coast Socialist party.[2] Just as the Socialists in Guinea were dominated by educated Fulani, and limited to that ethnic group, so the Ivory Coast socialist had an audience limited to the Bete. The other group was the Agni, who with their relations from Nkrumah's birthplace Nzima, on the Ghana frontier, became the basis of the *Parti Progressiste de la Côte d'Ivoire*, led by the Ponty-trained teacher, Kacou Aoulou.[3] For some ten years after 1945 the Bete-based Socialists and the Agni-based *Progressistes* opposed the PDCI, and fought unsuccessfully, 'to free themselves from the yoke of the Baule and the Dioula'.[4]

This first territorial election ever held in Ivory Coast was Houphouët's only narrow victory. During the 1946 campaign to the second *Constituante* he won by an overwhelming 21,099 out of 22,995 valid second college votes.[5] There were three reasons. First, Latrille was back as governor. Perhaps the sight of Houphouët riding about in the governor's car[6] had something to do with the decision of the Mossi chiefs not to oppose him during what were the last months of their administrative connexion with Abidjan. Second, in Paris Houphouët successfully sponsored the law which abolished forced labour. In most territories the man who took credit for the end of forced labour—Senghor in Senegal, Apithy in Dahomey—was widely acclaimed. Rejoicing was more fervent in Ivory Coast because Africans there had been subjected to some of the worst abuses of the system. As the candidate of the *Syndicat*, Houphouët had made the abolition of forced labour his special task and became in the countryside a hero and a liberator. This achievement was the beginning of a myth around Houphouët, the first truly national Ivory Coast tradition. Third, Houphouët's supporters worked hard to organize, and they profited from his prestige to build a party

---

[1] See Wallerstein, Immanuel, *The Emergence of Two West African Nations: Ghana and Ivory Coast*, Ph.D. thesis, Columbia University, New York, 1959.

[2] Immediately after the war he was editor of *La France Africaine*, a newspaper in Paris. *Annex 11348*, op. cit., pp. 465–71. He became the director of a private school, and head of the *Association des Contribuables Bétés*.

[3] It had loose ties with the MRP in France.

[4] Citation from private correspondence of a *Progressiste* leader.

[5] *Le Monde, Élections et referendums*, 1946, op. cit., p. 249.

[6] *Annex 11348*, op. cit., pp. 211 f.

structure. It was a testimony to their diligence, as well as the business sense of the *dioula* and Lebanese traders that by 1946 there were Houphouët pictures, perfume, lockets, and cloths on sale in the markets of Ivory Coast. And dances, legends, songs, and plays throughout the territory retold the tale of Houphouët's freeing of the workers.

Thus there was the basis for a mass party in Ivory Coast even before it was born, of consolidation of the existing town associations, which was the initial phase of party growth in Ivory Coast as in the other territories. In Abidjan as early as August 1945, just prior to municipal council elections, educated Africans unified in a *Bloc Africain*, the homonym of the Senegalese group of the same period. But while in Senegal the Socialist caucus gained control of the *Bloc*, in Ivory Coast it was the GEC caucus of men calling themselves *démocrates* who took control. Under their lead, the *Bloc* boycotted all European candidates for the municipal council of the *commune mixte* of Abidjan. The election was the first in which some 'subjects' could vote, and though both 'citizens' and 'subjects' had to be among the candidates, the vote was by single college. The *Bloc* successfully presented an all-African slate of nine 'subjects' and nine 'citizens'. This was the first electoral victory for the Africans, due largely to their united front against the Europeans.[1]

During the first campaign for the Constituent Assembly the unity among the town Africans of Abidjan broke for a short time, as both a Socialist and *Progressiste* nucleus opposed Houphouët's election. By 1946, however, the 'unity of action' of the *Bloc* was restored under the banner of a *Rassemblement Africain*. It became a party in the formal sense in April 1946 and took the name *Parti Démocratique de la Côte d'Ivoire*. It spread quickly, along lines of communication within Ivory Coast provided by the structure of the *Syndicat*. Even before the first interterritorial congress took place in Bamako in October 1946 the PDCI claimed more paid-up members than there were legally registered voters—some 65,000.[2] For not only economic but also political, social, and religious forces of revolt sought a channel of expression. Even religious dissidents like the Muslim Hamallists and the Christian Harrists gave their loyalty to the PDCI. This success of the PDCI, the wealth of its planter-leaders and the special status accorded Houphouët from his parliamentary fight against forced labour, explained why he became by acclamation the president of the interterritorial RDA. The power of the PDCI for at least a decade gave sustenance to the movement.

---

[1] d'Aby, op. cit., pp. 36–7, 49–50, 57.
[2] *Réveil*, 3 October 1946.

People knew that regardless of purpose 'if Houphouët asks (the Baules) today for five, ten, twenty million, he will have them within twenty-four or forty-eight hours'.[1] On various occasions PDCI leaders subsidized one or another *section* of the RDA, as these took root over the years throughout AOF (except Mauretania) and in parts of Equatorial Africa.

Rural discontent gave momentum to the PDCI and pushed the party to repeated electoral victories since 1945. Its candidates, returned uncontested to the 1946 Legislature, were picked with care for regional balance; Houphouët headed the list while Ouëzzin Coulibaly from the Bobo region and Kaboret Zinda from Ouagadougou completed it. Zinda was a 27-year-old African pharmacist, a Mossi son of the *chef de canton* from Koudougou, with traditional status challenging the Morho Naba's. When the PDCI nominated him in 1946 the Mossi chiefs agreed, and he came to be the youngest member of the French National Assembly. Then the chiefs, like the administration, turned against the RDA. In 1947 at a meeting held before the door of the palace of the Morho Naba, Zinda attacked him and his entourage, cited many abuses and claimed the French deformed chieftaincy. He challenged the chiefs, 'climb off your horses and walk with the people'. They walked out of the meeting. Shortly afterwards Zinda died, reputedly poisoned.[2] He was never replaced; Upper Volta became a separate territory and the PDCI had no formal part in the by-elections won overwhelmingly by the chiefly party, the *Union Voltaïque*.

The PDCI drew up yet another unity list for the elections to the first *conseil général*, which received 87 per cent. of the votes cast,[3] and won 25 out of the 27 second college seats; the other 2 were Agni, elected on the unity list, who then broke away. The care taken to keep an ethnic, professional, and status balance is evident from an analysis of the councillors for Ivory Coast proper—from the *conseil général* second college as it was after the 1948 by-elections replaced the 12 councillors who had been elected from Upper Voltan constituencies. Of the total, 21 had been educated at Ponty and 7 were teachers, 8 clerks, and 6 African doctors. Nine came from chiefly families and the rest were commoners. They represented 18 different ethnic groups; not more than 3 were members of a single ethnic group—and that only of Baule, Malinke and Agni.[4] Five were 'strangers' from Guinea, Soudan, Senegal, Upper Volta, and Dahomey. The choice of candidates for the first *conseil général* began

[1] *Annex 11348*, op. cit., Léon, p. 93.
[2] *Interafrique Presse*, 11–17 July 1960, p. 9.
[3] d'Aby, op. cit., p. 58
[4] See Appendix VIII: A for supporting statistical data.

the series of negotiations among ethnic and professional groups which henceforth preceded all direct elections in Ivory Coast. Since the PDCI remained the dominant party and when votes were counted honestly ran up overwhelming majorities, the real struggle for power among Africans in Ivory Coast took place within the party, when candidates were chosen, rather than in the actual voting.

Even in 1947, when the pressure for unity among Africans came from their common hostility to the Europeans, the educated leaders of two ethnic groups dissociated themselves from the PDCI, the Bete-Socialists and the largely Agni-*Progressistes*. Their withdrawal from the PDCI was precipitated by quarrels over nominations. The Agni took further issue with Houphouët over the nomination of his brother-in-law as chief in Abengourou, which led early in 1947 to incidents.[1] Agni and Bete disagreement with the leaders of the PDCI was a constant theme in post-war Ivory Coast politics, at least in part because of historic disagreements with neighbouring tribes.

In 1947 the educated leaders of the PDCI from the towns sought to formalize the structure. A permanent staff worked at territorial headquarters in Treichville, a suburb of Abidjan. In theory at least one member of the executive—the *comité directeur*—stayed at headquarters while at least three others toured the provinces. People snapped up party cards, first the agents of the *Syndicat* and the chiefs, then their followers. After Upper Volta was separated off, the PDCI claimed 350,000 members.[2] By 1950 the PDCI claimed to have 850,000 card-carrying members who presumably had paid 25 francs for the card and another 50 francs annual subscription fee.[3] These resources, together with the continuously generous response of the planter community to special appeals, made the Ivory Coast PDCI the richest party in French-speaking West Africa.

The fact was that popular support for the PDCI outstripped the capacities of the leaders to organize as they would have preferred. They tried to build according to a pattern agreed for all the territorial sections of the RDA—at the local level either rural *comités de village* or in the cities *comités de quartiers*; at the regional level *sous-sections* sent delegates to a territorial congress; which elected a *comité directeur*; which chose a smaller *bureau politique*. In theory the units were to be determined by geography, while the relationships among them was to be vertical, and by elected representatives. These principles were usually followed in the other territories.

[1] *Annex 11348*, op. cit., Josse, p. 931, and Houphouët, pp. 28-9.
[2] Ibid., Houphouët, p. 48.
[3] *Le Démocrate* 30 March 1950.

But in the Ivory Coast the crisis in the relations between Europeans and Africans led PDCI leaders to feel they had little time to spend on party organization. They already had a spontaneously evolving structure, along ethnic lines, and the organizers did not try to rebuild along the neighbourhood principle. Their immediate goal was to surmount the crisis; they tried to give direction to already formed groups; they would not risk further internal division by attacking within their own ranks. In their haste they also neglected holding annual territorial congresses and used the Treichville *soussection* for an 'interim' territorial executive. This, too, was organized along ethnic lines even though neighbourhoods were not. An effect was to institutionalize the ethnic principle, which later weakened the PDCI's ability to cope with mounting ethnic tensions.[1]

The sudden emergence of the *Syndicat*, the birth of the RDA and the adoption of reforms in the French Parliament, all these the European settlers in Ivory Coast considered to be defeats. Houphouët remarked of them:

Had they remained in France they would certainly have been among the Communists or the Socialists; but with a change in climate came a change in their social class; they were worse than those born reactionaries.[2]

Communications between Africans and the Europeans broke down, and debates between first and second college councillors in the *conseil général* were generally disorderly.[3] That its powers were inadequate was the only point on which both groups agreed. Fear and anger was behind such baseless rumours circulating among the Europeans like 'on Christmas eve (1946) the whites will all be slaughtered'.[4] Though there were no acts of violence by Africans against Europeans, nevertheless they took to sleeping 'with their revolvers cocked'.[5] Most settlers believed 'Paris' was responsible for the changes they hated, and so their spokesmen went with their case to Paris, to the meetings of the *États Généraux de la Colonisation Française*. By co-operating with the extensive lobby of French *colons* in all the French colonies, the Ivory Coast settlers became part of a powerful machine, and gained sympathetic attention from such Right-wing newspapers as *Climats* and *l'Aurore*.

As long as the French Communists remained in the French government the Ivory Coast settler had little success in obtaining

---

[1] See Aristide Zolberg, 'Effets de la structure d'un parti politique sur l'intégration nationale', *Cahiers d'Études Africaines*, October 1960, p. 140.
[2] *Annex 11348*, op. cit., p. 28.
[3] Conseil général de la Côte d'Ivoire, *Procès-verbaux des séances, mars 1947* Abidjan, 1947, p. 9.
[4] *Annex 11348*, op. cit., p. 31.
[5] Ibid., Orselli, p. 104.

official support in France against the RDA, even though they charged that it was Communist-dominated. There was French Communist influence, but it was rather in the nature of swimming with a tide they could not control. Later, the French Communists claimed their influence prevented the *Syndicat* from dominating Ivory Coast politics, and led to the formation of a mass party.[1] This claim seems exaggerated since the post-war reforms precipitated the birth of African parties everywhere and it is hardly likely the *Syndicat* leaders would have left the initiative in politics to others. During these formative years, a number of French Communists did act as advisors—one worked on the staff of the *conseil général*, another assisted at the birth of the CGT trade union movement in Ivory Coast while Communist lawyers, journalists, and technicians moved back and forth between Paris and the various capitals of French-speaking West Africa.[2] There is some evidence that the GEC of Abidjan met at least for a brief period in the offices of Lambert, the *chef de cabinet* of the governor, Latrille. But the French Communists were quite peripheral to the central fact that great popular enthusiasm for the idea of a real change in Ivory Coast became attached to the RDA.

The attitude of the French government towards the RDA altered after the tripartite alliance broke down in May 1947. The Vichy record of the settlers became less significant to a French government increasingly preoccupied with Communist opposition in France. Informed members of the French government did not go so far as to believe some of the more exaggerated statements of the European settlers—that Norwegian boats manned by Russians were unloading arms in Ivory Coast, for example.[3] Yet they were fearful, lest a revolt in Ivory Coast follow the Madagascar rebellion, and took measures to transfer Governor Latrille early in 1947, on the pretext he mismanaged the controversy surrounding the chieftaincy of Abengourou, and was responsible for incidents there.[4] His successor, Governor Orselli, held office only between February and October 1948, and though his instructions were to tighten control over the RDA, he instead claimed he tried to reconcile settlers and the RDA, and to woo the RDA from their Communist allies. The attempt failed. He blamed the settler attitude for this, claiming they caused trouble when he tried to have mixed dinner parties, when a *colon* found Africans did not get out of the way of his sports car fast enough, when Africans sat on white benches in movie houses of Abidjan,

---

[1] Barbé circular for the GEC's, October 1946, op. cit., p. 5.

[2] *Annex 11348*, op. cit., Orselli. pp. 112 f.

[3] Ibid., Houphouët, p. 34.

[4] d'Aby, op. cit., pp. 59 f.; Marc Rucart. *Climats*, 24 November 1959.

when he tried to allocate 20 per cent. of the imported refrigerators to Africans, when he allotted one of three American cars to the president of the *conseil général*, Auguste Denise, or when he tried to allocate a reasonable share of bread to Africans who had developed a taste for it.[1] Orselli summed up the settler attitude in his report of a snatch of dinner table conversation 'This matter cannot be settled here without 10,000 deaths.'[2]

As for the Communists, their tone also sharpened after they became free from the restraints of co-operating with the parliamentary majority in France. In May 1947 they entered on a phase of systematic opposition, and since they subordinated African policy to the French, they urged opposition upon the RDA. More French Communists devoted their energies to the RDA, as Communist lawyers, journalists, cameramen, politicians and other functionaries moved between Paris and Ivory Coast. The French Communists, under the lead of R. Barbé, wanted to consolidate their position and cautioned their African allies against Titoist deviation, against 'a certain autonomism, African, perhaps even territorial'.[3] Barbé and his comrades, instead of saying publicly, 'obey the constitution', as in 1946, said in 1948, 'it is time for mass action against reaction'.[4] A large Communist delegation attended the second interterritorial congress of the RDA in December–January 1949; in their speeches they made clear they connected events in Africa and the cold war in Europe. They conducted a seminar on techniques of protest, and produced a film on forced labour and its aftermath. (The administration later seized this.)[5]

French officials, between the settlers and the French Communists became convinced the RDA was a danger. The two extremes left no room for the neutral position, and this was observed in an RDA editorial.

To bring Africans together is a Russian plan. The Russians must be extraordinary people, geniuses, since everything which should make men happy, all that can diminish the exploitation of man by man, everything that can stop man from being a tool in the hands of man, is attributed to them.

The Bamako Congress? Russian plan. The formation of the RDA? Russian plan. United States of Africa? Russian plan. Do the people of France support the fight of the oppressed people? Russian plan. The Russians must really be geniuses since everything that is human is attributed to them.[6]

[1] *Annex 11348*, op. cit., Orselli, pp. 104 f.   [2] Ibid., p. 103.
[3] Barbé's circular 144 to the GEC groups, mimeographed, 20 October 1948.
[4] *Annex 11348*, op. cit., Monnet, p. 137.   [5] Ibid., Péchoux, p. 257.
[6] *Le Démocrate*, 19 December 1950.

The French government designated Governor Péchoux to Ivory Coast. He arrived in November 1948. It was his task to restore the 'prestige' of the administration—to stop the use of a *service d'ordre* at RDA meetings for arrogation of police powers; the 27 schools of the PDCI's *Ligue Contre l'Ignorance* for teaching without permission of the educational authorities; the use of party tribunals to settle differences for arrogation of judicial powers.[1] He used the law to break the power of the RDA, even at the risk of incidents.

The Incidents

Péchoux expelled the Communists from the administration, and sponsored individuals and groups in opposition to the RDA. His plan included preparing a defeat for the RDA in the 1951 elections to the French National Assembly. Confronted with the united front of Africans within the RDA, the administration adopted divisive tactics, at every level from the capital to the village. The administration found it impossible to build a single opposition party and so sponsored five—among Baule opposed to President Houphouët the *Union des Indépendants de la Côte d'Ivoire*; among Muslims living in the savannah the *Entente des Indépendants de la Côte d'Ivoire* led by Sékou Sanogo; in the southern lagoon area the *Bloc Démocratique Eburnéen* under the lead of former Senator Djaument. Two other parties existed since 1946—the *Progressistes* among Agni later joined by Abrong, and the Socialists among the Bété.

The next phase in the official campaign against the PDCI came with the arrest of most members of the *comité directeur* who were not covered by French parliamentary immunity. The circumstances were the following. To create the *Bloc Démocratique Eburnéen*, Etienne Djaument called a meeting for 30 January. He was angry that he was not renominated RDA Senator in November 1948, and Biaka Boda took his place. The BDE had police and official protection, and the place of the meeting, the Comacico meeting hall, was but a few yards away from the *Syndicat* in the predominantly RDA stronghold of Treichville, a suburb of Abidjan. At the 30 January meeting were some of Djaument's Sassandra kinsmen and a few supporters of the *Progressistes* and the Socialists. The bulk of the audience was RDA. After Djaument insulted Houphouët, Ouëzzin Coulibaly, and the secretary general of the PDCI, Auguste Denise, went across the road to escort Houphouët to the meeting. Houphouët seated himself comfortably on the stage and asked for a right to reply. Questions were all right, said Djaument, but not speeches. Houphouët led the boos, catcalls, and hisses which drowned out

---

[1] *Annex 11348*, op. cit., Raymond Lefèvre, *chef de cabinet* of Péchoux, pp. 211 f.; Péchoux, pp. 221 f. and 329 f.; and *Le Monde*, 8 April 1953.

Djaument's voice—then left the meeting, taking his followers with him. From the balcony of the *Syndicat* Houphouët told the crowd Governor Péchoux was really responsible for the insults, while in the hall Djaument adjourned the meeting until the 6th of February.[1]

In the interval Djaument, the administration and the RDA formulated plans. The administration wanted to demonstrate encouragement to RDA opponents.

Péchoux's *chef de cabinet*, Raymond Lefèvre, later stated:[2]

We believed . . . we could not tolerate the dictatorship of the RDA . . . and certain of being able to re-establish order the Governor accepted the risk of seeing reproduced, perhaps in a somewhat aggravated form, the events of the previous Sunday.

Djaument and his friends met in the European sections of town, at the Chamber of Commerce and at the business headquarters of Massiège & Ferras. Their confidence in official support was shown by the telegram they sent all over Ivory Coast on 2nd of February:

'BATTLE DESTRUCTION SOVIET RDA DECLARED—BLOCK ALL ACTION
SUPPORTERS KOMINFORM'[3]

As for the RDA, in a meeting on the 1st of February at their *Syndicat* headquarters, the leaders pointed out that in France people who disagreed with political speakers had the right to reply, else there were boos, catcalls, and hisses. Houphouët clearly wanted Djaument put in his place. But not by violence. He said 'even if M. Djaument wanted to insult in order to provoke the population, they should . . . content themselves with drowning out his traitorous voice'.[4] Meanwhile, he recalled general councillors Paraiso and Mockey from the interior for the meeting, and then left town to join Ouëzzin Coulibaly, the other deputy, on tour.

Denise, Mockey, and Paraiso asked Governor Péchoux to cancel the meeting on 6 February, since Djaument's followers were armed and planned trouble. Péchoux refused. On the day of the meeting an enormous crowd milled in the streets. Police and military trucks were at the hall which Djaument's supporters entered first. Paraiso slipped in some of his men who reported Djaument's supporters, armed, had taken up strategic positions. At 9:10 a.m. the RDA contingent entered. Paraiso told his men to throw away even ball point pens if they were without caps, and asked the police to search for arms.[5] This was done. In the hall trouble soon broke out. Houphouët claimed, 'The minority, just a few men, beat our unarmed militants

[1] *Annex 11348*, op. cit., Houphouët, p. 43.   [2] Ibid., p. 215.
[3] Ibid., Denise, p. 430.   [4] Ibid., p. 43.
[5] Ibid., Paraiso, p. 415.

with sticks and slippers, under the eyes of the indifferent police.'[1] Who beat, insulted, and pushed whom is not clear. The police decided to evacuate and the two groups left by different doors. The police protected Djaument's men against the hostile crowd. Paraiso, Mockey, and Rigo (a French Communist organizer of the CGT), carried on the shoulders of their supporters, led singing of the *Marseillaise*—but also ordered the crowd to make way for the 'traitors'.[2] By noon the hall was clear, and it seemed a serious incident had been averted.

But only seemed. By early afternoon crowds besieged the homes of RDA opponents in both Treichville and Adjamé. The secretary-general of the *Progressistes*, Kacou Aoulou, fleeing from pursuers, shot and wounded RDA supporter Sidibé, and when Aoulou took refuge in the house of Yapobé the crowd attacked and damaged it. People also attacked the house of superior chief Antonin Dioullo, another RDA opponent, and stole his 'two hundred year old throne'.[3] In the fracas his nephew was wounded and eventually died. The crowd also wrecked the headquarters and presses of the Progessives, 'while Paraiso danced a Dahomean dance'.[4]

By 3 p.m. the rioting ended. Forty-six Africans were arrested, 1 man was killed, 4 of the wounded were in hospital, while some 13 others were treated but discharged. Later the military patrolled the streets and reported 'the night was never before so calm in Abidjan'.[5] On 9 February the police arrested eight key leaders of the RDA, including Mockey and Paraiso, and kept them in jail for the duration of the repression.[6] The eight felt they were fighting for freedom, and nicknamed the paddy wagon which transported them to jail and court, as 'la liberté'.[7]

These arrests were but the first of the measures officials took against the educated leaders of the RDA. Charges were brought against the *Syndicat*.[8] The governor sued the RDA paper *Le Démocrate*, on more than fifty different counts (but since the editor Ouëzzin Coulibaly was a deputy, covered by immunity, the cases could not come up until after Coulibaly lost his seat in 1951). Officials alternated threats and bribes to make men leave the RDA. So many civil servants lost their jobs for political reasons, some even formed, during 1950, a *Syndicat des fonctionnaires sanctionnés pour raison politique*. Civil servants were so vulnerable to official pressure the

---

[1] *Annex 11348*, op. cit., Houphouët, p. 43.   [2] Ibid., Aoulou, pp. 225–6.
[3] Ibid., Dioullo, p. 235.   [4] *Le Monde*, 15 April 1953.
[5] Unpublished report by Greffier-en-chef Divay.
[6] The eight were Bernard Dadié, Mathieu Ekra, Sery Kore, Lama Camara, Jean Baptiste Mockey, Albert Paraiso, Philippe Veira, and Jacob Williams.
[7] *Annex 11348*, op. cit., Paraiso, p. 416.   [8] Ibid., Coulibaly, p. 1048.

RDA made it a rule they could not be party officers. As for the *conseil général*, at the ordinary budgetary session in the fall of 1949 the RDA majority refused to approve the budget. The Governor dissolved the council and called an extraordinary session. In the interval, pressures, arrests, bribery resulted in cutting the number of RDA councillors from 25 to less than 10. They simply disowned the letters of resignation from the *conseil général* which they had filed with the party at the time of their election, and instead officials published, broadcast, and posted everywhere news of their resignation from the party.[1]

Repressive measures were not confined to the educated. Major army and police movements occurred at any sign, real or imagined, of disorder. Africans considered a provocation the aggressively military celebrations, near Man, of the fiftieth anniversary of the French capture of the warrior Samory Touré.[2] In the countryside chiefs favourable to the RDA lost their offices—according to RDA estimates at least 300.[3] Governor Péchoux took special pains to woo the paramount chief of the Baule, Kouakou Anoublé. The Governor offered him 'a car, grooved rifles for his elders, and encouraged the publication in the unofficial organ of the government, *La Côte d'Ivoire* . . . his resignation from the RDA'. Kouakou Anoublé made a personal trip to Abidjan 'to denounce this fiction and to state publicly his devotion to the RDA'.[4]

Ordinary villagers were as much involved in the incidents as were the chiefs. Village chiefs were pitted against their superiors, and some incidents took place where historically French conquest had always met with African resistance. An example were the incidents in the northern village of Koumbala, among the Senoufo in the cercle of Korhogo. At the turn of the century a chief of the Palaka had been executed in Korhogo by the French for refusing to pay taxes. Since September 1948 there were new troubles over payment of taxes. Sikaly, chief of the Palaka, who favoured the RDA, refused to pay 4,000 francs cfa in taxes which he owed to his superior chief and cousin Ouattara, who opposed the RDA. Sikaly said, 'I pay only to Houphouët'. Officials claimed they made attempts to mediate, then to arrest Sikaly, but to no avail. At dawn on 26 February ten truckloads of Colonel Lacheroy's Alaouite troops (Syrian mercenaries) made a surprise attack on the small encampment of some hundred souls. Who fired first is a matter for controversy. The troops reported that when one of their three attacking groups was greeted by

---

[1] *Climats*, 24 November 1949, 12 and 19 January 1950.
[2] *Annex 11348*, op. cit., Léon, p. 95.
[3] *Climats*, 13–19 September 1951.
[4] *Annex 11348*, op. cit., Gadeau, p. 459.

stones, shots, and poisoned arrows, it fired without waiting for orders and that then the other two groups also opened fire. But the RDA denied the Palaka attacked first, pointing to the disparity in forces, arms, and the absence of evidence. On record were four deaths among the villagers, including chief Sikaly and one woman, two wounded villagers, and the arrest of all those who did not flee.[1] With some relish the settler paper *Climats* remarked 'thus the Africans learned that the sorcerer and the RDA lied when they said the teeth of the French are broken'.[2]

Officials raised taxes of villagers favouring the RDA. For example, on 14 March 1950, the elders in the village of Danane gathered 150,000 francs for the families of RDA prisoners. The administrator ordered their treasurer, al Hajj Sori Soumanhoro, to return the money, and then raised taxes which the elders had to produce.[3] Officials turned down the applications by RDA members for import licences to buy cars or other scarce goods. Before pilgrims could leave for Mecca they were required to sign resignations from the RDA. The spiritual leader of the Muslims of Tienne (Odienné) was told by officials he should leave the RDA because Houphouët was not a Muslim. He replied, 'and are you?' RDA supporters found, 'in order to ask for a gun permit one must begin with an *Indépendant* membership card'. In Ivory Coast guns are not only symbols of prestige but also necessary to planters who must keep animals from eating their crops. RDA members learned that 'to get an identity card (and the vote) one must show a card as an *Indépendant*, and the stupidity continues'.[4] Customs held up one million membership cards printed in France for the RDA for 'false declaration of contents'.[5] Officials protected opponents to the RDA, in spite of the many questionable methods they used. *Le Démocrate*, the PDCI paper, printed accounts like the following.

Agboville. In order to show his infinite attachment to the colonialist administration, M. N'Guessan Jean, Secretary of the *Progressistes* presented a lamb to the administrator who had just ended an incendiary anti-RDA speech. As he was about to put the lamb in his truck, a man ran up, furious, and snatched the lamb away. To N'Guessan he shouted, 'This lamb is mine. Who gave it to you? Mr. Administrator, this man is a thief. He stole my lamb. I press charges against him.' M. the administrator of Agboville, embarrassed, preferred to leave rather than arrest his friend. Of course he left the lamb behind. What a regime![6]

[1] *Annex 11348*, op. cit., Houphouët, p. 49, Douzon, p. 186, Péchoux, p. 259, military report, pp. 281 f.   [2] Marc Rucart. *Climats*, 1 December 1949.
[3] Letter in RDA archives, Ouëzzin Coulibaly to administrator, 18 March 1950.
[4] Both citations from *Le Démocrate*, 21 August 1950.
[5] *Annex 11348*, op. cit., Houphouët, pp. 49 f.
[6] *Le Démocrate*, 9 September 1950.

Dubious methods were also used to distribute the cards of parties other than the RDA. Some of the more enterprising Africans bought the cards of several parties, so as to be left undisturbed.[1]

Under this constant fire from the administration, PDCI tactics were at first purely defensive. The leaders still at liberty toured the provinces urging their followers not to reply 'to the provocation of the traitors'. The *parlementaires* wanted to avoid arrest, lest the movement remain without any leaders. They could be arrested, if caught in the act of breaking the law, or if the government convinced Parliament to lift immunity—for 'inciting rebellion' as in the case of the Malgasy deputies. The *parlementaires* explained this to their followers, who asked 'even if you wanted to, could you tell us to fight back?' The answer was 'no'. Villagers at times took matters into their own hands, and transmitted what they called 'silent orders', real or imagined. Meanwhile a debate took place within the RDA, about tactics. The Communist advisors urged direct action; and among the Africans one wing wanted to fight back, while another pointed to the defections from RDA ranks, urged conciliation, and suggested cutting links with the French Communists.

The 'fight back' wing won the debate.[2] By the end of 1949, RDA leaders urged their followers to demonstrate peacefully in front of official residences and prisons, to protest against the arrest of their leaders. Monjauze, administrator of the Abidjan district, found on visiting the villages under his jurisdiction that the inhabitants slipped away, leaving empty huts to greet him when he arrived. On 18 October a tussle took place at Dabou and Akradio between the administrator and the population. First the villagers recovered their leaders whom the administrator had arrested, then troop reinforcements arrived and arrested the RDA leaders as well as many of the followers.[3] In Abidjan the RDA organized large demonstrations and fishing boats in the lagoon carried banners printed with 'Free the innocents', 'We defend liberty', 'We resist oppression'.[4] Peaceful protests were organized throughout the territory, in Bouake, and as far north as Ferkéssedougou near the frontier of Upper Volta. There Marc Rucart, European first college senator from Upper Volta, reported that after he had addressed a large crowd for some fifteen minutes, suddenly, without a sound, most of his audience walked out. He thought a hurricane was expected. When he left too, his path was lined by hundreds of

---

[1] *Annex 11348*, op. cit., Filidori, p. 169.
[2] See Houphouët–d'Arboussier correspondence, op. cit., and *Annex 11348*, op. cit., Sanogo, pp. 479 f. and Houphouët, pp. 487 f.
[3] Ibid., Monjauze, pp. 239, 241–2.
[4] *Le Démocrate*, 3 March 1950.

children chanting RDA slogans.[1] Not only children but also women were active for the RDA since August 1949. They organized many demonstrations particularly during the week of 21 December in front of the prison in Grand Bassam, holding the eight arrested leaders, and before the Governor's palace. The point was, said Mme. Ouëzzin Coulibaly, an organizer of the women, 'to show they could keep up the work of their arrested menfolk'.[2] Senator Marc Rucart reported the women pushed back by guards from the prison, 'lay down on the sidewalk, undressed, and presented their two hundred derrieres to the gendarmes. A burst of water from fire hoses soon re-established reason out of this hysterical behaviour.'[3] RDA militants dubbed this 'la bataille des jets d'eau'.[4]

At the end of 1949, the party decided on several measures.[5] Between 12 and 27 December the eight imprisoned leaders at Grand Bassam went on a hunger strike while their followers demonstrated outside the jail.[6] This, advised by the Communists, never had the wholehearted approval of the RDA militants, particularly not of practicing Muslims. In contrast, all agreed on the boycott of all European goods between 15 December and 1 January. The RDA claimed a sharp decline in the profits of the European importers to one tenth of the normal amount,[7] while the administration claimed that in the long run profits were unaffected, that Africans stored purchases before the strike and quietly made purchases during the night for emergency needs.[8] Without warning for some days beginning 9 January domestic servants disappeared from the homes of Europeans, causing them to do unaccustomed work. From 15 to 19 January there was a boycott of the railroad, which appears to have been unsuccessful.[9] At the end of January there was a strike of fruit and vegetable vendors at the principal market patronized by European housewives.

Meanwhile, in the countryside, during the spring 'incident season', there were numerous demonstrations, mostly in the plantation belt. Quite serious incidents occurred in the Baule area, culminating at Dimbokro, 28–31 January. There was one attempt by officials to arrest President Houphouët, causing a wave of popular protest. It took place two days after the incidents of 22 January in Bouaflé. Houphouët arrived and stayed at the house of an African planter who had recently been arrested. To welcome him in the usual manner,

[1] *Climats*, 15 December 1949.   [2] Citation from an interview in 1956.
[3] *Climats*, 19 January 1950.
[4] I am indebted to Aristide Zolberg for this information.
[5] *Climats*, 15 December 1949.   [6] *Annex 11348*, op. cit., Monjauze, p. 246.
[7] Ibid., Houphouët, p. 52.   [8] Ibid., Monjauze, p. 247.
[9] Ibid., p. 249, also *Climats*, 16 February 1950.

the population from the surrounding villages camped around Houphouët's temporary residence. Among those paying their respects was a local RDA leader, Zoro Bi Tra, wanted by the administration. Shortly after his arrival in the house, soldiers surrounded it, and the assistant attorney-general, together with the captain in command of the troops, challenged Houphouët to turn over the man whom, they claimed, he was hiding. There were several hundred witnesses who knew Zoro Bi Tra was in the house, and Houphouët turned him over to the troops. At that moment, Houphouët could have been charged with *flagrant délit*, and arrested even though a French deputy.

He was not, perhaps simply out of oversight. Several days later, after Houphouët continued on his tour and had arrived at his personal estate at Yamoussoukrou, troops with the assistant attorney-general, demanded the right to enter and arrest Houphouët at 1 a.m. The porter at the estate, well instructed in French law, refused to allow the troops to enter at that hour. The troops retired, and the news of the attempt to arrest Houphouët travelled through the countryside. People started marching on Yamoussoukrou. All night and all day the marching continued, until the roads were blocked, for miles, by crowds. At 4 p.m. on 27 January, the assistant attorney-general again came to the estate; he was allowed to pass by the crowd and made his way in. Houphouët claimed parliamentary immunity from arrest. Houphouët's interpretation of the law was correct; he was not arrested, though the French Communist publicist who was with him was, 'for insulting a magistrate'. It is probable that had Houphouët not used his influence to prevent the crowd from touching the European magistrate, and further, had the magistrate not abandoned his attempt to arrest Houphouët, there would have been violence throughout the region.[1]

The incidents at Dimbokro were clearly connected with the charged atmosphere resulting from the attempted arrest. For Dimbokro is also in Baule country. European–African relations were bad, and both groups disliked the administrator, an Annamite mulatto named Montel. As early as February 1949 the administrator reported small incidents, when the RDA majority chased six chiefs out of their villages.[2] On 29 January 1950 the excited RDA supporters had not yet returned from the pilgrimage to Yamoussoukrou. At 5 a.m. Montel arrested the RDA leader Samba Ambroise, a trader and planter who had been in the *Syndicat*. It was Ambroise's

[1] *Annex 11348*, op. cit., Houphouët, p. 61, Léon, p. 87; Monnet, p. 141; Denise, p. 431; see also *Climats*, 22 June, 27 July, 31 August 1950.
[2] *Annex 11348*, op. cit., Léon, p. 77, and annex of documents submitted by Péchoux, p. 328.

fifth arrest in two years, this time for ordering that RDA opponents not be sold food at the market. Montel charged further that Ambroise, who had urged the confiscation of any imported goods bought during the boycott, had stolen goods in his possession.[1] Montel ordered a search of RDA headquarters and the arrest of several others also.

Then people massed in protest, and for some 48 hours the crowd in the market-place grew larger and larger. Some wore warrior fetishes, carried hoes and sticks. Homes, farms, and stores were deserted, as between two and four thousand demonstrated. Tension grew. The families of the Europeans took refuge at the official residence. The crowd wanted Samba back, and the administrator wanted to regain control. He called for troops which arrived by the 30th. The European territorial councillor Filidori wanted to avoid bloodshed and urged RDA secretary general Denise be called to speak to the crowd. But it was too late. At 2 p.m. on the 30th Montel ordered the troops to clear the market-place, ten minutes later the firing began,[2] and thirteen Africans were killed while the official estimate of the wounded varied between twenty and forty.[3] Some officials claimed the Africans fired first.[4] This the RDA hotly denied, and their lawyer (a Communist, Blanche Matarasso) claimed the Africans, unarmed and in flight were taken in a crossfire between troops and settlers.[5] Lt. Lefèbvre who with one other European officer commanded the troops admitted that they 'were not able to control the troops as well as might have been expected'.[6] The bodies were buried in a common grave early on the morning of the 31st; they were buried in separate graves only after autopsies were performed on 4 February. The records did not show if the bullets causing death came from military rifles or from weapons of the calibre owned by the white settlers.[7] A painting of the shootings at Dimbokro, by Ouëzzin Coulibaly, decorated RDA headquarters in Treichville. It became the special task of a group of paratroopers to confiscate it.

There was yet another serious incident in this region at about the same time—the death of the Baule Senator Biaka Boda. It illustrates the climate of fear and violence, and of baseless rumours of the time. Biaka Boda disappeared on the night of 28 January, when he was carrying a letter from Houphouët to the attorney-general at Bouaflé.

[1] *Annex 11348*, de Montera, p. 206, and Houphouët, p. 67.
[2] Ibid., Filidori, p. 166.
[3] Ibid., Péchoux's annex of medical report, p. 267, Matarasso, p. 173, de Montera, p. 206.
[4] Ibid., Houphouët, p. 69.   [5] Ibid., Matarasso, pp. 173, 185.
[6] Ibid., Lefèbvre, p. 688.   [7] Ibid., Péchoux's annex, p. 267.

His disappearance gave rise to a story sensational enough to attract a world-wide attention the incidents never received. The British student of French politics Peter Campbell,[1] and the American publicist John Gunther[2] both picked up statements perhaps in the American and the French press that Biaka Boda had been 'eaten by his constituents'. Campbell even embroidered the rumour by saying, 'His two wives believe he has been eaten by some of his cannibal constituents'. It is hard to be certain who first launched the rumour. Senator Marc Rucart, when charged, staunchly denied having given this item of information either to the American press or to French *Paris-Presse*. He certainly transmitted the rumour, as well as such others as Boda, fearing for his life, fled to Liberia, to Nigeria, even to Chicago.[3]

What were the facts? Boda's skeletal remains, and some of his clothes and papers were found. He had last been seen near the home of an Almamy in the vicinity of Daloa, where people were still excited over the attempt to arrest Houphouët. These facts came out at an official inquiry. The remaining facts, reconstructed by his successor as Senator, Ouëzzin Coulibaly, are the following. On the road near Daloa, Boda's car broke down. He sent his chauffeur for spare parts, and remained alone in the car, surrounded by the forest. It was night. He became afraid—for fear was in the air after the many incidents. To prevent opponents from acquiring his notes, he threw his notebook into the dense foliage, where it was later recovered. He then started to walk to the nearest village, to seek shelter. He was taken in by a local Muslim leader, an Almamy. During the night, the agents of the local chief—newly installed in office because of his opposition to the RDA—dragged Boda from sleep, and took him into the forest for questioning. A small, slight man, Boda died under the ill treatment he received at the hands of his questioners. These men became afraid; they were not certain that their action would be covered by the administration, and were afraid of vengeance from fervent RDA militants. So they left his body in the forest. The damp heat, together with ants and insects, caused Boda's corpse to disintegrate quickly; and therefore only the skeleton was found. In 1953 Boda was officially declared dead by a French court of inquiry. Nothing was said about the circumstances under which he met his death.

While the incidents in Baule country were the most serious, quite a few others took place, at Zénouala on 14 December 1949, Bouaké

---

[1] Campbell, 'Vérification . . .', op. cit., p. 68, n. 10.
[2] Gunther, John. *Inside Africa*, Harper & Bros., New York, 1955, p. 872.
[3] *Annex 11348*, op. cit., Rucart, pp. 1031 f.

on 2 January 1950, Daloa on the 5th, N'Gorko on the 6th, Adzopé on the 17th, and many other places. This was the general pattern. First Africans secure in the knowledge of administrative support quarrelled with RDA members. The opponents frequently belonged to different social groups than RDA members. The administrator following instructions, sided with the opponents and arrested the local RDA leaders whether or not they had been involved in the quarrel. Then the market-place filled with people, who appointed a delegation to ask for the release of the leaders. The official refused the request—and the crowd remained gathered at the market place. Responding to instructions, the hostility of the crowd, and sometimes to the urgings of local European settlers, the administrator called for troops which used force to disperse the unarmed crowd.

As the lines between Europeans and Africans were sharply drawn, the Churches became involved. Catholics were told of the incompatibility of Communism and Catholicism, in a pastoral letter by Monseigneur Thévenoud, Bishop of Ouagadougou, dated 3 May 1948. The explanations why conversions largely stopped during the repression, and most RDA militants who were Catholics left the Church, can be found in a letter from Ouëzzin Coulibaly. He wrote

'at Toumoudi, some Catholic comrades asked that a memorial mass be said for the thirteen relations who were shot at Dimbokro. The Reverend Father Rey, who officiated at the mass, was sent back to France the same week; he was not even allowed time to pack. . . . On 23 May our comrade Albert Yaya died, the leader of the RDA at Tabou. Five years ago he was married in church. The Catholic mission refused him the last sacrament and a Christian burial.'[1]

Not all the Catholic missionaries agreed with this policy of the Church. Wrote a missionary: 'It is true, for I must be honest, that the missionaries were lax in their duties and did not oppose the oppressors . . . Good priests, zealous, . . . but it must be said that the social side of the Church's teaching was largely overlooked by them.' There were those who discounted the exaggerated reports of Communist influence, and recognized that the incidents, explained mostly in terms of ethnic rivalries, 'certainly did not disturb the settlers, who rubbed their hands and said openly "let them kill each other" '.[2] They transmitted their views to left-wing Catholic circles in Paris, where by 1950 rare individuals like Mlle. Claude Gérard began to work on behalf of a new policy towards the RDA.

By spring 1950, the official records showed that 52 African men,

---

[1] From unpublished letter, 28 May 1950.
[2] Both citations from unpublished letter by Père Bidon, 7 January 1952.

women, and children had lost their lives, that several hundred more were wounded, and that some 3,000 were in jail.[1] But these figures are certainly too low since they do not account for the many casualties which administrators and RDA leaders were too busy to record. The incidents brought to the surface most of the controversies—about land and water, religion, tribes, economic interests, women, and chieftaincy—which existed in the heterogeneous Ivory Coast society. Indeed matters had gone so far that both the administration and the RDA found themselves enlisting support among witch-doctors. RDA funds were low, and Houphouët had already advanced 3 million francs cfa to the movement.[2] Both administrators and RDA leaders came to realize they were losing control and that the countryside was near anarchy. European planters were anxious to get back to planting. 'We all need peace now. The plantations which used to produce 6,000 tons of coffee now yield only 2,000, and next year none at all,' said their spokesman, Filidori, in the *conseil général*.[3] Robert Léon, a settler close to the PDCI, mentioned the high cost of the incidents—some 15 million francs cfa to bring the troops from Dakar and for the Alaouites alone. Then 'they build a bridge, on a road which has no commercial value, and will cost 15–20 million'.[4] Many Africans and Europeans in Ivory Coast were anxious to return to normal.

Since the spring of 1950 Houphouët was in Paris, engaged in political negotiations. The results were evident in the fall. Overseas Minister Mitterrand spoke of wanting to reduce the incidents to their true proportions, the 'divergence between tribes exploited by the Communist party in order to encourage disorder'.[5] The RDA *parlementaires*, for their party, after a lengthy internal debate, accepted Houphouët's thesis, 'we were wrong in allowing the use of the COMMUNIST PRETEXT as a justification for a retrograde policy and for division among Africans . . . the battle continues but without the pretext of Communism'.[6] The secretary-general of the RDA, Gabriel d'Arboussier did not want disaffiliation from the French Communists in Parliament, and he resigned under pressure from his colleagues before they issued, in September 1950, the communique announcing disaffiliation. This laid the basis for a new policy of co-operation, hard to implement because tension in Ivory Coast was high, and both the settlers and the French Communists tried to upset the new policy. The transition was awkward, and began

---

[1] *Esprit*, December 1951, p. 832, *Annex 11348*, op. cit., p. 288.
[2] Ibid., Houphouët, p. 47.   [3] Ibid., Filidori, p. 167.
[4] Ibid., Léon, p. 85.
[5] *Marchés Coloniaux*, 7 October 1950, p. 2373.
[6] Houphouët, 'Réponse a d'Arboussier', *Afrique Noire*, 24 July 1952.

publicly in Ivory Coast when the Overseas Minister invited the RDA deputies to attend the inaugural ceremonies of the newly completed port of Abidjan in February 1951.

When they heard this the settler extremists lamented, 'how completely the policy in Paris can destroy the patiently elaborate work of the men on the spot'.[1] The French Communists attacked 'the slave traders, the purveyors of prisoners who might call themselves Pleven, Queuille, René Mayer, Péchoux, Béchard and Co., as well as their accomplices, some of the RDA leaders like Houphouët-Boigny'.[2] The French Communist lawyers of the Secours Populaire who were in Ivory Coast urged the RDA prisoners to petition for amnesty, a policy they knew would delay action on the appeal then lodged in the courts, and therefore keep them in jail longer. The lawyers solicited from the RDA prisoners a letter asking the *parlementaires* not to attend the ceremonies at the port. With some difficulty deputy Ouëzzin Coulibaly convinced the prisoners of the need for the new policy, and argued, 'the port stays when the French go'.[3] Then the RDA dismissed the Communist lawyers, who had worked for a very small fee—150,000 francs cfa a month plus expenses while the usual fee was 500,000 francs cfa. The RDA view was, 'We could hardly keep and pay lawyers who stepped out of their role as our defenders and took it upon themselves to disapprove publicly of our political line'. At the same time the RDA *parlementaires* explained, 'we suffer from our knowledge that at the very moment when they repeated with us that we were not Communists, they had perhaps in the back of their minds the idea that they had us, without our knowledge, encircled. We suffer from the knowledge that in the eyes of Europeans we seem to remain eternally big children, who are to be enjoyed and easily led into changing their minds.'[4]

The RDA leaders attended the opening of the port, and for the first time in some years shared the same platform with the overseas minister and the governor, as well as with visiting dignitaries like Lamine Guèye of Senegal. The crowd of Abidjan came, though they showed their primary allegiance by leaving as soon as Houphouët left. Nevertheless, formally, peace was declared.

By May 1951, the French government transferred Governor

[1] *Climats*, 15 February 1951.
[2] *La Défense* (Secours Populaire), special issue on Ivory Coast trials, Paris, c. 1951.
[3] Private letter written from Ivory Coast by a non-Communist European close to the RDA, 9 August 1950.
[4] Both citations from 'To him or those who wrote this letter'; reply, probably written by Ouëzzin Coulibaly, to an attack upon the RDA *parlementaires* by African students in Paris, c. 1952.

Péchoux to Togo (where he was to carry on a repressive policy against the nationalist *Comité d'Unité Togolaise*). But it took longer to transfer the officials lower in the hierarchy who had been picked for their qualities in implementing a policy of repression. They stayed long enough to carry out the plan to falsify the results of the June 1951 parliamentary elections, with the assistance of chiefs appointed during the repression. Afterwards Prince Adingra, chief of the Abrong and President of the *Association des Chefs Coutumiers de la Côte d'Ivoire* remarked, 'did we not expend our energies without limit in order to assure the election of Sékou Sanogo, our deputy? Thus we took one seat from our political adversaries who lied when they said they were assured of total victory',[1] Though Houphouët was re-elected, officials recorded the defeat of Ouëzzin Coulibaly by Sanogo.

The techniques French officials used to falsify the 1951 Ivory Coast elections are worth examining since similar ones were used in other French-speaking territories.[2] There were such simple tactics as reducing Ouëzzin Coulibaly's audience among Upper Voltans in Ivory Coast, by emphasizing the points dividing Bobo from Mossi. There was a distinctly political flavour to Governor Péchoux's hospitality, for ten days, to a Mossi delegation of chiefs and *élus*.[3] Other techniques are summarized in the documents presented by the RDA to the credentials committee of the 1951 National Assembly, where they challenged, unsuccessfully, Sanogo's election. First, the administration named only opponents of the RDA to be members of the commissions charged with revising and correcting the electoral register and with supervising the distribution of cards among the electors. Hence members were officers of the Socialists, the two *Indépendant* parties, the *Progressistes*, and the president of the *Association des Chefs Coutumiers de la Côte d'Ivoire*. These men were well qualified to point out to the European members of the commissions the identity of the local RDA militants in each area. Second, men known to be RDA were crossed off the electoral register, even though they had been qualified to vote in previous elections. Known opponents of the RDA were enrolled even if their claims to the vote were unfounded in law. Third, in accordance with the enlarged franchise provisions of the 1951 electoral law, additional voters were placed on the rolls. In Ivory Coast the increase was no more than 1 per cent., 'while in Soudan the increase was 479 per cent., and even in the desert area of Mauretania the increase was 79 per cent'.[4] The largest increase in qualified voters—far out of proportion

[1] *Climats*, 13 September 1951.
[2] See Senghor's attack on the falsification, *Afrique Nouvelle*, 9–15 July 1950.
[3] *Climats*, 6 March 1951.   [4] From the RDA documents, 1951.

with the population figures—was in the Muslim area of Odienné, the Abrong area of Boundoukou, and the Agni area of Abengourou. In these areas, the RDA's opponents had some following. The increase in the number of those entitled to vote in the highly populated Baule and southern areas was negligible; indeed in some Baule areas the number decreased. Fourth, the local administrator in many areas announced his opposition to the RDA, restricted the movements of RDA campaigners and their right to call propaganda meetings, as well as covered the use of intimidating methods by RDA opponents. Fifth, though by law each party presenting candidates was entitled to be represented at the polls, in many areas officials excluded RDA representatives from the polls. In and around the polls, RDA voters were beaten, while the ballot papers of parties opposed to the RDA were distributed illegally in the market-place. Officials paid no attention to the legally required precautions to keep the vote secret.

The falsification of the 1951 elections ended the official repression of the PDCI. But the consequences were many, on relations among all groups in Ivory Coast—European and African—and were evident throughout the ten years preceding, in 1960, the independence, of Ivory Coast.

Division in Unity

The past left its legacy. One of the aims of the administration had been to restore its authority, yet in 1950 official prestige could hardly have been lower. 'To each burst of a gun is attached one name: that of the Governor Péchoux,'[1] said the secretary-general of the RDA, Denise, and the party paper spoke of 'the Proconsul ALIBABA, that great big wicked wolf'.[2] In African eyes the French institutions were discredited.

They have degraded the institutions by cynical collusion. They subordinate justice to a criminal policy: making war on men, women and children; destroying civilians pitilessly with bombs. They have degraded the institutions by setting up extraordinary courts, by discriminating against their political adversaries, against all those who fight for peace and liberty. They cover for thieves, high grade crooks, assassins, jail birds, all types of stooges bent on revenge against honest people whose only crime is their fight against colonialism and imperialism. They have violated the legal code . . . Judges have become deaf and blind towards the stooges' crimes, and exceptionally vigilant towards RDA militants, who are sentenced according to a pre-established table of sentences, like a table of prices . . . The prisons have become our schools in citizenship . . . You, in your

---

[1] *Annex 11348*, op. cit., Denise, p. 399.
[2] *Le Démocrate*, 15 December 1950.

folly, will have degraded your institutions, which one day, like you, will be swept out by the people, who want to live free and happy.[1]

The French authorities accepted, after the incidents, the power of the PDCI. It grew steadily clearer that the government of France would yield to each successive demand of the PDCI. When the PDCI informally vetoed an action the Governor was aware he could only resort to force—and Paris forbade this. First the French government replaced the officials who had been involved in the repression. Soon, like for the BDS of Senegal, the French government replaced any officials, including governors, who displeased the PDCI. By 1956, when Houphouët became a French minister, administrators knew their jobs depended upon the PDCI, and as a result backed down or asked the party for help when they had to implement unpopular decisions. As for the courts, judgements also reflected the new balance of power in Ivory Coast. Between 1951 and 1953 there were trials of PDCI militants involved in the incidents.[2] In 1950 the charges against the eight top RDA leaders were 'rebellion, complicity in rebellion, pillaging, and destruction'.[3] By 1953, however, in the words of Mê Josse, one of the lawyers for the prosecution, the charges 'had no further political content'.[4] In 1956 the French government sponsored a law lifting the political disqualifications of some 3,000 people who had been arrested during the incidents,[5] which made it possible for almost all to receive their political rewards over the next years.

The end of the incidents also marked a complete change in the position of the European settlers. The administration no longer was at their disposal, and they also became increasingly dependent upon the pleasure of the PDCI. The African planters had won their struggle. Yet they did not use their new political power directly against the economic position of French investors. On the contrary; after the incidents the territorial assembly even granted a long-term non-transferable lease to a French rubber plantation combine to transfer its activities from Vietnam to Ivory Coast. The PDCI took care to point out 'no *colon*, no (European) trader, no European civilian was disturbed (during the incidents), and yet their dispersal

---

[1] *Le Démocrate*, 4 August 1950.
[2] For reports of the trials, which took place between 1950 and 1953, see *Humanité*, 17 March 1950; *Climats*, 23 March and 6 April 1950; *Libération*, 25 June 1952; *France–Afrique*, 21 June and 10 July 1952; *la Côte d'Ivoire*, 12 July 1952; *Monde-Ouvrier*, 5–11 July and 9–15 August 1952; *l'Observateur*, 24 July 1952; *Témoignage Chrétien*, 25 July 1952; *la Défense*, 25 July–8 August 1952; *Afrique Informations*, 1 and 15 April 1953; *l'Observateur*, 9 April 1953; *le Monde*, 17 and 21 April 1953; *Monde-Ouvrier*, 11–17 April 1953; *France–Afrique*, 21 April 1953.
[3] From the unpublished records of the defence attorney.
[4] *France–Afrique*, 21 April 1953.   [5] Siriex, op. cit., p. 236.

P

in the forest made them very vulnerable'.[1] Increasingly, however, French economic interests centred on activities other than planting, and French companies took care to include PDCI planters and traders on their boards.

While the PDCI leaders acted on the belief that their economic interests and those of European settlers and investors coincided, they took care to change relations at the political and social level. The end of the repression opened a new era in social relations between Europeans and Africans. Gradually racial discrimination disappeared from the towns though as late as 1957 the *Cercle Sportif d'Abidjan* was reserved to Europeans only, and even then the only Africans invited to join were Félix Houphouët-Boigny and Ouëzzin Coulibaly. Indeed, to replace the *Sportif* at the top of Abidjan society, Governor Messmer in co-operation with RDA leaders sponsored the *Cercle d'Amitié*, where Europeans and Africans met. At about the same time a swimming pool in Abidjan still practised discrimination, and changed course only after the territorial assembly threatened to withdraw ground rights.

The settlers accepted the PDCI, and changed tactics to make relations as good as possible. Though some wanted to, they could not join the PDCI which after disaffiliating from the French Communists in Parliament made clear it wanted to remain an exclusively African party. Most settlers changed their party from RPF to the UDSR, with which the PDCI was allied in the French Parliament. For their part, until independence the PDCI leaders treated the settlers like a somewhat privileged ethnic minority. President Houphouët insisted that the PDCI sponsor some settlers in elections. Hence the 1952 'unity' list included 4 Europeans among 32 second college candidates; there were, however, at least 3 Africans among the 18 elected to the first college. Though in 1954 the proportion of Africans to Europeans living in the *commune mixte* of Abidjan was, roughly, 16:1, the PDCI sponsored the election by single college of 10 Europeans and 20 Africans to the city council.[2] Similar tactics were used in the 1956 municipal elections. In 1957 the territorial assembly elections, the first held by single electoral college, the PDCI sponsored 10 Europeans out of a total of 60, making the proportion of Europeans to Africans in Ivory Coast higher than in any other territory. The PDCI maintained this 'unity' tactic in the elections for the legislative assembly of April 1959 and abandoned it only after independence.

Determined PDCI co-operation with the European residents was

---

[1] RDA electoral manifesto, June 1951.
[2] *Afrique Informations*, 1 June 1954.

one of the concessions the PDCI leaders made to the French authorities. There were others. The militantly anti-colonial pronouncement disappeared, at least in the French language. The new emphasis was on constitutional methods and on reforms which simply extended already existing French policies—the Code du Travail, equality between African and European soldiers, the extension of the franchise, the single electoral college, municipal reforms, extended powers for the territorial assembly, and internal self government.[1] There was no challenge from Ivory Coast to France's rejection of independence. On the contrary, for a decade after the repression and especially after 1956 the PDCI leaders became loyal backers of French policy, pushing no faster than French officials were willing to go.

Even while the PDCI conciliated European residents and assured the French administration of their loyalty, the party leaders proceeded to consolidate the ground lost during the repression. Over the next decade there was a general settling of accounts, as the PDCI reasserted control over most Ivory Coast institutions. Loyal party men took the lead in associations of veterans, ethnic groups, *originaires* from a given region, professionals, businessmen, teachers, civil servants, workers, young people, indeed even ·sportsmen, musicians, market-women, and co-religionists. The civil service reinstated PDCI men, and promoted them. Customs released the PDCI cards impounded during the repression, which the party distributed during 1956. PDCI militants could again expect gun permits and import licences;[2] even ferry operators who had been loyal to the PDCI received medals for long service. Students who had lost their grants for political reasons again received aid. Many chiefs deposed for loyalty to the PDCI were restored to their posts. The PDCI made a point of defeating Sékou Sanogo when he stood in his native constituency for election to the 1952 territorial assembly. Governor Péchoux dropped his charges against Ouëzzin Coulibaly, whom the territorial assembly elected a Senator in 1953, a post again conferring the parliamentary immunity he lost in the rigged elections of 1951. In all the elections after 1952 the PDCI won overwhelming victories.[3]

Nevertheless after the crisis of the repression the PDCI, as an organization, was weaker than it had ever been, partly because it operated in new conditions. Unity was pressed less upon the party from the outside and therefore it had to find more cohesive forces

[1] RDA electoral manifesto, June 1951 elections.
[2] *Climats*, 7–13 April 1955.
[3] See the three articles by Aristide Zolberg in *West Africa*, 30 July, 6 and 20 August, 1960.

from within. The fact was, however, that conflicts within the Ivory Coast population became the single most important problem for the party, and holding together preoccupied the leaders of the PDCI. Among Africans the repression had led practically to civil war, as the many conflicts of interest and outlook which characterized the heterogeneous population of Ivory Coast came to the surface. Since the PDCI remained dominant and continued to attract mass support, the many conflicts came out within the party.

This was illustrated by the way people developed a new vocabulary to differentiate degrees of party loyalty. There were the 'hard' PDCI members loyal since 1945. At the territorial level this included the *parlementaires* with immunity, and the 'martyrs' in jail or otherwise penalized by the administration. There were the 'soft' members, including some wealthy planter-traders who simply withdrew from politics. As the repression progressed, moreover, and the PDCI was seen as the sole source of legitimacy, opposition to the party became tantamount to treason. Afterwards there was little room for the idea of a loyal opposition to take root. The terms 'traitor' or *administratif* came to refer to those who yielded under official pressure and organized one of the opposition parties. *Progréssiste* and *Indépendant* were used as terms of insults. (Later the terms 'ex-RDA-RDA' referred to those who quit the party during the repression but returned afterwards; neo-RDA came to refer to those not involved in the incidents at all—men away as students, soldiers, civil servants or traders, for example.)

The new vocabulary was a corollary of the incidents which set ethnic groups against each other, divided families, generations, indeed in some areas even caused the physical separation of villages into 'A' and 'B' sections—Sikensi, for example, in the subdivision of Bouafle.[1] The decision taken in Paris and Abidjan—that French officials and the PDCI would co-operate—could not simply arrest the revolutionary pressures in the countryside. Incidents continued with a momentum of their own. After the 1956 PDCI victory in elections to the French National Assembly, there followed a wave of *règlement des comptes* incidents in the villages. People felt certain the administration would never again falsify elections.

Among Muslims in Issia, for example, there were incidents when PDCI 'martyrs' refused 'traitors' the right of burial in their cemetery. On the Liberian frontier there were incidents between Wobe and Yacouba. In the vicinity of Man an age-group called the 'troops of the elephant' carried out a policy of revenge against former

[1] Gouvernement Général de l'AOF, Côte d'Ivoire, *Éducation de base*, 1955, mimeographed, pp. 19–20.

opponents. The elephant is the symbol of the RDA, but the 'troops' in Man were certainly not under orders from the territorial headquarters. They simply assumed the 'silent order' system of 1950 still applied—that even if the PDCI leaders wanted to they could not order revenge without risking prison. The 'troops' forced former opponents to pay large sums for the PDCI cards, destroyed property, and committed some acts of personal violence. The administrator placed those he considered responsible in jail, and called for help from the PDCI. Headquarters in Abidjan sent a delegation, which discovered the wrong people were in jail. Yet so great was local solidarity with the leaders of the 'troops' that the prisoners chose to stand trial rather than inform—they felt certain of acquittal.

Another example of the divisive heritage of the repression was events in Boundoukou on the frontier of Ghana. There were many historic differences between the Muslim *dioula* who were descendants of partisans of the nineteenth century warrior Samory Touré, and the animist majority of Abrong under their chief Prince Adingra. During the incidents the Muslims remained loyal to the PDCI, while the Abrong opposed the party. After 1951 the Abrong, 'traitors' in the eyes of the Muslim followers of the Almamy, once again joined the PDCI, and hence it was within the party that the many and ancient conflicts between the two groups became expressed.

Acting in part on the theory that unity among the leaders might arrest the conflicts among their kinsmen, President Houphouët proceeded to reunite the elite of 1945. To former opposition leaders he offered protection against popular pressure for revenge, and other incentives. In spite of protests from among his *militants* he insisted on including four former adversaries on the list for the territorial assembly of 1952. Even Prince Adingra hastened to take out a party card, became a territorial councillor, and went so far as to 'adopt' as his son Ouëzzin Coulibaly whose father had died. This process of restoring unity among the elite which had been divided in the repression led in 1961 to the designation of two of them—Tidiani Dem in 1959 and Kouakou Aoulou in 1961—ministers in Ivory Coast governments.

The new unity was fragile and only on the top layer of Ivory Coast society. Though the former opposition parties faded away without official support and without leaders, in the countryside the kinsmen of the former *adversaires* were usually the losers in the incidents designed to settle the accounts of the repression. When the party was born a symbol of opposition to authority, the leaders did not try to stop conflict but simply to co-ordinate and use it against the administration. After 1950 new considerations became paramount as the phase of transfer of power began and the party came on to the side of law and order. Yet the party organization was often unable to stop or resolve conflicts. It was hampered by changes among the leaders and the crumbling of the structure which were consequences of the repression.

The PDCI began as an alliance of most forces making for unity in Ivory Coast—the planters, migrants, *dioula* and other immigrant strangers, religious dissidents of both Muslim and Christian inspiration, civil servants, traders, professional people, even football players and veterans of French wars. The PDCI had done much to unify representatives of all ethnic groups, of modern and traditional cadres, strangers and *originaires*, planters and migrants, traders and their customers. But this alliance broke up; in 1952 the party could renominate only twelve outgoing territorial councillors. As President Houphouët reported to the July 1955 meeting of the Co-ordinating Committee of the interterritorial RDA, the PDCI lost 'first the chiefs, then the civil servants, the small traders whose livelihood depended upon the administration'. And the remaining territorial leaders found themselves deeply concerned what further violence 'might have occurred, if in a wave of zenophobic nationalism' they, 'the most responsible and educated Africans had been rejected by the population'.[1] The repression thus reduced further an already far too small group of educated leaders of the PDCI—by discrediting some, and removing others who died, went to jail or were sent to outlying districts. The result was a serious crisis of leadership at the territorial level.

There was also a crisis at the local level. The evidence so far available from the local turnover of leadership suggests there was a pattern in these conflicts. Particularly outside the areas dominated by Houphouët's Baule kinsmen, 'traitors' were often men with privileges to lose, and with a claim to traditional status among the *originaires*, the tribe owning the land. There was frequently no one in the village to replace them having the temperament, training, honesty, and background to run party affairs and settle conflicts. Often those who took their places as party leaders during the conflict were least suited to the responsibilities of peace. Moreover, it was not unusual for men whose claim to local land or status was uncertain, usually 'stranger', to use the occasion of the incidents to show loyalty and so rise. This pattern was suggested in the struggle for leadership in Boundoukou, Man Danané, Gagnoa, and Daloa, for example, where 'strangers' made dramatic sacrifices during the repression. The available evidence suggests another pattern, however, in predominantly Baule areas. There often the 'strangers' under

---

[1] From the RDA records of the Conakry meeting.

pressure from the administration were accusers of Baule 'martyrs' in the repression. For many Baule the ideas of 'traitor' and 'stranger' became closely associated, while in much of the rest of the country, the ideas of '*originaire*' and 'traitor' became linked.

Under the impact of the repression the party weakened also because its intermediate structure withered away. Many local and village committees of the PDCI which had emerged spontaneously after the war, though they continued to exist, were deeply involved in ethnic conflicts which the ethnic basis of local organization did little to reduce. Most formal links broke between the village committee and territorial headquarters in Abidjan. In the *sous-sections* it was hard to know which of many rival claimants to leadership had valid credentials.

The crisis of structure and leadership came to a head in December 1952, at the party conference in Treichville. The issues were many. The disorder of the *sous-sections* was evident from the presence of many rival delegations. Who were to be permanent employees of the party, and who would pay them? Few of the *sous-sections* had paid for all the cards they had ordered from headquarters, or for their subscriptions to *Afrique Noire* (the non-Communist RDA paper which succeeded *Réveil* in Dakar). Some militants were selling party cards at exhorbitant prices, extorting protection money from former enemies, and stealing party funds. There were debts. The president of the session of 21 December remarked, 'It is important that the party cards be sold before the collection of taxes. The enthusiasm of debate is being replaced by a progressive cooling in mass sentiment. There is discouragement among our militant comrades who are not satisfied in their requests addressed to the authorities . . .' Over and above the financial and administrative questions the most serious issue was who spoke for the PDCI? As President Denise remarked, 'the discouragement of the masses comes from the chill among the leaders. The matter can only be cured in the *comité directeur.*'[1]

The problem had a long history. In the PDCI as in the interterritorial RDA after the 1948 Abidjan congress the theory was the *élus* were subject to control by the *militants* in the *comité directeur*. Before the repression this rule was not much of an issue. The two groups interlocked, fresh elections kept changing *militants* into *élus*, and the two groups kept a common front against the Europeans. By 1949 most *militants* were fully convinced of the usefulness of the rule after they saw the majority of territorial councillors elected on the party ticket turn 'traitor'. But in 1950, the *parlementaires*

---

[1] Citations from records of the December 1952 PDCI Conference.

violated the rule. While party machinery in Ivory Coast crumbled they took it upon themselves to change to a policy of co-operation with the government. They did not refer this decision to the interterritorial co-ordinating committee until 1955. Nor did the PDCI *comité directeur* have an opportunity to express an opinion.

Behind the confusion of party institutions was the confusion of leadership resulting from the repression. Less than half of the *bureau politique* were legally free for political action. It was uncertain who was in the *comité directeur* as long as the credentials of rival *sous-section* leaders were not sorted out. As for the *élus*, most from the *conseil général* were in jail, retired from active politics, or 'traitors'. Then President Houphouët effectively chose as PDCI-supported candidates for the 1952 territorial assembly some who were 'soft' party members, 'traitors', and Europeans. This outraged many *militants* and 'martyrs'.

Hence at the conference of 1952 there was sharp protest against the way recent party decisions had been taken. Yet those who protested had difficulty proposing alternative procedures. Except for Ouëzzin Coulibaly—dubbed the 'Lion' of the repression—they were mostly second-rank leaders. The important 'martyrs' were still in jail. No one wanted to challenge Houphouët personally. Without an effective *bureau politique* they could not demand Houphouët submit decisions to its control, and they did not want to make the *bureau politique* effective by filling the seats temporarily vacated by the 'martyrs'. They could not propose a reorganization of the *bureau politique* until the many conflicting credentials at the level of the *sous-section* were settled, for only then could the *comité directeur* be truly representative, and elect a valid new *bureau politique*. Nor did the *militants* want to give formal authority to the new *élus*, or to the tiny group of *parlementaires*. There were long and stormy sessions, opened and closed by President Houphouët's appeals to unity. At the end, they came to only one conclusion: the party had to be reorganized. Ouëzzin Coulibaly was requested to do this in addition to his work as interterritorial RDA political director.

The fact was those who survived as territorial leaders of the PDCI became preoccupied with the transfer of power and took on governmental duties in France, West Africa, the territorial assembly, the Ivory Coast government, and the civil service. They did not reconstruct the party structure or even call a territorial congress until 1959. The members of the *comité directeur* and the *bureau politique* remained as in 1949; they sometimes co-opted a man to fill a vacancy. In theory the occasional conferences of *élus*, *sous-section* leaders, and members of the *comité directeur* chose candidates for election and took important decisions. But in practice power became progressively concentrated in the hands of President Houphouët.

He did not use his authority to halt this process. On the contrary. Houphouët often ignored disagreement with his policies from the PDCI *comité directeur*—for example, the demand he resign from the French government in 1956 unless African troops were immediately withdrawn from the Algerian war; or the rejection of his choice of the French UDSR leader Joseph Perrin as Senator from Ivory Coast in 1956. Houphouët went considerably further than most of his colleagues wanted, in conciliating European opinion in France and Africa, and in discarding the idea of eventual independence. Far from using his authority to institutionalize collective leadership and responsibility (as did for example Modibo Keïta, Mamadou Konaté, or Sékou Touré) Houphouët appealed over the heads of his own associates to the masses. The status of every other Ivory Coast leader became dependent upon his personal relationship with Houphouët, and no party decisions became final without him. This made running things in his frequent absences difficult. There were more effects. As increasingly the leadership became ossified, Houphouët alone could recruit new men to the party. There were no regular channels through which new individuals could rise in the ranks of the party, challenge the policy decisions taken at the top, express the growing number of grievances about corruption and nepotism, or settle the many ethnic and other conflicts which arose within the party community at the grass roots level.

Without structure or precedure, the approach to issues in practice was short-term and piecemeal. Conflict was accepted as natural, and the press, party leaders, *élus*, civil servants, and President Houphouët simply ignored it where possible. PDCI leaders were glad to take assistance, for example, for reconciling conflicts among the Baule in the PDCI, from paramount chief Kouakou Anoublé. Only the most serious matters came before President Houphouët, and the one other man with some authority to settle matters, Ouëzzin Coulibaly. In their piecemeal approach the PDCI leaders used to argue 'the RDA does not need you; you need the RDA'. It is not certain whether a more systematic approach to settling the many conflicts would have been any more successful in making the transition from revolutionary opposition to responsibility among the heterogeneous population of Ivory Coast.

In the midst of conflict all claimed loyalty to the RDA. Around the party the leaders wove a national myth, having as prime elements President Houphouët, the end of forced labour, and the victorious emergence from the repression. The party surrounded President Houphouët with veneration, as the sage whose wisdom knew no bounds, who had abolished forced labour and led his people from the repression to prosperity. Though hardly a partisan of any cult of personality, the poet Bernard Dadié, the son of a founder of the *Syndicat* and himself one of the eight martyrs of the 6 February incidents, expressed how people thought of Houphouët:

> . . .
> As *griot* of the century, on the *cora* of old Africa,
> Today in turmoil
> Through the cities and the prisons
> Under the baobabs at the crossroads
> > To each
> > I clamour
> > You are the Master!
>
> . . .
> You are the master
> It's you who plants the rice
> It's you who works the wool
> It is you who builds the mansions
> It's you who dies of hunger
> It is you who walks on knees
> It is you who sleeps under the stars
>
> . . .
> > To each
> > I clamour
> > You are the king of the factories
> > You are the king of the fields
> > You are the people
> > You are the master![1]

The use the party made of the repression was similar to the use Gaullists made of Resistance victory over Vichy. This could be observed, for example, at the ceremonies surrounding the inauguration of the regional PDCI headquarters at Agboville in the plantation belt during 1956. A large crowd attended, and from Abidjan came PDCI deputy Ouëzzin Coulibaly, secretary-general Auguste Denise, and a large group of party dignitaries. The land for the building belonged to Doudou Guèye, who gave it to the party shortly after the war; the PDCI put up only a temporary building. In 1950 officials ordered the party to build a permanent structure or forfeit the land. Volunteers put up a concrete structure in a month. Nevertheless, officials requisitioned the land, claiming the value of the building was too low to meet zoning laws. By 1956, however, the party resumed ownership of land and building. Hence the celebration, and many reminiscences. While people danced, sang, strutted around on

[1] Dadié, *Afrique debout*, op. cit., pp. 17–8, 'Tu es le maître' dedicated to Houphouët-Boigny.

stilts, brandishing Houphouët lockets and cloths as well as the *tricolor*, party officials made speeches in four languages. 'Yesterday they took the house; today they return it. The times change. The whites are like chameleons, while we remain the same. They have a special kind of character. They recognize and respect force.' Drums, cries of *'Vive RDA'*, and songs accompanied these statements. 'None dares to show he is not RDA.' The local 'martyrs' were praised, and individually applauded by the crowd. Finally a village elder poured a libation of gin, exorcized the evil spirits which took the house from the RDA, called for the continued presence of the good spirits which gave the house back to the RDA, and requested the village ancestors to protect the house forever.[1]

The myth of unity in Ivory Coast covered a studied disorder while for almost a decade the main energies of party leaders went into pressing forward on development. Rapid advances in education, health, and other social services accompanied the sharp rise in world prices due to the Korean War. The RDA received the credit for substantially reducing many causes for mass protest—subordinate status for Africans, low incomes, stagnant education, and other services. The government undertook many projects in the villages, and on display in Abidjan.

Development costs money, and increasingly the leaders of Ivory Coast chose policies towards African neighbours and France which resulted in bringing money in. AOF took money out, and since 1947 the territorial assembly of Ivory Coast objected. The objections and the sums grew after the boom of the Korean War; the share of Ivory Coast by 1955 was 30 per cent. of the imports and 50 per cent. of the exports of AOF.[2] In spite of a long record of backing federal ties within the interterritorial RDA at the governmental level, President Houphouët was the main African spokesman for the French policy of eliminating AOF. It was a painless way to increase greatly the assets of his government. It made possible in 1959 lower taxes for the rich and the elimination of the head tax for villagers. Most new wealth of Ivory Coast was still in the hands of a minority. In 1959 according to official statistics out of a total estimated population of three million Africans and 14,000 Europeans half were deemed 'active' but they had very unequal shares of wealth. The 'evolved' class of 12,000 had a total money revenue of ten milliard francs cfa; the 'intermediate' class of 280,000 had a total revenue of 29 milliards cfa; and finally those in 'traditional' society, some 1,300,000 active people had a revenue of only 25 milliards cfa.

[1] Based on personal observation, 1956.
[2] *AOF 1957*, op. cit., p. 134.

Thus less than 1 per cent. of the population had more than one-sixth of the wealth, and less than one-fifth of the population had more than half.[1]

Even while the PDCI leaders moved their country forward or development, they became part of the privileged 1 per cent., and many of the generation of 1945 lost their appetite for revolution. Like Muños-Marín of Puerto Rico, President Houphouët was not inclined to press the point of independence. The French connexion brought in capital. He was satisfied with the pace of transfer of power under the Loi-Cadre, pointed to the scarcity of trained cadres among Africans, and claimed that without development and more education independence was an empty dream.[2]

In this way the PDCI approached yet another crisis, both in its relations with its neighbours of Ghana and Guinea and internally. Cracks in the façade of unity internally were evident from the results of the 1957 territorial assembly elections. The PDCI won 58 of the 60 seats, and the two independents soon afterwards joined the party. All opposition groups together gained no more than 5 per cent. of the votes cast. But general discontent can be deduced if not proved from the abstention rate, 46 per cent.[3] The explanations for growing discontent are several.

Opposition to independence separated the PDCI from the university students returning home first in tens, then in hundreds. In their student politics many sharply opposed the new look of the RDA in October 1950, which was accompanied by the withering away of the RDA student organisation in Paris. Repeatedly, too, the *Association des Élèves et Étudiants de la Côte d'Ivoire* passed resolutions against the official policy of the PDCI.[4] Many, when back in Ivory Coast, considered the repression old history, and independence the burning issue. Many openly snickered at public meetings where President Houphouët spoke in favour of union, fraternity, and co-operation with France. At the same time they were totally dependent upon him for jobs and resented that Europeans still held many top civil service posts and still held elective offices. As student opposition mounted, the PDCI government slowed down Africanization. For a while between 1957 and 1959 it felt it could count on more loyalty from the Europeans than from the African intellectuals.

Nuclei of opposition groups began to crop up. The most

---

[1] *Interafrique Presse*, 11–17 July 1960, p. 17.
[2] See his *Discours et allocations*, April–May 1956, and October–November 1956, printed in pamphlet form by the Service d'Information de la Côte d'Ivoire.
[3] Zolberg in *West Africa*, op. cit., 30 July 1960.
[4] *Afrique Nouvelle*, 6 March 1959.

determined attack on the PDCI came from the *Front de Libération Noire-Kotoko* (FLN-Kotoko). It was led by a private school professor, A. N'Goh Bony, who according to RDA leaders had 'more pretensions than titles'.[1] His mimeographed paper *Attoungblan* was filled with anti-Semitic, anti-American and vaguely pro-Russian statements like:

These JEWISH COLONIALISTS, refugees from ISRAEL the WAR MONGER, as well as their new valets, the HIRED NEGROES become BOURGEOIS, openly mock the people as long as they can travel in AMERICAN CARS.[2]

More moderate was the criticism from the *Action Démocratique et Sociale de la Côte d'Ivoire*, a group of left-wing Catholic origins publishing *Action Démocratique*. They attacked unity, not in itself, but because:

Union before it is made around a man, regardless of how virtuous, must be made around a programme. . . .

and because:

Under the label of sections of the RDA people organize themselves by tribes. The road is barred to those who do not belong to the tribe in the race for prebends and political offices. . . . In many regions the *non-originaires* who have a future in commerce or administration are hated, execrated in the area by their brothers who know how to read and write. They are called strangers and are generally considered usurpers. They are the objects of cabals. Even some local *élus* excel in this sort of dishonourable plotting which divides Ivory Coasters among each other and Ivory Coasters from other Africans. Even some ministers are caught up in this complex of regionalism and weigh down their ministries with people whose only qualification is to belong to a tribe.[3]

Though President Houphouët included four returned students in the 1957 territorial assembly, and two in the first government, opposition grew among the intellectuals.

Opposition grew from trade unionists also. When the PDCI planter-politicians took over the government they represented the single largest employer of labour. Privately, also, their interests became those of employers, as they shared activities with European entrepreneurs and with the wealthier traders and transporters. Tension grew, and by January 1957 there were incidents in Treichville between workers calling themselves RDA and their RDA employers. The election of union leader Kissi Camille Gris to the territorial assembly, and of the railway workers' leader Gaston Fiankan to the ministry

[1] Ouëzzin Coulibaly in *Concorde*, 20 December 1956.
[2] *Attoungblan*, 11 November 1956.
[3] P. Kouame in *Action Démocratique*, 28 August 1957.

of labour, did not appreciably reduce the hostility of the workers. Soon this conflict took on political overtones. For President Sékou Touré of Guinea was also the key figure in UGTAN, the West African trade union movement; prior to the referendum the organization came out in favour of independence. By fall 1959, despite government appeals, the civil servants of Abidjan walked out on strikes and showed their feelings by tearing the name-plaque off the new model bridge, Pont Houphouët-Boigny.

Trouble built up in the countryside as well. Opposition to the PDCI from the Agni and Bete continued, and from these areas candidates opposed to the unity list ran in the 1957 elections. An opposition candidate ran in Boundoukou, also, where the 'martyrs' supporting the Almamy were outraged at the extent to which the party had reintegrated the Abrong. In 1955 a mission from the territorial assembly of Upper Volta uncovered evidence of mistreatment of migrants by African planters; their list evoked memories of the forced labour system:

> Imprisonment in dungeons, whipping for the least resistance or for work judged inadequate, non-payment of salaries, forced withholding of salaries to prevent flight, blows with sticks and dressing in ridiculous sisal sacks in case of attempts at flight, prizes given to a man who brings back a fugitive worker, excessive surveillance by overseers in the fields, and in the dormitories . . . to the extent that a worker could not go and relieve himself without being watched, obligations to work in order to be fed as long as the worker is not seriously ill, insufficient food. . . .[1]

As development advanced, there were more opponents, and not only students, salaried workers, and migrants. More and more people sought places in government office and in the machinery of the party. In Bouake, for example, though only 31 municipal councillors were elected, in November 1956 fully a thousand candidates sought the nomination. Inevitably the competition took on an ethnic form. As long as Ouëzzin Coulibaly remained alive (he died in September 1958), he worked to minimise ethnic friction among 'strangers' and *originaires*. In Bouake he scolded:

> And you, Africans, if you want an *originaire* of Ivory Coast to be separate from an *originaire* of Guinea and to be separate from an *originaire* from Soudan—where then will we go when you will be separated one from the other? . . . you who were born in Ivory Coast, respect well this sacred trust making your territory attract Africans from everywhere, like birds to a mirror. You are lucky that all Africans run towards you, and you know well the proverbial hospitality of our ancestors.[2]

[1] Mimeographed report, February 1955, written by Joseph Ouëdraogo, Henri Guissou, and others.
[2] *Concorde*, 15 November 1956.

Soon afterwards, that hospitality came to an end. Even before the break became open in the interterritorial RDA between Guinea, Soudan, and Ivory Coast, it already existed in the countryside of Ivory Coast. It came to the surface of national life when relations among the leaders in Abidjan, Conakry, and Bamako became strained.

Until then the RDA hardly stopped at frontiers. 'Strangers' carried news of the RDA from Ivory Coast to their kinsmen in Guinea, Soudan, and the other territories, thus contributing to the spread of the RDA in French-speaking West Africa. But after the dissolution of the RDA over the issues of federation and independence, the 'stranger'-*originaire* question in Ivory Coast took on new meaning. The quarrel became the occasion for *originaires* from the border areas discredited during the repression to re-establish their patriotism, while among the Baule the quarrel increased the already considerable suspicion of 'strangers'. The rise of xenophobia which followed in Ivory Coast was not unrelated to McCarthyism in the United States, where some of German–American ancestry whose patriotism during the Second World War was suspect, used the issue of anti-Communism to prove they were patriots who always knew who was the real enemy.

Originaires on the frontiers pointed out to their Baule countrymen the danger to the internal security of Ivory Coast from those known to have foreign connexions. The *Ligue des Originaires de la Côte d'Ivoire* which the government outlawed after its leader triggered in October 1958 serious incidents against Dahomean and other African strangers working in the towns of Ivory Coast, were but the lunatic fringe of a wider group. Xenophobia accompanied in 1958 and 1959 the transfer of power. Such men as the *dioula* representative Ladji Sidibé fell from the favour of President Houphouët; Jean Baptiste Mockey lost his posts as minister of interior and PDCI secretary-general at least in part because people suspected he was too close to disaffected youth, unions, the *dioula* and other 'strangers', and through them to Mali and Guinea.

Just before the 1958 referendum, President Houphouët added to the general suspicion of the loyalty of 'strangers'. Calling for a 'yes' vote in the referendum, he asked:

Would you have us in Ivory Coast and in Africa, novices in public affairs, who must ask aid from the Metropole and within the Community or from outside the Community . . . who must at all times keep the public order, indispensable if anyone of good will is to come to our aid, would you have us, out of immoderate love for democracy and liberty, accept that from frontiers near or far instructions be given to an irresponsible minority to endanger the regime we have freely chosen? Don't count on me for this.

If, after the choice, some people, whether white or black, *originaires* of the country or *non-originaires*, men or women, want to sap the bases of indispensable co-operation by accepting the role of paid agents, I don't give them twenty-four hours to leave the Ivory Coast forever.[1]

Thus until 1959 opposition grew from returned students, trade unions, disaffected 'martyrs'; tribalism grew also.

For a while the PDCI government used force against its opponents —arrested some, exiled others who went to Ghana or Guinea. Some six hundred civil servants were penalized for their strike. But at the same time the PDCI leaders gave way. They enlarged their ranks— and drew critics into the enlarged legislative assembly as well as the regional councils. Disaffected intellectuals were allowed to build their own organization, *Jeunesse RDA de la Côte d'Ivoire* (JRDACI), which became almost a party within the party. In 1959 there finally took place another PDCI congress, where many critics were drawn into the new *comité directeur*. The generation of 1945, though it still dominated Ivory Coast politics, ceased to monopolize all the posts. At the congress the party recognized its own contribution to ethnic fragmentation by resolving to reorganize the *sous-section* of Treichville on a neighbourhood basis.

As Mali became independent, President Houphouët became disenchanted with his experiment in Franco-African co-operation. In 1960, Ivory Coast briskly took leave of France and the Community and became independent. There came to Ivory Coast a new surge of unity, related, perhaps, to the fact that the 'martyrs' again saw continuity with the RDA tradition of 1946. They expressed it by excluding Europeans from the National Assembly of December 1960, and by blowing up the palace of the French governor. The chief goal remained development, and to end undue dependence on cocoa and coffee. The chief long term problem was unifying a heterogeneous population, and it compounded the difficulties of finding a possible successor to the man who held both party and state together— President Houphouët.

---

[1] 'Discours prononcé par M. Houphouët-Boigny, Ministre d'État, au Stade Géo-André à Abidjan, le 7 septembre 1958', Ministère de l'Intérieur, Service de l'Information, Abidjan.

PART SIX

Trade Unionists and Chiefs in Guinea

FROM the French standpoint, Senegal was a pilot colony politically and Ivory Coast economically. Guinea, too, was a pilot state, but from another standpoint. It pointed the way for the other French-speaking West African states by being the first to achieve total independence from France. An extraordinary conference of some 600 leaders of the *Parti Démocratique de Guinée* on 14 September acted upon General de Gaulle's declaration on 25 August 1958 that 'independence is at the disposal of Guinea'. 'Considering there cannot be for a dependent people the slightest hesitation in choosing between Independence and the proposed Community,' the PDG decided 'TO CHOOSE INDEPENDENCE BY VOTING "NO" IN THE REFERENDUM OF 28 SEPTEMBER'.[1] So certain were the PDG leaders of their following, they did not even campaign. The vote was 1,130,292 no against 56,959.[2] This result was made possible because the PDG was thoroughly rooted in town and countryside.

The PDG burst into power only after 1953. Before, Guinea was rather a sleepy backwater, as is evident from some statistics. The number of educated Africans in 1945 was tiny. For a population estimated in 1958 at $2\frac{1}{2}$ million[3] (and probably nearer 3 million) in 1937–8 less than 8,000 were in state elementary school and less than 200 in state primary school.[4] By 1947, in both state and private elementary schools, the number was only 11,000,[5] while in upper primary and secondary schools there were but 540 pupils or under half the number in Ivory Coast and about one-sixth the number in Senegal.[6] Even in 1957, just before Guinea became independent, not even 10 per cent. of the school-age children were actually in classes; the total number of primary school pupils, state and private, was

---

[1] All three citations from the resolution adopted at the conference, *La Liberté*, 24 September 1958, and reprinted in Territoire de la Guinée, *L'Action politique du Parti Démocratique de Guinée pour l'émancipation africaine*, by Sékou Touré Imprimerie du Gouvernement, Guinea, n.d., tome i, p. 206.
[2] République de Guinée, *L'Action politique du PDG–RDA Guinée pour l'émancipation et l'unité africaine dans l'indepéndance*, by Sékou Touré, tome 2, Imprimerie du Gouvernement, Conakry, *c.* 1959, p. 9, see also p. 198.
[3] *Outre-mer 1958*, op. cit., p. 831.
[4] *Annuaire Statistique*, tome 2, 1951, op. cit., p. 83.
[5] Ibid., p. 94.   [6] Ibid., p. 96.

still no more than 37,400;[1] only 21 took respectively the first and second parts of the *baccalauréat* examination; and in each only 15 passed.[2] Thus an acute shortage of modern cadres characterized Guinea.

The money economy also was rudimentary at the end of the Second World War. There was no African planter class as in Ivory Coast; and even after the resumption of world trade in 1947 the total value of exports from Guinea was one-fifth that of Senegal.[3] The number of inhabitants living in the towns was quite low—even Conakry, the capital and largest city was in 1945 estimated to have no more than 26,000.[4] In 1947, the 35,206 wage earners was less than half the number in Senegal; roughly one-third were trade union members.[5]

Regional Politics

Against the background of economic stagnation, limited education, and African inexperience with modern politics, it is understandable why the reforms of 1945 did not immediately precipitate great changes in Guinea. There were only stirrings of discontent, leading, for example, to incidents in the 'holy city' of Kankan inhabited by a Malinke Muslim majority and a Fulani minority.[6] These incidents were isolated, however, and in the absence of any organized parties had little meaning beyond the level of local politics.[7] Only limited changes followed the reforms in Guinea. For the first few years, 'elections were prepared and directed by the ethnic groups while none of the candidates could pretend to represent the entire territory'.[8]

The principal ethnic bloc in Guinea is Fulani;[9] a little more than a third of the total population is Fulani proper if those assimilated with them are counted together.[10] In the seventeenth and eighteenth centuries Fulani invaders came from the region of Macina in the present Republic of Mali, and in the name of Islam declared war on the diverse peoples most of whom now inhabit upper and lower Guinea. As victors, the Fulani occupied the plateau of the Fouta Djallon, concerned themselves with cattle, and lived in an almost

---

[1] *AOF 1957*, op. cit., p. 115.   [2] *Outre-mer 1958*, op. cit., p. 835.
[3] See Appendix XI.   [4] See Appendix IX.
[5] *Annuaire Statistique*, 1951, tome ii, op. cit., pp. 410 and 415, n. 1 and 2.
[6] Mamadou, Barry. 'Le Fouta Djalon', *L'Étudiant Afrique noire*, April 1957, p 12.   [7] See *La Liberté*, Conakry, 27 June 1955.
[8] Touré, Sékou. 'Rapport moral et politique', Les Assises du PDG, 23–26 janvier 1958, *L'Action politique du PDG* . . ., tome i, op. cit., p. 8.
[9] See the ethnic groups of Guinea, Map 5.
[10] The administrative estimate of the number of Fulani in Guinea was 870,000 out of a total of some 2½ million. Houis, Maurice. *Guinée française*, Édition Maritimes et Coloniales, Paris, 1953, p. 324. See also Richard-Molard, op. cit. pp. 95 and 99.

feudal society.[1] Their differences with their neighbours caused them on the whole to welcome the arrival of the Europeans. Hence French rule came fairly peacefully to the area, and disturbed the traditional political structure relatively little. There was not much modern economic development, and therefore the goals of the French administration were confined to keeping the peace and keeping up French prestige. A proud history, an aristocracy whose authority was reinforced by Islam and resistance to European education also served to set the Fulani somewhat apart from other Guineans.

Among the educated Fulani, there existed in 1943 the only really flourishing ethnic association. It was called the *Amicale Gilbert Vieillard* (AGV) after a French administrator of socialist leanings who studied and worked among the Fulani from the time of the Popular Front,[2] and who spoke of it as 'the land of "sterile stones, of famine, hunger and the badly dressed"'.[3] The AGV was the successor in Guinea to the Fulani club *Voix du Montagnard* which existed among students at the École Normale William-Ponty. Founded as a mutual aid and cultural group, the AGV took on political functions as well.[4] Its members discussed, for example, difficulties under Vichy, in their home villages and towns. The chiefs required total obeisance and would not recognize the special qualifications of Africans educated in French schools or in the French army. The AGV members complained that in 1945, 'arbitrarily expelled from their region by the chiefs in connivance with the former administrators, almost all the Fulani intellectuals were living in the coastal region of Guinea and particularly in Conakry.'[5]

There were less than a hundred educated Fulani in the AGV when they first heard of the prospect of elections from the Free French General Chervance-Bertin. A founder of *Combat*,[6] he flew to Guinea to solicit, successfully, the first college votes. The AGV decided they represented the biggest bloc of voters in the second college, and

---

[1] For brief descriptions of the feudal organization of Fulani society in the Fouta Djallon, see Barry Mamadou, op. cit., p. 12; Richard-Molard, op. cit., p. 99; Poirier and Leroi-Gourhan, op. cit., pp. 258–9; Abdoulaye Diallo (African doctor), in *L'AOF*, Dakar, 11, 15, 18, and 22 July 1947; Ba Kamanca Ollida in *Réveil*, Dakar, 23 September 1946. Gauthier, E. F., in *L'Afrique noire occidentale*, Larose, Paris, 1943, p. 171 calls the life of the Fulani chiefs 'la vie de chateau'. A longer description of Fulani feudal leaders is given by Marty, Paul. *L'Islam en Guinée*, Leroux, Paris, 1921, Chap. I.
[2] Most of his essays were printed in the *Bulletin du Comité d'Études Historiques et Scientifiques de l'AOF*.
[3] Gouilly, op. cit., p. 67, citing Gilbert Vieillard in 1940.
[4] See AGV statutes, mimeographed, 1953, Article 4.
[5] Tounkara Cellou, in *Le Populaire de Guinée*, 15 June 1956.
[6] See *Climats*, 27 December 1955.

wanted their favourite Barry Diawadou to be deputy. The son of the *chef de canton* at Dabola, Diawadou was then in his early thirties, Ponty-trained, and a government clerk. But the Fulani chiefs considered Diawadou a radical and a threat, and without them the AGV intellectuals could not produce the Fulani votes. After some heated debates, the intellectuals gave in to the chiefs and designated as candidate in the *Constituante* elections a man in his fifties, Yacine Diallo, a graduate of Ponty and a teacher. He was a favourite of the traditionalists, perhaps in part because he was older and of low traditional origins. In that first election 'the AGV . . . included all the sons of the Fouta, shoulder to shoulder behind their deputy Yacine Diallo; chiefs and intellectuals worked sincerely in the interests of the country'.[1]

Diallo won the election, but by a very narrow margin and because the representatives of the three other regions of Guinea were divided. There were the predominantly Malinke peoples of upper Guinea, about a fifth of the total population,[2] centering around Kankan. Their main representative was Lamine Ibrahima Kaba, a Muslim scholar and educator in his fifties. From the forest region bordering on Sierra Leone, Ivory Coast, and Liberia, the favourite son was Mamba Sano, of assimilated Malinke origins, a Ponty graduate and teacher. He came from the historic market town of Kissidougou, one of the bases the French used in the 1890s to launch their forces against the nineteenth century warrior Samory Touré.[3] The upper Guinea and forest regions co-operated on these two candidates.

In lower Guinea, as in most of the West African sea coast, lived people with the longest history of European contact; when the reforms came they felt specially qualified to take the initiative politically. But as elsewhere, their numbers did not match their aspirations for office. One coastal candidate was Amarah Soumah, graduate of the upper primary school in Conakry, a clerk and son of a chief of the Baga fishermen and farmers who owned the land on which Conakry was founded in 1889.[4] So popular was he among his kinsmen that in the market of Conakry the women found rice sold better when called after him. The second coastal candidate was Fodé Touré, who had, exceptionally, trained as a lawyer in Paris. He was a

---

[1] AGV Bureau directeur, Report of third congress at Mamou, January 1953, Conakry, mimeographed, p. 8.

[2] For background see Niane, Djibril Tamsir. 'Mise en place des populations de la Haute-Guinée', *Recherches Africaines*. Institut National de Recherche et de Documentation, Conakry, April–June 1960.

[3] Delafosse in Hanotaux and Martineau, op. cit., p. 209.

[4] Dollfus, O. 'Conakry en 1951–52. Étude humaine et économique', *Études Guinéennes*, IFAN, Conakry, no. 10–11, 1952, p. 6.

Soussou from Forecariah who had been president, in Bamako, of the town association *Foyer du Soudan*.

During the first eight years of elections candidates in Guinea spoke of tribe or region, not of nation. They 'went digging into history to find accusations to hurl against each other',[1] and chose the examples which divided. For example the AGV, at their 1953 congress, took care to freshen people's memories of Fulani victories in war against other ethnic groups in Guinea.[2] Only for immediate electoral purposes were the leaders of the regional groups willing to form alliances, which were most unstable. During the 1945 campaign, for example, hoping to reduce the chances of Yacine Diallo who had a plurality on the first ballot, the representatives from the three non-Fulani areas made a pact in favour of Mamba Sano on the second ballot. 'This seemed to be the first instance of "unity of action" against "regionalism" in Guinea,'[3] and it was not successful. Lamine Kaba insisted on running, received 1,711 votes, and as a consequence Yacine Diallo won with 5,774 votes against 5,065 for Mamba Sano.[4]

During this period of regional politics, only the AGV could point to some formal structure. Three congresses took place—in 1947, 1949, and 1953. A youth group existed for a short time, *Jeunesse AGV*. Briefly after 1951 deputy Yacine Diallo paid for a newspaper, the *Progrès Africain*. In 1953 the AGV could claim 35 sections, 14 with paid-up dues. Between April 1949 and January 1953, the AGV budget was published as 263,032.50 francs cfa.[5] Never good, 'Liaison between the headquarters and the sections progressively diminished until in July 1951 there only were rare exchanges of correspondence when exceptionally important events took place.'[6] The existence of a formal structure reflected the wishes of the Fulani elite, often thwarted by rural chiefs who were not eager to invite visits from townsmen whom they regarded as disrespectful and interfering. The geography in the Fouta Djallon favoured control by the chiefs. The density of population was low, people lived scattered rather than in clusters, markets were few, and the chiefs controlled the *missidé* or mosque area, one of the rare places of assembly. Against the will of the chiefs, there was little the educated Fulani in the AGV could do: without money they could not afford to hire staff or put out a newspaper. As long as they limited recruitment, by definition, to the Fulanis, growth of support for their modern views remained limited by the slow rate

---

[1] Magassouba, Moriba in *La Liberté*, 2 November 1954.
[2] Mimeographed records, AGV 1953 Congress, op. cit., p. 8.
[3] *La Liberté* article by Cissé Fodé, 27 June 1955.
[4] J.O.A.N.C. I, *Débats*, 21 February 1946, p. 424.
[5] Mimeographed records, AGV 1953 Congress, op. cit., p. 13.
[6] Ibid., p. 9.

of social change in the Fouta Djallon. To get the chiefs to produce the Fulani votes which made *élus* of the educated Fulani, the latter paid a high ideological price. Then AGV policy was best summed up by a chief attending the 1953 AGV congress—'Let us move carefully. No motions, no violence. Let us concentrate on corridor interventions. The administration frequently pays no attention to motions.'[1]

The other regional associations were less organized and also concerned themselves with privileges rather than principles. Some French officials referred to the regional associations not as parties but as *'syndicats de nantis'* (unions of those who feather their nests).[2] Success or failure in elections depended in large measure upon official chiefs whom French officials had little difficulty in influencing. Until 1954 the administration could and did rule largely in the pre-war manner.

Until 1954 each successful *parlementaire* was usually a rival of the others, backed by most of the voters from his own region and by an unstable combination from one or several of the other regions. Each election led to an 'agonizing reappraisal'[3] of the electoral alliances. For example, deputy Yacine Diallo had only sporadic support from the *Foyer de la Basse Guinée*. The *Foyer* was composed of the younger dissidents from lower Guinea, who in 1946 signed a pact with the chiefs of the Fouta known as 'the milk and the salt' or *khigné nou foukhé*.[4] The young men in the *Foyer* opposed the dominant group in lower Guinea, *Union de la Basse Guinée*. It in turn supported Amarah Soumah, usually entered into alliances with Mamba Sano of the forest region, and also combined with the *Union du Mandé*. It had been founded by several Malinke, including Sékou Touré, Keïta Koumandian, and Sinkoun Kaba, and, most important, Framoï Berété. The group was also known as the *Union Mandingue*.

On other occasions, however, as in 1953, the *Union du Mandé* supported Yacine Diallo. The AGV, for its part, supported Yacine Diallo in 1945 and 1946, opposed him and his chiefly backers until 1951, when it supported his rival from the forest region, Mamba Sano. In the election of 10 November 1946, Mamba Sano and the AGV president Barry Diawadou were on the single list[5] of the *Parti Socialiste de Guinée*. Only Sano won. The 1951 elections saw several other shifts in alliances and in the names of the regional groups. Thus Yacine Diallo created with Fodé Touré a *Union Franco-Guinéenne*, which was a co-ordinating committee in Conakry of his various

[1] Mimeographed records, AGV 1953 Congress, op. cit., p. 27.
[2] From interviews, February 1956, Conakry.
[3] *La Liberté*, 14 June 1955, editorial citing Foster Dulles' phrase.
[4] *La Liberté*, 27 June 1955.
[5] J.O.A.N., *Débats*, 25 February 1947, p. 471.

ethnic backers. Mamba Sano created a similar group, the *Comité d'Entente Guinéenne*, which included Amarah Soumah and Bangoura Karim, son of the chief of Coyah, from lower Guinea, Framoï Berété from upper Guinea and some Fulani chiefs.

The RDA *section* of Guinea was born against this background of regional associations in which higher African civil servants and official chiefs uneasily co-operated in choosing candidates for successive elections. As in the other territories, educated Africans in Guinea were concerned at the rejection in referendum of the April 1946 Constitution, and discussed the need for unity. Another party nucleus was born out of the *Groupe d'Études Communistes* (GEC) in Conakry, and took on the name *Parti Progressiste de Guinée* (PPG). It was 'the only political party in Guinea which in framework and programme was conceived so as to group together Africans and Europeans of good will;'[1] and it urged unity in the form of a *rassemblement*. The AGV, however, true to its socialist origins, spoke of a *bloc*. In the first Constitutante Yacine Diallo joined the Socialist group, and voted in favour of the April Constitution. Briefly in 1946 the PPG and the AGV worked together for the re-election of Yacine Diallo, while within each respectively French Communist and Socialist advisors tried to win influence. Like the other *parlementaires* who had become associated with the SFIO, Yacine Diallo signed the call issued by the African deputies for a *rassemblement*, which became the RDA at Bamako in October 1946. But Diallo decided not to attend the Bamako Congress, after the Socialist overseas minister Marius Moutet withdrew his approval. Some Guineans went to Bamako nevertheless: the GEC contingent in the PPG which included a few Frenchmen and a handful of young Africans, mostly in their twenties, having only primary school education, holding low ranks in the civil service, and some eleven representatives of ethnic groups.[1]

Back from Bamako, the Guinea delegates worked together organizing the 1946 elections to the first Legislature of the French National Assembly, but kept to methods, propaganda themes, and structures based on tribe or region. The PPG did not of itself turn into the RDA *section* of Guinea, but dissolved. Not until May 1947 was the Guinea section formally created—the *Parti Démocratique de Guinée* (PDG). The statutes were adopted at the first congress in June. Its *comité directeur*, where each ethnic group was represented, was then a co-ordinating committee. Sékou Touré, for example, represented the *Union Mandingue*. Later he spoke of:

[1] Touré. 'Rapport moral . . .', 23–26 janvier 1958, *L'Action politique du PDG . . .*, tome i, op. cit., p. 9.

The contradictions which existed in the methods and doctrines of the ethnic groups also existed inside the RDA movement of Guinea, and almost took away its true purpose. **This was to unite, in democratic organs and in units geographically defined, men and women of all races, of all religions, around a common programme for a common action.**[1] The fragile and (we must admit it) uniquely electoral bases of our new section did not resist the centrifugal activities of its own leaders, and the elections which followed . . . ended the myth of political unity theoretically symbolised by the existence of an RDA section. . . . Thus the Guinean section of the RDA broke apart, and only a small minority of democrats, who had resolutely placed their confidence in the future of the movement and defended its flag to prevent its total disappearance, could speak in its name and for its programme.[2]

While French officials made clear their disapproval of the RDA, only a tiny minority of educated Africans remained loyal to it and regionalism remained the chief obstacle to its growth.

The Trade Union Base

Initially few people in Guinea shared the interterritorial RDA's disapproval for 'opportunism'[3] of the regional associations uniting 'chiefs' and their educated allies. Most Guinean Ponty graduates sought to benefit immediately from the introduction of elections in Guinea, and so kept out of the RDA. They held the top civil service posts, and had the most to lose from official opposition to the RDA. This had been clear since the Bamako Congress, and became clearer during the official repression between 1949 and 1951. The PDG in Guinea remained tiny, and for the most part simply marked time. Sékou Touré's article in the RDA newspaper, *Réveil*, 'Guinea Stirs' on 14 November 1949, was more wish than reality:

> It stirs due to the push of the RDA . . . After the disastrous failure of all the racist groups which want to keep a perpetual and sterile division, our country understands that the RDA alone merits its confidence and support . . .[4]

A PDG conference in 1951 selected Sékou Touré as candidate for the parliamentary elections. When Mamba Sano won, the RDA claimed there was official pressure. The PDG was then a seed; and in Touré's words, 'if a seed is to grow, it must be put in favourable conditions'.[5]

[1] Sentence in heavy type in the original.   [2] Touré, tome 1, op. cit., pp. 9–10.
[3] From typescript of report by an interterritorial RDA mission to Guinea, spring 1947.
[4] Cited by Abdoulaye Ly. *Publications du P.R.A.–Sénégal sur le nationalisme dans l'ouest-africain*, no. 1, Dakar, 9 August 1959, p. 24.
[5] Sékou Touré. 'Rapport de doctrine et de politique générale', in *Le Cinquième Congrès National du Parti Démocratique de Guinée* (RDA) tenu à Conakry les 14,

To prepare the ground, most loyal PDG men turned to trade union work within the framework of the West African federation in the French *Confédération Générale du Travail*. The CGT link gave access to funds, travel, training, political experience and metropolitan allies against the local administration. In French law, also, trade unionists had special legal protection. The number of salaried workers in Guinea, though negligible in 1946, had increased rapidly by 1953.[1]

By then Guinea surpassed Dahomey as the third richest French West African territory. Exports which were 17,000 tons in 1944 were 155,000 tons in 1952 and 841,000 tons in 1953.[2] Iron mines started producing. In 1952 construction of bauxite installations on the islands of Loos off the coast of Conakry was finished, and production of washed and dried bauxite rose from 325,000 to 500,000 between 1953 and 1955. In the same period crude iron exports from the peninsula of Kaloum off Conakry rose from 400,000 tons to 650,000 tons.[3] More rich iron deposits were soon discovered on the Liberian border. Advance surveys indicated mineral deposits and water power potential in all regions except the Fouta Djallon. Studies begun in 1947 of hydro-electric installations at Konkouré, by 1953 established that a 5 million kilowatt annual capacity would probably allow Guinea to produce aluminium more cheaply than the projected Volta River scheme in Ghana.[4] Between 1952 and 1954 officials authorized the installation of 17 secondary industries, as compared with 21 in Ivory Coast.[5] The diamond fever of neighbouring Sierra Leone spread to the forest region of Guinea. The official figures, showing a rise from 50,000 carats in 1948 to 300,000 carats in 1955, did not take into account extensive smuggling.[6] The number of resident Europeans, sometimes a pointer to economic activity, rose from 4,035 in 1946, to 8,852 in 1955.[7] The Korean War brought a general rise in world market prices. As Governor Parisot indicated in his address to the territorial assembly, 1953 was a turning point; agricultural production rose and the exploitation of minerals was under way.[8]

Once Guinea's economic future was assured in minerals, the

15, 16, et 17 septembre 1959, tome iv, République de Guinée, Conakry, Imprimerie Nationale, p. 44.
[1] See Appendix X.
[2] See Appendix XI.
[3] *Annuaire Statistique*, 1956, op. cit., pp. 236–7.
[4] Moussa, Pierre. *Les Chances économiques de la communauté franco-africaine*, Armand Colin, Paris, 1957, pp. 236–8.
[5] *Annuaire Statistique*, 1956, op. cit., p. 230.   [6] Ibid., pp. 236–7.
[7] *Annuaire Statistique*, 1950, tome i, op. cit., p. 64 and ibid., 1956, tome i, p. 55.
[8] Guinée Française. *Assemblée Territoriale, session budgetaire 15 novembre au 14 décembre 1954*. Conakry, 1955, p. 5.

labour movement, though small, assumed new importance. In response to rumours of immediate wealth, Africans left their villages and came to the cities. Conakry's population rose sharply. Though official figures were 26,000 in 1945 and 34,000 in 1951, the real figures, particularly between the planting and harvesting seasons, were considerably higher. Conakry had a large floating population, including seasonal migrants.[1] By 1953 there were many who had come to Conakry but found no work. In the CGT they found an organization willing to help with their problems.

While increased economic activity brought more followers in Guinea to the CGT–RDA leaders, all the African trade unions were involved in disputes with the French government first over the adoption and later over the implementation of the Code du Travail.[2] The Guinea workers took the initiative and called for a *conférence intersyndicale* of all West African unions to meet in Dakar in October 1952. The conference adopted resolutions calling for 'vigorous and unified action of all African trade unions, which alone can defeat the forces opposed to the implementation of the Code du Travail'.[3] Workers throughout West Africa went on strike on 3 November, partly to end the long delays in Parliament, which finally adopted the Code on 15 December.

While the Code substituted a forty hour for a forty-eight hour week, the African deputies were unable to secure adoption by Parliament of a corresponding 20 per cent. rise in the hourly minimum wage. The French Government retained the power to determine its relationship to the shorter work week, and did not increase the minimum wage by 20 per cent. Guinea leaders again took the initiative by calling for a second *conférence intersyndicale*, which met in Bamako in March 1953 to determine 'methods and means of action' for a favourable implementation of the Code.[4] During 1953 the workers in one or another city were usually out on strike.[5] CGT–AOF secretary Diallo Seydou, a loyal RDA man since 1946, saw the unprecedented wave of activities as 'the result of accumulated discontent knowingly repressed for too long'.[6]

Union protest was most extensive in Guinea; workers throughout AOF sympathized and previously inactive villagers within Guinea

---

[1] Dollfus, op. cit., p. 9, also Appendix IX.
[2] For further details see *Afrique Informations*, 15 December 1953–1 January 1954.
[3] *Afrique Noire*, 16 October 1952; *le Prolétaire*, newspaper of the CGT union of Dakar, October 1952.
[4] *L'Ouvrier*, CGT newspaper in Guinea, 16 March 1953.
[5] For a list of the strikes in 1953 see *Afrique Informations*, 15 December–1 January 1954.
[6] *Le Facteur*, 14 January 1954, CGT postal union newspaper.

became involved in the already legendary strike of 1953. It began on 21 September with the workers in the private sector. The secretary-general of the CGT, which grouped most of the workers, was Sékou Touré, who had lost his civil service job because of his union work. He had only elementary schooling, was barely thirty, veteran of the GEC of Conakry and the Bamako RDA Congress. He cultivated his talents as an orator by speaking daily in different neighbourhoods of Conakry, giving the news and watchwords, maintaining determination and discipline among the strikers. The themes of his speeches in the daily town meetings were designed to break down ethnic differences, to point out how little tribe counted among workers. People from near-by villages brought food to the families of the strikers. The strike lasted a record-breaking sixty-six days and ended only on 25 November.[1]

In Guinea the impact of the strike was profound. The number of organized union members, only 4,600 at the beginning of 1953 rose to 20,000 in 1954 and 44,000 in 1955.[2] The union leaders of Guinea acquired fame and credit for the decree taken by French officials on 27 November, increasing the AOF minimum hourly wage by 20 per cent.[3] In Dakar, for example, the workers gave a standing ovation to Sékou Touré as representing 'the heroes of the workers' movement of Guinea'.[4] So solid was Touré's support among West African workers that the French CGT feared losing control and changed the statutes to provide for not one but three secretaries of the West African AOF–CGT co-ordinating committee. At the 1954 CGT–AOF meeting in Abidjan, Sékou Touré was elected one of the three (the others were Diallo Seydou of Mali and Bassirou Guèye of Senegal).

Within Guinea, the strike had most important political consequences, since the trade unionists also led the PDG. After the sixty-six-day strike, they had territorial fame, a recognized leader in Sékou Touré and the party entered a new phase. On the coast, the market women were selling whole loaves of bread as *'pain Sékou Touré'*, while cut-up slices, symbolizing the break-up of regional politics, were sold as *'pain Amarah Soumah'*. Within less than two years the PDG leaders displaced in elected office the leaders of the ethnic and regional associations; within four years they had destroyed also the *commandement indigène*, particularly the *chefs de canton*.

The PDG burst into prominence in Guinea during 1954 with a

---

[1] See *Afrique Informations*, 15 December–1 January 1954; and Sékou Touré's editorial in the federal CGT–AOF newspaper *Le Travailleur africain, c.* July 1955. President Touré in his 'Rapport Moral . . .' of January 1958, *L'Action politique du PDG . . .*, tome i, op. cit., p. 19, speaks of the 73-day strike.

[2] See Appendix X.   [3] *Afrique Noire*, 24–30 November 1953.

[4] Citation recorded at trade union meetings in January and February 1956.

speed rivalling the emergence of the PDCI in Ivory Coast some nine years earlier. There was, however, a different social and economic base. Guinea's economic development did not take the form of small farms, and the introduction of the cash economy did not mean as in Ivory Coast the formation of a rurally based African middle class. Guinea's wealth was in mining and potentially in industry. Though economic growth was rapid, most of the profits not invested in machinery went out of the country. The Guineans associated with the modern economy were for the most part labourers organized in the trade union movement; like the planters in the *Syndicat* who launched the PDCI–RDA of Ivory Coast the workers of Guinea proceeded to back their economic fight with a political one. The PDG–CGT leaders wanted Guineans to have a larger share of the wealth, and believed they could achieve this only by ending the colonial relationship. To them, in the first post-war decade, party and trade union were one. And though they achieved their first public successes as trade union leaders, they insisted

the trade union movement . . . must integrate itself as the nationalist revolutionary and not the reformist force within the context of other progressive political forces. Its role at every instant is political.[1]

The trade union experience of many PDG leaders affected their ideas as well as their style of living, speaking, writing, and acting. Since they held jobs low in the administrative hierarchy, they lived of necessity close to the people. Many had but irregular incomes; their housing was bad, few had cars, their clothes were simple. They relied on their colleagues or relations when in need, and made virtues of the labels pinned on them by their adversaries—'illiterates', 'vagrants', and 'badly dressed'.[2] The union background meant they prized more highly loyalty, discipline, and collective solidarity, than technical proficiency or job performance. Their union background assured their familiarity with the techniques of mass action and protest, with boycotts, strikes, and demonstrations. The PDG newspaper *La Liberté* did not err on the side of understatement. This, for example, was how they went about defending the interest of veterans who wanted higher pensions.

Every time a minister visits he pins medals of the Legion d'Honneur or the Étoile du Benin on the chests of old and loyal servants of France—to be certain no one seeks to raise their miserable pension. NO MEDAL FEEDS A MAN.[3]

They said of their adversaries 'let us pray for the damned souls who would sell mother and father for a title or an invitation'.[4] The French

[1] Diallo, Seydou. *La Liberté*, 11 December 1956.   [2] Ibid., 25 January 1955.
[3] Ibid., 2 November 1954.   [4] Ibid., 10 May 1955.

political vocabulary of the PDG leaders bore marked traces of the union experience. The PDG–CGT leaders became revolutionaries; they rejected the privileges the colonial system gave to the Europeans and to the small nucleus of Ponty-trained African *élus*. They recognized that not only the lower educational qualifications of Africans than of Europeans, but the entire colonial system kept Europeans in the top jobs and prevented Africans from outranking Europeans. The trade union experiences also made the CGT–PDG leaders modernizers, who rejected the traditionalist view that tribe or inherited status made men different. Finally, trade union work in Guinea and attendance at French and international trade union congresses deepened the inclination of the PDG–CGT leaders to seek the goal of equality.

After the strike the PDG burst to popularity as an expression of revolutionary protest in the villages. This kept the PDG–CGT leaders from accepting the Marxist formula that the workers were the vanguard of the revolution. Sékou Touré came to elaborate the thesis that 'the first great industry of Africa is agriculture,'[1] and to be increasingly reluctant to ask villagers for sacrifices so that the workers in the towns might have high wages. At first the PDG–CGT leaders, using Marxist categories drawn from CGT and GEC pamphlets, spoke largely in terms of 'the exploitation of capitalism and colonialism'. As the base of party support spread to the rural areas, they added 'chiefs and feudalism' to the list, and began to use words designed to harmonize with Muslim tradition.

Building National Support

The trade unions organized townspeople and these the PDG structure attached to an already existing rural base. As an interterritorial movement the RDA had the advantage not to divide the loyalties of peoples joined for centuries before the Europeans drew the frontiers. The party had dominated Ivory Coast politics since the end of the war and spread naturally across the forest from the frontier town of Nzo with the migrants who went to work on the farms of Ivory Coast, and with the African traders. These *dioula* regularly travelled the ancient routes of kola nuts, slaves, and Islam.[2] In the twentieth century kola and imported goods which entered at Abidjan moved along roads from the port of Abidjan to Man and Danané, through Beyla, Macenta, and Nzérékoré, from there to Bamako by way of Kankan; and sometimes from there through Bobo-Dioulasso back to Abidjan by way of Bouaké. The inhabitants of the forest, many belonging to

[1] *La Liberté*, 27 March 1956, reprinting his maiden speech to the French National Assembly.
[2] Cardaire, Marcel. 'L'Islam et le terroir africain', *Études Soudaniennes*, I.F.A.N., Soudan, 1954.

'headless' tribes, welcomed the RDA message of protest and change brought by the travellers. As early as 1947 Macenta elected the first and only RDA representative to the *conseil général*, Camara Kaman. In the 1952 territorial assembly Nzérékoré elected an RDA councillor Gnan Félix Mathos. Then in 1953 Sékou Touré won in a by-election in Beyla. He defeated, among others, the deputy Mamba Sano, and cited the victory as one more proof that the administration had falsified the elections of 1951.

The territorial assembly provided a convenient platform from which Sékou Touré attacked the established ethnic and regional party leaders. He was isolated among the *élus* and never won the votes within the assembly, but he won support outside. This is how he explained the budget of the territorial assembly, particularly the category of compulsory expenditures.

The white man is made of the same stuff as the black, he has the same blood. He came to us as a brother . . . and brought gifts as a brother . . . but lo! how surprising from a rich brother in Africa, he asked to be paid for his goods. . . . Then he did more. Of every five francs he took, all but 50 centimes went to maintain *himself* in style.[1]

Touré's lengthy muckraking speeches drew large crowds and he usually supplemented his remarks in the streets of Conakry. He considered himself a representative of the PDG, and travelled 'to account for his mandate to each village not of his electoral district, but rather of the entire Territory'.[2] On 12 April 1954, Sékou Touré once again opposed Yacine Diallo in the assembly, this time in a heated debate on the issue of allowances for the *parlementaires*. He claimed the *élus* already have a 'style of living which proved they were not short of money, since some construct new houses costing millions and others buy new cars'.[3] Feeling ran high against the increase in Conakry; nevertheless the assembly voted it. Shortly afterwards, Yacine Diallo died, and PDG supporters did not hesitate to point up the coincidence.

To replace Yacine there was a by-election in June. It was the occasion for a political realignment. The PDG launched an all-out campaign to elect Sékou Touré even while they claimed, after the experiences in 1951, to expect falsification again. Fear of the PDG organization, teamwork, methods, territorial structure, and growing popularity caused the ethnic and regional associations to change. In 1954 they unified, into a single party, territorial in scale, the *Bloc*

[1] Information based on interview, 1956.
[2] Touré. *L'Action politique du PDG* . . ., tome i, op. cit., p. 17.
[3] Guinée Française, Assemblée Territoriale, *Session ordinaire mars–avril 1954*. p.v. Conakry, 1954, p. 221.

Africain de Guinée (BAG). They altered their methods, too, held meetings and even for a while put out a newspaper, *la République*. For their candidate the BAG chose Barry Diawadou. He thus shifted position from the favourite of the Fulani intellectuals in the AGV, and became the spokesman of the traditionalists and neo-traditionalists. Meanwhile the AGV broke apart, mainly because the PDG attack on chiefs and tribal differences brought into the open issues which had troubled the organization from its beginning. The AGV radicals found they could not on the one hand reject tribal political structure—by saying to the Fulani chiefs that education and merit should count for more than lineage—and on the other hand keep the ethnic principle in recruiting. Some AGV men joined the BAG and backed Diawadou; others, including the president Diallo Abdoulaye (*huissier*), Balde Chaikhou, and Barry Ibrahima *dit* Barry III founded a new party, the *Démocratie Socialiste de Guinée* (DSG).

The hope of the DSG founders was to rid socialism in Guinea, until then associated with the AGV and with Yacine Diallo, of its regional origins. The new orientation was partly the work of Jean Paul Alata, a European accountant and treasury official who had previously helped to mount a socialist party in Cameroun. The DSG tried to be socialist in more than the parliamentary affiliations of its *élus*. The party published a newspaper, *Le Populaire de Guinée*, sponsored a marxist study group in Conakry, officially opposed tribe and caste differences, and backed equality for all. The party's candidate in the 1954 election, Barry III,[1] set himself directly against Fulani feudalism. His campaign met with some success, since in spite of official disapproval of opponents to Barry Diawadou, he ran up 7,995[2] votes. He did divide the Fulani voters, but had no appeal beyond the Fouta Region. Instead, the existence of the DSG contributed to keeping the PDG weak in the Fouta Djallon, by depriving it of those who might have been its best spokesmen there.

The PDG was well on the way to becoming a national party. In the coastal forest and upper regions of Guinea it gained the monopoly of those who favoured an anti-colonial and egalitarian policy. The PDG had acquired local representatives who urged their kinsmen to respond to the anti-tribal message 'that the misery which kills TOGBA of Macenta is the same as that of Samba of Upper Guinea, Soriba of lower Guinea, or Diallo of the Fouta Djallon'.[3]

Even before the PDG organizers came to the savannah region

---

[1] Barry III was one of the rare Guineans to become a member of the French civil service elite corps of *inspecteurs des contributions directes*. Drame Alioune was another. Both became ministers after independence.

[2] *Afrique Informations*, 15 March–1 April 1955.

[3] Savane Moricandian. *La Liberté*, 18 August 1954.

news of the party spread fast and among receptive peoples. This region, dominated by Kankan and including Kouroussa and Siguiri, had a long tradition of political, cultural, and religious unity. It was a base of the Mande ethnic family that spread in the western savannah and down into the forest, and included among others the Malinke, Bambara, and Dioula groups who lived in Ivory Coast, Guinea, and Mali. This was the tradition inherited by many leaders of the interterritorial RDA: Madeira Keïta, the first secretary-general of the PDG and later administrative secretary-general of the *Union Soudanaise*, who came from Kita, a town in Mali on the road between Siguiri and Bamako; Sékou Touré, who was born in Faranah on the border between the Guinea forest and savannah. His father's family considered as an ancestor the warrior-trader Samory Touré who organized the Mande resistance to European penetration. Samory Touré delayed European occupation for several decades, before French forces captured and exiled him in 1898, when he was already an old man. There was no scarcity of direct descendants of Samory Touré who made a practice of taking wives everywhere in his extensive travels. The mantle of succession fell upon Sékou Touré at least in part because he consciously emphasized the historical parallel of resistance against alien rule. Contemporary memories of Samory's empire helped the PDG build the sense of unity with which to overcome the separatism of the regional and ethnic political groups.

Skilful use of 'Samorism' brought the PDG support from among the descendants of those who had been associated with him. Most of the traders considered Samory one of themselves; he was reputed to have spent the early years of his life trading between Beyla and Macenta; even after he acquired a kingdom much of his wealth was connected with gold, kola, and slaves, and he was at the end of the nineteenth century the single largest buyer and seller in the area. Also associated with Samory were Muslim reformers and teachers, for he made war in the name of Islam; there were those who had been the administrators of his empire, and his soldiers or 'sofa',[1] both captive and free, whose numbers grew with each military victory. Though the Samory connexion was on the whole an asset to the PDG, at times it was a liability. In the later phase of his life when his power waned and he was under heavy siege from the Europeans, Samory's victories decreased and his name became associated with acts of cruelty still remembered by the descendants of those Africans who suffered. Similarly descendants of those captured by Samory's wars remained resentful. 'You will not sell us into slavery?' asked some of the older villagers of Sékou Touré during his first campaign in the forest. 'I am

---

[1] Delafosse in Hanotaux and Martineau, op. cit., pp. 200 f.

against all slavery,' was his reply.[1] This theme brought the PDG peripheral support even in the Fouta Djallon, in the *roundé* annexes to the Fulani villages, among 'captives' whose ancestors were sold by tradesmen dependent upon Samory. Among them organizers said, 'If Samory Touré can make you slaves, Sékou Touré can make you free.'[2] From the *roundé* came the votes the PDG had in the Fouta even in 1951, and a good proportion of the votes the PDG had there in the 1956 election.

Memory of unity under Samory eased the task assumed by the RDA leaders to demonstrate to villagers, at least 70 per cent. of whom were Muslim,[3] 'the total identity of the RDA's programme of emancipation . . . with the liberating principles of justice and hope in Islam'.[4] Samory had fought in the name of Islam, and many descendents of the *marabouts* associated with him still made religion their way of life. The Grand Chérif Fanta Mady, one of the most influential Muslim teachers in the western savannah, belonged to a family originally from northern Mali, and following the Kounta Qadriya tradition in Kankan. The Grand Chérif had an international following; among those who sought his advice was President Kwame Nkrumah of Ghana. During the last decades of his life Fanta Mady was a recluse and a mystic; his sway over his many followers was so great that he was reputed to have received on the average a million francs a day as tribute. This he redistributed to the poor. His father Karamoko Boubacar Sidiki Chérif had been the moral and spiritual guide of Almamy Samory, to whom he taught 'the Koran, theology, law, and Muslim philosophy'.[5] The number of the Karamoko's disciples grew with each of Samory's military victories, since he was chaplain-in-chief of the troops. The woman who became Fanta Mady's mother was given in marriage to his father by Samory, and as a boy Fanta Mady studied with Moctar Touré, one of Samory's sons. Fanta Mady's religious ideas harmonized with aquiescence to French rule, but his family history explains why he regarded the rise of the PDG with benevolent neutrality.

When Fanta Mady died in 1955 the PDG mourned and Sékou Touré praised him 'as the living example of a being who believes in God, who has faith in his function, and who treats as equal and brother every man, regardless of his colour or his origins'.[6]

---

[1] Information based on interviews.   [2] Ibid.

[3] *Tam-Tam*, March–May 1955, pp. 34–5.

[4] *La Liberté*, 28 December 1954.

[5] Lamine Kaba writing in *La Liberté*, 25 October 1955. Considerably more research is needed on this subject.

[6] *La Liberté*, 13 September 1955. See also ibid., 27 September and 1 November 1955.

The benevolent neutrality of Fanta Mady brought with it valuable backing in Kankan and the surrounding areas. Yet it also involved the PDG in a centuries old local rivalry between the Tourés and the Kabas. Among the Kabas there were several outstanding Muslim scholars who asserted a claim for primacy in Muslim circles of Kankan as soon as the question of succession to Fanta Mady was posed. There were within the Kaba family several feuds which helped explain why one member of the family, al Hajj Ibrahima Lamine Kaba was not only a fervent disciple of Fanta Mady who was usually associated with the Tourés, but also 'adopted' Sékou Touré as his son. Lamine Kaba was an elder, whose education had been mostly in Arabic and who had been during the war director of the *École Libre Franco-Arabe* in Dakar. There he claimed to be carrying out the wishes of the Grand Chérif by organizing prayers in favour of the Resistance cause. When the war ended Kaba was in his fifties. He returned to Kankan and there incidents occurred, involving Tourés, Kabas, and the various rival Muslim notables, for which the French authorities exiled him to Mauretania. He returned to become president of the Kankan *sous-section* of the PDG. In the long run the PDG did not accept that Lamine Kaba use his party position to strengthen his claims within the Kaba family. But in the first phase of the PDG's struggle to win elections the leaders ignored the issue, as well as conflicts between Lamine Kaba and the modernizing educated PDG leaders in Kankan. For the PDG leaders deliberately sought an

early victory over the instruments of colonialist reaction in the religious milieux. In fact the RDA was presented as anti-religious, atheist, Communist, and the forces of Islam which exercised a profound influence in our country were mobilized by the Administration in a fight against us. Happily, the profound knowledge of democratic principles in this religion, and the abuses of the supposedly religious chiefs, allowed us to alter the balance of forces, and even to identify the RDA with all the concepts of progress, of democracy and liberty even when they are of a religious order.[1]

To harmonize their revolutionary message, which they saw primarily in secular terms, with the precepts of Islam, the PDG leaders used several techniques, some of which they abandoned after 1957. Most party meetings included a recital of the Fatiha or opening *sura* of the Koran. The puritanism of Islam and of the revolution coincided in the refusal of Touré and many of his associates to take alcohol. On Friday, Sékou Touré attended religious services, at a different mosque. He made quite a production of this . . . chose an impeccably styled *boubou* and Muslim hat, and often found a supporter with a

[1] Touré. *L'Action politique du PDG* . . ., tome i, op. cit., p. 18.

matching car to drive him. Muslim reform leaders, trained in north African universities and eager to purify Islam, became associated with the PDG. A frequent member of Sékou Touré's entourage was Chérif Youssouf Nabhaniou, Professor of Arabic at Boke, who was a graduate of the Institut des Études Superieures Islamiques in Algiers. The Chérif, in a letter to the anti-RDA paper *La Nouvelle Guinée*, answered criticisms which had been made first of his ancestry and right to speak in the name of Islam, and second, of his associations with the RDA. He traced his ancestry back to 'Radissa Lalhbara, who founded Fez and upheld the precepts of Islam', and directly to 'Aliou (may the blessings of God be upon him), who is the husband of the daughter of the Prophet Mohammed (may God give him health), Fatouma-Diahrai-Bintou-Rassoulahi'. He also explained that he has been preaching the precepts of Islam in the mosques throughout Guinea; and that he believes those who challenge his views belong 'to the camp of those who oppose . . . the Muslim religion in all its grandeur, the Faith which no man may trample underfoot for political interests'.[1]

In the mosques, prayers drew an implied parallel between the community of the RDA and the community of Islam.

> God is great
> It is hard
> To bring unbelievers
> Into the brotherhood of believers
> But we need the die-hards
> To spur us on.[2]

On the coast, in the forest, and in upper Guinea, popular support for the PDG was expressed in dance and song. Sily, the elephant, was the symbol of the RDA.

> Sily is too strong
> He does not retreat
> When he is provoked.

Not all the songs simply praised the PDG and its candidate. One popular Mambo rhythm repeated a racist theme, and hurled insults at all Fulani, as well as at Barry Diawadou. To stop this Touré held numerous lengthy meetings. He spoke to the women.

---

[1] Full geneology registered at Kaolack, 5 August 1946, Folio 87 Case 979. *La Liberté*, 9 November 1954. After independence the Chérif became Guinea's diplomatic representative at Jiddah.
[2] For the texts of the PDG songs cited in this chapter I am indebted to M. Gadiri Mangue, who became Guinea's ambassador at Freetown. See my 'French Guinea's RDA Folk Songs', *West African Review*, August 1958.

'Will you do something for me? I know you are angry at Diawadou. Anger makes us stupid. Use the anger against me and so cure your anger. Do not play the song again. Do not dance the song again. Forget the song. The Fula is your brother. He is the most oppressed, the saddest, the poorest. Diawadou is not Fula. Diawadou is without a country. You are Fula. You are all races.'

The tendency to ethnic division, particularly between the Fulani and the rest, remained a serious problem to the PDG.

To overcome regionalism, the PDG leaders used a variety of techniques: symbols—of the elephant, Sily, 'who does not forget'; PDG banners and colours; clothes such as head-scarves, and the grey Muslim hat, somewhat like a fez (it came widely to represent the Guinean political position abroad). The women wore dresses cut of identical cloth. There were party songs, poems, dances, and slogans. To spread the party message, Sékou Touré and his associates used, in their words 'auto-suggestion'. Though the party regularly did publish a newspaper since 1950,[1] circulation in 1957 was still no more than 3,000; and there were only 6,000 copies even of the historic 24 September 1958 independence issue. The population of Guinea was largely illiterate, and communication was largely by word of mouth. The images and anecdotes of Sékou Touré's speeches were translated and re-translated into the many different languages and spread rapidly. PDG organizers used concrete examples from everyday life to hammer home the ideas that men are equal regardless of tribe or race, the need for unity, for faith in action, for discipline in the PDG. They mentioned often mother, the family, fertility, planting and harvesting, and God. PDG leaders paid special attention to women and children for these social categories cut across clan class, ethnic and regional divisions.

'My mother carried me. She carried me for twenty years and five months before my birth. My age is her age. The women are the fire of the RDA. When we want to make a knife we need iron, water and fire. The knife is Africa. We are the blacksmiths. We must use fire to make our knife. Our fire is our women. Our women mold us, carry us.

To point out that all men are equal, only the environment makes a difference, Touré said:

'Man is water. Put fire under the water. What is left at night?' 'Steam' answers the crowd. 'Take the water and put it into an ice box. What is left at night?' Answers the crowd 'Ice'. 'Is ice the same as steam?' Answers the crowd 'NO'. 'Is the water which made the steam the same as the water which made the ice?' Answers the crowd 'YES'. 'Man is like water, equal and alike at the beginning. Then some are heated and some are frozen and

---

[1] Before, *Coupe de bambou* came out occasionally.

so they become different. Just change the conditions, heat or freeze, and the original equality is again clear.' 'Do you think you are Soussou, Malinke, Bambara? No, you are water and you are equal. At sunset when you pray to God say over and over that each man is a brother, and that all men are equal.'

The point that men are equal but the environment is not, was repeated:

'Take twins. Separate them at birth and send one to Mecca for his education. He will speak Arabic, have much experience in the world, be accustomed to human society and to machines. Take the other. Put him alone in the forest. Bring them together when they are thirty and compare. One will know speech and the other not. One will crane his neck in awe when a plane passes overhead, wonder when the electricity is turned on, tremble when a car passes, shout when a pair of glasses is placed on his nose. The other will be perfectly at ease before this wealth of things. Does this mean God made the twins unequal?'

A variant of this theme was:

'Take a peanut. Break it open. Find two seeds inside. Plant one in the ground. Put the other on a table or in a drawer or under a drum or on a stone floor. The seed in the earth will sprout, the other will forever be dead. Does it mean God made the seeds differently, that God is unjust? No the seeds are equal, only the conditions surrounding them vary.

A man can be what he thinks he is, a slave is he who thinks himself a slave.

'Say to yourself I am Mamadou, boy of the Commandant. I am the same as Vincent Auriol the President of France, as the Governor, as the Commandant. Pinch the Commandant and he is hurt.' Do not let Auriol sleep, and he is tired. Give the Governor no food and he is hungry. You are the same. You are equal. If you tremble before the Commandant, before Auriol, before the Governor, then you insult God. He made men equal.'

The technique of making general points through particular anecdotes Sékou Touré developed first in the West African trade union context.

'If I wore a grey *boubou* and were called Amadou Guèye and spoke Wolof you would think me Senegalese. If I wore a white cloth and spoke Bambara and were called Mamadou Sissoko you would think me Soudanese. If I wore tan wool and spoke Fulani and were called Diallo Alpha you might think me Soudanese. If I wore khaki trousers and spoke Ewe you would think me Togolese. But I am called Sékou Touré and I am Soussou and I speak Soussou. But I also speak Bambara, and Malinke, and Wolof. . . . I change my clothes and I change my language. The clothes can change and the language can be learned. I am like you; I am a man like you; my race is African.'

The 1954 Election

Though the campaign of 1954 gave ample indications of the PDG's popularity, nevertheless French officials declared Diawadou elected. The PDG claimed falsification, and listed the techniques employed by Governor Parisot and his secretary-general Marchesseau. They made their political preferences public, and administrators in the countryside passed these preferences on at gatherings of villagers and *chefs de canton*. Diawadou's agents had a decided advantage because at election time they could take leave from their civil service jobs and they received official transport. Officials manipulated the electoral register, still limited to less than half a million. In 1951 when both ran unsuccessfully, most of Diawadou's votes came from the Fouta and most of Touré's from the forest. By 1954, 82,980 new electors were on the electoral register—72,056 of these were in the Fouta. Furthermore, in the *cercles* of Nzérékoré, Kankan, Gueckedou, Forecariah, and Siguiri, where the PDG was known to be particularly strong, 10,627 names were stricken from the electoral register. During the elections, the voting cards were not distributed by a commission, as prescribed by law, but mostly by the very *chefs de canton* who with their associates were also the local agents of Diawadou. Some made only Diawadou's ballot paper available to the voters. Some *chefs de canton* also presided at the polls where the secrecy required by law did not exist. At Kissidougou, for example, Diawadou's agent *chef de canton* Bendou Leno presided; at Dabola the father of Diawadou, *chef de canton* Almamy Barry Aguibou, presided. In many polling stations the PDG representatives though duly accredited were turned away; sometimes they were beaten. Illiterates manned many of the polling stations, men who could not write an official report or record the results. Administrators wrote in the figures as they saw fit, sent them by coded cable to Conakry where they were added under the personal supervision of the governor. Only global figures became public, and the PDG representatives at the time could obtain no official breakdown of the total: 147,701 for Diawadou, 85,906 for Touré; 7,995 for the socialists, 5 RPF and 16,000 for various independents.[1]

Many people refused to accept the official results. During the rest of 1954 and 1955, except in the Fouta Djallon, there were periodic incidents involving partisans of PDG and BAG. On the coast and in the forest people chased their chiefs out of villages and towns. Administration broke down as officials and the *élus* lost influence. Barry Diawadou required police protection in Conakry while large

---

[1] Figures from special number of 15 March–1 April 1955 of *Afrique Informations*.

crowds acclaimed Sékou Touré as 'the real chief', 'the real deputy'.[1] The PDG took care to demonstrate its preponderance. Sang the women:

> You are a new chief
> You are chosen as chief
> The people is with you
> You are a new chief
> Lift up your head
> Look at the sea of faces
> That answers when you call.

The reasons varied why Governor Parisot and his associates of the 'tough' school of French officials, took so active a part in the Guinea elections. Some saw the PDG as subversive because of its potential nationalism, and others because of its supposed Communist sympathies. The latter group argued that the PDG had never accepted the interterritorial RDA decision to disaffiliate from the French Communists in Parliament, and pointed out that no Guinean was among the RDA parlementarians who took the decision. The interterritorial RDA, therefore, stepped in to demonstrate solidarity with the PDG, prevent a repetition of the Ivory Coast incidents, and to undercut in Paris the influence of the French officials in Guinea who opposed the PDG. These tasks fell upon the political director, Ouëzzin Coulibaly, then a senator from Ivory Coast. He spent most of the year after the by-elections touring with Sékou Touré and helping to organize the PDG, and occasionally joining in where the PDG came to blows with chiefs and their clients. He used his status and immunity as a *parlementaire* to press local French officials to pay attention to the law. He prepared the way within the PDG also, for a shift from the tactics and vocabulary of total opposition to those of partial communication with French officials. Then in July 1955 the interterritorial RDA Co-ordinating Committee met for the first time since the RDA *parlementaires* broke with the French Communists, and deliberately chose Conakry as the place.

This meeting was the occasion Sékou Touré chose to begin breaking the West African trade unions from the French CGT and out of the Communist-dominated international, the World Federation of Trade Unions. A secret session of the Co-ordinating Committee began the pattern leading to the autonomy of all West African union, youth and party organizations from their French affiliates. The move revealed the frankly nationalist objectives of the Guinea RDA leaders, determined to build

---

[1] *L'Essor*, Bamako, 15–16 July 1954.

nationalist trade unionism . . . joined to two fundamental principles: nationalism and the unity and solidarity of the various social groups in the countries under foreign domination. The original element in this new trade unionism, which clearly differentiates it from Western trade unionism, is a strong determination to back political action in order to hasten the coming of national independence. This preoccupation with the political independence of the nation takes precedence over all social preoccupations.[1]

After the Conakry meeting Sékou Touré was well on the way to becoming, in French eyes, an *interlocuteur valable*. There had been political shifts in Paris. In June 1954 officials in Guinea were carrying out the 'tough' policy of the outgoing French government; but already the Mendès-France government was taking office. The new Overseas Minister Robert Buron, like the Governor-General of West Africa, Bernard Cornut-Gentille, favoured conciliating African nationalists. When the interterritorial RDA stepped between the PDG and French officials with the hope of avoiding more violence, the French government was receptive. In October 1954 Buron visited Conakry. By previous agreement the PDG organized a giant reception and demonstrated efficiency when the party without the police kept order and directed traffic. PDG women wore white dresses embroidered with Sily, the RDA elephant. Demonstrators carried giant placards which read *Vive RDA* on one side; *Vive le Ministre* on the other. The RDA took Buron's visit as a disavowal from Paris of Parisot's policy in Guinea. People taunted the BAG in song:

> The RDA is everywhere
> The saboteurs always said
> That they are the chiefs
> But a man is a chief
> If he is heard by the people.
> Sékou says he is not a chief
> But today they wisely gave him power.

Another song recalled that at a reception for Buron in the palace of the governor, there were not enough seats when Sékou Touré and his wife arrived. The Minister and the Governor-General offered their chairs. People sang:

> Sékou, your enemies are not yet tired
> But they forget
> That in Conakry
> Capital of Guinea
> You are the Governor
> Is it not true, comrades?
> It is as sure

[1] *La Liberté*, 11 December 1956.

As certain as the world
So true
That in Conakry
Sékou is Governor.

Buron's visit did not mean the immediate assumption of political office by the PDG leaders. The French Parliament validated Diawadou's credentials in January 1955, and new incidents broke out in Guinea. Repeatedly during 1955 Sékou Touré publicly thanked Governor Parisot for being against the PDG, claiming 'This allowed the PDG to become the organized champion of the people.'[1] The party turned to its own advantage many of the official measures designed to oppose it. Thus when French officials, in order to reduce tension in Conakry, decided to send the unemployed 'vagrants' back to the villages, the PDG urged people to take the free rides and use them for party propaganda. Trucks carried people chanting:

> They say the elephant does not exist
> But here is the elephant
> The elephant no one can beat.

The PDG used the wave of popular protest during 1955 in order to prepare for the next parliamentary elections. The leaders were well aware the party was weak among the Fulani. There were few Fulani or even Fulani-speaking people among the PDG. The party leaders tried to link with Sékou Touré on the PDG ticket for 1956 a man who could attract Fulani support—though publicly they disclaimed that ethnic considerations entered into the choice. They first invited DSG candidate Barry III to share the PDG ticket; when he declined, the PDG *conférence des cadres* of 1955 selected Diallo Sayfoulaye for the party ticket.

A Ponty *major* who had been a GEC member and an early stalwart of the RDA, he became a 'martyr' when French officials transferred him out of Guinea to Mali and Niger. He had important traditional credentials as well. He is the son of Alpha Bocar Diallo, dean of the *chefs de canton* in the Fouta Djallon. The PDG newspaper *la Liberté* was able to announce that 'like La Fayette on the night of 4 August 1789, Sayfoulaye renounced his privileges to join the democratic camp'.[2] His name signifies 'the sword of God;' one PDG electoral theme was to exploit the Koranic story in which his name figures. This is how Sékou Touré introduced him:

I shall tell you a story, a story you will recognize. I had a dream in which I saw the people of Guinea, in which I saw the people of the Fouta. I saw the chiefs of the Fouta as tyrants. I saw them use and abuse and beat and

[1] Citation from interviews.   [2] 27 December 1955.

oppress the people. I saw them decorating and gilding their many wives. Among them there was one chief (the *chef de canton* of the area where the speech was delivered). This chief had twenty chickens. One day he captured a hawk and put it among the twenty chickens. He chained the hawk, fed the hawk, and treated it as if it were a chicken. Then a stranger came to the village, a man the RDA educated. This stranger knew the hawk was not a chicken. He told the chief. 'This is a hawk, not a chicken. It is like treating a man like a pack horse; put him among pack horses yet he is still a man.' The chief disagreed with the stranger, Sayfoulaye. A fierce debate took place. To show what he meant Sayfoulaye lifted his sword in one hand, the chained hawk in the other. He looked up; the hawk looked at the sun and the sky. 'Prove you are still a hawk, or have you, as the chief says, alas, become a chicken? Choose between servitude and a free sky, your chain and the horizon.' He cut the chain. The hawk chose liberty.

'In the same way a man is not a pack horse. The chief must know as we all know. Man chooses liberty. The chief must accept or the chief will lose.'[1]

Through Sayfoulaye, whose family opposed his election and backed Diawadou, the PDG pointed out that not ethnic ties but only the family of the like-minded really counted.

During the 1956 campaign PDG *militants* concentrated their voluntary efforts. The youth wing of the party, the JRDA of Conakry, organized dances and other socials to raise funds. Since most of the electioneering came during Christmas vacation teachers in the party had time off. Many other civil servants took vacations without pay to work for the party. Traders and transporters put their cars at the disposal of the PDG. In villages and towns local party representatives fed, housed, and gave gas and oil to a stream of political visitors. It is difficult to estimate the cash value of these gifts in kind.

Since Conakry solidly favoured the PDG, and so did the Beyla area, the party leaders did no formal campaigning there. They asked the *militants* of Conakry to go to their villages and organize there. They asked the women of Conakry who had been among the most ardent supporters of the party to organize the coastal areas, and they asked the men from the coast to campaign in the Fouta Djallon.

The party leaders wanted to guard against a repetition of the Ivory Coast incidents. They stipulated that never one but at least two party leaders had to be involved in negotiations with French officials. They urged 'vigilance' against 'saboteurs', for they feared unwanted incidents. The vigilance at times passed out of the control of the party leaders, and popular fears of plots against the PDG were recorded in song.

[1] Information based in interviews.

You cannot know
In this mass of faces
Who are your friends
Who are your enemies.
Why are they here?
Is it to tarnish the RDA?
Surely this they cannot do.
For God is here.
Is it to perfect the RDA?
Then they have two helpers
Human help
Divine Help.
You are human.
You cannot tell the differences
Between your true friend
And your betrayer.

The PDG leaders expected, as in Ivory Coast, the use of bribery and corruption; they provided a simple answer.

'If they offer you money, take it and give it to the party. If they offer you transport to the polls take it and vote for the PDG. Is it not true, if you hear that they beat a man for the dream he had, it is because he explained his dream? The money they give you cannot buy you. Money can buy cloth, sandals, the work of a man. It cannot buy a man; it cannot buy his thoughts; it cannot buy his faith. The money was stolen from you. Take it, it is yours. Use it not for yourself but for your brothers, for the PDG.'[1]

The PDG leaders remained skeptical about Buron's assurances that the January 1956 elections would be honestly administered; they set up an elaborate party procedure for the watching of the polls. The PDG *bureau politique* instructed its poll-watchers: to show up in good time; to verify that ballot envelopes were empty and corresponded exactly with the number of electors; to see before voting began that the urn was empty, had no false bottom, was fastened by two dissimilar locks, that the keys were held respectively by the president of the electoral commission and the oldest assessor, and signed inside and out; to oppose the presence near the polls of any unauthorized persons, including guards or chiefs, who might unduly influence the voters; to denounce people who voted under assumed names or in the name of people dead or absent; to watch over the voting, the opening of the ballot envelopes and the counting and to require a record of all observations and protests; never to leave the polls without leaving a proxy, so as to prevent the substitution of a fraudulent urn; to avoid replying to provocations since incidents make such a substitution

[1] Citation based on interviews.

easy; in case of doubt to check that the urn was the originally signed one; to take immediate steps in case of fraud; to telegraph observations and results to the PDG *bureau politique* in Conakry; even to carry a torch in case the lights go out.[1]

The PDG Takes Over

The 1956 elections were relatively honest. The BAG vote, 131,678, only slightly less than it had been in 1954, was enough to elect Barry Diawadou. But the PDG was the victor. Two of its men became deputies—Sékou Touré and Diallo Sayfoulaye. The number of those entitled to vote more than doubled to become almost a million and a little more than half voted. The PDG vote had grown from 14.3 per cent. in 1951, 34.6 per cent. in 1954, to 62 per cent. in 1956. Since then elections were by universal suffrage and the PDG majority grew steadily: it won control of all the municipalities in 1956; 56 out of 60 seats for the territorial assembly of March 1957. (Three from the Fulani area of Pita went to the socialists.)[2] Under the Loi-Cadre reforms, the assembly voted for the first elected African ministry and Sékou Touré became vice-president of the new council of government.

The PDG took control of the legal organs of the state after an interval of struggle that left a legacy. The struggle strengthened the party in Guinea rather than weakened it, as in Ivory Coast. Part of the explanation lies in the different intensity of the repression. In Ivory Coast officials tried to by-pass parliamentary immunity and most of the territorial leaders of the PDCI were among the estimated 3,000 prisoners. The pressure left the PDCI almost without territorial leaders, while at the local level the repression led to a rapid turnover both among official chiefs and local party leaders. In Guinea, however, fewer PDG leaders became 'martyrs' and most of these were local. Sékou Touré gave figures to the July 1955 meeting of the RDA interterritorial Co-ordinating Committee: in one year 250 arrested, 118 wounded, and 6 dead.[3] The members of the PDG *bureau politique* remained at liberty even though none had parliamentary immunity.

[1] From the mimeographed party instructions, Conakry, 20 December 1955. They were signed by Couyate Diely Bocar, permanent employee of the party, and Keïta Nfamara, then 2nd secretary. Nfamara, a primary school graduate, worked as a clerk in the judiciary, and drafted the instructions. A Malinke from Kindia, he held a variety of ministerial portfolios in PDG governments.
[2] Figures from Direction des Affaires Politiques d'AOF, 1956, op. cit.; and Beaujeu-Garnier, Jacqueline. 'Essai de géographie électoral guinéenne', *Les Cahiers d'Outre-mer*, Bordeaux, October–December 1958.
[3] *La Liberté*, 16 August 1955.

The struggle confirmed the PDG *militants* in the conviction that they were on the side of history. It discredited French institutions. The PDG *militants* came to regard the formal constitution, laws, and decrees as the European, alien façade and only their party as truly African. The struggle helped unify people against the colonial system and propelled the leaders to adopt a frankly nationalist platform. The official record of tampering with the elections gave the PDG a solid moral advantage and made possible a representation of the rivalry between BAG and PDG as between truth and falsehood, nationalism and colonialism. The PDG leaders could claim their adversaries were disloyal to the real African tradition, and so could discredit as un-African both the 'intellectuals' who were the BAG *élus* and the 'chiefs' who were the local BAG representatives.

The struggle prolonged the period when the PDG was in opposition, and therefore in harmony with the revolutionary forces in the countryside. These forces knew no frontiers. Where the 'diamond fever' was spreading, in and around Sierra Leone, the *Sily Baga Society* took root; the PDG leaders called it RDA.[1] Outside the Fouta Djallon most people, often for contradictory reasons, were against all authority, and as Sékou Touré explained, 'anarchy itself served the emancipating movement, to the extent that it was directed against the colonial system'.[2] Party finances benefited from resistance against paying taxes, party justice was sometimes acceptable when that of chief or French judge was not. For a few years the PDG could concentrate on building a party organization while free of the responsibilities of keeping order, roads open and telephone lines functioning.

Electoral success by the PDG brought a sense of liberation. The PDG claimed 300,000 members in 1955;[3] by 1959 it was 800,000,[4] and in 1960, 857,000.[5] People volunteered their labour and it was not unusual for villagers to construct a road so that party organizers could reach them, or a shelter so that they might come to the main road to hear itinerant PDG spokesmen. Volunteer labour, dubbed *investissement humain*, was at the disposal of the new PDG government, which tried to harness the burst of popular enthusiasm to the

[1] After the citizens of French Guinea had been expelled from Sierra Leone in 1956, Sékou Touré and Diallo Sayfoulaye led a delegation to Freetown. A most interesting account of their voyage is in the 15 January 1957 issue of *La Liberté*.
[2] Touré, Sékou. 'Allocution de clôture de la conférence des cadres du PDG', of November 1958, *L'Action politique . . .*, tome ii, op. cit., p. 237.
[3] *Afrique Informations*, 15 April–1 May 1955.
[4] *La Liberté*, 4 March 1959.
[5] Touré, Sékou. *La Lutte du Parti Démocratique de Guinée pour l'émancipation africaine*, tome vi, République de Guinée, Conakry, 1961, p. 334 (report to Conakry conference).

building of roads, bridges, schools, party headquarters, and mosques.[1] Though perhaps not very efficient, voluntary labour indicated how close to the people the party had become.

At the same time the party took within itself the chief problems of Guinea: scarcity of trained leadership, absence of national social structures, ethnic fragmentation, and a very limited modern economy. In the countryside and city there was a turnover of leadership from BAG to RDA and a rejection of the existing authorities. The party was the only national institution people considered their own, and its popularity exceeded its ability to channel support; leaders found it easy to increase opposition but hard to discipline their followers. They preached responsibility of leaders to followers, partly by way of contrast with BAG methods, whose *élus* the PDG claimed 'had no direct ties with the masses, did not represent them, and as a result did not influence them'.[2] They emphasized the party was for all, not for the leaders. Therefore no man could nominate himself for office; he had to be nominated.

'A canoe is in the ocean. Ten men are in it. It springs a leak. All are in danger. Two men start bailing out the water. The other eight help. Does it mean the two are the first or most important, and that the eight work for the two? No, each man of the team works for the whole team.'[3]

In 1954 the party structure was rudimentary: the *bureau executif* of Conakry led the party of all of Guinea. Sékou Touré as secretary-general, Diallo Abdourahmane, Keïta Nfamara, Camara Bengaly, and al Hajj Mamadou Fofana—directed the planting of PDG committees in each village and locality.

After the electoral success of 1957, the leaders set about consolidating their power. They strengthened the party structure, asserted its control over administration, integrated all opposition parties into the PDG. A *bureau politique nationale* became elected at regular party congresses; it sent a stream of directives to the village and local committees. There were party conferences of cadres, whenever urgent matters needed discussion. A permanent staff worked at party headquarters, not only in Conakry, but increasingly also at the regional headquarters. The party youth wing, the JRDA, became strengthened and gained control over all Guinean youth organizations; the trade unions, also, unified into a single movement, as the party asserted control.

[1] Touré, tome vi, op. cit.. pp. 163–97; see also Touré, *L'Action du PDG* . . ., tome i, op. cit., p. 52; Touré, *Le Cinquième congrès national* . . ., tome iv, op. cit., pp. 136–7 and p. 41; Touré, Sékou. *La Planification économique*, tome v, République de Guinée, Conakry, 1960, p. 68.
[2] Touré, *L'Action politique du PDG* . . ., tome i, op. cit., p. 15.
[3] Information based on interviews, 1956.

PDG victory did not simply wipe out ethnic divisions, though the party had for the first time in Guinea history managed to span these differences. The shift from the BAG marked a change in the balance of ethnic groups within Guinea. Fulani influence decreased, and Malinke and Soussou townsmen had greater influence. Incidents which took place in Conakry in October 1956 showed how close to the surface ethnic differences still were. The PDG leaders took care to conciliate Fulani opinion, and blamed colonial rule for the division which still reigned among ethnic groups:

in this world there are but two races, that which dominates and exploits in an inhuman fashion . . . and that which is dominated and profoundly exploited, which includes all the colonised peoples to which belong the Almamys of the Fouta in the 'GALLES', the Fulani in their 'FOULASSOS' and 'MARGAS' and the 'MATCHOUBES' in their 'ROUNDES'. They should know that today more than ever before if they can have any secular hatred of any race, it is surely against the one which, trampling to the ground the 'TREATY OF PROTECTORATE OF THE FOUTA DJALLON', submitted them to the same system of daily humiliation and exploitation as their Soussou, Malinke, Toma, Guerze, Kissi, Koniaguis, Baga and Landouman brothers.[1]

Thus ethnic divisions drove the PDG leaders to greater nationalism.

To limit ethnic fragmentation, the PDG leaders adopted several other measures. They refused to recognize or accept ethnic or regional organizations in the party. They insisted—unlike the PDCI leaders of Ivory Coast—that local PDG committees be organized on a strict neighbourhood basis. This meant that in Conakry, where neighbourhoods included people of different origins, the local party structure mixed people. The PDG leaders publicly refused to mention a man's ethnic group or status; their very rigidity on this principle showed there was a problem. At the same time, the leaders took great care to keep balance within their ranks; the top four leaders reflected the four major regions—Sékou Touré the Malinke, Diallo Sayfoulaye the Fulani, Beavogui Lansana[2] the forest peoples, and Bengaly Camara the coastal Soussou.

Ethnic divisions also impelled the PDG leaders to weaken further the traditional leaders. In the countryside, defeat of the BAG also marked defeat of the 'chiefs' in local politics. As long as the PDG was in opposition, the leaders did not attack the chieftaincy collectively; instead they argued 'we are not against the chiefs, we are only against the bad chiefs'.[3] PDG organizers learned it was fruitful to investigate if there was a violation of pre-European tradition in the

---

[1] Moriba, Magassouba. *La Liberté*, 26 October 1956.
[2] An African doctor, he became minister of foreign affairs.
[3] Citation from interviews.

designation of the official chief, and to seek out his rival. They did not disdain chiefly backing; indeed during the July 1955 interterritorial RDA meeting in Conakry President Houphouët made it his special task 'to stretch out the hand of friendship to the chiefs'.[1] These were but temporary expedients. The close connexion between official chiefs, traditionalists, and the BAG served to discredit them in politics, and most PDG *militants* shared the ideas of Diallo Sayfoulaye:

the chieftaincy degraded by the colonial administration no longer represents the tradition which gave rise to the office. Many chiefs betrayed their functions by making themselves the servile instruments of the state, against the permanent interests of the people. Most were designated illegitimately and hold their posts only because they made themselves spokesmen and defenders of the colonial authorities. . . . Traditional chieftaincy as such no longer exists . . . and nothing can replace it.[2]

In most places it was clear the chiefs had lost their authority, and administrators were troubled. 'In each canton there is the problem of relations with the population, the transmission of orders and all the points of detail which are our work; right now we have great difficulty contacting nearly 100,000 people without intermediaries.'[3] One of the first actions of the PDG government was to call a conference of administrators to study how to eliminate the *chefs de canton* from local administration. On 31 December 1957 the change took place, administrators nominated from Conakry took the place of the *chefs*, and in May 1958 the PDG had a majority of 87.8 per cent. in elections for local advisory councils or *conseils de circonscription*.[4]

These elections eliminated 'chiefs' from local administration, but did not wipe out the influence of traditional leaders whose authority people still admitted. The PDG leaders made a deliberate attempt to integrate these into the party. One example was the family descended of al Hajj Umar Tall, the Toucouleur emperor who had used Dinguiraye as a base.[5] The PDG elected one member of this family, Habib Tall, vice-president of the assembly. Another, also the most important of the African trading community, Baïdy Guèye, became president in 1960 of the *conseil économique*. The PDG used a related technique with Lamine Kaba. After 1956 they would no longer accept that he use his party position to strengthen his claims within the Kaba family. In 1957 the PDG sponsored his election from Kankan to the territorial assembly, and there elected him a vice-president;

---

[1] Citation from interviews, 1955.   [2] *La Liberté*, 5 June 1956.
[3] *Conférence des commandants de cercle*, op. cit., Commandant de Siguiri, p. 45.
[4] Beaujeu-Garnier, op. cit., p. 317.
[5] *Conférence de commandants de cercle*, op. cit., Commandant de Dinguiraye, p. 27.

but they also undercut his position in Kankan and insisted he remain in residence in Conakry.[1]

The local government reforms, designed to consolidate party control over local administration, also increased the need for cadres. The reforms released yet further revolutionary forces in the countryside, and reinforced the pressures for early independence. People flocked to Conakry.[2] The PDG leaders knew the party was closer to the people than was the administration, and elaborated the doctrine of party supremacy over the government, with its corollary that party loyalty and ideology were supreme over the technical and seniority standards in the civil service. Yet the French governor still maintained French standards in key sectors of the civil service, while the shortage of African personnel sharply limited the pace of Africanization. The Loi-Cadre framework forced the PDG leaders to pay attention to French criteria for promotion; they knew they could strengthen administration or the party, but not both, for there were not cadres enough. In order to be able to introduce their own criteria for promotion, they had to overcome the limits on their powers. That meant independence.

The division of the educated men between PDG and BAG intensified the conflict between civil service and party criteria for promotion. The shift from BAG and PDG cadres meant a shift from more to less educated, from older to younger. This was a heritage of French pressure against the PDG in 1947 when Guineans with secondary schooling knew they risked their jobs unless they kept out of politics or backed a regional association. Hence the founders of the PDG were primary school products mostly and held low civil service jobs. By 1954 they were joined by the new products of the elementary and upper primary schools who also found little scope in the existing system. Most Ponty men were BAG, and there were only a handful of exceptions: Madeira Keïta, Keïta Fodéba, a teacher from Siguiri who built a ballet company of international fame before he became the first minister of interior of Guinea; Diane Lansana, a veterinary surgeon and cousin of Sékou Touré from Faranah who became general of the Guinea armed services; Diallo Sayfoulaye, and Abdoulaye Diallo, Fulani with family both in Mali and Guinea—Sayfoulaye was the first president of the National Assembly of Guinea, Abdoulaye built the CGT in Mali, was its first minister of labour, and after he voted against the 1958 constitution went to Guinea to become its first minister-resident in Ghana; Magassouba

---

[1] He died shortly after independence.

[2] By 1960 the population was estimated at 112,491. Touré, *La Lutte du PDG* . . ., tome vi, op. cit., p. 87.

Moriba, an African doctor from Kankan who became the first director of Guinea's *sûreté nationale*. This handful of Ponty men suffered for their politics. Some lost their jobs, were transferred to outlying districts or to other territories, or served jail sentences.

Their experience with the elite of 1945 gave to the PDG leaders prior to independence a conviction that self-made men were more reliable to the nation than highly educated ones. Observing that 'when a country is betrayed by its elite it dies or it invents another',[1] they prized ideological conviction above diplomas, which they felt Africans obtained only at the cost of their own identity. They held the existence of links with the mass of the population to be far more important than the fact or level of education. 'One cannot,' they observed, 'judge the quality of a State as a function of the individual qualities of the men who lead it.'[2]

University graduates were not involved in the competition for political power between BAG and PDG.[3] The first generation of university graduates was still studying in France or Dakar during the fighting phase of the PDG. Many students were near the age of PDG leaders. The students backed the PDG against the BAG, but after 1956 they found many grounds for criticism: the limited education of the new PDG ministers; their acceptance of the Loi-Cadre reforms.

The uneasy relations with the more educated Guineans propelled the PDG leaders towards independence. So did uneasy relations with the workers. Briefly workers accepted that there was an identity of interests with the new African PDG government; their leader Sékou Touré became head of the government, and Bengaly Camara became minister of labour. Friction grew, however. The government though African was still the single largest employer of labour. There were some brief strikes in spring of 1958.[4] The AOF union organization, UGTAN, called for immediate independence and an elected AOF African executive. Touré was formally the head of that movement, and knew that by ignoring that call he risked forfeiting his claim to lead the workers.

Pressure grew further early in 1958, when the new interterritorial *Parti du Regroupement Africain* (PRA) united all AOF parties except

---

[1] N'Diaye, Edge. *La Liberté*, 24 July 1956.
[2] Touré. 'Rapport de doctrine . . .,' September 1959, in *Le Cinquième congrès national . . .*, tome iv, op. cit., p. 48.
[3] In the mid-fifties Mê Paul Fabert was almost the only returned student; he led a one-man party, the *Union Démocratique et Sociale Africaine*, dedicated to building a West African federation of French and English speaking independent states. He became minister of justice after independence.
[4] See my article in *West Africa*, 5 April 1958.

the RDA,[1] and adopted a radical platform. In Guinea the PRA branch was born in May 1958 of a union between DSG and BAG. Then in July at Cotonou, the interterritorial congress of the PRA called for immediate independence. If they ignored this, Touré and his associates knew they were vulnerable to attack from left and right, within Guinea and outside. Yet, for some months, though their speeches were sharply critical of France,[2] the position of the PDG leaders towards the 1958 constitution was uncertain. When General de Gaulle came to Conakry on 25 August, he was received by a huge demonstration and a sharply worded speech by President Touré.[3] On 27 August in Dakar the UGTAN announced for a NO in the referendum. On 11 September Bakary Djibo, union and party leader from Niger, said NO. On 7 September Ouëzzin Coulibaly died in Paris. It was he who had kept the interterritorial RDA together in spite of internal differences. The break in the RDA remained. On 12 September Sékou Touré broke discipline with the interterritorial RDA, disregarded President Houphouët's orders for a YES, and demanded independence. 'We prefer poverty in liberty to riches in slavery.'[4] Once the NO decision was taken there was remarkable unity within Guinea. Barry III and Barry Diawadou joined the reorganized PDG government which took over the newly independent state. Their parties dissolved and members became integrated within the PDG.

The French government was not really prepared for the NO, and the first reaction was one of anger. French civil servants withdrew but made no provision to transfer files, and French administrators, judges, doctors, and other civil servants left confusion behind. For some months the terms of Guinea's relationship to France remained undefined. Only when the Guinea government made clear that it recognized the Provisional Government of the Republic of Algeria during the Monrovia Conference on 6 August 1959 was the break between Guinea and France final.

The uncertainty surrounding the departure of French officials and soldiers added to the problems of the PDG leaders as they became fully responsible. Guinea became a state before it was fully a nation.[5] Only the party was truly a national institution, and held people together with the theme of 'a common misery and a common destiny'.[6]

People expected great things of independence. There was a call for modernization even though there were few modernizers, more justice

---

[1] And the Mauretanians.   [2] See *Paris–Dakar*, 16 April 1958.
[3] Touré. *L'Action politique du PDG* . . ., tome i, op. cit., pp. 73 f.
[4] Ibid., op. cit., p. 94.
[5] Touré. *La Lutte du PDG* . . ., tome vi, op. cit., p. 429.
[6] Touré. *L'Action politique du PDG* . . ., tome i, op. cit., p. 14.

even though few judges, more administration even though few clerks, more maternities even though few doctors, more roads even though few engineers, more schools even though few teachers. Sergeants became majors, clerks became senior administrators, union leaders became ambassadors as Guinea became the first former French-speaking West African state to become a member of the United Nations.

PART SEVEN

Teachers and Chiefs in Mali

THERE are close connexions between Guinea and Mali (known as Soudan until 1960). A common savannah region joins the two states, and easy communications by land and by river facilitated the growth of political and cultural ties long before the Europeans came. In both Mali and Guinea there is a substantial group of Mande-speaking peoples, mostly Malinke and Bambara. Fulani who had migrated from the north-eastern part of Africa during the seventeenth century and cut through the Mande-speaking savannah areas, settled or herded cattle in the Fouta Djallon plateau of Guinea. Before France introduced a policy of cultural assimilation, the Fulani and Mande-speaking peoples were assimilating the different tribes of the region, partly by war, but mainly by providing uniform social, economic, and political systems.

The majority of the people in Mali and Guinea became brothers in Islam, a religion which for some thousand years has been descending from the north. There grew up a pre-European urban tradition represented by Gao, Timbuctu, Sikasso, Macina, and Kankan. Arabic studies and commerce flourished under the empires such as Ghana, Mali, and Gao, which were at their height respectively in the eleventh, fourteenth, and sixteenth centuries. Though relations among these overlapping empires were not always peaceful, on the whole they provided conditions favouring peaceful contact in the area stretching from the Sahara through the western savannah. Contact was favoured also by geography, specially by the Niger river, which rises in Guinea and cuts Mali in a great arch.

The modern states of Guinea and Mali share yet another historical tradition, that of resisting colonial conquest. There developed a renaissance during the eighteenth and early nineteenth centuries. The empires led by the families of the Toucouleur Muslim teacher al Hajj Umar Tall, and of the Malinke warrior-trader Samory Touré represented different forces, and at times relations between them were strained. Yet both empires represented obstacles to colonial rule, and France had to defeat these empires so as to make Guinea and Mali into colonies.

The names and the fact that a frontier exists at all between Guinea and Mali are of course legacies of colonial rule. Only Guinea has an outlet on the Atlantic and a share of the fertile forest zone that lines the West African coast. Therefore Guinea was more directly involved, in modern times, with the trans-Atlantic trading begun when the Portuguese ships came in the fifteenth century. The new trade routes of the ocean took on added significance with the slave trade, and gradually replaced the declining trans-Saharan caravan routes, which for millenia had brought landlocked Mali in contact with Mecca and the Mediterranean world. Mali, situated in the core of West Africa, has vast barren areas on the southern shore of the Sahara, known by the Arabic term *sahel*. Geography contributed to the relative cultural homogeneity of Mali, where there are not, as in Guinea, many small tribes such as those inhabiting coastal inlets and forest.

There are other differences between the two states. In Guinea the Fulani minority, more than a third of the total population, has responded more slowly to modernization than the rest. Mali too has a minority problem, but it involves fewer people. Many of the northern, primarily white nomads, who constitute about 7 per cent. of the population, see their past and perhaps their future with their neighbours in Algeria or Mauretania rather than with their Negro countrymen.[1] Another difference between the states is in the pace of modern economic development. Guinea has been more favoured, is rich in water power, iron, bauxite, and other minerals, and has already embarked on a road leading towards industrialization. Mali, on the other hand, limited by the high cost of transport, has been able to exploit very few modern sources of wealth or energy. Until recently, therefore, Mali remained largely a subsistence economy and exported little except some rice, peanuts, fish, hides, and meat products.

Though colonial rule was responsible for the fixing of the actual frontiers dividing the two states, it served to reinforce the ties between the inhabitants of the two states. For French rule imposed uniformity in policy and institutions. The men who became the post-war leaders of Guinea's and Mali's parties, trade unions, and youth organizations worked in a harmony which reflected their common history, social origins, education, and timetable of political reform. In both states the parties which first won elections were based upon the official chiefs, hastily assembled by French administrators and in 'spectacular collusion'[2] with them. 'Chiefs' not only filled the posts in the lowest rung of the administration, but for a decade took on the added function of representing Africans in elected assemblies. In

[1] Dupuis, J. 'Un Problème de minorité: les nomades dans l'état soudanais', *L'Afrique et L'Asie*, 50, 2, 1960, p. 22.
[2] Citation from an interview in 1956 with *Bloc Africain de Guinée* (BAG) leader Bangoura Karim.

both states most of the French officials who intervened directly in the organization of the first elections were Socialists, and this helps explain why the parties of 'chiefs' from both Mali and Guinea had parliamentary ties with the French socialists. The new role of 'chiefs' as the first *élus* was in part due to similarities in social structure in the two states. Where large scale pre-European empires existed, French administrators often disregarded the official doctrine of direct rule. They found it cheaper and more efficient to name as *chefs de canton* men who came from the traditional aristocracy. Hence these two categories overlapped both in Guinea and Mali, perhaps to the greatest extent among the Fulani. In both Mali and Guinea the French policy of recruiting some of the traditional aristocracy into the *commandement indigène* and then using it as the basis for the first political parties, helped produce among many 'chiefs' across ethnic lines a consciousness approximating that of class.

For some years the 'chiefs' and their candidates won majorities in elections. Partly in reaction, the African opposition, organizers of the Guinea and Mali *sections* of the RDA, themselves became class conscious. Even though they were relatively few in numbers they took on the tasks of modernizing and levelling African society. The US and PDG became instruments of social and economic as well as political revolution; the leaders were the most intent of the French-speaking West African leaders in driving towards independence.

There were several related reasons for this. First, the *Union Soudanaise* (US–RDA) and *Parti Démocratique de Guinée* (PDG–RDA) leaders, could achieve electoral victory only after defeating the 'chiefs', not only in territorial politics, but in the villages. This of necessity involved the RDA leaders in sharp controversy with the French officials who maintained the 'chiefs' in the bottom rung of the administration. Second, a decade in opposition gave US and PDG leaders opportunities to clarify their political ideas, to introduce ideological considerations into party activities, and to concentrate on party structure to an extent not possible for the party leaders who succeeded in election earlier. Third, a decade in opposition gave US and PDG leaders opportunity and cause to organize trade unions; in Guinea and Mali the history of the RDA and of the trade union movement is closely entwined. The union experience, which began within the framework of the French *Confédération Générale du Travail* (CGT) reinforced their tendency to use Marxist terminology. It also further marked them as modernizing townsmen who struggled against the French administration partly because it was the single largest employer of labour.

In view of the common background, both pre-European and post-war, in the RDA and in the West African CGT federation, co-operation was close between the leaders of the PDG and the US. It even took the form of exchanges among the top personnel. For example Madeira Keïta, the first secretary-general of the PDG, became Mali's first minister of interior, and the administrative secretary of the US. Abdoulaye Diallo, in Mali the first secretary-general of the CGT and the first minister of labour, became in 1958 Guinea's first minister-resident in Ghana. Demba Diallo first attended United Nations sessions as a delegate of Guinea; he was Mali's delegate after 1960.

In their approach to social revolution the leaders of Mali and Guinea faced similar limitations, in that the base of wealth remained narrow. Unlike Senegal and Ivory Coast where the export of coffee, cocoa, or peanuts produced something of an African middle class, in Mali and Guinea only a few traders and the civil servants had a money income. In the absence of extensive social and economic changes introduced by European rule, the leaders of Mali and Guinea built support for their mass parties out of pre-European forces of revolution, the universal and egalitarian currents in Islam, contemporary memories of past African unity, and resistance against French colonial rule. The US leaders of Mali had the special problem of being revolutionaries in a state that was even poorer than Guinea.

Poverty With Old Riches

Unlike the coastal states of West Africa, Mali had no appreciable spurt of economic activity after the Europeans came to rule. Some figures illustrate this point. In 1960, the average family income was $52 a year.[1] In 1945, while the total customs receipts of Senegal were listed at 66.5 million francs and for Guinea at 71.3 million, Soudan (Mali) was credited with a mere 17.1 million francs.[2] No one had done much prospecting for minerals, and certainly not in the Saharan region, where French rule among the nomad tribes was at best insecure. The area is vast—about twice that of metropolitan France—while the population is quite small, under four million according to a 1960 estimate.[3] Moreover, it spreads unevenly; a density of roughly ten to the square kilometre around the fertile banks of Niger, less than one tenth of one to the square kilometre in the northern zones on the border of the Sahara.[4]

[1] *Plan du projet de rapport*, Ministère du Plan et de l'Économie Rurale à l'Assemblée Nationale, M.B.R.P. Bamako, April 1961, mimeographed, Mali, p. 2, five year plan project.
[2] *Annuaire Statistique*, tome i, 1950, op. cit., p. 345.
[3] République du Mali, Ministère de l'Économie Rurale et du Plan, *Bulletin Statistique Mensuel*, 1961, Bulletin spécial, p. 25.
[4] Spitz, Georges. *Soudan français*, Éditions Maritimes & Coloniales, Paris, 1955, pp. 11 f.; *AOF 1957*, op. cit., pp. 97-9.

Soudan had a minimum budget. A governor to make any progress had to shame the authorities in Dakar into making appropriations. Governor Edmond Louveau, for example, began building the École des Travaux Publics of Bamako before he had credits in hand.[1]

The slow rate of economic growth was due partly to the high cost of transport. French officials regulated the AOF economy to subsidize the products grown near the sea coast. They cut roads which ended the isolation of the forest peoples, and brought to the world market the peanuts from Senegal, the cocoa and coffee from Ivory Coast. They favoured the flow of labour from the savannah states, and that included Mali, to the farms on the coast. Mali migrants went to Senegal, Guinea, and Ivory Coast as well as Ghana. 'Going to Kumasi'[2] was the purpose of many young men, travelling down the eastern and western branches of the Niger to trade, harvest, and earn bride or tax money.[3]

From the French standpoint, Mali was to service the coastal economies. Within Mali, the arrival of the Europeans meant the gradual transfer of the centres of economic activity from the old northern cities to the newer southern ones, the decline of the north and the growth of southern towns like the capital, Bamako, which had been a village until after French conquest. In 1910 the estimated population was 6,500. Over the next half century this multiplied by ten. The southward move of trade was gradual. In the twenties, Mopti, the market city on the Niger river, was the 'third largest city of Mali' and half the size of Bamako but it was only a fifth in the fifties. Mopti had been a *commune mixte* since 1922, but this status was withdrawn by 1938.[4] The northern shepherds could sell wool on the international market. But this and other trade disappeared before the Second World War, due both to foreign competition and to French direct or indirect subsidies to other goods.

The roads the Europeans built were at best rudimentary, and had as object the flow of goods and people to the coast, to Ivory Coast by way of Sikasso or Bougouni, to Guinea by way of Siguiri. The one substantial transport legacy of French rule was the Dakar–Niger railroad. It led from the port of Dakar to the border town of Kayes, to Bafoulabe, Kita and stopped short at Bamako on the banks of the

[1] Governor 1946–52; Socialist.
[2] *Barakéla*, organ of the *Union Régionale des Syndicats C.G.T. du Soudan*, 19–25 December 1955, mimeographed.
[3] Rouch, 1956, op. cit., pp. 33 f.; *Bulletin de l'Institut Français d'Afrique Noire*, Série B, July–October 1960, no. 3–4, Dakar.
[4] *AOF 1957*, op. cit., p. 95; *Annuaire Statistique*, tome i, 1949, op. cit., pp. 85–7; and 'Mopti', unpublished typescript, Paul Barlet, municipal archives of Mopti.

Niger. There was a plan to prolong to Mali the railroads beginning in Conakry and Abidjan and thus to make Mali the hub of a regional railroad network in the form of a wheel. The plan remained on paper and the Dakar–Niger was the main tie to the sea, France, and the international economy. The cost of transport was prohibitive: in 1960 a ton of imported cement, wholesale, cost about 5,000 cfa francs, double in Bamako, and two and a half times in Mopti.[1] Cattle and fish were among the major exports—but many cattle driven to the coast on the hoof lost weight and sickened, while fresh fish, in the absence of adequate refrigeration, was expensive or unavailable at any distance from the Niger river.

The one development project by French administrators was the Office du Niger, an irrigation scheme including a large dam across the Niger at Sansanding, near Segou. The scheme was conceived before 1919; the dam, begun in 1929 and fully functioning only since 1947, deflected the flood waters of the Niger river into its old, 'dead' delta of the interior, into natural channels, and made possible the growing of rice. The Office du Niger authorities gave land, capital, and tools to African settlers. Interruptions in construction, administration, and financing kept the size of this peasant community well below its estimated potential. In 1959 about 55,000 hectares were under cultivation and the figure could rise to be three times as high. There were slightly less than 10,000 able bodied men, making with their families a total of some 35,000 people working the land, while near Segou at the headquarters and workshops of the Office in Markala, there were some 3,000 wage earners. The Office did not work to full capacity, due largely to lack of capital and bad transport facilities within West Africa.[2]

In the future Mali could become the granary of West Africa[3] supplying rice as well as fish from the Niger river, meat and milk from cattle, and fruit and grain to neighbouring states. This depends on development, the existence of adequate transport and refrigeration and on a free flow of trade between Mali and her many neighbours—

[1] République du Sénégal, Service Statistique, *Bulletin Statistique et Économique Mensuel*, année 1962, no. 1, p. 19. République du Mali, Service Statistique, *Bulletin Statistique Mensuel*, April 1961, p. 17.

[2] Spitz, Georges. *Sansanding: les irrigations du Niger*. Société d'Éditions Géographiques Maritimes & Coloniales, Paris, 1949; and Chambre de Commerce d'Agriculture et d'Industrie de Bamako, République du Mali, *Éléments du bilan économique de l'année 1960*, Bamako, mimeographed, 1961; Office du Niger, *le Delta ressuscité*, Service de Documentation Économique, Paris and Segou, République du Niger, pamphlet, *c.* 1960.

[3] Kone, Jean-Marie. 'Rapport sur le paysannat', in Union Soudanaise, *Les Travaux du 4e congrès territorial* ténu a Bamako les 22, 23, et 24 septembre 1955, Bamako, mimeographed (henceforth cited as *1955 US Report*).

Algeria, Mauretania, Senegal, Guinea, Ivory Coast, Upper Volta, and Niger. The Republic of Mali was set back economically by the break-up first of the AOF federation in 1958, and then by the break-up of the Mali federation of Soudan and Senegal in 1960. The development of the Republic of Mali depends on the growth of the internal African market, on economic ties across the Sahara with an independent Algeria, Morocco, and Tunisia. Mali is central not only to any West African federation, but also to connexions between the Maghreb and West Africa.

Though these ties are rudimentary now, they were not before the industrial revolution allowed Europe to outstrip, with her machines, the technology of the rest of the world; export trucks and steamships turned Mali's landlocked location into an economic disadvantage. Until European navigators came to the coast, geography rather favoured the economic growth of Mali. The northern towns were terminals in the trans-Saharan trade, and redistributed southward cloth, amber, salt, arms, and ideas.[1] The salt mines of the *sahel* supplied the needs of men and cattle in the savannah and to some extent in the forest. Gold from the forest was sent to the north. The Niger river, though not navigable, facilitated transport over great distances. Trade and the river explained the prosperity of the ancient northern cities—Djenne, Gao, and Timbuctu among others. For nearly a thousand years Islam was the basis of urban culture and pilgrims went to Mecca. There were flourishing centres of Muslim learning and architecture. From the cities people crossed the savannah relatively easily; brush and flatlands beckoned traders, scholars, warriors, and adventurers, and made easier the formation of large-scale political units.

Islam had come across the desert.[2] It was the religion of the advisors of the Soninke empire of Ghana, the Mande rulers of Mali and the Songhai rulers of Gao. These medieval empires were at their height respectively in the twelfth, fourteenth, and sixteenth centuries.[3] Each declined in part due to attacks from north Africa. Even as the Mali empire dissolved and came under the aegis of Gao, the first European navigators arrived. Then came the European traders, and in the nineteenth century the soldiers, who paved the way for administrators. In 1892 the area received the label Soudan and became a colony of France, a name it held, on and off, until in September 1960,

---

[1] Bovill, E. W. *The Golden Trade of the Moors*, Oxford, 1958.
[2] Cardaire, op. cit.; Gouilly, op. cit.; vol. vi, vii, viii, and ix (vols. i–iv of Soudan series) of Paul Marty's *Études sur l'islam*, Paris, Éditions Ernest Leroux, 1920–2. (See bibliography for complete listing of Marty series.)
[3] A brilliant addition to knowledge is Raymond Mauny. *Tableau géographique de l'ouest-africain au moyen age*, IFAN, Dakar, 1961.

the inhabitants in Legislative Assembly declared themselves the Republic of Mali.[1]

The people of Mali have a strong sense of history and the European colonizers over a little more than three generations of rule disturbed family and institutional links relatively little. To the people from the richer forest states, Maliens proudly say 'our wealth is our civilization', though some young people say, with a touch of bitterness, 'you have export crops and dams and factories while we have our past'. That past, which included long experience with travel, with large states and the universal culture of Islam, left a heritage which affected the growth of post-war political parties.

There is an urban tradition, nourished in the older trading cities like Gao, Djenne, and Timbuctu; from these some people moved south, with the trade, to the newer cities of Mopti, Segou, and Bamako. Mahamane Alassane Haidara, a proper Timbuctuan and president of the National Assembly of Mali,[2] spoke of his city, located where the Sahara and the Niger River meet.

Like Carthage in antiquity, Timbuctu in the Middle Ages was a famous metropole which included practiced and rich businessmen, a refined and cultivated aristocracy, priests revered by a people of fervent piety. She knew a civilization whose brilliance shone outside the limits of Africa, to reach the great capitals of the Muslim East and the Christian West. Well before the discovery of America, she figures on the Catalan Atlas of Charles V, drawn by Gresques in 1375.

Like Carthage, gold, perfumes, ivory and spices poured out on her wharves; Asian and Mediterranean cloths and silks spread out on her market places; slaves coming from everywhere worked in her fields and led her caravans; steel from Toledo and Damascus armed her warriors; marabouts and writers in her temples and seminaries cared for the health of souls and the culture of the Spirit.

Always wooed for her riches, she was always jealous of her independence and of her liberty which she defended during her long history with admirable determination, against powerful enemies.

For her inhabitants, she was also the city of cities; to her they devoted a positive Cult; and all the rest of the world, in the eyes of her sons, was the land of barbarians.

Even in our days, we must admit, this feeling of attachment crops up spontaneously. When a Timbuctuan makes ready to tear himself away from her holy circle, to go far from her venerable walls with which he has never ceased to commune, he announces in a tone filled with disillusion

---

[1] Foltz thesis, op. cit., specially Chapters VI and VII.

[2] His family traces its ancestry to the Moroccans. Ponty-trained, a schoolteacher, he was one of the founders of the *Union Soudanaise-RDA*, and a senator in the French Council of the Republic.

and regret: 'I betake myself . . . to the bush' even if he goes to Bamako. . . .[1]

There is also an ancient tradition of public service—administrative skills, the habits of keeping written records in Arabic, of following predetermined procedures, making decisions collectively, separating public and family assets, using specialized knowledge to deal with special problems. More than a thousand years of experience with Islam deepened the judicial tradition; the claim 'it is not just' is a call to action in Mali. There is a puritan tradition, too, a preoccupation with morals and motives—perhaps a legacy of the puritanism of the Almoravides who first brought the Koran to the savannah. It is one of the elements explaining that 'sobriety characteristic of the whole sub-desert region',[2] which contrasts so sharply with the turbulence of the forest and coast. Contemporary party declarations of the *Union Soudanaise* show a concern with morals and honour—with collecting taxes in a dignified manner and avoiding unnecessary humiliation for citizens, for example.[3] Preoccupation with principles contributed to the disintegration of the Mali federation with Senegal in August 1960. The Senegalese rudely expelled Soudanese officials, who decided honour demanded a clean break with Senegal even though it meant a blockade of goods entering at the port of Dakar, terminus of Bamako's sole railroad link to the sea. Mali paid a high price for this blockade: the price of cement doubled, for example.[4] The leaders of Mali had to explain to their followers economic decline just at the time of independence, and call upon them to rely almost entirely upon the subsistence economy. Yet, at a special congress, the ruling party (*Union Soudanaise*) confirmed the blockade; a cloth banner proclaiming 'sooner death than dishonour' decorated the platform at the congress. These words, in Malinke, are said to have been sung in the twelfth century by the mother of the Mande emperor, the legendary Soundiatta.[5]

Mali, though landlocked, has a tradition of outside contact, of

---

[1] Citation from speech by Mahamane Alassane Haidara, 15 April 1961 at the inauguration of the new airport of Timbuctu. Mimeographed, Bamako, pp. 2–3.
[2] Paques, Vivian. *Les Bambara*, Presses Universitaires de France, Paris, 1954, p. 111.
[3] *1955 US Report*, op. cit., sous-section de Dravela.
[4] République du Mali, *Bulletin Statistique Mensuel*, April 1961, p. 17.
[5] Mamby Sidibé. *Notes Africaines*, 'Numéro Special, L'Empire du Mali', IFAN, Dakar, avril 1959, p. 42; and République du Mali, *Congrès extraordinaire de l'USRDA, 22 septembre 1960, Le Mali continu. . . .* Imprimerie du Gouvernement, p. 22, photograph. For a brilliant transcription of oral tradition about Soundiatta, see Djibril Tamsir Niang's *Soundjatta*, Présence Africaine, Paris, 1960; a rough bibliography is by Robert Pageard, 'Soundiatta Keïta et la tradition orale', *Présence Africaine*, xxxvi, 1961, pp. 51 f.

travel, accommodating strangers, and new ideas. President Haidara of Timbuctu expressed this too.

> We are the heirs of a long Muslim cultural tradition and of a humanism which by its characteristics reaches to the universal.
>
> Without renouncing her African character, Timbuctu has made a choice among the multiple civilizations with which she was in contact. Whites near or far, and Blacks of all origins, East like the West, have brought contributions to her.
>
> From the most various elements and from her own gifts she has elaborated a form of civilisation at once original and universal. Thus no stranger feels homesick there and her sons, regardless where they move, are well received and find something which is familiar to them.
>
> Not in our city will any apostle of NÉGRITUDE, this racism in reverse, or any fanatic of Hitlerian ideas, succeed. He would preach in the desert.[1]

There is a pride in study, poetry, and scholarship which endures in modern Mali. This tradition helps explain the relative homogeneity of the people living in the two connected 'core' areas of the successive medieval empires.

> First there is a common geographic core area extending along the Niger from present-day Ségou to the Niger bend and encircling whatever were the major trading centers for the Saharan export trade. . . . A secondary core further to the south and west is provided by the area under the influence of the . . . Mande-speaking peoples.[2]

Urban society became differentiated as individual scholarly and trading families stood out, inter-married and became related in ways that sometimes blotted out the original ethnic labels. Ethnic lines even in the countryside became blurred as across the open savannah and up and down the Niger River and its tributaries there were many migrations, wars, and successive kingdoms. So there are no simple ethnic frontiers. After a long history of changing political rulers:

> The successive influences are present less like a series of layers superimposed in strata, than like a succession of states continually modifying a structure at the base which is always evident, through its various metamorphoses.[3]

Each set of rulers assimilated a certain number of the ruled, withdrew and was succeeded yet by others who assimilated perhaps the same, perhaps others, while Islam and the relatively advanced technology of the various savannah kingdoms did their work of unifying diverse

[1] Haidara speech, 1961, op. cit., pp. 7–8. There is an obvious difference here with the ideas of the President of Senegal, Léopold Senghor.
[2] Foltz thesis, op. cit., pp. 11–2.
[3] Rouch, Jean. 'Contribution à l'histoire des Songhay'. *Mémoires de l'Institut Français d'Afrique Noire*, no. 29, IFAN-Dakar, 1953, p. 243.

groups. Languages spread and in most areas groups of different origin lived together.

Yet there are differences. In the *sahel* lives a largely white nomad minority, less than 10 per cent. of the total population. Some descend from raiders of the trans-Saharan caravans, and resist sedentarization. In the northern savannah are the Songhai, settled in the eastern arch of the Niger River both in Mali and across the river in Niger. In the north-eastern savannah live the Fulani, from whose capital, Macina, some migrated to the Fouta Djallon in Guinea.[1] Some of the Fulani are nomads, moving with their cattle from the floodwaters of the Niger. They dispute land rights with farmers and fishermen—Dogon, Bozo, Somono. In the central savannah live the Mande-Tan speaking groups—including Malinke, Bambara, Soninke, and Dioula. They speak variations of the languages of Soundiatta in the thirteenth century, and Samory in the nineteenth, as do the people of Kankan and Siguiri on the Niger River in Guinea. Islam, too, made its contribution to cultural homogeneity; more than 60 per cent.[2] of the people consider themselves Muslim, and most men who move from pasture, river, or farm to the city become Muslim as a matter of course.

Successive conquests and defeats favoured other alignments—ruling aristocrats, scholars and holy men, commoners and captives. Within each group there are yet further layers: the kind of aristocrat, his precise relationship to such ruling families as the Tall, Keïta, Dia, or Diallo. If the defeat in war is recent, the circumstances of defeat are important. Commoners differ according to wealth, town or country origins, nomad or sedentary; and according to professions—such as shepherd, warrior, fisherman, hunter, farmer; artisans like blacksmiths or cobblers and musicians are usually of lower caste. Scholars represent different Muslim traditions, Kounta Qadriya, or the Tidjaniya, or its offshoot the Hamalliya; usually the scholars are attached if not related to past or present ruling families: the Cisse and Fode, for example. Captives vary according to the type of work they do in hut, workshop or field, according to marriage, rewards for past services. Since people travel and scatter, often the fortunes differed in war and politics within the same family. Some members might be aristocrats, others commoners and other captives. Many Soudanese families—the Sissoko, for example, Diawara or Sylla—can be so differentiated.

Mali society had been changing steadily for thousands of years, and

[1] Marty. *L'Islam en Guinée, Fouta Djallon* (vol. iv of *Études sur l'islam*, op. cit.), p. 2; Bâ, Amadou Hampaté and Jacques Daget, *l'Empire peul du Macina*, IFAN. Soudan, 1955.
[2] *Tam-Tam*, op. cit., March–May, 1955, pp. 34–5. The figure is unreliable.

the sharp contrast in the pace of social change implied by the terms
traditional and modern, lose sense in this setting. The changes
initiated by the European colonizers may have been less profound than
the ones already at work in Mali, with which they did not identify.

In the eighteenth and nineteenth centuries the indigenous forces
of change contributed to a renaissance, represented in Mali by the
Toucouleur dynasty of al Hajj Umar Tall. A Muslim teacher and
preacher, he migrated from his birthplace in the Senegalese Fouta
Toro and built an empire. He and all but one of his sons resisted the
Europeans; it was said that unlike Samory he refused to sell slaves
to the Europeans, for to him they were infidels. The Europeans, at
the end of the nineteenth century did not forget that resistance.
They knew that some members of the Tall dynasty joined forces with
sons of Samory and the smaller dynasty of Traore from Sikasso—
indeed the Europeans sent some into exile together. Mountaga Tall
(d. 1955), son of Cheikh Ahmadou son of al Hajj Umar, was sent
into exile by the French to Timbuctu for six years. With him was
another direct relation of al Hajj Umar, two sons of Samory (who
had been captured in 1898), including Lama Touré, and two young
men of the family of the Traores of Sikasso.

Many enemies of the Talls, of Samory Touré and of the Traores
in varying degrees welcomed the Europeans. These included the
Fulani dynasties from Macina, traditional enemies of the Toucouleur,
and some of the Bambara and Minianka ruling groups from the vicinity of Bafoulabe, Bougouni, Koutiala, and San. They looked to the
Europeans for help against their African enemies. The people whom
the rival African ruling families fought to conquer had the relatively
peaceful occupations, mostly of farmers and fishermen, and lived in
the fertile islands formed by the flood waters of the Niger river.
Most were Bambara, Minianka, Senoufo, Bozo. Most were animist.

The Fulani, centred in the Macina area, were almost alone among
the leading Muslim families to join forces with the Europeans,
whom they saw as allies against the Toucouleur. The Fulani and
Toucouleur belonged to different Muslim traditions. Most, though
not all Fulani looked to teachers of the Kounta Qadriya denomination. The Toucouleur, however, accepted with al Hajj Umar Tall the
newer reforming path of Tidjaniya; his teachings came to be known
as Tidjaniya Omarien. The Toucouleur were by no means alone
to take the religious path traced out by Cheikh Tidjane; but they
were special because they made war and administered in its name.

Hence in Mali many families identified with the pre-European
empires, skilled in many generations of trading, conscious of an
ancient urban tradition, responsible for the progress of reform
Muslim movements, were involved in varying degrees with resisting

European rule. No wonder, therefore, the initial line-up of friends and foe to the French conquerors at the end of the nineteenth century continued to have meaning, both to the French and to Maliens. After the change from military to civil rule at the turn of the century, French officials tried to nominate to the new slots in the *commandement indigène* men allied to the groups who welcomed the Europeans, and opposed to the groups which had resisted conquest. The pattern was of course not neat. In the phase of conquest, and after, sometimes from ignorance, occasionally from an excess of zeal French soldiers punished and made enemies of those who had originally good reason to welcome the Europeans. Once established in Mali the Europeans did relatively little to solidify the position of those they had chosen as African allies. Though they did involve these allies in the *commandement indigène*, they saw the institution as temporary, to be replaced eventually by the regularly trained, mobile civil servants. The speed of this substitution was in Mali as elsewhere set by the speed of economic development. The process was favoured further by the post-war reforms prior to independence. There were yet other reasons why the position of the *commandement indigène* eroded considerably faster in Mali than might be expected from the slow rate of economic development. To keep costs down, French officials sent a minimum of European personnel, and gave the *commandement indigène* considerable leeway. They rarely bothered to intervene except to maintain order and the desire for calm took precedence over other elements of French policy. This led to contradictions at the local level or in individual instances of general policies.

The evidence on the Hamalliya movement is not yet fully assembled, and an adequate account of it remains to be written. Yet it could perhaps serve as an example. French officials repressed the Hamalliya movement between the wars less because it was unfriendly to France and more because the spread of the doctrines, seeking to purify Islam, led to clashes with entrenched local Muslim interests. In some localities Hamalliya was something of a revolutionary movement, calling for improvement in the status of women and an end to slavery. In other areas the Hamallists represented a quietist pacifist tendency within Tidjaniya. This strand, in harmony with French interests, was represented by 'le sage de Bandiagara', Tierno Bokar. He was related to the followers of Aguibou the son of al Hajj Umar Tall who had joined the French.[1] Partly from ignorance, partly to avoid trouble, the French ignored that Hamalliya challenged the authority which the Tall family and their allies continued to have in the sphere of religion after they had lost it in

[1] Bâ, Ahmadou Hampaté and Marcel Cardaire. *Tierno Bokar, le sage de Bandiagara*, Présence Africaine, Paris, 1957.

T

politics. The case is far from proven that French officials make blaming Hamallists for

the dead of Nioro (1923), of Kiffa (1924), of Kaedi (1930), the massacre of the Assaba (July 1940), added to the killing of the geologist Jacquet committed in 1937 by two notorious Hamallists, the assassination of two *goumiers* at Ain-Berbegha on 30 April 1942 and more recently, the kidnapping of a European foreman from the Dakar–Niger yard near Ouani (cercle of Gao) on 26 March 1949.[1]

Yet in these incidents, religion was probably one of many elements.

It seems that in each village, in each agglomeration there is 'in suspension' a certain number of causes for dissention. When the conflict bursts forth one can see the appearance of a 'precipitant' of these causes. The population finds itself divided into two opposing clans, taking sides on all the points on which there is a divergence of opinion in the village: then the conflict becomes total.[2]

Polarization was easy and 'chiefs' continued to decline since there existed alternative leaders whom most people knew and remembered. It was an able group, and included most of the old town elite and their allies—blacksmiths, traders, cobblers, and goldsmiths, as well as many Muslim teachers. Long before there were political parties, though in opposition to the colonizers, they took quickly to modern skills and ways. Some of the old trans-Saharan trading families took to the trans-Atlantic trade, and organized the movement to the coast of dried fish, cattle, or rice, the movement into the interior of colas, salt, matches, sugar, and cloth. Some kept Islamic scholarship alive and stayed in touch with the Muslim world. Soudanese pilgrims to Mecca encountered there descendants of the Ahmadou wing of the Tall family installed there since 1906 and preferring to live in exile after defeat by the French.[3] No full study yet exists of the many Koranic schools these religious scholars maintained. In time the old town elite as well as their *griots* and servants sent occasional representatives to the French schools. These were the groups from which sprang most of the new elite—the civil servants, railroad workers, and wage earners in the newer southern towns like Bamako, Kita, and Koulikoro and Sikasso. They stayed active—the Keïtas, Syllas, Kouyates, Diarras, Maigas. By excluding them for the most part from the *commandement indigène*, the French probably strengthened their position, and prepared the way for their political rebirth. The post-war reforms made possible for old leading groups to come to the fore again. This was of course not the whole story, but it helps explain some of the interesting features of the development of political parties in Mali after the war.

[1] CHEAM, *Notes et études sur l'islam. . .*, op. cit., pp. 184–5.   [2] Ibid., p. 40.
[3] Delafosse in Hanotaux and Martineau, op. cit., p. 195.

The Birth of Parties

The first political parties of Mali were built by those educated in French schools and involved in the money economy. It was a tiny group. In 1949 the official estimate was 38,322 were wage earners, half worked in Bamako and a sixth around the Office du Niger;[1] by 1957 the total rose only to 41,800.[2] As for those who had been to French schools, they were relatively fewer than in Guinea. The total number of Soudanese to go to any AOF secondary, upper primary or vocational school between 1905 and 1947 was only 836. Even in October 1946 there were only 18,574 pupils in Mali,[3] and in 1947 both in Mali and in Guinea less than 5 per cent. of the school-age children were in classrooms. Not until the 'fifties were there Maliens studying abroad, in universities, and not until the 'fifties did the first lycée classes open in Bamako, when the former École Primaire Supérieure Terrasson de Fougères expanded. The slow rate of growth of the educational facilities is shown by the fact that in 1961 only 10 per cent. of school-age children could find places in class-rooms, and at least 98 per cent. of the total population remained illiterate in French.[4]

The size of the educated group in Mali remained small partly because of migration across the many open borders. Peoples like the Senoufo, Bambara, Malinke, and Fulani, divided by the frontiers to the coastal states, often sent sons to learn and earn in Ivory Coast, Guinea, and Senegal. The Dakar–Niger railroad encouraged move-ments towards Senegal, as did jobs in the *gouvernement-général* in Dakar. Among those involved and growing wealthy in these moves were members of the Sylla, Bocoum, Diawara, and Deme families trading in Ivory Coast; the Soudanese wing of the great Senegalese family of Lamine Guèye, which included his nephew Bassirou Guèye and the family of General Soumare; the families of Diallo Abdoulaye and Madeira Keïta also formed Guinean connexions. There were yet further moves encouraged by French policy between the wars. Malien civil servants served in the neighbouring poorer states of Niger and Upper Volta. The Songhai people, divided by the Niger

[1] *Annuaire Statistique*, tome ii, 1951, op. cit., p. 438.
[2] *Outre-Mer 1958*, op. cit., pp. 208–9.
[3] *Discours par le Gouverneur Louveau, à la 1re session du conseil général du Soudan français*, 13 January 1947, Government Printers, Soudan, 1947, p. 13. Calcula-tion based on the relationship between 10 per cent. of the population, and the number of children attending school. See *Annuaire Statistique*, tome ii, 1951, op. cit., pp. 94–5.
[4] Ministère du Plan et de l'Économie Rurale, *Plan du project de rapport*, mimeo-graphed, Bamako, April 1961, op. cit., p. 11. The goal for 1965 was to place 17.9 per cent. school-age children in classrooms.

river between Niger and Mali, remained a single unit to French officials and African party leaders. It is there that Mamby Sidibé served as a teacher, and from there he became the first president of the Niger section of the RDA. From there, too, came Bakary Djibo, young founder of the RDA and trade union leader of Niger. Between 1932 and 1947 parts of Upper Volta were in Soudan. Mali's many frontiers thus have been flexible, and her cadres travelled widely.

A French-educated Malien who stayed home had little chance before the war to leave the path French officials set out for him in the civil service, unless he emigrated to one of the coastal states. He was relatively isolated, especially if his post was outside of Bamako. In relation to the Europeans, he was a subordinate. Most official chiefs could neither read nor write and knew little French; they regarded him with suspicion. It grew as before the Second World War African civil servants increasingly 'made certain political interventions in favour of individuals and groups', and wrote on their behalf to the capital, so going over the heads of local African or European authorities. This of necessity involved the African civil servants in local struggles for power. Like the official chief, 'the African interpreter was often against these interventions which diminished his influence in the eyes of the masses'. The interventions took courage, and locally caused a civil servant to be labelled 'as a dangerous individual and placed on the index by the Whites and the notables and the African chiefs who were not honest or were cruel to the people'. These were difficult years for an African civil servant, who lived in a professional world in which the most important events were promotions and decorations, or demerits and demotions; the whim of a superior could lead to immediate transfer and there was no appeal. Even continuing to read and write was risky. 'You receive too much correspondence and too many brochures on matters outside your province,'[1] said in 1916–17 a Commandant de Cercle in Fada N'Gourma (Upper Volta) to Mamby Sidibé early in his teaching career, and he regarded the statement as a threat. Ponty-trained Soudanese felt the contrast between these local conditions and the relative freedom of Dakar.

In the interior before the war African civil servants often turned for companionship to Muslim educators or marabouts, men who

---

[1] Citations from the personal papers of Mamby Sidibé, senior among the Mali teachers. He was born in 1891 when France was still conquering the area. Schooled first in his native region of Kita, then in Bafoulabe and at the École des Fils de Chefs at Kayes (1909), he finished at the École Normale d'Instituteurs of Saint-Louis, which was transferred to Gorée in March 1, 1913. In June he received his Certificat d'aptitude à l'enseignement dans les écoles de l'AOF, and was among the first 'Ponty' graduates.

remained outside of the French administrative framework, and who could give them information about their own past. They developed deep interests in their own history, and saw the contrast between the splendid past and the inter-war reality. They accumulated detailed local knowledge which after 1945 they put to good effect in building parties. Their information came from Arabic manuscripts and from the words of the *griot* whose hereditary business it was to record, remember, and repeat. Most families of any distinction in Mali had some *griot* clients—praise singers, minstrels, confidants, advisers, messengers, jokers, and scolds. *Griot* performed at births, puberty rites, marriages, funerals, and other important private and public events. After the war many *griot* worked for the parties as spies, publicists, and in other public relations capacities.

Practically all those educated in the schools of the Europeans became active in post-war politics, or their sons were, and most studied history before they worked for parties. The first graduates of the École des Fils des Chefs et d'Interprètes at Kayes—like the classmates Bassirou Bâ of Segou and the elder Keïta, produced sons who went to Ponty, founded the RDA and became ministers—respectively Ousmane Bâ and Modibo Keïta. Slightly younger was Mamby Sidibé (Ponty 1913), born in 1891 before the conquest of the Europeans; he put his historical knowledge to work first for the RDA and later in the ministry of information of Mali. Sidibé represented the animist and Muslim traditions of the Mali empire and made its history his special subject.

Slightly younger were men like Fily-Dabo Sissoko (Ponty 1918) and Mamadou Konaté (Ponty 1919). Sissoko counted Gabriel d'Arboussier among his students; he was a teacher, poet, and writer who represented the animist Bambara tradition,[1] and was but nominally a Muslim. He sought 'fleeting moments of immersion in nature, stolen instants at the secret meetings of the wise old men';[2] he studied and respected the spirits of land and water; he surrounded politics with animist ritual.[3] Mamadou Konaté inspired many generations of

---

[1] Bambara is used here, as many Maliens use it, to refer to animists among the Mande-Tan speaking groups.

[2] Sissoko, Fily-Dabo. *Crayons et portraits*, privately printed, Paris, c. 1950, p. 16. Among Sissoko's other writings are his reports printed in the Brazzaville records, op. cit.; and in the records of the 1937 *Congrès International de l'Évolution Culturelle des Peuples Coloniaux*, op. cit.; *Les Noirs et la culture*, pamphlet printed in New York, 1950, when Sissoko was in the French delegation to the United Nations; *Hamarkhis, poèmes du terroir africain*, Éditions de la Tour du Guet, Paris, 1955; *Une Page est tournée*, première série (Voix perdues) Dakar, Imprimerie Dìop 1959; and ibid., deuxième série (Voix sans écho), 1960.

[3] Speech by Félix Houphouët-Boigny, at the founding Congress of the RDA, Bamako, 1946, typescript.

students, including Félix Houphouët-Boigny, Mahamane Alassane Haidara (b. 1910) and Modibo Keïta (b. 1915); both were RDA founders. Even before the war Konaté's strength was less in writing than in direct action—with Ouëzzin Coulibaly of Upper Volta he organized, in 1937, the first African union of teachers. Sissoko and Konaté both came from Bafoulabe. But while the former was an official chief at Niambia and son of a pre-European chief, the latter was the son of Tieblimba, a policeman, a commoner of the Khalonke sub-group of the Malinke. After the war, when they became leaders of rival political parties this difference in their origins was of some interest.

Yet another tradition is represented by the Fulani-speaking scholars. The best known of these is Ahmadou Hampaté Bâ, whose writings on Macina history, and biography of the Hamallist sage Tierno Bokar, are unique works of scholarship.[1] Bâ spent many years as a consultant of the French administration on Muslim matters. The works of Ibrahima-Mamadou Ouane are mainly full of reminiscences about his family, the Aguibou wing of the Tall dynasty.[2] He was the youngest son of al Hajj Umar Tall, who turned against his brothers and joined forces with Archinard in the hope of French aid against his rivals to the succession. Aguibou alone of the Tall family received French protection, pensions, and privileges and even French citizenship.[3]

In the 'thirties, educated Africans with an interest in history could write and produce plays. They published, for example, the fact that villagers gave French administrators nicknames like *Tassouma*, the fire; *Bagama Bandiougou* or *Bandiougou*, a man who bullies without reason; *Tiaka-Tiaka*, nosy or he who goes everywhere; *Koumbiri*, he who always walks with his head bowed; *Zan Fato*, *Zan* the crazy one.[4] Colonial authorities rightly saw protest in the plays, acted out by pupils in Bandiagara, for example, based 'on the first steps of Soundiatta, Bakaridian, Samory',[5] all heroes of the past. The youth group *Art et Travail* in Bamako acted out similar themes.

During the Second World War, Vichy tightened the autocratic system again, discouraged African associations from working on

---

[1] See also his 'Culture peuhle,' *Présence Africaine*, no. spécial, viii, ix, x, Paris, juin–novembre 1956, pp. 85 f.; and 'Sur l'animisme', ibid., xxiv–xxv, Paris, fevrier–mai 1959, p. 142. He became director of the IFAN in Bamako on independence.
[2] *L'Enigme du Macina*, Regain—Monte Carlo, 1952, and *Les Filles de la Reine Cléopatre*, Les Paragraphes Litteraires de Paris, April 1961.
[3] Seydou Nourou Tall, grand *marabout* associated with Senghor's party in Senegal, belongs to the Aguibou wing of the family; so does the wife of Gabriel d'Arboussier.
[4] Listed, between 1930–2 by Mamby Sidibé in the *Révue d'Outre-mer*, according to his own bibliography.
[5] Sidibé, personal papers, op. cit.

historical subjects, and encouraged sports, particularly football. At Bandiagara, for example, Mamby Sidibé presided over an *association sportive*. 'At the time it was risky to take the lead,' he recounted. 'Sunday 9 November 1942 the *association sportive* of Mopti, better trained,' beats that of Bandiagara. Two days later the (European) administrator says dryly to Mamby Sidibé, 'Hand in your resignation.'[1] The Vichy administration also tried, without much success, to cut trade and migration with the English colonies. The logic behind this escaped most Maliens, who if they had a preference chose the Gaullist side as representative of the tradition of the Popular Front.

At the war's end, unity became the first goal, and among French civil servants socialists and communists urged Africans to adopt the rival formula of *bloc* or *rassemblement*. Initially there was much jockeying for position. Four elections took place before a hierarchy emerged among men who had been peers, and political lines were drawn into two parties which fought each other in each election under the Fourth Republic. The first steps towards the two-party pattern took place within the various town associations. Since 1937 there had existed an *Association des Lettrés du Soudan* of which Mamby Sidibé was the first president. It changed its name to *Foyer du Soudan*, and after Liberation Mamadou Konaté became its most influential president. Among younger people there existed *Art et Travail* led by Modibo Keïta and *Espérance* led by Fodé Touré. As early as 1944, a 'progressive' administrator, Auguste Marcoin, successfully urged the young people to merge into a single group, and they did so. For a short time there existed in Bamako a *Groupe d'Études Communistes* (GEC), under the guidance, among others, of the French Communist teacher Pierre Morlet.

There was much discussion who should represent the second college of Soudan–Niger at the 1945 constituent assemblies. Theoretically all the existing associations had come together in the *Foyer du Soudan*. Its members at first considered Fodé Touré as the best candidate, on the theory that since he had achieved the highest level of education— he was a graduate in law—he could best speak for Africans in Paris. But he had two handicaps: he was Guinean, and he spoke chiefly of constitutional questions. Fodé Touré in Mali, like Mê Binzème in Ivory Coast, misjudged what people wanted to hear. It was not subtle points of French law. They wanted to air specific local grievances, attack forced labour, expose the abuses of the black market, condemn the *indigènat*. Fodé Touré fell behind, and did not even run in 1945.

Locally educated Africans spoke of these issues; fully a dozen of

---

[1] Sidibé, personal papers, op. cit.

them ran in the first balloting of 21 October 1945. A few old citizens were among them—men like Tidjani Sidibé who became in 1947 director of the first Mali newspaper favourable to the RDA, *l'Observateur du Soudan*. Most of the candidates, however, were pre-war subjects. Mamby Sidibé had 271 votes and Hamani Diori 564; Modibo Keïta 937 votes, Tiemoko Diarra 503, Sall Ibrahima 1,433. In the second ballot on November 18 they all withdrew in favour of Mamadou Konaté. Later these men launched the RDA branches in Niger and in Mali. They had used the first ballot as a primary; those eligible to vote sorted out the new hierarchy. Thus as the larger group of voters and town dwellers took over, the members of the pre-war associations ceased to have a monopoly in the choice of candidates. From then on, the French-educated of Mali built proper parties, reaching out to the entire population.

On the second ballot, Konaté lost with 5,242 votes, and Fily-Dabo Sissoko won with 11,277; he easily won re-election to the second Constituent Assembly. In 1946 it was already clear the two men were to be rivals though it was not yet clear what forces would be behind them. The franchise of the second college was still very restricted mainly to town dwellers—the number who actually voted in Soudan–Niger for the constituent assemblies was about 25,000.[1] Sissoko at first attracted some town votes. 'Papa' Konaté, who had spent more than a decade teaching in the vicinity of Bamako, was personally known. Sissoko was known largely through his reputation, as one of the rare Africans who had drawn the attention of the Europeans. The *lettrés* knew Sissoko's writings. He came to Bamako only in 1945; and among his titles was that of vice-president of the *Association France–URSS* (AOF). He made what were then incendiary speeches—called for absolute equality in wages and before the law between Africans and Europeans, an end to forced labour, emancipation of women, equal educational programmes and facilities with those of France, 'the introduction of bilingual teaching (example USSR)'.[2] His speeches were filled with examples from Africa, Asia, and the Soviet Union.

In France, Sissoko first became *apparenté* through a Right-wing peasant group to the Radicals, which neutralized his vote in an assembly dominated by Socialists, Communists, and MRP. But he broke discipline with his group to vote colonial reforms, and was disappointed when the April 1946 constitution was rejected in referendum. In the second Constituent Assembly he joined men like Houphouët-Boigny and d'Arboussier, briefly, in the *Union Répub-*

[1] Figures from J.O.A.N.C. I, *Débats*, 17 January 1946, p. 108; J.O.A.N.C. II, *Débats*, 11 July 1946, p. 2667.
[2] From his 'Profession de foi', 21 September 1945, Bamako, Soudan-Imprimerie.

licain des Résistants (URR) group *apparenté* to the French Communist parliamentary party. In Africa, however, his backers followed a different course; they formed the *Parti Progressiste Soudanais* (PSP). Meanwhile most of the defeated candidates formed the *Bloc Soudanais*, inspired, like the *bloc* of Senegal, by the French Socialists. It included Mamadou Konaté, but was dominated by the old citizens, and led by a Martiniquan accountant, Jean Silvandre. Partly as a reaction the GEC contingent formed the *Parti Démocratique Soudanais* (PDS). Like its counterpart in Conakry, the PDS was designed chiefly to maintain GEC representation in any future moves towards unity.

These came in the manifesto from the second college deputies calling for a *rassemblement* leading in October 1946 to the founding Congress of the interterritorial *Rassemblement Démocratique Africain* (RDA). The Soudanese saw general recognition of their special geographic and cultural position in West Africa, in the way President Houphouët-Boigny explained 'the union which we have come to seal on the banks of the Niger, at the feet of (Mount) Koulouba in the empire of Soundiatta'.[1] But union in Bamako was made difficult because the cold war touched most Frenchmen, and French influence on African politics was still strong. The Socialists in the overseas ministry tried to stop the Congress, and the Governor as well as the Governor-General were both Socialists. Fily-Dabo Sissoko, soon to join the Socialists in the first French National Assembly, wanted to boycott the Congress, but his followers within Bamako would not let him, and he presided at the first session. His first words were:

'If I have accepted the presidency of the first session of your Congress.' Everyone shouted, 'You must say our Congress.' He replied, 'No, it is yours, because it is a Communist manoeuvre. I, I am French and a traditionalist. I do not want to be Communist.'[2]

From Mali, the PDP, the *Bloc*, and the PDS each had five delegates. The atmosphere of the Congress was infectious, and during the first round of anti-colonial speeches in AOF, the delegates of the three Mali parties decided to unify. 'In the midst of a disorder which was but the new order of things,'[3] a single *Union Soudanaise* (US) emerged. Technically, between November 1946 and January 1947, throughout the elections of the first legislature of the French National Assembly and the first Soudanese *conseil général*, the US executive included representatives from the three former parties. But the executive did not make the decisions; unity broke over the issue of

---

[1] Typescript of Houphouët's opening speech, op. cit., 1946.
[2] *Annex 11348*, op. cit., p. 469.
[3] *L'Observateur du Soudan*, 15 July 1947.

nominations. The PDS contingent wanted a unit slate of Sissoko, Konaté, and Gabriel d'Arboussier. Sissoko refused d'Arboussier on the grounds he was a Communist and revived the PSP. For the November 1946 National Assembly elections, Sissoko formed a single slate with Jean Silvandre, who dissolved his *Bloc*, and both won seats. On a separate slate Konaté ran and won the third Soudanese seat in the National Assembly. The split widened in the *conseil général* election, to which Sissoko's partisans won an overwhelming second college majority, and the *Union Soudanaise* managed to win only two seats. Then the party lines hardened, and for a dozen years the PSP and the *Union Soudanaise* were rivals dominating Mali politics.

US–PSP Rivalry

The electoral results in Figure 6 show that Mali voters changed their allegiances during the first dozen years after the war. As the

FIGURE 6
Mali Electoral Results

Dates of Elections	Sissoko	Konaté	Votes Cast[8]	Registered
21 October 1945[1] ANC	10,406	2,905	27,014	33,626
18 November 1945 ANC	11,277 E	5,242	24,474	33,643
2 June 1946[2] ANC	17,032 E	4,307	25,500	36,714

	PSP	US–RDA		
10 November 1946[3] AN	60,759 (2 E)	27,653 (1 E)	95,243	160,464
17 June 1951[4] AN	201,866 (3 E)	115,490 (1 E)	340,207	916,944
30 March 1952[5] TA	122,957 (27 E)	101,902 (13 E)	259,348	925,131
2 January 1956[6] AN	161,911 (2 E)	215,419 (2 E)	438,502	1,075,640
31 March 1957[7] TA	218,668 (6 E)	472,208 (64 E)	33.9%	2,090,048

[1] Soudan–Niger, 2e college, J.O.A.N.C. I, *Débats*, 17 January 1946, p. 108; until 1947 Soudan included a part of Upper-Volta.

[2] Soudan–Niger, 2e college, J.O.A.N.C. II, *Débats*, 11 July 1946, p. 2667.

[3] Le Monde, *Résultats* . . . 1947, op. cit., p. 240.

[4] *La Documentation française*, 1951 results, op. cit., p. 433.

[5] Direction des Affaires Politiques d'AOF, Dakar, 1956 (typewritten), 2e college.

[6] Directions des Affaires Politiques, Bamako, printed sheet, 1956.

[7] Single college; US includes votes of *Union des Populations de Bandiagara* councillors; *AOF 1957*, op. cit., pp. 36–7; *Outre-mer*, 1958, p. 36.

[8] Number voting does not correspond to the sum total of PSP–US votes, because this chart does not show the minor parties, nor the number of votes declared invalid.

E = Elected   ANC = French National Constituent Assembly
TA = Territorial Assembly   AN = French National Assembly

franchise grew from 160,464 registered voters in November 1946 to more than two million in 1957, the majority swung from the PSP to the *Union Soudanaise* (RDA). In November 1946 the PSP had a two-thirds majority; but by March 1957 the US had the two-thirds. The shift was gradual, and the US started from a respectable one-third minority, having since 1946 one deputy, Konaté, in Paris. In this the US differed from the PDG, which won no significant elected posts in Guinea for almost a decade before it burst into prominence.

The PSP started in 1945 with Sissoko as a deputy, added Silvandre in 1946, and Dicko in 1951. In the first *conseil général*, the PSP had an easy second college majority, since its men held all but the two US seats.[1] In the 1952 territorial assembly the PSP held 27 of the 40 second college seats. These majorities allowed the PSP a preponderant voice in designating the indirectly elected Soudanese members of the AOF grand council, the assembly of the French Union and the French Council of the Republic. By 1951, however, the US increased its percentage of the votes, and in 1952 it won 13 out of the 40 second college seats in the territorial assembly. After the 1952 territorial assembly elections, the US made a somewhat unexpected temporary alliance with the RPF of the first college. The US, for its part of the bargain, could elect as senator Mahamane Alassane Haidara who had swung his home town of Timbuctu to the US, and as councillor of the French Union Modibo Keïta, the party's secretary-general and leader of the younger generation.[2]

By the mid-'fifties the US headquarters knew that the political balance was changing: from Markala-Diamarabougou came reports, for example, that 'the RDA was a sacrilege and a crime, today it is the preferred song of children and women'; from Dire, that 'popular demonstrations, general assemblies, tam-tams at night on the occasion of marriages, baptisms, and circumcisions are no longer the monopoly of the PSP'; from Goundam, too, optimistic reports that 'the dark veil which covered the fearful mass of the interior of the *cercle* thus lifts higher and higher, to the benefit of the growing party'.[3]

This optimism was confirmed in the 1956 results. The balance between US and PSP reversed: the US won a majority of votes. The rival parties each had two deputies in Paris—Sissoko and Hamadoun Dicko for the PSP, Konaté and Modibo Keïta for the US. RDA president Houphouët was then a minister in the French government, Mamadou Konaté a vice-president of the National Assembly, and

---

[1] Keïta, Modibo. 'Rapport politique', typewritten, Bamako, 1947. Also *l'Essor*, 15 March 1957.

[2] Singaré, Abdoulaye. 'Rapport sur les activités des conseillers territoriaux', *1955 US Report*, op. cit.

[3] Both citations from ibid.

FIGURE 7

Social background of the PSP and US executives,
Mali (Soudan) 1956

	PSP Exec.	US Exec.
Total	12	15
Average Age	47	40
Religion		
Muslim	11	14
Protestant		1[a]
Catholic	1	
Education		
University	1	
Ponty	6	7
EPS Upper Primary	4	5
CEP Lower Primary	1	2
Literate		
Literate in Arabic		1
Profession		
Government Clerk	6	6
Teacher	2	3
RR Employee		3
Commercial Clerk	1	2
Lawyer	1	
Veterinary Assistant	1	
Chief	1	
Journalist		1
Ethnic Origins		
Malinke	3	6[b]
Bambara	2	3
Songhai	1	2
Sarakole	3	2
Fulani		2[d]
Mulatto	1	
Mossi	1[c]	
Toucouleur	1[d]	
Ethnic Status		
Chief or close relation	6	2
Commoner	5	11
'Griot'		2
Maraboutic family	1	

[a] Calls himself 'Protestant-animist'.   [b] 1 from Guinea.
[c] 1 from Upper Volta.   [d] 1 from Senegal.

Modibo Keïta an under-secretary of state. When Konaté died in
May 1956, his successor as deputy was Bocoum Barema (b. 1914)
who had worked to swing the Mopti area to the US. It won all the
municipal council seats in November 1956—in the *communes de
pleine exercise* of Bamako, Kayes, Mopti, and Ségou, and in Sikasso,

a *commune de moyen exercise*. The US majority became over-whelming in March 1957. Counting the seven territorial assembly seats won by the *Union des Populations de Bandiagara* which declared for the US, it had 64 seats and the PSP only 6. Sissoko, Dicko, and the other PSP standard bearers lost in their home localities. A freshly victorious US team took over in 1957 the first elected African govern-ment which led Mali to independence in 1960.

In 1946, the PSP won in all *cercles* but Kita, San, and Sikasso; in 1951 it gained Kita but lost both Gao and Bamako to the US, which held on to San and Sikasso. In 1952 the PSP gained back San but again lost Kita and lost Timbuctu to the US, which kept Gao, Bamako, and Sikasso. By 1956, the PSP had lost everywhere except Bafoulabé, Nioro, Macina (now separated from the *Office du Niger* at Ségou), Koutiala, Bougouni, and Goundam. In 1957 only Sissoko's home canton of Bafoulabé, together with Koutiala and the Fulani's stronghold of Macina remained faithful to the PSP; all the rest had swung to the US.

From these results some general points emerge—tentative, since the available data is scanty. The PSP and the US started as parties led by two small rival groups that shared a common background. Yet in successive elections, as the franchise widened and they became increasingly involved in local struggles for power, the PSP and US teams were pulled further apart. Interests locally became polarized into two quite well defined camps kept apart by differences, some of which were far older than the elections. Local issues counted more and more in elections, as people in the 'cellules de base' of the villages and town neighbourhoods disputed over who should lead, how, and for what ends.

Yet both parties were from the outset territorial in scale. There were of course in Mali, as elsewhere, signs of separatist sentiment, and occasionally ethnic and regional parties sprang up—among the people of Kayes on the border of Senegal, among the Dogon living in the cliffs of Bandiagara, among the white nomads in the north, among the Bambara of Ségou. The separatist groups usually wanted to gain representation for a favourite son—the *Union Kayesienne* born in October 1946, the *Union Dogon* in 1947, the *Union Peulh, Assimilés et Sympathisants* formed in 1948. In 1951 the first-college party, the RPF, made some progress among the northern nomads.[1] In 1956, Jean Silvandre tried to form a 'third force', to 'fight against the dictatorship of the *comités directeurs*',[2] he united some PSP and US candidates and favourite sons. He was not re-nominated by the

[1] Delval, J. 'Le RDA au Soudan français', *L'Afrique et L'Asie*, no. 16, iv, 1951, pp. 54 f.
[2] From his printed electoral manifesto.

PSP; second on his list was Tiemoko Diarra from Kayes whom the US had passed over in 1953 for Modibo Keïta as councillor of the French Union. Their *Mouvement Socialiste de Défense des Intérêts du Soudan* obtained less than 4 per cent. of the votes.[1]

These groups never lasted very long, and people involved in local controversies kept returning to the fold of one or the other of the two parties. Both US and PSP leaders were skilled enough in politics to know the value of keeping a rough correspondence between the geographic and ethnic origins of leaders and followers. This would not have been possible if there had not been sufficient homogeneity in Mali society; rural groups like artisans or *marabouts*—who cut across ethnic frontiers. There was a history of co-operation among ethnic groups on which the rival leaders could and did build their parties. This is not to say that regional and ethnic considerations were absent from party politics in post-war Mali, but rather that the pattern of relations among ethnic groups counted for more, and helped overcome the tendency of individual ethnic groups to go it alone. The whole system helped to channel regional and ethnic questions into either purely local or territorial parties.

The available electoral results suggest that the two parties began with different centres of gravity. The PSP from the start was stronger in the rural areas and away from the main axes of communication provided by the Niger river and the railroads; it drew support chiefly from among animists; and lasted longest among Bambara and Fulani. The US on the other hand made its first gains in the towns, grew along the railroad and the Niger river, and among most Muslim notables other than Fulani; the first rural support came from primarily Malinke and Songhai areas.

The data also suggests that in the countryside the attitude towards the French at the time of conquest had significance in the post-war elections. The centre of PSP strength was among the Bambara and the Fulani, whose official chiefs, because descended from those who welcomed the French, often had pre-European claims to rule. Sissoko spoke of himself as the son of a 'Malinke islamized animist, grandson of one of the fiercest resistors to al Hajj Umar'.[2] At the time of conquest, Sissoko was a young child, and his family had welcomed French help against their Toucouleur enemies. This enmity was their bond with the Fulani of the Macina area. It was from Macina that Almamy Koreissy, chief, territorial councillor, and grand councillor, drew his support. The third PSP deputy was his protegée, Hamadoun Dicko (b. 1924), also a Fulani, and son of

---

[1] Figures from Direction des Affaires Politiques, Dakar, 1956.
[2] Sissoko. *Les Noirs et la culture*, op. cit., p. 38.

the *chef de canton* of Douentza. Most Fulani rulers were from the beginning closely allied with the French. The conquest left a legacy also in the electoral results of Koutiala and Bougouni, loyal to the PSP even when the vote became universal. The Bambara and Minianka in majority in Koutiala had for long resisted the Tall who had overthrown the Bambara dynasty of Ségou, and subjugated them. Tall rule ended with French conquest. In Bougouni, the armies of Samory devastated the town at the end of the nineteenth century and the people had welcomed the French defeat of these armies. Bougouni for long resisted the RDA and identified it with Samory.

For the US leaders support came most easily in the countryside from those who kept alive resistance to French colonization, including supporters of the families of al Hajj Umar Tall and Samory Touré. The interterritorial character of the RDA helped to make this support possible, since Samory Touré's empire was based on Guinea and extended into Ivory Coast and Mali, while al Hajj Umar Tall's empire included parts of Guinea and Senegal. The connexion with these heroes was evident from the early backing given the US by Madany bin Mountaga Tall, a scholar living in Ségou, by his brother Salif Tall, who became first a territorial councillor and then a deputy in Mali's representative assembly. These two were related to two stalwarts of the PDG in Guinea: Baïdy Guèye, though born in Duinguiraye, traded in Bamako, then in Ivory Coast, and after 1958 traded again in Guinea. His relative, Habib Tall, joined the PDG, became a territorial councillor and then deputy of the representative assembly in Guinea. As for the Samory Touré connexion, Sékou Touré had achieved this with the PDG in Guinea, and campaigned in Mali. The Malinke dynasty of the Traorés,[1] rulers of Sikasso, had also resisted the Europeans. Samory had tried unsuccessfully to conquer Sikasso before, and the Traorés had received assistance from Ahmadou the son of al Hajj Umar Tall, then ruling in Ségou. Thus the Tall, Traoré, and Touré ruling families had not always seen eye to eye in the nineteenth century, but had in common resistance to the French.

It was the not always easy job of RDA leaders to keep the peace among the descendants of these three families. One way they tried was by taking again the oath of alliance of their ancestors. They did this in yet another way among the Malinke—by going back several centuries to the time of Soundiatta Keïta, the most illustrious

[1] The Ponty-trained schoolteacher Ray Autra belonged to the RDA from the beginning, and worked in organizing the union of teachers as well as the party in many territories. Since its independence he worked in the Centre National de Recherche Scientifique of Guinea. He descended from the Traorés (Ray Autra spoken backwards).

Mande emperor of them all. In the Malinke *griot* village of Kangaba the US had an early base; the reputed hut of Soundiatta Keïta became an object of special US attention. In April 1961 Mamby Sidibé publicized for the US 'la cérémonie rituelle du Camabolon', the rebuilding of Soundiatta Keïta's hut.[1] It is part of the tale now told of Soundiatta Keïta, that the families of Keïta, Konaté (a name that in the past changed to Keïta after a man was 40), and Kouyaté (a *griot* name attached to the Keïtas) never fight and always work together. Among the leadership of the US, the Malinkes held a strong position, and among them these three family names figured prominently.[2]

There are no simple connexions among the position at the time of conquest, the designation over a half century of the official chiefs, and the party affiliations of different cultural groups. The Diawara, for example, though they resisted the armies of al Hajj Umar Tall, for the most part joined the US, and part of the explanation lay in the fact that they resented their Fulani neighbours even more.[3] The urban Songhay also turned to the US fairly early; they are in a majority in Gao, and provide a substantial segment of the population of Timbuctu. Both these areas turned to the US in the 1951 and 1952 elections, the first held with a fairly broadly based franchise. When the French first came, the Songhai enjoyed something of a liberation from both Fulani and Tuareg invaders.[4] Yet brutalities accompanied French conquest there. In about 1906 near Anzourou there had been a Songhai uprising which the French severely repressed, and the people never forgot.[5] Moreover, under Vichy the Songhai, many of whom were traders, had yet other reasons to dislike the French for trying to stop trade with Ghana and Nigeria.[6]

The PSP attracted many descendants of those who had welcomed the French at the conquest, because there was often a family link to the *commandement indigène*. This group gave the PSP its initial

---

[1] Sidibé, personal papers, op. cit.
[2] Konaté was deputy and president of the party; Modibo Keïta was secretary-general and became prime minister; Madeira Keïta was minister of interior; Fadiala Keïta was political secretary of the party and became ambassador to Moscow; Seydou Badian Kouyaté became minister of rural economy.
[3] Boyer, G. 'Un Peuple de l'ouest-soudanais, Les Diawara', *Mémoires de l'Institut Français d'Afrique Noire*, no. 29, IFAN, Dakar, 1953.
[4] Rouch. 'Contribution à l'histoire des Songhay', op. cit., p. 236.
[5] From this area comes Bakary Djibo, Ponty graduate, CGT trade union leader in Niger, first secretary-general of the RDA of Niger. He rejected the decision of the interterritorial RDA in 1950 to disaffiliate from the French Communists; there was a break in the party, and he founded in 1951 the *Union Démocratique Nigérienne* (UDN).
[6] Rouch. 'Contributions . . .', op. cit., p. 238.

advantage in elections, and the PSP had a ready-made machine in the official chiefs whom French officials summoned to Bamako to prepare for elections. They came from all the regions, some 500 of them,[1] to discuss not only technical arrangements but candidates. One of their spokesmen was Almamy Koreissy—Fulani chief from Macina, born in 1910 and educated at Ponty as a teacher; he told how his colleagues finally decided to back 'a *chef de canton* like us, a teacher like some of us, who has suffered in his life, who knows human miseries; Fily-Dabo is a link between us and the elders; he can be a link between Africans and Frenchmen'.[2] Sissoko never forgot how much he depended upon the 'chiefs'. His electoral manifesto of September 1945 called for a reinforcement of 'the prestige of chiefs—precedence, deportment, decoration, housing, salaries'.[3] He did not try to build a party in the modern sense. He rarely took part in the proceedings of the National Assembly, but was roused to speech when Yacine Diallo of Guinea proposed (unsuccessfully) a law to give 'chiefs' security.

> I am a witness, I who represent a tradition of these chiefs who had twelve or thirteen centuries of history behind them, that they have asked and that they now ask of France that their status be respected. . . .[4]

Sissoko worked to stay in the good graces of the French officials who had the power to make or unmake a 'chief'. By definition this meant staying away from the RDA. In the first Legislature of the French National Assembly Sissoko made it clear that he wanted to be on the side of the French government by joining the Socialist group—then the party of the overseas minister, the governor-general, and Soudan's governor. When minister Moutet lost his seat as deputy in 1946, the PSP majority in the *conseil général* voted to make him a senator from Soudan.[5] And to succeed him the PSP voted for Pierre Bertaux, a Resistance leader until then unknown among Africans in the Soudan.

Official support and the backing of the 'chiefs' help explain why the programme of the PSP was limited, its organization rudimentary, and its leadership a loose confederation of grand electors united around the person of Fily-Dabo Sissoko. The 'chiefs' did not welcome interference from Bamako, not even from PSP agents. They did not want a party structure, since locally this could mean sharing power.

[1] Delval, 'Le RDA au Soudan français', op. cit.
[2] Interview with Almamy Koreissy, *Journal du Soudan*, 4 June 1955.
[3] From his *profession du foi*, 21 September 1945, op. cit.
[4] J.O.A.N., *Débats*, 9 August 1947, p. 4185.
[5] In his 'Rapport politique' to the first 1947 congress of the US, secretary-general Modibo Keïta charged the *conseil général* elections had been falsified to help allow the election of a man like Moutet. Op. cit.

U

Party press was rudimentary; only in 1955 did the European backers of Pierre Bertaux, for example, put out the *Journal du Soudan* from Paris, and its circulation was very limited.[1] Nominations were made in a way which reflected the personal leadership of Sissoko. He would consult chiefs, notables, and French authorities and announce a result. Before he announced Ya Doumbia as the PSP candidate for councillor of the French Union, for example, Sissoko went into the forest alone to contemplate, then foretold the election in the manner of a prophet. The PSP majority in the territorial assembly made the prophecy safe. The PSP represented the established forces within the existing system. PSP disputes centred around individual questions; issues and ideas or theories did not interest them much. They did not push for the extension of the franchise, though perhaps they were not fully aware of how much this was working against them. The PSP leaders were taken by surprise when the US won a majority in the 1956 vote, and by the Loi-Cadre reforms, permitting the US to form the first elected Soudanese government. Then the PSP finally reacted and tried to refurbish the party. Their defence under challenge was something like that of the BAG in Guinea after the RDA won there in 1956. And in Soudan also the defence came too late.

The defence took the form of creating the *Syndicat des Chefs Coutumiers*, of which Almamy Koreissy was the president. In the midst of the rapid political changes after 1956, however, even the more popular members of the *commandement indigène* wore out their welcome. Chiefly power had eroded under US attack,[2] and the PSP had no alternative machinery with which to reach the people. PSP fear of the US even led Sissoko to make the quite unrealistic proposal that a federal executive in Dakar totally replace the territorial executives in West Africa.[3] In great haste the PSP also tried to distribute party cards, mimeographed a paper, *Vérité*, and refurbished party structure. Younger men like Hamadoun Dicko and Ya Doumbia tried to reduce Sissoko's power in the party, make leadership collective and reduce chiefly influence. But it was too late. Thus it came about that the initial cause of PSP victory—official favour causing 'chiefs' to back PSP candidates—in the long run brought consequences in PSP policy, structure, leadership, and procedure which became causes of PSP defeat.

[1] The paper went out of circulation shortly after Bertaux was defeated in his bid for re-election by the councillor of the French Union Fillon. Bertaux unsuccessfully charged corruption by 'the public and private supporters of the candidate of the Rothschild bank'. *Journal du Soudan*, 2 July 1955.
[2] See *l'Essor*, January–April 1957, for particularly sharp attacks.
[3] *Le Monde*, 9 January 1958.

The US in 'Double Opposition'

Just as official favour and 'chiefly' leadership of the PSP went together, so did official disfavour and leadership by the more radically minded educated townsmen help explain why at first the US did badly in elections, yet finally won. Opposition gave common ground to groups in Mali society which otherwise were not necessarily compatible, and ten years in opposition gave enough time for these groups to build a solid party.

An example of the incompatibility was local politics near the Sansanding dam. There, in the neighbourhoods of Markala and Diamarabougou lived the new inhabitants who came to work for the Office du Niger, and the old ones, who included at Bozola fishermen with ancestral rights to the fish in the Niger. The dam, with its ladder which allowed the fish slowly and laboriously to pass through, reduced altogether the chance the fish had to escape the net or spear of the fishermen. Fishing according to the old rules would have killed next year's catch. To prevent this, the French authorities prohibited fishing in the immediate vicinity of the dam. The fishermen protested, and the PSP did not support them. The US had no trouble obtaining the votes of the new residents, but they had difficulty with the older ones. The US yielded to the needs of electoral opposition. They officially championed the ancestral rights of the fishermen. Only after the US came into power, did the contradiction in the US position come out. The fishermen claimed their rights, and the US leaders in Bamako, essentially modernizing in outlook, had to renege on the electoral promise.

For a decade, these contradictions did not come to the fore, and it was possible for opposition to occur on at least two distinct structural levels. It was 'double opposition', first at the territorial level, where Africans were in touch with European authorities and institutions, and second, at the local level, in the countryside. There opponents to the *commandement indigène* themselves had something of an organization and a history longer than that of parties, indeed than the French presence. The US gave an opportunity for the two levels of opposition to come together.

Because of 'double opposition', when the US came to power it did not mean simply the succession of its team of educated townsmen to the PSP. It meant also a turnover in the countryside, almost a social revolution, just when Mali took independence. 'Double opposition', added to the strength of the US and helped explain why though cities were small and wage earners few, it was the more rather than the less radically minded townsmen who finally took over after the war.

The more radically-minded civil servants were responsible for starting the party off in opposition, and until 1947 a few European Communists helped organize: Pierre Morlet, a teacher, for example, was a 'technical councillor' of the US *comité directeur*;[1] his contract, as well as that of postal inspector Fayette, were not renewed and they left Mali. The solid organizing work was done by a team of young men—Modibo Keïta, Jean Marie Koné, a teacher who was the first territorial councillor from Sikasso,[2] Abdoulaye Singaré, also a teacher descended from fishermen (*somono*) from the market town of Koulikoro.[3] There were young civil servants too—men like Idrissa Diarra, son of a petty trader, educated at the EPS Terrasson, who became political secretary of the party and who worked in the postal services;[4] Timbuctu Coulibaly[5] and Dramane Coulibaly[6] who had graduated from Ponty in the first part of the war; the former was a clerk in the administration, the latter in the Office du Niger. There were employees of the Dakar–Niger railroad, like Mamadou Sidibé,[7] Yacouba Maiga[8] and Tidiani Keïta.[9]

There were men who turned practically all their energies, after the war, to building the *Union Générale des Travailleurs du Soudan—*CGT: Marcel Planes, a European, and secretary of the postal union, left in the late 'forties;[10] Lazare Coulibaly, who led the construction workers, and Abdoulaye Diallo who became the vice-president of the World Federation of Trade Unions.[11] The numbers involved in the trade unions were never very large—about one third of the salaried workers, and thus, in 1957, approximately 14,000. Yet they counted. 'There was nothing surprising in the fact that the working class was a fundamental base of the RDA.'[12] The Dakar–Niger employees carried messages and packages and publications. The postal em-

---

[1] Mimeographed US/CD circular no. 29, Bamako, 1947.

[2] He was the first vice-president of the council of government of Soudan, later became vice-premier; he was also mayor of Sikasso.

[3] Minister of Education.

[4] He became deputy premier, and was the second-ranking person in independent Mali.

[5] Governor of Ségou; deputy from San to the Mali national assembly.

[6] Deputy to the Mali national assembly and mayor of Ségou.

[7] Deputy to the Mali national assembly and mayor of Kayes.

[8] Administrative secretary of the party and deputy to the Mali national assembly; originally *chef de gare* in Gao.

[9] In 1957 Soudan's minister of labour; in 1958 he became Guinea's minister-resident in Ghana.

[10] 'Chronique syndicale', c. 1947, mimeographed, part of the *Bulletin Mensuel d'Information* which the US published when it first started.

[11] Member (1935) of the *comité directeur*, EPS graduate, of Malinke peasant origin from Diafarabé.

[12] Keïta, Mamadou Fadiala. 'Rapport sur problème ouvrier et sur syndicat', Bamako, 19 September 1949, 2e congrès territoriale, typescript, p. 1.

ployees used slack periods to cable party messages to 'sure' militants. Most French officials touring the interior were driven by African chauffeurs, and these were among the first to be recruited into the unions. From the standpoint of the party, 'the chauffeurs were their best propaganda agents'.[1]

These urban groups, supplemented by their juniors still studying in school, constituted the radical wing of the party, those who posed issues sharply, wrote papers on economic and social as well as political issues. From among them came the *élus*, the party organizers, the delegates to national and international conferences, and the leaders of what came to be, first in fact and later also in name, the parallel organizations of the US, youth and labour. Mali's social structure did not lend itself to the organization of militant women's branches. There was an organization, but it was weak, and led essentially by wives of US party leaders. The elite among women was tiny, and 'it cannot and does not seem to want to play either the role of leaders or of emancipators which one might have the right to expect of it. . . .'[2]

The offices and places where the wage earners worked turned first to the US; the market-places turned soon after. The US gradually gained the support of more moderate town groups, of which the traders were among the most influential. They were in touch with the outside world—with Muslims in Mecca where they went as soon as they were able, and with the peddlers involved in the trade from the coastal states. And their men went often into Mali's interior. There was al Hajj Daouda Sako, a pious Muslim of Sarakole origins, unschooled in French, whose age and Arabic scholarship helped qualify him to be commissioner for conflicts in the US *comité directeur*. Some of the traders were of lower caste origins, attended Ponty and were fiercely egalitarian in outlook—Makane Macoumba, for example, was born a *griot*;[3] and the Fulani overlords in his home region considered Bocoum Barema inferior because he was born a *djavando*.[4] Many traders like these became wealthy and also took prominent places in the US. All were at one time members of the *comité directeur*. Al Hajj Dossolo Traoré, originally a trader from Kolokani, became treasurer of the party and was since 1957 questor of the assembly in Bamako. The traders made substantial contributions to the party, as well as to mosques and *medersas* where the US was soon

[1] Keïta, Mamadou Fadiala, op. cit., p. 4.
[2] Keïta, Mme. Hawa. 'Rapport sur les femmes', *1955 US Report*, op. cit.
[3] He became a deputy to the Mali national assembly. He never graduated from Ponty. Some of his family lived in Guinea.
[4] He became mayor of Mopti, deputy to the French and the Mali national assembly and minister of foreign affairs.

discussed. On most issues in the party the traders took moderate positions, but on the issue of equality among all men they were radicals. Many were self-made men who suffered from the disdain of aristocrats, and worked to wipe out the hereditary stigma of lower caste. Many had themselves difficulty in finding wives except among families of lower caste, or mulattoes.

The traders were closely responsive to the interterritorial ties of the US–RDA. It was Sikasso, on the trading route to Ivory Coast, which swung to the US at the same time Bamako did. The RDA councillors in Dakar knew their work for 'lifting the tax on colas was a resounding victory which the honest dioulas recognized as a victory of our leader, Konaté Mamadou, and of his party'.[1]

The traders had at their disposal a large, effective, and constantly functioning system of communication which touched each market-place, and in the rural areas, Mali's artisan population. Figures are uncertain, but the number of artisans working largely in the subsistence economy in Mali could be as high as 200,000—at least five times the number of wage earners, and living scattered throughout the country,[2] butchers, woodcutters, blacksmiths, tailors, cobblers, jewellers, spinners. There were others who responded early to the appeal of the US, made in the language of equality. In the countryside the US acquired the support of sub-layers of the population defeated in pre-European wars by the various disputing ruling families, both victors and vanquished, and hence of lower status. There were the '*bella*' in the north, mostly 'captives' of the nomad tribes. Of them the Mopti leaders of the US said, in their 1955 report to the party:

The administration is well aware that the Bella are still forced to pay and forced to work, in the full view of everyone, and that they are far from benefiting from the good works of a democratic France. In some regions of Gao, like Menaka and Doro, Victor Schoelcher would have shed bitter tears on seeing some sights . . . in a word the Bella is and remains a slave citizen over whom the 'white owners' have the right of life or death.

The Rassemblement Démocratique Africain, through the voice of its *parlementaires*, owes to itself bringing up the problem of the Bella in high places. For this it could hardly be accused of sowing the seeds of trouble, since it did not itself codify the law of 1848 [against slavery] nor the rights of man and the citizen.[3]

There were others in Soudan in similar positions: *rimaïbe* farmers under the Fulani, and *bozo* fishermen. These groups lived mainly in the north, where US representatives reported that forced labour con-

[1] *1955 US Report*, op. cit., sous-section of Medina-Coura.
[2] *Comptes économiques*, Ressources humaines en 1956, Rapport II, op. cit., p. 45.
[3] *1955 US Report*, op. cit.

tinued to exist.[1] Liberation, spreading the message of equality within the brotherhood of Islam, 'democratization of tribal society', were among the more important goals the radical US organizers from Bamako set for themselves in what they called the northern 'feudal' areas.[2] Many aristocrats in the rural areas still believed in social distinctions but supported the US because it opposed the *commandement indigène*. They agreed that 'the *Cheffrie Indigène* should be a direct emanation of the people and not imposed representatives, and furthermore that the Chiefs should stop being representatives of political parties'.[3]

It is the aristocrats who in many areas helped provide alternatives to the official chiefs, who agreed to be against 'the chiefs who are political agents',[4] and whose supporters constituted already organized groups responsive to the message of opposition of the US. Opposition hid the fact that the aristocrats did not necessarily agree with the decisions to cut hereditary privileges which the US took after it came to power in 1958, to suppress the *tribunaux coutumier* and hence the judicial role of the chiefs;[5] and in 1960, to 'liberate the people from the feudal power of the *chefs de canton*', by eliminating them altogether from local government. The US government left intact in the north '*chefs de tribu nomades*'.[6]

Tensions among the various elements in the party grew, as the party itself gathered momentum. Being together in opposition acted as a cement. It also had the effect of sorting out people willing to make sacrifices for their ideals, and it was these who became 'militants avertis de la première heure'.[7] Until the mid-'fifties, among the townsmen in touch with the administration, supporting the US meant genuine hardship. Civil servants like Modibo Keïta, Ibrahima Sall, Sango Ibrahima, Cantara Cissoko, and Mamadou Sangaré, all members of the *comité directeur*[8] were imprisoned, fired, demoted, not promoted, or transferred to areas remote from where they had political support. Modibo Keïta, for example, was transferred from

---

[1] *Barakéla*, 19–25 December 1955.
[2] Cours no. 11, August 1949, École territoriale de l'U.S., typed outline.
[3] Political Resolution, *1955 US Report*, op. cit.
[4] Political Resolution, 1952 US Congress, mimeographed.
[5] Economic and Social Resolution, August 1958 Congress.
[6] *L'Essor*, 4 June 1960, report by minister of interior Madeira Keïta.
[7] *1955 US Report*, op. cit., sous-section de Dravela.
[8] Sall, a Fulani of Senegalese origins, Ponty 1933, was a *greffier*, became a councillor of the French Union and supported the US, and was for a while *adjoint* to the mayor of Bamako, Modibo Keïta, effectively acting in his place. Sango Ibrahima, also a Ponty graduate, was a teacher of *griot* Songhai origins and came from Niafounke. Cantara Sissoko had worked for the Dakar–Niger railroad, and with Mamadou Sangaré for several years edited the party paper.

Sikasso to the north, to the village of Kabara near Timbuctu;[1] and in the mid 'forties, while in Paris, he was for a short time placed under arrest. PSP leaders could buy imported concrete to build solid houses while US men continued to live in the red clay *banco* dwellings of their ancestors; PSP leaders could ride in official cars while US men had to make their first rounds on bicycles or on foot.

In the countryside, too, it was at first hard to be a US supporter. The occasional chief who sided with the US—such as Fatagoura Traoré of Sikasso, lost his post and became a party martyr.[2] The US supporters knew official chiefs were PSP, and believed the justice they handed out, the *justice indigène*, was a 'veritable instrument of the PSP'.[3] Moreover, for almost ten years after the war the official chiefs still had power in the villages—often determinant in disputes over land, water, women, market rights, and even religious rights and obligations.[4] It took real courage to stand up to the official chiefs, and only powerful motives could cause men to risk chiefly reprisal by voting the US ticket.

The US men took great pride in their sacrifices. They developed a tradition of resistance and dedication to the party. The first paragraph of the US by-laws stated that each militant 'Must be an example for all, as much in his private life as in his work—the party cannot include elements whose morals or professional conscience could be criticised.'[5] The same theme of dedication closed Modibo Keïta's report to the 1952 congress of the US:

> Comrades, when you find yourselves ready to weaken, tell yourselves the eyes of the world are fixed upon you, a world which judges you, a world which depending upon your action will laugh at Africa or respect her; think of our hundreds of martyrs, whom we remember, those who have known prison and those who died, whose sacrifice shall not have been in vain and should urge us on; think of the hundreds of thousands of Africans whom we projected into the political arena in 1946 who count on us to tear them from the grasp of the colonialists and to guide them to a better future, who have confidence in us, for the construction of an Africa where words express real things and acts, an Africa drawing strength from the immense resources she hugs jealously to her breast, that will dazzle the world. 'We shall no longer be of this world,' some will say. But we shall have marked the road to be followed, we shall have known the first pricks of the thorns, for we shall have been the first to break the path.[6]

[1] In 1961, he inaugurated there Place Modibo Keïta, in memory of his exile 'during the colonial repression'. *Afrique Nouvelle*, 3 May 1961.
[2] He was reinstated in 1953. *1955 US Report*, op. cit., sous-section de Sikasso.
[3] Ibid., sous-section de Ségou.
[4] A bitter struggle took place over market rights in San.
[5] 1950 by-laws.
[6] 1952 rapport moral, 3rd congress, *Afrique Noire*, 16 October 1952.

From the beginning the party decreed there would be no meeting of intellectuals in a vacuum. Instead, the leaders challenged each other:

> We speak always of the masses. But have we penetrated the masses so as to know their way of life, so as to have wiped away the hostility with which they look at those who went to the schools of the French, and finally so as to have sensed their vital needs and measured the extent of their ability to resist oppression? How many comrades agree to enter a dark and smoky hut, to sit on a mat which in colour and crust resemble the earth, to dip by hand, without the slightest repugnance, into the doubtful platter of *tô* or of rice, to carry to lip and drink without fear the milk on which swims a thin layer of dust.[1]

Thus they made a virtue out of the need to live close to the people, eat and dress like them; and pointed out that poverty was the best proof of honesty. Their moral tone, dedication, and sense of sacrifice was in line with the puritan tradition of their Muslim ancestors—even if most French words printed in party reports and papers were in the secular political tradition of French socialism. 'We will prove that the Maliens of the XXth century are the worthy heirs of all those in the past who knew how to demonstrate to the world their culture, their civilisation, and their sense of organization.'[2]

US Organization

The *Union Soudanaise* managed to hold together different wings—Idrissa Diarra, administering secretary, called them 'the nuances which exist in the party'[3]—because it was remarkably well organized. The formal structure was like that of other territorial RDA *sections*—a grid leading upward from the *comité de village* in the countryside or the *comité de quartier* in the cities, to the regional *sous-section* (called *section* after independence in 1960) and from there to the *comité directeur* in Bamako, itself capped by a smaller *bureau politique*. All the *sous-sections* were represented at congresses that laid down the general policy to be executed by the *comité directeur*. The US was special in its operation: the attention leaders gave to day-to-day detail and the principles involved in them, for keeping a steady flow of information to and from the top and bottom, for inquiring into problems before taking action, for open criticism within the party, and for resolving most internal conflicts less by force than by debate, by votes and the consensus that decisions of the majority engage the whole party. From the beginning it was a party having regular statutes and by-laws; a party of rules rather than of men. From the beginning, militants agreed that it is not 'shouts of "Vive Konaté"

[1] Modibo Keïta's political report, *1955 US Report*, op. cit.
[2] Diarra, Idrissa. *1960 extraordinary US congress*, op. cit., p. 11.
[3] Ibid. p. 6.

. . . which will make our movement develop'. There was enthusiasm about Konaté—evident when his supporters carried him aloft and called him 'the only truly elected' deputy; or when they welcomed his return in 1955 from Paris by turning off the motor of his car and pushing it all the way to Bamako from the airport. At the same time militants agreed with Modibo Keïta's statement in 1947:

> Do not believe you will attract new supporters by saying the UNION SOUDANAISE is a good party, the Parti Progressiste is worthless, or that KONATÉ is a good deputy, Fily DABO is a valet of MOUTET. It is not that this is false, on the contrary, but the Soudanese people is more exacting than that and with good reason.
> . . . a political speech is well and good, but if you speak to a *somono* (fisherman), the division of the catch is worth ten political speeches.[1]

From the beginning, the leaders preached 'the party is not a serpent like some often say, for then the day that the present leaders are no more would be the end of the party'.[2] Rather the leaders tried to inculcate the principles of collective leadership. Idrissa Diarra explained this principle again at the 1955 congress:

> Regardless of the inherent value of our leaders, taken individually, the decisions which they are led to take alone risk being decisions steeped in error. We can never place enough emphasis on the need and effectiveness of team work. It is the only certain way to best avoid errors, to strangle personal politics, and to assure the duration of the Party. All problems must be studied together. During meetings each one has the right and duty to defend his point of view.
> The decisions taken by the majority become the decision of all and discipline demands its respect by all. It is during these fraternal discussions that cadres are formed, acquire the necessary political experience to avoid errors and to assure the march forwards of our Movement.[3]

Other US principles of leadership were the responsibility of leaders to followers, and the control of the party over the *élus*. From the interior came a constant stream of complaints that the *élus* did not visit often enough, provoking organizing secretary Idrissa Diarra to urge that local committees should not rely 'solely on parliamentary missionaries which the C.D. [*comité directeur*] or the B.P. [*bureau politique*] sends to them'.[4] Secretary-general Modibo Keïta hardly spent a solid week in Bamako and even after he became a parliamentarian he was rarely in Paris; he was usually on tour in the interior.

An indication that leadership in the party was responsible and

---

[1] 'Rapport d'organisation', typewritten, Bamako, 7 November 1947.
[2] Ibid., closing report, mimeographed, 9 November 1947.
[3] *1955 US Report*, op. cit.   [4] Ibid. Parentheses mine.

responsive was that over the first ten years, congresses changed the composition and numbers in the *comité directeur*, and more than two-thirds of the actual members changed also. 'Papa Konaté's' power, though recognized as supreme, was regularly and successfully challenged. Some of the crises turned around nominations. For example, in 1953 Konaté preferred Tiémoko Diatigui Diarra from the border town of Kayes as candidate for councillor of the French Union, but the *comité directeur* outvoted him, nominating Modibo Keïta; Diarra ran in spite of this and the party expelled him for 'characteristic indiscipline'.[1]

Agreement that leadership was collective carried the party also through other crises. When the RDA *parlementaires* disaffiliated in 1950 from the Communist parliamentary group, there was considerable opposition in Soudan. At the US congress of 1952 there was full debate on the matter. Secretary-general Modibo Keïta was himself not in full agreement with the action, but bowed to the wish of the majority, and defined the US position:

There is no change in our aims, no fundamental about face in the methods of our struggle but rather an adaptation in the form our methods take which is to say that we recognize the emancipation of Africa through the anti-colonial fight must take into account the international and above all local realities . . . a financial impasse, and the masses not carried along by an elite not always imbued with morality or trained politically.[2]

Since disaffiliation both youth organizations and the trade unions criticized the action, while elders like Mamby Sidibé defended it. He wrote, in an essay addressed 'To those who reproach the RDA for no longer publishing incendiary articles', that the young people should have patience, since 'we, the old ones, we do not want that one day you go to cry upon our tombs. Listen to us and let us prepare for you singing tomorrows'.[3] In view of the great divergences in outlook, it took skill to hold the party together. The question cropped up repeatedly in the *comité directeur*. At the 1952 congress Mamadou Fadiala Keïta was elected political secretary. He was an adopted son and son-in-law of Mamadou Konaté, and a brother-in-law of Idrissa Diarra. Hence a family as well as a political crisis brewed when it came to light that Fadiala Keïta did not follow the official position on the Communist issue. On 26 July 1955, the *comité directeur* relieved him of his post; the matter was reconsidered in September, but his explanations 'did not convince the comrades in the *bureau politique* that there were not profound divergences between him and

[1] *L'Essor*, 15 March 1957.
[2] September 1952 report, *Afrique Noire*, 16 October 1952.
[3] From original typescript.

the political line traced by our congress in 1952. . . .'[1] At the September 1955 congress the matter was aired, and Idrissa Diarra was elected political secretary of the party.

Collective leadership was perhaps the chief reason why the *Union Soudanaise* could overcome yet another serious crisis: the death of US president Konaté in May 1956. His authority had been very great. People had brought personal and moral issues for his decisions, not only political ones. His poverty and honesty were legendary and contributed to the respect with which even his rivals regarded him. Devout Muslims praised him as 'supporter of the faith, defender of widows, orphans, the sick, and the poor.'[2] His judgement had contributed to keeping peace within a party embracing many tendencies. He maintained that 'criticism and auto-criticism are the rule for each democratic movement that respects itself', but insisted that it is 'inside the party, during meetings and assemblies and congresses that this should take place. . . .'[3] He used his authority to reinforce the principle of collective leadership, not to undercut it, and in this way coped with criticism from left and right and with the pressure of the next generation, which moved up when Modibo Keïta took Konaté's place at the top. Immediately the leaders had to cope with the criticisms by yet the next generation, of the choice of Bocoum Barema as US candidate in the by-elections of July 1956.

The interterritorial RDA helped the US overcome the problem of succession, both by a great show of solidarity at Konaté's funeral, and by immediate aid in the electoral campaign. The other RDA sections were not electioneering at that time, and from Ivory Coast, Guinea, Upper Volta, and Niger volunteers came. Cars, trucks, gasoline, and money arrived chiefly from Ivory Coast, while from the frontier states came campaigners often of the same ethnic origins as the Soudanese voters. The US victory was overwhelming, and solidified Modibo Keïta's position.

Yet another crisis came in the relations between party and trade unions. The Soudanese CGT union leaders were dissatisfied with the RDA decision to break links with the French Communists in 1950, and in 1955, when at Sékou Touré's instigation the interterritorial RDA decided at its Conakry Co-ordinating Committee meeting to call for trade union disaffiliation from the French CGT, opposition was strongest from Soudan. Abdoulaye Diallo led that opposition, which the US leaders condemned at the fourth congress of September

---

[1] CDUS/no. 140, 'Circulaire', 9 September 1955, signed by Idrissa Diarra, sécrétaire à l'organisation, mimeographed.
[2] From a declaration in Arabic read from a scroll by a mourner at Konaté's funeral.
[3] 'Allocution de clôture', Konaté, *1955 US Report*, op. cit.

1955. The matter was debated inside the party, but did not come to the fore until the October 1956 municipal elections. By then, the CGT had stopped opposing African union autonomy. Yet the US refused to designate Abdoulaye Diallo a candidate. He ran, lost, and discovered that the unions had no strength against the party even in the capital. In the March 1957 territorial assembly elections, the US again did not nominate Abdoulaye Diallo, though he became the first minister of labour in June. Thus the party had disciplined him by taking away any independent base, and in fact co-opted him into the government while keeping him out of the *comité directeur*. As minister of labour he had to use up a good deal of his credit with the workers by explaining to them why the government could not meet their wishes.

Because there were many sources of conflict within the party, leaders tried to foresee them. One way was by launching trial balloons, and then waiting, while 'ça chuchote, ça chuchote'.[1] There were old men who frequented party headquarters, like al Hajj Bayokoro, who went from courtyard to courtyard, consulting, listening, and then reporting how people feel. Bamako was small enough to allow this kind of informal sampling of public opinion.

At the local level, also, leaders paid considerable attention to the forms. Where organizers had difficulty they went from hut to hut, 'porte à porte',[2] to explain in each family concession before trying to hold open assemblies, so as to discover 'the most effective means to recruit members'. Headquarters warned that:

> A section assembly should never last longer than two hours. The greatest attention should be given to matters of local interest. The general political speeches should be very short. Meetings should be alive and everyone should take part in the discussion. Every member can and should be used in a specific task. A section in which only a few militants work is a section which operates badly, where one has not posed local questions likely to interest everyone and where the organizers have not understood their role.[3]

Elections were regular, reporting back was customary, and there were frequent general assemblies. In Bambara areas grouping all families locally in a *ton* was traditional, and collective discussions were rooted in long practice, and taken over within the party in the southern areas. Most leaders of the local *comités* had not been to a French school. The local committees were urged to defend the economic interests of workers, farmers, artisans, labourers, traders, fishermen,

---

[1] Citation from interview.
[2] *1955 US Report*, sous-section de Niarela, op. cit., 1961.
[3] Both citations from US/Comité, Circulaire 22 bis, 16 September 1947, typewritten.

veterans, women, and youth.[1] At the same time US leaders paid considerable attention to the formalities; each *comité* had a *commission sociale* whose job it was to involve the party in the joys and griefs of each family. Mali was poor, and politics often turned around questions of deportment, propriety, and prestige rather than property.

One of the remarkable characteristics of the US was that records were kept, even at the local level, and quite elaborately at the level of the *sous-section*. *L'Essor*, the US newspaper, was perhaps the oldest party daily in the AOF—it came out regularly since 1949, and though the paper was of poor quality and the words mimeographed,[2] the contents showed that the party system of communication was excellent. The paper carried personal and general party news—of births and deaths as well as the results of elections, the texts of party reports, speeches and resolutions, attacks on the administration or the PSP. Circulation was small—some 800 in 1957, but copies were read aloud in many localities, and the paper was a remarkable achievement in a poor area where few read French. The *comité directeur* regularly sent out news and directives and received reports. Headquarters in Bamako were well informed, and usually filled with visitors who dropped by. When there were local difficulties Bamako sent out a *commission de conflits* to inquire and make judgements. Serious conflicts were settled in the *comité directeur*. In the US, as in successful parties elsewhere in West Africa, fraudulent claims in the name of the party were sometimes a problem. The US helped solve this by providing official emissaries with written *mandats de mission* or authorizations.

The party urged members to buy cards, from the outset, at 100 francs a year: half to be divided between the *comité* and the *soussection*, and half for headquarters. The land was poor, and it was always hard to bring the money in. In 1947, there were only 12,000 paid up members.[3] The fee was reduced to 50 francs, and again supposed to be divided between local and territorial headquarters.[4] The division did not always take place; and for a while, the *soussections* were urged to 'hire propaganda agents who keep for themselves 5 or 10 francs per card'.[5] There were special fund-raising appeals and parties, but much of the US activity was financed by gifts in kind. This was true for the congresses, which met roughly every two years, and the occasional territorial seminars like the école

---

[1] Keïta, Modibo. 'Rapport d'organisation', op. cit., 7 November 1947.
[2] After independence there was a printed weekly.
[3] US mimeographed circular, signed by Modibo Keïta, January 1947; 'Rapport d'organisation', 7 November 1947.
[4] Règlement intérieur, 2 January 1950, typescript.
[5] CD/US, 22 April 1949, Bamako, mimeographed, from Modibo Keïta.

territorial du RDA of 1949 (following the December 1948 interterritorial école de cadres of Abidjan). Party militants fed, housed,
and transported delegates often without accepting any money at all.

Thus the party took on more and more characteristics of the community in which it grew, and the tasks of governing even before it
had legal power. 'Le parti, c'est l'école,' was the US motto, and the
leaders used the time in opposition to school themselves for exercising
power. Hence they studied their own society, looked into questions
of causes and principles, and at the same time into concrete interests.

'we do not stop at the level of slogans or ready made formulae, we shall
innovate, beginning from the realities of Mali grafted on to successful
experience elsewhere'.[1]

It may be the US leaders acquired their taste for theory in Koranic
school. They kept this interest up, deepened it in Marxist study
classes, and many read at home or took correspondence courses to
make up for their lack of formal schooling. Their reports, speeches,
and resolutions show an interest in thinking ideas through for themselves. They took as their point of departure the rejection, at the
interterritorial RDA Congress, of the principle of assimilation. They
had an early concern with 'the value of Negro–African civilization
. . . and the contributions it can make to human civilization'.[2] It was
urban Malien civilization that came to the fore when they took
power.[3]

They prepared each election in minute detail, studied the results
of past elections, and made full use of their very limited resources.
They knew that delicate diplomacy was needed to tip the balance, in
each locality, from PSP support and that work was needed to keep
already acquired votes. Thus the US leaders laid the bases for the
electoral victories of 1956 and 1957, which allowed them to form the
first African government in Soudan.

Unity and Independence

At the third interterritorial RDA congress of 1957, US and PDG
representatives pressed for resolutions supporting independence and
West African federation. Yet when the referendum of September
1958 came, the US leaders after controversial internal debates
decided to vote YES. Guinea became independent alone and labour

[1] Modibo Keïta, *1960 extraordinary US congress*, op. cit., p. 16.
[2] RDA communiqué, Paris, February 1947, typescript.
[3] The extent to which the cities dominated the US was evident from the structure.
In 1956, for example, the *comité directeur* included the *bureau politique* and one
representative from each *sous-section*. There was a *sous-section* in each of the
12 neighbourhoods of Bamako, and it therefore equalled in representation 12
rural *sous-sections*.

minister Abdoulaye Diallo, who had again broken discipline and called for a NO, left for Conakry. Soudanese leaders claimed they voted YES so as to be able to move more quickly to independence within an African federation. The August 1958 congress confirmed this,[1] and Soudan pressed for a federation within West Africa, as well as for independence within the French Community. Only Senegal finally joined Soudan to form the Federation of Mali. The US made the second *de facto* break in the interterritorial RDA after Guinea's, and formed in 1959 with the UPS of Senegal the *Parti de la Fédération Africaine*. US friction with RDA President Houphouët grew, as the Soudanese differed more and more with his policy.

While the Mali federation formed in spite of French and inter-territorial RDA opposition, within Mali there was a new move to unify all the parties. During 1958 the PSP had tried to restore its position, through the interterritorial socialist movement, and briefly took on the new name of *Parti du Regroupement Soudanais* (PRS). By March 1959, however, Fily-Dabo Sissoko announced his party was dissolving to merge with the US, because the federation of Mali was 'the embryo of the United States of West Africa'.[2] For a few months Hamadoun Dicko led a rump under the name of the *Parti du Rassemblement du Soudan*, which included the Cadi of Timbuctu. But the group faded out of existence, Dicko too rallied to the US, and there was by 1960 a single unified party in Soudan in favour of independence.[3]

The absorption of the PSP by the US was relatively smooth, partly because the US leaders exercised the diplomacy they had practised in keeping their own party together. It took skill to hold together a party which grew to absorb most of Mali. There was tension between old and new town elites, townsmen and country-men, aristocrats and men of caste, even to some extent friction among ethnic groups. The existence of a chain linking all these various groups within a single party, dedicated to disciplined political action in line with an agreed programme, is a remarkable achievement. It became possible at least in part because the leaders, aware of the nature of their own society, considered themselves moderate revolu-tionaries, rejected a 'solution de force' which would have antagonized their own moderates, sought a 'solution mixte' to issues where prin-ciples were involved which might tear the party apart.

The likelihood of independence altered the problems of politics in Soudan, and leaders of both US and PSP recognized their differences were perpetuated by cleavages other than those produced only by

[1] *L'Essor*, 19 August 1958.   [2] *Afrique Nouvelle*, 17 April 1959.
[3] *Afrique Nouvelle*, 27 February 1959 and *Lettre africaine*, op. cit., 30 March 1959.

French rule. French policy added to the differences, but in Soudan official pressure on the US was never as sharp as it had been on the PDG in Guinea. Nor had there been the same degree of French interference in electoral results of Mali.

Since before their organized rivalry began in 1945, the territorial US and PSP leaders, whose active lives centred around Bamako, had shared a common background. There were only a few of them who had come from the same schools and similar jobs; they had intermarried and had similar standards of living. They had common hopes and values—respect for age, for the given word, for example, dislike of the pre-war colonial system which had not let them rise, desire for more education and for development. They showed a more lively interest in their African past than the leaders of parties in any other of the French-speaking West African states. Even in school before the war they were less involved in the temporary rejection of their own past than were their more assimilationist-minded colleagues from the coastal states. Both US and PSP were led by Ponty men, and dominated by the teachers among them. Sissoko and Konaté, elders and contemporaries who had taught most of their political associates, could always step across party lines, speak to each other and speak to their former students,[1] in spite of their political differences.

Understanding tempered the political differences. The US–RDA elders had long used their influence to soften the tendency of their younger followers to call PSP men 'traitors', and the rivalry between the parties, though sharp, had not attained the bitterness found in the politics of Guinea or Ivory Coast. There was a delicacy to US tactics, evident in a report to party headquarters from Kolokani that 'a few good words, a friendly hand-clasp in an administrative office, are enough to stabilise the political position of some people'.[2] The differences between the generations had always been an important element in Mali politics, and this continued to be true within each of the two rival parties. Across party lines contemporaries had common bonds, a common sense of time and of history. All these special characteristics of the elite in Mali may help to explain why the rivals remained comparatively polite to each other over about twelve years, and could at least superficially join forces just before independence.

It was after all alone that Soudan had to face the problems of independence. In August 1960 friction between Senegalese and

---

[1] *Vérité*, PSP newspaper, special edition of May 1956. Konaté had taught at the École Professionelle de Bamako (1919–23), École Diafarabé (1923–8), École Kolokani (1928–30), the École Primaire Supérieure of Bamako (1930–3), and the École Rurale of Bamako (1933–46).

[2] *1955 US Report*, op. cit., sous-section de Kolokani.

Soudanese leaders came to a head. The Senegalese forcibly sent back from Dakar to Bamako the Soudanese officials of the Mali federation. Many Soudanese who worked in Senegal, in private or public positions, on the Dakar–Niger railroad, left at the same time. The differences between PSP and US leaders were many: the US leaders attacked what they considered to be Senegalese corruption, reluctance for social reforms, unequal distribution of wealth, and lethargy over the question of independence. Nor could they accept the Senegalese support of French foreign policy, particularly the Algerian war. These were the basic issues, though the immediate difference was the US rejection of Senghor as the president of the Mali federation.

Pressure from Soudan helped impel Senegal and the other 'states within the Community' to press for its 'renovation', and so independence. The price of the break-up of the Mali federation was high. Transport was wholly disrupted, as the republic of Mali refused to use the Dakar–Niger railroad. They knew it was 'necessary to foresee the isolation of the Soudanese Republic'.[1] This was a bitter disappointment to leaders who understood Mali's development depended on overcoming the limitations of her geographic position, and on close economic relations with her neighbours. Mali leaders had 'hoped that autonomy was the most favorable period for realizing unity',[2] and just at independence, unity with neighbours had to be postponed.

In Bamako, streets and stadiums received new names—after Mamadou Konaté and Ouëzzin Coulibaly. In the north, Fort Bonnier became Fort Cheikh Sidi Bakaye, after the man who had fought Bonnier; Fort Aiguini became Fort Ahmed Baba after a Muslim saint.[3] And Modibo Keïta declared, to the first budgetary session of the National Assembly of Mali:

In giving the name of Mali to our young Republic we have sworn before history to rehabilitate the moral values which formerly made the grandeur of Africa. This oath my government will keep and that is why we refuse to be passive spectators before the great problems of the world or simple pawns on the international checker-board.[4]

[1] Modibo Keïta, *1960 extraordinary US congress*, op. cit., p. 16.
[2] Ibid., p. 15.   [3] *Afrique Nouvelle*, 3 May 1961.
[4] 21 December 1960, mimeographed, Bamako, p. 6.

PART EIGHT

From AOF Federation to Sovereign Nations

FOR more than half a century the French-speaking West African states had close ties resulting from their common frontiers, administration and constitution. The ties of the colonial era both solidified those from pre-colonial times of trade, commerce, religion, language, migrations, and encouraged connexions among the educated elite through their work and their political parties. Lacking a common geographic and administrative framework the English-speaking West African leaders never forged so close a set of links through their parties during the colonial era.

When through French initiative the AOF federation dissolved in 1959, so did the formal ties among parties and other voluntary organizations. Each of the eight governments adopted different laws and practices upon separate independence. After the experiment of the Mali federation failed in 1960, nothing remained of the former modern interterritorial structures. Yet the geography remains the same. The rural connexions among traders, divines, and fellow tribesmen remain in spite of hardened borders.

Pressures for closer unity appeared after independence. It is not impossible that links should be formed again among West African states along the traces which remain of the past political connexions.

Hence there is more than historical interest in recalling in this chapter the connexions among AOF parties under the Fourth Republic, and the various African responses to the dissolution of the federation. This allows an assessment of the prospect of closer connexions among the independent West African states.

Interterritorial Movements

Over a dozen years the interterritorial alignment of French-speaking West African parties shifted several times. The first and most important grouping was that of the RDA, begun in October 1946. The second was a move against the RDA, taken in 1948 with the formation of the *Indépendants d'Outre-Mer* (IOM) parliamentary group; in 1953 it tried to launch an extra-parliamentary movement. In 1957, as the Loi-Cadre was implemented, a third series of moves took place, in January, when IOM became *Convention Africaine* (CAF) and the Socialists in Africa tried to form the *Mouvement Socialiste Africain* (MSA); and in September, when the interterritorial RDA held its third congress. The following year the parties of AOF were more closely related than they were ever before, though not for long. Apart from the RDA, all other significant territorial party leaders except those of Mauretania assembled in a *Parti du Regroupement Africain* (PRA).[1]

The RDA was the most important. It was the first interterritorial movement in AOF, created before parties in territories other than Senegal or Ivory Coast had taken root. The 1946 Bamako Congress, therefore, was able to give direction to, and affect the structure, composition, and policies of associated territorial parties still in their formative stage. The RDA was the only interterritorial movement in French West Africa which drew a popular response at the local level. The RDA was the most stable of all the interterritorial movements; disciplined and highly organized. Finally, because of the circumstances surrounding the 1946 Bamako Congress, participation in and fidelity to the decisions made at the Congress remained a major theme in all subsequent discussions of interterritorial relations among African party leaders. It matters, when a party is started and who started it—for who joins and who refuses to join.

The other interterritorial movements were founded later largely out of reaction against the RDA, were loosely organized, and grew out of attempts to 'integrate at the summit'[2] already existing parties. The other movements were unstable alliances, among party leaders who had little else in common than that they were not in favour of the RDA.

The Bamako RDA Congress was called by all the tropical African second college representatives to the French Constituent Assemblies. This placed the Bamako Congress under the aegis of unity among African political leaders; it was later used to substantiate the RDA claim 'to embody the national will'.[3] The immediate reason for the call was fear of the French *réaction*, and, in particular, of the *États Généraux de la Colonisation*. The Congress emphasized the differences between the April and October Constitutions. 'We all agree that the (October) Constitution does not satisfy us,' said the reporter of the political commission, Jacob Williams.[4] The initiators of the

---

[1] These interterritorial political movements were not exclusively West African, but only the West African connexions are discussed here.
[2] From the typescript of Mamadou Dia's report to the 1953 IOM Congress at Bobo-Dioulasso, mimeographed, p. 1.
[3] Hodgkin. *Nationalism in Colonial Africa*, op. cit., p. 144.
[4] Both citations from the typescript of the report.

Congress wanted to prove that they relegated forced labour, the *indigénat*, and their subordinate position as French 'subjects' firmly to the past; that they intended henceforth to express, and to defend their own interests. The 800-odd delegates[1] declared their goal: 'the liberation of Africa from the odious tutelage—imperialism'.[2] To attain that goal, they proposed to use 'front' tactics in each territory, in order to prepare for the emergence of a single, united RDA.[3] The Congress laid the basis for the structure of the RDA and adopted statutes clarifying the principles of party organization. Two provisions of the statutes helped maintain unity and discipline. Article 2 established that only one RDA section could legally be recognized in each territory;[4] the IOM had a statutory provision permitting more than one affiliate from each territory,[5] its effectiveness and discipline were weakened as a result.[6] The interterritorial RDA was governed along federalist lines; Article 10 provided that each territorial section was 'fully autonomous, within the framework taken by the (interterritorial) *Rassemblement*'.[7] At territorial meetings, Article 10 was invoked to justify the need to conform to decisions taken by the interterritorial Congresses and Co-ordinating Committee meetings. At interterritorial meetings, Article 10 was used to permit divergences in the views and decisions of territorial RDA leaders; and thus to permit the movement to adjust to different local conditions. Although there was in practice a considerable divergence in the actual distribution of power within the RDA territorial sections, temporary French Communist influence encouraged the adoption of similar structural principles, and the use of identical organizational terminology in the various territories.[8]

The statutes were important, but not always heeded. One example was the procedure followed by the RDA *parlementaires* in Paris when they decided to disaffiliate from the French Communist group in Parliament. The RDA statutes, as revised at the second interterritorial Congress held in Abidjan in December 1948–January 1949, sharply reduced the power of the *parlementaires* inside the movement, and placed them firmly under the control of the Co-ordinating Committee.[9] Yet in 1950 the *parlementaires* took the decision to

[1] *Esprit*, December 1951.
[2] Typescript of Houphouët's second speech at the Congress. The full citation is . . . 'odious tutelage—imperialism and capitalism'.
[3] RDA 1948 pamphlet, op. cit., p. 25.
[4] RDA 1948 pamphlet, op. cit., p. 27.
[5] Article IV of the IOM statutes, as adopted at the 1953 Congress.
[6] In Upper Volta, for example, the IOM had two associated parties, the MPEA and PSEMA, which were rivals locally.
[7] RDA 1948 pamphlet, op. cit., p. 28.   [8] See figure 8, p. 304.
[9] From records of the meeting.

FIGURE 8

Territorial and Interterritorial Structure of the RDA

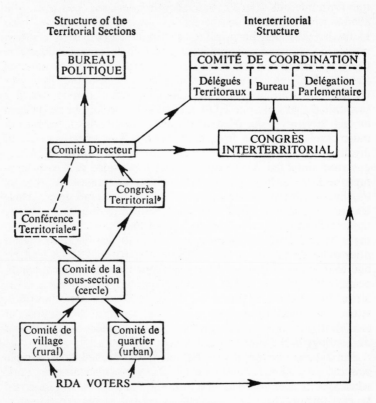

^a Equal number of delegates from each *sous-section*; usually the *conférence* was called by the *comité directeur* when a *congrès* was impractical.
^b Number of delegates proportional to membership in each *sous-section*.

disaffiliate without calling a Co-ordinating Committee meeting; indeed, uncertain if they would be supported at such a meeting, they did not call one until 1955, in Conakry, when the 1950 decision was finally regularized.

Although the most important French West African leaders were temporarily united when the call to Bamako was issued, and the Bamako Congress stressed the need for African unity, the 1946 Congress could not establish unity among African leaders. One reason was the position adopted by the administration. Moutet—well aware of the outcome of the territorial struggles for power between the GEC

supporters of the formula of *rassemblement,* and the Socialist sympathizers who conceived of unity within a *bloc*—indicated in no
uncertain terms his disapproval of the Congress; the leaders of the
non-Communist French parties followed suit. Moutet's attitude in
1946 was but one of a series of French official attitudes of opposition
to the RDA which culminated in the *répression.* What were the
results, for interterritorial relations among French West African
party leaders, of the fact that the administration took exception to
the RDA?

First, there was the effect on those who maintained their intention
to create the new movement. The official position strengthened ties
among those who gave their allegiance to the RDA. Among the
inner core of party leaders, the RDA became almost a religion;
loyalty to the party became the standard from which they judged their
own, and their associates' private as well as public actions. Official
pressure confirmed their conviction that they were the true spokesmen
of Africa; in the vanguard of those fighting against oppression; and
that their cause was just.

The second effect of official opposition was that the members of
the urban elite in the various territories had to make a choice—
prior to 1951—not only between supporting or opposing the RDA,
but also between its corresponding consequences, administrative
hostility or co-operation. It is possible to argue that in most territories the political leaders who made the decision either not to
attend the Bamako Congress, or to leave the RDA shortly after its
formation, did so principally because they were not prepared to face
the hostility of the administration.

Probably only the political leaders of Senegal, and small groups of
politically active Catholics in Dahomey and eastern Upper Volta,
refused to join the RDA movement out of other considerations. In
Senegal, Lamine Guèye enjoyed unique connexions with the French
Socialist party. He shared with the French Socialists a belief in the
necessity for Socialist discipline and a rejection of Communism. His
absence from Bamako can be interpreted as proof of his Socialist
loyalties rather than refusal to face official hostility. The rejection
by practising African Catholics of the RDA was as due to their
religious allegiance; for most members of the Catholic clergy
forbade their communicants any associations with the RDA prior
to 1950.

For several years, the territorial party leaders outside of the RDA
movement remained without any formal interterritorial ties. The constitutional framework did not favour the creation of such ties. The
members of the federal grand council were indirectly elected, usually
by unstable majorities within the territorial assemblies. The grand

council had little power or influence. Prior to 1956, African party leaders sought most diligently for allies in Paris, not in neighbouring African territories.

Thus it was in the French Parliament that the first tentative step was taken among some of these territorial leaders, for the creation of a parliamentary group in 1948, which eventually became the second AOF interterritorial formation—the IOM. The initiative came from the French MRP, and corresponded to the interests of the leaders of the newly formed BDS. For five years the IOM was purely a parliamentary alliance of some, not all the territorial leaders who rejected the RDA. In 1953 some of the ethnic leaders of Guinea, representatives of the *Union Voltaïque* in Upper Volta, a handful of politically active Africans in Dahomey, and later one of the two deputies elected through the chiefs and the administration in Niger, joined the BDS leaders in their attempt to transform the IOM into an extra-parliamentary movement.

The RDA leaders did not take a very cordial view of the existence of the IOM. After, as before disaffiliation from the French Communists, the RDA continued to hold the view that theirs was the only political organization which was the genuine expression of the African general will for emancipation. In retrospect, the role which the Senegalese BDS leaders played within the IOM proved to have more important, and more lasting effects on interterritorial relations among significant party leaders in AOF than the IOM organization itself. Only the participation of the BDS leaders in the IOM gave it weight or distinction; for the BDS was the only broadly backed, soundly constructed party associated with the IOM. At the same time, prior to 1956, the Ivory Coast section of the RDA was the only solidly implanted party associated with the interterritorial RDA. Therefore, the IOM–RDA rivalry took on more general overtones of rivalry for French West African leadership between the African representatives of Senegal and Ivory Coast.

Inside Senegal, the position enjoyed by the pre-war 'citizens' had a profound impact on post-war politics. The privileged position which most Senegalese living outside of Senegal enjoyed before the war, led many educated 'subjects' in the other territories to construct a stereotyped idea of the Senegalese; as men who assumed they were superior to other Africans; who believed theirs was a natural right to lead. Mamadou Dia, in his report to the 1949 BDS Congress, gave two reasons for the BDS refusal to join the RDA. One was the role of the Communists in the RDA. The second reason proved revealing: 'The RDA was born, but it did not have much attraction for the Senegalese masses. . . . It was born far away from the beaches of Senegal. Unhappily, the Senegalese, in his present state of mind, is only with difficulty permeable to local ideas which he did not initiate.'[1]

Within Senegal, the electoral victories of the BDS served in time to reduce the resentment the 'subjects' felt towards the 'citizens'. In the other territories, however, IOM–RDA rivalry did little to eradicate the unflattering pre-war stereotype of the Senegalese. The Ivory Coast leaders were at the head of the territory which by 1952 displaced Senegal from the place of economic pre-eminence in French West Africa. The Ivory Coast section of the RDA was the 'mother of the (interterritorial) RDA'.[2] Not surprisingly, therefore, stereotyped recollections of the pre-war role of the Senegalese continued in some measure to affect the judgement made by some Ivory Coast RDA leaders of the post-war interterritorial position adopted by the BDS.

The IOM did not assemble all the African party leaders who were opposed to the RDA. The political leaders of Mauretania did not join the IOM, as they joined no subsequent interterritorial movement. The leaders of UNIS in Niger, of the PSP in the Soudan, of the ethnic groups supporting Yacine Diallo in Guinea, joined the SFIO leaders of Senegal in maintaining some type of association with the French Socialists. Prior to 1957, their links with each other were informal, and tenuous. Still other territorial party leaders—Kango Ouëdraogo of the MDV in Upper Volta, Barry Diawadou of Guinea, Sourou Migan Apithy of Dahomey—were satisfied to remain without any steady interterritorial political associates until 1958. During the first post-war decade, the comparatively disciplined RDA and the loosely organized IOM were the only interterritorial political formations existing in French West Africa.

In July 1955, the RDA Co-ordinating Committee—meeting in Conakry for the first time since the beginning of the *répression*—made decisions which removed the last remaining suspicions in French official circles, of the attitude which the RDA leaders had towards the Communists. The Co-ordinating Committee expelled from the movement the UDN and UDS leaders who had refused to accept the 1950 decision to break links with the French Communists. The Committee also approved Sékou Touré's plan to break West African trade union links with the French CGT.[3] In January 1956 the RDA won widely in the parliamentary elections. This and the choice of Houphouët as a minister in successive French governments of the third Legislature suggested that the French administration had abandoned its previous opposition to the interterritorial RDA. The

[1] Typescript of the report.
[2] *Abidjan–Matin*, 22 October 1957, citing a speech by PDCI President Denise.
[3] From records of the meeting.

same electoral results demonstrated that the IOM was unsuccessful as an interterritorial movement; that the BDS leaders were practically the only IOM associates who had a mass following.

The Time to Decide

After the 1956 events altered the basis of African interterritorial relations, first stimulating and then discouraging close connexions. While nationalist pressure rose in Africa, French officials could no longer avoid further constitutional concessions. The adoption in Paris of first the Loi-Cadre and later the constitution of the Fifth Republic effectively broke up the West African federation. During the discussions on the Loi-Cadre in the French Parliament, it became clear that political power over African affairs was shifting from France to Africa, that henceforth relations among Africans would make more of a difference, and that the phase of direct French interference in African party politics was ending.

French policy was clear, but Africans had yet to define their position on the crucial issues of independence and federation. While busy setting up the very first elected African governments, they also had to reconsider their interterritorial party links. The original decision for or against joining the RDA had been made when the French administration interfered more directly in African party politics, and had indicated disapproval of the RDA. After the disapproval had disappeared, non-RDA leaders particularly felt the need to take stock. Early in 1956 IOM leaders tried to obtain RDA agreement on the creation of a new interterritorial movement. The attempt failed, mainly because the RDA leaders saw no reason to abandon their own tested organization and name, just after the electoral victory, just before they expected to consolidate their gains in municipal and territorial assembly elections, and while they alone were in regular consultation with the French government over the Loi-Cadre reforms.

In January 1957 Senegal's leaders of the BPS were fresh from the efforts of rejuvenating their party by the absorption of radical UDS leaders who had been expelled from the RDA in 1955. They took the initiative to revamp the IOM by building new interterritorial links with parties other than the RDA. Their hope, in creating the *Convention Africaine* around a radical programme, was to attract wider and deeper support—more territorial party leaders, and grass roots, rather than a summit response. The *Convention* meeting raised clearly, the issues—African independence, a strong French West African federation, the French war in Algeria—which had become the primary concern of Africans, regardless of their political affiliation. But the *Convention* was unable to attract as affiliates other parties than those which had been associated with the IOM. Indeed, in Upper Volta and in Dahomey, the *Convention* lost some former IOM associates to the RDA: respectively, the PSEMA and the UDD.

The limited audience of the *Convention* was partly because the French and Senegalese Socialists also tried, and also in January 1957, to reverse the decline in the fortune of the political groups with Socialist connexions. Most of the territorial parties joining the MSA at Conakry had been founded with French official support by the established members of the African elite: for example, the party of chiefs and higher civil servants of Niger, the *Bloc Nigérien d'Action* (BNA, formerly the *Union Nigérienne des Indépendants et Sympathisants*, UNIS).

One group joined the MSA which was in quite a different category: the young radicals associated with the CGT union leader, Bakary Djibo of Niger. Like the UDS of Senegal, his party, the *Union Démocratique Nigérienne* (UDN) had been read out of the interterritorial RDA at the 1955 Conakry meeting for refusal to conform to the interterritorial decision to disaffiliate from the Communists in 1950. Later Djibo opposed Sékou Touré's move to disaffiliate the African unions from the French CGT. In Niger, the UDN could count on about a quarter of the votes, while the BNA of the chiefs could count on slightly less than half. Djibo used the opportunity offered by the birth of the MSA to become allied with the chiefs. The alliance stood behind the first government of Niger and Djibo became the first vice-president.

Aside from strengthening Djibo in Niger, the creation of MSA and *Convention* did little to affect the outcome of the March 1957 elections.[1] In Ivory Coast, Guinea, and Soudan, the RDA gained overwhelming majorities; in Upper Volta, a bare majority; and in Niger and Dahomey, respectable minorities. As a result, the federal grand council was controlled, for the first time, by a comparatively disciplined and stable plurality of RDA leaders, who, in alliance with the representatives of Mauretania, gained control of the *bureau* of the grand council; Houphouët became president. Meanwhile, all who were not of the RDA felt increasingly isolated politically. They again revised their territorial tactics so as to attain a larger share in determining the outcome of the discussions about the future constitutional relationship between Africa and metropolitan France and among the African territories.

These two issues gave rise to great debate inside the RDA as well. The balance of power within it shifted. The phase of Ivory Coast

---

[1] See figure 9. p. 310.

FIGURE 9

Party affiliations of territorial councillors elected on 31 March 1957

(Numbers in brackets refer to party affiliations of *second college* councillors in the 1952–7 territorial assemblies. For the full names of the parties referred to by initials, see Appendix XII.)

Territories	1957 Interterritorial Affiliations[a]			Others	Total
	CAF	MSA	RDA		
Senegal	47 BPS (41)	12 PSAS (9)		1 Ind	60 (50)
Mauretania				33 UPM (15)	34 (16)
				1 Ind (1)	
Soudan		6 PSP (27)	64 (13)		70 (40)
Upper Volta	7 MPEA		37 (0)	26 NDV (6)	70 (40)
	(34 UV)				
Dahomey			7 (0)	35 PRD (19)	60 (32)
				18 Ind (13)	
Niger		41 (35 UNIS)	19 (0)		60 (35)
Ivory Coast			60 (28)	(4)	60 (32)
Guinea		3 (15)	56 (1)	1 (16)	60 (32)
Total	54	62	243	115	474

[a] The interterritorial alignment of 1957 was an approximation. Prior to 1957, the parties with loose Socialist attachments were not members of any organized interterritorial movement. In April 1958, CAF, MSA, and practically all 'others' except the UPM of Mauretania, announced their membership in the *Parti du Regroupement Africain* (PRA).

predominance came to an end at the September 1957 interterritorial Congress held in Bamako. The recent electoral successes of the Guinea and Soudan RDA sections gave weight to their arguments against Minister Houphouët-Boigny. He spoke for only a minority when he took a 'territorialist' position, and excluded independence. Sékou Touré spoke for the overwhelming majority when he took a 'federalist' position, and spoke of future AOF independence. At the 1957 Congress, there were more strains evident in the relations among the various RDA territorial leaders, than at any time since the 1950 break from the Communists. At the Congress, these profound differences on policy were temporarily patched up; Houphouët was once again elected the interterritorial president; and compromise resolutions were adopted. The RDA Congress favoured the 'democratization' of the federal organs of French West Africa, not specifically a federal executive; and stated both that 'the right to independence was an inalienable right', and that 'interdependence was the golden rule . . . of the Twentieth Century'.[1]

[1] *Interafrique Presse*, 4 October 1957.

Most RDA, *Convention* and MSA leaders could agree on these points, and it seemed the new conditions in African relations to France which followed the Loi-Cadre might bury the old issues that had given rise to African divisions. When Houphouët became president of the federal grand council in Dakar, there was speculation he might soften his opposition to a strong AOF. This was again suggested at the fusion meeting of African parties in Paris during February 1958 when all agreed (except the PAI of Senegal and the Mauretanians) on both independence and a federal executive of sorts. But the unity did not last. When the second conference of African parties took place in March in Dakar the RDA said they wanted to keep their name and their hierarchy; in other words, all the other parties were to join them. These were impossible conditions for the others. They created a new movement, the interterritorial *Parti du Regroupement Africain* (PRA)—'according to the principles and modalities of organic unity defined at the full Conférence de Regroupement des Partis Africains', which met in Paris on 17 February 1958[1]—while the MSA and *Convention* dissolved.

It looked, briefly, as if AOF were moving in the direction of a two-party system at the interterritorial level, of RDA and PRA. In July 1958 the PRA gained a new vitality at their founding congress in Cotonou, which the 'young Turks' dominated: Bakary Djibo of Niger, Abdoulaye Ly and Abdoulaye Guèye of Senegal. They forced a resolution through in favour of immediate independence, in spite of Senghor's disagreement. Thus both within the RDA and within the PRA the top leaders were defeated by their own rank and file, and a strong current of opinion in favour of independence was developing among Africans.

Once again French constitutional changes interrupted the course of African politics. As results, both the PRA and the RDA broke apart and there were substantial internal political changes within some of the territories. In May came the *coup* in Algiers, in June de Gaulle was invested, and during late summer and fall France and its dependencies were preoccupied by the crises out of which was born the Fifth Republic. Africans had little opportunity to express their views, except to vote 'yes' for the 1958 constitution, which expressly ruled out independence and broke up the African federations.

Senghor broke with the decision of the Cotonou PRA congress and called for a 'YES' vote, and since then was faced by opposition of youth, students, trade unionists, and 'young Turks'. Bakary Djibo, coalition president of the council of government in Niger, kept to the Cotonou decision and called for a 'NO'. Partly due to French pres-

[1] *Paris–Dakar*, 28 March 1958.

sure, his government coalition lost its support, the majority in Niger voted 'YES', and Djibo's government was dissolved. Later there were new elections, and a government was formed without Djibo, who had regrouped his followers in the newly-named *Sawaba* party (homeland in Hausa).[1] It was officially dissolved and he went into exile.

As for the RDA, it too broke in 1958 after twelve years of remarkable growth and unity on the issues of federation and independence. In spite of divisions inside the movement, President Houphouët did not call a meeting of the Co-ordinating Committee to discuss a common RDA policy on the referendum. Steps to call such a meeting had been begun by Political Director Ouëzzin Coulibaly, who was then also Ivory Coast deputy and president of the council of government of Upper Volta. But Ouëzzin Coulibaly died, unexpectedly, in Paris on 7 September, and his work of holding the movement together through crises was not taken up by anyone else. Most RDA leaders were by then too busy with offices in their parties, municipalities, territorial assemblies, and in the new territorial governments; they needed to organize the vote in their states and had little time left for inter-state matters.

Houphouët called for a YES, and RDA leaders in Niger, Upper Volta, and Dahomey agreed with him. Guinea, after some hesitation, decided NO. Soudan's US leaders agreed with the Guinea position, but for tactical considerations took a different course. There were still French bases in Soudan, and Senegal controlled the land lines of communication to the outside world. Thus in 1958 Guinea was alone to break out of the Community, and with this the interterritorial RDA broke apart. So did AOF. Parties ceased to be the channels connecting the various states; after 1958 relations among the 'ex-AOF' states moved into the realm of international relations.

Within each state the assumption of power by African governments crystallized the *status quo*. The parties which won majorities in the 1957 elections formed the governments and from then on could and did use force to keep their positions. After 1957 significant changes took place in those states—like Dahomey and Niger—where the party balance was precarious and no single party had come out ahead in the 1957 elections. Even those states, however, shared in the general pattern of moving fairly rapidly in the direction of single party systems.

Even as the old ties among the territories changed, within the new states, governments adopted new laws. Hence laws and institutions which had been uniform diverged and each state moved in its own direction. There was but one abortive last-minute attempt to halt this

---

[1] Sawaba was also the rallying cry of the Northern Elements Progressive Union (NEPU), the anti-traditionalist party in northern Nigeria.

process of 'Balkanization', with the creation of the Mali federation
and its party equivalent, the *Parti de la Fédération Africaine* (PFA).

The Mali Federation

In January 1959, meeting in Bamako, leaders of Dahomey, Senegal,
Soudan, and Upper Volta agreed to form a Mali federation. It
was their hope to prevent the total dissolution of 'ex-AOF', to form
by African initiative a nucleus for West African federation which
could cope with the economic problems of independence. After AOF
formally dissolved in April 1959, the leaders of the states meeting in
Bamako knew they would have great difficulty going it alone. Senegal,
which had long been outside of the RDA, was trying to join forces
with Soudan's government, entirely formed by the *Union Soudanaise-*
RDA; they tried to draw in Dahomey and Upper Volta, both with
relatively weak coalition governments. Pressure from both France
and Ivory Coast led Dahomey to withdraw in February, and Upper
Volta in March. Neither had any solid economic advantages in
trading with or through Soudan and Senegal. Upper Volta particularly had need of Ivory Coast ports for imports and exports and of
Ivory Coast farms to give jobs to migrant labourers. Ivory Coast had
only to threaten to interrupt the Abidjan–Ouagadougou railroad, for
Upper Volta to recognize the extent of its dependence.

By 24 March, when the PFA was formally organized in Dakar,
only the US–RDA and the UPS were seriously involved. The extent
to which the interterritorial RDA had been shattered was evident
from the public question: 'Must we break brutally also?' the US–
RDA leaders asked in their newspaper, *l'Essor*.

Measuring fully the consequences of our words we accuse M. Houphouët-
Boigny of poisoning Franco-African relations, of deliberately falsifying
them.

Clearly and before African and French opinion we take a forceful stand
against the discourteous and venomous proposals of a man who is no
longer among our friends, and whom we accuse of sabotaging both the
African Community and the Franco-African Community.

... The manoeuvre of presenting Guinea as anti-French is taken up
again by M. Houphouët and now addressed against the Federalists. ...
We affirm that the declarations of M. Houphouët-Boigny which in the
recent past provoked Guinea to stiffen its position, run the risk if they are
repeated and taken seriously of provoking a brutal reaction among the
Federalists.[1]

It had been a governmental decision to federate Soudan and
Senegal; links among parties, trade union, and youth organizations

[1] *Afrique Nouvelle*, 20 February 1959, citing *l'Essor*, 10 February 1959.

simply fell into place afterwards. Such links had become affairs of state. France and the other states of 'ex-AOF' opposed the Mali federation; even Guinea did so, on the ground that African unity could successfully be negotiated only among independent African states. The federation lived long enough to successfully pressure the de Gaulle government into granting total independence within the Community, but in the process developed too many strains to survive. In bitterness the former partners separated shortly after they became independent in 1960, as did all other states of former French West Africa.

Only vigorous and unified actions by the leaders of all the states of 'ex-AOF' could have prevented the total dissolution of the federation. But there had not been unity. Guinea, Senegal, and Soudan had been staffed by convinced 'federalists' who failed to achieve their goal in the autonomy stage. The leaders of Dahomey, Niger, and Upper Volta were undecided so the decision was taken for them in France; Mauretania and Ivory Coast were staffed by pronounced 'territorialists'. It is worth examining these positions somewhat more closely.

'Territorialists'

It is not difficult to discover why the leaders of Mauretania opposed strong West African federal organs of government. The majority of the population, less than three quarters of a million, are Moors who historically, geographically, and culturally are closer to their northern than to their southern neighbours.[1] They see a rich future as mineral and oil exporters and were encouraged when the International Bank loaned them $66 million in 1960. They had little contact with French education. The rudimentary political parties which developed among these proud, largely nomad, Muslim, Arabic-speaking peoples— mostly responsive to the authority of their traditional leaders—had few relations with the major party formations of AOF. The state schools, the civil service, the activities of the French Communist Party prior to 1950, the RDA, and the trade unions were the major forces tending towards binding 'ex-AOF' together. Mauretania was barely touched by any of these. Only the Negro minority living on the frontiers of Senegal and Soudan had any desires of the leaders in these two states for a strong federation[2]; they feared domination by majority of Moors.[3]

[1] Barbour, Neville, ed., *A Survey of North West Africa*, Oxford University Press, London, 1959, pp. 263–76.
[2] The Negro inhabitants of the Senegal river area were organized in the *Union Générale des Originaires de la Vallée du Fleuve* and active politically both in Senegal and in Mauretania.
[3] *Afrique Nouvelle*, 9 May 1958.

In the long run, it is likely the frontiers of southern Mauretania will be rectified. Nor can the western and northern frontiers of Mauretania be considered stable. Some spokesmen of the majority of the Mauretanian people have thought in terms of a 'Greater Mauretania', inclusive of what is now Rio de Oro.[1] Some have indicated interest in events in Cairo and Rabat.[2] Morocco claimed all of Mauretania, and put up an unsuccessful fight against the admission of Mauretania in the UN. France was ready to guarantee the integrity of Mauretania out of hope of sharing the mineral and oil wealth; a desire for a friendly neighbour in the Sahara during the Algerian War; a search for a place to evacuate Saharan resources if relations with the rest of North Africa should become worse. Most of these reasons ceased to be valid when Algeria became independent in 1962, and it became uncertain whether in the long run Mauretania would survive as a separate nation. The leaders counted on French readiness to support Mauretania as an independent buffer state.

The truth is that all of us here feel, in the bottom of our hearts, we don't want to have anything to do with Morocco; we don't want to have anything to do with AOF; we don't want to have anything to do with the Sahara (OCRS). We want to be free on our own, and to speak directly with France.[3]

The pull from the North is stronger, and neither in the interlude before independence nor after were Mauretanians inclined to accept federal institutions dominated by their southern Negro neighbours.

The indecision on federation of the Dahomean leaders had several explanations: geography, ethnic and group divisions, rudimentary regional parties, the absence of any strong links with the major inter-territorial parties, and economics. Dahomey is a long, narrow corridor, situated between the Autonomous Republic of Togo on the west, and Western Nigeria on the east; to the north lie Upper Volta and Niger. There are cultural affinities with the eastern and western neighbours, and a north–south division exists among the people; this was reflected by the predominantly regional parties which emerged. The members of the many varied social groups in Dahomey—both modern and traditional—were more conscious of their separate than of their common territorial identity.

[1] *Le Monde*, weekly, 13–19 and 20–26 March 1958.
[2] In 1958 two ministers in the council of government left their posts for Cairo. Dèye Ould Sidi Baba, minister of commerce, industry, and mines, and Mohamed El Moktar Ould Ba, minister of education and youth. They were excluded from the Mauretanian government. *Paris–Dakar*, 27 March 1958.
[3] From an interview recorded at the 1958 congress of Mauretanian parties by Simon Kiba and Alain des Mazery, *Afrique Nouvelle*, 9 May 1958. The OCRS is the Organisation Commune des Régions Sahariennes, an agency set up by the French Government in January 1957 to co-ordinate development in the Sahara.

In the southern rural areas, the more important of the rival leaders was Sourou Migan Apithy, whose local base was Porto Novo. He had attended the 1946 Congress of the RDA, but shortly afterwards broke with it and kept out of interterritorial alliances for more than a decade. He was regularly re-elected deputy to Paris, mostly with southern votes. In 1956 he and his colleagues of the *Parti Républicain du Dahomey* (PRD) took a definite stand against federation. The reason was chiefly economic. As part of '*opération hirondelle*' officials improved communications from the landlocked territory of Niger in an attempt to use Dahomey rather than Nigerian ports. As a result there were increased revenues for Dahomey and the territorial assembly, with a PRD majority, was reluctant to pay the money to the federation. By 1958, however, world prices of primary raw materials had fallen and Dahomey ceased to have surplus revenue. Then the PRD leaders changed their stand. They became members of the newly organized PRA which favoured federation.

On the whole, however, most southerners, including PRD supporters, had few cultural affinities with the peoples of French West Africa. Rather, as Ewe and Yoruba, they were respectively drawn towards Togo and Nigeria. In northern Dahomey, the supporters of still another regional party, the *Rassemblement Démocratique Dahoméen* (RDD) were culturally attracted as Djerma-Songhai or Mossi, to Niger and Upper Volta respectively.

Although the PRD leaders had an electoral majority in 1957, they did not have the support of most of the educated elite, of the trade unionists and youth leaders in the major towns of the south and centre of the territory. This elite divided their loyalty between the RDA and the former *Convention*. Though politically active and relatively highly educated, they did not—unlike most highly educated Africans in the other French West African territories—take the initiative in pressing for a strong federation. At least one explanation is that many members of this elite are part of an international urban coastal community, stretching from Takoradi in the west to Calabar in the east.[1] They have been more responsive to political events in Togo and British West Africa, than most other French-speaking West Africans. Their geographical position and ties of kinship made them uncertain about the desirability of a strong AOF federation.

Party names and support changed rapidly even after the Loi-Cadre started crystallizing political relationships inside most other states. Since the mid-'fifties, the *Union Démocratique Dahoméenne* (UDD, a branch of the RDA), led by Justin Ahomadegbe of Abomey, had growing support in the southern areas. In the 1957 elections it won a respectable minority position of 7 seats, and by April 1959 the

[1] See Tardits, Claude, *Porto-Novo*, Mouton & Co., Paris, La Haye, 1958.

withdrawal of Apithy's government from the Mali federation added to UDD support and it won a plurality of the votes. But in the assembly, there was another PRD majority in the 1959 elections, and the UDD vigorously protested. The issue of federation was but one of the many involved in the frequent changes of party names. The pre-dominantly regional parties combined and recombined; there were frequent political incidents. Attempts to bring the UDD and PRD together failed, though fusion of all the other parties at the summit was slowly taking place as Dahomey moved towards a single-party system under the leadership of Hubert Maga of the north: the *Parti Dahoméen de l'Unité* (PDU). Just after Dahomey became independent there were new elections, again gerrymandered, and the PDU won all the seats though the UDD had a third of the votes. The govern-ment banned the UDD in 1961, and jailed Ahomadegbe for about a year. In this way, Dahomey obtained a weak single party in the PDU.

Indecision about the issue of federation in Niger was also related to the weaknesses of the parties. Niger was a huge, sparsely settled inland territory, of about the same size as Soudan, but with far fewer people, about two and a half million.[1] In the capital, Niamey, lived less than 20,000 people. The very low density of population meant that people rarely came together long enough to make it easy to organize parties. The population was, however, homogeneous, and so the scale of parties tended towards the whole territory. Hamani Diori won the first elections; he came from western Niger. He became president and Bakary Djibo the secretary–general of the *Parti Pro-gressiste Nigérien* (PPN–RDA). Djibo's political support came from the eastern part of Niger, around Zinder. The PPN represented the modernizing groups, chauffeurs, camel drivers, wage earners, and people opposed to the official chiefs. To oppose the PPN, the chiefs with official support formed their own party, UNIS, which won in the 1952 and 1953 elections. Meanwhile, Djibo and Hamani Diori had broken when Djibo disagreed with the 1950 RDA disaffiliation from the French Communists. Djibo formed his own party, the UDN, and concentrated most of his efforts on CGT trade union work. In the late 'fifties he was the CGT representative in the Economic Council, a post which entitled him to a salary and a car, both rare assets in so poor a state as Niger.

In 1957 Djibo joined forces with the BNA, the party of the chiefs, so as to become head of the elected government of Niger. He urged that 'no French West African territory can exist solely on its own resources';[2] pressed for a strong federal government as well as inde-

---

[1] *Outre-mer 1958*, op. cit., p. 78.
[2] *Paris–Dakar*, 14 March 1958.

pendence, and for a NO vote. This policy was too radical for his chiefly allies, who responded to French urgings and broke the alliance. They switched to the PPN of Hamani Diori, and he became prime minister. After independence his party outlawed Bakary Djibo's party *Sawaba* and the PPN became the dominant single party of Niger.

Diori's PPN and Djibo's UDN had represented similar modernizing forces, respectively in western and eastern Niger. They had quarrelled in 1950 about issues which ceased to have any relevance in 1956. It might have been expected that the two parties unite; they did not because of past personal bitterness. They were perhaps more deeply divided than the people. The leaders of Niger were far too preoccupied struggling for power with each other to unify around either the issues of independence or federation. Niger too faced independence isolated and alone, without a seaport, railroad, or adequate roads, with a largely subsistence economy and dependent upon outside subsidies and personnel. Politically and economically the pull from the Federation of Nigeria was strong.

In Upper Volta party leaders were divided by regions and disagreed on fundamental issues. Of all the states of 'ex-AOF' it had the shortest history, since it was reconstituted only in 1947 after fifteen years as part of its neighbours, mainly Ivory Coast. There was little of a modern economy, and the railroad from Abidjan to Ouagadougou brought workers and little else to the coastal states. The main division was between east and west, and within each there was a further division between traditionalists and their opponents. The peoples of east and west were very different. In the east, around the capital Ouagadougou, lived approximately two million Mossi, largely animist except for an educated minority of Catholics, and mostly obedient to traditional rulers organized along feudal lines. In the west lived slightly less than two million Bobos and other fragmented, almost stateless peoples, largely Muslim in and around the town of Bobo-Dioulasso and animist in the rural areas. Not even the seasonal migration to Ghanaian and Ivory Coast farms by several hundred thousand labourers annually has effaced the political authority of the Mossi chiefs. The non-Mossi, however, had a long history of resistance to all forms of authority. The cultural, geographic, and economic ties between the people of the two regions were slender. Attempts to maintain on a territorial scale a unified party based on the chiefs have failed; the ethnic minority in the west even demanded separation from the Mossi east:[1] they looked rather to Ivory Coast or Mali.

The first party was the RDA, then a branch of the Ivory Coast

[1] 'À Propos des problèmes de la Haute Volta', *Esprit*, Paris, September 1953, signed D.O.

RDA–PDCI and centred largely around Bobo-Dioulasso. From there came both the political director of the interterritorial RDA, Ouëzzin Coulibaly and his wife. The RDA had little Mossi backing. To oppose it came the Mossi-sponsored *Union Voltaïque*, which had two goals, both reached, the establishment of a separate state, and extensions of the railroad to Ouagadougou. The UV won in the first round of elections, but after the second round divided in two: in the west the *Mouvement Populaire de l'Évolution Africaine* (MPEA) led by Nazi Boni and supported by official chiefs, and in the east, the *Parti Social d'Éducation des Masses Africaines* (PSEMA), backed by the Morho Naba and the other official Mossi chiefs subordinated to him. There was yet a fourth party, essentially regional in the east, the *Mouvement Démocratique Voltaïque* (MDV), centred around Ouahigouya. Michel Dorange, a former army officer and European trader, started the party in the late 'forties, first using veterans and local agents of his firm as party representatives. As the MDV grew, it combined radical opposition to the official chiefs with Mossi separatist sentiment for a traditional rival of the Morho Naba, the Yatenga Naba. They opposed French officials locally, but allied with Conservatives in Paris. The main African representative of the party was Kango Gérard Ouëdraogo, a relation of the Yatenga Naba.

After the Loi-Cadre was adopted in 1956, Ouëzzin Coulibaly negotiated with some difficulty an alliance between the RDA of the west and PSEMA of the east. This group, which eventually formed the *Parti Démocratique Unifié* (PDU–RDA), won a slender majority in the 1957 elections, and Ouëzzin Coulibaly headed the first African government. It was a summit alliance, dependent upon the person of Coulibaly, who was at least as much preoccupied with general inter-territorial affairs as with those of Upper Volta. He was a federalist, who believed 'France is but a scarecrow' in an atomic age.[1] Yet his first loyalty went to the RDA, and within it to President Houphouët, an outspoken territorialist. This relationship limited Coulibaly's willingness to defend a federalist position. He knew the extent to which Upper Volta was economically dependent on the states of the coast, especially Ivory Coast. Until Ouëzzin Coulibaly's death there was no clear expression of Upper Voltan opinion either on federation or on independence.

His successor, Maurice Yameogo from the Mossi area, had difficulty assuming power and did not chart a clear course on the issue of the Mali federation. Yameogo first swore allegiance to Mali, disavowed it after Ivory Coast and French pressure. There was some protest within Upper Volta, largely from the younger Catholic

[1] *Interafrique Presse*, 4 October 1957, p. 25, citing a speech by Ouëzzin Coulibaly at the Bamako Congress, 1957.

nationalists living in Ouagadougou and formerly supporters of PSEMA. Yameogo suppressed this opposition; and to control ethnic and regional separatism he forbade all kinds of ethnic associations—even sports or youth groups. Upper Volta also moved towards a single party system under the newly formed *Union Démocratique Voltaïque* (UDV). The UDV remained weak. Upper Volta had few assets: its labour, to send to the highest bidder either Ivory Coast or Ghana, a central geographical position, to bargain where there were plans for a new West African federation. These assets were not enough to bring funds for development, without which the economy could not grow and the modern elite remained static. Social changes seemed dependent upon events outside Upper Voltan borders. The pull of Ghana's Volta River development scheme was likely to grow.

Thus in Dahomey, Niger, and Upper Volta party leaders divided along regional lines and usually divided further between town and countryside; they spent the crucial time between 1956 and 1958 jockeying for power. The decisions on independence and federation were taken for them. Had these leaders had more time, might they have built mass parties comparable in strength to the dominant parties of Senegal, Ivory Coast, Guinea, or Mali? Perhaps. There were groups which could have become mass parties: the UDD of Dahomey, *Sawaba* of Niger, and the RDA of western Upper Volta. But these parties were still at the regional level when the Loi-Cadre reforms crystallized the *status quo*. Afterwards there seemed few, if any, opportunities to shift to new mass parties.

There did seem to be a connexion between the undecided positions on federation by party leaders in Dahomey, Upper Volta, and Niger, and the weak regional character of the various parties. The leaders of Ivory Coast were in a quite different position. They spoke for their people, for the oldest mass party of AOF which had contributed heavily to the interterritorial RDA, for the richest territory of AOF. When the PDCI, therefore, formally registered in April 1958 in territorial assembly opposition to a strong federal government, this was strong support for the French position in favour of Balkanization.[1]

Ivory Coast opposition to federation was old, and had economic as well as political reasons. As early as 1947 the first session of the Ivory Coast *conseil générale* refused to vote the budget, claiming among other reasons that 'the federal government has become a fifth wheel; its suppression will prevent the squandering of our assets'.[2] The refusal occurred during a period of bitter opposition between the RDA and the administration. Reluctance to pay money into the

[1] *West Africa*, 19 April 1958.
[2] *Annexe* no. 1, p. v. du 24 mars 1947, *Exposé du budget*, Abidjan, Ivory Coast, p. 1.

federal budget became stronger, as the territorial income rose with prices and production of coffee and cocoa. After 1952, the Ivory Coast contributed more than any other territory to the federal budget, and the sense of grievance of Ivory Coast leaders, against what they believed to be pouring money into a bottomless pit, became correspondingly stronger. They wanted to see the results of their new wealth.

The politics of the federation increased the PDCI reluctance. Until 1952 the PDCI had participated in the *bureau* of the federal grand council; but between 1952 and 1957, the RDA was excluded from all these elected federal posts. Most were held by Senegalese; which served to intensify resentment of the Ivory Coast leaders. For several decades prior to 1952 the Senegalese had paid the largest proportion of the costs of the federation; but they benefited from the prestige and profits and saw the evidence of daily activities, since the capital of Dakar was on their soil. Federal institutions and Senegalese domination became closely associated in the minds of most PDCI leaders.

Curiously, prior to 1958, while the Ivory Coast RDA leaders in their capacity as councillors in the territorial assembly indicated their reluctance to subsidize through the budget of the federation the poorer West African territories, as party leaders they made great efforts to help their party comrades in the other territories. The militants in the Ivory Coast RDA, and particularly the planters, gave freely of their resources to the interterritorial RDA and during several electoral campaigns helped RDA leaders of Guinea, Soudan, Niger, and Upper Volta. This was partly explained by acceptance of the personal authority of Houphouët. His generosity towards the Ivory Coast and interterritorial RDA was legendary; his requests to the planters for money met with immediate response. The loyalty of the Ivory Coast leaders to the interterritorial RDA was stronger than to the formal institutions of AOF. But the repeated attacks made within the interterritorial RDA since 1956 on the authority of president Houphouët eroded the commitment to the interterritorial movement within the PDCI. Guinean and Soudanese RDA leaders attacked Houphouët's policy steadily since 1957, and the PDCI leaders were quite ready to condemn them by the time of the referendum. He threw a challenge at the 'sorcerer's apprentice of false independence',[1] first Ghana, then Guinea.

Reluctance to pay subsidies to poorer states explained opposition to federation, while the desire for French subsidies explained the opposition to independence, and these two positions went hand in hand for Ivory Coast. Houphouët agreed with those who said 'every

[1] *Interafrique Presse*, 29 January 1960, p. 11, citing a speech by Houphouët at Duékoué on 22 January.

bridge they build remains', and who asked 'why pay for an army';[1] he believed Africans still have much to learn from France.[2] The Ivory Coast leaders achieved their goal of dissolving the federation, though they were caught somewhat by surprise at independence. Their state was better prepared than most, but it is doubtful they expected some of the effects.

Independence Ends Federation

Independence itself brought a host of new problems to the West African states; the problems became more serious because the eight governments of 'ex-AOF' had but a brief separate existence and limited capacities. Simultaneous division of AOF and independence upset the balance of forces within and among the states, educated men and countrymen, civil service and parties, parties and unions, towns and countryside, ethnic, religious, and professional groups.

The crisis in the civil service was made worse by the dissolution of the federation. Independence alone required considerable adjustments, to Africanization and the reduction of expatriate personnel, to the new standards of loyalty set by the African governments. In most states the African civil servants who had met high French technical standards were considered politically unreliable, a process which went further because some of the Africans holding the highest ranks held posts outside the states where they were born. Some members of the territorial services and many members of the federal services (which dissolved) or the French states services, found themselves foreigners and elected to go home. The new citizenship and civil service laws affected Senegalese and Dahomeans particularly, since roughly the disproportion in the nationalities serving in the civil services followed the disproportion in the nationalities educated in the schools. The troubles of many civil servants went further. Some had married while abroad, contracting, for example, 'Dakar–Niger' railroad marriages between Senegalese and Soudanese. In the midst of the general confusion about loyalty which accompanied the transfer of power, there were many strains put upon foreign marriages. Newly returned to their native lands, many civil servants found they had no established record with the dominant party and lost rank.

The break-up of the federation in most states worsened relations between the African governments and the trade unions, already strained, since the Loi Lamine Guèye and the Code du Travail, so urgently desired by African party and union leaders before the Loi-Cadre, afterwards made the wage bills of the first African govern-

[1] From remarks by Gabriel d'Arboussier at the Hansard Society Conference on West Africa, September 1957, Oxford, England.
[2] These were major themes of his speeches during 1956.

ments far too heavy. The government was the single largest employer, and tried to cut or keep level wage bills, while union leaders kept up pressures for higher wages. There were some strikes against African governments, and increased friction between civil servants. Most new African governments suspected the patriotism of their unions, since most were slow to dissolve federal connexions, had favoured a NO vote in the 1958 referendum, opposed Balkanization, and after the referendum, tried to keep within UGTAN. Pointing to the fact that Sékou Touré remained the head of UGTAN even after Guinea became independent, the other governments, still in the Community, forced their national unions to leave UGTAN, and used the issue of 'foreign' affiliations of the unions as one of several reasons to subordinate the unions to the governing party and the official foreign policy.

The break-up of the federation brought crisis into the lives of the most active supporters of the interterritorial RDA. It had been built by educated men having a common outlook based on the state schools, the colonial civil service, the trade unions, free trade among the states, the GEC's, the *répression*. Independence in division meant many of these *militants* had difficulty keeping a sense of continuity and achievement. Perhaps therefore in Guinea the PDG, in Ivory Coast the PDCI, in Mali the US still claimed the label of RDA.

In a more general sense town life was affected by AOF's dissolution. Most cities saw a decline in economic activity, and jobs became scarce just as the excitement and hope raised by independence attracted many people from the interior. Dakar, which had been the largest port and the seat of the federation, faced the sharpest recession. Economic and foreign exchange crises accompanied independence, which came during years when the world market price of West African exports was considerably lower than at the time of the Korean war. Separate independence for each state brought home the economic limits of the political independence. The poorer states became doubly conscious of their position as they lost federal subsidies. The richer states came to see the disadvantages of restricting their ports and industries largely to their own internal market. When AOF dissolved, the Ivory Coast leaders began to ask what had they lost, for example; previously, they had only studied how much they had given away because of federation.

Eight separate states meant new borders not even the colonial powers had watched. The result was more people had cause to resent the new African authorities. Independence brought some of this; the inauguration of the first African governments since the time of colonial conquest meant Africans again could and did use force against Africans. Countrymen who had looked upon African party leaders as spokesmen of opposition had to adjust to them as spokesmen of authority. One of the first acts of the African governments was to watch frontiers which previously had been open for centuries; they even instructed villagers on the old interterritorial frontiers to form border militia. To many of these villagers their ties across the border meant more than their ties with the people issuing instructions from their respective capital cities. For kinsmen belonging to border tribes, for migrants, traders, and pilgrims, travel became a problem.

When Guinea became independent the flow of migrants from the other French-speaking West African states almost stopped. When the Mali federation separated, the Republic of Mali tried to stop the flow of Soudanese *navetanes* (sharecroppers) to the peanut farms of Senegal. They stopped the railroad too, and railwaymen lost their jobs. Upper Volta recognized that it was in a position to bargain about its workers with Ivory Coast and Ghana, and proceeded to do so. These limits on migrants meant country people had less money to spend.

Traders whose families had carried goods over open borders for centuries—along the roads from Ivory Coast through Guinea to Mali and Upper Volta and back to Ivory Coast—found the trade declared illegal or subject to conflicting regulations on different sides of the border. As old trading patterns were interrupted, the traders indicated their displeasure to the new governments. They, like the civil servants, had constituted an interterritorial AOF community of modernizers. They had scattered relations as agents in different towns of the federation; their families and businesses were adversely affected by federal dissolution. The movement of peoples down the western branch of the Niger river, which had gone on for centuries before the French came, became subject to national regulation.

Under French rule, pilgrims had come from the entire area, freely. Animist communities were involved, like the adepts of the San religion[1] which fought the extension of Islam in the border region of Upper Volta and Soudan. Tidjani had been accustomed to make pilgrimages to Senegal, as did Mourides. The Chérif of Kankan in Guinea had adepts and disciples all over West Africa. People united within AOF and the brotherhood of Islam found it hard to accept that Muslims on the other side of the newly strengthened frontiers might not still be brothers. Hence the 'sharp cultural cleavage between the peoples of the Muslim . . . and the non-Muslim areas'[2] came closer to the surface. The strain was felt both

[1] Cardaire, op. cit., pp. 35 f.
[2] Coleman, James. 'The Problems of Political Integration in Emergent Africa' *The Western Political Quarterly*, March 1955, p. 54, n. 23.

in the predominantly Muslim states of Guinea, Mali, Mauretania, Senegal, and Niger, and in the predominantly non-Muslim states of Ivory Coast, Upper Volta, and Dahomey.

A state like Ivory Coast was in majority animist but had a substantial Muslim minority. On the frontier where the two cultural groups came together, the interterritorial RDA had managed to localize the conflicts of contact. The RDA break-up nationalized the local conflicts. For example, in Boundoukou, controversies between the Muslim Dioula supporting the Almamy and loyal to the RDA since 1946, and the Abrong responsive to the authority of the RDA only since the 'fifties, were localized after both groups came together within the RDA. The Dioula came to the RDA when the descendants of Samory's supporters revived the tradition of opposition to France. Culturally and politically they were Mande, like Sékou Touré. After Guinea took separate independence, Dioula loyalty to the RDA, though older than that of the Abrong, became suspect in Ivory Coast; the local cleavage gained national significance, and contributed to a general suspicion of 'strangers'.

Interterritorial party ties had made it possible for Songhai living between Mali and Niger, for Malinke between Guinea, Mali, and Ivory Coast, for Bobo between Upper Volta and Ivory Coast, to belong to the same RDA, to be proud of their ethnic and general African community. The interterritorial RDA had embraced the descendants of supporters of the Gao empire, of al Hajj Umar Tall, and of Samory. Samory at his height had an empire stretching from upper Guinea into Mali and from the forest region of Guinea into northern Ivory Coast. The empire of al Hajj Umar Tall embraced most of Mali, parts of Guinea and Senegal; the Tidjaniya Omarien school of Islam stemmed from his rule. Both rulers had resisted European penetration, and from this stemmed the RDA claim for the loyalty of descendants of their supporters. To prevent a revival of the elements of rivalry between Samory and the sons of al Hajj Umar Tall, the RDA even managed to 'make a pact of peace' against the French, reminiscent of the alliance between Lamba Tall and Mountaga Tall[1] with Samory. When AOF dissolved, so did the 'pact'.

Thus the break-up of the federation created conflicts of interest for the members of most professional groups. It created conflicts between ethnic and new national loyalties; it heightened differences between townsmen and countrymen. The strength of the major political parties had been to reconcile many of these conflicts. The break-up of the federation called into question the limited amount of integration of

[1] Information based on interviews. The nineteenth century alignment is mentioned by Paul Marty, *Études . . . Soudan*, vol. iv, p. 53 in *Études sur l'islam*, op. cit., vol. ix.

the post-European political units which the political parties had been able to effect, for the break-up changed the scale of the units. Most of these problems would have accompanied independence even if AOF borders had remained; changing them made the problems worse.

Facing these problems was something the eight governments had in common. At first there was more rather than less friction among them. In time, however, an understanding of common domestic problems caused the new governments to take a new look at their relations with each other.

West African Unity?

In the colonial era formal relations between AOF and other states, African or not, were set by France. There were, of course, a few exceptions at the level of parties, trade unions, and individuals. Some Mauretanian leaders talked things over with Moroccans and other North African nationalists. Top RDA leaders like Ouëzzin Coulibaly and Sékou Touré had talks with CPP leaders of Ghana. Tropical African leaders in Paris even while voting with the French government kept connexions with Algerian nationalist leaders engaged in the war against France. Africans used the opportunity of the pilgrimage to Mecca to discuss politics with Middle Eastern leaders, and many took part in ceremonial Muslim maledictions of the French army in Algeria. Yet at the formal level France set a uniform pattern.

The new African governments broke the previously uniform pattern of relations with each other and with their neighbours. Partly this was because independence came separately, at different times, to governments having different political and social bases, economic interests and connexions with France. The initial discrepancies, though perhaps not very great, gave rise to some disputes. There were troubles on the borders. In its first year of solitary existence, for example, Guinea feared a French plot based on Senegalese soil, and watched the Ivory Coast border with special attention.

To break its isolation, Guinea welcomed the offer of aid from Ghana, and the Ghana–Guinea union, begun in November 1958, marked the first African initiative to break down the barriers between former British and French colonies. Guinea went off the French franc standard, and the Republic of Mali set controls on its own franc. In 1961 the Republic of Mali joined the Ghana–Guinea–Mali union. The joint institutions of the union remained at the discussion stage, and the currencies had different values. The allies considered ending their separate sovereignties, and inserted enabling clauses into their various constitutions. But they stayed separate while wooing others to join them. They were especially interested in Upper Volta, which would have given them common borders and Ghana much needed labour.

Abroad the Ghana–Guinea–Mali union received the title 'radical' for several reasons. In relation to the rest of AOF, Guinea claimed the credit for breaking with France first, while the Republic of Mali claimed it had pushed the remaining states quickly towards independence. In relation to France, Mali and Guinea had less cordial relations than the other former territories, and labelled the continuation of close connexions with France on the part of Ivory Coast or Senegal 'un-African' and 'neo-colonialist'. They attacked the continued maintenance of French bases in tropical Africa, and the support which the other former French territories gave to France in the Algerian war. This dispute over Algeria was one of the main reasons why they took part in the larger grouping of African states, the Casablanca powers, which included the Algerian Provisional Government.

Meanwhile the remaining states of ex-AOF moved closer together. Ivory Coast took the initiative, in forming the *Conseil de l'Entente* with Dahomey, Niger, Upper Volta. When the *Entente* began, it was Ivory Coast's response to Senegal's membership in the Mali federation. The *Entente* was loose and existed as a group of independent states co-operating functionally—on air services, shipping, and related matters. Ivory Coast alone was comparatively rich and kept the co-operation of the others by offers of limited aid. The *Entente* had no common frontiers. Niger and Dahomey were too far away, and their economic interests seemed to lie more with Nigeria than with Ivory Coast. The *Entente* states were part of a larger grouping labelled abroad as 'moderates'. Friendly connexions with France were kept through the *Union Africaine et Malgache* (UAM) born in September 1961 of former French tropical African territories, including Cameroon and Togo. It dealt with questions like currency, transport, and other common technical services.[1] The UAM was part of another, larger grouping known as the Monrovia powers, which included among others Nigeria, Liberia, and Sierra Leone.

In the long run, these 'radical' and 'moderate' groupings—Mali federation, Ghana–Guinea–Mali Union, *Conseil de l'Entente*—seemed transitional. The divisions had originated in the circumstances surrounding the transfer of power from European to African. Yet both in France and in Africa these circumstances changed very quickly, pointing the way to the emergence of other kinds of African groupings and in 1963 of the continental Organization of African Unity.

[1] *Nations Nouvelle*, no. 2, UAM organ, n.d. (*c.* 1962).

French internal and external politics changed radically since 1958. When Algeria became independent in 1962 there ended the chief reason why France had followed a policy of subsidies and Balkanization in tropical Africa. Southern Saharan bases ceased to count as much. Economically, France's tropical African colonies had been profitable only to special interest groups, not to the French government. As the French economy became more deeply involved in the European Common Market, most French businessmen looked to European rather than to African markets. In France the sense of commitment diminished to subsidize above the world market price Senegalese peanuts, for example, or to help pay the administration bills of various tiny 'pocket-handkerchief' states which France had encouraged into separate independence. Instead, France used her influence with the European Economic Community to include her former dependent territories as associated states, and gave up her exclusive economic relationship.[1] By 1967, all 'ex-AOF' export prices were to be at the level of the world market, allowed to enter duty-free into the Common Market; Common Market manufactured goods were to have preferential rights in the associated African states.

In the light of these basic changes in Europe, most of the old differences among the states of 'ex-AOF' had less meaning. It mattered less that Guinea took her independence first, that the Republic of Mali was more aggressive in leaving the French Community, or that Ivory Coast had at first resisted independence. Currency arrangements inherited from the colonial era lost significance as western Europe negotiated new ones. The old economic divisions between French and English colonies were less important —differences in currencies, spare parts, railroad gauges, and administrative practices. For the future of African economic relations it mattered more that some new West African states were becoming associated with the Common Market, while others such as Guinea, and Ghana were not. Western Europe continued to be the chief seller of manufactured goods as well as the chief buyer in the West African states. A united West African policy towards the Common Market seemed likely to encourage economic unity among the West African states; a divided policy seemed likely to encourage economic divisions.

New problems in Africa, and a new pattern of relationships with Europe and the rest of the world, caused the African governments to reassess their foreign relations. Though the groups of 'moderates' and 'radicals' might be transitional, the need for larger units and closer relations seemed permanent. In the 'sixties, leaders of the states of 'ex-AOF' revived memories of the interterritorial RDA and other

[1] *New York Times*, 6 October 1962.

party connexions, and exchanged cordial visits to discuss closer unity. They deplored the divergences in their laws and institutions which followed separate independence. They began to work out a new pattern of links with each other and their neighbours.

Many issues remained to be settled. It seemed unlikely the broken units of AOF would reconstitute themselves. The colonial basis of division between English- and French-speaking West Africa had disappeared. The process of the stronger states attracting weaker ones had already begun. Prospects were good of a merger between Senegal and Gambia. Mauretania's separate existence seemed in doubt. Ghana attracted Togo and Upper Volta, Nigeria attracted Niger and Dahomey. Closer connexions among states of roughly equal size and importance were under consideration. Outside pressures, both from Europe and from the cold war participants, affected the prospects of African unity.

So did the common needs and limited resòurces for economic development. Most rivers watered several states, and water power of the Niger, Senegal, Volta, or Mono rivers was possible only with interstate co-operation. The scarcity of labour made co-operation on migration vital. Disease, locusts, and other pests could only be controlled through co-operation. The skeleton of a West African transport system, making possible the formation of a West African market, could be built only by united action of the various states.

These, then, were issues of the 'sixties. The form which West African co-operation would take remained to be seen. The important point was negotiations had begun. Most young Africans, who would in time take the succession from their elders, favoured closer African unity. They revived the theme used to good effect in building parties, the theme around which had been built interterritorial ties, the theme connecting them to the pan-Africanist tradition which they shared with their English-speaking neighbours. This was the theme of

union, a word like friendship, goodness, an abstract thing having no face, raising no concrete image in the mind. It goes into all sauces; it accomodates itself with all irreconcilables.[1]

[1] *La Liberté*, 23 November 1954.

PART NINE

Towards One Party States

ARE there any general statements that can be made about the growth of parties in French-speaking West Africa?[1] General statements can be made only tentatively, chiefly because the colonial era was brief and provided an unstable geographic, social, constitutional, and political framework. Even such basic parts of a political system as frontiers were less than a century old, created according to European criteria, and ignoring African cultural divisions. Frontiers continued to change. Upper Volta was reconstituted separately less than fifteen years before becoming independent; there were recent border shifts between Soudan and Mauretania; the Mali federation existed for less than two years; and the entire AOF federation broke into its territorial parts just before independence. The comparatively short history of the African parties also makes it hard to generalize. The oldest existing party was less than twenty years old at independence and had not yet faced the problems of succession to the 'founding fathers'. Significant rights to organize parties and vote came to French-speaking West Africa only after the Second World War, while power to legislate and execute decisions came after 1956. Until then, parties could legally exercise only the function of representation, and were effectively excluded from real responsibility. Once begun, formal institutional change took place very quickly and with sharp discontinuities. The franchise grew from practically zero to become universal; the power of elected representatives grew from purely consultative to legislative and eventually executive, while the place where power was exercised shifted from Paris to Africa.

In spite of these reasons for caution it is worth looking for a pattern. Parties were among the oldest existing national political institutions in the West African states, wholly Africanized long before governments and civil services; some still are not. Parties grew according to African specifications, for they had to and did become representative of the major forces in the total society. Formal governmental institutions, in contrast, were set up according to French specifications at least in part as a condition for French withdrawal. In the first years after independence Africans made many changes in

[1] Some of the material in this chapter was published in my article, 'Single-Party Systems in West Africa', *The American Political Science Review*, June 1961.

laws, the formal institutions of government, and in their constitutions. They usually moved towards presidential rule, instituted
emergency legal procedures allowing for summary justice, revised
local administration so as to achieve full control from the centre, and
eliminated municipal self-government. At the same time, though the
relationship of parties to the formal institutions altered, the parties
themselves continued to try to be representative of the major groups
in the society. These did not alter so quickly.

Thus in a period of great change there was some continuity in
party history, which this chapter seeks to explore. Most of the
generalizations apply to the period prior to independence. In relation
to the major parties, one basic distinction is drawn, between 'mass'
and 'patron' types. There is also a brief discussion of minor parties.
Attention is drawn to the emergence of single-party systems in each
of the states around the time of independence. In conclusion, and in
a most tentative manner, the parties are considered in the post-
independence framework of the new sovereign states. To illuminate
these distinctions it is necessary first to examine the society in which
the parties took root.

Modern and Traditional

The eight sovereign states which were formerly AOF were at an
earlier stage of economic and social history than the retiring colonial
powers. The specific figures are less reliable than the points they are
designed to illustrate. As a result of the reforms extended after the
Second World War, the vote became universal in a society where—
on a very rough average—15 per cent. could read or write, perhaps
3 per cent. were regular wage earners, and another 3 per cent.
employed away from their villages. Considerably more than half the
people's efforts still went into subsistence activity outside the exchange economy.[1] In Europe, by contrast, the vote became general
only after almost everyone was deeply involved in the market
economy. Indeed, not even the middle classes could vote until after
the emergence of the 'commercial civilization from the feudal, the
society based on contract from the society based on status'.[2] Not so
in West Africa. Although there is an educated elite—mainly clerks,
teachers, nurses, doctors, lawyers, and low-level technicians—only
in Senegal and Ivory Coast is there a growing minority of literate
Africans, self-employed in trade, transport, and farming for export.

[1] See Elliot Berg's, 'The Economic Basis of Political Choice in French West
Africa', *American Political Science Review*, June 1960, especially Table I on
p. 393.
[2] Clark, Colin. *The Conditions of Economic Progress*, Macmillan, London, 1951
ed., p. 567.

Several hundred different ethnic groups make up the approximately twenty-five million inhabitants of the new French-speaking West African nations. The educated minority is almost alone in seeing a clear interest in maintaining the present territorial frontiers, or in enlarging them, and in preventing tribal separatism from fragmenting the new nations. With a few exceptions, the existence of this elite, their size and even their distribution according to ethnic and geographic origins, were due to the forces of economic and social change accompanying the arrival of the Europeans in West Africa. Much more economic activity took place in the coastal and forest belt of West Africa, and the proportion of people educated from that region is far greater than from the savannah and sahel belts. This caused trouble both for parties and for nations. Northern Dahomeans, and Ivory Coasters, for example, resented having too many party organizers, too many civil servants, and too many government leaders come from the southern regions of their countries. Some seeds of the 1958 riots against Dahomeans in the Ivory Coast were planted before the war, when the French West African educational system trained an unusually high proportion of them.

It was, however, the political facts of colonial rule, and then the democratic reforms extending over some two decades, which sped up the process whereby the modern layer of African society acquired the lead politically, even though it was still so small a minority. The European powers enlarged the scale of West African political units from many tribal to the present territorial ones. Together with their new technology, they introduced or reinforced secular values such as equality and merit, weakened traditional religious sanction, and overthrew kinship as the main determinant of rank. Although the British believed in indirect rule and the French in direct rule, in varying degrees both undermined the secular authority of the pre-European authorities.

There were few areas in which the presence of the Europeans did not add yet another dimension to the already thorny issue of succession. Pre-war members of the *commandement indigène*—the official 'chiefs'—did not necessarily also have a traditional claim to high rank. These categories seem to have conflicted least and overlapped most in the savannah region of the western Sudan, where such historic pre-European empires as Mali and Ghana existed, and where in the nineteenth century the Europeans could not install their administrations until they had defeated the warrior-kings: Samory and the sons of al Hajj Umar Tall. But the official 'chiefs' were not regular mobile civil servants, since they were not recruited by standards of merit. Few were literate, and they were for the most part stationed among their kinsmen. In time, these official 'chiefs'

constituted a new stratum of the population in the countryside, and
they had a sense of corporate identity transcending the limits of
their different ethnic groups. Before 1945 the work of the 'chiefs'
conformed to custom only insofar as French officials permitted. After
1945 the secular authority of the 'chiefs', 'disarmed by the abolition of
the *indigénat*, forced labour', and citizenship laws, shrank with each
new reform.[1] At various times in various territories the 'chiefs'
formed unions, *syndicats*, to defend their interests, and in 1956 they
formed an AOF *Union Fédérale des Syndicats des Chefs Coutumiers*
under Almamy Koreissy of Soudan.[2] They were well aware that the
post-war reforms affected the 'prestige of the chiefs, precedence,
deportment, decoration, housing, salaries'.[3]

Awareness of corporate identity among 'chiefs' developed farthest
in Mali, Niger, the plateau and savannah regions of Guinea, and with
qualifications in Senegal. It became the basis for the more successful
'patron' parties, including those behind the governments which took
Niger and Mauretania to independence. In Mali and Guinea also,
the patron parties which won in the first post-war elections until
defeated, in 1956, by the *Union Soudanaise* and the *Parti Démocratique de Guinée* mass parties respectively, were based on these
'chiefs'. There was, indeed, a contradiction in French policy after the
war, which on the one hand produced reforms reducing the powers
of the *chefs de canton* and eliminating their claim to represent
Africans, and on the other hand encouraged the formation of
political parties based on the 'chiefs'. The reason was expediency.
When elections were first called the 'chiefs' could easily be summoned by officials who counted upon them to organize. Later French
officials hoped to use their control over the *chefs de canton* to slow
down the growth of nationalist sentiment.

In most territories the struggle against the colonial power only
partly masked another struggle, most acute in the countryside,
between traditionalists and modernizers. In Mali and Guinea the
mass party leaders, as soon as they were in a position to do so, consolidated their electoral victory by doing away altogether with the
official 'chiefs' and replacing them with regular civil servants. In a
state like Niger, however, the challenge to the 'chiefs' though offered
by *Sawaba* was not very successful.

Already before the war, educated Africans rather than traditional

---

[1] Citations from circular 9145, 25 September 1947, sent by French Overseas
Minister Marius Moutet to the French West African governor–general, and to
all the territorial governors. Typescript.
[2] *Paris–Dakar*, 8 December 1956.
[3] From the electoral manifesto of 5 September 1945, issued by *Parti Progressiste
Soudanais* leader, Fily-Dabo Sissoko.

or official 'chiefs' were increasingly sought out by their kinsmen to help them settle controversies with the Europeans and their laws. After the war, by the order in which they came as well as by their content, the reforms in West Africa facilitated the assumption of the political initiative by the educated elite. Most people took for granted that Africans elected to post-war representative posts would know how to read and write in French—if only to talk to the Europeans who had promulgated the reforms. Moreover, in most territories the franchise was initially weighted in favour of those who were able to identify themselves in the records kept by the colonial power—which meant the literate and those earning money, mainly the people in the regular civil service, and only to a lesser degree those recognized as candidates for official 'chief'. The reforms gave the educated Africans legal channels for organizing the expulsion of the colonial power. They had reason to want to. Most of them lived in towns, saw Europeans often and were directly affected by the discrimination—racial, cultural, social, and professional—which characterized the pre-war colonial system.

The post-war reforms further strengthened the position of the educated elite by synchronizing political developments in areas of unequal political pressure, and by forcing even those traditional leaders who could still count upon the following of their ethnic groups, as in Mauretania or parts of Niger, to select educated 'front men' for the new elective offices. Moreover, because the reforms extended over approximately two decades before full independence came, aspiring leaders had time to build records as nationalists, to champion opposition causes in the countryside, to build parties, and anchor their authority to some degree. Nationalism gave the educated elite a powerful theme: that of making all Africans once again masters in their own land. With a few exceptions this educated elite, rather than the traditional aristocrats or official 'chiefs', received the credit for expelling the European colonizers.

Major or minor parties, mass or patron ones, these educated men staffed them. They provided the candidates for the new government offices after the war; they took the seats in legislative assemblies, in cabinets, and public corporations; they filled the senior civil service posts. A majority were the first generation in their families to read or write a language other than Arabic. They had been trained in schools designed to produce only subordinates for Europeans in that phase of colonial history when all senior posts were reserved for Europeans. Many were only primary school graduates, a minority—significantly larger in Senegal which had better schools and was richer—went to secondary school, and only a tiny number graduated from universities.

Since most university places only opened up to West Africans after the war, there were few graduates available to take the first offices. The vast majority of these had to content themselves with second-level posts, usually in the civil service. Some, indeed, were in the peculiar position of working under African ministers who were contemporaries, but who had failed the secondary school or college entrance examinations, which had left them free to take part in the crucial first years of post-war political activity, and so they were 'founding fathers'. The mass franchise, in effect, added yet another reason why, for the modern elite, the standards of success in the schools of the Europeans were often the reverse of the standards of success in African elections. Under the pre-war conditions of total European control the most educated generally acquired the highest of the subordinate offices open to Africans. But after the war, when the villagers acquired the vote and so became arbiters in the competition for power among members of the elite, often those with primary school education spoke the language of the people and had the reactions to which the villagers responded.

While the state schools helped weaken ethnic and historic antagonisms, they also created new cleavages among the educated elite, which in some territories acquired political significance. For example, in post-war Guinea, most of those who had been pre-war students in the dominant French West African secondary school, the École Normale William-Ponty, wanted to keep the only paying jobs open to them. These were invariably in the civil service and so they had little alternative, prior to 1956, but to go into 'administrative' parties. Most of them joined one of the officially preferred regional patron parties. The mass party in Guinea, the *Parti Démocratique de Guinée*, was led by products of the lower state schools, who accused Ponty graduates of 'betraying the masses', and called them 'valets of the administration'. In the Gold Coast, also, political and educational cleavages were to some degree superimposed when the 'Standard VII boys' joined a radical breakaway from the more highly educated leaders of the *United Gold Coast Convention* (UGCC) and built the *Convention People's Party*. In Ivory Coast, by contrast, Ponty graduates took the lead both in the regional 'patron' parties, and in the mass party—the *Parti Démocratique de la Côte d'Ivoire*. There Ponty graduates found alternatives to administrative employment in cocoa and coffee farming. Consequently in the Ivory Coast political cleavages did not relate closely to differences in the diplomas achieved by members of the elite.

Among the elite there were other points of cleavage than those derived from differences in the level of education. Differences of generation also made for divisions, such as those which divided the

Senegalese leaders of the *Bloc Démocratique Sénégalais* (BDS) from those leading the Senegalese federation of the *Section Française de l'Internationale Ouvrière* (SFIO); or dividing the younger organizers of the *Union Soudanaise* from the older leaders of the *Parti Progressiste Soudanais*. There were differences also in ideology: Marxist-inspired for the *Parti Démocratique de Guinée* and the *Union Soudanaise*; a blend of Catholic and evolutionary socialist political doctrine for many leaders of the *Union Progressiste Sénégalaise*. These differences were sharpest in the minor parties organized by university trained graduates: dissident Marxist for some leaders of the *Parti de Régroupement Africain-*(PRA) *Sénégal*; close to orthodox Communism for the leaders of the Senegalese *Parti Africain de l'Indépendance* (PAI); an African version of Emmanuel Mounier's French Catholic social doctrine of *personnalisme* for those partici-pating in the *Mouvement Africain de Libération Nationale* (MLN). There were also differences in status, distinguishing in Senegal, for example, the pre-war privileged 'citizens' (SFIO) from the 'subjects' (*Bloc Démocratique Sénégalais*); the former had earlier access to education, more wealth often from the peanut trade, higher jobs in the civil service.

These differences within the modern elite were balanced, however, by a certain common outlook. They conceived of themselves as Africans rather than Malinke, for example. Their common experi-ences in schools, jobs, and in the money economy, in pre-war town associations, and with colonial administration gave them a homo-geneity. But no such common outlook linked all the elite to the mass of the population. There was, instead, a gradual separation, most marked among people several generations or several decades re-moved from the village—the 'citizens' of Senegal or many of the French-trained university graduates.

Mass and Patron Parties

Before independence, successive electoral results made clear that major parties could be classified broadly into 'mass' and 'patron' (or 'cadre' or 'personality')[1] types. The distinction has wide implica-tions for local branch organization, size of membership, structure, finance, and patterns of authority; it illuminates also variations in functions, social composition, and methods.

The main distinction between mass and patron parties lies not in the social origins of aspiring national leaders, and not in the scale

[1] 'Patron' parties and 'parties of personalities' were terms employed by Thomas Hodgkin, *Nationalism in Colonial Africa*, op. cit., and *African Political Parties*, Penguin Books, 1961; 'cadre' party was used by Maurice Duverger in his *Political Parties*, Methuen and Co., London, 1954.

of party organizations. It lies rather in the reply to the questions: How are the national leaders related to the rest of the population? On what groups and with what ideas and structures did they build parties? The distinction is perhaps best seen first at the local branch level.

Mass parties generally sought the adherence of every single individual. They wanted to enroll each man, woman, and even child, and so they had to establish local branches with headquarters, regular meetings, and elections for branch leaders. Examples are the *Parti Démocratique de la Côte d'Ivoire* (PDCI) or the *Parti Démocratique de Guinée* (PDG) of Guinea. The patron parties usually terminated their structure simply with the adherence of influential notables or patrons; these were mostly the officially recognized 'chiefs' or their direct representatives. Examples are the *Union Nigérienne des Indépendants et Sympathisants* (UNIS) of Niger, or *Parti Progressiste Soudanais* (PSP). Most patron parties did little to reach every individual in the community, and relied upon the 'patrons' for their local influence. Patron party agents rarely called mass meetings; they called upon the 'chiefs'. A defection from the local branch of a mass party rarely led to the distintegration of the branch. But the defection of a local notable from the patron party seriously weakened it in the locality.

Mass parties counted their members in hundreds of thousands. As early as 1950 the *Parti Démocratique de la Côte d'Ivoire* claimed 850,000 and in 1955 the *Parti Démocratique de Guinée* claimed 300,000 paid up members. First organized around an anti-colonial platform, mass parties called themselves 'the expression . . . of the will of the African masses'.[1]

Several structural concepts elaborated by Duverger and applied to Moroccan parties by Rézette[2] can be usefully employed in connexion with the tropical African parties. At least for a time, most mass parties were strongly articulated, relatively disciplined, and called forth considerable direct participation from members. The degree of course varied, descending in the following order: US, PDG, PDCI, UPS. Expulsions, demotions, fines, and other penalties were not uncommon.

The mass party community became far more differentiated than the simple two categories of leaders and voters, or patrons and clients, which characterized patron parties. The mass parties had established hierarchies, and though the lines separating the various categories of adherents were fluid, it was possible to distinguish party

---

[1] PDG electoral manifesto for the 2 January 1956 elections.
[2] Rézette, R. *Les Partis politiques marocains*, Colin, Paris, 1955.

élus or elected representatives, and members of the party bureaucracy at the territorial, regional, and local levels. T1 ey belonged to the wider category of *militants* willing to devote time and resources to party work. They were part of a still larger group of members who bought cards, themselves part of the wider group of party sympathizers who voted the party ticket.[1]

The leaders of mass parties emphasized organization partly because they opposed the established authorities and could not use established institutions. They usually created parallel women's and youth organizations, *organismes annexes*. They published newspapers, established central and regional headquarters, hired permanent staff, distributed membership cards, charged dues, and especially before independence, synchronized activities and shared personnel with African trade unions. The more effective their organization, the more mass party leaders were in a position to implement their decisions. *Union Soudanaise* and *Parti Démocratique de Guinée* leaders, for example, regarded their mass parties as 'weapons'[2] designed to achieve independence and economic development with the greatest speed possible.

In contrast, most patron parties—*Parti Progressiste Soudanais* and *Union Nigérienne des Indépendants et Sympathisants*—were weakly articulated, comparatively undisciplined, with little if any direct membership participation. This difference in structure between mass and patron parties is one of several reasons why though mass parties took the place of patron parties with a regularity suggesting a definite pattern before independence, no mass party was ever replaced in free election. Mass parties took power in Senegal, Guinea, Mali, and Ivory Coast, while in Niger, Upper Volta, and Dahomey mass parties were growing though patron parties had majorities.

In view of the small money income of most Africans it was remarkable that in some years mass parties sold hundreds of thousands of cards costing roughly 100 francs cfa each. These periods of intense party loyalty alternated with others when people were less inclined to spend money. Mass party resources came also from profits at party festivals, *tam-tams*, dances, receptions, which were the West African counterparts of the $100 a plate dinners of the Democratic and Republican parties in the United States. Profits were usually shared between the local and territorial treasuries. The PDCI could count on the assets of the *Syndicat Agricole Africain*, while the PDG

---

[1] Duverger, op. cit., chapter ii.
[2] Apter, David E. and Rosberg, Carl G. 'Nationalism and Models of Political Change in Africa', *The Political Economy of Contemporary Africa*, Symposia Studies Series #1, The National Institute of Social and Behavioral Science, George Washington University, 1959, p. 8.

of Guinea, the US of Soudan and the UDN of Niger could count on
the resources of the territorial CGT unions. Special contributions
came to the PDCI from African coffee and cocoa farmers, and to the
other mass parties from many African traders. Contributions from
other sources such as Lebanese traders, European businessmen, or
the colonial authorities usually did not come until after it became
clear that the mass parties were going to form the governments. The
largest contribution to the resources of the mass parties came not in
money but in kind. The mass parties could count upon local branches
to produce insignia, decorations, and cloth for demonstrations, to
build platforms and even party headquarters. Party-sponsored
travellers received free hospitality, free rides, the loan of a car, and
gifts of gasoline. Even where hundreds of party delegates to conferences came together the community provided food and housing.

The leaders of some patron parties, such as the Socialists of Ivory
Coast and the PSP of Soudan, at times tried to sell membership cards
after they saw the successful use of this money-raising technique by
their mass party rivals. But patron parties found few individual
buyers for their cards, because people who voted the party ticket did
so not out of a sense of loyalty to the party, but to the local notable
who happened to represent it. Patron parties were generally financed
by the patrons from their own resources, or from outside gifts.
French officials frequently provided subsidies in the form of transport, housing, printing facilities, and official channels of communication like telephone, telegraph, and radio. The PSP of Soudan received
contributions from European business interests which wanted
economic or political favours.

Not all but some of the mass parties had both institutionalized and
collective leadership, as did the *Union Progressiste Sénégalaise*, the
Union Soudanaise and the *Parti Démocratique de Guinée*. Elections
were fairly regular; *élus* and officers gave some account of their
stewardship to the members; discipline received serious attention; a
predetermined procedure was followed for the making of important
decisions. Patron parties, and a mass party such as the *Party Démocratique de la Côte d'Ivoire* after 1952 had essentially personal leadership; leaders made decisions and reconciled conflicts in ways un-
fettered by pre-arranged rules, either as individuals or as a group.
The parties with institutionalized leadership could deal more
smoothly with the problems posed by renewal and succession.

To an understanding of the authority pattern within the parties, a
modified notion of charisma is sometimes useful,[1] provided it is not
understood simply as 'the polar opposite of formal and traditional

[1] Apter, op. cit.

bonds',[1] or taken to mean the total 'absence of any defined hierarchy'.[2] Thus some, but not all, mass party top-level leaders—Sékou Touré of the *Parti Démocratique de Guinée* and Mamadou Konaté (d. 1956) of the *Union Soudanaise*—enjoyed a type of charisma which was limited both by the constitutional procedure they themselves insisted upon within their mass parties, and by the power exercised to a greater or lesser extent by other groups and individuals within the party. Other leaders, particularly of patron parties—such as Fily-Dabo Sissoko of the *Parti Progressiste Soudanais* and Sourou Migan Apithy of the *Parti Républicain du Dahomey* (PRD)—used their charisma comparatively unchecked by procedure, though limited by the power and influence of the 'patrons'. This was also true for some mass party leaders, such as Félix Houphouët-Boigny of the *Parti Démocratique de la Côte d'Ivoire*. Still other leaders, like Lamine Kaba of the Kankan region of Guinea, enjoyed charisma only within a locality considerably smaller than a territory. Their gift, usually recognized by only one ethnic group, came to be regarded as a threat to national party discipline. The notion of charisma, insofar as it points out that in some instances extraordinary qualities are ascribed to an individual, is a useful starting point for further investigation. But it is only a starting point, perhaps sharper than the idea Carlyle expressed with 'Find in a country the Ablest Man . . . raise him to the supreme place . . . what he tells us to do must be precisely the wisest, fittest. . . .'[3]

In illuminating the function of the parties, the mass patron party distinction also has meaning. Patron parties fulfilled but the minimum tasks assigned by the formal institutions. Patron parties integrated only patrons. These parties were interested in the individual only insofar as he happened to be included in the franchise, provided candidates for election and the minimum machinery for bringing the voter to the polls. Before independence patron parties made few attempts to perform even the function of political educator and explain the post-war reforms to the population.

By contrast, the functions of mass parties such as the *Parti Démocratique de la Côte d'Ivoire*, the *Parti Démocratique de Guinée*, the *Union Soudanaise*, or the *Union Progressiste Sénégalaise* were far more complex and varied. On occasion, prior to acquiring govern-

---

[1] Weber, Max. 'The Sociology of Charismatic Authority', *From Max Weber*, H. H. Gerth & C. Wright Mills, editors, Routledge & Kegan Paul, Ltd., London, 1952, p. 250.

[2] Worsley, Peter. *The Trumpet Shall Sound*, MacGibbon & Kee, London, 1957, p. 271.

[3] Carlyle, Thomas. 'The Hero as King', *On Heroes and Hero Worship*, Ward & Lock Co., London, 1900, p. 262.

ment responsibilities, mass parties disregarded, indeed replaced the existing legal institutions. The UPS of Senegal, which never directly challenged the French administration did little of this. In contrast, the PDCI of Ivory Coast and the PDG of Guinea by-passed the police and army with its own personnel for keeping order; together with the US they by-passed the colonial courts with party machinery for settling all types of disputes. These three parties found their best sales figures for party cards prior to independence coincided with rural hold-ups in the payment of taxes. People decided they would rather contribute to their own party than to the colonial administration. To the extent these mass parties for a time substituted, or proposed to, their structure for that of the state, they performed a revolutionary function. (In West Africa, unlike Cameroon or Algeria, none waged guerrilla war.) For some time mass parties, far more than the legal institutions conceived in Paris, were considered to be legitimate by the population. By agreeing to work at least partly within the post-war representative institutions, therefore, these parties legitimized them, rather than vice-versa. Coincidentally, these parties acted as national 'melting pots', educating people to be African. To the extent that they provided a new social framework for people no longer firmly rooted in a stable ethnic tradition, they can be termed 'parties of social integration'.[1] They and their affiliates were interested in everything from the cradle to the grave—in birth, initiation, religion, marriage, divorce, dancing, song, plays, feuds, debts, land, migration, death, public order—not only in electoral success.

Ethnic and Status Arithmetic

How the mass parties performed this integrating function was evident from an analysis of the modern and traditional status and the ethnic origins of national and local leaders. This analysis is particularly important, since the process by which independence was achieved in West Africa gave occasion for shifts in the distribution of power not only between Europeans and Africans, but also within African society—between modern and traditional elite, within each of these groups, and in the links connecting them with the mass of the population.

This process is perhaps best approached with the relatively simple question—what group or sub-group predominated in the major parties? Trade unionists predominated within the *Parti Démocratique de Guinée* and were of great significance in the *Union Soudanaise* and

[1] Neumann, Sigmund. *Modern Political Parties*, University of Chicago Press, Chicago, 1956, p. 404.

Sawaba of Niger. African planters formed the *Parti Démocratique de la Côte d'Ivoire*. The educated former 'subjects' constructed the *Bloc Démocratique Sénégalaise* to challenge, in effect, the 'citizen'-led socialists. These groups were in the modern categories of the population, a feature all mass parties had in common and shared with but those few 'patron' parties based on a pre-war town elite.

Who predominated in those patron parties resting on important village personalities? The distinction between mass and patron parties, already made in relation to local party structure, was less neat in fact than in definition. When first organizing, aspiring mass party leaders did not disdain to accept the backing of a local important personage—an official chief, a traditional aristocrat, a Muslim *marabout* or an animist sage. But partly because most mass parties were born after the war either as or out of anti-colonial 'congresses',[1] local important persons in West Africa connected with the colonial establishment usually held aloof until the mass party was itself becoming the establishment. Then many 'shifted their rifles from one shoulder to the other'.[2] Most important local persons without modern education who became identified with the mass parties during the height of the independence struggle—*la lutte anti-impérialiste*—had special reasons for lining up against the colonial administration, usually connected with events surrounding the conquest, with a local quarrel over chieftaincy, prestige, or property. Many rivals to the official 'chiefs', at village or regional level, joined the mass parties at an early stage. However, when such a personality became included locally within the mass party, the methods of the mass party worked to control his local influence, to make of him but one among many. There were, of course, variations in degree, related to mass party structure and to the type of tribal political organization.

Where there was an educated urban middle class, also identified both for cultural and economic reasons with the colonial power, they too hesitated before becoming associated with the radical, anti-colonial mass parties, usually initiated by younger, less educated men, less acceptable to the Europeans. A clear example of this was in Senegal, where pre-war 'subjects' shortly after they acquired the vote in 1945, broke from the 'citizen'-dominated SFIO to organize their *Bloc Démocratique Sénégalais*. Similarly in Gold Coast the younger, more radical men broke from the *United Gold Coast Convention* to organize the *Convention People's Party*.

Thus in some areas, in spite of their many differences, a pre-war

---

[1] Hodgkin. *Nationalism in Colonial Africa*, op. cit., p. 144.
[2] Keïta, Madeira. 'Le Parti unique en Afrique', *Présence Africaine*, February–March, 1960, pp. 19–20.

town elite holding the highest positions permitted Africans in the colonial system, and the official 'chiefs' already conscious that the presence of the Europeans stabilized their position, made common cause in patron parties against mass party leaders. This process, in which 'haves' lined up against their 'have not' challengers was evident from the epithets exchanged at election time. Urban patron party leaders called mass party leaders 'vagrants' (Guinea), in the countryside of Mali patrons underlined that their rivals were 'slaves' or 'strangers'. Mass party leaders, for their part, hurled labels like 'union of featherbedders' and 'stooges' at the patron party leaders.

In varying degrees, the nationalist struggle helped stir up 'loyalty' issues, national and local, with as a frequent result yet another cause for disintegration in an already fragile society. For where they could, those lower on the traditional or modern social scale used the issue of nationalism to strengthen their own position through the mass parties. And those with privileges to lose, as in Niger, showed signs of preferring rule by the Europeans to rule by the *talakawa* (commoners in Hausa). Especially in the countryside, showing loyalty to the mass party, when it was under pressure from the colonial power, was one way to compensate for a weak claim to belonging to the local ethnic group—for immigrant Dioula 'strangers' in Ivory Coast, to show they were as loyal, for example, as the *originaires* who first came to the area.

Given the low percentage of educated elite in relation to the rest of the population, and the fact that both in mass and in patron parties a network of kinship connects leaders and followers, it follows that leaders of both mass and patron parties which are territorial in scale have gone through the first and simplest stage of 'ethnic arithmetic': they kept a rough correspondence between the ethnic origins of leaders and followers. This correspondence is at least as important in Africa as in Boston or New York City politics. Defeating a patron party which has not been through this first stage, was relatively easy for mass party leaders—as when, for example, the *Bloc Démocratique Sénégalais* used 'favourite sons' in the Casamance region of Senegal, to defeat the SFIO which was locally and territorially dominated by Wolof and Lebou from Dakar or Saint-Louis. Leaders who tried to build national parties failed when they did not have among their ranks representatives of the most important ethnic groups. The Socialist party of Guinea was in this category. It grew from the Fulani club at the École Normale William-Ponty and never really succeeded in broadening the ethnic base, even though it underwent several important changes, from ethnic to a nationalist ideology. Too many of one ethnic group, too few of another, caused difficulties for any party. The *Parti Démocratique de la Côte d'Ivoire* had relatively little trouble with ethnic separatism from the Baule, while the *Convention People's Party* had considerable difficulty with the Ashanti. These two ethnic groups, traditionally related, occupy similar historic and geographic positions in their respective states, produce most of the coffee and/or cocoa and so have the most wealth. The PDCI from the beginning had Baule associated with it through the person of their Baule leader, Félix Houphouët-Boigny, while in Ghana the CPP started and, except in the revolutionary years of 1949–50, remained without similar support among the Ashanti.

While patron parties leaders, once through this first simple phase of 'ethnic arithmetic', generally stopped their calculations there, the leaders of mass parties had but begun. They tried to use their party organizations in order to awaken a wider, national sense of community. They appealed to particular categories existing within, or cutting across ethnic groups—a technique suitable to recruiting in a mobile, changing society. Youth and women were of course two such categories which mass parties emphasized heavily. It was already pointed out that in many villages mass party organizers went to rivals of official 'chiefs'; from these they discovered local grievances. They often appealed to rural underprivileged groups. For example, the *Parti Démocratique de Guinée* first gained a following in the Fouta Djallon plateau not among the Fulani majority, but rather among the 'captives' living in the ancillary villages (*roundé*). They appealed to rural scribes, whose modern skills set them apart. There were those who had travelled, often 'strangers' who were among the most recent immigrants to a flourishing agricultural area. In some areas they went to veterans—in Senegal, for example. There were religious dissidents—Harrists in the Ivory Coast, Hamallists in Mali. There were in some areas Muslim proselytizers opposed by the 'chief'—either because he was animist, or because though Muslim he nevertheless felt his secular position under attack. There were camel drivers, chauffeurs, transporters, and peddlers—such as the *dioula* traders of Western Upper Volta, Mali, Guinea, and Ivory Coast, or some 'Hausa' traders of Ghana and Nigeria. And, of course, there were those who earned money income for growing coffee, cocoa, peanuts, or bananas, became restless with tradition; then young men no longer listened to the old, women made money trading in the market-place, and people responded to the appeals against established authorities made by the mass party organizers.

Of course, people in these non-ethnic social categories were still in a minority; most had some roots in a tribal community and they too wanted party leaders of roughly similar origins to their own. Even while they rejected the principle that ethnic considerations should enter into the selection of party office holders, mass party leaders were still well aware they needed associates who were kinsmen of those they sought as followers. Indeed, conflicts among ethnic groups were often sharper in mass than in patron parties, since mass parties made a continuous attempt to propagate modern values and diminish the weight of ethnic exclusiveness. For example, since their 1956 victories, both *Union Soudanaise* and *Parti Démocratique de Guinée* leaders had the habit of deliberately scrambling the ethnic origins of party propagandists and their audiences. Men from the Guinea coast campaigned in the forest and Fouta Djallon; men from Upper Guinea in the forest. All these tactics had the purpose of encouraging people to relate themselves directly to the party.

Conflicts between modern and traditional leaders were also sharper in mass than patron parties since most mass parties were egalitarian by policy. The traditional upper-class standing of Sékou Touré or Modibo Keïta, for example, was important for the high popular esteem given to them. The *Parti Démocratique de Guinée* began to make headway among the Fulani after Diallo Sayfoulaye, the son of an important Fulani chief, 'like La Fayette . . . left his privileges to join the democratic cause'.[1] Félix Houphouët-Boigny, in the militant years of the *Parti Démocratique de la Côte d'Ivoire* prior to 1952, used his prestige as official chief, and not only as a doctor and wealthy planter, in order to entrench the PDCI in the countryside. On the whole, they used their nobility to preach equality.

The majority of the national and regional leadership in patron parties is of traditional upper class status, while the majority of the mass party national and regional leadership is of commoner origin. But mass parties have a surprisingly large number of people with high traditional status as the top national party leaders. And patron parties have an exceptionally large number of prime ministers, or officials holding the first post in the modern institutions, with low traditional status. (Is this a method of chiefly control, reminiscent of their habit, at the turn of the century, to send not their own but sons of slaves to the schools of the Europeans?) Of low traditional status is Joseph Conombo, who was until 1956 deputy to the French National Assembly from Upper Volta, elected through a patron party based on the Mossi chiefs. So was Yacine Diallo (d. 1954), Guinea deputy to the French National Assembly representing the then dominant patron party alliance, and more specifically the Fulani chiefs. So is Hubert Maga, first President of Dahomey, who represented a regional patron party strong in the north. It is as if 'princes' fear least the competition of 'captives'; while villagers, first hearing equality preached, learn fastest from 'princes'.

[1] *La Liberté*, 22 December 1955.

Thus within mass parties, not only ethnic origins but also ethnic status continued to count, often causing more conflict precisely because it is usual mass party ideology to ignore or challenge these differences. Yet men with high modern but low traditional qualifications—Ponty graduates of *griot* descent, for example, lawyers descended of 'captives'—were rarely put forward by local mass party branches as candidates for elective office. In varying degrees, mass party national leaders maintained a continuous pressure in favour of such nominations, as of West Indians and other 'strangers', to prove they believed in equality. So as to be able to maintain this pressure, mass party leaders often preferred multi-member to single-member constituencies in legislative assembly elections. Where ten seats were to be filled, local branch members were more inclined to accept that national headquarters designate some candidates, than where only one seat was involved.

Though they tried much harder than patron party leaders, mass party leaders did not always succeed in avoiding institutionalizing ethnic differences. In the long run, friction among ethnic groups in Ivory Coast may have been intensified by the *Parti Démocratique de la Côte d'Ivoire*'s decision to organize local branches on an ethnic, rather than a neighbourhood principle. This distinguished the PDCI local structure from that of most other mass parties. The *Union Soudanaise*, the *Parti Démocratique de Guinée*, and the *Union Progressiste Sénégalaise*, for example, made strenuous efforts to mix ethnic groups at the local level—and did so at least to the extent that neighbourhoods did. The PDCI decision was a recognition of the way people actually communicated in Ivory Coast, a concession to reality, unwillingly made by many educated leaders because they knew they might need to assemble their followers rapidly. This practice was challenged by a PDCI Congress resolution in 1959, as yet unimplemented.[1]

The various methods used by mass and patron parties further illustrate the differences between them. Patron parties adopted methods respectful of established authority. Prior to 1957 these generally avoided the techniques of protest, offered few if any personal services to supporters, were little concerned with party symbols. The mass parties, prior to achieving government majorities, employed techniques related to their revolutionary, legitimizing, educational, and social integration functions. Demonstrations, strikes, boycotts, occasional violence were revolutionary techniques. The parties paid considerable attention to creating new national symbols: insignia, colours, slogans, party cloth for women to wear. Mass party choices

[1] *Abidjan-Matin*, 18 June 1959. See A. R. Zolberg, op. cit., p. 140.

of symbols and slogans were based on sound insight into popular responses, and repetition is at the heart of African oratory, as of drumming and dance. 'Vote the elephant; he is wise and never forgets.' The *Parti Démocratique de Guinée* and the *Parti Démocratique de la Côte d'Ivoire* painted the elephant on walls and roofs and streets and cars. In the savannah, however, the *Union Soudanaise* never made much of the fact that the elephant was its symbol also; for US opponents said, with effect 'the elephant eats your crops and leaves you destitute'. Elaborating on the meaning of the *Bloc Démocratique Sénégalais* party colours, Léopold Senghor of Senegal wrote 'Green is for the Muslim majority, the colour of the Prophet's flag; green is for the Christian minority, the colour of hope; green is for the animists, the symbol of youth and the irrepressible force of Black Africa'.[1] And using the elimination of forced labour to their ends, aspiring mass party *Union Démocratique Nigérienne* leaders in Niger whose ballot carried the picture of a camel, warned people not to vote for UNIS, the patron party which had a yellow ballot bearing the picture of a stick and a basket. 'Vote for the camel, and you will be as free as he,' they said, well acquainted with that ornery beast. And they added, 'The yellow ballot is a stick and a basket; if you vote for it forced labour will come back.'

All the important French-speaking West African party leaders except those of Mauretania favoured the lay state. Yet religious ceremonies were associated with party activities. In predominantly Muslim areas, particularly Mali, Niger, and Guinea, most leaders generally observed the fast of Ramadan, rarely smoked, and never drank in public, went to Friday prayer meetings, began to wear the *boubou*—a flowing caftan or robe—and hats modelled on the fez or turban. At *Parti Démocratique de la Côte d'Ivoire* meetings libation was often poured. Prior to many *Parti Démocratique de Guinée* meetings the *Fatiha*, or opening *sura* of the Koran was intoned.

In the Name of God, the Merciful, the Compassionate Praise belongs to God, the Lord of all Being, the All-merciful, the All-compassionate, the Master of the Day of Doom. Thee only we serve; to Thee alone we pray for succour. Guide us in the straight path, the path of those whom Thou hath blessed, not of those against whom Thou art wrathful, nor of those who are astray.[2]

Personal oratory was one of the most effective educational techniques. Campaigning against the Guinea regional patron parties Sékou Touré explained, 'I am Diallo the shepherd from the Fouta, I am Mamba

---

[1] *Condition Humaine*, 30 November 1948.
[2] Arthur J. Arberry's translation, *The Koran Interpreted*, vol. i, George Allen & Unwin, London, 1955, p. 29.

the planter from Nzérékoré, Keïta the rice grower from Siguiri, Soumah the fisherman from the coast, I am African, I am every man.' Both because they believed it, and because the 'important people' in the countryside opposed them, most mass party organizers preached equality. 'Vincent Auriol and Lamine both die if they go hungry' or 'three men want to go to Bamako. The governor goes by plane, Mamba by bicycle, Yacine on foot. Who arrives first?' 'The governor,' shouts the crowd. 'Next?' 'Mamba.' 'Then?' 'Yacine.' In such dialogue leaders communicated the idea that the environment accounts for most human differences.

The identification of the mass party with the community before independence was emphasized not only by party sponsorship of baptisms, weddings, or funerals, but also by the existence of an informal party social security system which resulted in support for indigent partisans, legal advice for imprisoned militants, payment of medical bills for the sick, food and housing for families of party widows or grass widows. On occasion the mass parties could count on free labour even for the construction of bridges, roads, mosques, and schools—on popular good will that *Parti Démocratique de Guinée* and *Union Soudanaise* leaders termed human investment—*investissement humain*—and included in their inventory of economic resources.

Minor Parties

The division into mass and patron types is applicable to the more important parties—those with a substantial membership and scale. There were, however, many other parties. If parties are defined as all groups calling themselves parties or generally so called, and seeking political power, then from the time they became legal to independence some hundred parties were born in French-speaking West Africa.

Why so many parties? First, to allow for experimentation, discovery and turnover. Most voluntary organizations took on party labels and became the instruments for competition among educated Africans who had previously been peers. With the partial exception of Senegal and perhaps Ivory Coast the early elections of 1945 and 1946 were more in the nature of primaries, eliminating and selecting candidates before structured parties emerged. There was no other way to do this, and the men who did well in those elections had a head start. It was comparatively easy and cheap to form a new party, when the electorate was small and competition was among individuals and their backers rather than among organized parties. Some such 'one man shows' continued to crop up even after the first elections—like the *Union Démocratique et Sociale Africaine* (UDSA) of Guinea or the *Front de Libération Noire* (*Kotoko*) of Ivory Coast. But most 'one man shows' disappeared by merging into larger groups as it became clear to the competing candidates that to win in elections they needed a party organization, finance, procedure, and some agreement on principles even before the elections.

Another reason for the large number of parties was that in the countryside some ethnic parties emerged, especially when the rural franchise suddenly widened in the 1951 elections—groups like the *Union Dogon*, the *Union Lobi*, or the Socialists among the Bete. Where ethnic parties were based on urban areas they usually rested on the tribes originally owning the land—like the *Rassemblement Démocratique Sénégalais* among the Lebou of Dakar. These ethnic parties at best existed long enough to elect one or two men to the territorial assembly, and then petered out or joined with parties territorial in scale. There were a few other types of minor parties: rump groups left out after mergers or reorganizations like the *Parti Socialiste Sénégalais*; splinter groups built by men negotiating to join a larger party like the *Socialistes Unitaires* of Senegal; groups representing a disaffected and defeated minority within a larger party, like the *Parti de Solidarité Sénégalaise* of some 'clan' leaders and rural personalities. These minor parties had mostly curiosity value; they rarely succeeded in electing even a municipal council representative.

There was, especially in the first years of elections, a fairly large number of regional parties—like the Fulani-based *Démocratie Socialiste de Guinée*, or in Casamance the *Mouvement Autonome de la Casamance*. Frequently regional groups divided further between those based in countryside or town, like the *Union de la Basse Guinée* and the *Foyer de la Basse Guinée* respectively. Regional parties usually managed to assemble representatives of more than one ethnic group, and can be seen as steps towards parties territorial in scale. There was, in fact, a clear trend both in the direction of reducing the number of parties and enlarging their scale to territorial frontiers. By the time the Loi-Cadre was in force parties everywhere except Upper Volta and Dahomey, and, with some qualification, Niger, had enlarged to the territorial frontiers. Why?

The first reason was the political system. As the franchise enlarged, parties of very limited appeal lost. The administration was territorially organized and deputies to the French National Assembly had the most influence. Territorial and municipal council representatives had less power or prestige. The post-war colonial reforms by their sequence and nature favoured reducing the number of parties and enlarging their scale. Second, parties territorial in scale emerged easily where for cultural and historic reasons the population was relatively homogeneous, as in Mauretania, Mali, and with qualification, Niger. Upper Volta and Dahomey, in contrast, had relatively heterogenous populations. Third, economic change introduced by the Europeans and accompanied by social change produced new social strata which cut across ethnic categories and responded to appeals to build territorial parties: workers in Guinea, farmers, migrants, and civil servants in Ivory Coast, traders and civil servants in Senegal. Fourth, in some areas social change took place after colonial rule began, even without marked economic change—as in Mali and Niger, where groups with an interest in breaking out of regional and provincial limits and forming territorial parties won elections.

There is one other reason for the trend in the direction of regional or territorial parties: the political intentions, dedication, skill, and methods of the political elite in each territory. The way in which rival political leaders went about building parties, and dealing with such obstacles to unity as ethnic, religious, geographic, cultural, professional, and other divisions affected party scale. In Dahomey, for example, the educated rival party leaders themselves remained divided and this contributed to the divisions among their followers. In Mali, the skill in harmonizing differences, the internal discipline and unity of party leaders, particularly of the *Union Soudanaise*, contributed to the growth and maintenance of parties on a territorial scale.

Therefore, few parties born actually survived. Instead they reorganized, split, merged, died, and otherwise underwent changes which resulted in reducing their numbers and extending the scale to territorial frontiers. The more important parties survived and engaged in the sharp struggle for power which accompanied the installation of the first governments under the Loi-Cadre. The struggle was resolved, near the time of independence, when in each of the new states a single party system came into existence or was in the process of doing so. The single parties tried hard to dominate for some time regardless whether opposition parties were allowed to exist alongside. In the states of Senegal, Guinea, Ivory Coast, and Mali mass parties, while in the states of Upper Volta, Niger, Dahomey, and Mauretania patron parties dominated.

Single-Party System

Until independence, consecutive electoral results pointed up that the only definite changes in parties which took place were from mass to patron party majority, but never the reverse. The only exception was Ivory Coast, where the *Parti Démocratique de la Côte d'Ivoire* rode to power in 1946, then lost in a series of elections and by-elections between 1949 and 1952, but only because the French administration had tampered with the ballot. Officially in those years the allied patron parties of Ivory Coast won, but as soon as people could once more register their vote freely the PDCI resumed its monopoly of offices. There was no evidence, however, that the turnover from patron to mass party would continue after independence. Though conditions altered it is nevertheless worth asking what were the distinctions evident at that time.

At independence, the distinction had validity in relation to three issues: degree of popular consent, degree to which party leaders held reform in the direction of social equality to be important; degree of opportunity to express dissenting views inside or outside the dominant party. The degree was least in the patron party states of Dahomey, Upper Volta, Niger, and Mauretania. In these states the main opposition groups were outlawed, the organization of the dominant party was but rudimentary and so it had no capacity to push for reforms nor to channel the expression of dissenting views; from the beginning the governments had to use force against rising discontent and criticism.

In the single party states based on the mass parties there was at independence evidence of widespread consent. During at least a brief period the national and the party communities were indistinguishable; the mass party reflected the 'general will'. This was usually just prior to taking over responsibility for governing, but after using to advantage being in opposition. Discontent was the common denominator. Typical of the instructions national mass party leaders gave to local leaders were, 'Go and talk to the peasants in the field'. 'Tell Abdoulaye his daughter cannot be forced to marry the old chief.' 'Tell the peasants not to sell their crops at that ruinous price.' 'Defend Pango's palm trees against destruction by the administrator.' 'Speak up for Binta's right to cultivate the land the chief claims.' While not all the questions were settled, villagers found a national platform in the mass party which they had never known. Mass party organizers sought out grievances, expressed them in the market-place, co-ordinated them. They blamed European rule for forced labour, taxes, abuses of official 'chiefs', racial discrimination, poverty. Out of these grievances they welded their massive demonstrations against colonial rule. Most patron party leaders were too linked with the established authorities to play this muckraking role.

Muckraking paid. Mass party membership was open to all, and practically all sought to acquire it. This characteristic at the level of recruitment distinguished West African states based on the mass party, from states based on single parties confining their membership —as most fascist or Communist parties do—to a selected group. The widespread influence and number of followers of the mass parties at their peak, their national character long before the institutions of government were controlled by Africans, their success in acquiring the credit for the national revolution—all these bore out the mass party claim to represent the entire population. This helps explain why many West African mass party leaders saw little contradiction between claiming to be democratic, and insisting on the existence of but a single, mass based party. It was the African version of that 'sole and central power which governs the whole community, by its direct influence',[1] which de Tocqueville observed in the nineteenth-century American idea of the state.

Consent in West African mass party states was made possible, further, by party organization and procedure. Direct democracy is impossible except on the scale of the village—whether in New England, U.S.A., or the region of Banfora, Upper Volta. Mass parties, in varying degrees, have developed the organization which publicized and encouraged the mass discussion of important issues on a larger scale. Local branches involved the many rather than honoured the few, and mass party leaders tried to use traditional organizations in order to reach individuals. They were often more effective than the civil service. Leaders were chosen by voting. In the thoroughly organized mass parties, institutionalized leadership was also collective. Set procedures were followed for the making of decisions and leaders were expected to report back.

Mass party states, moreover, encouraged social equality. The modern elite, themselves in favour of such values as merit rather than birth as the determinant of rank, were in a stronger position in the mass party states. Furthermore, most mass party leaders rose from low positions in the modern or the traditional social scale, and favoured social equality. Of course, to bridge the gap between the educated and the mass of the population, all parties had to use both ethnic and status arithmetic. Unlike patron party leaders, however, mass party leaders tried to use this in order to blur ethnic differences and weaken inherited status differences.

Within mass parties there were, in varying degrees, conditions in which opposition was possible. Among the elite in Africa, there was enough consensus about the rules of the political game to make it possible for them to disagree without coming, too often, to blows. In pre-war Senegal, as in nineteenth century Britain or present Southern Rhodesia and South Africa, the vote, and controversies among the several parties remained confined to a few who speak the same language and fight for similar interests. This consensus disappeared when the franchise expanded rapidly. At the present stage of African social history, the mass party organization made it possible for people to disagree within it, without necessarily triggering incidents endangering the rule of the elite and the stability of the state.

[1] de Tocqueville, Alexis. *Democracy in America*, Oxford, London, 1952, pp. 550–1.

Opportunities for expressing opposition varied. Discussion was widespread and frank within the best-organized mass parties, the *Union Soudanaise*, for example, where leaders have on occasions been outvoted on important issues. Not only individual disagreement was possible under the party umbrella, but also organized disagreement by *tendances*—such as trade union, youth, students, and cultural organizations, and even the civil service. In the less organized mass party states, such as Ivory Coast and Senegal, these modern associations quickly became foci of opposition outside of the mass party, though not necessarily calling themselves parties.

The opportunity to express opposition through rival political organizations also varied. Specified parties or types of parties were outlawed in most states. Organized opposition was excluded in effect, where it was a matter of doctrine to insist on the single party, the *parti unique*, and on its identity with both the popular will and with the state. It was less excluded where leaders justify the single party for empirical reasons as a *parti unifié*, making common cause in the national emergency.

While single-party systems in mass and patron party states differed at the time of independence, the leaders of both types of states faced some similar problems. Confining disagreements to the issues at hand is difficult in a society where only the members of the elite born of different ethnic groups are able to speak directly to each other in French. Even where the organization of a mass party was a 'spider's web' villagers often had different values than national leaders. President Sékou Touré spoke of this to the Fifth Congress of the *Parti Démocratique de Guinée* in September 1959:

. . . democracy, within our Party, is not a democracy of clan or family, but a basic democracy to which the entire population contributes directly and freely . . . the old forms of social democracy anchored in the villages often influence the party militants, who believe themselves authorized to violate the new individual forms prescribed within the PDG. Therefore at each new election for officers, dissensions arise within the Movement. This occurs because we have not yet accomplished our work.[1]

As long as kinship is an important link between the educated and their rural constituents, division among the elite on such constitutional matters as federalism, independence, or the position of 'chiefs' —is often taken by their kinsmen as a signal for settling entirely unrelated traditional issues over land, women, or water. This was one of the dynamics behind the Ivory Coast incidents of 1949–52. In the

[1] Touré, *Le Cinquième congrès national* . . ., tome iv, op. cit., pp. 43–4.

relatively integrated societies of North America or Western Europe, plurality is quite rightly counted among the democratic virtues. In Africa today, it is rather a vice.

That is why many Africans justified the existence of single-party states on the grounds that a national emergency exists. The struggle for independence is 'not the concern of a day, a year, or an age; posterity are virtually involved in the contest . . .'[1] These words of Tom Paine reflect the African sense of history.[2] Africans argue the plural 'party system under imperialist domination is synonomous with a sterile division that profits only those who want to see to it that their privileges continue'.[3] This is the logic of a community at war, considering an *administratif* to be like a 'quisling'. Most Africans carried their sense of urgency into the post-independence era, and consider unity necessary in order rapidly to 'install the apparatus of the State, at the service of economic development, of social and cultural development'.[4]

New Problems

Though the difference between single party states of the mass and patron types was considerable at the time of independence, it was not certain whether afterwards the distinction remained valid. At best it turned on a difference in degree, and some parties fell between the two categories. Were the *Parti Démocratique de la Côte d'Ivoire* or the *Union Progressiste Sénégalaise* losing their mass party characteristics and becoming patron party types? The efficiency of both organizations declined, so did interest in social equality; there were many signs of rising discontent among youth, students, workers, and civil servants; the parties had difficulties with ethnic separatist pressures. Both parties obtained mass support at the local level in the 'forties, when there was the most significant turnover of leadership at the local level. Both parties, for different reasons, blurred the controversies between modern and traditional leaders. Both were old mass parties, and the dominant national leaders had been in power for almost a generation. Their public offices were taking precedence over party work. To a growing segment of the population, not directly involved in the struggle which brought the two parties to power, the

[1] Paine, Thomas. 'Common Sense', in *The Political Writings*, vol. i, Investigator Office, Boston, 1856, p. 33.
[2] For a most interesting discussion of the new history of West Africa, see Immanuel Wallerstein, 'The New History: The Search for National Identity in West Africa', *Présence Africaine*, French and English editions, Paris, October 1960.
[3] Adandé, Alexander. 'In the Phase of National Reconstruction the Fusion of Parties Becomes a Categorical Imperative,' address at the Congress for Cultural Freedom Conference, Ibadan, March 1959, mimeographed, F/413, p. 3.
[4] Keïta, Madeira. op. cit., p. 9.

leaders represented the establishment. The difference between mass and patron party states was more evident after independence, with the US of Mali and the PDG of Guinea. These parties had electoral majorities and took over leadership both at the national and at the local levels only since the late 'fifties; shortly after independence most people still felt they were involved in a social as well as a political revolution. In both Mali and Guinea, party hierarchy seemed to take precedence over the government hierarchy.

After independence there was an entirely new framework within which the parties operated. New problems confronting both mass and patron party governments made it appear at least for a time that the distinction was eroding between mass and patron party types. Within a few years it was possible for the popularity of a once widely acclaimed mass based government to disappear, for it to become regarded rather as representative of the *status quo*; thus some mass parties acquired patron party attributes. At the same time some patron parties after independence encouraged a turnover of leadership at the local level, a move away from domination by the patrons and towards wider mass participation as well as more formal structure and procedure, hence to acquire mass party attributes.

All the states, including mass party ones, found it hard to continue to reflect the 'general will'. The unifying nationalist struggle was over, and many controversies came to the fore. There was a great difference between what people expected of independence and what occurred. In every state there were financial difficulties due to an immediate shortage of foreign exchange, a reduction or elimination of French subsidies, a fall in the world market price of exports. There was a crisis in the civil service—expatriates left; the dominant political party in varying degrees suspected the loyalty and standards of African higher civil servants trained or promoted by the Europeans; Africanization of the civil service was usually accompanied by a repolitization in favour of the governing party; in addition as standards of political loyalty took precedence over standards of performance problems of corruption cropped up; there were charges of nepotism as some men promoted their kinsmen rather than men chosen on the basis of merit. The crisis in the civil service usually made worse the financial and economic crisis following independence since the capacity to implement changes depended on the efficiency of government servants.

To help solve the post-independence economic problems the new states usually raised tariffs and export duties; tried to control trading across African borders; and the activities of the traders. The result was that many African traders previously among the best supporters became critics of the nationalist governments. The governments also tried to reduce or hold level the salaries of workers, and became involved in struggles with the unions.

As support from among the modern sectors of the population declined, many governments were thrown back upon the rural elements for support. This shifted the balance against the modernizing townsmen. In the countryside, too, there were critics of the new governments. Some subsistence farmers had hoped taxes would no longer be collected; fishermen like the *somono* living near Ségou of Mali hoped to be able to fish near the Sansanding dam; some Muslim scholars hoped Islam would become the state religion—most such groups were disappointed after independence. Signs of ethnic separatism multiplied, particularly on international frontiers; and rural friction intensified, for example between 'strangers' or Dioula and the original owners of the land. Villagers looked with suspicion upon townsmen who came as representatives of the central authorities. In varying degrees townsmen caught in financial difficulties due to the readjustments of the modern economy after independence, became more dependent upon their rural kinsmen and the subsistence economy for supplies.

Thus after independence there were new conditions, making it necessary to pose new questions. There were, first, questions about the relationship of the dominant party to the institutions of state: to army, police, civil service, courts, to the national assembly and ministries. Immediately after independence the fear of anarchy made the new African governments as quick to institute special courts and security laws as was the United States to adopt Alien and Sedition Acts in 1798. All manipulated electoral procedures to obtain overwhelming majorities—though not all went so far as Dahomey where there was but a single list for the elections to the National Assembly and the whole nation became a single constituency. All the governments imprisoned some opponents and held secrét or public political trials. All the governments became more dependent on the army and police, as in many states there were plots or fears of plots. Some opposition groups began planning their campaigns underground.

There were, second, questions about proceedings inside the single dominant party: frequency of meetings, the existence of conditions of internal democracy, opportunities for resolving peacefully problems of succession and renewal. In most states the inner core of party leaders accumulated offices both inside the party and inside the government; in some states government affairs drew their attention from the party. There were, third, questions about the existence of opposition groups, their opportunities to function and eventually to challenge successfully the group in power.

Whether outlawed or not, opposition groups could be identified.

'One-man shows', rump groups, expatriate groups and minor ethnic parties had little potential on the national scene. Some significant opposition came from the defeated mass parties—*Sawaba* in Niger, for example. There were also the opposition groups of 'young Turks', mainly town dwellers differently educated or younger than the men leading the dominant parties: *An Nahda al Watenia al Mauritania* (Party of the National Renaissance of Mauretania), *Parti du Regroupement Africain-Sénégal*, and the *Parti Africain de l'Indépendance* of Senegal. With the possible exception of the PAI, these parties had no conscious elitist theory governing recruitment, but in practice their audience was still confined to the modern elite, to youth and student and trade union groups. Particularly when the party in power was of a mass type, most of the 'young Turks' alternated between opposing it, and joining it in order to constitute a 'party within a party'. On occasion they became allied with dissident groups from among the 'founding fathers'. Most of the 'young Turks' began their political careers concerned with post-independence problems. Thus they were not, like most leaders of the dominant single party, of the generation to whom the *indigénat*, force labour, racial discrimination, and displacing the European administrators were major concerns. The 'young Turks' were nationalists and modernizers. They had little appetite for ethnic, separatist opposition, and constituted the actual or potential national opposition.

There were, finally, questions of programme and ideology. African party leaders knew they needed fresh ideas to fill the gap left by the achievement of independence, to set the post-independence goals and guides to action. They needed new policies to preserve the sense of community which had been successfully harnessed to the struggle for independence.

This struggle had inspired the first generation of African party leaders. They hoped to enlarge the area of dignity, freedom, and welfare of their people. Some showed their intention to promote social as well as political reforms just after independence: marriage laws raising the legal age women may marry and insisting on their right to consent; land reforms; laws modernizing rural justice, reducing or eliminating the power of 'chiefs', and opening the way to equal status for 'captives' and other lower strata of society; educational reforms. Most of these reforms caused bitter controversies between modernizers and traditionalists, between townsmen and villagers. Only economic development can help resolve these controversies.

On development depends the capacity to implement the social reforms already on the statute books and agreement on yet other reforms. Without development, there can only be a new *status quo* around which society hardens into castes. Mobility is possible only with economic growth. On development depends the realization of the hopes of the first generation of French-speaking West African party leaders, and the capacity of their sons to do better. This thought may have impelled Sékou Touré to say 'Our party is identified with our people. Our regime has the virtue of being the expression of a people within a party. . . . But we do not know the realities of tomorrow.'[1]

[1] *Afrique Nouvelle*, 20–27 November 1963, reporting a speech at a meeting between the *bureau politique* and the National Assembly.

Bibliography

Professor Kenneth E. Robinson's 'A Survey of the Background Material for the Study of Government in French Tropical Africa', *The American Political Science Review*, vol. i, no. 1, March 1956, is a valuable starting point.

I. GENERAL PUBLISHED MATERIALS
(a) Not specifically on Africa

BROGAN, D. W., *The Development of Modern France*, Hamish Hamilton, London, 1940.

BERLIA, GEORGES, *Les Constitution et lois principales de la France depuis 1789*, Librairie Générale de Droit et Jurisprudence, Paris, 1952 (7e édition).

CAMPBELL, PETER, 'Discipline and Loyalty in the French Parliament During the Pinay Government', *Political Studies*, vol. i, no. 3, Oxford, 1953.

—— *French Electoral Systems and Elections 1789–1957*, Faber, London, 1958.

—— 'Vérification des Pouvoirs in the French National Assembly', *Political Studies*, vol. i, no. 1, Oxford, February 1953.

CHAPMAN, BRIAN, *Introduction to French Local Government*, Allen and Unwin, London, 1953.

CÉSAIRE, AIMÉE, *Discours sur le colonialisme*, Présence Africaine, Paris, 1955.

CLARK, COLIN, *The Conditions of Economic Progress*, Macmillan, London, 1951.

DUVERGER, MAURICE, *Les Partis politiques*, Librarie Armand Colin, Paris, 1951. Translated in English as *Political Parties*, Methuen, London, 1954.

EMERSON, RUPERT, *From Empire to Nation*, Harvard University Press, Cambridge, 1960.

JANSSENS, J., 'Le Conseil d'état a cinq ans', *Révue Nouvelle*, 13 October 1953.

LACHAPELLE, G., *Élections législatives*, Paris, 1928, 1932, 1936.

LIDDERDALE, D. W. S., *The Parliament of France*, The Hansard Society, London, 1951.

LE MONDE, ed., *Élections et référendums des 13 oct. 10 et 24 nov. et 8 dec., 1946*, Le Monde, Paris, 1947.

—— *Élections et référendums des 21 octobre 1945, 5 mai et 2 juin 1946*, Le Monde, Paris, 1946.

NEUMANN, Sigmund, *Modern Political Parties*, University of Chicago Press, Chicago, 1956.

PICKLES, DOROTHY, *French Politics*, Royal Institute of International Affairs, Oxford University Press, London, 1953.

THOMSON, DAVID, *Democracy in France*, 2nd edition, Oxford University Press, London, 1952.

WILLIAMS, PHILIP, *Politics in Post-War France*, 2nd edition, Longmans, London, 1958.

WRIGHT, GORDON, *The Reshaping of French Democracy*, Methuen, London, 1950.

(b) General Books on Africa

Des Africanistes russes parlent, Présence Africaine, Paris, 1960.

APTER, DAVID B., *The Gold Coast in Transition*, Princeton University Press, Princeton, 1955.

—— and ROSBERG, CARL G., 'Nationalism and Models of Political Change in Africa', *The Political Economy of Contemporary Africa*, Symposia Studies Series 1, The National Institute of Social and Behavioral Science, George Washington University, Washington, D.C., 1959. (Pamphlet.)

BARBOUR, NEVILL, ed., *A Survey of Northwest Africa*, Oxford University Press, London, 1959.

BOVILL, B. W., *The Golden Trade of the Moors*, Oxford University Press, London, 1958.

CARTER, GWENDOLEN, ed., *African One-Party States*, Cornell University Press, New York, 1962.

COLEMAN, JAMES S., 'The Emergence of African Political Parties', *Africa Today*, edited by C. Grove Haines, Johns Hopkins Press, Baltimore, 1955.

—— *Nigeria*, University of California Press, Los Angeles, 1958.

—— 'The Problem of Political Integration in Emergent Africa', *The Western Political Quarterly*, March 1955.

La Conscience chrétienne et les nationalismes, Pierre Horay, Paris, 1958.

DECRAENE, PHILIPPE, *Le Panafricanisme*, Presses Universitaires de France, Paris, 1961.

GARIGUE, PHILIP, 'Changing Political Leadership in West Africa', *Africa*, vol. xxiv, no. 3, Oxford University Press, London, July 1954.

HODGKIN, THOMAS, *African Political Parties*, Penguin Books, London, 1961.

—— *Nationalism in Colonial Africa*, Frederick Muller, Man and Society Series, London, 1956.

—— 'A Note on West African Political Parties', *What are the Problems of Parliamentary Government in West Africa?* The Hansard Society, London, 1958.

HAILEY, LORD W. M., *An African Survey*, Oxford University Press, London, 1938.

—— Ibid., Revised 1956, Oxford University Press, London, 1957.

JULIEN, CHARLES-ANDRÉ, *L'Afrique du nord en marche*, Julliard, Paris, 1952.

NKRUMAH, KWAME, *Ghana: The Autobiography of Kwame Nkrumah*, Thomas Nelson, London, 1957.

LEROI-GOURHAN, ANDRÉ, et POIRIER, JEAN, *Ethnologie de l'Union française*, Tome Premier, Afrique, Presses Universitaires de France, Paris, 1953.

LEYS, COLIN, *European Politics in Southern Rhodesia*, Clarendon Press, Oxford, 1959.

RÉZETTE, ROBERT, *Les Partis politiques marocains*, Armand Colin, Paris, 1955.

WALLERSTEIN, IMMANUEL, *Africa—The Politics of Independence*, Vintage Books, New York, 1961.

WALLERSTEIN, IMMANUEL, 'Ethnicity and National Integration in West Africa', *Cahiers d'Études Africaines* 3, 1960.
—— 'The New History: The Search for a National Identity in West Africa', *Présence Africaine*, French and English editions, October 1960.

(c) French Colonial Policy

AFRICANUS, *L'Afrique noire devant l'indépendance*, Plon, Paris, 1958.
ALDUY, P., *Union française et mission de la France*, Fasquelle, Paris, 1948.
BARBÉ, R., 'Où va l'Union française?', *Cahiers du Communisme*, May 1947.
—— 'Les Problèmes de l'Union française', *Cahiers du Communisme*, October 1946.
BLANCHET, ANDRÉ, *L'Itinéraire des partis africains depuis Bamako*, Plon, Paris, 1958.
BRIN, H. L., *La Nationalité française dans les territoires d'outre-mer*, Recueil Sirey, Paris, 1954.
Congrès International de l'Évolution Culturelle des Peuples Coloniaux, 26–27–28 septembre 1937, Rapports et Compte Rendu, Paris, 1938, Exposition Internationale de Paris, 1937.
DESCHAMPS, HUBERT, *L'Éveil politique africain*, Presses Universitaires de France, Paris, 1952.
—— *Méthodes et doctrines coloniales de la France*, Librairie Armand Colin, Paris, 1953.
—— *L'Union française*, Éditions Berger-Levrault, Paris, 1952.
DEVÈZE, MICHEL, *La France d'outre-mer*, Librairie Hachette, Paris, 1948.
EHRHARD, J., *Le Destin du colonialisme*, Éditions Eyrolles, Paris, 1958.
FOLLIET, JOSEPH, *Le Travail forcé aux colonies*, Éditions du Cerf, Paris, c. 1936.
GAYET, G., 'Évolutions récente des collèges électoraux en Afrique occidentale', *Comptes Rendus Mensuels des Séances de l'Académie des Sciences Coloniales*, Paris, February 1952.
GROS, CH., *Ce qu'il faut savoir sur le statut des municipalités africaines et malgaches*, rue Barye, Paris 17, c. 1957.
GONIDEC, P. F., 'Les Assemblées locales des territoires d'outre-mer', *Révue Juridique et Politique de l'Union Française*, no. 3, 1952.
——*Droit d'outre-mer*, tome i et ii, Éditions Montchrestien, Paris, 1957 and 1960.
—— 'L'Évolution des territoires d'outre-mer depuis 1946', series, in *Révue Juridique et Politique de l'Union Française*, 1957, 1958.
GUÈYE, LAMINE, *Étapes et perspectives de l'Union française*, Éditions de l'Union Française, Paris, 1955.
HOLLEAUX, A., 'Les Élections aux assemblées dans les territoires d'outre-mer', *Révue Juridique et Politique de l'Union Française*, no. 1, January–March 1956.
LACOUTURE, JEAN, *Cinq hommes et la France*, Éditions du Seuil, Paris, 1961.
LAMPUÉ, PIERRE, 'Pour une réforme de l'Union française', *Les Cahiers de la République*, May–June 1957.

LAVERGNE, BERNARD, *Afrique du Nord et Afrique Noire*, Larose, Paris, 1956.

LUCHAIRE, F., 'Les Institutions politiques et administratives des territoires d'outre-mer après la loi cadre', *Révue Juridique et Politique de l'Union Française*, no. 2, April–June 1958.

MERLE, MARCEL, 'La Communauté franco-africaine', *Révue de l'Action Populaire*, June 1960.

MITTERRAND, FRANÇOIS, *Aux frontières de l'Union française*, Julliard, Paris, 1953.

—— *Présence française et abandon*, Plon, Paris, 1957.

MOUSSA, PIERRE, *Les Chances économiques de la communauté Franco-africaine*, Armand Colin, Paris, 1957.

—— *Les Nations prolétaires*, Presses Universitaires de France, Paris, 1959.

OUDARD, GEORGES, editor, *Union Française 1953*, Julliard, Paris. Ibid., 1954, 1955, 1956, 1957, and 1958.

ROBINSON, KENNETH, 'French Africa and the French Union', *Africa Today*, edited by C. Grove Haines, Johns Hopkins Press, Baltimore, 1955.

—— 'Local Government Reform in French Tropical Africa', *Journal of African Administration*, October 1956.

—— 'Constitutional Reform in French Tropical Africa', *Political Studies*, vol. vi, no. 1, February 1958.

—— 'Political Development in French West Africa', *Africa in the Modern World*, edited by Calvin Stillman, University of Chicago Press, Chicago, 1955.

—— 'The Public Law of Overseas France Since the War', *Journal of Comparative Legislation*, third series, vol. xxxii, 1950. Reprint no. 1a, Institute of Colonial Studies, Oxford, England.

ROLLAND, LOUIS, et PIERRE LAMPUÉ, *Précis de droit des pays d'outre-mer*, 2nd edition, Librairie Dalloz, Paris, 1952.

ROSSILLION, CLAUDE, *Le Régime législatif de la France d'outre-mer*, Éditions de l'Union Française, Paris, 1953.

SANNER, P., 'Budgets et fiscalité des territoires d'outre-mer', *Révue d'Économie Politique*, 1952.

SÉCRÉTARIAT SOCIAL D'OUTRE-MER, *Code du travail des territoires d'outre-mer: Guide de l'usager*, Société d'Éditions Africaines, Paris, n.d.

THIAM, DOUDOU, *La Portée de la citoyenneté française dans les territoires d'outre-mer*, Société d'Éditions Africaines, Paris, 1953.

II. BOOKS AND ARTICLES ON FRENCH-SPEAKING TROPICAL AFRICA

(a) By Africans

The single most important collection of writings by French-speaking Africans has come from the presses of Présence Africaine in Paris. Organized in the late 'forties by the former Senegalese senator Alioune Diop, the organization has not only published, fairly regularly, a magazine of interesting articles, but it has also stimulated and published African writings.

D'ABY, F. J. AMON, *La Côte d'Ivoire dans la cité africaine*, Larose, Paris, 1951.

D'ARBOUSSIER, GABRIEL, *L'Afrique vers l'unité*, Éditions Saint-Paul, Paris, 1961.

AUTRA, RAY, 'Historique de l'enseignement en A.O.F.', in *Présence Africaine*, February–March 1956.

BÂ, AHMADOU HAMPATÉ, 'Culture peuhle', *Présence Africaine*, no. spécial, June–November 1956.

—— 'Sur l'animisme', *Présence Africaine*, Paris, February–May 1959.

—— and CARDAIRE, MARCEL, *Tierno Bokar, le sage de Bandiagara*, Présence Africaine, Paris, 1957.

—— and DAGET, JAQUES, *L'Empire peul du Macina*, Études Soudanaises, I.F.A.N., Soudan, 1955.

BOULNOIS, JEAN and HAMA, BOUBOU, *Empire de Gao: Histoire, coutumes et magie des Sonrai*, Adrien-Maisonneuve, Paris, 1954.

DADIÉ, BERNARD, *Afrique débout*, Pierre Seghers, Paris, 1950.

—— *Climbié*, Éditions Seghers, Paris, 1956.

—— 'Misère de l'enseignement en A.O.F.', *Présence Africaine*, December 1956–January 1957.

DIA, MAMADOU, *Contributions à l'étude du mouvement cooperatif en Afrique noire*, Clermont-Ferrand, Paris, 1952.

—— *L'Économie africaine*, Presses Universitaires de France, Paris, 1957.

—— *Nations africaines et solidarité mondiale*, Presses Universitaires de France, Paris, 1960.

—— *Réflexions sur l'économie de l'Afrique noire*, Éditions Africaines, Paris, c. 1954.

DIOP, CHEIKH ANTA, *L'Afrique noire précoloniale*, Présence Africaine, Paris, 1960.

—— *Les Fondements culturels, techniques et industriels d'un futur état fédéral d'Afrique noire*, Présence Africaine, Paris, 1960.

—— *Nations nègres et culture*, Présence Africaine, Paris, 1955.

—— *L'Unité culturelle de l'Afrique noire*, Présence Africaine, Paris, 1959.

DIOP, MAJHEMOUT, *Contribution à l'étude des problèmes politiques en Afrique noire*, Présence Africaine, Paris, 1958.

KABORET, GOMKOUDOUGOU, 'Caractère "féodal" du système politique mossi', *Cahiers d'Études Africaines* 8, Mouton & Co., Paris, 1962.

KANE, CHEIKH HAMIDOU, *L'Aventure ambiguë*, Julliard, Paris, 1961.

KEÏTA, MADEIRA, 'Le Parti unique en Afrique', *Présence Africaine*, February–March, 1960.

Ki-Zerbo's section on Africa in GENET, L., REMOND, R., CHAUSSU, P., MARCET, A., and KI-ZERBO, J., *Le Monde contemporain*, Hatier, Paris, 1962.

LY, ABDOULAYE, *La Compagnie du Sénégal*, Présence Africaine, Paris, 1958.

—— *Les Masses africaines et l'actuelle condition humaine*, Présence Africaine, Paris, 1956.

—— 'Mercenaires noirs', Présence Africaine, Paris, 1957.

NIANE, DJIBRIL TAMSIR, 'Mise en place des populations de la Haute-Guinée', *Recherches Africaines*, Institut National de Recherche et de Documentation, Conakry, April–June 1960.

—— 'Soundjatta', Présence Africaine, Paris, 1960.

—— and SURET-CANALE, J., *Histoire de l'Afrique occidentale*, Éditions du Ministère Nationale de la République de Guinée, Conakry, 1960.

OUANE, IBRAHIMA MAMADOU, *Les Filles de la Reine Cléopatra*, Les Paragraphes Littéraires de Paris, April, 1961.

—— *L'Enigme du Macina*, Regain-Monte Carlo, 1952.

Recontres 47, Des Prêtres noirs s'interrogent, Éditions du Cerf, Paris, 1957.

SAR, A., FOFANA, I., and BANNY, K., 'Esprit et situation de l'enseignement en Afrique noire', *Présence Africaine*, December 1956–January 1957, Paris.

SOCÉ, OUSMANE, *Mirages de Paris*, Nouvelles Éditions Latines, Paris, n.d.

—— *Karim*, Éditions 'France–Afrique', Paris, 1949.

SENGHOR, LÉOPOLD, ed., *Anthologie de la nouvelle poésie nègre et malgache de langue française*, Presses Universitaires de France, Paris, 1948.

SIDIBÉ, MAMBY, *Notes Africaines*, 'Numéro Special, L'Empire du Mali', I.F.A.N., Dakar, April 1959.

SISSOKO, FILY-DABO, *Crayons et portraits*, no publisher, Paris, c: 1950.

—— *Harmakhis*, Éditions de la Tour de Guet, Paris, 1955.

—— *Les Noirs et la culture*, no publisher, New York, 1950.

—— *Une Page est tournée*, première série, voix perdues, Imprimerie Diop, Dakar, 1959.

—— Ibid., deuxième série, voix sans écho, Imprimerie Diop, Dakar, 1960.

TEVOEDJRE, ALBERT, *L'Afrique revoltée*, Présence Africaine, Paris, 1958.

(b) By non-Africans

The semi-governmental Institut Français d'Afrique Noire (I.F.A.N.) encouraged many scholarly works on Africa, mainly in the natural sciences before the Second World War, and increasingly in the social sciences since then. The I.F.A.N. had connexions with the Musée de l'Homme in Paris, its African headquarters were in Dakar under the federation, and it maintained branches in the various territories. Since independence the structure has been decentralized, and Guinea cut its links with the French organization, substituting for it the Institut National de Recherche et de Documentation in Conakry.

I.F.A.N. published studies have included books, a series of *mémoires*, its *Bulletin de l'I.F.A.N.*, *Notes Africaines*, and occasional publications of the various territorial branches. The *Cartes Ethno-démographiques de l'Afrique occidentale*, published by the I.F.A.N. in Dakar, have been particularly useful.

ANSPRENGER, FRANZ, *Politik im Schwarzen Afrika*, Westdeutscher Verlag, Köln und Opladen, 1961.

AOF 1957, Côte d'Ivoire, Encyclopédie d'Outre-mer, Paris. (Pamphlet.)

BALANDIER, GEORGES, 'La Situation coloniale: approche théorique', *Cahiers Internationaux de Sociologie*, vol. xi, Paris, 1951.
—— *Sociologie actuelle de l'Afrique noire*, Presses Universitaires de France, Paris, 1955.
—— *Sociologie des Brazzavilles noires*, Cahiers de la Fondation Nationale des Sciences Politiques, Librairie Armand Colin, Paris, 1955, no. 67.
BALANDIER, GEORGES ET MERCIER, P., *Les Pêcheurs lébou*, Études Sénégalaises no. 3, Centre I.F.A.N., Saint-Louis, Sénégal, 1952.
BEAUJEU-GARNIER, JACQUELINE, 'Essai de géographie électorale guinéenne', *Les Cahiers d'Outre-mer*, no. 44, Bordeaux, October–December 1958.
BERG, ELLIOT, 'The Economic Basis of Political Choice in French West Africa', *The American Political Science Review*, June 1960.
—— 'French West Africa' in *Labor and Economic Development*, ed. by Walter Galenson, Wiley, New York, 1959.
BOYER, G., 'Un Peuple de l'ouest soudanais, Les Diawara', *Mémoires de l'Institut Français d'Afrique Noire*, no. 29, I.F.A.N., Dakar, 1953.
BOUCHARD, R. O., JOSEPH, *L'Église en Afrique noire*, La Palatine, Paris, 1958.
BUELL, R. L., *The Native Problem in Africa*, 2 vols. Macmillan, New York, 1928.
CARDAIRE, MARCEL, *L'Islam et le terroir africain*, Études Soudaniennes, I.F.A.N., Soudan, 1954.
CENTRE DE HAUTES ÉTUDES ADMINISTRATIVES SUR L'AFRIQUE ET L'ASIE MODERNES, *Notes et études sur l'islam en Afrique noire*, Peyronnet, Paris, 1962.
COLEMAN, JAMES, *Togoland*, International Conciliation 509, Carnegie Endowment for International Peace, New York, September 1956.
CORBY, C., 'Le Grand conseil de l'AOF', *L'Afrique et L'Asie*, no. 22, 1953.
DELAFOSSE, MAURICE, 'Afrique Occidentale Française', in Hanotaux, Gabriel and Martineau, Alfred, *Histoire des colonies françaises et de l'expansion de la France dans le monde*, tome iv, Société de l'Histoire Nationale, Plon, Paris, 1931.
DELAVIGNETTE, ROBERT, *Freedom and Authority in French West Africa*, Oxford University Press, London, 1950 (translation of *Service Africain*, Paris, 1946).
DELVAL, J., 'Le RDA au Soudan français', *L'Afrique et L'Asie*, no. 16, iv, 1951.
DOLLFUS, O., 'Conakry en 1951–1952. Étude humaine et économique', *Etudes Guinéennes*, I.F.A.N., Conakry, no. 10–11, 1952.
DUMONT, RENÉ, *L'Afrique noire est mal partie*, Éditions du Seuil, Paris, 1962.
DUPUIS, J., 'Un problème de minorité: les nomades dans l'état soudanais', *L'Afrique et L'Asie*, no. 50, 2, 1960.
GAMBLE, DAVID P., *The Wolof of Senegambia*, International African Institute, London, 1957.
GAUTIER, E. F., *L'Afrique Noire Occidentale*, Larose, Paris, 1943.
GOUILLY, ALPHONSE, *L'Islam dans l'Afrique Occidentale Française*, Larose, Paris, 1952.
GRIVOT, R., *Réactions dahoméennes*, Berger-Levrault, Paris, 1954.

GUERNIER, EUGÈNE, *Afrique Occidentale Française*, Encyclopédie Coloniael et Maritime, Paris, 1949 (2 vols.).

HODGKIN, T., and SCHACHTER, R., *French-Speaking West Africa in Transition*, International Conciliation 528, Carnegie Endowment for International Peace, May 1960.

HOUIS, MAURICE, *Guinée française*, Éditions Maritimes et Coloniales, Paris, 1953.

JACOBSON, ALFRED, 'L'Afrique Occidentale', in *La France d'outre-mer: sa situation actuelle*, Plon, Paris, 1953.

JAHN, JANHEINZ, *Muntu—the New African Culture*, Press, New York, 1961.

KÖBBEN, A. J. F., *Le Planteur noir:* Essai d'une ethnographie d'aspect, Études Eburnéennes, vol. v, I.F.A.N., Centre de Côte d'Ivoire, 1956.

MARTY, PAUL, *Études sur l'islam*, Éditions Ernest Leroux, Paris, 1915–26:
I. *L'Islam en Mauritanie et en Sénégal*
II. & III. *Études sur l'islam au Sénégal.*
IV. *L'Islam en Guinée*, Fouta Djallon.
V. *L'Émirat des Tarzas.*
VI., VII., VIII., IX. *Études sur l'islam et les tribus du Soudan.*
X. *La Vie des maures.*
XI. *Études sur l'islam et les tribus maures.*
XII. *Études sur l'islam en Côte d'Ivoire.*
Études sur l'islam au Dahomey.

MAUNY, RAYMOND, *Tableau géographique de l'ouest-africain au moyen age*, I.F.A.N., Dakar, 1961.

MILCENT, ERNEST, *L'AOF entre en scène*, Bibliothèque de l'Homme d'-Action, Éditions Témoignage Chrétien, Paris, 1958.

NEWBURY, C. W., 'The Formation of the Government General of French West Africa', *The Journal of African History*, vol. i, no. 1, Cambridge University Press, London, 1960.

PAGEARD, ROBERT, 'Soundiatta Keïta et la tradition orale', *Présence Africaine*, vol. xxxvi, 1961.

PAQUES, VIVIANA, *Les Bambara*, Presses Universitaires de France, Paris, 1954.

Présentation de la Côte d'Ivoire, I.F.A.N., Abidjan, 1953.

RICHARD-MOLARD, JACQUES, *Afrique Occidentale Française*, Collection l'Union Française, Éditions Berger-Levrault, Paris, 1952.

ROBINSON, KENNETH E., and MACKENZIE, W. J. M., eds., *Five Elections in Africa*, Clarendon Press, Oxford, 1960.

ROUCH, JEAN, *Contribution à l'histoire des Songhay*, Mémoires de l'Institut Français d'Afrique Noire, No. 29, I.F.A.N., Dakar, 1953.

—— 'Migrations au Ghana', *Journal de la Société des Africanistes*, tome xxvi, fasc. I and II, Musée de l'Homme, Paris, 1956.

SCHACHTER, RUTH, 'French Guinea's RDA Songs', *West African Review*, August 1958.

—— 'Single Party Systems in West Africa', *The American Political Science Review*, June 1961.

SECRÉTARIAT SOCIAL DE DAKAR, *Manuel pratique du syndicaliste*, Librairie Clairafrique, Dakar, 1956.

Séré de Rivières, Edmond, *Le Sénégal-Dakar*, Éditions Maritimes et Coloniales, Paris, 1953.
—— *Niger*, Éditions Maritimes et Coloniales, Paris, 1952.
Siriex, Paul-Henri, *Une Afrique nouvelle: A.O.F. 1957*, Plon, Paris, 1957.
Skinner, Elliott P., 'Christianity and Islam among the Mossi', *American Anthropologist*, vol. 60, no. 6, part 1, December 1958, 1102–19.
Spitz, Georges, *Sansanding: les irrigations du Niger*, Société d'Éditions Géographiques Maritimes et Coloniales, Paris, 1949.
—— *Soudan français*, Éditions Maritimes et Coloniales, Paris, 1955.
Sophie, Ulrich, *Le Gouverneur Général Félix Éboué*, Larose, Paris, 1950.
Suret-Canale, J., *Afrique noire*, Éditions Sociales, Paris, 1958.
Tardits, Claude, *Porto-Novo*, Mouton, Paris, 1958.
Thompson, Virginia and Adloff, Richard, *French West Africa*, University Press, Stanford, 1958.
Trimingham, J. Spencer, *Islam in West Africa*, Clarendon Press, Oxford, 1959.
Zolberg, Aristide, 'Effets de la structure d'un parti politique sur l'intégration nationale', *Cahiers d'Études Africaines*, October 1960.

III. OFFICIAL DOCUMENTS

The *Journal Officiel* of the Fourth Republic was a valuable source of information. Particularly useful were the *Débats Parlementaires de l'Assemblée Nationale, du Conseil de la République*, and de *l'Assemblée de l'Union Française*. An introductory guide to the *Journal Officiel* is 'Les Journaux Officiels de la République Française, étude historique et analytique', *La Documentation Française*, 7 May 1953, no. 1738, Paris.

Various reports issued by the committees of the National Assembly, the Council of the Republic and the Assembly of the French Union were indispensable: for example, the *Rapport fait au nom de la commission chargée d'enquêter sur les incidents survenus en Côte d'Ivoire*, Assemblée Nationale no. 11348, annexe au procès-verbal de la séance du 21 novembre 1950 (3 vols); or the *Rapport fait au nom de l'intercommission sur . . . la réforme de la structure de l'Union française*, annexe au procès verbal de la 1ʳᵉ séance du 22 mars 1955, no. 104, Assemblée de l'Union Française.

The National Assembly, Council of the Republic and Assembly of the French Union published annually a pamphlet listing the names of members, with some biographical information, including the breakdown by parties and commissions. Other useful official publications include some of La Documentation Française, such as 'l'Évolution récente des institutions politiques dans les Territoires d'outre-mer et Territoires associés', 11 March 1954, no. 1847; or ibid., *Les Élections législatives du 17 juin 1951*, Paris, 1951. *La Conférence africaine française*, Brazzaville, Commissariat aux Colonies, Alger, 1944, recorded the debates about reforms immediately before Liberation.

For a brief period the *Journal Officiel de la Communauté* was published in Paris. The *Journal Officiel de l'AOF*, and of each of the territories, has also proved valuable. The records of the *Grand Conseil d'A.O.F.* were published, albeit irregularly; the records of the various commissions of the *grand conseil* contained much valuable data. The *Annuaire du Grande Conseil et des Assemblées Territoriales*, published by the Direction des Affaires Politiques, listed the members of the various representative assemblies in French West Africa, usually with some biographical data, and information on party affiliations.

The records of the territorial assemblies were usually published, after some delay, in most of the territories. The annual reports of the governors to the territorial assemblies—of which the *Rapport presenté à la session budgétaire 1955 de l'Assemblée Territoriale de la Côte d'Ivoire*, Gouverneur Messmer, was one of the best examples—usually made some mention of the political situation. Occasionally reports were issued by members of territorial assembly committees, such as the 'Rapport de la mission de l'Assemblée Territoriale en Côte d'Ivoire, février 1955' (mimeographed, Ouagadougou, Upper Volta).

At irregular intervals the Gouvernement-Général in Dakar published legal documents, such as *Textes de l'indigénat en A.O.F.*, issued in 1926; the result of surveys made in co-operation with territorial services: such as *Éducation de base 1955* (Côte d'Ivoire, Service des Affaires Sociales), *Enquête agricole de Bouaké* (Côte d'Ivoire, 1954), *Enquête nutrition-niveau de vie Bongouanou 1955–6* (Côte d'Ivoire), *Étude sur la société Adioukrou et la région de Dabou* (Côte d'Ivoire 1954–5), *Mission démographique de Guinée*, Études agricoles et économiques de quatre villages de Guinée française (1955–6, Guinée). These occasional documents were either issued as pamphlets or mimeographed.

Probably the single most valuable statistical reference on French West Africa was the *Annuaire Statistique de l'A.O.F.* Published by the Gouvernement-Général at Dakar, volumes have appeared between the wars and since, in 1946, 1950, and 1951, in 1956 and 1957. As successors to the *Annuaire Statistique*, the Haut Commissariat de la République en AOF, Direction Générale des Services Économiques et du Plan, and the Direction des Services de la Statistique Générale et de la Mécanographie published *AOF 1957*, Imprimerie Paul Dupont, Paris, 1957; and the Services Statistiques d'Outre-mer put out *Outre-mer 1958*, Imprimerie Paul Dupont, Paris, 1959. The Haut Commissariat Général à Dakar also published a most useful series of studies in the *Comptes économiques de l'Afrique Occidentale Française* which has come out successively in Dakar and Paris since 1959. The statistical data assembled in the *Annuaires* was produced by the territorial representatives of the Service de la Statistique. In most territories a *Bulletin Statistique* appeared regularly in mimeographed form.

These figures were used in the various development plans which the African states drew up as they became independent. For example, Senegal's mimeographed *Rapport général sur les perspectives de développement du Sénégal* (2ᵉ édition, Dakar, juillet 1960) came out in two volumes, and contained many appendices and maps. The United Nations and the various specialized agencies republished many of the official French, overseas, and independent African state statistics and reports. There is, for example, United Nations E/CN.14/125/ADD. 1, *African Statistics*, Annex to the Economic Bulletin for Africa, vol. ii, no. 1, January 1962. The budgets and economic reports considered by the various representative assemblies were also useful.

In some territories, the Service de l'Information was particularly active; as a result, such documents as *Discours et allocations prononcés par M. le Ministre Houphouët-Boigny* (2 pamphlets, Côte d'Ivoire, April–May 1956 and October–November 1956) were published. There were territorial reports on various subjects, such as *La Conférence des commandants de cercle* (Conakry, 25–27 July 1957). Some territorial administrations published local newspapers: *Niger-Information, La Nouvelle Guinée*. There were, of course, many typewritten or mimeographed administrative records. Two examples: typewritten reports of the Inspecteurs des Colonies and the Inspecteurs de Travail; and ministerial circulars to the territorial governments.

With the transfer of power the publications in each of the states became more numerous, since they took over previously federal services. Statistics were published by official services and such semi-official bodies as the Chambres Économiques or Chambres de Commerce. For example, there was Chambre de Commerce, d'Agriculture et d'Industrie de Bamako, République du Mali, *Eléments du bilan économique de l'année 1960*, Bamako, 1961. The foreign ministries published speeches of government officials and ministers. The information services pushed speeches and reports, such as Senghor, Léopold, *Conférence de presse du 23 août 1960*, Ministère de l'Information, République du Sénégal, Dakar, 1960; or Territoire de Guinée, *Textes des interviews accordées aux représentants de la presse par le Président Sékou Touré*, Conakry, Imprimerie Nationale, September 1959. In Guinea the information ministry published a newspaper, *Horoya*; and it took on the work of an *Agence Guinéenne de Presse*, while the Bureau de Presse published a mimeographed *Bulletin d'Information de la Présidence*. Most of the new states published at least in mimeographed form the debates of the various National Assemblies and committees. Some of the more specialized territorial services put out irregularly reports and pamphlets, such as Office du Niger, *Le Delta ressuscité*, Service de Documentation Économique, Paris and Ségou, République du Mali, *c.* 1960.

After independence, as single parties took over in the various African governments, the line between party and government documents began to fade. This was evident, for example, in the series of publications put out in Conakry, most of them under the name of Sékou Touré, which were collections of party and government reports. The first two volumes were republished by Présence Africaine in Paris in 1959, under the title of *L'Expérience guinéenne et l'unité africaine*.

Territoire de la Guinée (par M. Sékou Touré), *L'Action politique du Parti Démocratique de Guinée pour l'émancipation africaine*, Conakry, Imprimerie du Gouvernement, n.d. (probably 1958), Dépôt légal 138, tome i.

RÉPUBLIQUE DE GUINÉE (PAR SÉKOU TOURÉ), *L'Action politique du P.D.G.–R.D.A. Guinée pour l'émancipation et l'unité africaine dans l'indépendance*, probably Conakry, Imprimerie Nationale, n.d. (*c.* 1959), no. 345, tome ii.

TOURÉ, SÉKOU, *L'Action du Parti Démocratique de Guinée et lutte pour l'émancipation africaine*, Paris, Présence Africaine, 1959, tome iii.

RÉPUBLIQUE DE GUINÉE, *Le Cinquième congrès national du Parti Démocratique de Guinée (R.D.A.):* Tenu à Conakry les 14, 15, 16, et 17 septembre 1959, Conakry, Imprimerie Nationale, n.d., Dépôt légal no. 187, tome iv.

RÉPUBLIQUE DE GUINÉE, *L'Action politique du Parti Démocratique de Guinée: La Planification économique.* (Plan triennal de Développement Économique et Social de la République de Guinée, Conférence Nationale des cadres des 2 au 5 avril 1960 à Kankan), Imprimerie Nationale, Conakry, 1960, Dépôt légal no. 25, tome v.

TOURÉ, SÉKOU, *La Lutte du Parti Démocratique de Guinée pour l'émancipation africaine*, République de Guinée, Conakry, 1961, tome vi.

IV. PAPERS AND JOURNALS PUBLISHED OUTSIDE AFRICA

Some have come out only occasionally; some deal with Africa only occasionally; unless otherwise indicated, the place of publication is Paris.

Africa—published in U.K.
L'Afrique.
Afrique Action—published in Tunis.
L'Afrique et L'Asie.
L'Afrique Force Ouvrière.
Afrique Information.
Agence France-Presse—section Afrique.
L'Ami du Peuple.
Bulletin de l'Association pour l'étude des problèmes de l'Union française.
Bulletin Catholique International.
Bulletin Intérieur du Parti Socialiste S.F.I.O.
Bulletin du Comité d'Études Historiques et Scientifiques de l'AOF—1916–38.
Cahiers du Communisme.
Cahiers d'Études Africaines.
Bulletin d'Information de l'Union Française—MRP.
Cahiers Internationaux de Sociologie—annual.
Les Cahiers d'Outre-mer—published in Bordeaux.
Les Cahiers de la République.
Climats—settler lobby.
Civilisations—published in Brussels.
Combat—Socialist.
La Défense—Secours Populaire—Communist.
Démocratie Nouvelle—Communist.
Esprit.

L'Étudiant Afrique Noire—Fédération des Étudiants d'Afrique Noire en France.
Hommes et Mondes.
Humanité—Communist.
Information and Documents on Africa—Christian Gilbert Newsletter.
Interafrique Presse.
The Journal of African History—published in U.K.
Libération.
Marchés Coloniaux du Monde—changed name to *Marchés Tropicaux du Monde* in 1956.
Le Monde.
Monde-Ouvrier.
Nations Nouvelles—organe de Liason de l'Union Africaine et Malgache.
La Nouvelle Critique.
La Nouvelle Révue Française d'Outre-mer.
L'Observateur.
Politique Étrangère.
Le Populaire—SFIO.
Présence Africaine—African cultural review.
La Quinzaine—left-wing Catholic.
Révue de l'Action Populaire—Catholic.
Révue d'Économie Politique.
Révue Juridique et Politique de l'Union Française.
Témoignage Chrétien—Catholic.
Tam-Tam—Bulletin des Étudiants Catholiques en France.
La Voix de l'Afrique Noire—étudiants en France du RDA.
West Africa—published in London.

V. PAPERS AND JOURNALS PUBLISHED IN AFRICA

Most came out irregularly. Many were mimeographed.

(a) Directed by Europeans

Abidjan-Matin—settlers, Abidjan.
Afrique Nouvelle—White Fathers, Dakar.
La Concorde—pro-PDCI, Abidjan.
La Côte d'Ivoire—settler, Ivory Coast.
Les Échos de l'Afrique Noire—'poujadist', Dakar.
France-Afrique—settlers, Abidjan.
Genèse—Bulletin of the Association William-Ponty, Dakar.
Journal du Combattant et Victime de Guerre—later, *Voix des Combattants* —Union Fédérale des Anciens Combattants, Dakar.
Le Journal du Soudan—PSP, Bamako.
Paris-Dakar, Dakar.
La Presse de Guinée, Conakry.
Servir Pour Agir—Catholic Mission, Centre Culturel Daniel Brottier, Dakar.
Soudan-Matin—Bamako.

(b) *African Party Papers*

L'Action—MPS, Dakar.
Action Démocratique—Action Démocratique et Sociale de la Côte d'Ivoire, Abidjan.
Afrique Noire—interterritorial RDA, Dakar.
L'AOF—SFIO, Dakar.
Attoungblan—FLN, Ivory Coast.
Azalat—Sawaba newspaper, Niger.
Le Bloc—BPA, Cotonou.
La Casamance—MFDC–BDS, Ziguinchor, Senegal.
Communauté—Mouvement Nationaliste Africain, Dakar.
La Condition Humaine—BDS, Dakar.
Le Démocrate—PDCI, Abidjan.
Le Démocrate—UDN, Niamey.
Clarté—PSS, Dakar.
Daho-Matin—UDD–RDA, Cotonou.
L'Essor—US, Bamako.
L'Éveil de l'Afrique—IOM nucleus, Cotonou.
L'Étendard—PFA, Dahomey.
Fraternité—PDCI, Abidjan.
Gaskya (Truth)—clandestine paper of Sawaba, successor to Azalat.
L'Indépendance Africaine—PRA, Dakar.
La Liberté—PDG, Conakry.
Le Mali—MLN, Dakar.
Momsarev (Independence)—PAI, Senegal.
Unité Africain—UPS organ, Dakar.
Le Niger—PPN, Niamey.
L'Observateur—PSEMA, Ouagadougou.
L'Observateur du Soudan—predecessor to *l'Essor*, Bamako.
Le Périscope Africain—pre-war, Senegal.
Le Phare du Sénégal—socialist, Rufisque.
Le Populaire de Guinée—socialist, Conakry.
Le Progrès—pre-war, Senegal.
Progrès Africain—AGV, Conakry.
Le Regroupement—UPS, Dakar.
Rélations Africaines—socialist, Saint-Louis.
Réalités Africaines—Senegalese intellectuals.
La Révue Africaine—pre-war, Senegalese.
Réveil—interterritorial RDA, Dakar.
Réveil d'Aujourd'hui—UDS, Dakar.
Le Sénégal—Mouvement Autonomist Africain, Dakar.
L'Unité—BPS, Dakar.
Vérité—PSP, Bamako.

(c) Trade Union Papers

Barakéla—CGT, Soudan.

Bulletin de Liason des Travailleurs des Pays Coloniaux—published in Paris by the CGT to maintain liaison in AOF.

Enseignants d'Afrique Noire—CGT–AOF teachers, Conakry.

Liaison—CFTC–AOF, Dakar.

Le Facteur—CGT federal postal workers, Dakar.

L'Ouvrier—CGT, Guinea.

Le Postier—autonomous federal postal workers, Dakar.

Le Prolétaire—CGT, Senegal.

SUEL-Liason—Syndicat Unique de l'Enseignement Laic du Sénégal et de la Mauritanie, autonomous teachers, Dakar.

Talaka—CGT, Niger.

Le Travail—CGT, Dahomey.

Le Travailleur Africain—CGT–AOF, Dakar.

Le Travailleur d'Afrique Noire—UGTAN–AOF, Dakar.

Le Travailleur Ivoirien—CGT, Ivory Coast.

Tribune d'Administration Générale—CGT–AOF, civil servants, Dakar.

La Voix des Travailleurs—CGTA–AOF (dissident CGT leaders who broke from the CGT in 1956), Dakar.

(d) Youth Papers

Dakar-Étudiant—Association Générale des Étudiants de Dakar, Dakar.

Jeunesse Liaison—Conseil de le Jeunesse du Sénégal.

Le Jeune Sénégal—pre-war Senegalese youth publication.

Le Réveil Islamique—Union Culturelle Musulmane, Dakar.

Tribune des Jeunes du Soudan Français—Union des Jeunes du Soudan Français, Bamako.

Vers l'Islam—Association Musulmane des Étudiants Africains, Dakar.

La Voix des Jeunes—Rassemblement des Jeunesses Démocratiques d'Afrique, Dakar.

La Voix des Jeunes—Unité d'Action des Jeunes de Guinée.

VI. PARTY RECORDS

Printing and mimeographing facilities were scarce and usually controlled by the French administration; therefore few of the better organized mass parties had access to printing facilities prior to 1957. Many party documents were published in newspapers. Occasionally parties issued reports of party meetings, in printed pamphlet, mimeographed or typewritten form. Some examples were RDA typed records of interterritorial congresses, mimeographed records of the 1948 and 1949 study course and congress resolutions and proceedings of RDA *Comité de Coordination* meetings; the *Union Soudanaise* mimeographed records of party congresses; PDG records of party conferences; MDV records of the 1956 congress; IOM records of the 1950 *Journées d'Études*, and the 1953 Bobo–Dioulasso Congress; the January 1957 records of the *Convention Africaine* Congress; and the 1953 records of the third AGV Congress in Guinea.

The 1948 pamphlet *Le Rassemblement Démocratique Africain dans la lutte anti-impérialiste*, Impressions Rapides, Paris, published some RDA documents issued prior to 1949.

Persistent searches for manifestos, records of public speeches, and reports of party officers frequently brought good results, such as access to GEC papers and to the typewritten records of the *États Généraux de la Colonisation Française*. The individual party leaders, their friends, and the secretarial staff at some party headquarters preserved many interesting documents, particularly for the US of Soudan, the PDG of Guinea, the BDS–BPS–UPS of Senegal, and the interterritorial RDA. Prior to 1950, while Gabriel d'Arboussier was RDA secretary-general, he issued frequent reports of the Co-ordinating Committee and the territorial sections of the movement. The Houphouët–d'Arboussier correspondence of 1952 threw considerable light on the problems and the distribution of power within the interterritorial RDA. One of Houphouët's letters was printed in *Afrique Noire*, 24 July 1952; d'Arboussier's first letter of May–June 1952 and his second letter of September 1952 were issued in pamphlet form in Paris. Mamadou Dia's typewritten reports, lengthy and detailed, to the annual BDS congresses in Senegal were previous sources of information. So were occasional pamphlets like Ray Autra's *Considérations sur la Loi-Cadre*, UDD, Porto Novo, *c.* 1957. Most significant parties have issued their statutes and by-laws in mimeographed form. The electoral *dossiers* submitted to the *vérification de pouvoir* committees of the French National Assembly by various African parties—where available—contain much valuable information.

After 1957 African party leaders had easier access to printing and duplicating facilities, and more pamphlets, party records, and resolutions became available. Some examples were the conference records of the 1957 meeting in Dakar of the *Convention Africain*; the manifesto of the Mouvement Africain de Libération Nationale, *Libérons l'Afrique*, printed in Paris and issued in Dakar, 25 August 1958; the records of the *Congrès Constitutif du Parti de la Fédération Africaine*, Dakar, 1–3 July 1959; the *Plate-forme du PRA-Sénégal*, Dakar, 5 July 1959; *Publications du PRA-Sénégal sur le nationalisme dans l'Ouest-Africain*, Dakar, 9 August 1959, par Abdoulaye Ly; Congrès Extraordinaire de l'U.S.R.D.A., *Le Mali continue*, Bamako, 22 September 1960.

VII. UNPUBLISHED MANUSCRIPTS

BERG, ELLIOT, 'The Recruitment of a Labor Force in Sub-Sahara Africa', doctoral dissertation for Harvard University, Cambridge, 1960.

GUÈYE, LAMINE, 'De la situation politique des sénégalais originaires des communes de plein exercice, telle qu'elle résulte des lois des 19 octobre 1915, 29 septembre 1916, et de la jurisprudence antérieure', Doctoral dissertation, La Vie Universitaire, Paris, 1921.

FOLTZ, WILLIAM J., 'From French West Africa to the Mali Federation', Yale University, New Haven, 1963, doctoral dissertation.

Fréchou, Hubert, 'Les Plantations européennes en Côte d'Ivoire, Thesis typescript, University of Bordeaux, c. 1955.

Diakate, Amadou Lamine, 'Le Nègre de demain ou la civilisation de synthèse' (Conférence prononcée à Rufisque), c. 1953.

Wallerstein, I. M., 'The Emergence of Two West African Nations: Ghana and Ivory Coast', Ph.D. thesis, Sociology, typescript, Columbia University, 1959. (To be published as The Road to Independence: Ghana and Ivory Coast, Mouton & Co., Paris.)

APPENDICES

APPENDIX I

*French Prime Ministers and Overseas Ministers Under the Fourth
Republic*

Date of Investiture	Premier and Party	Overseas Minister and Party
	Provisional Government	
1. 10.9.44–13.11.45	De Gaulle (n.p.)	Pleven (n.p.) Giacobbi
	Election of 21 October 1945, ANCI	
2. 21.11.45–22.1.46	De Gaulle	Soustelle, UDSR
3. 26.1.46–11.6.46	Gouin, SFIO	Moutet, SFIO
	Election of 2 June 1946, ANC II	
4. 23.6.46–28.11.46	Bidault, MRP	Moutet, SFIO
	Election of 10 November 1946	
	1st Legislature	
5. 16.12.46–16.1.47	Blum, SFIO (not M.P.)	Moutet (in C.R.)
6. 22.1.47–22.10.47	Ramadier, SFIO	,, (,,)
7. 22.10.47–19.11.47	,,	
8. 24.11.47–19.7.48	Schuman, MRP	Coste-Floret, MRP
9. 26.7.48–28.8.48	Marie, Rad.	,, ,,
10. 5.9.48–7.9.48	Schuman, MRP	,, ,,
11. 11.9.48–6.10.49	Queuille, Rad.	,, ,,
12. 29.10.49–24.6.50	Bidault, MRP	Letourneau, MRP
13. 2.7.50–4.7.50	Queuille, Rad.	Coste-Floret, MRP
14. 12.7.50–28.2.51	Pleven, UDSR	Mitterrand, UDSR
15. 10.3.51–10.7.51	Queuille, Rad.	,, ,,
	Election of 17 June 1951	
	2nd Legislature	
16. 10.8.51–7.1.52	Pleven, UDSR	Jacquinot, Ind. Rep.
17. 20.1.52–29.2.52	Faure, Rad.	,, ,,
18. 8.3.52–23.12.52	Pinay, Ind. Rep.	Pflimlin, MRP
19. 8.1.53–21.5.53	R. Meyer	Jacquinot, Ind. Rep.
20. 27.6.53–12.6.54	Daniel, Ind. Rep.	,, ,,
21. 18.6.54–5.2.55	Mendès-France, Rad.	Buron, MRP ,,
22. 23.2.55–3.1.56	Faure, Rad.	P.-H. Teitgen, MRP
	Election of 2 January 1956	
	3rd Legislature	
23. 1.2.56–21.5.57	Mollet, SFIO	Defferre, SFIO
24. 13.6.57–30.9.57	Bourgès-Manoury, Rad.	Jacquet, SFIO
25. 3.11.57–15.4.58	Gaillard, Rad.	,,
26. 14.5.58–28.4.58	Pflimlin, MRP	Colin, MRP
27. 1.6.58–	de Gaulle (n.p.)	Cornut-Gentille (n.p.)

n.p. = no party

APPENDIX II

French Constitutions

A. CONSTITUTION OF THE FRENCH REPUBLIC, OF 19 APRIL 1946

(The text was adopted by the National Assembly by 309 votes against 249. It was rejected in the referendum of 5 May 1946 by 10,584,359 votes against 9,454,034. The translation of articles of the draft Constitution relevant to the French Union is my own.[1])

Declarations of the Rights of Man

On the morrow of the victory gained by the Free Peoples over the régimes which have attempted to subjugate and degrade the human person, and which have just bathed the entire world in blood, the French people, faithful to the principles of 1789—the charter of its liberation—solemnly reaffirms once again that every human being possesses inalienable and sacred rights, on which no law can infringe, and decides, as in 1793, 1795, and 1848, to inscribe these at the head of its Constitution.

The Republic guarantees to all men and all women living within the French Union the right to the individual and collective exercise of the liberties and rights cited below:

12. On penal matters, identity of jurisdiction within the framework of the same territory is guaranteed to all the inhabitants of the French Union. . . .

18. Without other conditions than those of ability, aptitude and talent, access to the public service is open to all subjects[2] of the French Union enjoying the political rights attached by the present Constitution to the title of citizen.

Access to all private professions, posts, and occupations is open under the same conditions to all subjects[2] of the French Union and in the absence of particular regulations made by law, to all persons legally resident in the French Union.

In equality of work, of function, of grade, of category, of responsibility, everyone has the right to equality in material and moral benefits. . . .

Institutions

40. France is a Republic, indivisible, democratic, and social.

41. France forms with the overseas territories on the one hand and with the associated states on the other hand, a Union freely consented to.[3]

44. All subjects of the French Union enjoy the rights and freedoms of

[1] Text taken from *Les Constitutions et lois principales de la France depuis 1789*, Librarie Générale de Droit et Jurisprudence, Paris 1952, pp. 518–33. . . .

[2] *Ressortissants.*   [3] *Librement consentie.*

CC

the human person, guaranteed by Articles 1 through 39 of the present Constitution.

All French nationals and subjects of the metropole and the overseas territories enjoy the rights of citizenship.

45. The natives[1] of the overseas territories for whom the law recognizes personal status,[2] preserve their personal status so long as they do not renounce it.

This status cannot in any case constitute a reason for refusing or limiting the rights and freedoms guaranteed by Articles 1 through 39 of the present Constitution. . . .

48. The overseas territories elect representatives to the National Assembly under conditions fixed by electoral laws.

49. Electors are all adult French nationals and subjects of both sexes who enjoy their civil and political rights.

Adults are those who reach twenty years of age. . . .

52. War cannot be declared without previous consent from the National Assembly and previous consultation of the Council of the French Union. . . .

61. The members of the National Assembly cannot be members of the Council of the French Union or of the Economic Council. . . .

66. The National Assembly alone has the right to legislate. It cannot delegate this right in whole or in part to anyone.

Without contrary provision, the laws of the Republic are applicable to the overseas departments and territories. . . .

71. The Council of the French Union is composed of councillors elected by the general councils of the departments of the metropole and by the general councils or territorial assemblies of the overseas departments and territories.

72. The Council of the French Union is elected for four years.

Its sessions are public and its minutes are published *in extenso* in a special bulletin.

The Council of the French Union sits at the same time as the National Assembly. It cannot prolong its session beyond the time foreseen for the second reading of the texts which it considers.

73. The Council of the French Union deliberates upon the projects or proposals which are submitted to it for opinion, whether upon its own demand or by the Council of Ministers or by the National Assembly.

It gives its opinion during the month following transmission by the National Assembly. When the National Assembly declares urgency, the Council of the French Union gives its opinion within the same time limit as that foreseen for the debates of the National Assembly by the rules of the latter.

If the opinion of the Council of the French Union conforms, or if it has not been given within the time limit foreseen in the preceding paragraph, the law is promulgated according to the text voted by the National Assembly.

---

[1] *Originaires.* . . .   [2] *Statut personnel.* . . .

If the opinion does not conform, the National Assembly examines the project or proposal in a second reading. It legislates definitively and supremely on the amendments proposed by the Council of the French Union.

74. The speeches made within the Council of the French Union as well as the reports and all other documents printed by order of the Council of the French Union cannot give rise to any action.

During the tenure of his mandate no councillor can be prosecuted on matters of criminal law or misdemeanour, without the authorization of the National Assembly given after consultation of the Council of the French Union, except in the case of *flagrant délit*.[1] The detention or prosecution of a councillor is suspended if the National Assembly requires it.

The councillors of the French Union receive an indemnity as fixed by the law.

75. The members of the Council of the French Union cannot belong to the Economic Council. . . .

The President of the Republic

95. He represents the permanent interests of the French Union and presides at formal national occasions. . . .

The Local Collectivities

114. The French Republic, one and indivisible, recognizes the existence of territorial collectivities.

These collectivities are the communes and departments, the overseas territories and federations. They administer themselves freely in conformity with the law of the nation.

115. The law fixes the framework, the extent, the eventual regrouping and organization of the communes and departments, overseas territories and federations. . . .

119. The particular interests of the territories are administered and managed by local assemblies, elected by universal and direct suffrage. Their electoral system, composition and competence are determined by special laws assuring the liberty of the vote.

Those of the territories which form a group or a federation elect an Assembly whose composition and competence is fixed by special laws.

120. The Minister in charge of all the problems of overseas France is assisted by a resident Under-Secretary of State for every federation or group of territories.

The latter watches over the application of the laws. He co-ordinates the public services of the French Union and controls the work of the local administrations.

He is responsible for the maintenance of order and for the defence of the group or federation of territories.

[1] Being caught in the act.

B. CONSTITUTION OF THE FRENCH REPUBLIC OF 28 OCTOBER 1946

The text is my adaptation of Peter Williams' (op. cit., pp. 423–35) revision of the English translation issued by the French Embassy in London. The Articles below refer to overseas France.

Preamble

... France, together with the overseas peoples, forms a Union founded upon equality of rights and of duties, without distinction of race or of religion.

The French Union is composed of nations and peoples who pool or co-ordinate their resources and their efforts to develop their respective civilizations, to increase their well-being, and to ensure their security.

Faithful to her traditional mission, France proposes to lead the peoples of whom she has assumed charge to a state of freedom in which they administer themselves and conduct their own affairs democratically; rejecting any form of colonial rule based upon arbitrary power, she guarantees to all equal access to the public service, and the individual or collective exercise of the rights and liberties proclaimed or confirmed above. . . .

Article 1. France is a Republic, indivisible, laic, democratic, and social. . . .

Article 24. No one can belong to the National Assembly and to the Council of the Republic.

Members of Parliament cannot belong either to the Economic Council or to the Assembly of the French Union.

CHAPTER 8

THE FRENCH UNION

Section I

PRINCIPLES

Article 60. The French Union consists, on the one hand, of the French Republic, which comprises Metropolitan France, the overseas *départements* and territories, and on the other hand, of the associated territories and States.

Article 61. The position of the States associated with the French Union is settled for each of them by the act which defines their relations with France.

Article 62. The members of the French Union pool all the means at their disposal, to guarantee the protection of the whole of the Union. The government of the Republic assumes the co-ordination of these means and the control of the policy apt to prepare and ensure this protection.

Section II

ORGANIZATION

Article 63. The central organisms of the French Union are: the Presidency, the High Council, and the Assembly.

Article 64. The President of the French Republic is the President of the French Union, of which he represents the permanent interests.

Article 65. The High Council of the French Union is composed—under the presidency of the President of the Union—of a delegation of the French government and of the representation which each of the associated States has the power of accrediting to the President of the Union.

Its function is to assist the government in the general management of the Union.

Article 66. The Assembly of the French Union consists half of members representing Metropolitan France, and half of members representing the overseas *départements* and territories and the associated States.

An organic law will determine in which conditions the different sections of the population can be represented.

Article 67. The members of the Assembly of the Union are elected by the territorial assemblies as far as the overseas *départements* and territories are concerned; they are elected, as far as Metropolitan France is concerned, two-thirds by members of the National Assembly representing the mother country, and one-third by the members of the Council of the Republic representing the mother country.

Article 68. The associated States can designate delegates to the Assembly of the Union within limits and conditions defined by a law and an internal act of each State.

Article 69. The President of the French Union convenes the Assembly of the French Union and closes its sessions. He must convene it when so requested by half its members.

The Assembly of the French Union cannot sit during the interruption of the sessions of Parliament.

Article 70. The rules of Articles 8, 10, 21, 22, and 23 are applicable to the Assembly of the French Union in the same conditions as in the case of the Council of the Republic.

Article 71. The Assembly of the French Union deliberates upon the projects or proposals which are submitted to it for opinion,[1] by the National Assembly, or the government of the French Republic, or the governments of the associated States.

The Assembly is qualified to pronounce itself on motions submitted by one of its members, and, if it decides to consider them, to charge its *bureau* to transmit them to the National Assembly. It can make proposals to the French government and High Council of the French Union.

To be receivable, the motions mentioned in the preceding paragraph must relate to legislation concerning overseas territories.

[1] *Avis.*

Article 72. In overseas territories, legislative power belongs to Parliament, in matters of criminal law, the organization of public freedoms, and political and administrative organization.

In all other matters, French law is applicable in overseas territories only under special provisions, or if it has been extended by decree to overseas territories after consultation of the Assembly of the Union.

In addition, by derogation from Article 13, special provisions for each territory can be decreed in Council of Ministers by the President of the Republic after previous consultation of the Assembly of the Union.

Section III

OVERSEAS DEPARTMENTS AND TERRITORIES

Article 73. The legislative system of the overseas *départements* is the same as that of the metropolitan *départements*, excepting in certain cases defined by law.

Article 74. The overseas territories are endowed with a special statute, taking into account their particular interests within the framework of the general interests of the Republic.

The statute and the internal organization of each overseas territory or of each group of territories are determined by the law after consultation with the Assembly of the French Union and of the territorial Assemblies.

Article 75. The respective statutes of the members of the Republic and of the French Union are liable to evolve.[1]

Statutory amendments and the passage from one category to another within the framework set forth in Article 60, can only be brought about by a law voted by Parliament, following consultation of the territorial Assemblies and of the Assembly of the Union.

Article 76. The representative of the government in each territory or group of territories is the trustee of the powers of the Republic. He is the head of the administration of the territory.

He is responsible for his action before the government.

Article 77. An elected Assembly is instituted in each territory. The electoral procedure, the composition and the powers of this Assembly are fixed by law.

Article 78. In groups of territories, the management of common interests is entrusted to an Assembly consisting of members elected by the territorial Assemblies. Its composition and its powers are fixed by law.

Article 79. The overseas territories elect representatives to the National Assembly and to the Council of the Republic in conditions fixed by law.

Article 80. All subjects[2] of overseas territories are citizens, on the same basis as French nationals of the mother country or of overseas territories. Special laws shall determine the conditions in which they will exercise their rights as citizens.

Article 81. All French nationals[2] and subjects[3] of the French Union are

---

[1] In original: '*susceptibles d'évolution*'.　　　　[2] *Nationaux.*
[3] *Ressortissants.*

citizens of the French Union, a title which ensures for them the enjoyment of the rights and freedoms guaranteed by the Preamble to the present Constitution.

Article 82. Citizens who do not enjoy French civilian status preserve their personal status so long as they do not renounce it.

This status cannot, in any case, constitute a ground for refusing or restricting the rights and liberties attached to French citizenship. . . .

Article 85. The French Republic, one and indivisible, recognizes the existence of territorial collectivities.

These collectivities are the communes and *départements*, the overseas territories.

Article 86. The framework, the extent, the eventual regrouping and organization of the communes and *départements*, and territories overseas, are fixed by law.

C. CONSTITUTION OF THE FIFTH REPUBLIC, ADOPTED BY THE REFERENDUM OF 28 SEPTEMBER 1958 AND PROMULGATED ON 4 OCTOBER 1958[1]

Preamble

The French people hereby solemnly proclaims its attachment to the Rights of Man and the principles of national sovereignty as defined by the Declaration of 1789, reaffirmed and complemented by the Preamble of the Constitution of 1946.

By virtue of these principles and that of the free determination of peoples, the Republic hereby offers to the Overseas Territories that express the desire to adhere to them, new institutions based on the common ideal of liberty, equality, and fraternity, and conceived with a view to their democratic evolution.

Article 1

The Republic and the peoples of the Overseas Territories who, by an act of free determination, adopt the present Constitution thereby institute a Community.

The Community shall be based on the equality and the solidarity of the peoples composing it.

TITLE II

THE PRESIDENT OF THE REPUBLIC

Article 5

The President of the Republic shall see that the Constitution is respected. He shall ensure, by his arbitration, the regular functioning of the governmental authorities, as well as the continuance of the State.

He shall be the guarantor of national independence, of the integrity of the territory, and of respect for Community agreements and treaties.

[1] Translation of the French Embassy Press and Information Division, New York.

Article 6

The President of the Republic shall be elected for seven years by an electoral college comprising the members of Parliament, of the General Councils, and of the Assemblies of the Overseas Territories, as well as the elected representatives of the municipal councils.

These representatives shall be:

—the mayor for communes of fewer than 1,000 inhabitants;

—the mayor and the first deputy mayor for communes of from 1,000 to 2,000 inhabitants;

—the mayor, first deputy mayor and a municipal councillor chosen according to the order in which he appears on the council list for communes of from 2,001 to 2,500 inhabitants;

—the mayor and the first two deputy mayors for communes of from 2,501 to 3,000 inhabitants;

—the mayor, the first two deputy mayors and three municipal councillors chosen according to the order in which they appear on the council list for communes of from 3,001 to 6,000 inhabitants;

—the mayor, the first two deputy mayors and six municipal councillors chosen according to the order in which they appear on the council list for communes of from 6,001 to 9,000 inhabitants;

—all the municipal councillors for communes of more than 9,000 inhabitants;

—in addition, for communes of more than 30,000 inhabitants, delegates appointed by the municipal council in the ratio of one delegate for every 1,000 inhabitants above 30,000.

In the Overseas Territories of the Republic, the elected representatives of the councils of the administrative units shall also form part of the electoral college under the conditions to be determined by an organic law.

The participation of member States of the Community in the electoral college for the President of the Republic shall be determined by agreement between the Republic and the member States of the Community.

The procedures implementing the present article shall be determined by an organic law. . . .

Article 11

The President of the Republic, on the proposal of the Government during (Parliamentary) sessions, or on joint motion of the two assemblies, published in the *Journal Officiel*, may submit to a referendum any bill dealing with the organization of the governmental authorities, entailing approval of a Community agreement, or providing for authorization to ratify a treaty that, without being contrary to the Constitution, might affect the functioning of (existing) institutions.

When the referendum decides in favour of the bill, the President of the Republic shall promulgate it within the time limit stipulated in the preceding article. . . .

Article 13

The President of the Republic shall sign the ordinances and decrees decided upon in the Council of Ministers.

He shall make appointments to the civil and military posts of the State.

Councillors of State, the Grand Chancellor of the Legion of Honour, Ambassadors and envoys extraordinary, Master Councillors of the Audit Office, prefects, representatives of the Government in the Overseas Territories, general officers, rectors of academies (regional divisions of the public educational system), and directors of central administrations shall be appointed in meetings of the Council of Ministers.

An organic law shall determine the other posts to be filled in meetings of the Council of Ministers, as well as the conditions under which the power of the President of the Republic to make appointments to office may be delegated by him and exercised in his name. . . .

TITLE XI

ON TERRITORIAL UNITS

Article 72

The territorial units of the Republic are the communes, the Departments, the Overseas Territories. Other territorial units may be created by law.

These units shall be free to govern themselves through elected councils and under the conditions stipulated by law.

In the departments and the territories, the Delegate of the Government shall be responsible for the national interests, for administrative supervision and for seeing that the laws are respected.

Article 73

Measures of adjustment required by the particular situation of the Overseas Departments may be taken with regard to their legislative system and administrative organization.

Article 74

The Overseas Territories of the Republic shall have a special organization, which takes into account their own interests within the general interests of the Republic. This organization shall be defined and modified by law after consultation with the Territorial Assembly concerned.

Article 75

Citizens of the Republic who do not have ordinary civil status, the only status referred to in Article 34, may keep their personal status as long as they have not renounced it.

Article 76

The Overseas Territories may retain their status within the Republic.

If they express the desire to do so by a decision of their Territorial

Assemblies taken within the time limit set in the first paragraph of Article 91, they shall become Overseas Departments of the Republic or member States of the Community, either in groups or as single units. . . .

ON THE COMMUNITY

Article 77

In the Community instituted by the present Constitution, the States shall enjoy autonomy; they shall administer themselves and manage their own affairs democratically and freely.

There shall be only one citizenship in the Community.

All citizens shall be equal before the law, whatever their origin, their race, and their religion. They shall have the same duties.

Article 78

The Community's jurisdiction shall extend over foreign policy, defence, currency, common economic and financial policy, as well as over policy on strategic raw materials.

It shall include, in addition, except in the case of specific agreements, the supervision of the tribunals, higher education, the general organization of external transportation and transportation within the Community, as well as of telecommunication.

Special agreements may create other common jurisdictions or regulate any transfer of jurisdiction from the Community to one of its members.

Article 79

The member States shall benefit from the provisions of Article 77 as soon as they have exercised the choice provided for in Article 76.

Until the measures required for implementation of the present title go into force, matters within the common jurisdiction shall be regulated by the Republic.

Article 80

The President of the Republic shall preside over and represent the Community.

The institutional organs of the Community shall be an Executive Council, a Senate, and a Court of Arbitration.

Article 81

The member States of the Community shall participate in the election of the President according to the conditions stipulated in Article 6.

The President of the Republic, in his capacity as President of the Community, shall be represented in each State of the Community.

Article 82

The Executive Council of the Community shall be presided over by the President of the Community. It shall consist of the Premier of the Republic, the heads of Government of each of the member States of the Community, and the ministers responsible for the common affairs of the Community.

The Executive Council shall organize the co-operation of members of the Community at Government and administrative levels.

The organization and procedure of the Executive Council shall be determined by an organic law.

Article 83

The Senate of the Community shall be composed of delegates whom the Parliament of the Republic and the legislative assemblies of the other members of the Community shall choose from among their own membership. The number of delegates of each State shall be determined according to its population and the responsibilities it assumes in the Community.

The Senate of the Community shall hold two sessions a year, which shall be opened and closed by the President of the Community and may not last longer than one month each.

The Senate of the Community, when called upon by the President of the Community, shall deliberate on the common economic and financial policy before laws on these matters are voted upon by the Parliament of the Republic and, should circumstances so require, by the legislative assemblies of the other members of the Community.

The Senate of the Community shall examine the acts and treaties or international agreements, which are specified in Articles 35 and 53, and which commit the Community.

The Senate of the Community shall make executory decisions in the domains in which it has received delegation of power from the legislative assemblies of the members of the Community. These decisions shall be promulgated in the same form as the law in the territory of each of the States concerned.

An organic law shall determine the composition of the Senate and its rules of procedure.

Article 84

A Court of Arbitration of the Community shall rule on litigations occurring among members of the Community.

Its composition and its jurisdiction shall be determined by an organic law.

Article 85[1]

By derogation from the procedure provided for in Article 89, the provisions of the present title that concern the functioning of the common institutions shall be amendable by identical laws passed by the Parliament of the Republic and by the Senate of the Community.

Constitutional law 4 June 1960: The provisions of the present title can also be amended by agreements concluded with all the States of the Community; the new provisions are implemented under the conditions required by the Constitution of each State.

[1] As revised by the Constitutional Law of 4 June 1960 (my translation).

Article 86[1]

A change of status of a member State of the Community may be requested, either by the Republic, or by a resolution of the legislative assembly of the State concerned confirmed by a local referendum, the organization and supervision of which shall be ensured by the institutions of the Community. The procedures governing this change shall be determined by an agreement approved by the Parliament of the Republic and the legislative assembly concerned.

Under the same conditions, a member State of the Community may become independent. It shall thereby cease to belong to the Community.

Constitutional Law 4 June 1960: A member state of the Community may also, by way of agreements, become independent without thereby ceasing to belong to the Community.

An independent State not a member of the Community may, by way of agreements, join the Community without ceasing to be independent.

The position of these States within the Community is determined by the agreements concluded to this end, notably the agreements cited in the above clauses as well as, where applicable, the agreements mentioned in the second clause of article 85.

Article 87

The special agreements made for the implementation of the present title shall be approved by the Parliament of the Republic and the legislative assembly concerned.

TITLE XIII

ON AGREEMENTS OF ASSOCIATION

Article 88

The Republic or the Community may make agreements with States that wish to associate themselves with the Community in order to develop their own civilizations.

TITLE XIV

ON AMENDMENT

Article 89

The initiative for amending the Constitution shall belong both to the President of the Republic on the proposal of the Premier and to the members of Parliament.

The Government or Parliamentary bill for amendment must be passed by the two assemblies in identical terms. The amendment shall become definitive after approval by a referendum.

[1] As revised by the Constitutional Law of 4 June 1960 (my translation).

Nevertheless, the proposed amendment shall not be submitted to a referendum when the President of the Republic decides to submit it to Parliament convened in Congress; in this case, the proposed amendment shall be approved only if it is accepted by a three-fifths majority of the votes cast. The Secretariat of the Congress shall be that of the National Assembly.

No amendment procedure may be undertaken or followed when the integrity of the territory is in jeopardy.

The republican form of government shall not be subject to amendment.

TITLE XV

TEMPORARY PROVISIONS

Article 90

The ordinary session of Parliament is suspended. The mandate of the members of the present National Assembly shall expire on the day that the Assembly elected under the present Constitution convenes.

Until this meeting, the Government alone shall have the authority to convene Parliament.

The mandate of the members of the Assembly of the French Union shall expire at the same time as the mandate of the members of the present National Assembly.

Article 91

The institutions of the Republic, provided for by the present Constitution, shall be established within four months after its promulgation.

This time limit shall be extended to six months for the institutions of the Community.

The powers of the President of the Republic now in office shall expire only when the results of the election provided for in Articles 6 and 7 of the present Constitution are proclaimed.

The member States of the Community shall participate in this first election under the conditions derived from their status at the date of the promulgation of the Constitution.

The established authorities shall continue to exercise their functions in these States according to the laws and regulations applicable when the Constitution becomes operative, until the authorities provided for by their new régimes are set up.

Until it is definitively constituted, the Senate shall consist of the present members of the Council of the Republic. The organic laws that determine the definitive composition of the Senate must be passed before July 31, 1959.

The powers conferred on the Constitutional Council by Articles 58 and 59 of the Constitution shall be exercised, until this Council is set up, by a committee composed of the Vice President of the Council of State, as chairman, the First President of the Court of Cassation, and the First President of the Audit Office.

The people of the member States of the Community shall continue to be represented in Parliament until the measures necessary to the implementation of Title XII have been put into effect.

Article 92

The legislative measures necessary for the setting up of the institutions and, until they are set up, for the functioning of the governmental authorities, shall be taken in meetings of the Council of Ministers, after consultation with the Council of State, in the form of ordinances having the force of law.

During the time limit set in the first paragraph of Article 91, the Government shall be authorized to determine, by ordinances having the force of law and passed in the same way, the system of elections to the assemblies provided for by the Constitution.

During the same period and under the same conditions, the Government may also adopt measures, in all matters, which it may deem necessary to the life of the nation, the protection of citizens or the safeguarding of liberties.

APPENDIX III

West African Members of French National Assembly Under the Fourth Republic and their French Parliamentary Groups *

*app. = apparenté   n.p. = no party

Territory	ANC I 21 October 1945	ANC II 2 June 1946	1st Legislature 10 November 1946	2nd Legislature 17 June 1951	3rd Legislature 2 January 1956[10]
Senegal	Lamine Guèye,[1] SFIO Senghor,[2] SFIO	Lamine Guèye,[1] SFIO Senghor,[2] SFIO	Lamine Guèye, SFIO Senghor, SFIO, IOM	Senghor, IOM Abbas Guèye, IOM	Senghor, IOM *app.* MRP Dia, IOM *app.* MRP
Mauretania			H-O Babana, SFIO, *app.* UDSR	Mokhtar, URAS	Mokhtar, MRP
Ivory Coast	Reste,[1] Rad. Houphouët-Boigny,[2] RDA, URR	Schock,[1] *app.* MRP Houphouët-Boigny,[2] URR	Houphouët-Boigny, URR, *app.* UDSR Kabore-Zinda,[5] URR Coulibaly, URR, *app.* UDSR	Houphouët-Boigny, RDA, *app.* UDSR Sanogo, *app.* MRP	Houphouët-Boigny, RDA *app.* UDSR Coulibaly, RDA *app.* UDSR[9]
Upper Volta[3]			Guissou, IOM[3] Nazi Boni, IOM M. Ouédraogo, IOM	Guissou, IOM Conombo, IOM Nazi Boni, IOM M. Ouédraogo, IOM	G. K. Ouédraogo, *app.* RS Nazi Boni, IOM *app.* MRP Conombo, NP Guissou, NP
Soudan	Kaouza,[1] UDSR	Lattes,[1] MRP	Sissoko, SFIO Silvandre, SFIO Konaté, URR, *app.* UDSR	Sissoko, SFIO Konaté, RDA *app.* UDSR Silvandre, SFIO Dicko, SFIO	Konaté,[7] RDA *app.* UDSR Bocoum, RDA *app.* UDSR Keita, RDA *app.* UDSR Sissoko, SFIO Dicko, SFIO
Niger	Sissoko,[2] URR	Sissoko,[2] URR	Diori, URR, *app.* UDSR	Condat, UDSR Zodi, IOM	Diori, RDA *app.* UDSR Condat, UDSR

APPENDIX III (contd)

West African Members of French National Assembly Under the Fourth Republic and their French Parliamentary Groups

*app. = apparenté   n.p. = no party

Territory	ANC I 21 October 1945	ANC II 2 June 1946	1st Legislature 10 November 1946	2nd Legislature 17 June 1951	3rd Legislature 2 January 1956[10]
Guinea	Chevance,[1] UDSR	Ferracci,[1] SFIO	Y. Diallo, SFIO	Y. Diallo,[6] SFIO	Touré, RDA app. UDSR
	Y. Diallo,[2] SFIO	Y. Diallo,[2] SFIO	Sano, URR, IOM	Liurette, SFIO	S. Diallo, RDA app. UDSR
				Sano, IOM	Diawadou, Rad.[8]
				Diawadou, Rad.	
Dahomey	R. P. Bertho,[1] MRP	R. P. Bertho,[1] MRP	Apithy, SFIO, IOM	Apithy, app. Ind. Rep.	Apithy, app. IPAS
	Apithy,[2] SFIO	Apithy,[2] SFIO Voting with Togo[4]		Maga, IOM	Maga, IOM app. MRP

[1] First college of citizens.
[2] Second college of subjects.
[4] Voted with Togo Nov. 1945-6.
[5] d. June 1947; not replaced.
[7] d. 1956; replaced by Bocoum.
[8] Edgar Faure wing of Rad.

[3] Elections held 27 June 1948.
[6] d. 1954; replaced by Diawadou.
[9] d. Sept. 1958; not replaced.

[10] In office until birth of the organs of the Community under the Fifth Republic in April 1959. The exceptions were the deputies of Guinea who left the National Assembly when Guinea became independent in September 1958.

APPENDIX IV

Party Strength in the French National Assembly Under the Fourth Republic

Election Date	CP	SFIO	MRP	Party Groups Rad.	UDSR	Cons.	RPF	Others	Total
21.10.45	161	150	150	28	29	64		4	586
2.6.46	153	129	169	32	21	67		15	586
10.11.46	183	105	167	43	27	71		22	618
17.6.51	101	107	96	76	19	98	120	10	627
2.1.56	150	100	80	87		97	RS Pouj 22 52 + 3	5	596

Sources:

The first three from Wright, op. cit., p. 262; the fourth from Williams, op. cit., p. 447; the fifth from Campbell, *French Electoral Systems and Elections 1789–1957*, op. cit., p. 125, supplemented by the official lists of 1956.

The Franchise: Voters Registered (R)

Territory	I. Referendum 21 Oct. 1945		II. Election 21 Oct. 1945		III. Referendum 5 May 1946		IV. Election 2 June 1946	
	R.	V.	R.	V.	R.	V.	R.	V.
Senegal	44,292a	26,732a	44,292a	26,695 a	46,075a	31,930a	46,985a	32,753a
		1st quest. 25,772 yes 332 no				28,975 yes 2,666 no		
Mauretania		2nd quest. 12,790 yes 13,280 no	25,188b	20,376b			28,461b	21,281b
Ivory Coast	3,646a	2,730a	3,646a	2,990a	3,836a	1,920a	4,271a	2,674a
		1st quest. 2,420 yes 194 no				768 yes 1,099 no		
Upper Volta		2nd quest. 1,782 yes 812 no	31,384b	25,835b			37,888b	23,994b
Soudan	3,243a	2,573a	3,243a	2,578a	3,314a	1,923a	3,484a	2,148a
		1st quest. 2,404 yes 74 no				883 yes 958 no		
Niger		2nd quest. 2,107 yes 356 no	33,626b	27,014b			36,714b	25,500b
Guinea	1,944a	1,429a	1,944a	1,418a	1,910a	1,022a	2,098a	1,342a
		1st quest. 1,318 yes 26 no				491 yes 500 no		
		2nd quest. 1,090 yes 243 no	16,233b	12,829b			22,522b	18,492b
Dahomey[2]	1,279a	1,068a	1,279a	1,103a	1,502a	852a	1,577a	833a
		1st quest. 1,006 yes 27 no				373 yes 463 no		
		2nd quest. 945 yes 83 no	11,599b	9,057b	11,962		11,962b	9,069b

Including Togo

a First college French 'citizens'.
b Second college French 'subjects'.

[1] All election figures are for National Assembly, except those for 1947, which are for elections for the territorial assemblies. Figures given refer to the first ballot. Only first college 'citizens' voted in the referenda.
[2] Dahomey–Togo voted together until November 1946.
[3] Elections were held 27 June 1948; figures taken from J.O.A.N., *Débats*, 22 March 1949.
[4] Percentage of those registered voting.

V

and Voting (V) in French West Africa, 1945–57[1]

V. Referendum 13 Oct. 1946		VI. Election 10 Nov. 1946		VII. Election 17 June 1951		VIII. Election 2 Jan. 1956		IX. Election 31 March 1957	
R.	V.	R.	V.	R.	V.	R.	V.	R.	V.[4]
53,859a	30,911a	192,861	130,691	665,280	316,166	835,035	457,014	1,063,946	54·6
	28,278 yes 2,557 no	16,271	9,539	135,586	52,181	217,717	127,480	376,017	71·7
4,442a	2,305a	187,904	127,670	189,154	111,287	890,515	586,654	1,482,862	54·9
	668 yes 1,612 no	140,339a	87,318	334,149	251,138	978,087	633,965	1,904,658	51·6
3,749a	1,921a	160,464	95,243	916,944	340,207	1,075,640	438,502	2,090,048	33·9
	859 yes 1,029 no	57,276	26,159	94,968	56,594	697,488	311,361	1,234,914	28·6
2,310a	1,235a	131,309	96,099	393,628	224,182	976,662	569,319	1,376,048	55·6
	563 yes 652 no								
1,697a	806a	57,153	33,573	332,867	147,350	384,643	182,430	673,058	43·3
	212 yes 568 no								

Sources:
I–VI: Le Monde, ed., *Élections et referendums*, 1946, op. cit., pp. 248–52; ibid., des 13 oct., 10 et 24 nov. et 8 dec. 1946, Le Monde, Paris, 1947, pp. 238–41.
VII: *Les Élections législatives du 17 juin 1951*. La Documentation Française, Paris, 1951.
VIII: Unpublished manuscript from Direction des Affaires Politiques, Gouvernement Général, Dakar, 1956.
IX: *AOF 1957*, op. cit., pp. 36–7.

APPENDIX VI

A. REFERENDA, 1945-1946

Dates	Electorate of Overseas France			Total Metropolitan and Overseas Electorate		
	Registered	Voting	Valid Votes	Registered	Voting	Valid Votes
Referendum 21 Oct. 1945	1,122,130	699,701	quest. 1 626,878 yes / 28,464 no	25,744,992	20,353,985	quest. 1 18,584,746 yes / 699,136 no
			quest. 2 477,061 yes / 177,694 no			quest. 2 12,794,943 yes / 6,449,206 no
Election 21 Oct. 1945	2,752,572	1,623,284	1,589,159	27,375,434	21,280,887	20,778,958
Referendum 5 May 1946	1,172,297	671,967	344,263 yes / 311,773 no	25,829,425	20,567,378	9,454,034 yes / 10,584,359 no
Election 2 June 1946	2,837,258	1,630,699	1,603,503	27,534,207	21,845,899	21,484,244
Referendum 13 Oct. 1946	1,238,733	599,217	258,438 yes / 335,090 no	26,311,643	17,792,008	9,297,470 yes / 8,165,459 no
Election 10 Nov. 1946	3,506,489	1,922,258	1,898,217	28,559,422	21,487,955	21,101,287

Source:
Le Monde, ed., *Élections et referendums*, 1946, op. cit., p. 260; ibid., 1947, op. cit., p. 252.
Second college voters for members of the Constituent Assemblies did not vote in referendum; this accounts for the difference of more than a million voters registered between referendum and election. Note that this difference is about equal to the margin defeating the April Constitution, and adopting the October Constitution.

B. REFERENDUM ON THE CONSTITUTION
FIFTH REPUBLIC, 28 SEPTEMBER 1958

Territories	Registered	Voting	Yes	No
Senegal	1,110,823	893,251	870,362	21,901
Mauretania	382,870	322,451	302,018	19,126
Soudan	2,142,266	972,197	945,586	23,875
Ivory Coast	1,636,533	1,596,610	1,595,286	216
Dahomey	775,170	431,407	418,963	9,246
Guinea	1,408,500	1,203,875	56,981	1,136,324
Niger	1,320,174	493,953	372,383	102,395
Upper Volta	1,914,908	1,431,167	1,415,651	11,687

Source:

Outre-mer 1958, op. cit., p. 45.

APPENDIX VII

Area and Population, AOF[1]

Territory	Area[2] (sq. km.)	Europeans[2]	Africans[2]	Total[2]
AOF Total	4,634	88.2	18,982	19,070
Senegal	197	48.6	2,270	2,319
Soudan	1,204	7.4	3,701	3,708
Guinea	246	9.5	2,482	2,491
Ivory Coast	322	11.6	2,471	2,483
Dahomey	116	2.8	1,710	1,713
Niger	1,189	3.0	2,412	2,415
Mauretania	1,086	1.6	614	615
Upper Volta	274	3.7	3,322	3,326

[1] Source: *Outre-mer 1958*, op. cit., p. 78. Later statistical samples suggest these official figures may underestimate by 25 per cent.
[2] In thousands.

APPENDIX VIII

The Social Background of Some French-Speaking West African Political Leaders

INTRODUCTORY COMMENTS

The following data were gathered during a field trip in 1956. There was no time for the questionnaire method. The data come from usually reliable members of each organization studied. In spite of the goodwill of my informants it is possible that errors have crept in, especially about age and status in traditional society. Moreover time limits and the existence of a tense political climate in some territories mean the data are incomplete. I present them in spite of their limitations, with the caution that they allow only rough, not detailed generalizations.

Of the members of the territorial assemblies only the second colleges were studied. The full names of parties are given in Appendix XII. 'Ex-RDA' refers to men elected on an RDA list who left the party during the repression. RR refers to the railway employees important in the trade union movement. Among my original categories was 'veteran'. It turned out to be irrelevant at the level of territorial leaders. Veterans of French armed services, mostly non-commissioned, often went back to the village. Their political role must be studied at the local level.

'Teachers' refers to secondary and normal school graduates as well as monitors who graduated only from primary school. 'African doctors' are graduates of Ponty secondary school. Doctors trained at a university are listed as 'MD'. It was easier to label a man Muslim or Catholic than to define the label. Some recorded as Muslims adhere to animist practices and beliefs. Some recorded as Catholics have several wives.

No more than a handful of women played active political roles at the territorial level. None were members of territorial assemblies. Occasionally, as in Guinea or the Ivory Coast, they were members of party executives, but only in the formal sense. Yet they were very active at the local level. It seems that, with a few exceptions such as Mme. Ouëzzin Coulibaly in the Ivory Coast and Upper Volta, educated women were either unwilling or unable to make direct contact with the mass of the population.

The category 'chiefs' perhaps hides more than it shows. I recorded as my informants designated. In parts of Niger, Upper Volta, Mali, and Guinea, where large pre-European states existed, my informants agreed that they ascribed 'chiefly' origins to those who had a traditional claim and to those who were simply members of the *commandement indigène*. On the whole there the two categories overlapped. But in those parts of the Ivory Coast, Guinea, Upper Volta, and Senegal where pre-European political units were often small, traditional chieftaincy existed only at the village level, and was frequently not hereditary. Hence when my informants said a man was of chiefly origin they frequently meant nothing more than that there was a connexion, within living memory, with a village chief, or with a member of the *commandement indigène* in an area where there were no aristocrats by tradition.

A. IVORY COAST

Members of the 1947–52 and 1952–7 territorial assembly; Members of the RDA (PDCI) executive who were not also élus, *1950–6; Members of the full RDA territorial executive, including territorial councillors and* parlementaires, *(1956)*

	1947–52 TA[17]	1952–7 TA	RDA Exec. 1950–6	RDA Exec. All 1956
Total	27	32[10]	10	36
Religion				
Muslim	9	12	2	12
Catholic	18	14	8	23
European		4		
Animist		2		1
Party[15]				
RDA	13	19	10[14]	36
ex-RDA	12[1]	5		
Others	2[2]	4		
European		4		
Education				
University			1	2
Ponty	21[16]	14	5	19
EPS—Upper Primary	2	7	2	10
CEP—Lower Primary	3	2	2	3
Literate		4		2
Illiterate		1		
Europeans		4		
Profess. School	1			
Profession				
Teacher[3]	7	6[12]		6
Clerks, govt.	8	6	5	11
African Doctor	6	5	1	4
MD				1
RR worker	2	2		2
Lawyer			1	1
Pharmacist	1			1
Business Clerk	1	1		1
Timber Merchant	1			
Planter-trader	1	7[13]		6
Housewife			2	2
Chief		1		
European		4[11]		
Poet			1	1
Ethnic Origin				
Baule	3	4	2	7
Malinke	3[4]	6[4]	3[5]	6[4, 6]
Fulani	2[5]	2[5]		3[5]
Agni	3	1	2	3
Senoufo	1	1		1
Bete	2	3		3

	1947–52 TA[17]	1952–7 TA	PDCI Exec. 1950	PDCI Exec. All 1956
Ethnic Origin				
Kulango	1	1		
Samogo	1[6]	1[6]		1[6]
Bobo		1[6]		
Wolof	1[7]	1[7]		
Toucouleur		1[7]		1[7]
Mulatto	1	1	1	2
Apollonian (W. Zima)	1		1	2
Abrong		1		
Neyo	2			
Abure		1	1	2
Krumen	1			
Bambara				2[6]
Yacouba	1	1		1
Dioula	1			
Ebrie	1			
Alladien		1		1
Abey	1	1		
European		4		
Creole	1[8]			1[8]
Ethnic Status				
Chief's Family[9]	9	14	6	11
Commoner	18	13	4	25
Griot		1		
European		4		

[1] Of the 12, 4 were clerks, 4 teachers, 3 African doctors, and 1 a timber merchant from Senegal. Therefore 11 depended on government service for their salaries.
[2] Both Agni.
[3] Plus 2 former teachers in 1951, listed here as government clerk and planter; 1 former teacher in 1956 listed as planter.
[4] 1 a 'stranger' from Guinea.
[5] 1 a 'stranger' from Soudan.
[6] 1 a 'stranger' from Upper Volta.
[7] 1 a 'stranger' from Senegal.
[8] 1 a 'stranger' from Dahomey.
[9] Includes village chiefs and many without traditional titles.
[10] 12 were re-elected.
[11] 1 planter, 1 engineer, 1 journalist, 1 administrator.
[12] 1 teacher in a private school.
[13] 5 have Ponty or EPS-level education, but left the civil service to become planters.
[14] 2 are women, wives of RDA leaders.
[15] The concept of RDA membership became complicated because of the repression. There are the 'martyrs', the 'hard' members, 'soft' members, and ex-members. The 'neo'-RDA are those who were not involved in the repression.
[16] 20 of the 21 were elected on the RDA unity ticket.
[17] The Upper Volta representatives, who sat during 1947–8, are not included.

B. MALI (Soudan)
Members[1] of the 1947–52 territorial assembly

	TA 1947–52		TA 1947–52
Total	28[11]	*Education*	
Average Age	49	Ponty	10
Religion		EPS Terrasson	5
Muslim	27[2]	EPS Katibougou	1
Animist	1[3]	Primary	6
Party		Unknown	6
PSP	22[4]	*Ethnic Origin*	
RDA	5[5]	Sarakole	5
Independent	1[6]	Fulani	5
Profession		Bambara	4
Chef de canton	8[7]	Malinke	3
Government Clerk	8	Songhai	2
Teacher	6	Dogon	1
Business Clerk	3[8]	Toucouleur	1
African Doctor	2	Unknown	7
Trader	1	*Ethnic Status*	
		Family of Chiefs	10
		Family of Marabouts	2[9]
		Commoner	9[10]
		Unknown	7

[1] My information is complete only for 21 members.
[2] Including a former Christian.
[3] Fily-Dabo Sissoko PSP, calls himself animist first and Muslim second.
[4] Including a Dogon chief who later supported the regional *Union Dogon*.
[5] Including a Bambara representative from Segou, elected on a PSP ticket.
[6] A Bambara chief from Kayes.
[7] Including 2 former teachers.
[8] 1 former government clerk.
[9] Including the Imam of Mopti.
[10] Including all 5 RDA.
[11] Two seats were vacant in 1951.

C. UPPER VOLTA
Members of the 1948-52, and 1952-7 territorial assembly

	TA 1948-52	TA 1952-7		TA 1948-52	TA 1952-7
Total	40	40[6]	*Profession*		
Average Age	45	46	Nurse		3
Religion			Interpreter	2	2
			Teacher	10	5
Muslim	9	1[8]	Veterinary Officer	2	3
Catholic[2]	18	24	Agricultural Officer	1	
Animist	11	13	Farmer		1
Protestant	1	1	Business Clerk	1	
European[1]	1	1	None	1	2
Party			Trade Unionist		2
UV	24	23	Veteran		1
ex-RDA	8[3]	1	European[1]	1	1
RDA	6	1[4]	*Ethnic Origin*		
Lobi (ethnic)	1		Mossi	15	21 [7]
Dorange (later			Fulani	5	1
MDV)	1	6	Bobo	6	5
MPEA		10	Gourounssi	3	2
Education			Lobi	2	3
University		1	Gourmanche	2	3
Ponty	12	7	Boussanga	2	1
EPS Upper Primary	18	13	Fulani-Mossi	1	
CEP Lower Primary	3	6	Djerma (Sonrai)	1	
Literate	1	3	Samogo	1	2
Illiterate	4	5[5]	Gouin	1	1
Mission Schools	1	3	European[1]	1	1
Professional School		1	*Ethnic Status*		
European[1]	1	1	Family of Chief	18	16
Profession			Commoner	19	21
Government Clerk	16	11	Captive	1	1
Doctor, MD		1	Blacksmith	1	1
Chief	6	8	European[1]	1	1

[1] Dorange, former army officer and trader.

[2] Ranging from members who were merely baptized to practising Catholics. One chief counts his wives by the score.

[3] 4 were chiefs or their close relations.

[4] An ex-RDA man who returned to the RDA as a result of pressure from his constituents in Banfora.

[5] Chiefs, their representatives, and one army veteran on a pension.

[6] Only 14 of the members in 1951 were re-elected.

[7] The rise was in part from among the Mossi supporters of the Yatenga Naba, organized by Dorange.

[8] The fall in Muslims and rise in Catholics was linked with the rise in Mossi and fall in Fulani and Djerma, who were RDA and eliminated during the 1952 elections.

D. NIGER

Members of the 1947–52, and 1952–7, territorial assembly;
Members of the territorial executive of the RDA (PPN) of 1956

	Niger 1947–52 TA	Niger 1952–7 TA	Niger RDA Exec.
Total	20	24 [8]	31
Average Age	46	48	40
Religion			
Muslim	20	24	31
Animist			
Catholic			
Protestant			
Parties	15 UNIS 3 RDA 2 ex-RDA	All 24 UNIS	All 31 in RDA
Profession			
Government Clerk	8	10	15
Teacher	2	3	2
Nurse		2	
Agricultural Officer	1	1	
Parlementaire [1]		1	
African Doctor	1	1	
Chief	6	2	
Notable		3	
European		1	
Interpreter	2		
Veterinary Officer			3
Petty Trader			3
Marabout			2
Farmer			2
Tailor			1
Chauffeur			1
On pension			2
Education			
Baccalaureat		1	
Ponty	5 [7]	2	3
EPS Upper Primary	4	12	10
CEP Lower Primary	5	2	4
Literate	3 [2]	6	2
Literate in Arabic			2
Vocational School			1
Illiterate	3		9
European		1 [3]	
Ethnic Origin			
Hausa	3	3	1
Goberawa	3	1	
Djerma (Sonrai)	2	3	11 [5]
Beriberi	2	2	
Tuareg	1		
Daura	1		
Sonrai	1	5	9
Maduri	1		2
Daghira	1		
Bambara	1		1

	1947–52 TA	1952–7 TA	RDA Exec.
Ethnic Origin			
Targi	2	1	
Fulani	2	4[4]	3[4]
Kelgres			1
Soudie		2	
Sarakole			2
European		1	
Mulatto		1	
Wolof (Senegal)		1	
Gouroussi			1
Ethnic Status			
Family of Chief	14	15	9[6]
Family of Marabouts			3
Commoner	6	9	18
Lower Caste			1

[1] No other profession.
[2] One from the *École des Fils des Chiefs*.
[3] Education unknown.
[4] One Soudanese Fulani.
[5] 5 rivals to the chiefs holding office.
[6] 1 Djerma 'captive' nobleman.
[7] 4 out of the 5 Ponty men were RDA or ex-RDA.
[8] Not *one* member of the 1947–51 territorial assembly was re-elected.

E. SENEGAL

Members of the 1946–52, and 1952–7 territorial assembly (TA);
Members of BDS executive, 1956; Members of SFIO executive, 1956

	1946–52 TA	1952–7 TA	BDS Élus	BDS Branch Leaders	Total BDS Exec. 1956	SFIO Exec. 1956
Total	50[1]	50[21]	39[17]	46[18]	85	54[22]
Average Age	50	42[11]	40	40	40	52[27]
Religion						
Muslim	28	38	28	40	68	49
Catholic	22[2]	12[12]	11	6	17	2
Unknown						3
Party						
SFIO	32	9[13]				54
ex-SFIO/BDS	17[3]	41				
BDS			39	46	85	
Others	1[4]					
Education						
University	9	6	5	5	10	3[13]
Lycée	3	2	2	1	3	
Ponty	9	16	14	13	27	9
EPS Upper Primary	2	10	5	7	12	7
CEP Lower Primary	1	9	7	10	17	
Literate	2	3	1	5	6	3
Illiterate				2	2	1
Vocational Schools				2	2	
Alford Veterinary[5]	3					3
Unknown	21[6]		3	1	4	28
Europeans		4	2		2	
Profession						
Trader	13[7]	4	4	3	7	2
Teacher	8	15	12	14	26	2
Lawyer	6[8]	6[13]	3	1	4	3[13]
Government Clerk	4	6	5	11	16	10[25,26]
Business Clerk	4	2		4	4	1
Municipal Employee	3[9]					4[23]
Journalist	2					
Veterinary Doctor	3	1				3
European Businessman	2	3[15]	2[19]		2	
Crop Inspector[10]	1	3	3		3	
Professor	1	1	1	2	3	
African Doctor	1	2	2	2	4	4
RR Employee	1	3[14]	3[14]	3	6	3
Pharmacist	1		1	1	2	
Farmer		1				
Nurse		1	1		1	
Bailiff		1	1		1	1
Veterinary Officer		1	1		1	
Co-op. Director				1	1	
Printer				1	1	
None				1	1	

	1946–52 TA	1952–7 TA	BDS Élus	BDS Branch Leaders	Total BDS Exec. 1956	SFIO Exec. 1956
Profession						
MD				1	1	
Veterinary Nurse				1	1	
Housewife						2[24]
Chief						1
Workers						2
Unknown						16
Ethnic Origin						
Wolof	16	12[16]	9[16]	24[20]	33	15
Mulatto	7	4	5	1	6	
Lebou	6	6	1	8[20]	9	9
European	6	4	2		2	1
Toucouleur	4	11	11	3	14	8
Serere	4	4	4	3	7	
Mandiaque	1			1	1	
West Indian	1					
Diola	1	3	3	3	6	
Fulani		2	2	2	4	
Portuguese Creole				1	1	
Unknown	4	4	2		2	21
Pre-war Status						
Pre-war Citizen	35					23
Pre-war 'Subject'	7					4
Unknown	8					27
Ethnic Status						
Mulatto/European	13	8	7	1	8	1
Family of Chiefs	1	2	4	1	5	7
Griots		1	1	4	5	
Shoemaker				1	1	
Jeweller	1	1	1	1	2	2
Marabout Family						4[29]
Commoner	35	34	26	38	64	
Unknown		4				35
Citizen 'bourgeois'[28]						5

[1] 7 had been in the pre-war *conseil coloniale*.
[2] Including 6 Europeans.
[3] Of the 17, 10 were Catholic, 5 Mulatto, 1 European, 2 Toucouleur, 2 Wolof, 2 Lebou, 2 Serere, 1 Diola, 2 unknown.
[4] A European supporter of the RDA.
[5] The French school for veterinary doctors at Alford.
[6] All 21 were literate, but where they were educated was unknown to my informants; most in this group were not natives of Senegal.
[7] 1 was a Mulatto ship-owner.
[8] 1 European; 2 Mulatto.
[9] 1 mayor; 1 municipal secretary; 1 municipal agent.
[10] Of groundnuts.
[11] Average age for 9 SFIO, 52; for 41 others, 40.
[12] Including 4 Europeans.
[13] Including 1 European.
[14] Including the leader of the RR trade union.
[15] 1 RR manager; 1 factory owner; 1 trader.
[16] 1 Wolof-Sarakole.

[17] 37 Territorial Assembly members (of these 26 were natives of their electoral districts); and 2 *parlementaires*: 1 European administrator; 1 Mulatto pharmacist (indirectly elected).

[18] 8 from the BDS youth movement, MJBDS.

[19] 1 Administrator; 1 businessman.

[20] The rise is because Dakar and Saint-Louis are Socialist strongholds, and therefore many BDS leaders from the cities are not *élus*.

[21] 15 from 1946–52 Assembly were re-elected.

[22] 8 were territorial councillors.

[23] Including a former teacher.

[24] Representing women.

[25] 1 representing Socialist Youth.

[26] 1 representing FO trade unions in the *Conseil Économique*.

[27] Based on 31 known ages.

[28] This category was used by my SFIO informant.

[29] 2 from key Muslim Mouride families.

F. GUINEA

Members of the 1947–52 Territorial Assembly (incomplete; 16 out of total 24 in second college)

	1947–52 TA
Total	16
Average Age	46
Religion	
Muslim	13
Animist	3
Profession	
Teacher	5
Chief	4
Business clerk	3
Government clerk	2
Agricultural officer	1
Lawyer	1
Education	
Paris	1
Ponty	6
EPS	7[1]
CEP	1
Literate	1
Ethnic Origin	
Fulani	7
Soussou	3
Malinke	3
Toma	1
Baga	1
Koranko	1
Party	
A.G.V.	4[3]
Union Basse Guinée	3[6]
Entente Guinéenne	4[4]
Union Mandingue	2
Socialiste-Rénovation	1[5]
Union Forestière	2[2]
RDA	1
Ethnic Status	
Family of chiefs	12
Commoners	4

[1] 5 in Conakry and 2 at Katibougou.
[2] Including one forest chief who had been RDA.
[3] Fulani group calling itself Socialist, but opposed to Yacine Diallo, who was Socialist in Parliament.
[4] Including pro-Diallo Fulani, who called themselves Socialist and opposed AGV.
[5] Including anti-Diallo inhabitants of the lower region of Guinea.
[6] Including pro-Diallo inhabitants of the lower region of Guinea.

APPENDIX IX
French West African Cities, 1916–56
Total Population

	1916 (units)	1936 (units)	1945 (units)	1950 (units)	1955–6 (thousands)	Non-African Population 1955–6 (units)
Senegal						
Dakar	19,800	92,000	132,000	250,000	234.8	34,013
Rufisque	12,600	20,000	43,000	34,000	39.8	2,680
Saint-Louis	22,800	33,100	51,000	60,000	37.1	1,281
Kaolack	1,500	40,000	30,000	38,500	48.4	1,587
Thies	3,000	16,300	24,000	38,700	42.1	2,997
Diourbel	2,200	16,000	13,000	14,300	20.6	555
Louga	1,500	4,400	12,000	15,200	13.2	366
Ziguinchor	1,500	8,000	10,000	16,100	22.4	407
Soudan						
Bamako	8,700	22,500	37,000	—	62.9	3,579
Kayes	5,800	12,500	19,000	24,000	19.6	387
Segou	7,300	7,700	14,000	15,500	17.4	439
Sikasso	7,800	11,900	13,000	19,600	13.6	70
Mopti	3,532[3]	3,800	—	—	12.7	176
Mauretania						
Tidjikdja	—	—	6,000	5,900	6.0	6
Kaedi	—	3,200	5,000	6,900	8.5	25
Atar	—	4,600	3,000	5,300	4.7	150
Guinea						
Conakry	7,100	13,600	26,000	38,100	34.8[1]	2,970
Mamou	—	3,900	—	—	5.1	326
Kankan	7,200	9,800	14,000	18,400	24.6	450
Siguiri	6,016[3]	7,400	11,000	11,100	11.4	26
Labe	—	9,000	11,000	10,600	11.8	152
Nzerekore	—	—	—	—	10.8	287
Kindia	4,526[3]	7,600	7,000	12,100	13.0	432

Total Population

	1916 (units)	1936 (units)	1945 (units)	1950 (units)	1955–6 (thousands)	Non-African Population 1955–6 (units)
Ivory Coast						
.Abidjan	700	17,500	46,000	86,400	127.6	8,553
.Grand-Bassam	3,000	4,900	—	8,600	9.7	340
.Bouake	3,600	3,300	22,000	32,800	42.1	917
Korhogo	4,978[3]	—	—	—	13.2	104
Agboville	—	5,300	7,000	7,600	7.5	557
Mankono	1,550[3]	—	7,000	7,000	7.4	198
Upper-Volta						
.Bobo-Dioulasso	—	10,000	28,000	39,000	41.7	1,617
.Ouagadougou	—	14,200	18,000	29,800	31.7	1,105
Koudougou	—	15,900	19,000	15,900	8.8[2]	84
Ouahigouya	—	—	—	7,000[4]	8.7	86
Dahomey						
.Porto-Novo	20,000	23,500	29,000	28,800	31.5	490
.Cotonou	2,500	6,500	19,000	19,800	57.9	1,428
.Ouidah	10,500	10,500	14,000	13,900	14.0	83
.Abomey	12,000	11,300	12,000	16,800	18.9	69
.Parakou	—	—	—	—	5.7	225
Niger						
.Niamey	—	5,000	7,000	9,400	17.2	1,374
.Zinder	5,851[3]	10,500	12,000	13,000	13.3	504
Tahoua	8,662[2]	12,600	12,000	10,900	12.4	59
Maradi	6,539[3]	8,100	8,000	8,900	10.1	222

EE2

[1] In 1958, 52,256 inhabitants, including 4,856 Europeans. *Paris–Dakar*, 9 April 1958.
[2] With surrounding villages—20,000 in 1955.
[3] In 1921.
[4] In 1948.

Key:
    Dot (.) = *Commune de plein exercise* (1957).

Sources:
    Service Statistique d'AOF, 1956; *Outre-Mer 1958*, op. cit., pp. 80–1.

APPENDIX X[1]

African Trade Union Members in French West Africa
(One third of wage earners)

Territories	1952 Sector		1953 Sector		1954 Sector		1955 Sector	
	Public	Private	Public	Private	Public	Private	Public	Private
Senegal	1,315	34,520	3,030	43,525	5,345	49,120	5,500	50,200
Mauretania	400	500	450	550	450	600	530	700
Guinea	1,000	2,000	1,000	3,600	4,000	15,000	4,300	40,000
Ivory Coast	2,435	7,417	5,087	9,305	5,490	12,215	6,960	14,670
Dahomey	6,045	5,923	6,711	6,179	8,485	8,777	8,740	9,061
Upper Volta	1,251	1,700	1,426	3,260	1,187	4,162	1,224	4,704
Soudan	540	875	780	1,110	930	1,590	5,666	12,678
Niger							980	1,600
Total AOF	12,986	52,935	18,484	67,529	25,887	91,464	33,900	133,613[a]

Wage Earners—Totals

Territories	1957 Africans and Europeans			1947	
	Public	Private	Total	Africans	Europeans
Senegal	20,750	79,550	100,300	71,301	9,563
Mauretania	3,050	1,750	4,800	2,511	86
Guinea	15,600	93,800	109,400	35,206	759
Ivory Coast	28,000	143,000	171,000[b]	76,629	1,169
Dahomey	8,125	13,900	22,000	12,046	421
Upper Volta	11,700	12,850	24,500	[d]	[d]
Soudan	15,560	26,200	41,800	29,028	619
Niger	6,375	7,200	13,600	4,945	58
Total AOF	109,160	378,250	487,400[c]	231,666	12,675

[1] Sources:
Inspection de Travail, Dakar, June 1956.
Annuaire Statistique., tome ii, 1951, op. cit., pp. 409–10; *Outre-mer 1958*, op. cit., pp. 207–10.
These figures are only estimates.

[a] 150,000 in 1957.
[b] Including 90,000 agricultural workers.
[c] In 1954, 372,547, including 20,034 Europeans and of these ⅓ worked in the public sector.
[d] Figures included in Ivory Coast.

APPENDIX XI

Foreign Trade per Territory in French West Africa—1944-58

Units: (A) = *quantity* in thousands of tons.
(B) = *value* in millions of francs CFA.

(a) Including Upper Volta.
(b) Dahomey and Niger.

IMPORTS

A. Quantity

Years	Senegal Soudan Mauretania	Guinea	Ivory Coast	Upper Volta	Dahomey	Niger	Total
1944	233	9	17 (a)		12	4	275
1945	299	8	25 (a)		10	3	345
1946	300	26	35 (a)		24	11	396
1947	457	43	65 (a)		24	6	595
1948	481	43	108 (a)		37	9	678
1949	613	78	153 (a)		63	12	919
1950	671	99	222 (a)		64	14	1,070
1951	844	141	333	22	114	17	1,471
1952	671	160	352	21	103	22	1,329
1953	663	143	322	25	75	26	1,254
1954	696	135	426	25	138 (b)		1,420
1955	725	155	448	20	141 (b)		1,489
1956	769	158	476 (a)		142 (b)		1,545
1957	874	192	479	16.7	122	36.7	1,722
1958	787	276	476	17	122	39.4	1,712

B. Value

Years	Senegal Soudan Mauretania	Guinea	Ivory Coast	Upper Volta	Dahomey	Niger	Total
1944	1,718	73	177 (a)		50	59	2,077
1945	2,514	153	439 (a)		97	208	3,411
1946	4,087	484	941 (a)		266	213	5,991
1947	8,357	985	1,773 (a)		604	197	11,916
1948	12,734	1,767	3,881 (a)		1,116	343	19,841
1949	20,783	3,104	7,693 (a)		2,242	657	34,479
1950	24,437	4,166	10,675 (a)		2,137	755	42,170
1951	33,931	6,234	15,372	1,342	3,564	893	61,336
1952	32,346	6,720	15,591	1,520	3,775	1,241	61,193
1953	30,858	6,295	12,453	1,400	2,874	1,362	55,242
1954	33,689	6,482	19,340	1,291	5,645 (b)		66,447
1955	34,535	6,437	19,005	1,666	5,556 (b)		67,199
1956	34,780	6,638	19,981 (a)		5,262 (b)		66,661
1957	41,002	9,250	19,512	1,612	4,269	1,872	77,517
1958	43,774	12,999	22,827	1,800	4,323	2,298	88,021

APPENDIX XI

Foreign Trade per Territory in French West Africa—1944-58

Units: (A) = *quantity* in thousands of tons.
(B) = *value* in millions of francs CFA.

(a) Including Upper Volta.
(b) Dahomey and Niger.

EXPORTS

Years	Senegal Soudan Mauretania	Guinea	Ivory Coast	Upper Volta	Dahomey	Niger	Total
A. Quantity							
1944	163	17	71 (a)		53	8	312
1945	168	15	101 (a)		44	19	347
1946	271	23	127 (a)		31	13	465
1947	304	51	142 (a)		36	44	577
1948	389	59	224 (a)		72	49	796
1949	354	87	265 (a)		75	38	816
1950	367	89	295 (a)		75	27	853
1951	332	102	283	28	60	51	856
1952	399	155	239	22	62	69	946
1953	508	841	295	29	78	59	1,810
1954	553	1,183	310	25	140 (b)		2,211
1955	468	1,262	388	33	165 (b)		2,316
1956	593	1,421	509 (a)		202 (b)		2,725
1957	706	1,511	506	30.8	78.0	75	2,907
1958	749	701	650	38.3	98.0	105	2,331
B. Value							
1944	877	136	528 (a)		163	22	1,726
1945	1,354	157	818 (a)		148	49	2,526
1946	2,511	316	1,063 (a)		173	58	4,121
1947	4,017	840	1,934 (a)		339	366	7,496
1948	9,887	1,158	5,197 (a)		1,515	715	18,472
1949	12,889	1,663	10,269 (a)		1,881	703	27,405
1950	12,557	1,878	13,767 (a)		2,233	530	30,965
1951	13,627	2,730	17,481	798	2,810	1,257	38,703
1952	14,168	3,014	18,815	614	1,939	1,616	40,166
1953	18,443	4,025	19,085	883	2,606	1,741	46,783
1954	20,997	4,672	27,310	751	4,506 (b)		58,236
1955	16,029	5,091	25,585	940	5,501 (b)		53,146
1956	21,085	5,075	27,285 (a)		6,571 (b)		60,016
1957	24,976	5,121	24,426	897	2,447	2,601	60,468
1958	28,801	4,875	31,492	1,131	3,371	3,818	73,488

Sources:

For 1944–53 *Annuaire Statistique,* 1956, tome i, op. cit., p. 268.
For 1954 and 1955, Ivory Coast: Messmer 1955 Report, op. cit., p. 7.
Bulletin de la Statistique de la Côte d'Ivoire, Abidjan, 1955, p. 1, and its August Annex, pp. 95-7, for Upper Volta.
For 1954 and 1955, *Bulletin Statistique, Sénégal et Mauritanie,* no. 2, Saint-Louis, April 1956.
For Guinea, 1954, *Bulletin Statistique de la Guinée,* no. 5, 1955, pp. 17-8.
For the rest: *AOF* 1957, op. cit., p. 133; and *Outre-mer* 1958, op. cit., pp. 724, 732, 743, 751, 763, 772, 838.

APPENDIX XII

French West African Parties and their Leaders

This list includes the interterritorial and territorial parties of any importance, but not all the regional parties and one-man shows under their
various names. Parties which formed the territorial Government
majorities in 1962 are indicated by (G).

DAHOMEY

(1) 1945–6—*Electoral nuclei:*

Comités Électoraux [sic]:
The territorial leaders were the old town elite: Victor Patterson,
Paul Hazoumé, Azango, Père Nicoué—known as the *Conseil des
Anciens.* Local support was based on ethnic groups: e.g. the
Groupement des Fon d'Abomey. These local groups were the basis
of the UPD, BPD, and GEND.

(2) *Central and southern parties:*

BPD—*Bloc Populaire Dahoméen:* led by Justin Ahomadegbe and
Emile Poisson; created 1946; merged into UDD in 1955.

PRD—*Parti Républicain du Dahomey:* led by Sourou Migan Apithy;
founded in 1951.

UDD—*Union Démocratique Dahoméenne:* led by Justin Ahomadegbe;
absorbed BPD and UPD rump groups; created *c.* 1955, and RDA
section since 1956; dissolved by decree 10 April 1961.

(3) *Northern parties:*

GEND—*Groupement Ethnique du Nord—Dahomey:* led by Hubert
Maga and Paul Darboux; created 1951, from dissident wing of
UPD.

MDD—*Mouvement Démocratique du Dahomey:* IOM; new name,
from 1952, of GEND; led by Hubert Maga.

Défense des Intérêts Economiques: led by Paul Darboux; anti-Maga
Northern regional party; created 1956; also known as *Indépendants
du Nord.*

RDD—*Rassemblement Démocratique Dahoméen:* created in August
1957, through a merger of Maga's MDD and Darboux's independents.

UNIDAHO—*Union des Indépendants du Dahomey:* created in April
1958, when the supporters of Darboux left the RDD.

(4) *Southern one-man shows:*

MSA—*Mouvement Socialiste Africain:* created in 1957; led by Flavien
Campbell and Hyacinthe de Silva.

Indépendants des Partis Politiques: led 1951 by Quenum Possy; led 1956 by Antoine Toko.

RPF—*Rassemblement du Peuple Français:* led in 1951 by Victor d'Assomption.

CAF (nucleus)—Several members of the younger generation from the old town elite, led by Senator Emile Derlin Zinsou; merged into PPD–PFA (see p. 425).

MLN—Dahomey: intellectuals of Left-wing Catholic training; created 1959 (see p. 423).

PRSB—*Parti de la Révolution Socialiste du Benin:* founded in 1959 by intellectuals close to the PAI of Senegal, for Dahomey and Togo.

(5) *Territorial parties:*

UPD—*Union Progressiste Dahoméenne:* created 1946–7, was RDA section until 1948 when became IOM; led by same men as *Comités Electoraux,* plus Sourou Migan Apithy, Emile Derlin Zinsou, Hubert Maga; split in 1951, when PRD and GEND broke away; southern rump group merged into UDD in 1955.

FAD—*Front d'Action Démocratique:* temporary alliance, in February and March 1958, of the RDD and the UDD; the alliance was dissolved in March 1958.

PPD—*Parti Populaire du Dahomey:* founded 1959 by Emile Zinsou, briefly succeeded in merging all parties but UDD, as Apithy and Maga groups came together at first congress, November 1959.

PND—*Parti Nationaliste du Dahomey:* founded March 1960 by fusion of Apithy's PRD with the PPD.

PDU—*Parti Dahoméen de l'Unité:* created to support Maga's national ticket in the presidential elections of December 1960, to include all groups except the UDD. During crisis at end of 1963, replaced by a *parti national* led by Ahomadegbe, Maga and Apithy. (G)

GUINEA

(1) *Territorial parties and alliances:*

PPG—*Parti Progressiste de Guinée:* outgrowth of *Groupe d'Études Communistes;* forerunner of PDG; created in 1946 and dissolved in 1947.

PDG—*Parti Démocratique de Guinée:* RDA; led by Sékou Touré; built on CGT nucleus of trade unionists; founded in June 1947. (G)

UFG—*Union Franco-Guinéenne:* vaguely socialist electoral alliance; most active in 1951 elections; led by Yacine Diallo (deceased, 1954) and Albert Liurette. Dissolved *c.* 1954.

CEG—*Comité d'Entente Guinéenne:* 1951 electoral alliance, led by Mamba Sano, and grouping his supporters, the *Union de la Basse Guinée, Union Mandingue,* and the Fulani chiefs. Dissolved *c.* 1954.

BAG—*Bloc Africain de Guinée:* founded 1954; led by deputy Barry Diawadou and Keïta Koumandian; allied the rump groups of the regional parties. In 1958 briefly called *Union Progressiste de Guinée;* merged with PDG in 1958.

(2) *Ethnic and regional parties, and one-man shows:*

AGV—*Amicale Gilbert Vieillard:* born *c.* 1943, vaguely socialist political group among Fulani of Fouta Djallon; led by Mê Diallo Abdoulaye and Barry Diawadou; split between BAG and DSG in 1954.

DSG—*Démocratie Socialiste de Guinée:* MSA, founded 1954; led by Ibrahima Barry (*dit* Barry III): merged into PDG in 1958.

Union de la Basse Guinée, or *Fraternelle de la Basse Guinée,* or *Comité de la Basse Guinée:* regional political group led by Bangoura Karim and Amara Soumah; absorbed by BAG.

Foyer de la Basse Guinée: young opponents of the above, in 1953; absorbed by BAG.

Union du Mandé: Malinké ethnic group; absorbed into BAG; led by Framoï Bareté; also called *Union Mandingue;* absorbed by BAG.

Union Forestière: regional group, led by Fara Touré, and Traoré Nestor; split in three parts in 1954; PDG, BAG, and *Indépendants d'Action Sociale et Économique.*

UDSA—*Union Démocratique et Sociale Africaine:* one-man show, with pan-African programme; created in 1954 by Mê Paul Fabert. Absorbed by PDG in 1958.

IVORY COAST

(1) *1944–6 Party nuclei:*

Bloc Africain: anti-European alliance, led by Houphouët, for 1945 Abidjan municipal elections; also called *Union Républicain Antifasciste;* dissolved after elections.

Rassemblement Africain: 1946 predecessor of the RDA; contained an uneasy alliance of RDA–PDCI leaders, headed by Houphouët, and of PPCI leaders, headed by Kacou Aoulou; dissolved by the end of 1946.

Comité d'Action Patriotique de la Côte d'Ivoire: 1945 predecessor of the PPCI, led by Aoulou, and Mê Binzème.

Union Voltaïque: organization of Mossi and pro-separatist Upper Volta people in Ivory Coast, 1945–7. The creation of Upper Volta as a separate territory in 1947 ended the relevance of the *Union Voltaïque* in Ivory Coast politics; led by Zébango Pohi.

'*Six Cercles de l'Ouest':* component part of *Rassemblement Démocratique,* led by Etienne Djaument, which was the predecessor to the BDE.

(2) *Parties:*

PDCI—*Parti Démocratique de la Côte d'Ivoire:* led by Felix Houphouët-Boigny and Auguste Denise, RDA; built on *Syndicat
Agricole Africain* nucleus of planters. (G)

PPCI—*Parti Progressiste de la Côte d'Ivoire:* led by Kacou Aoulou,
1946–56; based on some Agni groups. Merged with PDCI in 1956.

Union des Indépendants de la Côte d'Ivoire: created *c.* 1949, with
administrative sponsorship, to oppose the RDA; based upon
some Baule groups from the region of Toumodi; led by N'da
Koffi. Dissolved by 1952.

Entente des Indépendants de la Côte d'Ivoire: created *c.* 1949, with
administrative sponsorship, to oppose the RDA; based upon the
Idéal d'Odienné, a Muslim organization in the north-west of
Ivory Coast; led by Sékou Sanogo. The PPCI, the *Entente* and the
Union of independents, were the bases for the *Union Française* list
on which Sékou Sanogo was elected deputy from Ivory Coast in
1951. Dissolved by 1952.

BDE—*Bloc Démocratique Eburnéen:* anti-RDA southern party, led by
Etienne Djaument; created in 1948; dissolved in 1956.

MSA or *SFIO-Socialistes:* led by Dignan Bailly; strong regionally
among the Bété in the Gagnoa region. Changed to MSA in 1957.

RPF—*Rassemblement du Peuple Français:* party of the anti-RDA
Europeans, led by Commandant André Ply. Dissolved. Most
Europeans transferred their support after 1952 to the

UDSR—*Union Démocratique et Socialiste de la Résistance*, led by MM.
Purrey and Charles Borg, Europeans favourable to the RDA.

(3) *Nuclei of African opposition to the PDCI after 1956:*

Ethnic opposition, regionally based:

MSA—led by Dignan Bailly at Gagnoa (see p. 426).

Group led by former territorial councillor Boa Amoakon at Abengourou, in opposition over old questions of 'chiefly' succession.

Muslim opposition (against animist pro-RDA Prince Adingra),
centred around the Almamy and the mosque, in Boundoukou.

Partly ethnic opposition, called RDA *Mutaciste*, by some of the
officers at the *Mutualité des Autochtones de la Côte d'Ivoire* of
Bouaké.

Regional opposition, led mostly by graduates, left wing:

FLN—*Front de Libération Noire* (Kotoko), mostly around Abidjan,
led by teacher Goh Boni.

Intérêts Économiques et Sociaux: led by lawyer Assi Camille Adam,
at Agboville.

Bloc Populaire: Daloa, among the Bété, vaguely socialist.

Vérité du Peuple: led by anti-RDA territorial councillors Germain
Diarro Gnadji, postal employee, and Arsène Usher Assouan,
lawyer; both later joined the RDA in the territorial assembly.

Action Démocratique et Sociale de la Côte d'Ivoire: founded in July 1957 by men favourable to the *Convention*, and linked with the Ivory Coast branch of the *Confédération Africaine des Travailleurs Croyants*, the Catholic trade union.

Mouvement de Libération de la Côte d'Ivoire: Adam Assi, Pres., headquarters for a while in Conakry; created in 1959; exile group.

MAURETANIA

EM—*Entente Mauritanienne:* led by Horma Ould Babana, deputy 1946–51; defeated by the officially sponsored UPM in 1951 and 1956. In 1956 Babana went into voluntary exile in Cairo and Rabat; some supporters of the *Entente* fused with UPM in 1958.

Istiqlal: sections existed in the north of Mauretania.

UPM—*Union Progressiste Mauritanienne:* led by Sidi el Mokhtar.

Jeunesse Mauritanienne: ran under *Indépendant* ticket 1956; led by Mohamed Jiddou; some members joined UPM, others went into voluntary exile in Cairo and Rabat. Succeeded by

Nahda—*An Nahda al Watenia el Mauritania:* Party of the renaissance of the Mauretanian nation; created *c.* 1958, opposed to the PRM, based on Atar; favours union with northern neighbours; outlawed on 26 October 1960.

PRM—*Parti du Regroupement Mauritanien:* enlarged governing party, successor to UPM, created after the 1958 referendum.

UNM—*Union Nationale Mauritanienne:* founded shortly before March 1959 elections by former PRM members not nominated for office; favoured links with southern neighbours. PFA.

Union Socialiste des Musulmans Mauritaniens: founded Feb. 1960 at Atar 'to work for total independence'; by Ahmed Ould Kerkoub, Sidi Ould Abass.

Hiss Chaelo—*Parti du Peuple Mauritanien:* national unity party formed December 1961. (G)

MALI (SOUDAN)

(1) *Nuclei of parties, 1945–6:*

Parti Démocratique du Soudan: built around core of *Groupe d'Études Communistes*; absorbed into US in 1946.

Bloc Soudanaise: inspired by Senegalese SFIO; nucleus of PSP; led by Jean Silvandre.

(2) *Territorial parties:*

US—*Union Soudanaise:* RDA; led by Mamadou Konaté (deceased, 1956) and Modibo Keïta; founded in 1946. (G)

PSP or PPS—*Parti Soudanais Progressiste:* MSA; founded by Fily-Dabo Sissoko in 1946; became in 1958

PRS—*Parti du Regroupement Soudanais,* PRA; dissolved 1959 and joined the US, under leadership of Fily-Dabo Sissoko.

PRS—*Parti du Rassemblement du Soudan:* Dicko rump group; wanted to prevent merger of PPS with US; included the Cadi of Timbuctu. Faded out.

(3) *Regional parties and one-man shows:*

Mouvement Socialiste de Défense des Intérêts du Soudan: dissident socialist group; led by Jean Silvandre 1955–6; in 1958, Silvandre joined the US.

Union Dogon: regional party; led by Sékou Kansai; split in 1956–7 into the two parties listed immediately below. Dissolved by arrêté 15 May 1959.

Union Populaire de Bandiagara: pro-RDA regional party; led by Sékou Kansai and Dolo Somine; joined US.

Action Dogon-Peulh: 1957 regional party; led by Hammadoun Dicko, pro-PSP.

Action Progressiste Indépendante de Défense des Intérêts Economiques du Soudan, also known as list for *Bloc Démocratique Soudanais:* regional group led by Traoré Tidiane and Diarra Thiémoko; fused in 1956 with US.

Union Démocratique Ségovienne: founded 1958; dissolved arrêté 5 February 1959; president Moussa Diarra was arrested.

PAI—(see p. 423) some trace of activity in Gao; led by Bâ Amadou Seydou, a former teacher at the École Name des Ifora among nomad tribes.

Association Arabo-Berbère; or *Association des Originaires du Sahara,* as well as *Nahda* (see Mauretania) expressed regional sentiment among nomad white minority.

NIGER

PPN—*Parti Progressiste Nigérien:* RDA; led by Boubou Hama and Hamani Diori; founded in 1946. (G)

UDN—*Union Démocratique Nigérienne:* led by Bakary Djibo, former PPN secretary-general who opposed RDA disaffiliation from the Communists in 1950; created in 1951; merged with BNA to form MSA in 1956–7.

UNIS—*Union Nigérienne des Indépendants et Sympathisants:* officially sponsored party of chiefs led by Issoufou Seydou Djermakoye, Mahamane Condat and Zodi Ikhia; created c. 1948; led by Zodi Ikhia (IOM) since 1955, when the chiefs left to form the

BNA—*Bloc Nigérien d'Action:* led by Issoufou Seydou Djermakoye and Condat; started in 1955; party of chiefs; 'merged' into MSA in 1956–7; allied with PPN in 1958. (G)

UPN—*Union Progressiste Nigérienne:* formed in 1953 by Condat; dissolved in 1955.

MSM or MSA—*Mouvement Socialiste Nigérien* or *Africain:* result of BNA and UDN fusion in 1956–7; led by Bakary Djibo. Succeeded by

Sawaba—Successor to UDN, led by Bakary Djibo in PRA and PFA since 1958; outlawed 1959.

Union pour la Communauté Franco-Africaine: PPN-BNA alliance. (G)

SENEGAL

(1) *Pre-war cliques:*

Parti Diagnist: clique led by Blaise Diagne, 1914–34.

Parti de l'Opposition: interwar clique of opponents to *Diagnists.*

Parti Dioufist: clique led by Galandou Diouf; 1934–40.

PSS—*Parti Socialiste Sénégalais:* founded by Lamine Guèye *c.* 1928; it petered out in 1945.

(2) *Territorial parties:*

Bloc Africain: post-war 1944–6 popular movement; absorbed by SFIO in 1946.

SFIO—*Section Française de l'Internationale Ouvrière—Fédération du Sénégal:* led by Lamine Guèye; founded in 1936; dissolved in 1957, and changed into

PSAS—*Parti Sénégalais d'Action Socialiste:* created in 1957; MSA, led by Lamine Guèye, Ousmane Socé Diop, Abbas Guèye.

Socialistes Unitaires: created among pro-fusion Socialists in 1956; fused into BPS.

MSUS—*Mouvement Socialiste d'Union Sénégalaise:* created among pro-fusion Socialists in 1957; led by Ousmane Socé Diop; merged into UPS in 1958.

UDS—*Union Démocratique Sénégalaise:* RDA section of Senegal from 1946–50; opposed .1950 Communist disaffiliation by RDA; expelled in July 1955 from interterritorial RDA; fused in 1956 into BPS; led by Abdoulaye Guèye, Camara Latyr, James Benoît.

BDS—*Bloc Démocratique Sénégalais:* led by Léopold Sédar Senghor and Mamadou Dia; created in 1948; changed into

BPS—*Bloc Populaire Sénégalais,* after fusion of BDS with UDS, MAC, and *Socialistes Unitaires,* in 1956; led by Senghor and Dia.

UPS—*Union Progressiste Sénégalais:* led by Lamine Guèye and Léopold Sédar Senghor; created in April 1958, out of the former BPS, PSAS, and MSUS, and in 1959, MPS. (G)

MPS—*Mouvement Populaire Sénégalais:* RDA section started in 1955; led by Doudou Guèye; dissolved 1959, when UPS organized PFA.

PAI—*Parti Africain de l'Indépendance:* created in September 1957 by extreme left wing among returned graduates; favoured immediate independence; Marxist; led by Diallo Oumar and Diop Majhmoud.

MLN—*Mouvement Africain de Libération Nationale:* created August 1958 by Catholic trained intellectuals Albert Tevoedjre and Joseph Ki Zerbo.

PRA-Sénégal—*Parti du Regroupement Africain—Sénégal:* created September 1958 by dissidents in the UPS who wanted to vote NO in referendum; included intellectuals Abdoulaye Ly and Assene Seck, former UPS and trade unionists Abdoulaye Guèye.

(3) *Regional parties and one-man shows:*

RDS—*Rassemblement Démocratique Sénégalais:* one-man show, started by Abbas Guèye in 1955; some support among Lebous; allied with SFIO in 1956; fused into PSAS in 1957.

MAC—*Mouvement Autonome de la Casamance:* regional group led by Guibril Sarr and Assane Seck; allied with SFIO in 1955–6; merged into BPS in 1956.

MFDC—*Mouvement des Forces Démocratiques de la Casamance:* regional group, merged into BDS in 1954; led by Ibou Diallo, BDS senator since 1956.

Parti Travailliste Saloum-Saloum: regional one-man show in Sine-Saloum, led by Djim Momar Guèye; returned to BDS in 1956.

Front Démocratique Thièssois: Abdul Karim Sow's regional one-man show at Thiès; allied with MPS in 1956.

PSS—*Parti de Solidarité Sénégalaise:* created in 1959 to oppose independence in the Mali federation; led by Ibrahima Seydou N'Daw, Cheikh Amadou Tidiane Sy and other Tidjanist *marabouts*; outlawed in 1959 by the UPS government.

BMS—*Bloc des Masses Sénégalaises:* founded in 1961 by Cheikh Anta Diop; one wing fused with UPS in 1963.

UPPER VOLTA

UV—*Union pour la Défense des Intérêts de la Haute Volta:* created in 1945; also called *Union Voltaïque:* led by Joseph Conombo, Henri Guissou; supported by chiefs; IOM; broke into PSEMA and MPEA in 1954.

PDV—*Parti Démocratique Voltaïque:* created in 1948; RDA; led by Djibril Vinama and Dr. Ali Barraud; strong in Bobo–Dioulasso area; 1956 merged with the PSEMA to form the PDU.

Indépendants de l'Union Française, also called *liste Évolution Voltaïque;* pro-RPF; strong among Mossi loyal to Yatenga Naba in Ouahigouya area; led by European, Michel Dorange; changed name in 1956 to

MDV—*Mouvement Démocratique Voltaïque:* led by Gerard Kango Ouëdraogo; in 1951 sponsored *liste Progressiste;* strong in Mossi Ouahigouya area; created in 1956 around Dorange's Independents; became

MRV—*Mouvement de Regroupement Voltaïque:* rump group of PRA, led by Gerard Ouëdraogo, after Conombo left PRA to join RDA and Nazi Boni left to join PFA; organized August 1959; in October 1959 Blaise Bassoleth succeeded Gerard Ouëdraogo as secretary-general.

MPEA—*Mouvement Populaire d'Évolution Africaine:* led by Nazi Boni; around area of Bobo–Dioulasso; started in 1954; part of IOM, PRA, and PFA. Succeeded by

PNV—*Parti National Voltaïque:* PFA section created by Nazi Boni and Laurent Bandaogo; outlawed by decree 7 October 1959; succeeded by
PRL—*Parti Républicain de la Liberté:* outlawed for PFA propaganda.
PSEMA—*Parti Social d'Éducation des Masses Africaines:* led by Henri Guissou and Dr. Joseph Conombo; strong in Mossi Ouagadougou area; started in 1954; part of IOM; merged in 1956 with PDV to form PDU. In 1957 the party was briefly re-established by Conombo, but without Guissou. Faded out in 1959.
PDU—*Parti Démocratique Unifié:* PDV–PSEMA union created in 1956; started by Ouëzzin Coulibaly (d. 1958), Henri Guissou, Ousmane Bâ and Djibril Vinama; became territorial section of RDA in 1957; Maurice Yameogo succeeded Coulibaly in 1958. Became in 1959
UDV—*Union Démocratique Voltaïgue.* (G)
Union des Indépendants du Pays Lobi: pre-1951 Lobi ethnic group, led by Dabiré Ditte; merged with MPEA.
RDA–Orthodoxe—One-man show, opposing PDU, formed in 1959 by Joseph Ouëdraogo.
PAP—*Parti d'Action Paysanne:* founded in March 1960; Gabriel Ouëdraogo, Pres.

INTERTERRITORIAL

RDA—*Rassemblement Démocratique Africain:* created in October 1946; led by Félix Houphouët-Boigny; territorial branches were:

Dahomey: *Union Démocratique Dahoméenne* (to 1960).
Guinea: *Parti Démocratique de Guinée* (until 1958).
Ivory Coast: *Parti Démocratique de la Côte d'Ivoire.*
Niger: *Parti Progressiste Nigérien.*
Senegal: *Mouvement Populaire Sénégalais* (to 1959).
Soudan;   *Union Soudanaise* (until 1959).
Upper Volta: *Parti Démocratique Unifié.*

IOM—*Indépendants d'Outre-mer:* created in 1948; led by Léopold Sédar Senghor; associated territorial parties were:

Dahomey: *Union Progressiste Dahoméenne.*
Guinea: No party; former deputy Mamba Sano, and former Senator Rafaél Saller, were members of IOM parliamentary groups.
Senegal: *Bloc Démocratique Sénégalais.*
Upper Volta: *Union Voltaïque:* which divided into the *Parti Social d'Éducation des Masses Africaines* and *Mouvement Populaire d'Évolution Africaine.*

CAF—*Convention Africaine:* succeeded IOM in January 1957; led by Léopold Sédar Senghor; associated parties were:

Niger: *Union Nigérienne des Indépendants et Sympathisants.*
Upper Volta: *Mouvement Populaire d'Évolution Africaine.*
Guinea: CAF. nucleus.
Dahomey: CAF. nucleus.
Ivory Coast: CAF. nucleus.

MSA—*Mouvement Socialiste Africain:* founded in January 1957; led by Lamine Guèye and Bakary Djibo; member parties were:

Dahomey: MSA.
Guinea: *Démocratie Socialiste de Guinée.*
Ivory Coast: MSA.
Niger: MSA.
Senegal: *Parti Sénégalais d'Action Socialiste.*
Soudan: *Parti Soudanais Progressiste.*

PRA—*Parti du Regroupement Africain:* founded in March 1958; led by Léopold Sédar Senghor and Lamine Guèye; united interterritorial CAF and MSA; associated territorial parties were:

Upper Volta: *Mouvement Démocratique Voltaïque.*
             Parti Social d'Éducation des Masses Africaines.
Guinea: *Bloc Africain de Guinée.*
Dahomey: *Regroupement Démocratique* ⎫
             Dahoméen   ⎬ Briefly united in *Parti*
             Parti Républicain du   ⎭ *Populaire du Dahomey.*
             Dahomey
Senegal: *Union Progressiste Sénégalaise.*
Soudan: *Parti du Regroupement Soudanais,* dissolved July 1959.

PFA—*Parti de la Fédération Africaine:* its birth in 1959 marked the break-up of the interterritorial RDA and PRA; created by Léopold Senghor and Modibo Keïta; supported the Mali federation and dissolved with it in 1960; associated parties were:

Senegal: *Union Progressiste Sénégalais.*
Soudan: *Union Soudanaise.*
Niger: *Sawaba* (outlawed).
Dahomey: *Parti Populaire du Dahomey.*
Upper Volta: *Parti National Voltaïque* (outlawed).

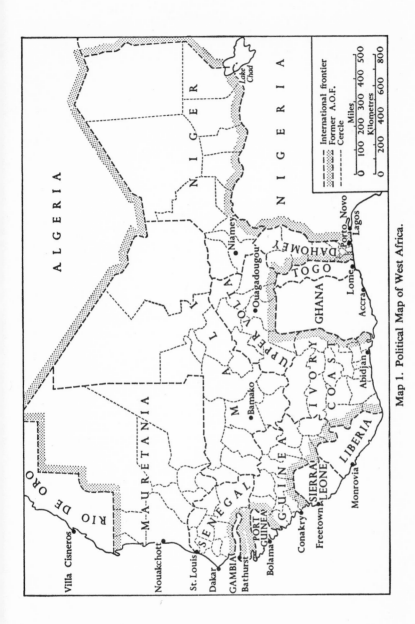

Map 1. Political Map of West Africa.

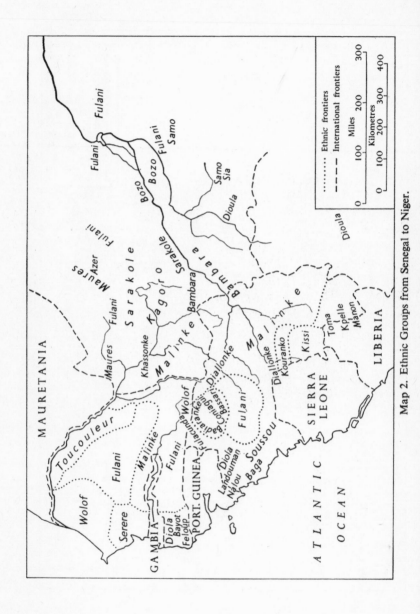

Map 2. Ethnic Groups from Senegal to Niger.

428

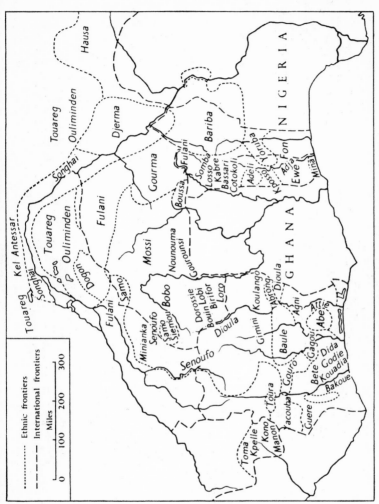

Map 3. Ethnic Groups from Niger to the Altantic.

429

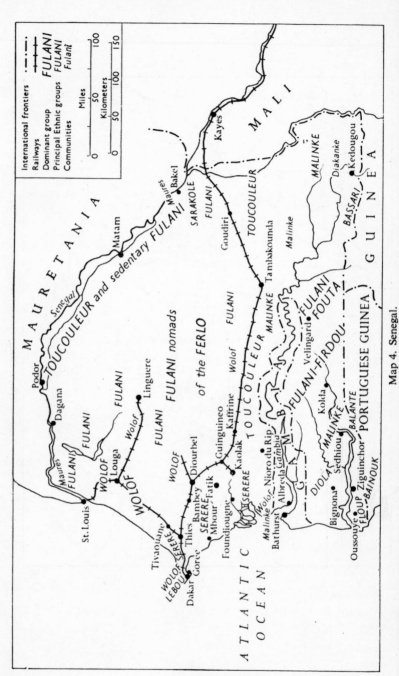

Map 4. Senegal.

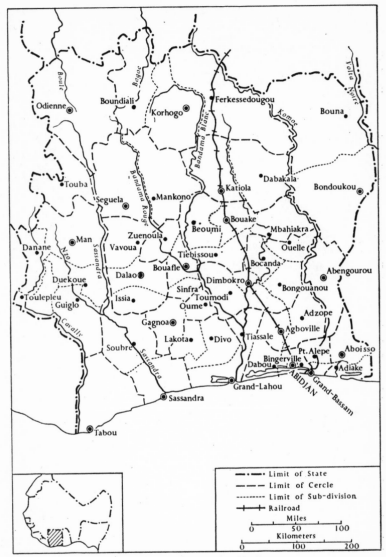

Map 5. Political Map of Ivory Coast.

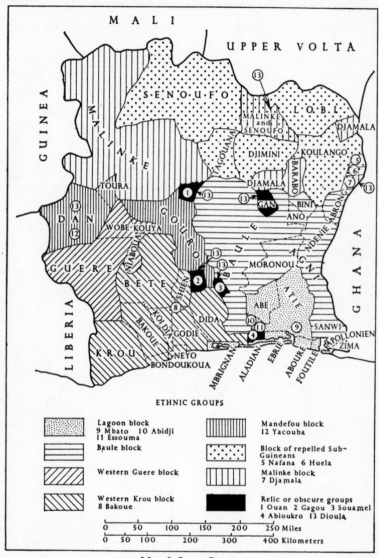

ETHNIC GROUPS

Lagoon block	Mandefou block
9 Mbato 10 Abidji	12 Yacouba
11 Essouma	
Baule block	Block of repelled Sub-Guineans
	5 Nafana 6 Huela
Western Guere block	Malinke block
	7 Djamala
Western Krou block	Relic or obscure groups
8 Bakoue	1 Ouan 2 Gagou 3 Souamel
	4 Abioukro 13 Dioula

0   50   100   150   200   250 Miles
0 50 100   200   300   400 Kilometers

Map 6. Ivory Coast.

432

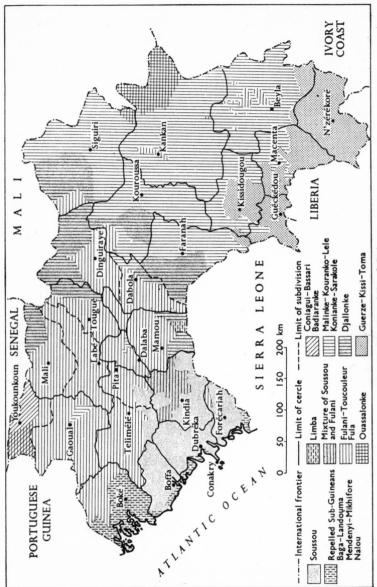

Map 7. The Republic of Guinea.

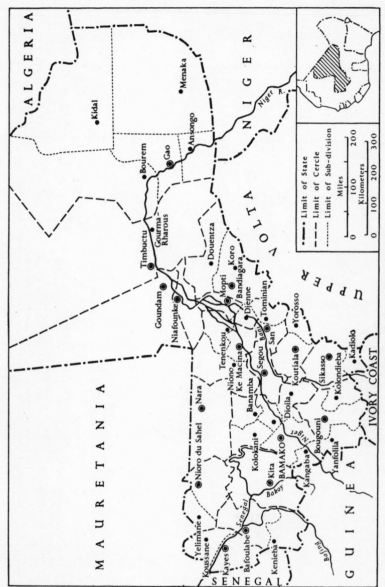

Map 8. Political Map of Mali.

ALGERIA

NIGER

Niger R.

•Kidal

•Menaka

•Bourem
Gao● •Ansongo

Gourma-
Rharous

Timbuctu

Douentza

Koro
●Goundam   Mopti● ●Bandiagara   UPPER VOLTA
Niafounké●   Djenne

Tenenkou   San ●Tominian   Yorosso
Nione   Ke Macina   Ségou● Bani   ●Koutiala   Kadiolo●
Banamba   Dioila   ●Sikasso ●Kolondieba
Nara   Kolokani   Niger   Bougouni
●Nioro du Sahel   Dioila   Yanfolila●   IVORY COAST

Kita●   BAMAKO
Bakoy   Kangaba●

Yélimané●   Senegal
Koussane●   Bafoulabé●   Kénieba●
●Kayes

MAURETANIA

GUINEA

SENEGAL

Limit of State
Limit of Cercle
Limit of Sub-division

Miles
0   100   200   300
Kilometers
0   100   200

Index